NOVA
GEO PRIZM
1985-90

All U.S. and Canadian models of Chevrolet Nova and GEO Prizm

Pesident GARY R. INGERSOLL
Senior Vice President Book Publishing and Research RONALD A. HOXTER
Vice President and General Manager JOHN P. KUSHNERICK
Editor-in-Chief KERRY A. FREEMAN, S.A.E.
Managing Editor DEAN F. MORGANTINI, S.A.E.
Senior Editor RICHARD J. RIVELE, S.A.E.
Senior Editor W. CALVIN SETTLE, JR., S.A.E.
Editor JIM TAYLOR

CHILTON BOOK COMPANY
Radnor, Pennsylvania
19089

CONTENTS

DRIVE TRAIN

SUSPENSION and STEERING

BRAKES

BODY

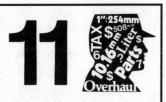

MECHANIC'S DATA

SAFETY NOTICE

Proper service and repair procedures are vital to the safe, reliable operation of all motor vehicles, as well as the personal safety of those performing repairs. This book outlines procedures for servicing and repairing vehicles using safe, effective methods. The procedures contain many NOTES, CAUTIONS and WARNINGS which should be followed along with standard safety procedures to eliminate the possibility of personal injury or improper service which could damage the vehicle or compromise its safety.

It is important to note that repair procedures and techniques, tools and parts for servicing motor vehicles, as well as the skill and experience of the individual performing the work vary widely. It is not possible to anticipate all of the conceivable ways or conditions under which vehicles may be serviced, or to provide cautions as to all of the possible hazards that may result. Standard and accepted safety precautions and equipment should be used during cutting, grinding, chiseling, prying, or any other process that can cause material removal or projectiles.

Some procedures require the use of tools specially designed for a specific purpose. Before substituting another tool or procedure, you must be completely satisfied that neither your personal safety, nor the performance of the vehicle will be endangered.

Although the information in this guide is based on industry sources and is as complete as possible at the time of publication, the possibility exists that the manufacturer made later changes which could not be included here. While striving for total accuracy, Chilton Book Company cannot assume responsibility for any errors, changes, or omissions that may occur in the compilation of this data.

PART NUMBERS

Part numbers listed in this reference are not recommendations by Chilton for any product by brand name. They are references that can be used with interchange manuals and aftermarket supplier catalogs to locate each brand supplier's discrete part number.

SPECIAL TOOLS

Special tools are recommended by the vehicle manufacturer to perform their specific job. Use has been kept to a minimum, but where absolutely necessary, they are referred to in the text by the part number of the tool manufacturer. These tools can be purchased, under the appropriate part number, from your Chevrolet or GEO dealer or regional distributor or an equivalent tool can be purchased locally from a tool supplier or parts outlet. Before substituting any tool for the one recommended, read the SAFETY NOTICE at the top of this page.

ACKNOWLEDGMENTS

Chilton Book Company expresses appreciation to the General Motors Corporation, Detroit, Michigan; Toyota Motor Corporation, Torrence, California; and Del Chevrolet Inc., 1644 Lancaster Ave., Paoli, PA 19301, for their generous assistance.

Information has been selected from Chevrolet shop manuals, owner's manuals, service bulletins, data books and technical training manuals.

Manufactured in the United States of America
1234567890   8765432109

Chilton's Repair Manual: Chevrolet Nova/GEO Prizm 1985–90
ISBN 0-8019-7948-X PBK.
Library of Congress Catalog Card No. 88-43192

General Information and Maintenance

HOW TO USE THIS BOOK

Chilton's Repair & Tune-Up Guide for the Chevrolet Nova and Prizm is intended to help you learn more about the inner workings of your car and save you money on its upkeep and operation.

The first two chapters will be the most used since they contain maintenance and tune-up information and procedures. Studies have shown that a properly tuned and maintained car can get at least 10% better gas mileage (which translates into lower operating costs); periodic maintenance will catch minor problems before they turn into major repair bills.

The other chapters deal with the more complex systems of your car. Operating systems from engine through brakes are covered to the extent that the average do-it-yourselfer becomes mechanically involved. This book will not explain such things as rebuilding the automatic transmission for the simple reason that the expertise required and the investment in special tools make this task uneconomical. It will give you the detailed instructions to help you change your own brake pads and shoes, tune the engine, replace spark plugs and filters, and do many more jobs that will save you money, give you personal satisfaction and help you avoid expensive problems.

A secondary purpose of this book is a reference guide for owners who want to understand their car and/or their mechanics better. In this case, no tools at all are required. Knowing just what a particular repair job requires in parts and labor time will allow you to evaluate whether or not you're getting a fair price quote and help decipher itemized bills from a repair shop. Simply reading through the book about a particular repair will introduce you to vocabulary and part names; this will allow you to "speak the language" better when discussing the car and its repair.

Before attempting any repairs or service on your car, read through the entire procedure outlined in the appropriate chapter. This will give you the overall view of what tools and supplies will be required. There is nothing more frustrating than having to walk to the bus stop on Monday morning because you were short one gasket on Sunday afternoon. So read ahead and plan ahead. Each operation should be approached logically and all procedures thoroughly understood before attempting any work.

Some special tools that may be required can often be rented from local automotive jobbers or places specializing in renting tools and equipment. Check the yellow pages of your phone book.

All chapters contain adjustments, maintenance, removal and installation procedures, and overhaul procedures. When overhaul is not considered practical, we tell you how to remove the failed part and then how to install the new or rebuilt replacement. In this way, you at least save the labor costs. Backyard overhaul of some components (such as the alternator or water pump) is just not practical, but the removal and installation procedure is often simple and well within the capabilities of the average car owner.

Two basic mechanic's rules should be mentioned here. First, whenever the LEFT side of the car or engine is referred to, it is meant to specify the DRIVER'S side of the car. Conversely, the RIGHT side of the car means the PASSENGER'S side. Second, all screws and bolts are removed by turning counterclockwise, and tightened by turning clockwise.

Safety is always the most important rule. Constantly be aware of the dangers involved in working on or around an automobile and take proper precautions to avoid the risk of personal injury or damage to the vehicle. See the section in this chapter Servicing Your Vehicle Safely and the SAFETY NOTICE on the acknowledgement page before attempting any service procedures and pay attention to the instructions provided. There are 3 common mistakes in mechanical work:

1. Incorrect order of assembly, disassembly or adjustment. When taking something apart or putting it together, doing things in the wrong order usually just costs you extra time; however it CAN break something. Read the entire procedure before beginning disassembly. Do everything in the order in which the instructions say you should do it, even if you can't immediately see a reason for it.

When you're taking apart something that is very intricate (for example a carburetor), you might want to draw a picture of how it looks when assembled at one point in order to make sure you get everything back in its proper position. A sketch or diagram is also highly recommended before removing vacuum hoses or wiring connectors.

We will supply exploded views whenever possible, but sometimes the job requires more attention to detail than an illustration provides. When making adjustments (especially tune-up adjustments), do them in order. One adjustment often affects another and you cannot expect satisfactory results unless each adjustment is made only when it cannot be changed by any other.

2. Over- or under-tightening nuts and bolt. The amount of rotational force applied to a bolt is called torque and can be measured in numerical units. In this country, the most common unit of measure is the foot-pound (ft.lb.); you may also encounter inch-pounds and Newton-meters.

While it is more common for overtorquing to cause damage, undertorquing can cause a fastener to vibrate loose and cause serious damage, especially when dealing with aluminum parts. Pay attention to torque specifications and use a torque wrench in assembly. If a torque figure is not available, remember that if you are using the right tool to do the job, you will probably not have to strain yourself to get a fastener tight enough. The pitch of most threads is so slight that the tension you put on the wrench will be multiplied many times in actual force on what you are tightening.

A good example of critical torque can be seen in the case of spark plug installation, especially where you are putting the plug into an aluminum cylinder head. Too little torque can fail to crush the gasket, causing leakage of combustion gases and consequent overheating of the plug and engine parts. Too much torque can damage the threads or distort the plug, which changes the spark gap to the electrode. Since more and more manufacturers are using aluminum in their engine and chassis parts to save

weight, a torque wrench should be in any serious do-it-yourselfers' tool box.

There are many commercial chemical products available for ensuring that fasteners won't come loose, even if they are not torqued just right (a very common brand is Loctite®). If you're worried about getting something together tight enough to hold, but loose enough to avoid mechanical damage during assembly, one of these products might offer substantial insurance. Read the label on the package and make sure the product is compatible with the materials fluids, etc. involved before choosing one.

3. Crossthreading. This occurs when a part such as a bolt is screwed into a nut or casting at the wrong angle and forced, causing the threads to become damaged. Crossthreading is more likely to occur if access if difficult. It helps to clean and lubricate fasteners and to start threading the nut or bolt with your fingers. If you encounter resistance, unscrew the part and start over again at a different angle until it can be inserted and turned several times without much effort.

Keep in mind that many parts, especially spark plugs, use tapered threads so that gentle turning will automatically bring the part you're threading to the proper angle if you don't force it. Don't put a wrench on the part until it's been turned in a couple of times by hand. If you suddenly encounter resistance and the part has not seated fully, don't force it. Pull it back out and make sure it's clean and threading properly.

Always take your time and be patient; once you have some experience, working on your car will become an enjoyable hobby.

TOOLS AND EQUIPMENT

Naturally, without the proper tools and equipment it is impossible to properly service you vehicle. It would be impossible to catalog each tool that you would need to perform every operation in this book. It would also be unwise for the amateur to rush out and buy any expensive set of tools on the theory that he may need one or more of them at sometime.

The best approach is to proceed slowly, gathering together a good quality set of those tools that are used most frequently. Don't be misled by the low cost of bargain tools. It is far better to spend a little more for better quality. Forged wrenches, 10 or 12 point sockets and fine tooth ratchets are by far preferable to their less expensive counterparts. As any good mechanic can tell you, there are few worse experiences than trying to work on a car with bad tools. Your monetary savings will be far outweighed by frustration and mangled knuckles.

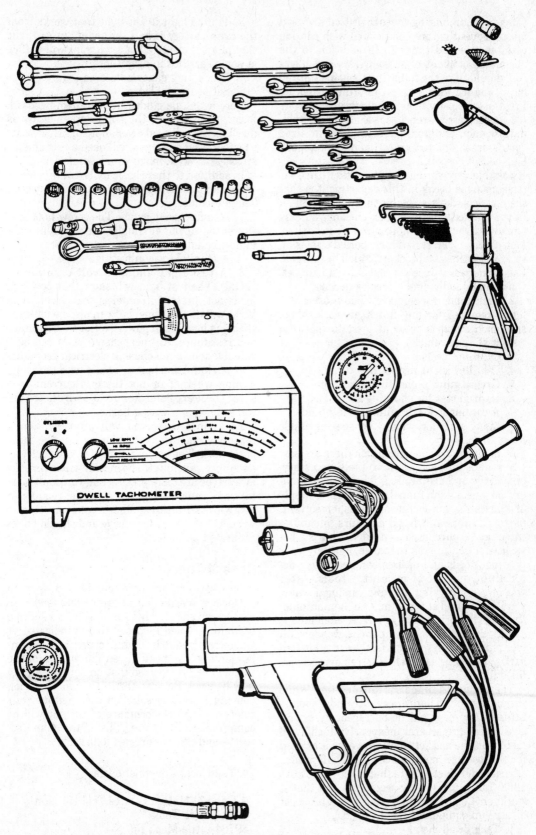

You need only a basic assortment of hand tools for most maintenance and repair jobs

Begin accumulating those tools that are used most frequently; those associated with routine maintenance and tune-up. In addition to the normal assortment of screwdrivers and pliers you should have the following tools for routine maintenance jobs (your Chevrolet Nova or Prizm uses mostly metric fasteners):

1. SAE/Metric wrenches, sockets and combination open-end/box-end wrenches in sizes from 1/8 in. (3mm) to 3/4 in. (19mm); and a spark plug socket ($^{13}/_{16}$ in.)

If possible, buy various length socket drive extensions. One break in this department is that the metric sockets available in the U.S. will all fit the ratchet handles and extensions you may already have (1/4 in., 3/8 in., and 1/2 in. drive). Many retail chain stores have periodic sales on sets of wrenches and sockets. Much like a set of fine dinnerware, once you have the starter set, you can add individual pieces as needed.

2. Jackstands for support. These are absolutely required for any undercar work. Make sure each stand is rated at least to the total weight of your vehicle.

3. Oil filter wrench

4. Oil filter spout for pouring oil

5. Grease gun for chassis lubrication

6. Hydrometer for checking the battery.

7. A container for draining oil and fluids.

8. Many rags for wiping up the inevitable mess.

In addition to the above items there are several others that are not absolutely necessary, but handy to have around. These include oil-dry, a transmission funnel and the usual supply of lubricants, antifreeze and washer solvent, parts cleaners and hand cleaners, although these can be purchased as needed. This is a basic list for routine maintenance, but only your personal needs and desires can accurately determine your list of necessary tools. After you've been working on your car for a while, you'll be amazed at the number of non-automotive tools living in your tool box. A small mirror can see up and under a component, wooden golf tees plug vacuum lines perfectly and a kitchen turkey baster is excellent for removing overfilled fluids.

The second list of tools is for tune-ups. While the tools involved here are slightly more sophisticated, they need not be outrageously expensive. There are several inexpensive tach/dwell meters on the market that are every bit as good for the average mechanic as a $400.00 professional model. Just be sure that it goes to at least 1,200-1,500 rpm on the tach scale and that it works on 4,6 and 8 cylinder engines. A basic list of tune-up equipment could include:

1. Tach-dwell meter

2. Spark plug wrench

3. Timing light (a DC light that works from the car's battery is best, although an AC light that plugs into 110V house current will suffice at some sacrifice in brightness)

4. Spark plug gauge/adjusting tools

5. Set of feeler blades

Here again, be guided by your own needs. A feeler blade will set the point gap as easily as dwell meter will read dwell, but slightly less accurately. And since you will need a tachometer anyway . . . well, make your own decision.

In addition to these basic tools, there are several other tools and gauges you may find useful. These include:

1. A compression gauge. The screw-in type is slower to use, but eliminates the possibility of a faulty reading due to escaping pressure

2. A manifold vacuum gauge

3. A test light and/or a volt-ohm meter (VOM). The test light will show that power is (or is not) present in an electrical circuit. The VOM will do the same, but can also be used for checking how much power (voltage), continuity and resistance. An inexpensive VOM can be a valuable tool when chasing electrical gremlins.

4. An induction meter. This is used for determining whether or not there is current in a wire. These are handy for use if a wire is broken somewhere in a wiring harness.

As a final note, you will probably find a torque wrench necessary for all but the most basic work. The beam type models are perfectly adequate, although the newer click (breakaway) type are more precise, and you don't have to crane your neck to see a torque reading in awkward situations. The breakaway torque wrenches are more expensive and should be recalibrated periodically.

Special Tools

Special tools are occasionally necessary to perform a specific job or are recommended to make a job easier. Their use has been kept to a minimum. When a special tool is indicated, it will be referred to by manufacturer's part number, and, where possible, an illustration of the tool will be provided so that an equivalent tool may be used. Before substituting another tool, you must be fully satisfied that neither your safety nor the performance of the car will be compromised by its use. A list of tool manufacturers and their addresses follows:

• Your local Chevrolet dealer

• General Motors Service Tool Division
Kent-Moore Tools
29784 Little Mack Rd.
Roseville, MI. 48066

● Snap-on Tools Corp.
Kenosha, Wisconsin 53141

● CP/Matco Tools
4403 Allen Rd.
Stow, Ohio 44224

SERVICING YOUR VEHICLE SAFELY

It is virtually impossible to anticipate all of the hazards involved with automotive maintenance and service, but care and common sense will prevent most accidents.

The rules of safety for mechanics range from "don't smoke around gasoline" to "use the proper tool for the job." The trick to avoiding injuries is to develop safe work habits and take every possible precaution.

Dos

● Do keep a fire extinguisher and first aid kit within easy reach. Know how to use them before you need them.

● Do wear safety glasses or goggles when cutting, drilling, grinding or prying, even if you have 20-20 vision. If you wear glasses for the sake of vision, they should be made of hardened glass that can serve also as safety glasses, or wear safety goggles over your regular glasses.

● Do shield your eyes whenever you work around the battery. Batteries contain sulphuric acid. In case of contact with the eyes or skin, flush the area with water or a mixture of water and baking soda and get medical attention immediately.

● Do work neatly. A few minutes spent clearing a workbench or setting up a small table for tools is well worth the effort. Make yourself put tools back on the table when not in use; doing so means you won't have to grope around on the floor for that wrench you need right now. Protect your car while working on it with fender covers. If you don't wish to buy a fender cover, an old blanket makes a usable substitute.

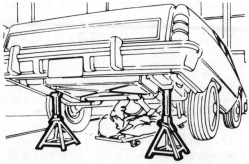

Always use jackstands when working under the car

● Do use safety stands for any undercar service. Jacks are for raising vehicles; safety stands are for making sure the vehicle stays raised until you want it to come down. Whenever the car is raised, block the wheels remaining on the ground and set the parking brake.

● Do use adequate ventilation when working with any chemicals or hazardous materials. Like carbon monoxide, the abestos dust resulting from brake lining wear can be poisonous in sufficient quantities.

● Do disconnect the negative battery cable when working on the electrical system. The secondary ignition system can contain up to 40,000 volts.

● Do follow manufacturer's directions whenever working with potentially hazardous materials. Both brake fluid and antifreeze are poisonous if taken internally. Housepets and small animals are attracted to the odor and taste of engine coolant (antifreeze). It is a highly poisonous mixture of chemicals; special care must be taken to protect open containers and spillage. If a housepet drinks any amount of coolant, it is a "drop everything" emergency--seek immediate veterinary care.

● Do properly maintain your tools. Loose hammerheads, mushroomed punches and chisels, frayed or poorly grounded electrical cords, excessively worn screwdrivers, spread wrenches (open end), cracked sockets, slipping ratchets, or faulty droplight sockets can cause accidents. Working on your own car is not supposed to be a painful experience.

● Do use the proper size and type of tool for the job being done.

● Do, when possible, pull on a wrench handle rather than push on it, and adjust your stance to prevent a fall.

● Do use socket, open-end or box-end wrenches where possible. They are made to a precise measurement and will fit the hardware exactly. If you must use an adjustable wrench, be sure that the jaws are tightly closed on the nut or bolt and pulled so that the face is on the side of the fixed jaw.

● Do select a wrench or socket that fits the nut or bolt. The wrench or socket should sit straight, not cocked.

● Do strike squarely with a hammer; avoid glancing blows.

● Do set the parking brake and block the drive wheels if the work requires the engine running.

Don'ts

● Don't run an engine in a garage or anywhere else without proper ventilation--EVER! Carbon monoxide is poisonous; it takes a long time to leave the human body and you can build up a deadly supply of it in your system by simply breathing in a little every day. You may not realize you are slowly poisoning yourself. Always use power vents, windows, fans or open the garage doors.

Carbon monoxide is odorless and colorless. Your senses cannot detect its presence. Early symptoms of monoxide poisoning include headache, irritability, improper vision (blurred or hard to focus) and/or drowsiness. When you notice any of these symptoms in yourself or your helpers, stop working immediately and get to fresh, outside air. Ventilate the work area thoroughly before returning to the car.

• Don't work around moving parts while wearing a necktie or other loose clothing. Short sleeves are much safer than long, loose sleeves; hard-toed shoes with neoprene soles protect your feet and give a better grip on slippery surface. Jewelry (watches, fancy belt buckles, beads or body adornment of any kind) is not safe working around a car. Long hair should be hidden under a hat or cap.

• Don't use pockets for toolboxes. A fall or bump can drive a screwdriver deep into your body. Even a wiping cloth hanging from the back pocket can wrap around a spinning shaft or fan.

• Don't smoke when working around gasoline, cleaning solvent or other flammable material. Assume that all liquids and sprays are flammable unless specifically labled otherwise.

• Don't disconnect either terminal from the battery while the engine is running. Modern cars contain many solid-state components and "black-box" computers. You will not get a second chance with solid-state failures; you will get to buy some very expensive replacement parts.

• Don't smoke when working around the battery. When the battery is being charged, it gives off explosive hydrogen gas.

• Don't use gasoline, kerosene or solvents to wash your hands; there are excellent soaps available. Gasoline contains lead, and lead can enter the body through a cut, accumulating in the body until you are very ill. Gasoline also removes all the natural oils from the skin so that bone-dry hands will suck up oil and grease.

• Don't service the air conditioning system unless you are equipped with the necessary tools and training. The refrigerant, R-12, is extremely cold when compressed, and when released into the air will instantly freeze any surface it contacts, including your eyes. Although the refrigerant is normally non-toxic, R-12 becomes a deadly poisonous gas in the presence of an open flame. One good whiff of the vapors from burning refrigerant can be fatal.

HISTORY

Built in Freemont, California, by the New United Motor Manufacturing, Inc., and bought by Chevrolet under the terms of a joint venture agreement between General Motors and Toyota Motors, the Nova borrows its dimensions and many mechanical components from the Toyota Corolla.

Toyota was responsible for designing and engineering the manufacturing layout, coordinating the acquisition and installation of equipment and the implementation of the production system. Production management is handled jointly by Toyota and Chevrolet; Chevrolet handles the distribution and marketing the products of the joint venture.

Built in two body styles only, the 4-door sedan and the 5-door hatchback originally came equipped with the 1587 cc 4A-LC engine. This engine is virtually ideal for a car of this size, offering reasonable performance in a front wheel drive package, economy and simplicity of repair. Additionally, the cars have independent suspension at all four wheels, front disc brakes, and a list of interior amenities. The Novas could be had in either the base or CL levels; the CL package included further niceties such as remote fuel door release, tilt-wheel steering column and velour interior.

For 1988, the 4-door sedan was given an optional twin-cam 16 valve motor. This 4A-GE motor is derivative of the original, but gives noticably more horsepower due to better "breathing" of the engine and better fuel control from the new fuel injection system.

In 1989, the Nova was restyled completely and christened Prizm. The product line was brought under the Geo banner, under which Chevrolet has grouped its foreign and import products. The 1989 Prizm is still offered in two body styles and now comes with the twin-cam 102 horsepower 4A-FE motor as standard equipment. The top of the line is designated LSi and includes trim and option upgrades such as dual side mirrors, different wheel covers and a rear window wiper/washer on the hatchbacks.

SERIAL NUMBER IDENTIFICATION

Vehicle

The vehicle identification number (VIN) is located on a stamped plate which is attached to the left side of the instrument panel. This plate is visible through the windshield.

The VIN is also stamped on a plate in the engine compartment (usually located on the firewall) and a third VIN plated is attached to the drivers door post.

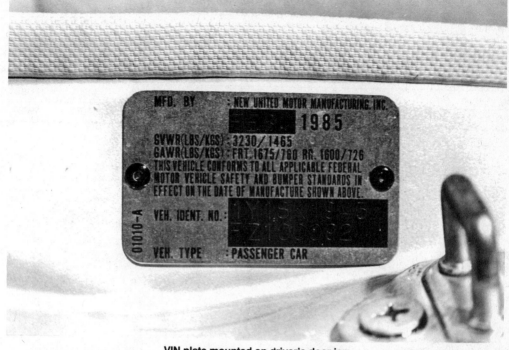

VIN plate mounted on driver's door jam

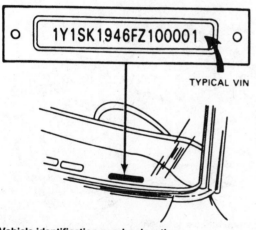

TYPICAL VIN

Vehicle identification number location

The serial number is a 17 digit format. The first three digits are the Work Manufacturer Identification number. The next five digits are the Vehicle Description Section. The remaining nine numbers are the production numbers.

Engine

The engine serial number consists of an engine series identification number, followed by a seven digit production number.

Transaxle

The manual and automatic transaxle identification numbers are stamped into the top of

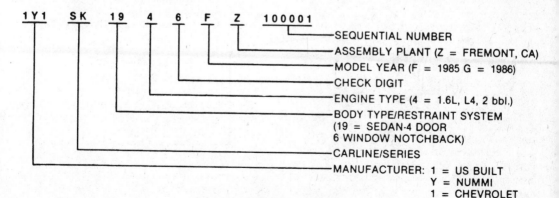

Vehicle identification number codes

Engine Identification Chart

No. of Cylinders and Cu. In. Displacement	Actual Displacement			Fuel System	Type	Built by	Engine Code	Years
	Cu. In.	CC	Liters					
4-97	96.86	1587.4	1.6	2-bbl	OHC	Toyota	4A-LC	1985–88
4-97	96.86	1587.4	1.6	Injected	OHC	Toyota	4A-GE	1988
4-97	96.86	1587.4	1.6	Injected	OHC	Toyota	4A-FE	1989–90

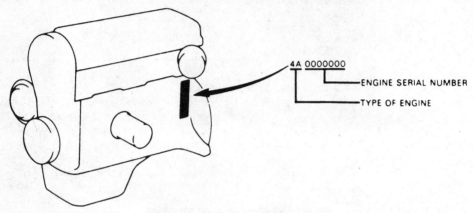

4A 0000000

ENGINE SERIAL NUMBER

TYPE OF ENGINE

Engine identification number location

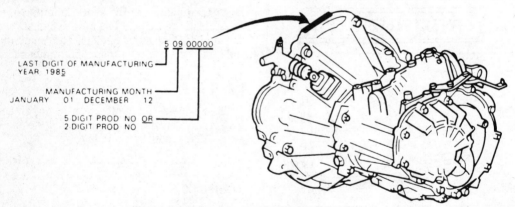

5 09 00000

LAST DIGIT OF MANUFACTURING YEAR 1985

MANUFACTURING MONTH
JANUARY 01 DECEMBER 12

5 DIGIT PROD NO OR
2 DIGIT PROD NO

Manual transaxle identification number location

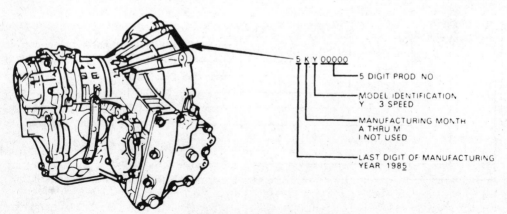

5 K Y 00000

5 DIGIT PROD NO

MODEL IDENTIFICATION
Y 3 SPEED

MANUFACTURING MONTH
A THRU M
I NOT USED

LAST DIGIT OF MANUFACTURING YEAR 1985

Automatic transaxle identification number

Manual Transmission Application Chart

Transmission Types	Years	Models
5-Speed, full synchro	1985–90	Nova and Prizm

Automatic Transmission Application Chart

Transmission	Years	Models
A131L-3 speed	1985–88	Carbureted Nova
A240E-3 speed w/overdrive	1988	Fuel Inj. Nova
A131L-3 speed	1989–90	All Prizm

the casing, on the clutch/torque converter housing end of the transaxle.

ROUTINE MAINTENANCE

Jacking and Supporting the Car

While not every maintenance operation requires you to get under the car, many do. Even if you're not working under the car, it may be necessary to remove a wheel or gain access to a low component. Proper support of the car is critical to your safety during these operations.

The car should only be lifted with a proper jack. While the scissors jack in the trunk may be used, a floor (hydraulic) jack is recommended for its additional load-carrying capability. An added benefit is that the floor jack can be used to lift one end of the car; the scissors jack can only raise one corner at a time. When purchasing a floor jack, make sure its weight rating is at least equal to the TOTAL weight of your car. Since the Nova/Prizm cars are currently in the 2300 lb. range, a 1½ ton capacity jack will suffice.

Correct placement of the jack is essential to the success of the project. Only lift the car at the designated jacking points on the body or frame. These reinforced locations will support the weight of the car during the elevation. Any other points, such as the floor pan, engine oil pan or suspension will not.

Before lifting the car, make sure the surrounding area is clear. If any wheels are to be removed, loosen the wheel lugs two or three turns while the wheel is on the ground. Place a wheel chock behind a wheel on the opposite side (or at the opposite end) of the car. Once the car is elevated, immediately place jackstands under the support points. Make sure the stands are on a firm, level footing and will not shift under load. Lower the jack until the weight of the car is supported on the stand, not on the jack.

These simple preliminary steps cannot be stressed often enough. Each year many people are maimed or killed because their car fell on them. A hydraulic jack cannot be trusted to stay elevated--always use jackstands, even for a quickie repair.

Air Cleaner

REMOVAL AND INSTALLATION

All the dust and grit present in the air is kept out of the engine by means of the air filter element. Proper maintenance is vital, as a clogged element not only restricts the air flow and thus the power, but can also cause premature engine wear.

The filter element should be cleaned or replaced every 7,500 miles, or more often if the car is driven under dry, dusty conditions. Remove the filter element and using low pressure compressed air, blow the dirt out.

NOTE: *The filter element used on the Chevrolet Nova/Prizm is of the dry, disposable type. It should never be washed, soaked or oiled.*

The filter element should be replaced every 30,000 miles, or more often under dry dusty conditions.

Carbureted engines

1. Unfasten the wing nut and clips on the top of the air filter housing and lift off the top.
2. Lift out the air filter element; clean or replace it.
3. Install the air filter, making sure the element is correctly centered. If a new element is being installed, make certain the height of the new one is identical to the old one. Proper sealing between the top of the housing and the filter is essential.

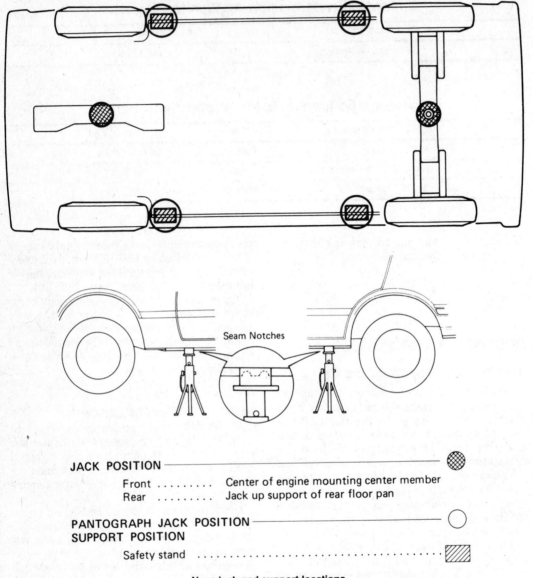

Seam Notches

JACK POSITION ——————————————————————————— ⊛

    Front ....   Center of engine mounting center member
    Rear ....   Jack up support of rear floor pan

PANTOGRAPH JACK POSITION ———————————————— ◯
SUPPORT POSITION

    Safety stand .... ▨

Nova jack and support locations

4. Reinstall the top of the housing and attach the clips. Install the wing nut and tighten it snugly with your fingers.

Fuel Injected Engines

1. The air cleaner housing is located on the left front fender, just ahead of the shock tower. Locate and carefully remove the screws holding the top half to the bottom half of the housing.

2. Lift the top of the casing just enough to remove the old filter. Be careful of other wires and hoses in the area.

3. Install the new filter, making sure it is properly positioned in the housing.

4. Reinstall the cover and install the retaining screws.

Fuel Filter
REMOVAL AND INSTALLATION

The fuel filter is located on the firewall. The element inside the filter reduces the flow speed of the fuel causing dirt particles that are heavier than gasoline to settle to the bottom. The lighter particles are filtered by the element.

Carbureted Engine

CAUTION: *Gasoline is hazardous and extremely flammable. Remove the hoses slowly and contain spillage. Observe no smoking/no open flame precautions. Have a Class B-C (dry powder) fire extinguisher within arm's reach at all times.*

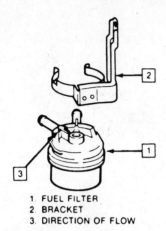

1. FUEL FILTER
2. BRACKET
3. DIRECTION OF FLOW

Fuel filter and mounting bracket

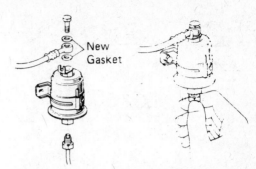

Replacing the fuel filter for the fuel injection system

1. Remove the fuel filler cap.
2. Note the routing of inlet and outlet lines and the direction of flow as marked by the arrow on the filter. With a pair of pliers, shift the clips on the inlet and outlet hoses back and well away from the connections on the filter.
3. Disconnect the fuel lines, using a twisting motion to break them loose. Pull the filter out of its retaining clip. Plug the lines immediately to prevent spillage.
4. Install the filter in the holder. When reconnecting the fuel lines, make sure the hoses are connected to the correct ports on the filter.(The arrow on the filter indicates direction of flow and points towards the carburetor.)

Install the hose clips to the inside of the bulged sections of the fuel filter connections, and not right at the ends of the fuel lines. Start the engine and check for leaks.
5. Install the fuel filler cap.

Fuel Injected Engines

CAUTION: *The fuel system is under pressure. Release pressure slowly and contain spillage. Observe no smoking/no open flame precautions. Have a Class B-C (dry powder) fire extinguisher within arm's reach at all times. Perform this procedure only on a cold motor.*
1. Disconnect the negative battery cable.
2. Relieve the pressure in the fuel line as follows:

   a. Fit a wrench of the exact size onto the upper line connection and fit a second wrench on the flats of the filter. This counterholding arrangement will prevent the filter and lines from turning during removal.

   b. Wrap the upper filter area in layers of rags to absorb spray and spillage.

   c. Slowly loosen the bolt holding the line to the filter. When the pressure is equalized, re-

move the bolt and the line. Plug the line immediately.
3. Again using two wrenches, disconnect the lower line to the filter. Be prepared to deal with fuel spillage. Be very careful not to crimp or bend the fuel line. Plug the line immediately.
4. Remove the filter from its holder and install a new one.
5. Apply a thin coat of oil to the threads and connect the bottom fuel line to the filter. Always begin the threads by hand, then tighten to 22 ft.lbs.
6. Install the uppper line with NEW gaskets. Make sure the line is held within the forked bracket on the filter and begin the bolt by hand to insure proper threading.
7. Tighten the bolt to 22 ft.lbs. Reconnect the negative battery cable.
8. Start the engine and check for leaks. (The engine may require a longer period of cranking until it starts due to loss of fuel pressure.)

PCV Valve

The PCV (Positive Crankcase Ventilation) valve regulates crankcase (oilpan) ventilation during the various engine operating conditions. At high vacuum (idle speed and partial load range) it will open slightly and at low vacuum (full throttle) it will open fully. This causes vapor to be removed from the crankcase by the engine vacuum and then sucked into the combustion chamber where it is burned.

REMOVAL AND INSTALLATION

1. Check the ventilation hoses for leaks or clogging. Clean or replace as necessary.
2. Locate the PCV valve in the valve cover. Remove the valve.
3. Blow into the engine end of the valve. There should be a free passage of air through the valve.
CAUTION: *Do not suck air through the PCV valve. Petroleum substances inside the valve may be harmful to your health.*
4. Blow through the intake manifold side of

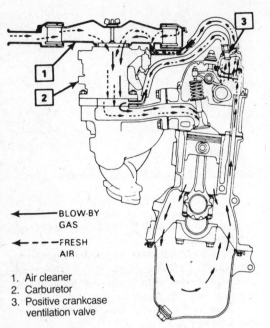

← BLOW-BY GAS

← - - -FRESH AIR

1. Air cleaner
2. Carburetor
3. Positive crankcase ventilation valve

Positive crankcase ventilation system

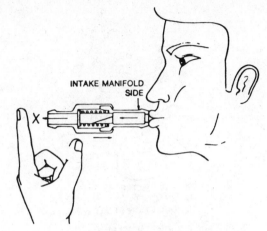

Air should not pass through the PCV valve when blowing through the intake manifold side

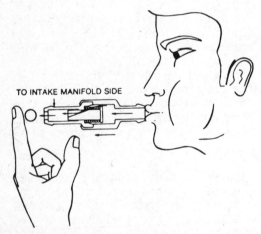

Air should pass through the PCV valve when blowing into the crankcase side

the valve. There should be little or no passage of air through the valve.

5. If the PCV valve failed either of the preceding two checks, it will require replacement.

6. Install the valve firmly into the valve cover. Connect the hose(s) and make sure there are no leaks around the hose connections.

NOTE: *The fuel injected engines do not have a PCV valve. A hose runs from the valve cover to the intake manifold. The hose must be checked periodically for any signs of cracking or looseness.*

Evaporative Canister
OPERATION

The evaporative control system reduces hydrocarbon emissions by storing and then routing fuel vapor from the fuel tank and the carburetor's float chamber through the charcoal canister to the intake manifold for combustion in the cylinders at the proper time.

When the ignition is OFF, hydrocarbons from the carburetor float chamber pass through the de-energized outer vent control valve and into the charcoal canister. Vapors from the fuel tank also pass into the charcoal canister through a check valve located on the canister.

When the ignition is switched ON, but the engine is NOT running, the outer vent control valve is energized blocking the movement of fuel vapor from the carburetor's float chamber. Vapors from the fuel tank can still flow and be stored in the charcoal canister.

Check the evaporation control system every 15,000 miles. Check the fuel and vapor lines and the vacuum hoses for proper connections and correct routing, as well as condition. Replace clogged, damaged or deteriorated parts as necessary, using only hoses marked fuel resistant or "EVAP". If the charcoal canister is clogged, it may be cleaned using low pressure compressed air. The entire canister should be replaced every 5 years/60,000 miles.

REMOVAL AND INSTALLATION--ALL ENGINES

1. Diagram or label the hoses running to the canister. Incorrect reassembly will affect driveability. Remove the hoses from the cannister.

2. Remove the charcoal canister from the vehicle.

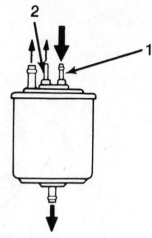

1. TANK PIPE
2. PURGE PIPE

Checking the charcoal canister

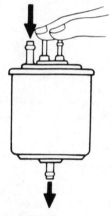

Cleaning the charcoal canister

3. Visually check the charcoal canister for cracks or damage.

4. Check for a clogged filter and stuck check valve. Using low pressure compressed air, blow into the tank pipe and check that the air flows freely and without resistance from the other pipes. If the airflow is not free and unrestricted, replace the canister.

5. Clean the filter in the canister by blowing 43 psi of compressed air into the pipe to the outer vent control valve (see illustration) while holding the other upper canister pipes closed.

NOTE: *Do not attempt to wash or flush the charcoal canister. Also be sure that no activated carbon comes out of the canister.*

6. Reinstall the canister on its mounts and connect the hoses to their proper ports.

Battery

All Novas and Prizms are equipped with maintenance free batteries, which do not re-

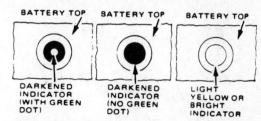

Examples of battery "eye" on maintenance free batteries. A flashlight may be needed to determine the color in low light conditions

quire normal attention as far as fluid level checks are concerned. However, the terminals require periodic cleaning, which should be performed at least once a year.

The sealed top battery cannot be checked for charge in the normal manner, since there is no provision for access to the electrolyte. To check the condition of the battery:

FLUID LEVEL

1. If the indicator eye on top of the battery is dark, the battery has enough fluid. If the eye is light, the electrolyte level is too low and the battery must be replaced.

2. If the green dot appears in the middle of the eye, the battery is sufficiently charged. If no green dot is visible, charge the battery at a low rate. The green dot will appear when the battery is at 65% of full charge; in some cases the battery may need charging even if the grren dot is visible.

CAUTION: *Do not charge the Nova battery for more than 50 amp/hours or the Prizm battery for more than 75 amp/hours. (Number of charging amps x number of hours on charger = amp/hours. Example: Charger set for 10amp rate of charge--do not charge longer than 5 hours. 10x5 = 50.)*

If the green dot appears, or if the electrolyte squirts out of the vent hole stop the charge.
NOTE: *It may be necessary to tip the battery from side to side to get the green dot to appear after charging.*

CABLES AND CLAMPS

At least twice a year, clean the side terminals and cable ends. Loosen the clamp bolts (you may have to brush off any corrosion with baking soda and water solution if they are really messy) and remove the cables, negative cable first.

There is a special cleaning tool available for cleaning side terminal batteries. When using this tool, make sure you get the terminal and the cable ends clean and shiny. Any oxidation, corrosion or foreign material will prevent a

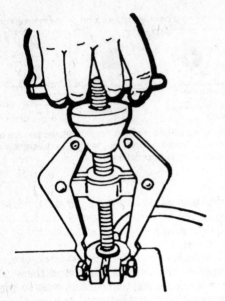

Special pullers are available to remove cable clamps

Clean the inside of the clamps with a wire brush, or the special tool

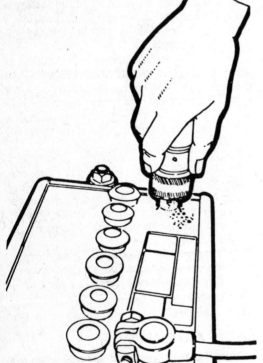

Clean the battery posts with a wire brush, or the special tool shown

sound electrical connection and inhibit either starting or charging.

Check the battery tray and wash it off with warm soapy water, rinse and dry. Any rust should be sanded away, and the tray given at least two coats of a quality anti-rust paint.

Drive Belts

INSPECTION

The drive belts are used to transfer power from the crankshaft at the bottom of the motor to another component which needs to be turned. The belts are generally made of rubber and fabric layers and are subject to deterioration from wear, heat, and chemicals.

To inspect the belts, make sure the engine is off and the key removed from the ignition. (This eliminates any chance of surprises while

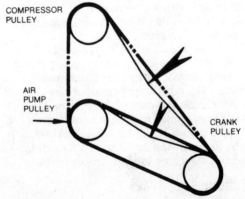

Air pump drive belt tension checking locations with and without A/C

1. Loosen the pivot bolt

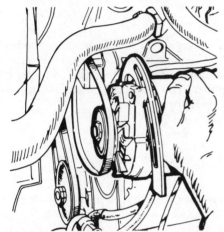

2. Push the component inwards

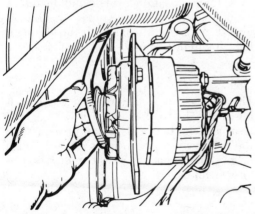

3. Slip the old belt off and the new one on

you've got your hands on potentially moving parts). Select a long section of a belt and examine it closely. There should be no signs of fraying, cracking or chunking on either the top surface or the working faces. Anything that doesn't look right isn't right.

Continue checking all the belts in the same fashion. If you're checking the longest sections,

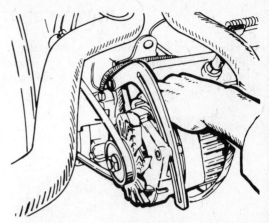

4. Pull outwards to tension the belt

you're seeing a representative section of the belt. If you wish, start the engine and shut it off again; the belts will come to rest in another position and other sections may be viewed.

Considering the speed at which the belts turn, and the importance of what they drive (alternator, water pump, power steering, etc.), any flaw found in a belt should be viewed as a potential catastrophe with your name written on it. Replace the belt before it chooses to break on a cold, rainy night.

CHECKING TENSION AND ADJUSTMENT

The belt tension on most driven components is adjusted by moving the component (alternator, power steering pump, etc.) within the range of a slotted bracket. Some late model air conditioner compressor drive belts are adjusted by varying the number of discs between the halves of the crankshaft pulley.

Check the belt tension every 6 months or 10,000 miles. Push in on the drive belt about midway between the crankshaft pulley and the driven component. If the belt deflects more than 9/16 inch or less than 3/8 inch, adjustment is required.

1. Loosen the adjustment nut and bolt in the slotted bracket. Slightly loosen the pivot bolt(s).

2. Pull (don't pry) the component outward (away from the motor) to increase tension. Push inward to reduce tension. Tighten the adjusting nut and bolt and the pivot bolt.

3. Components such as the power steering pump and some air conditioner compressors, may be mounted with a double slotted adjusting bracket using a threaded bolt or bolts and locknuts to adjust and maintain tension. Loosen the locknut(s) and slightly loosen the bolt(s) in the slotted groove(s), turn the threaded adjustment bolt(s) in or out to gain correct tension. Tighten locknuts and slotted bracket bolts.

4. Recheck the drive belt tension, readjust if necessary.

HOW TO SPOT WORN V-BELTS

V-Belts are vital to efficient engine operation—they drive the fan, water pump and other accessories. They require little maintenance (occasional tightening) but they will not last forever. Slipping or failure of the V-belt will lead to overheating. If your V-belt looks like any of these, it should be replaced.

This belt has deep cracks, which cause it to flex. Too much flexing leads to heat build-up and premature failure. These cracks can be caused by using the belt on a pulley that is too small. Notched belts are available for small diameter pulleys.

Cracking or weathering

Oil and grease on a belt can cause the belt's rubber compounds to soften and separate from the reinforcing cords that hold the belt together. The belt will first slip, then finally fail altogether.

Softening (grease and oil)

Glazing is caused by a belt that is slipping. A slipping belt can cause a run-down battery, erratic power steering, overheating or poor accessory performance. The more the belt slips, the more glazing will be built up on the surface of the belt. The more the belt is glazed, the more it will slip. If the glazing is light, tighten the belt.

Glazing

The cover of this belt is worn off and is peeling away. The reinforcing cords will begin to wear and the belt will shortly break. When the belt cover wears in spots or has a rough jagged appearance, check the pulley grooves for roughness.

Worn cover

This belt is on the verge of breaking and leaving you stranded. The layers of the belt are separating and the reinforcing cords are exposed. It's just a matter of time before it breaks completely.

Separation

REPLACEMENT

If a belt must be replaced, the driven unit must be loosened and moved to its extreme loosest position, generally by moving it toward the center of the motor. After removing the old belt, check the pulleys for dirt or built-up material which could affect belt contact. Carefully install the new belt, remembering that it is new and unused--it may appear to be just a little too small to fit over the pulley flanges. Fit the belt over the largest pulley (usually the crankshaft pulley at the bottom center of the motor) first, then work on the smaller one(s). Gentle pressure in the direction of rotation is helpful. Some belts run around a third or idler pulley, which acts as an additional pivot in the belt's path. It may be possible to loosen the idler pulley as well as the main component, making your job much easier. Depending on which belt(s) you are changing, it may be necessary to loosen or remove other interfering belts to get at the one(s) you want.

When buying replacement belts, remember that the fit is critical according to the length of the belt ("diameter"), the width of the belt, the depth of the belt and the angle or profile of the V shape. The belt shape should exactly match the shape of the pulley; belts that are not an exact match can cause noise, slippage and premature failure.

After the new belt is installed, draw tension on it by moving the driven unit away from the motor and tighten its mounting bolts. This is sometimes a three or four-handed job; you may find an assistant helpful. Make sure that all the bolts you loosened get retightened and that any other loosened belts also have the correct tension. A new belt can be expected to stretch a bit after installation so be prepared to re-adjust your new belt, if needed, within the first hundred miles of use.

Hoses

Replacing hoses requires draining the cooling system. This potentially messy job involves working under the car and handling antifreeze, a slippery, smelly, stain-making chemical. Have a large drain pan or bucket available along with healthy supply of rags. Be prepared to deal with fluid spills immediately. See the previous list of Do's and Don'ts for other hints.

1. Drain the cooling system. This is always done with the motor cold. Attempting to drain hot coolant is very foolish; you can be badly scalded.

   a. Remove the radiator cap.

   b. Position the drain pan under the drain cock on the bottom of the radiator. Addition-

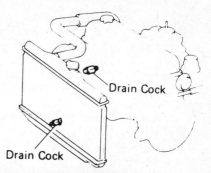

Location of draincocks for the cooling system. Never drain hot coolant—wait for the engine to cool

ally, the Nova/Prizm engines have a drain cock on the side of the engine block, near the oil filter. This may be opened to aid in draining the cooling system. If for some reason the radiator drain cock can't be used, you can loosen and remove the lower radiator hose at its joint to the radiator.

   c. If the lower hose is to be used as the drain, loosen the clamp on the hose and slide it back so it's out of the way. Gently break the grip of the hose on its fitting by twisting or prying with a suitable tool. Do not exert too much force or you will damage the radiator fitting. As the hose loosens, you can expect a gush of fluid to come out--be ready.

Remove the hose end from the radiator and direct the hose into the drain pan. You now have fluid running from both the hose and the radiator.

   d. When the system stops draining, proceed with replacement of the damaged hose. WARNING: *Housepets and small animals are attracted to the odor and taste of engine coolant (antifreeze). It is a highly poisonous mixture of chemicals; special care must be taken to protect open containers and spillage.*

2. Loosen the hose clamps on the damaged hose with a screwdriver and slide the clamps either off the hose altogether or in toward center.

3. Break the grip of the hose at both ends by prying it free with a suitable tool or by twisting it with your hand.

4. Remove the hose.

5. Install a new hose. A small amount of soapy water on the inside of the hose end will ease installation.

NOTE: *Radiator hoses should be routed with no kinks and, when installed, should be in the same position as the original. If other than specified hose is used, make sure it does not rub against either the engine or the frame while the engine is running, as this may wear a hole in the hose. Contact points may be in-*

sulated with a piece of sponge or foam; plastic wire ties are particularly handy for this job.

6. Slide the hose clamps back into position and retighten. When tightening the clamps, tighten them enough to seal in the coolant but not so much that the clamp cuts into the hose or causes it internal damage. If a clamp shows signs of any damage (bent, too loose, hard to tighten, etc) now is the time to replace it. A good rule of thumb is that a new hose is always worth new clamps.

NOTE: *Make sure that the hose clamps are beyond the bead and placed in the center of the clamping surface before tightening them.*

7. Either reinstall the lower radiator hose and secure its clamp or close the drain cocks on the side of the engine block and bottom of the radiator.

8. Fill the system with coolant. Chevrolet strongly recommends the coolant mixture be a 50-50 mix of antifreeze and water. This mixture gives best combination of anti-freeze and anti-boil characteristics for year-round driving.

9. Replace and tighten the radiator cap. Start the engine and check visually for leaks. Allow the engine to warm up fully and continue to check your work for signs of leakage. A very small leak may not be noticed until the system develops internal pressure.

Leaks at hose ends are generally clamp related and can be cured by snugging the clamp. Larger leaks may require removing the hose again--to do this you MUST WAIT UNTIL THE ENGINE HAS COOLED DOWN, GENERALLY A PERIOD OF HOURS. NEVER UNCAP A HOT RADIATOR. After all leaks are cured, check the coolant level in the radiator (with the engine cold) and top up as necessary.

Air Conditioning

NOTE: *This book contains simple testing procedures for your NOVA's or PRIZM's air conditioning system. More comprehensive testing, diagnosis and service procedures may be found in CHILTON'S GUIDE TO AIR CONDITIONING SERVICE AND REPAIR, book part number 7580, available from your local retailer.*

SAFETY PRECAUTIONS

There are two particular hazards associated with air conditioning systems and they both relate to refrigerant gas.

The refrigerant (generic designation: R-12, trade name: Freon, a registered trademark of the DuPont Co.) is an extremely cold substance. When exposed to air, it will instantly freeze any surface it comes in contact with, including your eyes.

The other hazard relates to fire. Although normally non-toxic, refrigerant gas becomes highly poisonous in the presence of an open flame. One good whiff of the vapor formed by refrigerant can be fatal. Keep all forms of fire (including cigarettes) well clear of the air conditioning system.

Further, it is being established that the chemicals in R-12 (dichlorodifluoromethane) contribute to the damage occuring in the upper atmosphere. The time may soon come when sophisticated recovery equipment will be necessary to prevent the release of this gas when working on an air condiitoning system. Any repair work should be left to a professional. DO NOT, under any circumstances, attempt to loosen or tighten any fittings or perform any work other than that outlined here.

SYSTEM CHECKS

A lot of A/C problems can be avoided by simply running the air conditioner at least once a week, regardless of the season. simply let the system run for at least 5 minutes a week (even in the winter), and you'll keep the internal parts lubricated as well as preventing the hoses from hardening.

Checking For Oil Leaks

Refrigerant leaks show up only as oily areas on the various components because the compressor oil is transported around the entire system along with the refrigerant. Look for oily spots on all the hoses and lines, and especially on the hose and tube connections. If there are oily deposits, the system may have a leak, and you should have it checked by a qualified repairman.

A small area of oil on the front of the compressor is normal and no cause for alarm.

Check the Compressor Belt

The compressor drive belt should be checked frequently for tension and condition. Refer to the section in this chapter on "Belts".

Keep the Condenser Clear

The condenser is mounted in front of the radiator (and is often mistaken for the radiator). It serves to remove heat from the air conditioning system and cool the refrigerant. Proper air flow through the condenser is critical to the operation of the system.

Periodically inspect the front of the condenser for bent fins or foreign material (dirt, bugs, leaves, etc.). If any cooling fins are bent, straighten them carefully with needle nose pliers. You can remove any debris with a stiff bristle brush or hose.

HOW TO SPOT BAD HOSES

Both the upper and lower radiator hoses are called upon to perform difficult jobs in an inhospitable environment. They are subject to nearly 18 psi at under hood temperatures often over 280°F., and must circulate nearly 7500 gallons of coolant an hour—3 good reasons to have good hoses.

A good test for any hose is to feel it for soft or spongy spots. Frequently these will appear as swollen areas of the hose. The most likely cause is oil soaking. This hose could burst at any time, when hot or under pressure.

Swollen hose

Cracked hoses can usually be seen but feel the hoses to be sure they have not hardened; a prime cause of cracking. This hose has cracked down to the reinforcing cords and could split at any of the cracks.

Cracked hose

Weakened clamps frequently are the cause of hose and cooling system failure. The connection between the pipe and hose has deteriorated enough to allow coolant to escape when the engine is hot.

Frayed hose end (due to weak clamp)

Debris, rust and scale in the cooling system can cause the inside of a hose to weaken. This can usually be felt on the outside of the hose as soft or thinner areas.

Debris in cooling system

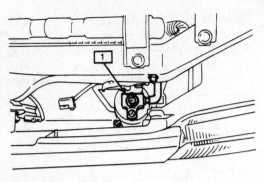

1 SIGHT GLASS

Location of receiver-dryer and sight glass on 89–90 Prizm

Refrigerant Level Check

The first order of business when checking the refrigerant is to find the sight glass. It is located in the head of the receiver/drier. On Novas, it's located to the left of the radiator, just behind the left headlights. On the Prizm, it's still behind the headlight, but in front of the condenser. Once you've found it, wipe it clean and proceed as follows:

1. With the engine and the air conditioning system running, look for the flow of refrigerant through the sight glass. If the air conditioner is working properly, you'll be able to see a continuous flow of clear refrigerant through the sight

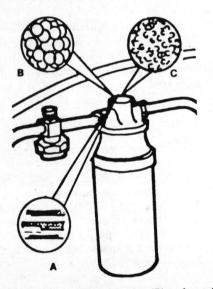

Oil streaks (A), constant bubbles (B) or foam (C) indicate there is not enough refrigerant in the system. Occasional bubbles during initial operation is normal. A clear sight glass indicates a proper charge of refrigerant or no refrigerant at all, which can be determined by the presence of cold air at the outlets in the car. If the glass is clouded with a milky white substance, have the receiver/drier checked professionally

glass, with perhaps an occasional bubble at very high temperatures.

2. Cycle the air conditioner on and off to make sure what you are seeing is refrigerant. Since the refrigerant is clear, it is possible to mistake a completely discharged system for one that is fully charged. Turn the system off and watch the sight glass. If there is refrigerant in the system, you'll see bubbles during the off cycle. If you observe no bubbles when the system is running and the air flow from the unit in the car is delivering cold air, everything is OK.

3. If you observe bubbles in the sight glass while the system is operating, the system is low on refrigerant. Have it checked by a professional.

4. Oil streaks in the sight glass are an indication of trouble. Most of the time, if you see oil in the sight glass, it will appear as series of streaks, although occasionally it may be a solid stream of oil.

In either case, it means that part of the charge has been lost. This is almost always accompanied by a reduction in cold air output within the car.

GAUGE SETS

Before attempting any charge-related work, you will need a set of A/C gauges. These are generally available from good parts suppliers and automotive tool suppliers. Generally described, this tool is a set of two gauges and three hoses. By connecting the proper hoses to the car's system, the gauges can be used to "see" the air conditioning system at work. The gauge set is also used to discharge and recharge the system.

Additionally, if a component must be removed from the system, a vacuum pump will be needed to evacuate (draw vacuum) within the system to eliminate any moisture which has entered during repairs. These pumps can be purchased outright; many find it easier to rent one from a supplier on an as-needed basis.

Small cans of refrigerant will be needed; make sure you purchase enough meet the capacity of the system. Since the refrigerant is measured by weight (generally in ounces), you'll need a small scale to weigh the refrigerant can(s) as the system is recharged.

DISCHARGING THE SYSTEM

CAUTION: *Wear protective goggles and gloves before proceeding with repairs.*

Connecting and disconnecting the gauges should always be done with the engine off to prevent injury from moving parts. To hook up the gauges, first make sure that the valves on the gauges are turned to the closed (off) position. The hose from the low-pressure gauge will

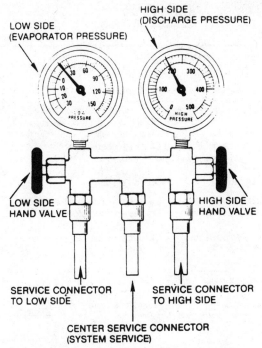

LOW SIDE
(EVAPORATOR PRESSURE)

HIGH SIDE
(DISCHARGE PRESSURE)

LOW SIDE
HAND VALVE

HIGH SIDE
HAND VALVE

SERVICE CONNECTOR
TO LOW SIDE

SERVICE CONNECTOR
TO HIGH SIDE

CENTER SERVICE CONNECTOR
(SYSTEM SERVICE)

Typical set of manifold gauges for the air conditioning system

attach to the low pressure side (suction) of the A/C system.

The Prizm has this connection on the compressor; it's labled "S". The fuel-injected Nova's low pressure connector is found in the piping on the firewall--it's the line that does NOT connect to the receiver-drier. Carbureted Novas have the low pressure connection in a vertical section of the A/C tubing on the right side of the engine near the fender; it's the line that couples to another short piece running to the compressor.

Once found, unscrew the dust cap from the valve and quickly connect the threaded fitting from the gauge hose.

Now connect the high pressure guage to the high pressure (discharge) side of the system. The connecting ports will be in the same area as the low pressure connectors.

WARNING: *Connect the hose quickly and carefully. Pressurized refrigerant will escape during the connecting procedure.*

To discharge the system:

1. Place the center hose of the gauge set into a container.

2. Slowly open the valve on the low-pressure gauge to allow refrigerant to flow into the container. You should just hear a light hissing, indicating a slow discharge from the system. If you empty the system too quickly you will drain the lubricating oil as well. This oil is critical to the system's well being and replacing it is not

within the scope of this book. If no discharge occurs, first check for proper hose hook-up. If all checks of your hook-up are OK, you may be attempting to discharge an already empty system.

3. Close the gauge valve when the gauge indicates zero pressure in the system. There should be very little, if any, oil in your drainage container. You have now discharged the system.

If you wish to thoroughly evacuate the system, follow the lettered steps below.

1. Confirm that high and low pressure hoses are correctly attached and secure on their fittings. Confirm that gauge valves are closed. Connect the center hose from the gauge set to the vacuum pump.

2. Start the vacuum pump, then open both gauge valves slowly and at the same time.

3. Run the pump until the low pressure gauge shows 28 in. of vacuum. Note the time that 28 in. is reached; if the temperature is above 85°F, run the pump another 30 minutes. If the temperature is below 85°F, run the pump another 50 minutes. The target value of 28 in. of vacuum is valid at or close to sea level. For every 1000 feet of altitude in your area, reduce the expected reading by 1 in. of vacuum. Example: At 2000 feet above sea level, you would expect a reading of 26 in. of vacuum.

4. When the pump has been run for the proper period of time, and the proper gauge readings have been maintained, close both gauge valves and shut off the pump. Disconnect the hose from the vacuum pump. The air conditioning system has now been evacuated and sealed. A system which is not leaking should hold this vacuum with the pump off.

RECHARGING THE SYSTEM

1. Confirm that the high and low pressure hoses are correctly connected and secure on their fittings. Confirm that the gauge valves are closed.

2. Attach the center hose to the R-12 refrigerant source, usually a 16-ounce can. Make sure the control valve for the can is closed before connecting.

3. Hang or position the can so that it stays upright during the remaining procedures. DO NOT turn the can upside down or on its side during charging. Severe damage to the system can occur.

4. Open the low pressure valve; make sure the high pressure valve is firmly closed.

5. Open the vehicle front doors, start the engine, and set the blower fan on top speed with the air conditioning controls ON and set for maximum cooling. Run the engine at 1000 rpm and begin filling the system. Use the scale to de-

Troubleshooting Basic Air Conditioning Problems

Problem	Cause	Solution
There's little or no air coming from the vents (and you're sure it's on)	• The A/C fuse is blown • Broken or loose wires or connections • The on/off switch is defective	• Check and/or replace fuse • Check and/or repair connections • Replace switch
The air coming from the vents is not cool enough	• Windows and air vent wings open • The compressor belt is slipping • Heater is on • Condenser is clogged with debris • Refrigerant has escaped through a leak in the system • Receiver/drier is plugged	• Close windows and vent wings • Tighten or replace compressor belt • Shut heater off • Clean the condenser • Check system • Service system
The air has an odor	• Vacuum system is disrupted • Odor producing substances on the evaporator case • Condensation has collected in the bottom of the evaporator housing	• Have the system checked/repaired • Clean the evaporator case • Clean the evaporator housing drains
System is noisy or vibrating	• Compressor belt or mountings loose • Air in the system	• Tighten or replace belt; tighten mounting bolts • Have the system serviced

Sight glass condition
  Constant bubbles, foam or oil streaks
  Clear sight glass, but no cold air
  Clear sight glass, but air is cold
  Clouded with milky fluid
	• Undercharged system
	• No refrigerant at all
	• System is OK
	• Receiver drier is leaking dessicant
		• Charge the system
		• Check and charge the system
		• Have system checked

Large difference in temperature of lines	• System undercharged	• Charge and leak test the system
Compressor noise	• Broken valves • Overcharged • Incorrect oil level • Piston slap • Broken rings • Drive belt pulley bolts are loose	• Replace the valve plate • Discharge, evacuate and install the correct charge • Isolate the compressor and check the oil level. Correct as necessary. • Replace the compressor • Replace the compressor • Tighten with the correct torque specification
Excessive vibration	• Incorrect belt tension • Clutch loose • Overcharged • Pulley is misaligned	• Adjust the belt tension • Tighten the clutch • Discharge, evacuate and install the correct charge • Align the pulley
Condensation dripping in the passenger compartment	• Drain hose plugged or improperly positioned • Insulation removed or improperly installed	• Clean the drain hose and check for proper installation • Replace the insulation on the expansion valve and hoses
Frozen evaporator coil	• Faulty thermostat • Thermostat capillary tube improperly installed • Thermostat not adjusted properly	• Replace the thermostat • Install the capillary tube correctly • Adjust the thermostat
Low side low—high side low	• System refrigerant is low • Expansion valve is restricted	• Evacuate, leak test and charge the system • Replace the expansion valve
Low side high—high side low	• Internal leak in the compressor—worn	• Remove the compressor cylinder head and inspect the compressor. Replace the valve plate assembly if necessary. If the compressor pistons, rings or

Troubleshooting Basic Air Conditioning Problems (cont.)

Problem	Cause	Solution
Low side high—high side low (cont.)		cylinders are excessively worn or scored replace the compressor
	• Cylinder head gasket is leaking	• Install a replacement cylinder head gasket
	• Expansion valve is defective	• Replace the expansion valve
	• Drive belt slipping	• Adjust the belt tension
Low side high—high side high	• Condenser fins obstructed	• Clean the condenser fins
	• Air in the system	• Evacuate, leak test and charge the system
	• Expansion valve is defective	• Replace the expansion valve
	• Loose or worn fan belts	• Adjust or replace the belts as necessary
Low side low—high side high	• Expansion valve is defective	• Replace the expansion valve
	• Restriction in the refrigerant hose	• Check the hose for kinks—replace if necessary
	• Restriction in the receiver/drier	• Replace the receiver/drier
	• Restriction in the condenser	• Replace the condenser
Low side and high side normal (inadequate cooling)	• Air in the system	• Evacuate, leak test and charge the system
	• Moisture in the system	• Evacuate, leak test and charge the system

termine total weight delivered into the system. DO NOT exceed the specified charge weight.

Change cans as necessary to achieve the correct total. Remember to shut off the can control valve before changing the can.

REFRIGERANT QUANTITIES:
All Nova and Prizm models, 1985-90
1.3 - 1.7 lbs

6. When the correct weight has been delivered into the system, shut off the can control valve. Run the engine for an additonal 30 seconds to clear the lines and gauges.

7. With the engine running, disconnect the low side hose from the connecting port. Then disconnect the high pressure side; hold the fitting down and unscrew it rapidly to avoid loss of refrigerant.

CAUTION: *NEVER disconnect any gauge hose at any fitting except the connecting port. Sudden loss of refrigerant could result.*

8. Replace the protective dust caps on the line fittings and shut off the engine.

Windshield Wipers

Intense heat and ultra-violet rays from the sun, snow, ice and frost,road oils, acid rain, and industrial pollution all combine quickly to deteriorate the rubber wiper refills. One pass on a frosty windshield can reduce a new set of refills to an unusable condition. The refills should be replaced about twice a year or whenever they begin to streak or chatter on wet glass.

Blade life can be prolonged by frequent cleanings of the glass with a rag and a commer-cial glass cleaner. The use of a ammonia based cleaner will ease the removal of built-up road oils and grease from the glass. Ammonia based cleaners are harmful to painted surfaces. Be careful when applying them and don't fill the washer jug with an ammonia based solvent; when used it will run onto the painted bodywork.

WINDSHIELD WASHER ADJUSTMENT

The washer spray direction can be adjusted by inserting a pin into the nozzle and turning it to the desired position.

WIPER BLADE REPLACEMENT

Normally, if the wipers are not cleaning the windshield properly, only the refill has to be replaced. The blade and arm usually require replacement only in the event of damage. It is only necessary (except on Tridon refills) to remove the arm or the blade to replace the refill (rubber part), though you may have to position the arm higher on the glass. You can do this by turning the ignition switch on and operating the wiper. When they are positioned where they are accessible, turn the ignition switch off.

There are several types of refills and your vehicle could have any kind, since aftermarket blades and arms may not use exactly the same type refill as the original equipment.

1. Lift the wiper arm off the glass.

2. Depress the release lever on the center bridge and remove the blade from the arm.

3. Lift the tab and pinch the end bridge to release it from the center bridge.

4. Slide the end bridge from the wiper blade and the wiper blade from the opposite end bridge.

5. Install a new element and be sure the tab on the end bridge is down to lock the element in place. Check each release point for positive engagement.

Most Trico styles use a release button that is pushed down to allow the refill to slide out of the release jaws. The new refill slides in and locks in place.

Some Trico refills are removed by locating where the metal backing strip or the refill is wider. Insert a small screwdriver blade between the frame and the metal backing strip. Press down to release the refill from the retaining tab.

The Anco style is unlocked at one end by squeezing two metal tabs, and the refill is slid out of the frame jaws. When the new refill is installed, the tabs will click into place, locking the refill.

The polycarbonate type is held in place by a locking lever that is pushed downward out of the groove in the arm to free the refill. When the new refill is installed, it will lock in place automatically.

The Tridon refill has a plastic backing strip with a notch about an inch from the end. Hold the blade (frame) on a hard surface so that frame is tightly bowed. Grip the tip of the backing strip and pull up while twisting counterclockwise. The backing strip will snap out of the retaining tab. Do this for the remaining tabs

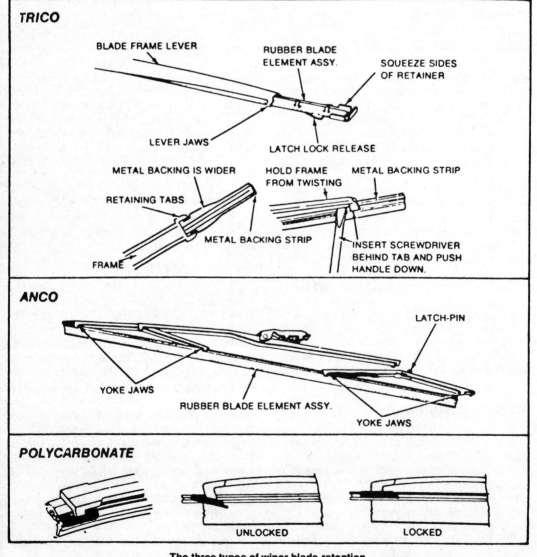

The three types of wiper blade retention

until the refill is free of the arm. The length of these refills is molded into the end and they should be replaced with identical types.

No matter which type of refill you use, be sure that all of the frame claws engage the refill. Before operating the wipers, be sure that no part of the metal frame is contacting the windshield.

Tires and Wheels

Common sense and good driving habits will afford maximum tire life. Fast starts, sudden stops and hard cornering are hard on tires and will shorten their useful life span. If you start at normal speeds, allow yourself sufficient time to stop, and take corners at a reasonable speed, the life of your tires will increase greatly. Also make sure that you don't overload your vehicle or run with incorrect pressure in the tires. Both of these practices increase tread wear.

Inspect your tires frequently. Be especially careful to watch for bubbles in the tread or side wall, deep cuts, or underinflation. Remove any

A penny works as well as anything for checking tread depth; when the top of Lincoln's head is visible, it's time for new tires

Tread wear indicators will appear when the tire is worn out

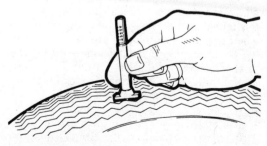

Tread depth can also be checked with an inexpensive gauge

tires with bubbles. If the cuts are so deep that they penetrate to the cords, discard the tire. Any cut in the sidewall of a radial tire renders it unsafe. Also look for uneven tread wear patterns that indicate that the front end is out of alignment or that the tires are out of balance.

TIRE ROTATION

So that the tires wear more uniformly, it is recommended that the tires be rotated every 7,500 miles. This can only be done when all four tires are of the same size and load rating capacity. Any abnormal wear should be investigated and the cause corrected.

Radial tires may be cross-switched; newer production methods have eliminated the need to keep them on one side of the car. Studded snow tires will lose their studs if their direction of rotation is reversed.

NOTE: *Mark the wheel position or direction of rotation on radial studded snow tires before removal.*

CAUTION: *Avoid overtightening the lug nuts or the brake disc or drum may become permanently distorted. Alloy wheels can be cracked by overtightening. The specified lug nut torque is 76 ft. lbs. for Nova and Prizm cars. Always tighten the nuts in a criss-cross pattern.*

TIRE DESIGN

When buying new tires, you should keep the following points in mind, especially if you are switching to larger tires or a different profile series (50, 60, 70, 78):

1. All four tires should be of the same construction type. Radial, bias, or bias-belted tires should not be mixed. Radial tires are highly recommended for their excellent handling and fuel mileage characteristics. All Novas and Prisms are delivered with radial tires as standard equipment.

2. The wheels must be the correct width for

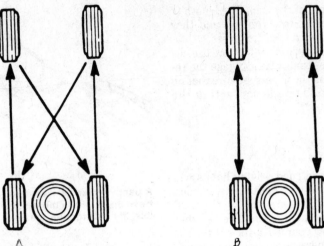

Tire rotation patterns. 'A' is recommended, 'B' is acceptable. Note that the spare tire is not used in the rotation

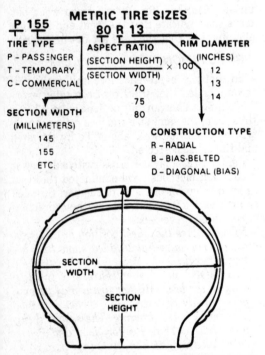

METRIC TIRE SIZES

P 155   80 R 13

TIRE TYPE
P – PASSENGER
T – TEMPORARY
C – COMMERCIAL

ASPECT RATIO
(SECTION HEIGHT)
———————— × 100
(SECTION WIDTH)
     70
     75
     80

RIM DIAMETER
(INCHES)
12
13
14

SECTION WIDTH
(MILLIMETERS)
145
155
ETC.

CONSTRUCTION TYPE
R – RADIAL
B – BIAS-BELTED
D – DIAGONAL (BIAS)

SECTION WIDTH

SECTION HEIGHT

Common (P-Metric) tire coding. A performance code such as H or V may appear before the R; the designation 'M+S' may appear at the end of the code to indicate a snow or all-season tire

the tire. Tire dealers have charts of tire and wheel compatibility. A mismatch can cause sloppy handling and rapid tread wear. The tread width should match the rim width (inside bead to inside bead) within an inch. For radial tires the rim width should be 80% or less of the tire (not tread) width. The illustration gives an example of a tire size designation number.

3. The height (mounted diameter) of the new tires can change speedometer accuracy, engine speed per given road speed, fuel mileage, acceleration, and ground clearance. Tire manufacturers furnish full measurement specifications to their dealers.

4. The spare tire should be usable, at least for low speed operation, with the new tires. Novas and Prizms use a space-saving spare tire mounted on a special wheel. This wheel and tire is for emergency use only. Never try to mount a regular tire on a special spare wheel.

5. There shouldn't be any body interference when the car is loaded, on bumps or in turning through maximum range.

TIRE INFLATION

The importance of proper tire inflation cannot be overemphasized. A tire employs air under pressure as part of its structure. It is designed around the supporting strength of air at a specified pressure. For this reason, improper inflation drastically reduces the tire's ability to perform as it was intended. A tire will lose some air in day-to-day use; having to add a few pounds of air periodically is not necessarily a sign of a leaking tire.

Tire pressures should be checked regularly with a reliable pressure gauge. Too often the gauge on the end of the air hose at your corner garage is not accurate enough because it suffers too much abuse. Always check tire pressure when the tires are cold, as pressure increases with temperature. If you must move the vehicle to check the tire inflation, do not drive more than a mile before checking. A cold tire is one that has not been driven for a period of about three hours.

CAUTION: *Never exceed the maximum tire pressure embossed on the tire. This maximum pressure is rarely the correct pressure for everyday driving. Consult your owners'*

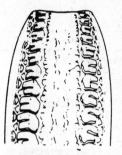

- **DRIVE WHEEL HEAVY ACCELERATION**
- **OVERINFLATION**

- **HARD CORNERING**
- **UNDERINFLATION**
- **LACK OF ROTATION**

Examples of inflation-related tire wear patterns. As little as two pounds under specification can induce premature wear

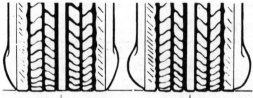

PROPERLY INFLATED   IMPROPERLY INFLATED

RADIAL TIRE

Radial tires have a characteristic sidewall bulge; don't try to measure tire pressure by looking at the tire. Use a quality air gauge

manual for the proper tire pressures for your vehicle.

CARE OF SPECIAL WHEELS

If you have invested money in magnesium, aluminum alloy or sport wheels, special precautions should be taken to make sure your investment is not wasted and that your special wheels look good for the lifetime of the car.

Special wheels are easily scratched and/or damaged. Occasionally check the rims for cracking, impact damage or air leaks. If any of these ae found, replace the wheel. In order to prevent this type of damage, and the costly replacement of a special wheel, observe the following precautions:

- Use extra care not to damage the wheels during removal, installation, balancing, etc. After removal of the wheels from the car, place them on a mat or other protective surface. If they are to be stored for any length of time, suppport them on strips of wood. Never store tires upright--the tread will develop flat spots.
- While driving, watch for sharp obstacles.
- When washing, use a mild detergent and water. Avoid cleansers with abrasives or the use of hard brushes. There are many cleaners and polishes for special wheels. Use them.
- If possible, remove your special wheels from the car during the winter months. Salt and sand used for snow removal can severly damage the finish.

Troubleshooting Basic Wheel Problems

Problem	Cause	Solution
The car's front end vibrates at high speed	• The wheels are out of balance • Wheels are out of alignment	• Have wheels balanced • Have wheel alignment checked/adjusted
Car pulls to either side	• Wheels are out of alignment • Unequal tire pressure • Different size tires or wheels	• Have wheel alignment checked/adjusted • Check/adjust tire pressure • Change tires or wheels to same size
The car's wheel(s) wobbles	• Loose wheel lug nuts • Wheels out of balance • Damaged wheel • Wheels are out of alignment • Worn or damaged ball joint • Excessive play in the steering linkage (usually due to worn parts) • Defective shock absorber	• Tighten wheel lug nuts • Have tires balanced • Raise car and spin the wheel. If the wheel is bent, it should be replaced • Have wheel alignment checked/adjusted • Check ball joints • Check steering linkage • Check shock absorbers
Tires wear unevenly or prematurely	• Incorrect wheel size • Wheels are out of balance • Wheels are out of alignment	• Check if wheel and tire size are compatible • Have wheels balanced • Have wheel alignment checked/adjusted

Troubleshooting Basic Tire Problems

Problem	Cause	Solution
The car's front end vibrates at high speeds and the steering wheel shakes	• Wheels out of balance • Front end needs aligning	• Have wheels balanced • Have front end alignment checked
The car pulls to one side while cruising	• Unequal tire pressure (car will usually pull to the low side) • Mismatched tires • Front end needs aligning	• Check/adjust tire pressure • Be sure tires are of the same type and size • Have front end alignment checked
Abnormal, excessive or uneven tire wear See "How to Read Tire Wear"	• Infrequent tire rotation • Improper tire pressure • Sudden stops/starts or high speed on curves	• Rotate tires more frequently to equalize wear • Check/adjust pressure • Correct driving habits
Tire squeals	• Improper tire pressure • Front end needs aligning	• Check/adjust tire pressure • Have front end alignment checked

Tire Size Comparison Chart

"Letter" sizes			Inch Sizes	Metric-inch Sizes		
"60 Series"	"70 Series"	"78 Series"	1965–77	"60 Series"	"70 Series"	"80 Series"
			5.50-12, 5.60-12	165/60-12	165/70-12	155-12
		Y78-12	6.00-12			
		W78-13	5.20-13	165/60-13	145/70-13	135-13
		Y78-13	5.60-13	175/60-13	155/70-13	145-13
			6.15-13	185/60-13	165/70-13	155-13, P155/80-13
A60-13	A70-13	A78-13	6.40-13	195/60-13	175/70-13	165-13
B60-13	B70-13	B78-13	6.70-13	205/60-13	185/70-13	175-13
			6.90-13			
C60-13	C70-13	C78-13	7.00-13	215/60-13	195/70-13	185-13
D60-13	D70-13	D78-13	7.25-13			
E60-13	E70-13	E78-13	7.75-13			195-13
			5.20-14	165/60-14	145/70-14	135-14
			5.60-14	175/60-14	155/70-14	145-14
			5.90-14			
A60-14	A70-14	A78-14	6.15-14	185/60-14	165/70-14	155-14
	B70-14	B78-14	6.45-14	195/60-14	175/70-14	165-14
	C70-14	C78-14	6.95-14	205/60-14	185/70-14	175-14
D60-14	D70-14	D78-14				
E60-14	E70-14	E78-14	7.35-14	215/60-14	195/70-14	185-14
F60-14	F70-14	F78-14, F83-14	7.75-14	225/60-14	200/70-14	195-14
G60-14	G70-14	G77-14, G78-14	8.25-14	235/60-14	205/70-14	205-14
H60-14	H70-14	H78-14	8.55-14	245/60-14	215/70-14	215-14
J60-14	J70-14	J78-14	8.85-14	255/60-14	225/70-14	225-14
L60-14	L70-14		9.15-14	265/60-14	235/70-14	
	A70-15	A78-15	5.60-15	185/60-15	165/70-15	155-15
B60-15	B70-15	B78-15	6.35-15	195/60-15	175/70-15	165-15
C60-15	C70-15	C78-15	6.85-15	205/60-15	185/70-15	175-15
	D70-15	D78-15				
E60-15	E70-15	E78-15	7.35-15	215/60-15	195/70-15	185-15
F60-15	F70-15	F78-15	7.75-15	225/60-15	205/70-15	195-15
G60-15	G70-15	G78-15	8.15-15/8.25-15	235/60-15	215/70-15	205-15
H60-15	H70-15	H78-15	8.45-15/8.55-15	245/60-15	225/70-15	215-15
J60-15	J70-15	J78-15	8.85-15/8.90-15	255/60-15	235/70-15	225-15
	K70-15		9.00-15	265/60-15	245/70-15	230-15
L60-15	L70-15	L78-15, L84-15	9.15-15			235-15
	M70-15	M78-15				255-15
		N78-15				

Note: Every size tire is not listed and many size comparisons are approximate, based on load ratings. Wider tires than those supplied new with the vehicle, should always be checked for clearance.

• Make sure that the recommended lug nut torque is never exceeded or the wheel may crack. Never use snow chains on special wheels; severe scratching will occur.

FLUID AND LUBRICANTS

Fuel and Engine Oil Recommendations

FUEL

All Chevrolet Novas and Prizms use unleaded fuel of 91 research octane (RON) or higher. Regular leaded fuel may not be used in these models because they are equipped with a catalytic converter for emission control purposes. Leaded fuel will render the converter useless, raising the emission content of the exhaust to illegal and environmentally unacceptable levels. It will also block the converter passages, increasing exhaust back pressure; in extreme cases, exhaust blockage will be raised to the point where the engine will not run.

Fuels of the same octane rating have varying anti-knock qualities. Thus if your engine knocks or pings, try switching brands of gasoline before trying a more expensive higher octane fuel.

Your engine's fuel requirements can change with time, due to carbon buildup which changes the compression ratio. If switching brands or

grades of gas doesn't work, check the ignition timing. If it is necessary to retard timing from specifications, don't change it more than about four degrees. Retarding the timing will reduce power output and fuel mileage, and increase engine temperature.

ENGINE OIL

The SAE (Society of Automotive Engineers) grade number indicates the viscosity of the engine oil, or its ability to lubricate under a given temperature. The lower the SAE grade number, the lighter the oil; the lower the viscosity, the easier it is to crank the engine in cold weather.

Oil viscosities should be chosen from the oils recommended for the lowest anticipated temperatures during the oil change interval. Multiviscosity oils (10W-30, 20W-50 etc.) offer the important advantage of being adaptable to temperature extremes. They allow easy starting at low temperatures, yet they give good protection at high speeds and engine temperatures. This is a decided advantage in changeable climates or in long distance touring.

The API (American Petroleum Institute) designation indicates the classification of engine oil for use under given operating conditions. Only oils designated for Service SE/SF, or just SF, should be used. These oils provide maximum engine protection. Both the SAE grade number and the API designation can be found on the top of a can of oil.

For recommended oil viscosities, refer to the chart. Note that the 10W-30 and 10W-40 grade

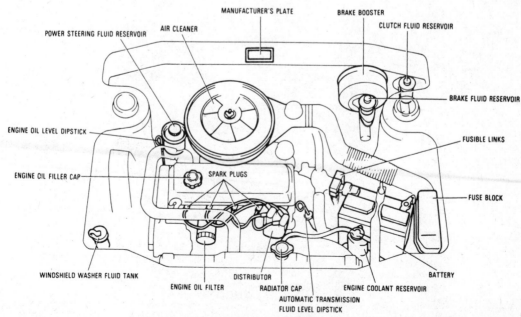

Engine compartment fluid check location, 4A-LC engine

oils are not recommended for sustained high speed driving when the temperature rises above the indicated limit.

NOTE: *Non-detergent or straight mineral oils should not be used. Oil viscosities should be chosen from those oils recommended for the lowest anticipated temperatures during the oil change interval.*

Engine

OIL LEVEL CHECK

CAUTION: *Prolonged and repeated skin contact with used engine oil, with no effort to remove the oil, can be harmful.*

Always follow these simple precautions when handling used motor oil:

• Avoid prolonged skin contact with used motor oil.

• Remove oil from skin by washing thoroughly with soap and water or waterless hand cleaner. Do not use gasoline, thinners or other solvents.

• Avoid prolonged skin contact with oil soaked clothing.

The engine oil should be checked on a regular basis, ideally at each fuel stop. If the car is used for trailer towing, or for heavy-duty use, it would be wise to check it more often.

When checking the oil level, it is best that the oil be at operating temperature, although checking the level immediately after stopping will give a false reading because not all of the oil will have drained back into the crankcase. Be sure that the car is on a level surface, allowing time for all of the oil to drain back into the crankcase.

1. Open the hood and locate the dipstick. It is located on the right hand (passenger's side) of the engine.

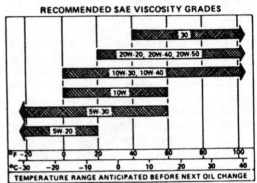

RECOMMENDED SAE VISCOSITY GRADES

NOTICE: Do not use SAE 5W-20 oils for continuous high-speed driving.

Oil viscosity chart

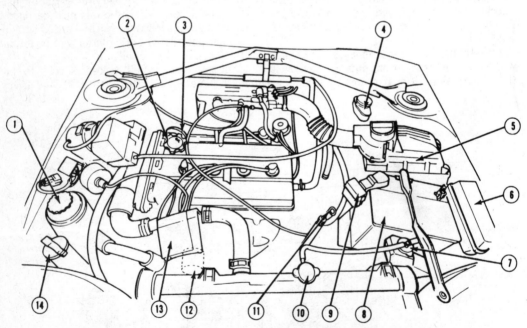

1. Power steering fluid reservoir
2. Engine oil filler cap
3. Engine oil dipstick
4. Brake fluid reservoir
5. Air filter
6. Fuse block
7. Coolant recovery tank
8. Battery
9. Fusible links
10. Radiator cap
11. Transmission fluid level dipstick
12. Oil filter
13. Distributor
14. Windshield washer reservoir

Engine compartment fluid check locations, 4A-GE and 4A-FE engines

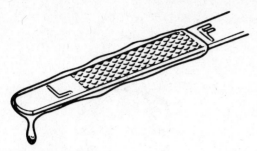

Typical oil dipstick

2. Remove the dipstick and wipe it clean with a rag.

3. Insert the dipstick fully into the tube and remove it again. Hold the dipstick horizontally and read the oil level on the dipstick. The level should be between the F (Full) and L (Low) marks. If the oil level is at or below the L mark, sufficient oil should be added to restore the level to the proper place. Oil is added through the capped opening in the top of the valve cover.

4. Replace the dipstick and check the level after adding oil. Be careful not to overfill the crankcase.

ENGINE OIL AND FILTER CHANGE

The engine oil and oil filter should always be changed together. To skip an oil filter change is to leave a quart of contaminated oil in the engine as well as a contaminated filter. Engine oil and filter must be changed at least as specified in the Maintenance Intervals chart.

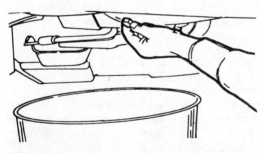

By keeping an inward pressure on the drain plug as you unscrew it, the oil won't escape past the threads

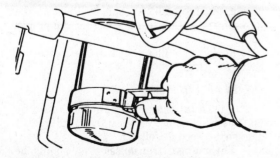

Remove the oil filter with a strap wrench

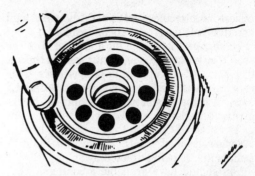

Lubricate the gasket on the new filter with clean engine oil. A dry gasket may not make a good seal and will allow the filter to leak

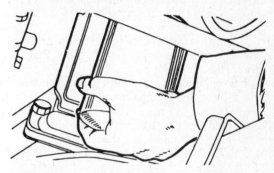

Install the new oil filter by hand

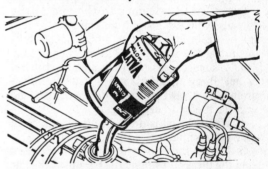

Add oil through the cylinder head cover only

NOTE: *Certain operating conditions may warrant more frequent changes. If the vehicle is used for short trips, water condensation and low-temperature deposits may make it necessary to change the oil sooner. If the vehicle is used mostly in stop-and-go city traffic, corrosive acids and high-temperature deposits may necessitate shorter oil changing intervals. The shorter intervals are also true for industrial or rural areas where high concentration of dust contaminate the oil. Cars used for carrying heavy loads, pulling trailers, or in mountainous areas may also need more frequent oil and filter changes.*

The type of motors used in the Nova and Prism--overhead camshaft--are particularly sensitive to proper lubrication with clean oil. Don't risk an expensive repair by neglecting the easiest maintenance on the car. Change the oil and filter regularly--it's cheap insurance.

To change the engine oil and filter, the car should be parked on a level surface and the engine should be at operating temperature. This is to ensure that foreign matter will be drained away with the oil and not left behind in the engine to form sludge, which will happen if the engine is drained cold. Oil that is slightly brownish when drained is a good sign that the contaminants are being drained away.

You should have available a container that will hold at least five quarts, a wrench to fit the oil drain plug, a spout for pouring in new oil and some rags to clean up the inevitable mess. If the filter is being replaced, you will also need a band wrench to fit the filter.

1. Position the car on a level surface and set the parking brake or block the wheels. Slide a drain pan under the oil drain plug.

2. From under the car, loosen, but do not remove the oil drain plug. Cover your hand with a heavy rag or glove and slowly unscrew the drain plug. Push the plug against the threads to prevent oil from leaking past the threads.

CAUTION: *The engine oil will be hot. Keep your arms, face and hands away from the oil as it drains out.*

3. As the plug comes to the end of the threads, whisk it away from the hole, letting the oil drain into the pan, which hopefully is still under the drain plug. This method usually avoids the messy task of reaching into a tub full of hot, dirty oil to retrieve a usually elusive drain plug. Crawl out from under the car and wait for the oil to drain.

4. When the oil is drained, install the drain plug and tighten it.

5. Loosen the filter with a band wrench and spin the filter off by hand. Be careful of the one quart of hot, dirty oil that inevitably overflows the filter.

6. Coat the rubber gasket on a new filter with clean engine oil and install the filter. Screw the filter onto the mounting stud and tighten according to the directions on the filter. Do not overtighten the filter; it may rupture under pressure and instantly deliver 5 quarts of oil onto the ground.

7. Refill the engine with the specified amount of clean engine oil. Be sure to use the proper viscosity. Pour the oil in through the opening in the valve cover.

8. Run the engine for several minutes, checking for oil pressure and leaks. The oil warning light on the dash should go out after a few seconds of engine operation. A few minutes after the engine is shut off, check the level of the oil and add if necessary.

NOTE: *Please dispose of used motor oil*

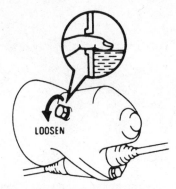

Checking the oil level with your finger

properly. Do not throw it in the trash or pour it on the ground. Take it to your dealer or local service station for recycling.

Manual Transaxle

FLUID RECOMMENDATIONS

The specified gear lubricant for all Nova and Prizm cars is SAE 75W-90 or SAE 80W-90 GL-5.

FLUID LEVEL CHECK

The oil in the manual transmission should be checked at least every 15,000 miles and replaced every 25,000-30,000 miles.

1. With the car parked on a level surface, remove the filler plug from the side of the transaxle housing.

2. If the lubricant begins to trickle out of the hole, there is enough lubricant. Otherwise, carefully insert your fingers (watch out for sharp threads) and check to see if the oil is up to the edge of the hole.

CAUTION: *Used motor oil may cause skin cancer if repeatedly left in contact with the skin for prolonged periods. Although this is unlikely unless you handle oil on a daily basis, it is wise to thoroughly wash your hands with soap and water immediately after handling used motor oil.*

3. If not, add oil through the hole until the level is at the edge of the hole. Most gear lubricants come in a plastic squeeze bottle with a nozzle, making additions simple. Refer to the Recommended Lubricants chart for the proper oil.

4. Replace the filler plug, run the engine and check for leaks.

DRAIN AND REFILL

The manual transmission oil should be changed at least every 30,0000 miles. To change, proceed as follows:

1. The manual transmission oil should be hot before it is drained. If the car is driven until

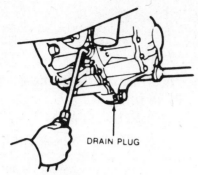

Manual transaxle refill

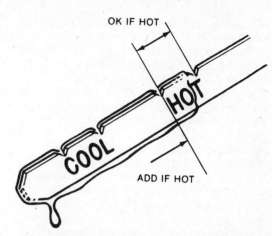

OK IF HOT

HOT

COOL

ADD IF HOT

Always checks automatic transmission fluid when fully warmed up. The fluid level should always be between the notches

the engine is at normal operating temperature, the oil should be hot enough.

2. Remove the cover under the left hand side of the engine. You may wish to jack and support the car to gain access and make the work easier. The car will need to be lowered onto level ground before refilling the transaxle with fresh oil.

3. Remove the filler plug to provide a vent. If the car is elevated, you may encounter spillage as the fill plug is removed.

4. Locate the drain plug on the bottom of the transaxle. Place a large container underneath the transaxle and remove the plug.

CAUTION: *The oil will be hot. Protect your hands and arms.*

5. Allow the oil to drain completely. Clean off the plug and reinstall it.
Tighten it until it is just snug. If the car is elevated, lower it to a level position.

6. Fill the transaxle with SAE 75W-90 or 80W-90 gear oil. This usually comes in a plastic squeeze bottle with a long nozzle; otherwise you can use an oil siphon gun available at most auto parts stores. Refer to the Capacities Chart for the proper amount of oil to put in.

7. Add new oil until it begins to run out of the filler hole.

8. Replace the filler plug, drive the car for a few minutes, stop, and check for leaks.

NOTE: *Please dispose of used oil properly. Do not throw it in the trash or pour it on the ground. Take it to your dealer or local service station for recycling.*

Automatic Transmission

FLUID RECOMMENDATIONS

The correct automatic transmission fluid for all Nova and Prizm cars is Dexron® II. There are no acceptable substitutes; internal damage may result if other fluids are used.

FLUID LEVEL CHECK

Check the automatic transmission fluid level at least every 5,000 miles (more often if possi-

ble). The dipstick is in the engine compartment between the battery and the distributor.

The fluid level should be checked only when the transmission is hot (normal operating temperature). The transmission is considered hot after about 20 miles of highway driving.

1. Park the car on a level surface with the engine idling. Shift the transmission into Neutral and set the parking brake.

2. Remove the dipstick, wipe it clean and reinsert it firmly. Be sure that it has been pushed all the way in. Remove the dipstick and check the fluid level while holding it horizontally. With the engine running, the fluid level should be between the notches in the "HOT" range on the dipstick.

3. If the fluid level is below the second notch, add Dexron® II automatic transmission fluid through the dipstick tube. This is easily done with the aid of a long-necked funnel. Check the level often as you are filling the transmission. Be extremely careful not to overfill it. Overfilling will cause slippage, seal damage and overheating. Approximately one pint of ATF will raise the level from one notch to the other.

WARNING: *The fluid on the dipstick should always be a bright red color. If it is discolored (black or brown), or smells burnt, serious transmission troubles, probably due to overheating, should be suspected. The transmission should be inspected by a qualified service technician to locate the cause of burnt fluid.*

DRAIN AND REFILL

The automatic transmission fluid should be changed at least every 30,000 miles. If the car is normally used in severe service, such as stop-and-go driving, trailer towing or the like, the interval should be halved. The fluid should be hot before it is drained; a 20 minute drive will accomplish this.

The automatic transmission has a drain plug so that if you're in a hurry, you can simply remove the plug, drain the fluid, replace the plug, and then refill the transaxle. Although this method is fine, a slightly longer procedure may be more effective on Novas and is required for Prizms.

1. Remove the plug and drain the fluid. When the fluid stops coming out of the drain hole, loosen the pan retaining screws until the pan can be pulled down at one corner. If the pan is stuck, tap the edges lightly with a plastic mallet to loosen it; DON't pry it or wedge a screwdriver into the seam. Lower the corner of the pan and allow the remaining fluid to drain out.

2. After the pan has drained completely, remove the pan retaining screws and then remove the pan and gasket.

3. Clean the pan thoroughly and allow it to air dry. If you wipe it out with a rag you run the risk of leaving bits of lint in the pan which will clog the tiny hydraulic passages in the transaxle.

4. With the pan removed on Prizm vehicles, the transmission filter is visible. The filter should be changed any time the transmission oil is drained. Remove the three bolts holding the filter and remove the filter.

WARNING: *The bolts are three different lengths and must be reinstalled in their correct locations. Take great care not to interchange them.*

5. Clean the mating surfaces for the oil pan and the filter; make sure all traces of the old gasket material is removed.

6. On Prizms, install the new filter. Install the three bolts in their correct locations and tighten only to 7½ ft. lbs. (89 inch-lbs.)

7. Install the pan using a new gasket.

8. Install the drain plug.

9. It is a good idea to measure the amount of fluid drained from the transaxle to determine the correct amount of fresh fluid to the be added. This is because some parts of the transaxle may not drain completely.

NOTE: *Do not overfill the transaxle. The automatic transaxle and the differential are separate units.*

10. With the engine off, add new Dexron® II fluid through the dipstick tube. The refill capacity is 2.4 quarts.

11. Start the engine and shift the gear selector into all positions from P through L, allowing each gear to engage momentarily. Shift into P. DO NOT race the engine.

12. With the engine idling, check the fluid level. Add fluid up to the COOL level on the dipstick.

NOTE: *Please dispose of used oil properly. Do not throw it in the trash or pour it on the ground. Take it to your dealer or local service station for recycling.*

Automatic Transmission Differential (Final Drive Unit)
FLUID RECOMMENDATIONS

The correct automatic transmission differential fluid for all Nova and Prizm cars is Dexron® II. There are no acceptable substitutes; internal damage may result if other fluids are used.

FLUID LEVEL CHECK

The oil in the differential should be checked at least every 5,000 miles and replaced every 20,000 miles.

1. With the car parked on a level surface, remove the filler plug from the SIDE of the differential.

NOTE: *The plug on the bottom of the differential is the drain plug.*

WARNING:
Do not confuse the differential filler plug with the filler plug for the transaxle.

2. If the lubricant begins to trickle out of the hole, there is enough lubricant. Otherwise, carefully insert your finger (watch out for sharp threads) and check to see if the oil is up to the edge of the hole.

CAUTION: *Used oil may cause skin cancer if repeatedly left in contact with the skin for prolonged periods. Although this is unlikely unless you handle oil on a daily basis, it is wise to thoroughly wash your hands with soap and water immediately after handling used oil.*

3. If the oil is not up to level, add oil through the hole until the level is at the edge of the hole. Most gear lubricants come in a plastic squeeze bottle with a nozzle, making additions simple. The differential uses Dexron® II automatic transmission fluid.

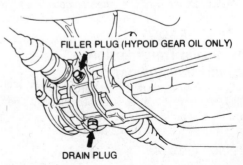

Filler and drain plug locations on the front differential

4. Replace the filler plug, run the engine and check for leaks.

DRAIN AND REFILL

The fluid in the differential should be changed at least every 20,000 miles.
To drain and fill the differential, proceed as follows:

1. Park the vehicle on a level surface. Set the parking brake.
2. Remove the filler (upper) plug. Place a container which is large enough to catch all of the differential fluid under the drain plug.
3. Remove the drain (lower) plug and allow all of the oil to drain into the container.
4. Install the drain plug. Tighten it so that it will not leak, but do not overtighten.
5. Refill with 1.5 quarts of Dexron® II automatic transmission fluid. Be sure that the level reaches the bottom of the filler plug.
6. Replace the filler plug, run the engine and check for leaks.

NOTE: *Please dispose of used oil properly. Do not throw it in the trash or pour it on the ground. Take it to your dealer or local service station for recycling.*

Cooling System

FLUID RECOMMENDATIONS

The correct coolant for the Nova and Prizm is any permanent, high quality ethylene glycol antifreeze mixed in a 50-50 concentration with water. This mixture gives the best combination of anti-freeze and anti-boil characteristics within the engine. Do not run the system filled with straight antifreeze or straight water; temperature extremes could damage the engine. For example, undiluted antifreeze will freeze at −8°F while a 50-50 mixture of antifreeze and tapwater freezes at −34°F.

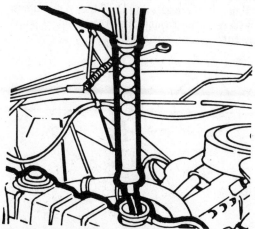

The freezing protection rating can be checked with an antifreeze tester

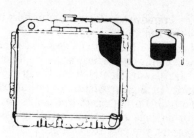

Check the coolant lever in the expansion tank

FLUID LEVEL CHECK

CAUTION: *Always allow the car to sit and cool for an hour or so (longer is better) before removing the radiator cap. To avoid injury when working on a warm engine, cover the radiator cap with a thick cloth and turn it slowly counterclockwise until the pressure begins to escape.*

Never remove the radiator cap until the expansion tank cap is removed. After the pressure is completely removed, remove the cap. Never remove the cap until the pressure is gone.

It's best to check the coolant level when the engine is cold. The radiator coolant level should be between the LOW and the FULL lines on the expansion tank when the engine is cold. If low, check for leakage and add coolant up to the FULL line but do not overfill it. There must be room in the jug for normal expansion of hot fluids.

DRAIN AND REFILL

The engine coolant should be changed every 30,000 miles or three years, whichever comes first. Replacing the coolant is necessary to remove the scale, rust and chemical by-products which build up in the system. This potentially messy job involves working under the car and handling antifreeze, a slippery, smelly, stain-making chemical. Have a large drain pan or bucket available along with healthy supply of rags. Be prepared to deal with fluid spills immediately. See the previous list of Do's and Don'ts for other hints.

1. Draining the cooling system is always done with the motor cold. Attempting to drain hot coolant is very foolish; you can be badly scalded.
2. Remove the radiator cap.
3. Position the drain pan under the drain cock on the bottom of the radiator. Additionally, the Nova/Prizm engines have a drain cock on the side of the engine block, near the oil filter. This should be opened to aid in draining the cooling system completely. If for some reason the radiator drain cock can't be used, you can

loosen and remove the lower radiator hose at its joint to the radiator.

4. If the lower hose is to be used as the drain, loosen the clamp on the hose and slide it back so it's out of the way. Gently break the grip of the hose on its fitting by twisting or prying with a suitable tool. Do not exert too much force or you will damage the radiator fitting. As the hose loosens, you can expect a gush of fluid to come out--be ready.

Remove the hose end from the radiator and direct the hose into the drain pan. You now have fluid running from both the hose and the radiator.

WARNING: *Housepets and small animals are attracted to the odor and taste of engine coolant (antifreeze). It is a highly poisonous mixture of chemicals; special care must be taken to protect open containers and spillage.*

5. When the system stops draining, close both draincocks.

6. In a bucket or similar large container, mix a 50-50 solution of antifreeze and water. Using a funnel, fill the radiator with this solution. Allow time for the fluid to run through the hoses and into the engine.

7. Fill the radiator to just below the neck. With the radiator cap off, start the engine and let it idle; this will circulate the coolant and begin to eliminate air in the system. Top up the radiator as the level drops.

8. When the level is reasonably stable, shut the engine off, and replace the radiator cap. Fill the expansion tank to a level halfway between the LOW and FULL lines and cap the expansion tank.

9. Drive the car for 10 or 15 minutes; the temperature gauge should be fully within the normal operating range. It is helpful to set the heater to its hottest setting while driving--this circulates the coolant throughout the entire system and helps eliminate air bubbles.

10. After the engine has cooled (2-3 hours), check the level in the radiator and the expansion tank, topping up as necessary.

CLEANING AND FLUSHING THE COOLING SYSTEM

Proceed with draining the system as outlined above. When the system has drained, reconnect any hoses close the radiator draincock. Move the temperature control for the heater to its hottest position; this allows the heater core to be flushed as well. Using a garden hose or bucket, fill the radiator and allow the water to run out the engine drain cock. Continue until the water runs clear. Be sure to clean the expansion tank as well.

If the system is badly contaminated with rust or scale, you can use a commercial flushing solu-tion to clean it out. Follow the manufacturer's instructions. Some causes of rust are air in the system, failure to change the coolant regularly, use of excessively hard or soft water, and/or failure to use the correct mix of antifreeze and water.

After the system has been flushed, continue with the refill procedures outlined above. Check the condition of the radiator cap and its gasket, replacing the cap if anything looks improper.

Brake and Clutch Master Cylinders
FLUID RECOMMENDATIONS

Both the hydraulic brake system and the hydraulic clutch system use brake fluid in the lines. Select a quality fluid meeting DOT 3 or DOT 4 specifications. DO NOT use brake fluid from previously opened containers which have been sitting around for any length of time--it will have absorbed enough moisture from the air to make it useless.

FLUID LEVEL CHECK

The brake and clutch master cylinders are located under the hood in the left rear section of the engine compartment. They are made of translucent plastic so that the levels may be checked without removing the tops. The fluid level in both reservoirs should be checked at least every 5,000 miles. The fluid level should be maintained at the uppermost mark on the side of the reservoir. Any sudden decrease in the level indicates a possible leak in the system and should be checked out immediately.

NOTE: *Normal brake wear will cause the fluid level to drop over a period of time. The fluid isn't leaking--it's simply relocated within the system.*

When making additions of brake or clutch fluid, use only fresh, uncontaminated brake fluid meeting or exceeding DOT 3 or 4 standards. Be careful not to spill any brake fluid on painted surfaces, as it eats paint.

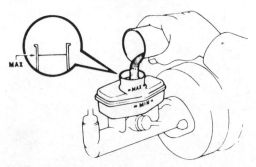

Always fill the master cylinder slowly so as not to create air bubbles in the system

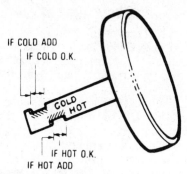

IF COLD ADD
IF COLD O.K.

COLD HOT

IF HOT O.K.
IF HOT ADD

Power steering pump dipstick

Before removing the caps to either reservoir, wipe off the cap area with a rag. This helps prevent dirt from entering the system. Do not allow the master cylinder reservoir to remain open any longer than necessary; brake fluid absorbs moisture from the air, reducing its effectiveness and causing corrosion in the lines.

Power Steering Pump
FLUID RECOMMENDATIONS

The correct fluid for the power steering system is Dexron® II automatic transmission fluid. There are no acceptable substitutes; any other fluid may damage the system.

FLUID LEVEL CHECK

The fluid level in the power steering reservoir should be checked at least every 5,000 miles. The vehicle should be parked on level ground, with the engine warm and running at normal idle. Remove the filler cap and check the level on the dipsticks; it should be within the HOT area on the dipstick. If the level is low, add Dexron® II ATF until the proper level is achieved.

Look down in the reservoir and check for evidence of foaming or which indicates the existence of air in the system. The power steering system does not "consume" fluid in normal use; any sign of fluid loss or air in the system should be treated as a potential problem.

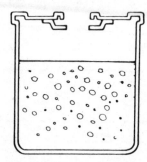

Foaming or emulsification indicates air in the system

The power steering fluid does not require replacement during the normal life of the car.

Chassis Greasing

The Nova and Prizm do not require routine chassis lubrication. All of the suspension joints are permanently lubricated and sealed during assembly.

Body Lubrication

There is no set period recommended for body lubrication; however, it is a good idea to lubricate the following body points at least once a year, especially in the fall before cold weather.

After lubricating a body part, be sure that all the excess lubricant has been wiped off, especially in any area of the car which may come in contact with clothing.

Wheel Bearings
REMOVAL, INSTALLATION AND REPACKING

The wheel bearings at both the front and rear of the car are permanently sealed and pressed into place. They are considered life-of-the-car components and are only replaced in the event of mechanical failure. There is no maintenance required on the wheel bearings.

Replacement of the bearings--a difficult task involving several special tools and a hydraulic press--is discussed in Chapter 8.

TRAILER TOWING

General recommendations

When towing a trailer, your car will handle differently than without the trailer. The three main causes of trailer-related accidents are driver error (notably failure to anticipate and react earlier than usual), excessive speed and improper loading.

Since the Nova and Prizm are front wheel drive cars, attaching the load of a trailer to the rear bumper creates special problems. As the weight of the trailer is hooked to the rear, the rear of the car is forced downwards. At the same time the front of the car rises, resulting in less weight on the drive wheels. This lightened, nose-up attitude has a definite effect on the "go, stop and turn" functions of the tires. Wet and/or slippery roads compound this problem since the tires have already lost some of their grip. You must alter your driving style when towing; moderate speeds and anticipation of problems are required.

Always check the trailer lighting before departing. Double check the hitch and its safety chains. Remember that the trailer makes the car tail-heavy; braking distances are increased and acceleration is slower. Chevrolet states that you should not exceed 45 mph when towing with these cars due to the increase in trailer sway at higher speeds.

Simply being conscious of the trailer at all times will go a long way to making your trip a safe one. Wider turns, extra length and a greater exposure to cross-winds need to be in your mind every minute.

When parking the car with the trailer, seek level ground if possible. If the unit must be parked on a slope, make sure the parking brake is firmly set and the transmission is set either in PARK (automatic) or first or reverse (manual). Always use wheel chocks on at least one vehicle wheel and one trailer wheel when parking, whether on a slope or not.

Necessary Equipment

Use only a hitch which is recommended by the manufacturer for your car and conforms to the weight requirements of the trailer. The hitch should be firmly bolted to the rear bumper but should not interfere with the motion of the energy absorbing bumper. Do not use axle-mounted hitches as they will place undue loads on the rear suspension, wheel bearings and tires. It is recommended by Chevrolet that the hitch be removed when not in use to prevent additional damage in the event of a rear end collision.

Wiring connections will need to be made from the car to the trailer. Minimum lighting requirements include tail lights, brake lights and turn signals. Some trailers now include sidemarker and reverse lights as well.

NOTE: *The additional turn signals may cause the system to flash very slowly or not at all. this can be cured by installing a heavy-duty turn signal flasher.*

Electric trailer brakes are recommended for any trailer over 1000 lbs. Your local laws may require brakes on trailers over a specific weight. Consult your dealer or a reputable repair facility for the correct wiring hook-ups.

TRAILER AND TONGUE WEIGHT

The total weight of the trailer and its load must NOT exceed 1400 lbs. The tongue weight (weight on the hitch) must not exceed 140 lbs or 10% of the total trailer weight, whichever is less.

The trailer must be loaded so that about 60% of the total load is in the front half of the trailer. Make sure that any load is secured in place; a sudden weight shift can radically upset the handling of the trailer and the tow vehicle.

As a further caution, the TOTAL weight of the vehicle and trailer (including passengers, luggage, hitch, trailer and cargo) cannot exceed the Gross Vehicle Weight Rating (GVWR) shown on the manufacturer's plate on the left door jamb.

PUSHING AND TOWING

Push Starting

Although Chevrolet recommends against it, all Novas equipped with a manual transaxle can be pushed started, although more than one car has received a dented fender or bumper from this operation. Push starting can develop extremely hot exhaust pulses which can damage the catalytic converter.

If push starting is the last resort, turn the ignition switch to the ON position, push in the clutch pedal, put the gear shift lever in second or third gear and partially depress the gas pedal. As the car begins to pick up momentum while being pushed, release the clutch pedal. Be prepared for the engine to start and the car to accelerate. As soon as the engine is running, push in the clutch and stop the car, keeping the engine running until it has smoothed out and warmed up a bit. As a rule, if the car hasn't started after two or three tries at pushing, it isn't going to.

CAUTION: *Never attempt to push start the car while it is in reverse.*

Novas that are equipped with an automatic transmission can not be push started no matter how far or how fast they are pushed. Attempt-

Capacities Chart

Year	Engine (cc)	Crankcase Including Filter (qt.)	Transmission (qt.)		Diff (pt.)	Fuel Tank (gal.)	Cooling System (qt.)
			5-sp	Auto *			w/ or wo/AC
1985–89	1587	3.5	2.7	2.6	1.5	13.2	6.3
1988	158 4A-GE	3.5	—	2.7	1.5	13.2	6.3

* Drain and refill capacity.

JUMP STARTING A DEAD BATTERY

The chemical reaction in a battery produces explosive hydrogen gas. This is the safe way to jump start a dead battery, reducing the chances of an accidental spark that could cause an explosion.

Jump Starting Precautions

1. Be sure both batteries are of the same voltage.
2. Be sure both batteries are of the same polarity (have the same grounded terminal).
3. Be sure the vehicles are not touching.
4. Be sure the vent cap holes are not obstructed.
5. Do not smoke or allow sparks around the battery.
6. In cold weather, check for frozen electrolyte in the battery. Do not jump start a frozen battery.
7. Do not allow electrolyte on your skin or clothing.
8. Be sure the electrolyte is not frozen.
CAUTION: *Make certain that the ignition key, in the vehicle with the dead battery, is in the OFF position. Connecting cables to vehicles with on-board computers will result in computer destruction if the key is not in the OFF position.*

Jump Starting Procedure

1. Determine voltages of the two batteries; they must be the same.
2. Bring the starting vehicle close (they must not touch) so that the batteries can be reached easily.
3. Turn off all accessories and both engines. Put both cars in Neutral or Park and set the handbrake.
4. Cover the cell caps with a rag—do not cover terminals.
5. If the terminals on the run-down battery are heavily corroded, clean them.
6. Identify the positive and negative posts on both batteries and connect the cables in the order shown.
7. Start the engine of the starting vehicle and run it at fast idle. Try to start the car with the dead battery. Crank it for no more than 10 seconds at a time and let it cool off for 20 seconds in between tries.
8. If it doesn't start in 3 tries, there is something else wrong.
9. Disconnect the cables in the reverse order.
10. Replace the cell covers and dispose of the rags.

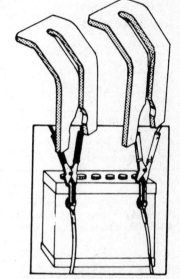

Side terminal batteries occasionally pose a problem when connecting jumper cables. There frequently isn't enough room to clamp the cables without touching sheet metal. Side terminal adaptors are available to alleviate this problem and should be removed after use.

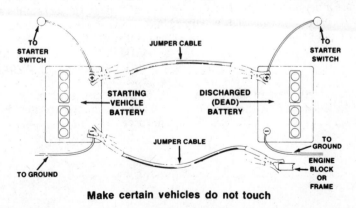

TO STARTER SWITCH

JUMPER CABLE

TO STARTER SWITCH

STARTING VEHICLE BATTERY

DISCHARGED (DEAD) BATTERY

JUMPER CABLE

TO GROUND

TO GROUND

ENGINE BLOCK OR FRAME

Make certain vehicles do not touch

Maintenance Intervals Chart

Miles x 1000 or months of age	5	10	15	20	25	30	35	40	45	50	55	60
Engine oil and filter	R	R	R	R	R	R	R	R	R	R	R	R
Body lubrication		T		T		T		T		T		T
Engine idle speed		I				I						I
Engine coolant						R						R
Spark plugs						R						R
Air filter		I		I		R		I		I		R
Valve clearance						I						I
Engine drive belts		I				I						I
Charcoal canister												I
Fuel lines and connections			I			I			I			I
Fuel filter cap gasket												R
Exhaust system			I			I			I			I
Engine timing belt												R
Wheels and tires	I	I	I	I	I	I	I	I	I	I	I	I
Brakes	I	I	I	I	I	I	I	I	I	I	I	I
Fluid levels check		T		T		T		T		T		T
Transmission fluid	I	I	I	I	I	R	I	I	I	I	I	R
Adjust clutch free play		T		T		T		T		T		T

R: Replace
T: Interval shown or at least twice a year
I: Inspect and clean, adjust, repair, service or replace as necessary
REMINDER: These are maximum intervals, not to be exceeded. More frequent maintenance and inspection may be required depending on usage of the vehicle.

ing to do so will severely damage the transmission and possibly the catalytic converter.

Towing

Novas and Prizms should be towed with the front (drive) wheels in the air. Do not tow the vehicle with the front wheels or all four wheels on the ground; transmission damage will result. In the event of wheel, tire or suspension damage to the rear, the car must be transported on a flatbed carrier.

Additionally, care must be taken not to damage the driveshafts, boots or suspension when hooking up towing equipment.

JACKING

There are certain safety precautions which should be observed when jacking the vehicle. They are as follows:

1. Always jack the car on a level surface.
2. Set the parking brake if the front wheels are to be raised. This will keep the car from rolling backward off the jack.
3. If the rear wheels are to be raised, block the front wheels to keep the car from rolling forward.
4. Block the wheel diagonally opposite the one which is being raised.
5. If the vehicle is being raised in order to work underneath it, support it with jackstands. DO NOT place the jackstands against the sheet metal panels beneath the car or they will become distorted.
CAUTION: *Do not work beneath a vehicle supported only by a jack. Always use jackstands.*
6. Do not use a bumper jack to raise the vehicle; the bumpers are not designed for this purpose.

Engine Performance and Tune-Up

2

TUNE-UP PROCEDURES

Neither tune-up nor troubleshooting can be considered independently since each has direct bearing on the other.

NOTE: *The procedures contained in this section are specific procedures applicable to your Nova or Prizm.*

An engine tune-up is a service designed to restore the maximum power, performance, economy and reliability in an engine, and at the same time, assure the owner of a complete check and lasting results in efficiency and trouble-free performance. Engine tune-up becomes increasingly important each year, to ensure that pollutant levels are in compliance with federal emissions standards.

It is advisable to follow definite and thorough tune-up procedures. Tune-up consists of three separate steps:

1. Analysis, the process of determining whether normal wear is responsible for performance loss, and whether parts require replacement or service

2. Parts Replacement or Service

3. Adjustment, where engine adjustments are returned to the original factory specifications after the installation and/or servicing of parts.

The extent of an engine tune-up is usually determined by the mileage or length of time since the previous service, although the type of driving and the general mechanical condition of the engine must be considered. Specific maintenance should also be performed at regular intervals, depending on operating conditions.

Troubleshooting is a logical sequence of procedures designed to lead the owner or service technician to the particular cause of trouble. The troubleshooting section of this manual is general in nature, yet specific enough to locate many problems. While the apparent cause of trouble, in many cases, is worn or damaged parts, performance problems are less obvious.

The first job is to locate the problem and cause. Once the problem has been isolated, refer to the appropriate section for repair, removal or adjustment procedures.

It is advisable to read the entire chapter before beginning a tune-up, although those who are more familiar with tune-up procedures may wish to go directly to the instructions.

Spark Plugs

A typical spark plug consists of a metal shell surrounding a ceramic insulator. A metal electrode extends downward through the center of the insulator and protrudes a small distance. Located at the end of the plug and attached to the side of the outer metal shell is the side electrode. The side electrode bends in at a 90° angle so that its tip is even with, and parallel to, the tip of the center electrode.

The distance between these two electrodes (measured in thousandths of an inch) is called the spark plug gap. The spark plug in no way produces a spark but merely provides a gap across which the current can arc. The coil produces anywhere from 20,000 to 40,000 volts which travels to the distributor where it is sent through the spark plug wire to the spark plug. The current passes along the center electrode and jumps to the gap to the side electrode, and, in so doing, ignites the air/fuel mixture in the combustion chamber.

SPARK PLUG HEAT RANGE

Spark plug heat range is the ability of the plug to dissipate heat. The longer the insulator (or the farther it extends into the engine), the hotter the plug will operate; the shorter the insulator the cooler it will operate. A plug that absorbs little heat and remains too cool will quickly accumulate deposits of oil and carbon since it

Troubleshooting Engine Performance

Problem	Cause	Solution
Hard starting (engine cranks normally)	• Binding linkage, choke valve or choke piston	• Repair as necessary
	• Restricted choke vacuum diaphragm	• Clean passages
	• Improper fuel level	• Adjust float level
	• Dirty, worn or faulty needle valve and seat	• Repair as necessary
	• Float sticking	• Repair as necessary
	• Faulty fuel pump	• Replace fuel pump
	• Incorrect choke cover adjustment	• Adjust choke cover
	• Inadequate choke unloader adjustment	• Adjust choke unloader
	• Faulty ignition coil	• Test and replace as necessary
	• Improper spark plug gap	• Adjust gap
	• Incorrect ignition timing	• Adjust timing
	• Incorrect valve timing	• Check valve timing; repair as necessary
Rough idle or stalling	• Incorrect curb or fast idle speed	• Adjust curb or fast idle speed
	• Incorrect ignition timing	• Adjust timing to specification
	• Improper feedback system operation	• Refer to Chapter 4
	• Improper fast idle cam adjustment	• Adjust fast idle cam
	• Faulty EGR valve operation	• Test EGR system and replace as necessary
	• Faulty PCV valve air flow	• Test PCV valve and replace as necessary
	• Choke binding	• Locate and eliminate binding condition
	• Faulty TAC vacuum motor or valve	• Repair as necessary
	• Air leak into manifold vacuum	• Inspect manifold vacuum connections and repair as necessary
	• Improper fuel level	• Adjust fuel level
	• Faulty distributor rotor or cap	• Replace rotor or cap
	• Improperly seated valves	• Test cylinder compression, repair as necessary
	• Incorrect ignition wiring	• Inspect wiring and correct as necessary
	• Faulty ignition coil	• Test coil and replace as necessary
	• Restricted air vent or idle passages	• Clean passages
	• Restricted air cleaner	• Clean or replace air cleaner filler element
	• Faulty choke vacuum diaphragm	• Repair as necessary
Faulty low-speed operation	• Restricted idle transfer slots	• Clean transfer slots
	• Restricted idle air vents and passages	• Clean air vents and passages
	• Restricted air cleaner	• Clean or replace air cleaner filter element
	• Improper fuel level	• Adjust fuel level
	• Faulty spark plugs	• Clean or replace spark plugs
	• Dirty, corroded, or loose ignition secondary circuit wire connections	• Clean or tighten secondary circuit wire connections
	• Improper feedback system operation	• Refer to Chapter 4
	• Faulty ignition coil high voltage wire	• Replace ignition coil high voltage wire
	• Faulty distributor cap	• Replace cap
Faulty acceleration	• Improper accelerator pump stroke	• Adjust accelerator pump stroke
	• Incorrect ignition timing	• Adjust timing
	• Inoperative pump discharge check ball or needle	• Clean or replace as necessary
	• Worn or damaged pump diaphragm or piston	• Replace diaphragm or piston

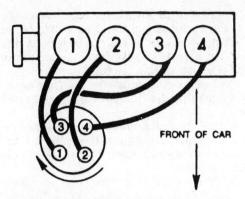

4A-GE and 4A-FE engines. Firing order 1-3-4-2

FRONT OF CAR

Electronic Ignition

Electronic ignition systems offer many advances over the conventional breaker point ignition system. By eliminating the points, maintenance requirements are greatly reduced. An electronic ignition system is capable of producing much higher voltage, which in turn aids in starting, reduces spark fouling and provides better emission control.

NOTE: *This book contains simple testing procedures for your Nova or Prizm's electronic ignition. More comprehensive testing on this system and other electronic control systems on your car can be found in*

CHILTON'S ELECTRONIC ENGINE CONTROLS MANUAL, book number 7781, available at your local retailer.

The system on the Nova consists of a distributor with a signal generator, an ignition coil and an electronic igniter. The signal generator is used to activate the electronic components of the ignition. It is located in the distributor and consists of three main components; the signal rotor, the pick-up coil and the permanent magnet. The signal rotor (not to be confused with the normal rotor) revolves with the distributor shaft, while the pickup coil and the permanent magnet are stationary. As the signal rotor spins, the teeth on it pass a projection leading from the pickup coil. As they pass, voltage is allowed to flow through the system, firing the spark plugs. There is no physical contact and no electrical arcing, hence no need to replace burnt or worn parts.

Service consists of inspection of the distributor cap, rotor and the ignition wires, replacing them as necessary. In addition, the air gap between the signal rotor and the projection on the pickup coil should be checked periodically.

CHECKING THE AIR GAP

4A-LC Engine, Carbureted Nova

1. Remove the distributor cap. Inspect the cap for cracks, carbon tracks or a worn center contact. Cracks in the cap can be very hard to

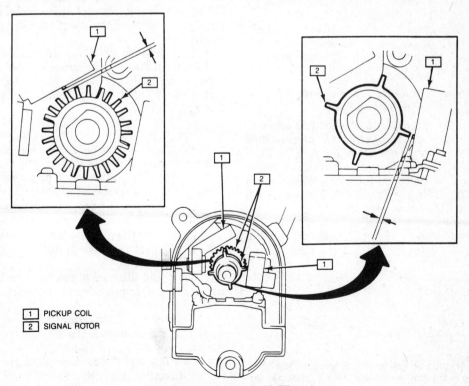

1 PICKUP COIL
2 SIGNAL ROTOR

Checking the air gap on 4A-FE engines

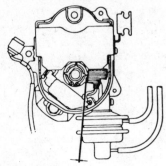

Checking the air gap

see. They are usually hairline thin and run in odd directions within the cap.

Replace the cap if necessary, transferring the wires one at a time from the old cap to the new one.

2. Pull the ignition rotor (not the signal rotor) straight up and remove it. Replace it if the contacts are worn, burned or pitted. Do not file the contacts.

3. Turn the engine over (you may use a socket wrench on the front pulley bolt to do this) until the projection on the pickup coil is directly opposite the signal rotor tooth.

4. Get a non-ferrous (paper, brass, or plastic) feeler gauge of 0.012 in. (0.3mm), and insert it into the pick-up air gap. DO NOT use an ordinary metal feeler gauge! The gauge should just touch either side of the gap. The permissible range is 0.008–0.016 in. (0.20–0.40mm).

NOTE: *The air gap on the Nova is not adjustable. If the gap is not within specifications, the pick-up coil (igniter) must be replaced.*

4A-GE Engine--Fuel-injected Nova and 4A-FE Engine--Fuel-injected Prizm

These electronically controlled fuel injection systems rely on the Electronic Control Module (ECM) for proper operation. Because the ECM needs to receive information from the distributor (and to control its function), there are two pickup coils in the distributor. Make sure you measure the gap to each coil.

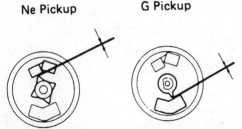

Ne Pickup   **G Pickup**

Measuring the air gap on 4A-GE engines. The "Ne" pickup is the rpm sensor and the "G" pickup is the crank angle (engine position) sensor

1. Remove the distributor cap. Inspect the cap for cracks, carbon tracks or a worn center contact. Cracks in the cap can be very hard to see. They are usually hairline thin and run in odd directions within the cap.

Replace the cap if necessary, transferring the wires one at a time from the old cap to the new one.

2. Pull the ignition rotor (not the signal rotor) straight up and remove it. Replace it if the contacts are worn, burned or pitted. Do not file the contacts.

3. Turn the engine over (you may use a socket wrench on the front pulley bolt to do this) until the projection on the pickup coil is directly opposite a signal rotor tooth.

4. Get a non-ferrous (paper, brass, or plastic) feeler gauge of 0.012 in. (0.3mm), and insert it into the air gaps between the signal rotor and the pickup coil projections on each side. DO NOT use an ordinary metal feeler gauge! The gauge should just touch either side of the gap. The permissible range is 0.008–0.016 in. (0.2–0.4mm).

5. The air gap is totally non-adjustable. Should it be out of specification, the entire distributor must be replaced.

PARTS REPLACEMENT

The two most commonly replaced parts in the distributor (aside from the cap and rotor as maintenance) will be the signal generator and the igniter. Replacement of any internal piece requires removal of the distributor from the engine.

NOTE: *The distributor on the 4A-FE (Prizm) engine contains no replaceable parts except the ignition coil. Any other failed item in the distributor requires replacement of the complete unit.*

Distributor Removal

WARNING: Once the distributor is removed, the engine should not be turned or moved out of position. Should this occur, please refer to the Distributor section of Chapter Three.

4A-LC Engine

1. Disconnect the negative battery cable.

2. Disconnect the distributor wire at its connector.

3. Label and disconnect the vacuum hoses running to the vacuum advance unit on the side of the distributor.

4. Remove the distributor cap (leave the spark plug wires connected) and swing it out of the way.

5. Carefully note the position of the distributor rotor relative to the distributor housing; a mark made on the casing will be helpful during

reassembly. Use a marker or tape so the mark doesn't rub off during the handling of the case.

6. Remove the distributor holddown bolts.

7. Carefully pull the distributor out until it stops turning counter-clockwise.

8. If the engine has not been moved out of position, align the rotor with the mark you made earlier and reinstall the distributor. Position it carefully and make sure the drive gear engages properly within the engine. Complete the installation by following steps 1-6 above in reverse order.

9. Check and reset the engine timing. Please refer to the Ignition Timing section later in this chapter.

4A-GE Engine

1. Label and disconnect the coil and spark plug wiring at the distributor cap.

2. Disconnect the distributor wire at its connector.

3. Remove the distributor holddown bolts. Before moving or disturbuing the distributor, mark the position of the distributor relative to the engine. Use a marker or tape so the mark doesn't rub off during the handling of the case.

4. Remove the distributor from the engine.

5. Remove the O-ring from the distributor shaft.

6. If the engine has not been moved out of position, align the rotor with the mark you made earlier and reinstall the distributor. Position it carefully and make sure the drive gear engages properly within the engine. Complete the installation by following steps 1-5 above in reverse order. For complete reinstallation instructions, please refer to the Distributor section in Chapter 3.

4A-FE Engine

1. Disconnect the negative battery cable.

2. Disconnect all electrical connections at the distributor, including the plug wires.

3. Remove the distributor cap.

4. Mark the position of the distributor case relative to the engine. Use a marker or tape so the mark doesn't rub off during the handling of the case. Also mark the position of the distributor rotor relative to the case.

5. Remove the distributor mounting bolts.

6. Remove the distributor from the engine and remove the O-ring from the distributor shaft.

7. If the engine has not been moved out of position, align the rotor with the mark you made earlier and reinstall the distributor. Position it carefully and make sure the drive gear engages properly within the engine. Complete the installation by following steps 1-6 above in reverse order.

Igniter and Signal Rotor Replacement

4A-LC and 4A-GE ENGINE

1. Remove the distributor as outlined above. Make certain the negative battery cable is disconnected before beginning the work.

2. Rmove the packing and distributor rotor.

3. Remove the dust cover over the distributor components and remove the dust cover over the ignition coil.

4. Remove the nuts and disconnect the wiring from the ignition coil.

5. Remove the four screws and remove the ignition coil from the distributor.

6. At the igniter terminals, disconnect the wiring from the connecting points.

7. Loosen and remove the two screws holding the igniter and remove it from the distributor.

8. If the signal rotor is to be replaced, use a screwdriver and CAREFULLY pry the rotor and spring up and off the shaft. When replacing the rotor, use a small bearing driver or long

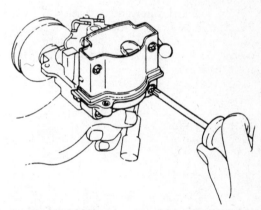

The coil is easily removed with the distributor off the car

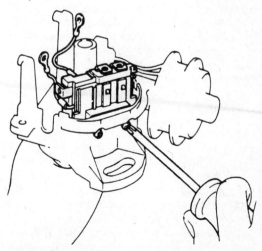

Removing the igniter

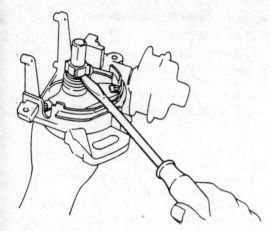

Carefully pry the signal rotor off the shaft. Don't damage the shaft or distributor housing

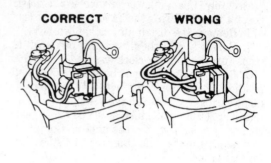

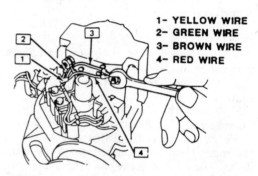

1- YELLOW WIRE
2- GREEN WIRE
3- BROWN WIRE
4- RED WIRE

socket to fit over the shaft on top of the signal rotor. Tap gently; the force will be equally distributed and the rotor will slide evenly into place.

9. Install the igniter and connect its wiring. Pay particular attention to the correct routing of the wiring within the housing. There is one correct position only; any other wiring placements risk damage.

10. Install the ignition coil and secure its wiring. Again, watch the wiring postions.

11. Reinstall the dust covers, the packing and distributor rotor.

12. Reinstall the distributor and set the engine timing.

Ignition Timing

Ignition timing is the measurement (in degrees) of crankshaft position at the instant the spark plug fires. Ignition timing is adjusted by loosening the distributor locking device and turning the distributor in the engine.

It takes a fraction of a second for the spark from the plug to completely ignite the mixture in the cylinder. Because of this, the spark plug must fire before the piston reaches TDC (top dead center, the highest point in its travel), if the mixture is to be completely ignited as the piston passes TDC. This measurement is given in degrees (of crankshaft rotation) before the piston reaches top dead center (BTDC). If the ignition timing setting for your engine is seven degrees BTDC, this means that the spark plug must fire at a time when the piston for that cylinder is 7 degrees before top dead center of its compression stroke. However, this only holds true while your engine is at idle speed.

As you accelerate from idle, the speed of your engine (rpm) increases. The increase in rpm means that the pistons are now traveling up

Correct wiring placement is required during reassembly. The spinning rotor can cut a wire almost instnatly. Above: wiring path for igniter; below: color code and placement for ignition coil wiring

and down much faster. Because of this, the spark plugs will have to fire even sooner if the mixture is to be completely ignited as the piston passes TDC. To accomplish this, the distributor incorporates means to advance the timing of the spark as the engine speed increases.

The distributor in your carbureted Nova has two means of advancing the ignition timing. One is called centrifugal advance and is actuated by weights in the distributor. The other is called vacuum advance and is controlled by the larger circular housing on the side of the distributor.

In addition, some distributors have a vacuum-retard mechanism which is contained in the same housing on the side of the distributor as the vacuum advance. The function of this mechanism is to retard the timing of the ignition spark under certain engine conditions. The causes more complete burning of the air/fuel mixture in the cylinder and consequently lowers exhaust emissions.

Because these mechanisms change ignition timing, it is necessary to disconnect and plug the vacuum lines from the distributor when setting the basic ignition timing.

The fuel injected Nova and all Prizms have

neither a centrifugal advance nor a vacuum unit. All the timing changes are controlled electronically by the ECM. This solid state "brain" receives data from many sensors (including the distributor), and commands changes in spark timing (and other functions) based on immediate driving conditions. This instant response allows the engine to be kept at peak performance and economy throughout the driving cycle. Basic timing can still be checked and adjusted on these motors.

If the ignition timing is set too far advanced (BTDC), the ignition and expansion of the air/fuel mixture in the cylinder will try to force the piston down while it is still traveling upward. This causes engine ping, a sound which resembles marbles being dropped into an empty tin can. If the ignition timing is too far retarded (after, or ATDC), the piston will have already started down on the power stroke when the air/fuel mixture ignites and expands. This will cause the piston to be forced down only a portion of its travel. This results in poor engine performance and lack of power.

Ignition timing adjustment is checked with a timing light. This instrument is connected to the number one (No. 1) spark plug of the engine. The timing light flashes every time an electrical current is sent from the distributor through the no. 1 spark plug wire to the spark plug. The crankshaft pulley and the front cover of the engine are marked with a timing pointer and a timing scale.

When the timing pointer is aligned with the 0 mark on the timing scale, the piston in the No. 1 cylinder is at TDC of it compression stroke. With the engine running, and the timing light aimed at the timing pointer and timing scale, the stroboscopic (periodic) flashes from the timing light will allow you to check the ignition timing setting of the engine. The timing light flashes every time the spark plug in the No. 1 cylinder of the engine fires. Since the flash from the timing light makes the crankshaft pulley seem to stand still for a moment, you will be able to read the exact position of the piston in the No. 1 cylinder on the timing scale on the front of the engine.

If you're buying a timing light, make sure the unit you select is rated for electronic or solid-state ignitions. Generally, these lights have two wires which connect to the battery with alligator clips and a third wire which connects to no. 1 plug wire. The best lights have an inductive pick-up on the third wire; this allows you to simply clip the small box over the wire. Older lights may require the removal of the plug wire and the installation of an inline adapter. Since the spark plugs in the twin-cam engines (4A-GE and 4A-FE) are in deep wells, rigging the

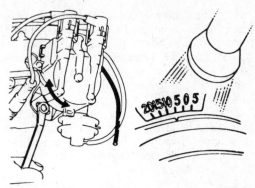

Ignition timing adjustment and mark location, carbureted Nova (4A-LC engine)

adapter can be difficult. Buy quality the first time and the tool will give lasting results and ease of use.

CHECKING AND ADJUSTMENT

4A-LC Engine--Carbureted Nova

The 4A-LC engine requires a special tachometer hook-up to the service connector wire coming out of the distributor. As many tachometers are not compatible with this hook-up, we recommend that you consult with the manufacturer or salesman before purchasing a certain type.

WARNING: *NEVER allow the ignition coil terminal to become grounded; severe and expensive damage can occur to the coil and/or igniter!*

1. Warm the engine to normal operating temperature. Do not attempt to check timing or idle on a cold motor--all the readings will be different. Connect a tachometer and check the engine idle speed to be sure it is within the specification given in the Tune-Up Specifications chart at the beginning of this chapter. Adjust the idle if needed and shut the engine off.

2. If the timing marks are difficult to see, use a dab of paint or chalk to make them more visible.

3. Connect a timing light according to the manufacturer's instructions.

4. Label and disconnect the vacuum line(s) from the distributor vacuum unit. Plug (them) with a pencil or golf tee(s).

5. Be sure that the timing light wires are clear of the fan and start the engine.

6. Allow the engine to run at the specified idle speed with the gearshift in Neutral.

CAUTION: *Be sure that the parking brake is set and the wheels are blocked to prevent the car from rolling in either direction.*

7. Point the timing light at the marks on the tab alongside the crank pulley. With the engine at idle, timing should be at the specification given on the Tune-Up Specification Chart at the beginning of the chapter.

8. If the timing is not at the specification, loosen the bolts at the base of the distributor just enough so that the distributor can be turned. Turn the distributor to advance or retard the timing as required. Once the proper marks are seen to align with the timing light, timing is correct.

9. Stop the engine and tighten the bolts. Start the engine and recheck the timing. Stop the engine; disconnect the tachometer and the timing light. Connect the vacuum line(s) to the distributor vacuum unit.

4A-GE Engine--Fuel Injected Nova

The 4A-GE engine requires a special tachometer hook-up to the service connector wire coming out of the distributor. As many tachometers are not compatible with this hook-up, we recommend that you consult with the manufacturer or salesman before purchasing a certain type.

WARNING: *NEVER allow the ignition coil terminal to become grounded; severe and expensive damage can occur to the coil and/or igniter.*

1. Warm the engine to normal operating temperature. Do not attempt to check timing or idle on a cold motor--all the readings will be different.

2. Using a small jumper wire, short both terminals of the Check Engine connector located near the wiper motor.

3. Connect a tachometer and check the engine idle speed to be sure it is within the specification given in the Tune-Up Specifications chart at the beginning of this chapter. Adjust the idle if needed and shut the engine off.

4. If the timing marks are difficult to see, use a dab of paint or chalk to make them more visible.

5. Connect a timing light according to the manufacturer's instructions.

6. Start the engine and use the timing light to observe the timing marks. With the jumper wire in the connector the timing should be 10° BTDC with the engine fully warmed up and the

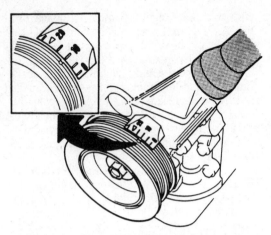

Ignition timing marks, 4A-GE engine. Note the small notch on the pulley; this is the mark to align with the degree scale

transmission in Neutral. If the timing is not correct, loosen the bolts at the distributor just enough so that the distributor can be turned. Turn the distributor to advance or retard the timing as required. Once the proper marks are seen to align with the timing light, timing is correct.

7. Without changing the position of the distributor, tighten the distributor bolts and double check the timing with the light.

8. Disconnect the jumper wire at the Check Engine connector.

9. Check the timing again with the light. Manual transmission cars should now show timing in excess of 16° BTDC and automatic transmission cars more than 12° BTDC. If necessary, repeat the timing adjustment procedure.

10. Shut the engine off and disconnect all test equipment.

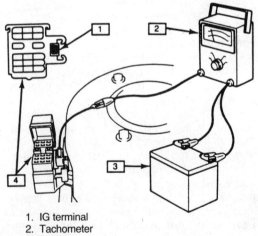

1. IG terminal
2. Tachometer
3. Battery
4. Diagnostic connector

Correct tachometer hook-up, '89–90 Prizm

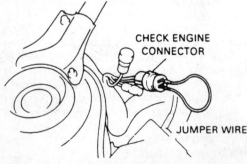

CHECK ENGINE CONNECTOR

JUMPER WIRE

Jumper wire must be installed to check the timing on fuel injected Novas (4A-GE engine)

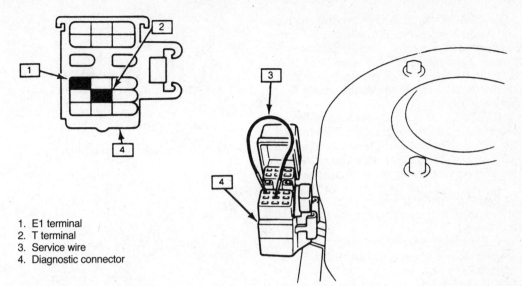

1. E1 terminal
2. T terminal
3. Service wire
4. Diagnostic connector

Checking the timing on the Prizm requires shorting the E₁ and T terminals at the diagnostic connector—see text for details

4A-FE Engine--Fuel Injected Prizm

The 4A-FE engine requires a special tachometer hook-up to the service connector port on the left shock tower. As many tachometers are not compatible with this hook-up, we recommend that you consult with the manufacturer or salesman before purchasing a certain type.

WARNING: *NEVER allow the tachometer terminal to become grounded; severe and expensive damage can occur to the coil and/or igniter.*

1. Warm the engine to normal operating temperature. Turn all electrical accessories off.

2. Connect a tachometer and check the engine idle speed to be sure it is within the specification given in the Tune-Up Specifications chart at the beginning of this chapter. Adjust the idle if needed and shut the engine off.

3. Connect a timing light according to the manufacturer's instructions.

4. Remove the cap on the diagnostic connector. Using a small jumper wire, short terminals E1 and T together.

5. Start the engine and use the timing light to observe the timing marks. With the jumper wire in the connector, the timing should be at the specification listed on the Vehicle Emis-

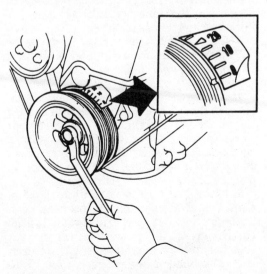

Timing marks, 4A-FE engine

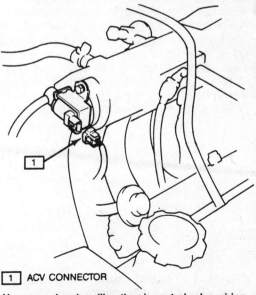

1 ACV CONNECTOR

Use care when handling the air control valve wiring. The connector has a locking device which must be released before removal

sions Label located under the hood. If the timing is not correct, loosen the bolts at the distributor just enough so that the distributor can be turned. Turn the distributor to advance or retard the timing as required. Once the proper marks are seen to align with the timing light, timing is correct.

6. Without changing the position of the distributor, tighten the distributor bolts to 14 ft. lbs. and double check the timing with the light.

7. Remove the jumper wire from the diagnostic connector and reinstall the cap.

8. Disconnect the air control valve (ACV) connector at the intake manifold.

9. Recheck the timing; it should be 10° BTDC.

10. Reconnect the ACV connector.

11. Shut the engine off and disconnect all test equipment.

Valve Lash

Valve lash is one factor which determines how far the intake and exhaust valves will open into the cylinder. If the valve clearance is too large, part of the motion of the camshaft will be used up in removing excessive clearance, thus the valves will not be opened far enough. This condition has two effects, the valve train components will emit a tapping noise as they take up the excessive clearance, and the engine will perform poorly, due to a smaller amount of air/fuel mixture admitted to the cylinders. The less the exhaust valves open, the greater the back pressure in the cylinder.

If the valve clearance is too small, the intake and exhaust valves will not fully seat on the cylinder head when they close. When a valve seats on the cylinder head it does two things, sealing the combustion chamber so none of the gases in the cylinder can escape and cooling itself by transferring some of the heat it absorbed from the combustion process. Therefore, if the valve clearance is too small, the engine will run poorly (due to gases escaping from the combustion chamber), and the valves will overheat and warp.

NOTE: *While all valve adjustments must be as accurate as possible, it is better to have the valve adjustment slightly loose than slightly tight, as burnt valves may result from overly tight adjustments.*

ADJUSTMENT

4A-LC Engine--Carbureted Nova

1. Start the engine and run it until it reaches normal operating temperature.

2. Stop the engine. Remove the air cleaner assembly. Remove the valve cover.

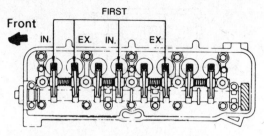

Adjust these valves first on 4A-LC engines

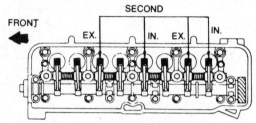

Adjust these valves second on 4A-LC engines

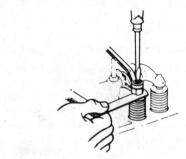

Checking the valve lash

CAUTION: *Be careful when removing components; the engine will be hot.*

3. Turn the crankshaft until the pointer or notch on the pulley aligns with the **O** or the **T** mark on the timing scale. This will ensure that the engine is at TDC. Turning the engine (with a wrench on the crankshaft bolt) is much easier if the spark plugs are removed.

NOTE: *Check that the rocker arms on the No. 1 cylinder are loose and those on the No. 4 cylinder are tight. If not, turn the crankshaft one complete revolution (360°).*

4. Using a feeler gauge, check the clearance between the bottom of the rocker arm and the top of the valve stem. This measurement should correspond to the one given in the Tune-Up Specifications Chart in this chapter. Check only the valves listed under First in the accompanying illustrations for your engine.

5. If the clearance is not within specifications, the valves will require adjustment. Loosen the locknut on the rocker arm and, still holding the nut with an open end wrench, turn the adjustment screw to achieve the correct clearance. This is a detail-oriented job; work for exact clearance.

6. Once the correct clearance is achieved, keep the adjustment screw from turning with your screwdriver, and then tighten the locknut. Recheck the valve clearance. If it's proper, proceed to the next valve as shown on the diagram.

7. After the correct four valves have been adjusted, turn the engine one complete revolution (360°) and adjust the remaining valves. Follow steps 4-6 and use the valve arrangement illustration marked Second.

8. Use a new gasket and then install the valve cover. Install any other components which were removed for access to the cover.

9. Start the engine. Listen for any excessive tapping (indicating a loosened rocker) and check the valve cover for any signs of oil leaks.

4A-GE Engine--Fuel Injected Nova
4A-FE Engine--All Prizm

WARNING: *The use of the correct special tools or their equivalent is REQUIRED for this procedure. The valve adjustment requires removal of the adjusting shims (Tool kit J-37141 or equivalent) and accurate measurement of the shims with a micrometer. A selection of replacement shims is also required. Do not attempt this procedure if you are not equipped with the proper tools.*

NOTE: *Valves on this motor are adjusted with the motor cold. Do not attempt adjustment if the engine has been run within the previous 4 hours. An overnight cooling period is recommended.*

1. Remove the valve cover following procedures discussed in Chapter Three.

2. Turn the crankshaft to align the groove in the crankshaft pulley with the **0** mark on the timing belt cover. Removing the spark plugs makes this easier, but is not required.

3. Check that the lifters on no.1 cylinder are loose and those on no.4 are tight. If not, turn the crankshaft pulley one full revolution (360°).

4. Using the feeler gauge, measure the clearance on the four valves shown in the diagram labled First Pass. Make a WRITTEN record of any measurements which are not within specification.

5. Rotate the crankshaft pulley one full turn (360°) and check the clearance on the other four valves. These are shown on the diagram labled Second Pass. Any measurements not within specification should be added to your WRITTEN record.

6. For ANY given valve needing adjustment:

    a. Turn the crankshaft pulley until the camshaft lobe points upward over the valve. This takes the tension off the valve and spring.

    b. Using the forked tool, press the valve lifter downward and hold it there.

Some tool kits require a second tool for holding the lifter in place, allowing the first to be removed

    c. Using small magnetic tools, remove the adjusting shim from the top of the lifter.

    d. Use the micrometer and measure the thickness of the shim removed. Determine

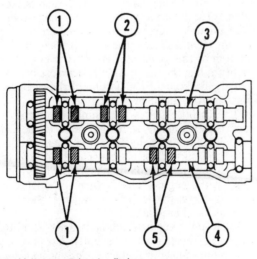

1. Valves—number 1 cylinder
2. Valves—number 2 cylinder
3. Intake camshaft
4. Exhaust camshaft
5. Valves—number 3 cylinder

First pass when checking valve clearance on twin cam, fuel injected engines (4A-GE and 4A-FE engines)

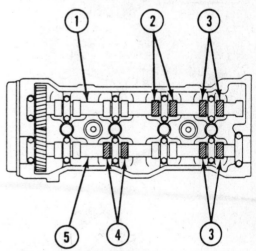

1. Intake camshaft
2. Valves—number 3 cylinder
3. Valves—number 4 cylinder
4. Valves—number 2 cylinder
5. Exhaust camshaft

Second pass when checking valve clearance on twin cam engines requires the crankshaft to be rotated 360°

the thickness of the new shim using the formula below or the selection charts. For the purposes of the following formulae, T = Thickness of the old shim; A = Valve clearance measured; N = Thickness of the new shim

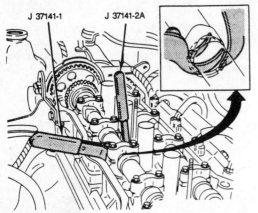

Use the correct tools to depress and hold down the valve lifter

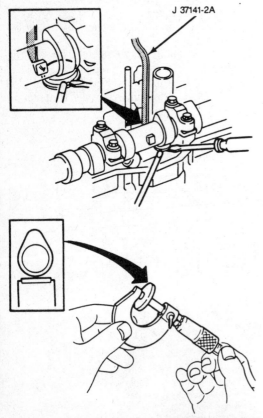

Carefully remove the shim to be replaced (above) with a small screwdriver and magnetic tools. Clean and dry the shim before measuring with the micrometer (below)

- For the intake side (camshaft nearest to the intake manifold):
N = T + (A − 0.20mm or 0.008 in.)

- For the exhaust side (camshaft nearest to the exhaust manifold):
N = T + (A − 0.25mm or 0.010 in.)

e. Select a shim closest to the calculated thickness. Use the lifter depressor tool to press down the lifter and install the shim. Shims are available in 17 sizes from 2.50mm (0.0984 in.) to 3.30mm (0.1299 in.). The standard increment is 0.05mm (0.002 in.)

f. Repeat steps a through e for each valve needing adjustment.

7. Reinstall the valve cover, following the procedures outlined in Chapter One.

8. Check and adjust the timing and idle speed, following the procedures outlined in this chapter.

Idle Speeds and Mixture Adjustment
CARBURETED NOVA

This section contains only adjustments as they normally apply to engine tune-up. Descriptions of the carburetor and fuel systems and complete adjustment procedures can be found in Chapter 5.

When the engine in your NOVA is running, air/fuel mixture from the carburetor is being drawn into the engine by a partial vacuum created by the downward movement of the pistons. The amount of air/fuel mixture that enters the engine is controlled by the throttle plates in the bottom of the carburetor. When the engine is not running, the throttle plates are closed, completely blocking off the bottom of the carburetor from the inside of the engine.

The throttle plates are connected, through the throttle linkage, to the gas pedal inside the car. What you actually are doing when you depress the gas pedal is opening the throttle plate in the carburetor to admit more air/fuel mixture to the engine. The further you open the throttle plates in the carburetor, the higher the engine speed becomes.

To keep the engine is idling, it is necessary to open the throttle plates slightly. To prevent having to keep your foot on the gas pedal when the engine is idling, an idle speed adjusting screw is included on the carburetor. This screw has the same effect as keeping your foot on the gas pedal--it holds the throttle plate open just a bit. When the screw is turned in, it opens the throttle, raising the idle speed of the engine. This screw is called the curb idle adjusting

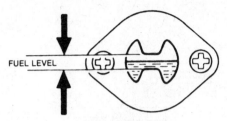

Check the fuel level in the float bowl

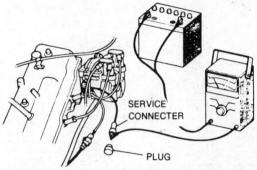

Special service connector required for tachometer hook-up

screw, and the procedures in this section will tell you how to adjust it.

When you first start the car after an overnight period, the cold motor requires a different air-fuel mixture to run properly. Because of the different mixture, the idle speed must be higher during cold engine operation. This High Idle (sometimes called cold idle or fast idle) speed is also adjustable and should be checked periodically. If the high idle is too low, the car will bog and stall until it warms up. If the high idle is set too high, the engine is wasting fuel and suffering increased and premature wear.

Before performing any carburetor adjustments, ALL of the following conditions must be met:

- All accessories are switched off
- Ignition timing is set correctly and all vacuum lines are connected
- Transmission in Neutral and engine warmed up to normal operating temperature
- Choke opened fully
- Fuel level in carburetor sight glass at the correct level. If the level is too high or low, adjust the float level as explained in Chapter Five.
- Tachometer installed with the '+ connector running to the service connector.

Curb Idle Speed Adjustment

Once all the above conditions are met, the curb idle can be adjusted by turning the adjusting knob at the rear of the carburetor. It has a knurled plastic head that may be gripped with the fingers (no screwdriver required) but may be hard to get at under the air cleaner housing. Turn the knob clockwise to raise the idle and counter-clockwise to lower it. Keep a close eye on the tachometer while turning the knob; sometimes a small change in the adjustor causes a big change in the idle speed. Adjust the idle speed to the rpm shown in the Tune-Up Specifications chart at the beginning of this chapter.

Idle Mixture Adjustment

To conform with Federal regulations, the idle mixture adjusting screw is adjusted at the factory and plugged with a steel plug by the manufacturer. Under normal conditions there should be no need to remove this plug.

When troubleshooting rough idle, check all other possible causes before attempting to adjust the idle mixture. Only if no other factors are found to be at fault should the idle mixture be adjusted. Since this repair involves removal of the carburetor, it is recommended that the car be thoroughly checked on an exhaust emissions analyzer as part of the diagnostic procedure before committing to the repair. If you perform this repair incorrectly or if the idle mixture is not the cause of your problem, you may cause the car to become uncertifiable under Federal and State or Provincial emission laws.

1. Following the procedures given in Chapter Five, remove the carburetor.

2. Using the following procedure remove the Mixture Adjusting Screw plug (MAS plug).

   a. Plug all of the carburetor ports to prevent the entry of steel particles when drilling.

   b. Mark the center of the plug with a punch.

   c. Drill a 6mm hole in the center of the plug. As there is only 1mm clearance between the plug and the screw below it, drill carefully

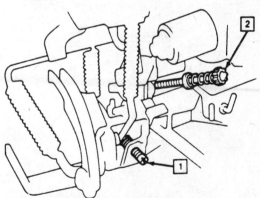

1. FAST IDLE ADJUSTING SCREW
2. IDLE ADJUSTING SCREW

Curb idle and fast idle adjusting screws are located on the firewall side of the carburetor

Exhaust Valve adjusting shim selection chart

Main chart — Installed Shim Thickness (mm)

Measured Clearance (mm)	2.500	2.525	2.550	2.575	2.600	2.620	2.625	2.640	2.650	2.660	2.675	2.680	2.700	2.720	2.725	2.740	2.750	2.760	2.775	2.780	2.800	2.820	2.825	2.840	2.850	2.860	2.875	2.880	2.900	2.920	2.925	2.940	2.950	2.960	2.975	2.980	3.000	3.020	3.025	3.040	3.050	3.060	3.075	3.080	3.100	3.120	3.125	3.140	3.150	3.160	3.175	3.180	3.200	3.220	3.225	3.250
0.000 – 0.009												02	02	02	02	02	04	04	04	06	06	06	06	08	08	08	08	10	10	10	10	12	12	12	14	14	14	14	16	16	16	18	18	18	18	18	20	20	20	22	22					
0.010 – 0.025										02	02	02	02	04	04	04	06	06	06	06	08	08	08	08	10	10	10	10	12	12	12	14	14	14	14	16	16	16	16	18	18	18	18	20	20	20	22	22	22	22					
0.026 – 0.040								02	02	02	02	04	04	04	06	06	06	06	08	08	08	08	10	10	10	10	12	12	12	12	14	14	14	14	16	16	16	16	18	18	18	18	18	20	20	20	22	22	22	22	24				
0.041 – 0.050							02	02	02	02	04	04	04	06	06	06	06	08	08	08	08	10	10	10	10	12	12	12	12	14	14	14	14	16	16	16	16	18	18	18	18	18	20	20	20	22	22	22	22	24					
0.051 – 0.070						02	02	02	02	04	04	04	06	06	06	06	08	08	08	08	10	10	10	10	12	12	12	12	14	14	14	14	16	16	16	16	18	18	18	18	20	20	20	20	22	22	22	22	24	24					
0.071 – 0.090				02	02	02	02	04	04	04	06	06	06	06	08	08	08	08	10	10	10	10	12	12	12	12	14	14	14	14	16	16	16	16	18	18	18	18	20	20	20	20	22	22	22	22	24	24	26					
0.091 – 0.100			02	02	02	02	04	04	04	06	06	06	06	08	08	08	08	10	10	10	10	12	12	12	12	14	14	14	14	16	16	16	16	18	18	18	18	20	20	20	20	22	22	22	22	24	24	26	26					
0.101 – 0.120		02	02	02	02	04	04	04	06	06	06	06	08	08	08	08	10	10	10	10	12	12	12	12	14	14	14	14	16	16	16	16	18	18	18	18	20	20	20	20	22	22	22	22	24	24	26	26						
0.121 – 0.140	02	02	02	04	04	04	04	06	06	06	06	08	08	08	08	10	10	10	10	12	12	12	12	14	14	14	14	16	16	16	16	18	18	18	18	20	20	20	20	22	22	22	24	24	24	26	26	28					
0.141 – 0.150	02	02	02	04	04	04	06	06	06	06	08	08	08	08	10	10	10	10	12	12	12	12	14	14	14	14	16	16	16	16	18	18	18	18	20	20	20	22	22	22	24	24	24	26	26	28						
0.151 – 0.170	02	02	04	04	04	06	06	06	06	08	08	08	08	10	10	10	10	12	12	12	12	14	14	14	14	16	16	16	16	18	18	18	18	20	20	20	20	22	22	22	24	24	24	26	26	28	28					
0.171 – 0.190	02	02	04	04	04	06	06	06	08	08	08	08	10	10	10	10	12	12	12	12	14	14	14	16	16	16	16	18	18	18	18	20	20	20	20	22	22	22	24	24	24	26	26	26	28	28	30					
0.191 – 0.199	02	02	04	04	04	06	06	06	08	08	08	08	10	10	10	10	12	12	12	12	14	14	14	16	16	16	16	18	18	18	18	20	20	20	20	22	22	22	24	24	24	26	26	26	28	28	30	30				
0.200 – 0.300																																																						
0.301 – 0.320	04	06	06	08	08	10	10	10	10	12	12	12	14	14	14	14	16	16	16	18	18	18	18	20	20	20	22	22	22	22	24	24	24	26	26	26	26	28	28	28	30	30	30	30	32	32	32	34	34	34				
0.321 – 0.325	04	06	06	08	08	10	10	10	10	12	12	12	14	14	14	14	16	16	16	18	18	18	18	20	20	20	20	22	22	22	24	24	24	26	26	26	28	28	28	30	30	30	30	32	32	32	34	34					
0.326 – 0.340	06	06	08	08	10	10	10	12	12	12	12	14	14	14	14	16	16	16	18	18	18	18	20	20	20	20	22	22	22	24	24	24	26	26	28	28	28	30	30	30	32	32	32	32	34	34						
0.341 – 0.350	06	06	08	08	10	10	10	12	12	12	14	14	14	14	16	16	16	18	18	18	18	20	20	20	20	22	22	22	24	24	24	26	26	26	28	28	28	30	30	30	32	32	32	34	34							
0.351 – 0.370	06	08	08	10	10	12	12	12	12	14	14	14	16	16	16	16	18	18	18	18	20	20	20	22	22	22	24	24	24	26	26	28	28	28	30	30	30	32	32	32	34	34										
0.371 – 0.375	06	08	08	10	10	12	12	12	12	14	14	14	16	16	16	16	18	18	18	18	20	20	20	22	22	22	24	24	24	26	26	28	28	30	30	30	32	32	32	34	34											
0.376 – 0.390	08	08	10	10	12	12	12	14	14	14	14	16	16	16	18	18	18	18	20	20	20	22	22	22	24	24	24	26	26	26	28	28	30	30	30	32	32	32	34	34	34											
0.391 – 0.400	08	08	10	10	12	12	14	14	14	14	16	16	16	18	18	18	18	20	20	20	22	22	22	24	24	26	26	26	28	28	30	30	30	30	32	32	32	34	34	34												
0.401 – 0.420	08	10	10	12	12	14	14	14	14	16	16	16	18	18	18	18	20	20	20	22	22	22	24	24	24	26	26	28	28	28	30	30	30	30	32	32	32	34	34	34												
0.421 – 0.425	08	10	10	12	12	14	14	14	16	16	16	18	18	18	18	20	20	20	22	22	22	24	24	24	26	26	26	28	28	30	30	30	30	32	32	32	34	34	34													
0.426 – 0.440	10	10	12	12	14	14	14	16	16	16	18	18	18	18	20	20	20	22	22	22	24	24	24	26	26	28	28	28	30	30	30	32	32	32	34	34	34															
0.441 – 0.450	10	10	12	12	14	14	14	16	16	16	18	18	18	18	20	20	20	22	22	22	24	24	24	26	26	28	28	28	30	30	30	32	32	32	34	34	34															
0.451 – 0.470	10	12	12	14	14	16	16	16	18	18	18	20	20	20	22	22	22	24	24	24	26	26	26	28	28	28	30	30	32	32	32	32	34	34	34																
0.471 – 0.475	10	12	12	14	14	16	16	16	18	18	18	20	20	20	22	22	22	24	24	24	26	26	26	28	28	28	30	30	30	32	32	32	34	34	34																
0.476 – 0.490	12	12	14	14	16	16	16	18	18	18	20	20	20	22	22	22	24	24	24	26	26	26	28	28	28	30	30	30	32	32	32	34	34	34																	
0.491 – 0.500	12	12	14	14	16	16	16	18	18	18	20	20	20	22	22	22	24	24	26	26	26	28	28	28	30	30	30	30	32	32	34	34	34	34																	
0.501 – 0.520	12	14	14	16	16	18	18	18	18	20	20	20	22	22	22	22	24	24	24	26	26	26	28	28	28	30	30	30	30	32	32	34	34	34	34																
0.521 – 0.525	12	14	14	16	16	18	18	18	18	20	20	20	22	22	22	22	24	24	24	26	26	26	28	28	28	30	30	30	32	32	32	32	34	34	34																
0.526 – 0.540	14	14	16	16	18	18	18	18	20	20	20	22	22	22	22	24	24	24	26	26	26	28	28	28	30	30	30	30	32	32	34	34	34	34																	
0.541 – 0.550	14	14	16	16	18	18	18	20	20	20	20	22	22	22	24	24	24	24	26	26	28	28	28	28	30	30	32	32	32	32	34	34	34																		
0.551 – 0.570	14	16	16	18	18	20	20	20	22	22	22	24	24	24	24	26	26	26	28	28	28	30	30	30	32	32	32	32	34	34	34																			
0.571 – 0.575	14	16	16	18	18	20	20	20	22	22	22	24	24	24	24	26	26	26	28	28	28	30	30	30	32	32	32	32	34	34	34																			
0.576 – 0.590	16	16	18	18	20	20	20	22	22	22	24	24	24	26	26	26	28	28	28	30	30	30	32	32	32	32	34	34	34																					
0.591 – 0.600	16	16	18	18	20	20	20	22	22	22	24	24	24	26	26	26	28	28	28	30	30	30	32	32	32	32	34	34	34																					
0.601 – 0.620	16	18	18	20	20	22	22	22	22	24	24	24	26	26	26	26	28	28	28	30	30	30	32	32	32	34	34	34	34																					
0.621 – 0.625	16	18	18	20	20	22	22	22	24	24	24	26	26	26	28	28	28	30	30	30	32	32	32	34	34	34																								
0.626 – 0.640	18	18	20	20	22	22	22	24	24	24	26	26	26	28	28	28	28	30	30	30	32	32	32	34	34	34																								
0.641 – 0.650	18	18	20	20	22	22	22	24	24	24	26	26	26	28	28	28	28	30	30	30	32	32	32	32	34	34	34																							
0.651 – 0.670	18	20	20	22	22	24	24	24	24	26	26	26	28	28	28	28	30	30	30	32	32	32	32	34	34	34																								
0.671 – 0.675	18	20	20	22	22	24	24	24	24	26	26	26	28	28	28	30	30	30	30	32	32	32	34	34	34																									
0.676 – 0.690	20	20	22	22	24	24	24	24	26	26	26	28	28	28	30	30	30	30	32	32	32	34	34	34																										
0.691 – 0.700	20	20	22	22	24	24	24	26	26	26	28	28	28	30	30	30	30	32	32	32	34	34	34	34																										
0.701 – 0.720	20	22	22	24	24	26	26	26	28	28	28	30	30	30	30	32	32	32	34	34	34																													
0.721 – 0.725	20	22	22	24	24	26	26	26	28	28	28	30	30	30	30	32	32	32	34	34	34																													
0.726 – 0.740	22	22	24	24	26	26	26	28	28	28	30	30	30	32	32	32	32	34	34	34																														
0.741 – 0.750	22	22	24	24	26	26	26	28	28	28	30	30	30	32	32	32	32	34	34	34																														
0.751 – 0.770	22	24	24	26	26	28	28	28	30	30	30	32	32	32	32	34	34	34																																
0.771 – 0.775	22	24	24	26	26	28	28	28	30	30	30	32	32	32	32	34	34	34																																
0.776 – 0.790	24	24	26	26	28	28	28	30	30	30	32	32	32	32	34	34	34																																	
0.791 – 0.800	24	24	26	26	28	28	30	30	30	30	32	32	32	34	34	34	34																																	
0.801 – 0.820	24	26	26	28	28	30	30	30	30	32	32	32	34	34	34	34																																		
0.821 – 0.825	24	26	26	28	28	30	30	30	32	32	32	34	34	34																																			
0.826 – 0.840	26	26	28	28	30	30	30	32	32	32	32	34	34	34																																			
0.841 – 0.850	26	26	28	28	30	30	30	32	32	32	32	34	34	34																																			
0.851 – 0.870	26	28	28	30	30	32	32	32	32	34	34	34																																					
0.871 – 0.875	26	28	28	30	30	32	32	32	32	34	34	34																																					
0.876 – 0.890	28	28	30	30	32	32	32	34	34	34																																						
0.891 – 0.900	28	28	30	30	32	32	32	34	34	34																																						
0.901 – 0.925	28	30	30	32	32	34	34	34																																								
0.926 – 0.950	30	30	32	32	34	34	34																																									
0.951 – 0.975	30	32	32	34	34																																										
0.976 – 1.000	32	32	34	34																																											
1.001 – 1.025	32	34	34																																												
1.026 – 1.050	34	34																																													
1.051 – 1.075	34																																														

AVAILABLE SHIMS mm (in)

Shim No.	Thickness	Shim No.	Thickness
02	2.500 (0.0984)	20	2.950 (0.1161)
04	2.550 (0.1004)	22	3.000 (0.1181)
06	2.600 (0.1024)	24	3.050 (0.1201)
08	2.650 (0.1043)	26	3.100 (0.1220)
10	2.700 (0.1063)	28	3.150 (0.1240)
12	2.750 (0.1083)	30	3.200 (0.1260)
14	2.800 (0.1102)	32	3.250 (0.1280)
16	2.850 (0.1122)	34	3.300 (0.1299)
18	2.900 (0.1142)		

Exhaust valve clearance (cold):
0.20 – 0.30 mm (0.008 – 0.012

Example: A 2.800 mm shim is installed and t
measured clearance is 0.450 mm.
Replace the 2.800 mm shim with
shim No. 22 (3.000 mm).

Installed Shim Thickness (mm) — chart columns (top row):
2.500, 2.525, 2.550, 2.575, 2.600, 2.620, 2.625, 2.640, 2.650, 2.660, 2.675, 2.680, 2.700, 2.720, 2.725, 2.740, 2.750, 2.760, 2.775, 2.780, 2.800, 2.820, 2.825, 2.840, 2.850, 2.860, 2.875, 2.880, 2.900, 2.920, 2.925, 2.940, 2.950, 2.960, 2.975, 2.980, 3.000, 3.020, 3.025, 3.040, 3.050, 3.060, 3.075, 3.080, 3.100, 3.120, 3.125, 3.140, 3.150, 3.160, 3.175, 3.200, 3.225, 3.250, 3.275, 3.300

Measured clearance (mm) — chart rows (left column):

− 0.009	− 0.025	− 0.029	− 0.040	− 0.050	− 0.070	− 0.075	− 0.090	− 0.100	− 0.120	− 0.125	− 0.140	− 0.149
0 − 0.250	− 0.270	− 0.275	− 0.290	− 0.300	− 0.320	− 0.325	− 0.340	− 0.350	− 0.370	− 0.375	− 0.390	− 0.400
− 0.420	− 0.425	− 0.440	− 0.450	− 0.470	− 0.475	− 0.490	− 0.500	− 0.520	− 0.525	− 0.540	− 0.550	− 0.570
− 0.575	− 0.590	− 0.600	− 0.620	− 0.625	− 0.640	− 0.650	− 0.670	− 0.675	− 0.690	− 0.700	− 0.720	− 0.725
− 0.740	− 0.750	− 0.770	− 0.775	− 0.790	− 0.800	− 0.820	− 0.825	− 0.840	− 0.850	− 0.870	− 0.875	− 0.890
− 0.900	− 0.925	− 0.950	− 0.975	− 1.000	− 1.025							

(The chart body consists of shim number codes — 02, 04, 06, 08, 10, 12, 14, 16, 18, 20, 22, 24, 26, 28, 30, 32, 34 — at the intersection of each measured clearance row and installed shim thickness column.)

AVAILABLE SHIMS

Shim No.	Thickness	Shim No.	Thickness
02	2.500 (0.0984)	20	2.950 (0.1161)
04	2.550 (0.1004)	22	3.000 (0.1181)
06	2.600 (0.1024)	24	3.050 (0.1201)
08	2.650 (0.1043)	26	3.100 (0.1220)
10	2.700 (0.1063)	28	3.150 (0.1240)
12	2.750 (0.1083)	30	3.200 (0.1260)
14	2.800 (0.1102)	32	3.250 (0.1280)
16	2.850 (0.1122)	34	3.300 (0.1299)
18	2.900 (0.1142)		

Intake valve clearance (cold):
0.15 − 0.25 mm (0.006 − 0.010 in.)

Example: A 2.800 mm shim is installed and the measured clearance is 0.450 mm. Replace the 2.800 mm shim with shim No. 24 (3.050 mm).

Intake Valve adjusting shim selection chart

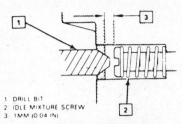

1 DRILL BIT
2 IDLE MIXTURE SCREW
3 1MM (0 04 IN)

Drilling the mixture adjusting screw plug

and slowly to avoid drilling onto the screw. The drill may force the plug off at any time.

d. Through the hole in the plug, fully screw in the mixture adjusting screw with a screwdriver.

NOTE: *Be careful not to damage the screw tip by tightening the screw too tight.*

e. Use a 7mm drill to force the plug off.

3. Inspect the mixture adjusting screw as follows:

a. Blow off any steel particles with compressed air.

b. Remove the screw and inspect it. If the drill has gnawed into the screw top or if the tapered portion is damaged, replace the screw.

4. Reinstall the mixture adjusting screw. Fully seat the idle mixture adjusting screw and then back it out 3¼ turns.

NOTE: *Be careful not to damage the screw tip by tightening the screw too tight.*

5. Reinstall the carburetor on the engine. Reconnect the vacuum hoses to their proper locations.

6. Reinstall the air cleaner.

7. Adjust the idle speed and mixture as follows:

a. Check the following initial conditions:
- The air cleaner is installed
- The engine is at normal operating temperature
- The choke is fully open
- All accessories are switch off

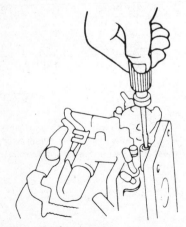

Seating the adjusting screw

- All vacuum lines are connected
- The ignition timing is correct
- The transaxle is in neutral (N)
- The float level is correct
- The front wheels are pointed straight ahead (power stering equipped vehicles)

b. Start the engine

c. Turn the mixture adjustment screw slowly until the maximum idle speed is obtained. The preliminary adjustment of 3¼ turn should be fairly close.

d. Set the idle speed by turning the idle speed adjusting screw. The idle mixture speed should be as shown on either the underhood Emissions Label or the Tune-Up Specifications chart at the beginning of this chapter.

e. Before moving to the next step, repeat adjustments (c) and (d) until the maximum speed will not raise any further no matter how much the idle mixture adjusting screw is adjusted.

f. Final adjust to 650 rpm by turning the mixture adjusting screw.

g. Final adjust the idle speed to specification by turning the idle adjusting screw.

8. Reinstall the mixture adjusting screw plugs. Remove the air cleaner and the EGR vacuum modulator bracket. With the tapered end of the plug facing inward, tap in the plug until it is even with the carburetor surface.

9. Reinstall the EGR vacuum modulator bracket and the air cleaner.

Adjusting High Idle

1. Stop the engine and remove the air cleaner and its housing.

2. Plug the hot idle compensator hose. It's the hose that runs from the lower front part of the carburetor body to a small valve on the air cleaner housing. If not plugged, it will create a vacuum leak causing either a rough idle or stalling.

3. On the left side of the engine, between the block and the firewall, find the vacuum valve with five hoses connected to it. One hose will be in a separate position and four will be in line. This is the thermo vacuum switching valve (TVSV). Of the four hoses in line, one will be labled ' M '; it's usually the second one from the upper or outer end of the valve.

4. Give the hose on the M port a half-turn and remove it from the port. Plug the port (not the hose) with an airtight plug to prevent vacuum leaks.

5. Hold the throttle plate open slightly (you can move the linkage with your fingers or pull gently on the accelerator cable) and move the choke plate to its fully closed position. Hold the choke closed as you release the throttle cable.

6. Start the engine but DO NOT move the gas pedal or the accelerator cable. The engine has been fooled into thinking it's cold--the choke is set and the high idle is engaged. If you move the accelerator, you'll undo everything set up in the prevous five steps.

7. Adjust the high idle by turning the Fast Idle adjusting screw; it's located just to the left and below the curb idle adjusting screw. You'll need a short, narrow screwdriver to adjust the screw. Set the fast idle to 3000 rpm.

CAUTION: *The engine is running at high speed. Beware of moving parts and hot surfaces.*

8. When the fast idle is set correctly, shut the engine off. Remove the plug from the M port of the TVSV and reconnect its hose. Remove the plug from the hot idle compensator hose.

9. Reinstall the air clearner housing and the filter; connect the hose.

FUEL INJECTED NOVA AND PRIZM

Adjusting Idle Speed

One of the merits of electronic fuel injection is that it requires so little adjustment. The computer (ECM) does most of the work in compensating for changes in climate, engine temperature, electrical load and driving conditions. The curb idle on the fuel injected Nova and Prizms should be checked periodically but not adjusted unless off spec by more than 50 rpm. If you are a compulsive tinkerer who feels that "the idle can be adjusted, therefore it must be adjusted", please don't.

If the idle is too far outside its normal range, the computer will see it as a problem (too much or too little air being taken in for the speed of the engine) and attempt to compensate by changing the amount of fuel being delivered. This can lead to wild surging and extremely bizarre idle behavior, making the car virtually undrivable. This is one area in which the old rule of Don't fix it if it isn't broken, applies.

The idle speed adjusting screw is located on the side of the throttle body. You can find the the throttle body by following the accelerator cable to its end. The adjusting screw may have a cap over it to prevent casual meddling. If so, pop the cap off with a small screwdriver.

With the engine fully warmed up, properly connect a tachometer. Make sure that all the electrical accessories on the car are turned off and remove the cap over the adjustor screw, if there is one. Start the engine and use a screwdriver to turn the screw. The idle speed should be as shown on the underhood Emissions Label or in the Tune-Up Specifications chart at the beginning of this chapter.

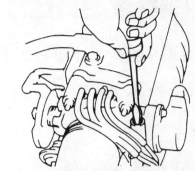

Idle adjuster location, fuel injected Nova

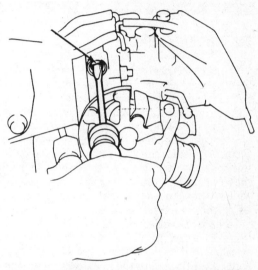

Location of idle adjusting screw, fuel injected Prizm

If for any reason the idle cannot be brought into specification by this adjustment, return the screw to its original setting and follow other diagnostic procedures to find the real cause of the problem. Do not try to cure other problems with this adjustment.

Mixture Adjustment

The air/fuel ratio burned within the engine is controlled by the ECM, based on information delivered by the various sensors on the engine. It is not adjustable as a routine maintenance item. The easiest way to check the air/fuel mixture is to put the car through a tailpipe emissions test. Whether or not this is required in your area, it's a good way of putting numbers on the combustion efficiency of the engine. The engine can only burn so much fuel; if too much is being delivered, it will show up on the test as unburned hydrocarbons (HC).

Putting the car through this test once a year from the time it is newly acquired can provide an excellent baseline for diagnosing future problems.

Engine and Engine Overhaul

3

ENGINE ELECTRICAL

For any electrical system to operate, it must make a complete circuit. This simply means that the power flow from the battery must make a complete circle. When an electrical component is operating, power flows from the battery to the components, passes through the component (load) causing it to function, and returns to the battery through the ground path of the circuit. This ground may be either another wire or the actual metal part of the car upon which the component is mounted.

Perhaps the easiest way to visualize this is to think of connecting a light bulb with two wires attached to it to the battery. If one of the two wires was attached to the negative (–) post of the battery and the other wire to the positive (+) post, the light bulb would light and the circuit would be complete. Electricity could follow a path from the battery to the bulb and back to the battery. Its not hard to see that with longer wires on our light bulb, it could be mounted anywhere on the car. Further, one wire could be fitted with a switch so that the light could be turned on and off at will. Various other items could be added to our primitive circuit to make the light flash, become brighter or dimmer under certain conditions or advise the user that it's burned out.

Some automotive components don't use a wire to battery--they ground to the metal of the car through their mounting points. The electrical current runs through the chassis of the vehicle and returns to the battery through the ground (–) cable; if you look, you'll see that the battery ground cable connects between the battery and the body of the car.

Every complete circuit must include a load--something to use the electricity coming from the source. If you were to connect a wire between the two terminals of the battery (DON'T do this) without the light bulb, the battery would attempt to deliver its entire power supply from one pole to another almost instantly. This is a short circuit. The electricity is taking a short-cut to get to ground and is not being used by any load in the circuit. This sudden and uncontrolled electrical flow can cause great damage to other components in the circuit and can develop a tremendous amount of heat. A short in an automotive wiring harness can develop sufficient heat to melt the insulation on all the surrounding wires and reduce a multi-wire cable to one sad lump of plastic and copper. Two common causes of shorts are broken insulation (thereby exposing the wire to contact with surrounding metal surfaces) or a failed switch (the pins inside the switch come out of place, touch each other and reroute the electricity).

Some electrical components which require a large amount of current to operate also have a relay in their circuit. Since these circuits carry a large amount of current (amperage or amps), the thickness of the wire in the circuit (wire gauge) is also greater. If this large wire were connected from the load to the control switch on the dash, the switch would have to carry the high amperage load and the dash would be twice as large to accommodate wiring harnesses as thick as your wrist. To prevent these problems, a relay is used. The large wires in the circuit are connected from the battery to one side of the relay and from the opposite side of the relay to the load. The relay is normally open, preventing current from passing through the circuit. An additional, smaller wire is connected from the relay to the control switch for the circuit. When the control switch is turned on, it grounds the smaller wire to the relay and completes its circuit. The main switch inside the relay close, sending power to the component without routing the main power through the inside of the car. Some common circuits which may use relays are the horn, headlights, starter and rear window defogger systems.

It is possible for larger surges of current to pass through the electrical system of your car. If this surge of current were to reach the load in the circuit, it could burn it out or severely damage it. To prevent this, fuse and/or circuit breakers and/or fusible links are connected into the supply wires of the electrical system. These items are nothing more than a built-in weak spot in the system. It's much easier to go to a known location (the fusebox) to see why a circuit is inoperative than to dissect 15 feet of wiring under the dashboard, looking for what happened.

When an electrical current of excessive power passes through the fuse, the fuse blows and breaks the circuit, preventing the passage of current and protecting the components.

A circuit breaker is basically a self-repairing fuse. It will open the circuit in the same fashion as a fuse, but when either the short is removed or the surge subsides, the circuit breaker resets itself and does not need replacement.

A fuse link (fusible link or main link) is a wire that acts as a fuse. It is normally connected between the starter relay and the main wiring harness under the hood. Since the starter is the highest electrical draw on the car, an internal short during starter use could direct about 130 amps into the wrong places. Consider the damage potential of introducing this current into a system whose wiring is rated at 15 amps and you'll understand the need for protection. Since this link is very early in the electrical path, it's the first place to look if nothing on the car works but the battery seems to be charged and is properly connected.

Electrical problems generally fall into one of three areas:

1. The component that is not functioning is not receiving current.

2. The component is receiving power but not using it or using it incorrectly (component failure).

3. The component is improperly grounded.

The circuit can be can be checked with a test light and a jumper wire. The test light is a device that looks like a pointed screwdriver with a wire on one end and a bulb in its handle. A jumper wire is simply a piece of wire with alligator clips on each end. If a component is not working, you must follow a systematic plan to determine which of the three causes is the villain.

1. Turn on the switch that controls the item not working.

NOTE: *Some items only work when the ignition switch is turned on.*

2. Disconnect the the power supply wire from the component.

3. Attach the ground wire on the test light to a good metal ground.

4. Touch the end probe of the test light to the power wire; if there is current in the wire, the light in the test light will come on. You have now established that current is getting to the component.

5. Turn the ignition or dash switch off and reconnect the wire to the component.

If the test light does not go on, then the problem is between the battery and the component. This includes all the switches, fuses, relays and the battery itself. Next place to look is the fusebox; check carefully either by eye or by using the test light across the fuse clips. The easiest way to check is to simply replace the fuse. If the fuse is blown, and upon replacement, immediately blows again, there is a short between the fuse and the component. This is generally (not always) a sign of an internal short in the component. Disconnect the power wire at the component again and replace the fuse; if the fuse holds, the component is the problem.

If all the fuses are good and the component is not receiving power, find the switch for the circuit. Bypass the switch with the jumper wire. This is done by connecting one end of the jumper to the power wire coming into the switch and the other end to the wire leaving the switch. If the component comes to life, the switch has failed.

WARNING: *Never substitute the jumper for the component. The circuit needs the electrical load of the component. If you bypass it, you cause a short circuit.*

Checking the ground for any circuit can mean tracing wires to the body, cleaning connections or tightening mounting bolts for the component itself. If the jumper wire can be connected to the case of the component or the ground connector, you can ground the other end to a piece of clean, solid metal on the car. Again, if the component starts working, you've found the problem.

It should be noted that generally the last place to look for an electrical problem is in the wiring itself. Unless the car has undergone unusual circumstances (major bodywork, flood damage, improper repairs, etc.) the wiring is not likely to change its condition. A systematic search through the fuse, the connectors and switches and the component itself will almost always yield an answer. Loose and/or corroded connectors--particularly in ground circuits--are becoming a larger problem in modern cars. The computers and on-board electronic (solid state) systems are highly sensitive to improper grounds and will change their function drastically if one occurs.

Remember that for any electrical circuit to work, ALL the connections must be clean and tight.

BATTERY AND STARTING SYSTEM

Basic Operating Principles

The battery is the first link in the chain of mechanisms which work together to provide cranking of the automobile engine. In most modern cars, the battery is a lead/acid electrochemical device consisting of six 2v subsections (cells) connected in series so the unit is capable of producing approximately 12v of electrical pressure. Each subsection consists of a series of positive and negative plates held a short distance apart in a solution of sulfuric acid and water.

The two types of plates are of dissimilar metals. This causes a chemical reaction to be set up, and it is this reaction which produces current flow from the battery when its positive and negative terminals are connected to an electrical appliance such as a lamp or motor. The continued transfer of electrons would eventually convert the sulfuric acid to water, and make the two plates identical in chemical composition. As electrical energy is removed from the battery, its voltage output tends to drop. Thus, measuring battery voltage and battery electrolyte composition are two ways of checking the ability of the unit to supply power. During the starting of the engine, electrical energy is removed from the battery. However, if the charging circuit is in good condition and the operating conditions are normal, the power removed from the battery will be replaced by the generator (or alternator) which will force electrons back through the battery, reversing the normal flow, and restoring the battery to its original chemical state.

The battery and starting motor are linked by very heavy electrical cables designed to minimize resistance to the flow of current. Generally, the major power supply cable that leaves the battery goes directly to the starter, while other electrical system needs are supplied by a smaller cable. During starter operation, power flows from the battery to the starter and is grounded through the car's frame and the battery's negative ground strap.

The starting motor is a specially designed, direct current electric motor capable of producing a very great amount of power for its size. One thing that allows the motor to produce a great deal of power is its tremendous rotating speed. It drives the engine through a tiny pinion gear (attached to the starter's armature), which drives the very large flywheel ring gear at a greatly reduced speed. Another factor allowing it to produce so much power is that only intermittent operation is required of it. Thus, little allowance for air circulation is required, and the windings can be built into a very small space.

The starter solenoid is a magnetic device which employs the small current supplied by the start circuit of the ignition switch. This magnetic action moves a plunger which mechanically engages the starter and closes the heavy switch connecting it to the battery. The starting switch circuit consists of the starting switch contained within the ignition switch, a transmission neutral safety switch or clutch pedal switch, and the wiring necessary to connect these in series with the starter solenoid or relay.

The pinion, a small gear, is mounted to a one-way drive clutch. This clutch is splined to the starter armature shaft. When the ignition switch is moved to the **start** position, the solenoid plunger slides the pinion toward the flywheel ring gear via a collar and spring. If the teeth on the pinion and flywheel match properly, the pinion will engage the flywheel immediately. If the gear teeth butt one another, the spring will be compressed and will force the gears to mesh as soon as the starter turns far enough to allow them to do so. As the solenoid plunger reaches the end of its travel, it closes the contacts that connect the battery and starter and then the engine is cranked.

As soon as the engine starts, the flywheel ring gear begins turning fast enough to drive the pinion at an extremely high rate of speed. At this point, the one-way clutch begins allowing the pinion to spin faster than the starter shaft so that the starter will not operate at excessive speed. When the ignition switch is released from the starter position, the solenoid is de-energized, and a spring pulls the gear out of mesh interrupting the current flow to the starter.

Some starters employ a separate relay, mounted away from the starter, to switch the motor and solenoid current on and off. The relay replaces the solenoid electrical switch, but does not eliminate the need for a solenoid mounted on the starter used to mechanically engage the starter drive gears. The relay is used to reduce the amount of current the starting switch must carry.

THE CHARGING SYSTEM

Basic Operating Principles

The automobile charging system provides electrical power for operation of the vehicle's ignition and starting systems and all the electrical accessories. The battery services as an electrical surge or storage tank, storing (in chemical form) the energy originally produced by the engine driven generator. The system also provides a means of regulating generator output to protect the battery from being overcharged and to avoid excessive voltage to the accessories.

The storage battery is a chemical device incorporating parallel lead plates in a tank containing a sulfuric acid/water solution. Adjacent plates are slightly dissimilar, and the chemical reaction of the two dissimilar plates produces electrical energy when the battery is connected to a load such as the starter motor. The chemical reaction is reversible, so that when the generator is producing a voltage (electrical pressure) greater than that produced by the battery, electricity is forced into the battery, and the battery is returned to its fully charged state.

The vehicle's generator is driven mechanically, through V-belts, by the engine crankshaft. It consists of two coils of fine wire, one stationary (the stator), and one movable (the rotor). The rotor may also be known as the armature, and consists of fine wire wrapped around an iron core which is mounted on a shaft. The electricity which flows through the two coils of wire (provided initially by the battery in some cases) creates an intense magnetic field around both rotor and stator, and the interaction between the two fields creates voltage, allowing the generator to power the accessories and charge the battery.

There are two types of generators: the earlier is the direct current (DC) type. The current produced by the DC generator is generated in the armature and carried off the spinning armature by stationary brushes contacting the commutator. The commutator is a series of smooth metal contact plates on the end of the armature. The commutator plates, which are separated from one another by a very short gap, are connected to the armature circuits so that current will flow in one direction only in the wires carrying the generator output. The generator stator consists of two stationary coils of wire which draw some of the output current from the generator to form a powerful magnetic field and create the interaction of fields which generates the voltage. The generator field is wired in series with the regulator.

Newer automobiles use alternating current generators or alternators, because they are more efficient, can be rotated at higher speeds, and have fewer brush problems. In an alternator, the field rotates while all the current produced passes only through the stator winding. The brushes bear against continuous slip rings rather than a commutator. This causes the current produced to periodically reverse the direction of its flow. Diodes (electrical one-way valves) block the flow of current from traveling in the wrong direction. A series of diodes is wired together to permit the alternating flow of the stator to be rectified back to 12 volts DC for use by the vehicles's electrical system.

The regulator consists of several circuits. Each circuit has a core, or magnetic coil of wire, which operates a switch. Each switch is connected to ground through one or more resistors. The coil of wire responds directly to system voltage. When the voltage reaches the required level, the magnetic field created by the winding of wire closes the switch and inserts a resistance into the generator field circuit, thus reducing the output. The contacts of the switch cycle open and close many times each second to precisely control voltage. On many newer cars, the regulating function is performed by solid-state (rather than mechanical) components. The regulator is often built in to the alternator; this system is termed an integrated or internal regulator.

While alternators are self-limiting as far as maximum current is concerned, DC generators employ a current regulating circuit which responds directly to the total amount of current flowing through the generator circuit rather than to the output voltage. The current regulator is similar to the voltage regulator except that all system current must flow through the energizing coil on its way to the various accessories.

Ignition Coil

TESTING

NOTE: *This test requires the use of an ohmeter. When using this tool, make sure the scale is set properly for the range of resistance you expect to encounter during the test. Always perform these tests with the ignition OFF.*

4A-LC and 4A-GE Engines

1. Disconnect the distributor cap and set it aside. The spark plug wires may be left attached to the cap. Remove the rotor and the dust cover(s).

2. Using the ohmeter, measure the resistance between the positive (+) and negative (−) terminals on the coil. The resistance on the primary side of the coil (when cold) should be:

- 4A-LC
    1985: 0.3–0.5Ω
    1986–88: 0.4–0.5Ω
- 4A-GE
    All: 0.5–0.7Ω

3. Using the ohmeter, measure the resistance between the positive terminal and the

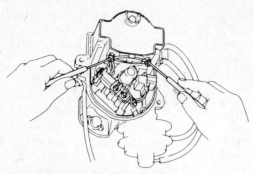

Checking the coil primary resistance

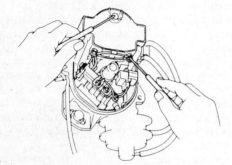

Checking the coil secondary resistance

center (high tension) terminal. (This is the terminal to which the coil attaches in the cap.) The resistance on the secondary side should be:

- 4A-LC
  1985: 7500–10,500Ω
  1986–88: 7500–10,400Ω
- 4A-GE
  All: 11,000–16,000Ω

4. Coils measuring outside either of these ranges must be replaced.

4A-FE Engine

1. Remove the distributor cap, the rotor and the dust cover.

2. Turn the ignition to the RUN position.(Ignition is on but engine is off). Measure the voltage (not ohms!) between the positive (+) terminal of the coil and any good ground. Look for voltage equal to battery voltage, approximately 12 volts. If voltage is low, and the battery is known to be good, check the wiring harness to the battery and the connector to the coil.

3. Turn the ignition OFF.

4. Using the ohmmeter, measure the resistance across the primary side of the coil. touch the probes of the meter to the + and − terminals on the coil and read the meter. Correct resistance is 1.3 - 1.6 ohms

5. Measure the resistance of the secondary side of the coil. Touch one probe to the + terminal and the other to the center

tap (high tension port). Correct resistance is 10,400 - 14,000 ohms.

6. Coils measuring outside either of these ranges must be replaced.

REMOVAL AND INSTALLATION

External coils (coils which are not built into the distributor) are easily replaced by the following procedure:

1. Make certain the ignition is off and the key is removed.

2. Disconnect the high tension wire (running between the coil and the distributor) from the coil.

3. Label and disconnect the low tension wires from the coil.

4. Loosen the coil bracket and remove the coil. Install the new coil and tighten the bracket.

5. Attach the low tension wires first, then the coil wire.

The internal coils found within the distributor can be changed without removing the distributor. A selection of various short screwdrivers may be required for access to the screws.

1. Disconnect the negative battery cable.

2. Remove the distributor cap with the wires attached and set it aside.

3. Remove the rotor and the dust cover(s).

4. Remove the nuts and disconnect the wires from the terminals on the coil.

5. Remove the four retaining screws and remove the coil. Note that later cars have a gasket below the coil--remove it carefully to avoid damage.

6. Install the coil, paying close attention to the gasket and its placement.

7. Connect the wiring to the coil and be careful of the routing of the wires.

8. Install the dust cover(s), the rotor and the cap.

9. Reconnect the battery.

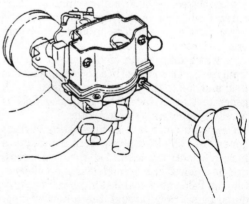

The coil is easily removed with the distributor off the car

Distributor

REMOVAL AND INSTALLATION

WARNING: *Once the distributor is removed, the engine should not be turned or moved out of position. Should this occur, please refer to the end of this section.*

4A-LC Engine

1. Disconnect the negative battery cable.
2. Disconnect the distributor wire at its connector.
3. Label and disconnect the vacuum hoses running to the vacuum advance unit on the side of the distributor.
4. Remove the distributor cap (leave the spark plug wires connected) and swing it out of the way.
5. Carefully note the position of the distributor rotor relative to the distributor housing; a mark made on the casing will be helpful during reassembly. Use a marker or tape so the mark doesn't rub off during the handling of the case.
6. Remove the distributor hold-down bolts.
7. Carefully pull the distributor out until it stops turning counterclockwise.
8. If the engine has not been moved out of position, align the rotor with the mark you made earlier and reinstall the distributor. Position it carefully and make sure the drive gear engages properly within the engine. Install the holding bolts.
9. Install the distributor cap and re-attach the vacuum lines to their correct ports.
10. Install the wiring to the distributor, and connect the battery cable.
11. Check and adjust the timing as necessary.

4A-GE Engine

1. Disconnect the negative battery cable.
2. Label and disconnect the coil and spark plug wiring at the distributor cap.
3. Disconnect the distributor wire at its connector.
4. Remove the distributor hold-down bolts. Before moving or disturbing the distributor, mark the position of the distributor relative to

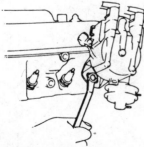

Loosen the pinch bolt and then pull the distributor straight out

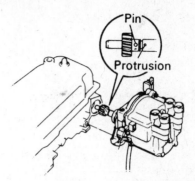

Distributor alignment

the engine and the position of the rotor relative to the case. Use a marker or tape so the mark doesn't rub off during the handling of the case.
5. Remove the distributor from the engine.
6. Remove the O-ring from the distributor shaft.
7. If the engine has not been moved out of position, align the rotor with the mark you made earlier and reinstall the distributor. Position it carefully and make sure the drive gear engages properly within the engine. Install the holding bolts.
8. Reconnect the wiring and the spark plug wires. Connect the negative battery cable.
9. Check and adjust the timing as necessary

4A-FE Engine

1. Disconnect the negative battery cable.
2. Disconnect all electrical connections at the distributor, including the plug wires.
3. Remove the distributor cap.
4. Mark the position of the distributor case relative to the engine. Use a marker or tape so the mark doesn't rub off during the handling of the case. Also mark the position of the distributor rotor relative to the case.
5. Remove the distributor mounting bolts.
6. Remove the distributor from the engine and remove the O-ring from the distributor shaft.
7. If the engine has not been moved out of position, align the rotor with the mark you made earlier and reinstall the distributor. Position it carefully and make sure the drive gear engages properly within the engine. Install the holding bolts.
8. Reconnect the wiring and the spark plug wires. Connect the negative battery cable.
9. Check and adjust the timing as necessary.

Installation - Timing Lost

If the engine has been cranked, dismantled or the timing otherwise lost while the distributor was out, proceed as follows:
1. Remove the No. 1 spark plug.
2. Place your finger over the spark plug hole

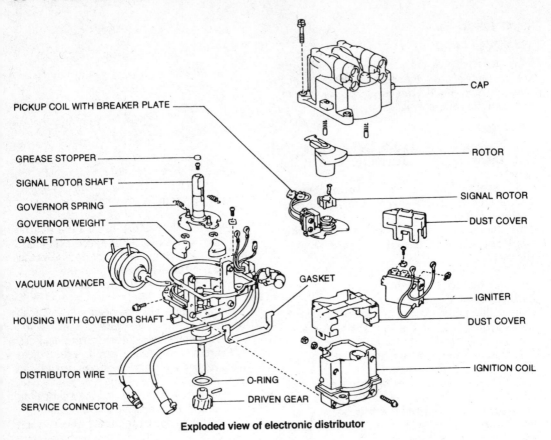

PICKUP COIL WITH BREAKER PLATE

CAP

GREASE STOPPER

ROTOR

SIGNAL ROTOR SHAFT

GOVERNOR SPRING

GOVERNOR WEIGHT

SIGNAL ROTOR

GASKET

DUST COVER

VACUUM ADVANCER

GASKET

IGNITER

HOUSING WITH GOVERNOR SHAFT

DUST COVER

DISTRIBUTOR WIRE

IGNITION COIL

O-RING

SERVICE CONNECTOR

DRIVEN GEAR

Exploded view of electronic distributor

and rotate the crankshaft clockwise to TDC (Top Dead Center). Watch the timing marks on the pulley; as they approach the zero point, you should feel pressure (compression) on your finger. If not, turn the crankshaft another full rotation and line up the marks.

NOTE: *The spark plugs on the 4A-GE and 4A-FE engines are in deep wells; use a screwdriver handle to plug the hole and feel the compression.*

3. Install the spark plug.

4. Observing the alignment marks made during removal, reinstall the distributor.

Igniter (Ignition Module)
REMOVAL AND INSTALLATION
4A-LC and 4A-GE ENGINE

NOTE: *The distributor on the 4A-FE (Prizm) engine contains no replaceable parts except the ignition coil. Any other failed item in the distributor requires replacement of the complete unit.*

1. Remove the distributor as outlined above. Make certain the negative battery cable is disconnected before beginning the work.

2. Rmove the packing and distributor rotor.

3. Remove the dust cover over the distribu-

tor components and remove the dust cover over the ignition coil.

4. Remove the nuts and disconnect the wiring from the ignition coil.

5. Remove the four screws and remove the ignition coil from the distributor.

6. At the igniter terminals, disconnect the wiring from the connecting points.

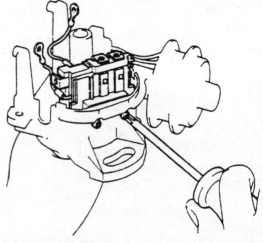

Removing the igniter

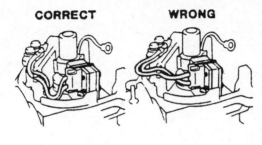

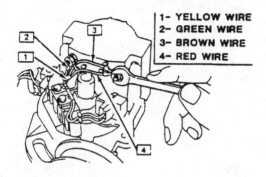

1- YELLOW WIRE
2- GREEN WIRE
3- BROWN WIRE
4- RED WIRE

Correct wiring placement is required during reassembly. The spinning rotor can cut a wire almost instnatly. Above: wiring path for igniter; below: color code and placement for ignition coil wiring

7. Loosen and remove the two screws holding the igniter and remove it from the distributor.

8. Install the igniter and connect its wiring. Pay particular attention to the correct routing of the wiring within the housing. There is one correct position only; any other wiring placements risk damage.

9. Install the ignition coil and secure its wiring. Again, watch the wiring postions.

10. Reinstall the dust covers, the packing and distributor rotor.

11. Reinstall the distributor and set the engine timing.

Alternator

ALTERNATOR PRECAUTIONS

Several precautions must be observed with alternator equipped vehicles to avoid damaging the unit. They are as follows:

1. If the battery is removed or disconnected for any reason, make sure that it is reconnected with the correct polarity. Reversing the battery connections may result in damage to the one-way rectifiers.

2. When utilizing a booster battery as a starting aid, always connect it as follows: positive to positive, and negative (booster battery) to a good ground on the engine of the car being started.

3. Never use a fast charger as a booster to start a car with an alternator.

4. When servicing the battery with a fast charger, always disconnect the car battery cables.

5. Never attempt to polarize an alternator.

6. Never apply more than 12 volts when attempting to jump start the vehicle. Many road service vehicles use two baateries connected in series to provide power--this 24 volt surge can destroy an electrical system instantly.

7. Do not use test lamps of more than 12 volts (V) for checking diode continuity.

8. Do not short across or ground any of the terminals on the alternator.

9. The polarity of the battery, alternator, and regulator must be matched and considered before making any electrical connections within the system.

10. Never disconnect the alternator or the battery with the engine running.

11. Disconnect the battery terminals when performing any service on the electrical system. This will eliminate the possibility of accidental reversal of polarity.

12. Disconnect the battery ground cable if arc welding (such as body repair) is to be done on any part of the car.

Noise from an alternator may be caused by a loose drive pulley, a loose belt, loose mounting bolts, worn or dirty bearings or worn internal parts. A high frequency whine that is heard at high engine speed or full alternator output is acceptable and should not be considered a sign of alternator failure.

REMOVAL AND INSTALLATION

All Nova and Prizm

1. Disconnect the negative battery cable. CAUTION: *Failure to disconnect the battery can cause personal injury and damage to the car. If a tool is accidentally shorted at the al-*

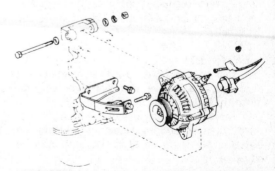

Alternator removal and installation; Nova shown, Prizm similar

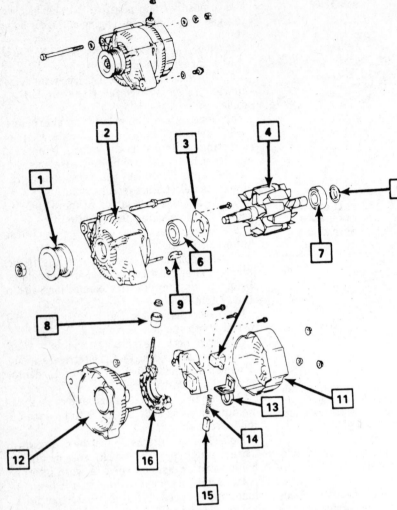

1. Pulley
2. Drive end frame
3. Retainer
4. Rotor
5. Bearing cover
6. Front bearing
7. Rear bearing
8. Terminal insulator
9. Rubber insulator
   IC regulator
10. Brush holder
11. Rear end cover
12. Rear end frame
13. Cover
14. Spring
15. Brush
16. Rectifier holder

Exploded view of the Nova alternator

ternator, it can become hot enough to cause a serious burn.

2. Disconnect the large connector from the alternator.

3. Remove the nut and the single wire from the alternator.

4. Loosen the adjusting lock bolt (Prizm, lower bolt) and pivot (upper) bolt. Remove the drive belt.

NOTE: *It may be necessary to remove other belts for access.*

5. Remove the lower bolt first, support the alternator and remove the upper pivot bolt. Remove the alternator from the car.

6. Installation is reverse of the above procedure. When reinstalling, remember to leave the bolts finger tight so that the belt may be adjusted.

7. Make sure that the plugs and connectors are properly seated and secure in their mounts.

Regulator
REMOVAL AND INSTALLATION

The voltage regulator is contained within the alternator. It is called an IC type (Integrated Circuit). The alternator must be removed to replace the regulator.

1. Disconnect the negative battery cable.

2. Remove the alternator.

3. Support the alternator on a workbench, pulley end down but not resting on the pulley.

4. At the side of the alternator, remove the nut and the plastic terminal insulator.

5. Remove the three nuts and remove the end cover.

6. Remove the five screws and carefully remove the brush holder and then the IC regulator. Be careful to keep track of various small parts (washers, etc)--they will be needed during reassembly.

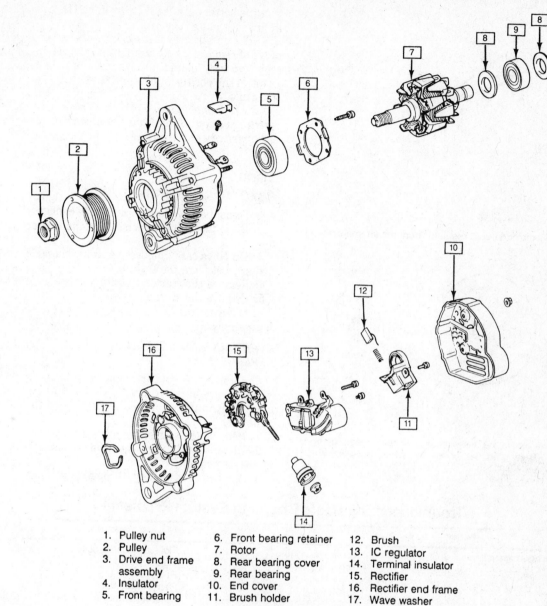

1. Pulley nut
2. Pulley
3. Drive end frame assembly
4. Insulator
5. Front bearing
6. Front bearing retainer
7. Rotor
8. Rear bearing cover
9. Rear bearing
10. End cover
11. Brush holder
12. Brush
13. IC regulator
14. Terminal insulator
15. Rectifier
16. Rectifier end frame
17. Wave washer

Exploded view of the Prizm alternator

7. When reinstalling, place the cover over the brush holder. Install the regulator and the brush holder onto the alternator and secure them with the five screws. Make sure the brush holder's cover doesn't slip to one side during installation.

8. Before reinstalling the rear cover, check that the gap between the bush holder and the connector is at least 1mm. After confirming this gap, install the rear alternator cover and its three nuts.

9. Install the terminal insulator and its nut. Hold the alternator horizontally and spin the pulley by hand. Make sure everything turns smoothly and there is no sign of noise or binding.

Battery

REMOVAL AND INSTALLATION

1. Disconnect the negative battery cable.
2. Disconnect the positive battery cable.
3. On Nova cars, remove the bolt holding the battery retainer and remove the retainer. On Prizms, remove the front retainer bolt first, then the rear retainer bolt and the retainer.
4. Remove the battery. You are reminded

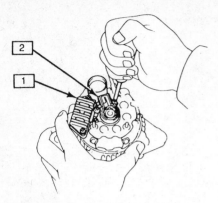

1. IC regulator
2. Brush holder

Removing the IC regulator from the alternator

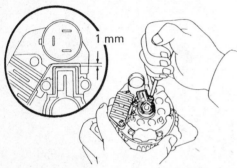

Maintain the minimum clearance between the brush holder and the connector when reassembling. 1 mm = 0.004 in

that the battery is a fairly heavy item. Use care in lifting it out of the car.

5. The new battery is installed in the reverse order of removal. Make certain that the retainer is correctly placed and its bolts are tight. Connect the positive cable first, then the negative cable.

NOTE: *Removing the battery may require resetting various digital equipment such as radio memory and the clock.*

Starter

REMOVAL AND INSTALLATION

1. Disconnect the negative battery cable.
2. Disconnect all the wiring from the starter terminals.
3. On Nova cars, remove the transaxle cable and bracket from the transaxle.
4. Remove the starter mounting bolts.
5. Remove the starter.
6. Reassemble in reverse order of disassembly.

OVERHAUL AND SOLENOID REPLACEMENT

The starter solenoid or magnetic switch is an integral part of the starter. It cannot be replaced without complete disassembly of the switch.

1. Remove the starter from the car.
2. Disconnect the wire lead from the magnetic switch terminal.
3. Remove the two long, through bolts hold-

Troubleshooting Basic Charging System Problems

Problem	Cause	Solution
Noisy alternator	• Loose mountings • Loose drive pulley • Worn bearings • Brush noise • Internal circuits shorted (High pitched whine)	• Tighten mounting bolts • Tighten pulley • Replace alternator • Replace alternator • Replace alternator
Squeal when starting engine or accelerating	• Glazed or loose belt	• Replace or adjust belt
Indicator light remains on or ammeter indicates discharge (engine running)	• Broken fan belt • Broken or disconnected wires • Internal alternator problems • Defective voltage regulator	• Install belt • Repair or connect wiring • Replace alternator • Replace voltage regulator
Car light bulbs continually burn out— battery needs water continually	• Alternator/regulator overcharging	• Replace voltage regulator/alternator
Car lights flare on acceleration	• Battery low • Internal alternator/regulator problems	• Charge or replace battery • Replace alternator/regulator
Low voltage output (alternator light flickers continually or ammeter needle wanders)	• Loose or worn belt • Dirty or corroded connections • Internal alternator/regulator problems	• Replace or adjust belt • Clean or replace connections • Replace alternator or regulator

Alternator Specifications

| | | Alternator | | |
| | | Field Current @ 12v (amps) | Output (amps) | Regulated Volts @ 75°F |
Year	Engine (cc)			
1985	1587	10	30	13.9–15.1
1986	1587	10	30	13.9–15.1
1987	1587	10	30	13.9–15.1
1988	1587	10	30	13.9–15.1
1989	1587	10	60	13.5–14.8
1990	1587	10	60	13.5–14.8

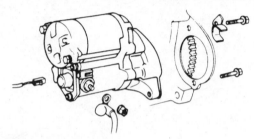

Starter motor removal

ing the field frame to the magnetic switch. Pull out the field frame with the armature from the magnetic switch.

3. On 1.0kw (1000 watt) starters, remove the felt seal. On 1.4kw starters, remove the O-ring.

4. To remove the starter housing from the magnetic switch assembly:

    a. For 1.0 kw starters, remove the two screws and remove the starter housing with the idler gear and clutch assembly.

    b. For 1.4kw units, remove the two screws and remove the starter housing with the pinion gear, idler and clutch assembly.

5. Using a magnetic tool, remove the spring and steel ball from the clutch shaft hole.

6. Remove the end cover from the field frame.

7. On 1.4kw units, remove the O-ring.

8. Use a small screwdriver or steel wire to separate the brush springs and remove the brushes from the holder.

9. Pull the brush holder off the field frame.

10. Remove the armature from the field frame.

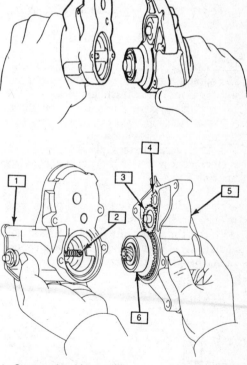

1. Starter solenoid assembly
2. Spring
3. Idler gear
4. Pinion gear
5. Drive housing
6. Clutch and drive assembly

Disassembly of the magnetic switch (solenoid) from the drive housing

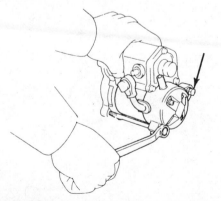

Separate the starter components by removing the two through bolts

11. Perform testing and repairs as necessary:

a. Measure the length of the brushes. If they are less than the acceptable minimum length, replace them with new brushes.

Standard Length:
- 1.0kw – 13mm
- 1.4kw – 15mm

Minimum Length:
- 1.0kw – 8.5mm
- 1.4kw – 10mm

b. Check the magnetic switch by performing the pull-in coil open circuit test. Using an ohmeter, check for continuity between terminal 50 and terminal C. If there is no continuity, replace the magnetic switch.

c. Check the hold in coil of the magnetic switch. Use the ohmeter to check for continuity between terminal 50 and the body (case) of the unit. If there is no continuity, replace the switch.

12. To reassemble the starter, apply high-temperature grease to the armature bearings and insert the armature into the field frame.

13. Use a screwdriver or a steel wire to hold the brush spring back and install the brushes into the holder(s).

WARNING: *Make certain the positive wires to the brushes are not grounded or touching surrounding parts.*

14. For 1.4kw starters, install the O-ring on the field frame.

15. Install the end cover on the field frame.

16. Apply grease to the ball and spring and insert them into the clutch shaft hole.

17. Install the gears and clutch assembly to the starter housing. Apply grease to the gear and clutch assemblies and:

a. For 1.0kw starters, place the clutch assembly, idler gear and bearing in the starter housing.

b. For 1.4kw starters, place the clutch asembly, idler gear, bearing and pinion gear in the starter housing.

18. Insert the spring into the clutch shaft hole and place the starter housing onto the magnetic switch. Install the two screws.

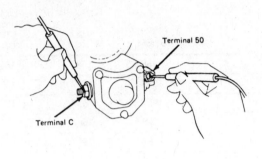

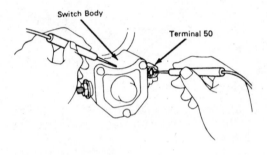

Performing the pull-in test (upper) and the hold-in test (below) will check the function of the solenoid

19. On 1.0kw units, install the felt seal on the armature shaft. On 1.4kw units, install the O-ring on the field frame.

20. Install the field frame with armature onto the magnetic switch assembly and install the two through bolts.

NOTE: *There is a protrusion or tab on each part; make sure you line them up correctly.*

21. Connect the wire to the terminal on the magnetic switch.

22. Reinstall the starter on the vehicle.

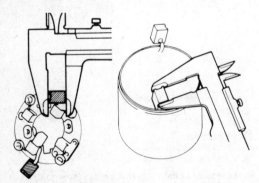

Checking the brush length

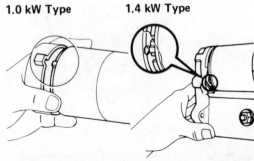

Match the field frame protrusion during reassembly

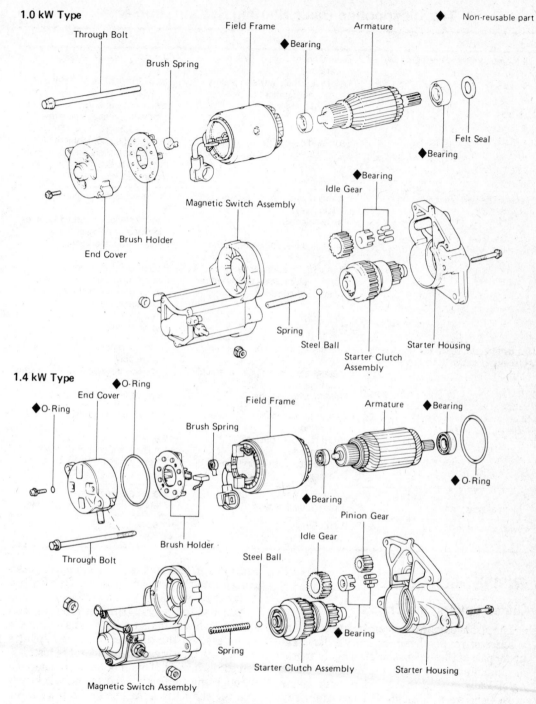

Exploded view of starter motors

Starter Specifications

	Lock Test		No-Load Test			Brush Tension (lbs.)
Year	Amps	Volts	Amps	Volts	RPM	
1985–88	NOT RECOMMENDED		90	11.5	3,500+	3.9–5.3
1989–90	NOT RECOMMENDED		90	11.5	5,800+	4.0–5.5

Troubleshooting Basic Starting System Problems

Problem	Cause	Solution
Starter motor rotates engine slowly	• Battery charge low or battery defective	• Charge or replace battery
	• Defective circuit between battery and starter motor	• Clean and tighten, or replace cables
	• Low load current	• Bench-test starter motor. Inspect for worn brushes and weak brush springs.
	• High load current	• Bench-test starter motor. Check engine for friction, drag or coolant in cylinders. Check ring gear-to-pinion gear clearance.
Starter motor will not rotate engine	• Battery charge low or battery defective	• Charge or replace battery
	• Faulty solenoid	• Check solenoid ground. Repair or replace as necessary.
	• Damage drive pinion gear or ring gear	• Replace damaged gear(s)
	• Starter motor engagement weak	• Bench-test starter motor
	• Starter motor rotates slowly with high load current	• Inspect drive yoke pull-down and point gap, check for worn end bushings, check ring gear clearance
	• Engine seized	• Repair engine
Starter motor drive will not engage (solenoid known to be good)	• Defective contact point assembly	• Repair or replace contact point assembly
	• Inadequate contact point assembly ground	• Repair connection at ground screw
	• Defective hold-in coil	• Replace field winding assembly
Starter motor drive will not disengage	• Starter motor loose on flywheel housing	• Tighten mounting bolts
	• Worn drive end busing	• Replace bushing
	• Damaged ring gear teeth	• Replace ring gear or driveplate
	• Drive yoke return spring broken or missing	• Replace spring
Starter motor drive disengages prematurely	• Weak drive assembly thrust spring	• Replace drive mechanism
	• Hold-in coil defective	• Replace field winding assembly
Low load current	• Worn brushes	• Replace brushes
	• Weak brush springs	• Replace springs

ENGINE MECHANICAL

Understanding the Engine

The piston engine is a metal block containing a series of round chambers or cylinders. The upper part of the engine block is usually an iron or aluminum- alloy casting. The casting forms outer walls around the cylinders with hollow areas in between, through which coolant circulates. The lower block provides a numer of rigid mounting points for the crankshaft and its bearings. The lower block is referred to as the crankcase.

The crankshaft is a long, steel shaft mounted at the bottom of the engine and free to turn in its mounts. The mounting points (generally four to seven) and the bearings for the crankshaft are called main bearings. The crankshaft is the shaft which is made to turn through the function of the engine; this motion is then passed into the transmission/transaxle and on to the drive wheels.

Attached to the crankshaft are the connecting rods which run up to the pistons within the cylinders. As the air/fuel mixture explodes within the tightly sealed cylinder, the piston is forced downward. This motion is transferrred through the connecting rod to the crankshaft and the shaft turns. As one piston finishes its power stroke, its next upward journey forces the burnt gasses out of the cylinder through the now-open exhaust valve. By the top of the stroke, the exhaust valve has closed and the intake valve has begun to open, allowing the fresh air/fuel charge to be sucked into the cylinder by the downward stroke of the piston. The intake valve closes, the piston once again comes back up and compresses the charge in the closed cylinder. At the top (approximately) of this stroke the spark plug fires, the charge explodes and another power stroke takes place. If you count the piston motions in between power strokes, you'll see why automotive engines are called four-stroke or four-cycle engines.

While one cylinder is performing this cycle, all the others are also contributing; but in different timing. Obviously, all the cylinders cannot fire at once or the power flow would not be steady. As any one cylinder is on its power stroke, another is on its exhaust stroke, another on intake and another on compression. These constant power pulses keep the crank turning; a large round flywheel attached to the end of the crankshaft provides a stable mass to smooth out the rotation.

At the top of the engine, the cylinder head(s) provide tight covers for the cylinders. They contain machined chambers into which the fuel charge is forced as the piston reaches the top of its travel. These combustion chambers contain at least one intake and one exhaust valve which are opened and closed through the action of the camshaft. The spark plugs are screwed into the cylinder head so that the tips of the plugs protrude into the chamber.

Since the timing of the valve action (opening and closing) is critical to the combustion process, the camshaft is driven by the crankshaft via a belt or chain. The valves are operated either by pushrods (called overhead valves--the valves are above the cam) or by the direct action of the cam pushing on the valves (overhead cam).

Lubricating oil is stored in a pan or sump at the bottom of the engine. It is force fed to all the parts of the engine by the oil pump which may be driven off wither the crank or the cam shaft. The oil lubricates the entire engine by travelling through passages in the block and head. Additionally, the circulation of the oil provides 25-40% of the engine cooling.

If all this seems very complicated, keep in mind that the sole purpose of any motor--gas, diesel, electric, solar, etc--is to turn a shaft. The motion of the shaft is then harnessed to perform a task such as pumping water, moving the car, etc. Accomplishing this shaft-turning in an automotive engine requires many supporting systems such as fuel delivery, exhaust handling, lubrication, cooling, starting, etc. Operation of these systems involve principles of mechanics, vacuum, electronics, etc. Being able to identify a problem by what system is involved will allow you to begin accurate diagnosis of the symptoms and causes.

Engine Overhaul Tips

Most engine overhaul procedures are fairly standard. In addition to specific parts replace-ment procedures and complete specifications for your individual engine, this chapter also is a guide to accepted rebuilding procedures. Examples of standard rebuilding practice are shown and should be used along with specific details concerning your particular engine.

Competent and accurate machine shop services will ensure maximum performance, reliability and engine life.

In most instances it is more profitable for the do-it-yourself mechanic to remove, clean and inspect the component, buy the necessary parts and deliver these to a shop for actual machine work.

On the other hand, much of the rebuilding work (crankshaft, block, bearings, piston rods, and other components) is well within the scope of the do-it-yourself mechanic. Patience, proper tools, and common sense coupled a basic understanding of the motor can yield satisfying and economical results.

TOOLS

The tools required for an engine overhaul or parts replacement will depend on the depth of your involvement. With a few exceptions, they will be the tools found in a mechanic's tool kit (see Chapter 1). More in-depth work will require any or all of the following:
- A dial indicator (reading in thousandths) mounted on a universal base
- Micrometers and telescope gauges
- Jaw and screw-type pullers
- Gasket scrapers; the best are wood or plastic
- Valve spring compressor
- Ring groove cleaner
- Piston ring expander and compressor
- Ridge reamer
- Cylinder hone or glaze breaker
- Plastigage®
- Engine stand

The use of most of these tools is illustrated in this chapter. Many can be rented for a one-time use from a local parts jobber or tool supply house specializing in automotive work.

Occasionally, the use of special tools is called for. See the information on Special Tools and Safety Notice in the front of this book before substituting another tool.

INSPECTION TECHNIQUES

Procedures and specifications are given in this chapter for inspecting, cleaning and assessing the wear limits of most major components. Other procedures such as Magnaflux® and Zyglo® can be used to locate material flaws and stress cracks. Magnaflux® is a magnetic process applicable only to ferrous (iron and steel) materials. The Zyglo® process coats the material with a fluorescent dye penetrant and can be used on any material. Checks for suspected surface cracks can be more readily made using spot check dye. The dye is sprayed onto the suspected area, wiped off and the area sprayed with a developer. Cracks will show up brightly.

OVERHAUL TIPS

Aluminum has become extremely popular for use in engines, due to its low weight. Observe the following precautions when handling aluminum parts:
• Never hot tank aluminum parts (the caustic hot tank solution will eat the aluminum.)
• Remove all aluminum parts (identification tag, etc.) from engine parts prior to the tanking.
• Always coat threads lightly with engine oil or anti-seize compounds before installation to prevent seizure.
• Never overtighten bolts or spark plugs especially in aluminum threads.

Stripped threads in any component can be repaired using any of several commercial repair kits (Heli-Coil®, Microdot®, Keenserts®, etc.).

When assembling the engine, any parts that will be in frictional contact must be prelubed to provide lubrication at initial start-up. Any product specifically formulated for this purpose can be used, but engine oil is not recommended as a prelube.

When semi-permanent (locked, but removable) installation of bolts or nuts is desired, threads should be cleaned and coated with Loctite® or other similar, commercial non-hardening sealant.

REPAIRING DAMAGED THREADS

Several methods of repairing damaged threads are available. Heli-Coil® (shown here), Keenserts® and Microdot® are among the most widely used. All involve basically the same principle--drilling out stripped threads, tapping the hole and installing a prewound insert--making

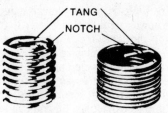

Standard thread repair insert (left) and spark plug thread insert (right)

Drill out the damaged threads with specified drill. Drill completely through the hole or to the bottom of a blind hole

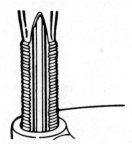

With the tap supplied, tap the hole to receive the thread insert. Keep the tap well oiled and back it out frequently to avoid clogging the threads

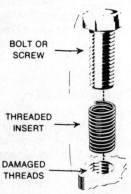

Damaged bolt holes can be repaired with thread repair inserts

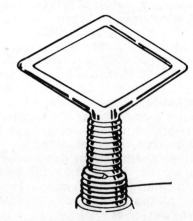

Screw the threaded insert onto the installation tool until the tang engages the slot. Screw the insert into the tapped hole until it is ¼–½ turn below the top surface. After installation break off the tang with a hammer and punch

welding, plugging and oversize fasteners unnecessary.

Two types of thread repair inserts are usually supplied: a standard type for most Inch Coarse, Inch Fine, Metric Course and Metric Fine thread sizes and a spark plug type to fit most spark plug port sizes. Consult the individual manufacturer's catalog to determine exact applications. Typical thread repair kits will contain a selection of prewound threaded inserts, a tap (corresponding to the outside diameter threads of the insert) and an installation tool. Spark plug inserts usually differ because they require a tap equipped with pilot threads and a combined reamer/tap section. Most manufacturers also supply blister-packed thread repair inserts separately in addition to a master kit containing a variety of taps and inserts plus installation tools.

Before effecting a repair to a threaded hole, remove any snapped, broken or damaged bolts or studs. Penetrating oil can be used to free frozen threads. The offending item can be removed with locking pliers or with a screw or stud extractor. After the hole is clear, the thread can be repaired, as shown in the series of accompanying illustrations.

Checking Engine Compression

A noticeable lack of engine power, excessive oil consumption and/or poor fuel mileage measured over an extended period are all indicators of internal engine wear. Worn piston rings, scored or worn cylinder bores, leaking head gaskets, sticking or burnt valves and worn valve seats are all possible culprits here. A check of each cylinder's compression will help you locate the problems.

As mentioned in the Tools and Equipment section of Chapter 1, a screw-in type compression gauge is more accurate that the type you simply hold against the spark plug hole, although it takes slightly longer to use. It's worth it to obtain a more accurate reading. Follow the procedures below.

Gasoline Engines

1. Warm up the engine to normal operating temperature.
2. Remove all the spark plugs.
3. Disconnect the high tension lead from the ignition coil.
4. Fully open the throttle either by operating the carburetor throttle linkage by hand or by having an assistant floor the accelerator pedal.
5. Screw the compression gauge into the No.1 spark plug hole until the fitting is snug.
WARNING: *Be careful not to crossthread the plug hole. On aluminum cylinder heads use*

extra care, as the threads in these heads are easily ruined.

6. Ask an assistant to depress the accelerator pedal fully on both carbureted and fuel injected vehicles. Then, while you read the compression gauge, ask the assistant to crank the engine two or three times in short bursts using the ignition switch.

7. Read the compression gauge at the end of each series of cranks, and record the highest of these readings. Repeat this procedure for each of the engine's cylinders. As a general rule, new motors will have compression on the order of 150-170 pounds per square inch (psi). This number will decrease with age and wear. The number of pounds of pressure that your test shows is not as important as the evenness between all the cylinders. Many cars run very well with all cylinders at 105 psi. The lower number simply shows a general deterioration internally. This car probably burns a little oil and may be a bit harder to start, but based on these numbers doesn't warrant an engine tear-down yet.

Compare the highest reading of all the cylinders. Any variation of more than 10% should be considered a sign of potential trouble. For example, if your compression readings for cylinders 1 through 4 were: 135 psi, 125 psi, 90 psi and 125 psi, it would be fair to say that cylinder number three is not working efficiently and is almost certainly the cause of your oil burning, rough idle or poor fuel mileage.

8. If a cylinder is unusually low, pour a tablespoon of clean engine oil into the cylinder through the spark plug hole and repeat the compression test. If the compression comes up after adding the oil, it appears that the cylinder's piston rings or bore are damaged or worn. If the pressure remains low, the valves may not be seating properly (a valve job is needed), or the head gasket may be blown near that cylinder. If compression in any two adjacent cylinders is low, and if the addition of oil doesn't help the compression, there is leakage past the head gasket. Oil and coolant in the combustion chamber can result from this problem. There may be evidence of water droplets on the engine dipstick when a head gasket has blown.

Engine
REMOVAL AND INSTALLATION
4A-LC

NOTE: *All wires and hoses should be labled at the time of removal. The amount of time saved during reassembly makes the extra effort well worthwhile.*

1. Disconnect the negative battery cable.

Troubleshooting Engine Mechanical Problems

Problem	Cause	Solution
External oil leaks	• Fuel pump gasket broken or improperly seated	• Replace gasket
	• Cylinder head cover RTV sealant broken or improperly seated	• Replace sealant; inspect cylinder head cover sealant flange and cylinder head sealant surface for distortion and cracks
	• Oil filler cap leaking or missing	• Replace cap
	• Oil filter gasket broken or improperly seated	• Replace oil filter
	• Oil pan side gasket broken, improperly seated or opening in RTV sealant	• Replace gasket or repair opening in sealant; inspect oil pan gasket flange for distortion
	• Oil pan front oil seal broken or improperly seated	• Replace seal; inspect timing case cover and oil pan seal flange for distortion
	• Oil pan rear oil seal broken or improperly seated	• Replace seal; inspect oil pan rear oil seal flange; inspect rear main bearing cap for cracks, plugged oil return channels, or distortion in seal groove
	• Timing case cover oil seal broken or improperly seated	• Replace seal
	• Excess oil pressure because of restricted PCV valve	• Replace PCV valve
	• Oil pan drain plug loose or has stripped threads	• Repair as necessary and tighten
	• Rear oil gallery plug loose	• Use appropriate sealant on gallery plug and tighten
	• Rear camshaft plug loose or improperly seated	• Seat camshaft plug or replace and seal, as necessary
	• Distributor base gasket damaged	• Replace gasket
Excessive oil consumption	• Oil level too high	• Drain oil to specified level
	• Oil with wrong viscosity being used	• Replace with specified oil
	• PCV valve stuck closed	• Replace PCV valve
	• Valve stem oil deflectors (or seals) are damaged, missing, or incorrect type	• Replace valve stem oil deflectors
	• Valve stems or valve guides worn	• Measure stem-to-guide clearance and repair as necessary
	• Poorly fitted or missing valve cover baffles	• Replace valve cover
	• Piston rings broken or missing	• Replace broken or missing rings
	• Scuffed piston	• Replace piston
	• Incorrect piston ring gap	• Measure ring gap, repair as necessary
	• Piston rings sticking or excessively loose in grooves	• Measure ring side clearance, repair as necessary
	• Compression rings installed upside down	• Repair as necessary
	• Cylinder walls worn, scored, or glazed	• Repair as necessary
	• Piston ring gaps not properly staggered	• Repair as necessary
	• Excessive main or connecting rod bearing clearance	• Measure bearing clearance, repair as necessary
No oil pressure	• Low oil level	• Add oil to correct level
	• Oil pressure gauge, warning lamp or sending unit inaccurate	• Replace oil pressure gauge or warning lamp
	• Oil pump malfunction	• Replace oil pump
	• Oil pressure relief valve sticking	• Remove and inspect oil pressure relief valve assembly
	• Oil passages on pressure side of pump obstructed	• Inspect oil passages for obstruction

Troubleshooting Engine Mechanical Problems (cont.)

Problem	Cause	Solution
No oil pressure (cont.)	• Oil pickup screen or tube obstructed • Loose oil inlet tube	• Inspect oil pickup for obstruction • Tighten or seal inlet tube
Low oil pressure	• Low oil level • Inaccurate gauge, warning lamp or sending unit • Oil excessively thin because of dilution, poor quality, or improper grade • Excessive oil temperature • Oil pressure relief spring weak or sticking • Oil inlet tube and screen assembly has restriction or air leak • Excessive oil pump clearance • Excessive main, rod, or camshaft bearing clearance	• Add oil to correct level • Replace oil pressure gauge or warning lamp • Drain and refill crankcase with recommended oil • Correct cause of overheating engine • Remove and inspect oil pressure relief valve assembly • Remove and inspect oil inlet tube and screen assembly. (Fill inlet tube with lacquer thinner to locate leaks.) • Measure clearances • Measure bearing clearances, repair as necessary
High oil pressure	• Improper oil viscosity • Oil pressure gauge or sending unit inaccurate • Oil pressure relief valve sticking closed	• Drain and refill crankcase with correct viscosity oil • Replace oil pressure gauge • Remove and inspect oil pressure relief valve assembly
Main bearing noise	• Insufficient oil supply • Main bearing clearance excessive • Bearing insert missing • Crankshaft end play excessive • Improperly tightened main bearing cap bolts • Loose flywheel or drive plate • Loose or damaged vibration damper	• Inspect for low oil level and low oil pressure • Measure main bearing clearance, repair as necessary • Replace missing insert • Measure end play, repair as necessary • Tighten bolts with specified torque • Tighten flywheel or drive plate attaching bolts • Repair as necessary
Connecting rod bearing noise	• Insufficient oil supply • Carbon build-up on piston • Bearing clearance excessive or bearing missing • Crankshaft connecting rod journal out-of-round • Misaligned connecting rod or cap • Connecting rod bolts tightened improperly	• Inspect for low oil level and low oil pressure • Remove carbon from piston crown • Measure clearance, repair as necessary • Measure journal dimensions, repair or replace as necessary • Repair as necessary • Tighten bolts with specified torque
Piston noise	• Piston-to-cylinder wall clearance excessive (scuffed piston) • Cylinder walls excessively tapered or out-of-round • Piston ring broken • Loose or seized piston pin • Connecting rods misaligned • Piston ring side clearance excessively loose or tight • Carbon build-up on piston is excessive	• Measure clearance and examine piston • Measure cylinder wall dimensions, rebore cylinder • Replace all rings on piston • Measure piston-to-pin clearance, repair as necessary • Measure rod alignment, straighten or replace • Measure ring side clearance, repair as necessary • Remove carbon from piston

Troubleshooting Engine Mechanical Problems (cont.)

Problem	Cause	Solution
Valve actuating component noise	• Insufficient oil supply	• Check for: (a) Low oil level (b) Low oil pressure (c) Plugged push rods (d) Wrong hydraulic tappets (e) Restricted oil gallery (f) Excessive tappet to bore clearance
	• Push rods worn or bent	• Replace worn or bent push rods
	• Rocker arms or pivots worn	• Replace worn rocker arms or pivots
	• Foreign objects or chips in hydraulic tappets	• Clean tappets
	• Excessive tappet leak-down	• Replace valve tappet
	• Tappet face worn	• Replace tappet; inspect corresponding cam lobe for wear
	• Broken or cocked valve springs	• Properly seat cocked springs; replace broken springs
	• Stem-to-guide clearance excessive	• Measure stem-to-guide clearance, repair as required
	• Valve bent	• Replace valve
	• Loose rocker arms	• Tighten bolts with specified torque
	• Valve seat runout excessive	• Regrind valve seat/valves
	• Missing valve lock	• Install valve lock
	• Push rod rubbing or contacting cylinder head	• Remove cylinder head and remove obstruction in head
	• Excessive engine oil (four-cylinder engine)	• Correct oil level

General Engine Specifications

Year	Engine	Fuel System Type	SAE Net Horsepower @ rpm	SAE Net Torque ft. lbs. @ rpm	Bore x Stroke	Comp. Ratio	Oil Press. psi. @ 2000 rpm
1985–88	4A-LC	2-bbl.	70 @ 4800	85 @ 2800	3.19 x 3.03	9.0:1	34
1988	4A-GE	Inj.	88 @ 6600	98 @ 4800	3.19 x 3.03	9.4:1	57
1989–90	4A-FE	Inj.	102 @ 5800	101 @ 4800	3.19 x 3.03	9.5:1	57

Valve Specifications

Year	Engine	Seat Angle (deg)	Face Angle (deg)	Spring Test Pressure (lbs. @ in.)	Spring Installed Height (in.)	Stem to Guide Clearance (in.)		Stem Diameter (in.)	
						Intake	Exhaust	Intake	Exhaust
1985–88	4A-LC	45	44.5	46 @ 1.52	1.52	0.0031	0.0039	0.2744	0.2742
1988	4A-GE	45	44.5	32 @ 1.36	1.36	0.0031	0.0039	0.2350	0.2348
1989–90	4A-FE	45	45.5	32 @ 1.36	1.36	0.0031	0.0039	0.2350	0.2348

Camshaft Specifications

All measurements in inches

Year	Engine	Journal Diameter					Bearing Clearance	Elevation		End Play
		1	2	3	4	5		Int.	Exh.	
1985–88	4A-LC	1.1015–1.1022					0.0015	1.5409		0.0098
1988	4A-GE	1.0610–1.0616					0.0014	1.3862		0.0118
1989–90	4A-FE	0.9035–0.9041					0.0014	1.3457	1.3587	0.0043

Troubleshooting the Cooling System

Problem	Cause	Solution
High temperature gauge indication— overheating	• Coolant level low	• Replenish coolant
	• Fan belt loose	• Adjust fan belt tension
	• Radiator hose(s) collapsed	• Replace hose(s)
	• Radiator airflow blocked	• Remove restriction (bug screen, fog lamps, etc.)
	• Faulty radiator cap	• Replace radiator cap
	• Ignition timing incorrect	• Adjust ignition timing
	• Idle speed low	• Adjust idle speed
	• Air trapped in cooling system	• Purge air
	• Heavy traffic driving	• Operate at fast idle in neutral intermittently to cool engine
	• Incorrect cooling system component(s) installed	• Install proper component(s)
	• Faulty thermostat	• Replace thermostat
	• Water pump shaft broken or impeller loose	• Replace water pump
	• Radiator tubes clogged	• Flush radiator
	• Cooling system clogged	• Flush system
	• Casting flash in cooling passages	• Repair or replace as necessary. Flash may be visible by removing cooling system components or removing core plugs.
	• Brakes dragging	• Repair brakes
	• Excessive engine friction	• Repair engine
	• Antifreeze concentration over 68%	• Lower antifreeze concentration percentage
	• Missing air seals	• Replace air seals
	• Faulty gauge or sending unit	• Repair or replace faulty component
	• Loss of coolant flow caused by leakage or foaming	• Repair or replace leaking component, replace coolant
	• Viscous fan drive failed	• Replace unit
Low temperature indication— undercooling	• Thermostat stuck open	• Replace thermostat
	• Faulty gauge or sending unit	• Repair or replace faulty component
Coolant loss—boilover	• Overfilled cooling system	• Reduce coolant level to proper specification
	• Quick shutdown after hard (hot) run	• Allow engine to run at fast idle prior to shutdown
	• Air in system resulting in occasional "burping" of coolant	• Purge system
	• Insufficient antifreeze allowing coolant boiling point to be too low	• Add antifreeze to raise boiling point
	• Antifreeze deteriorated because of age or contamination	• Replace coolant
	• Leaks due to loose hose clamps, loose nuts, bolts, drain plugs, faulty hoses, or defective radiator	• Pressure test system to locate source of leak(s) then repair as necessary
	• Faulty head gasket	• Replace head gasket
	• Cracked head, manifold, or block	• Replace as necessary
	• Faulty radiator cap	• Replace cap
Coolant entry into crankcase or cylinder(s)	• Faulty head gasket	• Replace head gasket
	• Crack in head, manifold or block	• Replace as necessary
Coolant recovery system inoperative	• Coolant level low	• Replenish coolant to FULL mark
	• Leak in system	• Pressure test to isolate leak and repair as necessary
	• Pressure cap not tight or seal missing, or leaking	• Repair as necessary
	• Pressure cap defective	• Replace cap
	• Overflow tube clogged or leaking	• Repair as necessary
	• Recovery bottle vent restricted	• Remove restriction

Troubleshooting the Cooling System (cont.)

Problem	Cause	Solution
Noise	• Fan contacting shroud	• Reposition shroud and inspect engine mounts
	• Loose water pump impeller	• Replace pump
	• Glazed fan belt	• Apply silicone or replace belt
	• Loose fan belt	• Adjust fan belt tension
	• Rough surface on drive pulley	• Replace pulley
	• Water pump bearing worn	• Remove belt to isolate. Replace pump.
	• Belt alignment	• Check pulley alignment. Repair as necessary.
No coolant flow through heater core	• Restricted return inlet in water pump	• Remove restriction
	• Heater hose collapsed or restricted	• Remove restriction or replace hose
	• Restricted heater core	• Remove restriction or replace core
	• Restricted outlet in thermostat housing	• Remove flash or restriction
	• Intake manifold bypass hole in cylinder head restricted	• Remove restriction
	• Faulty heater control valve	• Replace valve
	• Intake manifold coolant passage restricted	• Remove restriction or replace intake manifold

NOTE: *Immediately after shutdown, the engine enters a condition known as heat soak. This is caused by the cooling system being inoperative while engine temperature is still high. If coolant temperature rises above boiling point, expansion and pressure may push some coolant out of the radiator overflow tube. If this does not occur frequently it is considered normal.*

2. Drain the cooling system and save the coolant for reuse.

CAUTION: *When draining the coolant, keep in mind that cats and dogs are attracted by the ethylene glycol antifreeze, and are quite likely to drink any that is left in an uncovered container or in puddles on the ground. This will prove fatal in sufficient quantity. Always drain the coolant into a sealable container. Coolant should be reused unless it is contaminated or several years old.*

3. Drain the engine oil and the transmission oil.

CAUTION: *Used motor oil may cause skin cancer if repeatedly left in contact with the skin for prolonged periods. Although this is unlikely unless you handle oil on a daily basis, it is wise to thoroughly wash your hands with soap and water immediately after handling used motor oil.*

4. With the help of an assistant, remove the hood from the car. Be careful not to damage the paint finish.

5. Remove the air cleaner assembly from the carburetor.

6. Disconnect the upper radiator hose from the engine and remove the overflow hose.

7. Remove the coolant hose at the cylinder head rear coolant pipe and remove the coolant hose at the thermostat housing.

8. Remove the fuel hoses from the fuel pump.

9. Loosen the adjustor(s) and remove the alternator belt, the power steering and/or air conditioning drive belts depending on equipment.

10. Label and remove all wiring running to

Piston and Ring Specifications

All measurements in inches

		Ring Gap			Ring Side Clearance			
Year	Engine	#1 Compr.	#2 Compr.	Oil Control	#1 Compr.	#2 Compr.	Oil Control	Piston Clearance
1985–88	4A-LC	0.0079–0.0138	0.0059–0.0118	0.0118–0.0354	0.0012–0.0028	0.0008–0.0024	snug	0.0039–0.0047
1988	4A-GE	0.0098–0.0185	0.0079–0.0165	0.0059–0.0205	0.0016–0.0031	0.0012–0.0028	snug	0.0039–0.0047
1989–90	4A-FE	0.0098–0.0138	0.0059–0.0018	0.0039–0.0236	0.0020–0.0031	0.0012–0.028	snug	0.0024–0.0031

Troubleshooting the Serpentine Drive Belt

Problem	Cause	Solution
Tension sheeting fabric failure (woven fabric on outside circumference of belt has cracked or separated from body of belt)	• Grooved or backside idler pulley diameters are less than minimum recommended • Tension sheeting contacting (rubbing) stationary object • Excessive heat causing woven fabric to age • Tension sheeting splice has fractured	• Replace pulley(s) not conforming to specification • Correct rubbing condition • Replace belt • Replace belt
Noise (objectional squeal, squeak, or rumble is heard or felt while drive belt is in operation)	• Belt slippage • Bearing noise • Belt misalignment • Belt-to-pulley mismatch • Driven component inducing vibration • System resonant frequency inducing vibration	• Adjust belt • Locate and repair • Align belt/pulley(s) • Install correct belt • Locate defective driven component and repair • Vary belt tension within specifications. Replace belt.
Rib chunking (one or more ribs has separated from belt body)	• Foreign objects imbedded in pulley grooves • Installation damage • Drive loads in excess of design specifications • Insufficient internal belt adhesion	• Remove foreign objects from pulley grooves • Replace belt • Adjust belt tension • Replace belt
Rib or belt wear (belt ribs contact bottom of pulley grooves)	• Pulley(s) misaligned • Mismatch of belt and pulley groove widths • Abrasive environment • Rusted pulley(s) • Sharp or jagged pulley groove tips • Rubber deteriorated	• Align pulley(s) • Replace belt • Replace belt • Clean rust from pulley(s) • Replace pulley • Replace belt
Longitudinal belt cracking (cracks between two ribs)	• Belt has mistracked from pulley groove • Pulley groove tip has worn away rubber-to-tensile member	• Replace belt • Replace belt
Belt slips	• Belt slipping because of insufficient tension • Belt or pulley subjected to substance (belt dressing, oil, ethylene glycol) that has reduced friction • Driven component bearing failure • Belt glazed and hardened from heat and excessive slippage	• Adjust tension • Replace belt and clean pulleys • Replace faulty component bearing • Replace belt
"Groove jumping" (belt does not maintain correct position on pulley, or turns over and/or runs off pulleys)	• Insufficient belt tension • Pulley(s) not within design tolerance • Foreign object(s) in grooves • Excessive belt speed • Pulley misalignment • Belt-to-pulley profile mismatched • Belt cordline is distorted	• Adjust belt tension • Replace pulley(s) • Remove foreign objects from grooves • Avoid excessive engine acceleration • Align pulley(s) • Install correct belt • Replace belt
Belt broken (Note: identify and correct problem before replacement belt is installed)	• Excessive tension • Tensile members damaged during belt installation • Belt turnover • Severe pulley misalignment • Bracket, pulley, or bearing failure	• Replace belt and adjust tension to specification • Replace belt • Replace belt • Align pulley(s) • Replace defective component and belt

Troubleshooting the Serpentine Drive Belt (cont.)

Problem	Cause	Solution
Cord edge failure (tensile member exposed at edges of belt or separated from belt body)	• Excessive tension • Drive pulley misalignment • Belt contacting stationary object • Pulley irregularities • Improper pulley construction • Insufficient adhesion between tensile member and rubber matrix	• Adjust belt tension • Align pulley • Correct as necessary • Replace pulley • Replace pulley • Replace belt and adjust tension to specifications
Sporadic rib cracking (multiple cracks in belt ribs at random intervals)	• Ribbed pulley(s) diameter less than minimum specification • Backside bend flat pulley(s) diameter less than minimum • Excessive heat condition causing rubber to harden • Excessive belt thickness • Belt overcured • Excessive tension	• Replace pulley(s) • Replace pulley(s) • Correct heat condition as necessary • Replace belt • Replace belt • Adjust belt tension

Torque Specifications
(in ft. lbs.)

Year	Engine	Cyl. Head	Conn. Rod	Main Bearing	Crankshaft Damper	Flywheel	Manifold	
							Intake	Exhaust
1985–88	4A-LC	44	36	44	87	58	18	18
1988	4A-GE	22	36	44	101	58	20	18
1989–90	4A-FE	44	36	44	87	58-manual 47-auto	14	18

the motor. Be careful when unhooking wiring connectors; many have locking devices which must be released.

11. Label and disconnect vacuum hoses. Make sure your labels contain accurate information for reconnecting both ends of the hose. Make sure the labels will stay put on the hoses.

12. Disconnect the wiring at the transaxle.

13. Disconnect the speedometer cable at the transaxle.

14. Safely elevate and support the vehicle on jackstands.

15. Disconnect the exhaust pipe from the manifold. Be ready to deal with rusty hardware.

16. Disconnect the air hose at the converter pipe, if so equipped.

17. Loosen and remove the transaxle cooler lines at the radiator.

18. Remove the left and right undercovers (splash shields) under the car.

19. If so equipped, remove the power steering pump from its mounts and lay it aside. Leave the hoses attached. The pump may be hung on a piece of stiff wire to be kept out of the way.

20. If so equipped, remove the air conditioning compressor from its mounts and position out of the way. DO NOT loosen any hoses or fittings--simply move the compressor out of the way. It may be hung from a piece of stiff wire to be kept out of the way.

21. Disconnect the cable and bracket from the transaxle.

22. Disconnect the steering knuckles at the lower control arms.

23. Have an assistant step on the brake pedal while you loosen the nuts and bolts holding the driveshafts to the transaxle. Let the disconnected shafts hang down clear of the transaxle.

24. Remove the flywheel cover. If equipped with an automatic transmission, remove the flexplate-to-torque converter bolts.

25. Disconnect the front and rear mounts at the crossmember by first removing the two bolt covers and removing the two bolts at each mount. Remove the center crossmember under the engine.

26. Remove the clip and washer holding the shift cable; disconnect the cable at the outer shift lever or outer selector lever.

27. Lower the vehicle to the ground. Remove the radiator and fan assembly.

28. Install the engine hoist to the lifting bracket on the engine. Keep the wiring harness in front of the chain. Draw tension on the hoist

enough to support the engine but no more. Double check the hoist attachments before proceeding.

29. Remove the through bolt to the right side engine mount.

30. Remove the left side transaxle mount bolt and remove the mount.

31. Lift the engine and transaxle assembly out of the engine compartment, proceding slowly and watching for any interference. Pay particular attention to not damagine the right side engine mount, the power steering housing and the neutral safety switch. Make sure wiring, hoses and cables are clear of the engine.

32. Support the engine assembly on a suitable stand; do not allow it to remain on the hoist for any length of time.

To install:

33. Lower the engine and transaxle into the car, paying attention to clearance and proper position.

34. Install the left side transaxle mount and its bolt.

35. Install and tighten the right side through bolt for the motor mount.

36. When the engine is securely mounted within the car, the lifting devices may be removed. Replace the radiator and fan assembly.

37. Safely elevate and support the vehicle on jackstands.

38. Install the center crossmember and connect the shift cable.

39. Connect the front and rear mountings for the crossmember and reinstall the bolt covers.

40. Install the flywheel-to-torque converter bolts. Tighten them to the final specification in 3 steps: first, all to 20 ft. lbs; next, all to 40 ft. lbs. and finally all to 58 ft. lbs.

41. Replace the flywheel cover.

42. Connect the driveshafts to the transaxle; correct tightness is 27 ft. lbs.

43. Reconnect the steering knuckles to the lower control arms.

44. Reattach the cable and bracket to the transaxle.

45. Depending on equipment, reinstall the power steering pump and/or the air conditioning compressor. Tighten the mounting bolts enough to hold the unit in place but no more; the belts will be installed later.

46. Install the left and right splash shields (under covers).

47. Reconnect the transmission cooler lines to the radiator and connect the air hose at the conveter pipe.

48. Connect the exhaust pipe to the manifold and tighten the bolts to 46 ft. lbs

49. Lower the vehicle to the ground; reconnect the speedometer cable at the transaxle.

50. Paying close attention to proper routing and labeling, connect the wiring and vacuum hoses to the engine.

51. Install the drive belts (alternator, power steering and air conditioning) and make sure the belts are properly seated on the pulleys. Adjust the belts to the correct tension and tighten the bolts.

52. Connect the fuel hoses at the fuel pump. Use new clamps if necessary.

53. Attach the coolant hoses: at the thermostat housing, at the cylinder head rear pipe, at the overflow, and at the outlet for the upper hose. Insure that the hoses are firmly over the ports; use new clamps wherever needed.

54. Install the air cleaner assembly onto the carburetor.

55. Have an assistant help reinstall the hood. Make sure its is properly adjusted and secure.

56. Refill the transmission with the proper fluid.

57. Refill the engine oil to the proper level.

58. Refill the engine coolant with the proper amount of fluid.

59. Double check all installation items, paying particular attention to loose hoses or hanging wires, untightened nuts, poor routing of hoses and wires (too tight or rubbing) and tools left in the engine area.

4A-GE

NOTE: *All wires and hoses should be labled at the time of removal. The amount of time saved during reassembly makes the extra effort well worthwhile.*

1. Disconnect the negative battery cable.

2. With a helper remove the hood from the car. Use care not to damage the paint finsh on the bodywork.

3. Drain the engine oil.

CAUTION: *Used motor oil may cause skin cancer if repeatedly left in contact with the skin for prolonged periods. Although this is unlikely unless you handle oil on a daily basis, it is wise to thoroughly wash your hands with soap and water immediately after handling used motor oil.*

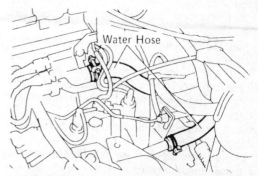

Location of the hoses at the water inlet housing

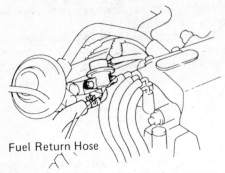

Fuel Return Hose

Location of the fuel return hose at the pressure regulator

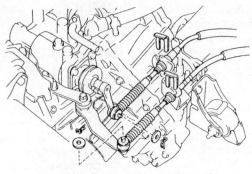

Removing the control cables at the transaxle

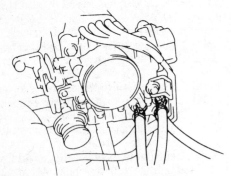

Disconnect the heater and air hoses from the air valve

4. Drain the cooling system. Save the coolant for reuse.

CAUTION: *When draining the coolant, keep in mind that cats and dogs are attracted by the ethylene glycol antifreeze, and are quite likely to drink any that is left in an uncovered container or in puddles on the ground. This will prove fatal in sufficient quantity. Always drain the coolant into a sealable container. Coolant should be reused unless it is contaminated or several years old.*

5. Drain the transaxle oil.

6. Remove the air cleaner assembly.

7. Remove the coolant reservoir tank and remove the PCV hose.

8. Remove the heater hoses from the water inlet housing.

9. Disconnect the fuel inlet hose from the fuel filter.

CAUTION: *The fuel system is under pressure. Release pressure slowly and contain spillage. Observe no smoking/no open flame precautions. Have a Class B-C (dry powder) fire extinguisher within arm's reach at all times.*

10. Disconnect the heater and air hoses from the air valve.

11. Remove the fuel return hose from the pressure regulator.

12. If equipped with a manual transaxle, re-

move the slave cylinder from the housing. Loosen the mounting bolts and move the cylinder out of the way but do not loosen or remove the fluid hose running to the cylinder.

13. Disconnect the vacuum hose running to the charcoal cannister.

14. Disconnect the shift control cable, the speedometer cable (at the trans) and the accelerator cable (at the throttle body).

15. If the car has cruise control, disconnect the cables. Remove the cruise control actuator by:

a. Disconnecting the vacuum hose,

b. Removing the cover and the three bolts,

c. Disconnecting the actuator connector and removing the actuator.

16. Remove the ignition coil.

17. Remove the main engine wiring harness in the following steps:

a. Inside the car, remove the right side cowl (kick) panel.

b. Disconnect the connectors at junction block 4.

c. Remove the cover over the Electronic Control Module (ECM) and carefully disconnect the ECM plugs.

d. Pull the main wiring harness into the engine compartment.

18. Disconnect the wiring at the number 2 junction block in the engine compartment.

19. Remove the engine and transaxle ground straps.

20. Disconnect the washer change valve connector.

21. Remove the wiring at the cruise control vacuum pump connector and the vacuum switch connector.

22. Remove the hose from the brake vacuum booster.

23. Depending on equipment, remove the air conditioning compressor and/or the power steering pump. Note that the units are to be removed from their mounts and placed out of the way--hoses and lines DO NOT disconnect from the units.

a. Remove the power steering pump pulley nut.

b. Loosen the idler pulley adjusting bolt and pulley bolt.

c. Remove the four compressor mounting bolts.

d. Move the compressor aside and suspend it from stiff wire out of the way.

e. Loosen the compressor bracket bolts.

f. Disconnect the oil pressure connector.

g. Loosen the power steering pump lock bolts and pivot bolts.

h. Remove the pump and its bracket; suspend it out of the way with a piece of stiff wire.

24. Safely elevate the vehicle and support on jackstands. Double check the stands and make sure the vehicle is solidly supported.

25. Remove the splash shields under the car.

26. Disconnect the oil cooler hoses.

27. Disconnect the exhaust pipe from the exhaust manifold.

28. Carefully disconnect the wiring from the oxygen sensor.

29. Remove the cover under the flywheel.

30. Remove the front and rear motor mounts from the center crossmember.

31. Remove the center crossmember.

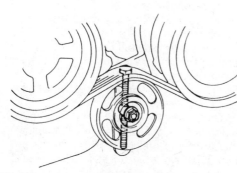

The idler pulley adjuster is behind the pulley

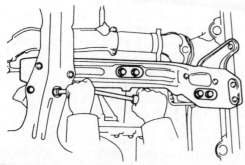

Removing the engine mounts from the crossmember

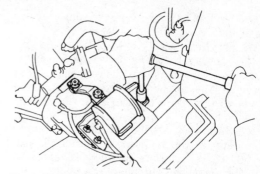

Removing the left side engine mount at the transaxle

32. Disconnect the right side control arm at the steering knuckle.

33. Disconnect the driveshafts from the transaxle.

34. Lower the vehicle to the ground. Install the engine hoist to the lifting bracket on the engine. Hang the engine wires and hoses on the lift chain. Take tension on the hoist sufficient to support the motor; double check all hoist attaching points.

35. Disconnect the right side engine mount by removing the bolt.

36. Disconnect the left side motor mount from the transaxle bracket.

37. Lift the engine and transaxle from the vehicle.

WARNING: *Be careful to avoid hitting the steering box and the throttle position sensor.*

38. Support the engine assembly on a suitable stand; do not allow it to remain on the hoist for any length of time.

39. Disconnect the radiator fan temperature switch connector.

40. Disconnect the start injector time switch.

41. Remove the vacuum hoses from the Bi-metal Vacuum Switching Valves (BVSV).

42. Remove the hoses from the water bypass valves and remove the water inlet housing assembly.

43. Label and remove the wiring connectors from the reverse switch, the water temperature sensor, and the water temperature switch. On cars with automatic transmissions remove the wiring to the neutral safety switch and the transaxle solenoid.

44. If equipped with automatic transmission, remove the six torque converter- to-flexplate bolts.

45. Remove the starter along with its cable and connector.

46. Support the transaxle, remove the retaining bolts in the case and remove the transaxle from the engine. Pull the unit straight off the engine; do not allow it to hang partially removed on the shaft. Keep the automatic trans-

axle level; if it tilts forward the converter may fall off.

To install:

47. Before reinstalling the engine in the car, several components must be rettached or connected. Install the transaxle to the engine; tighten the 12mm bolts to 47 ft. lbs and the 10mm bolts to 34 ft. lbs

48. Install the starter, its cable and connector. Tighten the mounting bolts to 29 ft. lbs.

50. Install the six torque converter-to-flexplate bolts on automatic transaxles. Tighten the bolts to 20 ft. lbs

51. Attach the wiring to the reverse light switch, the water temperature sensor and the water temperature switch.

52. Connect the hoses to the water bypass pipes and the wiring to the start injector time switch and the radiator fan temperature switch.

53. On automatic transaxle vehicles, connect the wiring to the neutral safety switch and the transmission solenoid.

54. Reinstall the water inlet housing assembly and connect the vacuum hoses to the BVSVs.

55. Attach the lifting mechanism to the engine; drape the hoses and wires on the chain.

56. Lower the engine and transaxle into place in the vehicle. Be careful not to hit the power steering gear housing or the throttle position sensor.

57. Install the right motor mount and through bolt; tighten it to 58 ft. lbs.

58. Install the left mount and attach it to the transaxle bracket. When the engine is securely mounted in the car, the lifting equipment may be removed.

59. Safely elevate and support the vehicle on jackstands.

60. Connect the driveshafts to the transaxle. Tighten the bolts to 27 ft. lbs.

61. Attach the right side control arm to the steering knuckle and tighten the bolts and nuts to 47 ft. lbs.

62. Replace the cover under the flywheel.

63. Install the engine mount center crossmember, tightening the bolts to 29 ft. lbs.

64. Install the front and rear mounts onto the crossmember. Tighten the mount bolts to 35 ft.lbs and the front and rear through bolts to 58 ft. lbs.

65. Using new gaskets and nuts, connect the exhaust pipe to the exhaust manifold; correct torque is 46 ft. lbs.

66. Connect the wiring to the oxygen sensor and attach the oil cooler lines.

67. Lower the vehicle from its stands to the ground.

68. Install the power steering pump and pulley with its bracket. Tighten the lock bolt and the pivot bolt.

69. Connect the wiring to the oil pressure unit.

70. Install the compressor bracket, the compressor and the belt. Tighten the pulley bolt on the power steering pump to 28 ft. lbs.

71. Install the drive belts and adjust them to the proper tension. Make certain each belt is properly fitted on its pulleys.

72. Connect the vacuum hose to the brake booster.

73. Install the wiring to the No.2 junction block. Connect the cable from the starter to the positive battery terminal and connect the engine and transaxle ground straps. DO NOT connect the negative battery cable at this time.

74. Attach the connectors for the washer change valve, and, if equipped, the cruise control vacuum pump and vacuum switch.

75. Connect the main engine wiring harness by:

　　a. Feeding the two connectors from the engine compartment back into the passenger compartment,

　　b. Connecting the ECM connector(s) and replacing the cover,

　　c. Connecting the wiring to the No.4 junction block and

　　d. Replacing the right side kick panel.

76. Reinstall the ignition coil.

77. If so, equipped install the cruise control actuator.

78. Connect or reinstall the cables for the accelerator, the cruise control, the speedometer and the shifter.

79. Install the vacuum hose to charcoal cannister.

80. On cars with manual transaxles, attach the clutch slave cylinder to the bell housing.

81. Attach the fuel return hose to the pressure regulator, the heater and air hoses to the air valve and the fuel hose to the fuel filter.

82. Connect the heater hoses to the water inlet housing.

83. Reinstall the PCV hose, the coolant reservoir and the air cleaner assembly.

84. Fill the transaxle with the correct amount of fresh oil, and fill the engine with fresh oil.

85. Fill the cooling system with the proper amount of fluid.

86. Double check all installation items, paying particular attention to loose hoses or hanging wires, untightened nuts, poor routing of hoses and wires (too tight or rubbing) and tools left in the engine area.

87. Connect the negative battery cable.

88. Start the engine and allow it to approach normal operating temperature. Check carefully for leaks. Shut the engine off.

89. Elevate the front end of the car, support on jackstands and install the splash shields below the car.

90. Lower the car to the ground. With your helper, install the hood and adjust it for proper fit and latching.

4A-FE

1. Remove the hood. Have a helper assist you and be careful not to damage the painted bodywork.

2. Disconnect the negative battery cable, then the positive battery cable and remove the battery.

3. Raise the vehicle and safely support it on jackstands.

4. Remove the left and right splash shields.

5. Drain the engine oil and the transmission oil.

CAUTION: *Used motor oil may cause skin cancer if repeatedly left in contact with the skin for prolonged periods. Although this is unlikely unless you handle oil on a daily basis, it is wise to thoroughly wash your hands with soap and water immediately after handling used motor oil.*

6. Drain the engine coolant and save it in closed containers for reuse.

CAUTION: *When draining the coolant, keep in mind that cats and dogs are attracted by the ethylene glycol antifreeze, and are quite likely to drink any that is left in an uncovered container or in puddles on the ground. This will prove fatal in sufficient quantity. Always drain the coolant into a sealable container. Coolant should be reused unless it is contaminated or several years old.*

7. Remove the air cleaner hose and the air cleaner assembly.

8. Remove the coolant reservoir. Remove the radiator and fan assembly.

9. Disconnect the accelerator cable and if equipped with automatic transaxle,the throttle cable.

10. Disconnect and remove the cruise control actuator.

11. Label and disconnect the main engine wiring harness from its related sensors and switches.

12. Remove the ground strap connector and its bolt. Disconnect the wiring to the vacuum sensor, the oxygen sensor and the air conditioning compressor.

13. Label and disconnect the brake booster vacuum hose, the power steering vacuum hose, the charcoal cannister vacuum hose and the vacuum switch vacuum hose.

14. Carefully disconnect the fuel inlet and return lines.

CAUTION: *The fuel system is under pres-*

Prizm fuel inlet line

sure. Release pressure slowly and contain spillage. Observe no smoking/no open flame precautions. Have a Class B-C (dry powder) fire extinguisher within arm's reach at all times.

15. Disconnect the heater hoses.

16. Loosen the power steering pump mounting bolt and through bolt. Remove the drive belt.

17. Remove the four bolts holding the air conditioner compressor and remove the compressor. DO NOT loosen or remove any lines or hoses. Move the compressor out of the way and hang it from a piece of stiff wire.

18. Disconnect the speedometer cable from the transaxle.

19. On cars with manual transmissions, unbolt the clutch slave cylinder from the bell housing and move the cylinder out of the way. Don't disconnect any lines or hoses. Disconnect the shift control cables by removing the two clips, the washers and retainers.

20. On cars with automatic transmissions, remove the clip and retainer and separate the control cable from the shift lever.

21. Elevate the car and support it safely on jackstands.

22. Remove the two bolts from the exhaust pipe flange and separate the pipe from the exhaust manifold.

23. Remove the nuts and bolts and separate the driveshafts from the transaxle.

24. Remove the through bolt from the rear transaxle mount.

25. Remove the nuts from the center transaxle mount and the rear mount.

26. Lower the vehicle to the ground and attach the lifting equipment to the brackets on the engine. Take tension on the hoist line or chain just enough to support the motor but no more. Hang the engine wires and hoses on the chain or cable.

27. Remove the three exhaust hanger bracket nuts and the hanger. Remove the two center crossmember-to-main crossmember bolts. Re-

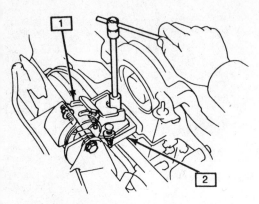

1. Engine mount
2. Engine mount bracket

Removing the engine mount-to-bracket bolt

move the three center crossmember-to-radiator support bolts.

CAUTION: *Support the crossmembers with a jack or jackstands when loosening the bolts. The pieces are heavy and could fall on you.*

28. Remove the eight crossmember-to-body bolts, then remove the two bolts holding the control arm brackets to the underbody. Remove the two center mount-to-transaxle bolts and remove the mount. Carefully lower the center mount and crossmember and remove from under the car.

29. At the left engine mount, remove the three bolts and the bracket, then remove the bolt, two nuts, through bolt and mounting. Remove the three bolts and the air cleaner bracket.

30. Loosen and remove the five bolts and disconnect the mounting bracket from the transaxle bracket. Remove the through bolt and mounting.

31. Carefully and slowly raise the engine and transaxle assembly out of the car. Tilt the transaxle down to clear the right engine mount. Be careful not to hit the steering gear housing. Make sure the engine is clear of all wiring, lines and hoses.

32. Support the engine assembly on a suitable stand; do not allow it to remain on the hoist for any length of time.

33. With the engine properly supported, disconnect the reverse light switch and the neutral safety switch (automatic trans).

34. Remove the rear end cover plate.

35. For automatic transaxles, remove the six torque converter mounting bolts.

36. Remove the starter.

37. Support the transaxle, remove the retaining bolts in the case and remove the transaxle from the engine. Pull the unit straight off the engine; do not allow it to hang partially re-

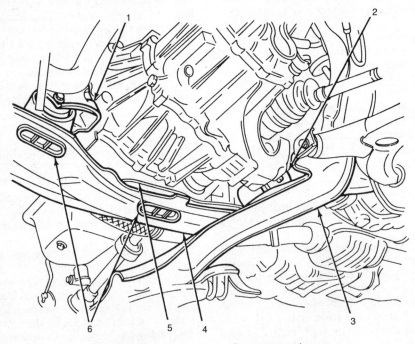

1. Front transaxle mount
2. Rear transaxle mount
3. Main crossmember
4. Center support
5. Center transaxle mount
6. Mount bolt shields

Detail of the crossmember and center support. Prizm with 4A-FE engine shown

moved on the shaft. Keep the automatic transaxle level; if it tilts forward the converter may fall off.

To install:

38. Before reinstalling the engine in the car, several components must be rettached or connected. Install the transaxle to the engine; tighten the 12mm bolts to 47 ft. lbs and the 10mm bolts to 34 ft. lbs

39. Install the starter, its cable and connector. Tighten the mounting bolts to 29 ft. lbs.

40. Install the six torque converter-to-flexplate bolts on automatic transaxles. Tighten the bolts to 20 ft. lbs.

41. Install the rear cover plate and connect the wiring to the reverse light swich and the neutral safety switch (automatic trans.).

42. Attach the chain hoist or lift apparatus to the engine and lower it into the engine compartment. Before it is completely in position, attach the power steering pump and its through bolt to the motor.

NOTE: *Tilt the transaxle downward and lower the engine to clear the left motor mount. As before, be careful not to hit the power steering housing (rack) or the throttle postion sensor.*

43. Level the engine and align each mount with its bracket.

44. Install the right mounting insulator (bushing) to the engine bracket with the two nuts and bolt. Tighten the bolt temporarily.

45. Align the right insulator with the body bracket and install the through bolt and nut. Temporarily tighten the nut and bolt.

46. Align the left mounting insulator with the transaxle case bracket. Temporarily install the three bracket bolts.

47. With the engine held in place by these mounts, repeat steps 44, 45 and 46, tightening the bolts to the following tightness. Step 44: 38 ft. lbs.; step 45: 64 ft. lbs.; step 46: 35 ft. lbs.

48. Install the left sidemounting support with its two bolts; tighten them to 15 ft. lbs.

49. With the engine securely mounted in the car, the lifting equipment may be removed. Elevate the car and support it on jackstands.

50. Install the center mount to the transaxle with its two bolts and tighten them to 45 ft. lbs.

51. Position the center mount over the front and rear studs and start two nuts on the center mount only. Loosely install the three center support-to-radiator support bolts.

52. Loosely install the two front mount bolts. Raise the main crossmember into place over the rear studs and align all the underbody bolts.

53. Install the two rear mount nuts; leave them loose.

54. Loosely install the eight underbody bolts, the lower control arm bracket bolts, the two center support-to-crossmember bolts and the exhaust hanger bracket and nuts.

55. With everything loose, but in place, make a second pass over all the nuts and bolts tightening them to the following specifications:
- Crossmember-to-underbody bolts: 152 ft. lbs
- Lower control arm bracket-to-underbody bolts: 94 ft. lbs.
- Center support-to-radiator support: 45 ft. lbs
- Center support-to-crossmember: 45 ft. lbs.
- Front, center and rear mount bolts: 45 ft. lbs.
- Exhaust hanger bracket nuts: 9 ft. lbs (115 INCH lbs.)

56. Install the rear transaxle mount and tighten its bolt to 64 ft. lbs

57. Install the nuts on the center transaxle mount and tighten them to 45 ft. lbs

58. Reconnect the driveshafts to the transaxle.

59. Using a new gasket, connect the exhaust pipe to the manifold and install the exhaust pipe bolts, tightening them to 18 ft. lbs

60. Lower the vehicle to the ground.

61. Either connect the control cables to the shift outer lever and selector lever and attach the control cables to manual transaxles or reconnect the control cable to the shift lever and install the clip and retainer on automatic transaxles. If equipped with manual transaxle, reattach the clutch slave cylinder to its mount.

62. Attach the speedometer cable to the transaxle.

63. Install the air conditioning compressor and drive belt if so equipped.

64. Install the power steering pump, pivot bolt and drive belt if so equipped. Adjust the belts to the correct tension.

65. Install the fuel inlet and outlet lines.

66. Connect the heater hoses. Make sure they are in the correct positions and that the clamps are in sound condition.

67. Connect the vacuum hoses to the vacuum switch, the charcoal canister, the vacuum sensor, the power steering and the brake booster.

68. Connect the wiring to the air conditioning, the oxygen sensor and the vacuum sensor.

69. Observing the labels made at the time of disassembly, reconnect the main engine harness to its sensors and switches. Work carefully and make sure each connector is properly matched and firmly seated.

70. Install the ground strap connector and its bolt; connect the wiring at the No.2 junction block in the engine compartment.

71. Install the cruise control actuator if so equipped.

72. Connect the accelerator cable and throttle cable (automatic) to their brackets.

73. Install the radiator and cooling fan assembly. Install the overflow reservoir.

74. Install the air cleaner assembly and the air intake hose.

75. Install the battery. Connect the positive cable to the starter terminal, then to the battery. DO NOT connect the negative battery cable at this time.

76. Fill the transmission with the correct amount of fresh fluid.

77. Refill the engine coolant.

78. Fill the engine with the correct amount of fresh oil.

79. Double check all installation items, paying particular attention to loose hoses or hanging wires, untightened nuts, poor routing of hoses and wires (too tight or rubbing) and tools left in the engine area.

80. Connect the negative battery cable. Start the engine and allow it to idle. As the engine warms up, shift the automatic transmission into each gear range allowing it to engage momentarily. After each gear has been selected, put the shifter in PARK and check the transmission fluid level.

81. Shut the engine off and check the engine area carefully for leaks, particularly around any line or hose which was disconnected during removal.

82. Elevate and support the front end of the car on jackstands. Replace the left and right splash shields and lower the vehicle.

83. With the help of an assistant, reinstall the hood. Adjust the hood for proper fit and latching.

Valve Cover (Cam Cover or Rocker Arm Cover)

REMOVAL AND INSTALLATION

4A-LC

1. Disconnect the negative battery cable.
2. Remove the air cleaner assembly.
3. Disconnect the PCV hose.
4. Disconnect the accelerator cable.
5. Disconnect the wire harness.
6. Remove the upper timing belt cover bolts and the cover. Remove the two valve cover bolts.
7. Remove the valve cover and its gasket.
NOTE: *If the cover is stuck in place, tap a corner with a plastic or rubber mallet. Don't pry the cover up; it will deform and leak.*
8. Clean the mating surfaces on the head and the cover; install a new gasket.
9. Place the cover and gasket in position on the head. Make sure the cover is straight and that the rubber bushings are on the studs.

10. Install the cover nuts and the upper belt cover with its bolts. Tighten the cover nuts to 15 ft. lbs.

11. Connect the wiring harness, the accelerator cable and the PCV hose.

12. Install the air cleaner assembly and connect the negative battery cable.

13. Start the engine and check for leaks after the engine has warmed up. Minor leaks may be cured by slightly snugging the cover bolts and the timing belt cover bolts. Any leak that is still present after about a ¼ turn CANNOT be cured by further tightening. Remove the cover again and either reposition or replace the gasket.

4A-GE

1. Disconnect the negative battery cable.
2. Disconnect or remove the PCV valve, the accelerator cable and the wiring harness.
3. Disconnect the spark plug wires at the plugs and disconnect the wiring to the noise filter.
4. Disconnect the oil pressure sender wire and, if equipped with air conditioning, the wire to the compressor.
5. Remove the center cover (between the cam covers) and its gasket.
6. Remove the cap nuts, the rubber seals and remove the valve covers.
NOTE: *If the cover is stuck in place. tap a corner with a plastic or rubber mallet. Don't pry the cover up; it will deform and leak.*
7. Clean the mating surfaces of the head and the covers.
8. Apply RTV sealant to the cylinder head before reassembly. This step is REQUIRED to prevent oil leakage.
9. Install the covers with new gaskets. Install the seals and the cap nut, making sure everything is properly seated. tighten the cap nuts to 15 ft. lbs.
10. Install the center cover with its gasket.
11. Connect the wiring to the oil pressure sender and the compressor, if equipped.

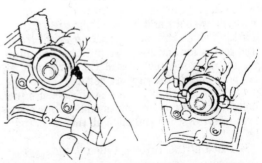

Apply sealant to these points before reinstalling the Nova 4A-LC valve cover

12. Connect the wiring to the noise filter and install the spark plug wires.

13. Connect, in this order, the wiring harness, the accelerator cable, the PCV valve and the negative battery cable.

14. Start the engine and check for leaks after the engine has warmed up. Minor leaks may be cured by slightly snugging the cover bolts. Any leak that is still present after about a ¼ turn CANNOT be cured by further tightening. Remove the cover again and either reposition or replace the gasket.

4A-FE

1. Disconnect the negative battery cable.

2. Disconnect the PCV and the vacuum hose.

3. Loosen the engine wiring harness running over the upper timing belt cover for easier access to the valve cover.

4. Remove the spark plug wires from the spark plugs.

5. Remove the three cap nuts, the seals below them and remove the valve cover.

6. Clean the mating surfaces of the head and the cover. Install a new gasket before installing the valve cover.

7. Apply RTV sealant to the cylinder head before reassembly. This step is REQUIRED to prevent oil leakage.

8. Install the covers with new gaskets. Install the seals and the cap nut, making sure everything is properly seated. Tighten the cap nuts to 15 ft. lbs.

9. Reconnect the spark plug wires and reposition the wiring harness over the timing belt cover.

10. Connect the vacuum hose, the PCV and the negative battery cable.

11. Start the engine and check for leaks after the engine has warmed up. Minor leaks may be cured by slightly snugging the cover bolts. Any leak that is still present after about a ¼ turn CANNOT be cured by further tightening. Remove the cover again and either reposition or replace the gasket.

Rocker Arms and Shafts
REMOVAL AND INSTALLATION
4A-LC

1. Remove the valve cover as described previously.

2. Loosen each rocker support bolt little-by-little, in three steps, in the proper sequence.

3. Remove the bolts and remove the rocker assembly from the head. Inspect the valve contacting surfaces for wear. Inspect the rocker-to-shaft clearance by wiggling the rocker on the shaft. Play should be virtually none; any noticeable motion requires replacement of the rocker arms and/or the shaft.

4. Disassemble the rockers from the shaft. Check the contact surfaces for signs of visible wear or scoring.

5. Using either an inside micrometer or a dial indicator, measure the inside diameter of the rocker arm. Using a regular micrometer, measure the diameter of the shaft. Maximum allowable difference (oil clearance) between the two measurements is 0.06mm.

6. After replacing any needed parts, loosen the adjusting screw lock nuts.

7. The rocker shaft has oil holes in it. When assembling the rockers onto the shaft, make sure the holes point to the left, the right and down. (Said another way, when viewed from the end of the shaft, the oil holes are at 3, 6 and 9 o'clock.)

WARNING: *Failure to observe this positioning will cause the rockers to starve for oil, causing expensive and premature wear.*

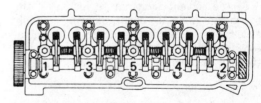

Rocker support bolt loosening sequence

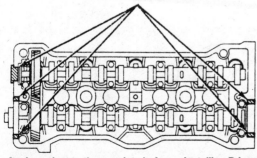

Apply sealant to these points before reinstalling Prizm valve cover

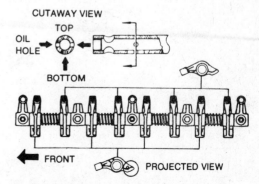

Oil hole positioning

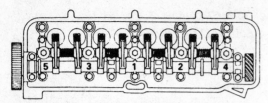

Tighten the rocker support bolts in this sequence

8. Install the rocker assembly on the head. Tighten the retaining bolts in three steps and in the correct sequence. Torque the bolts to 18 ft. lbs on the third pass.

9. Set the motor to TDC and adjust the valves, using the procedures discussed in Chapter 2.

4A-GE and 4A-FE

The twin camshaft motors (one cam for the intake valves and one for the exhaust valves) use direct-acting cams; that is, the lobes of the camshaft act directly on the valve mechanism. These engines do not have rocker arms.

Thermostat

REMOVAL AND INSTALLATION

All Models

The thermostat and its built-in by-pass valve is installed on the inlet side of the water pump. Its purpose is to prevent overheating of the coolant by controlling the flow into the engine from the radiator. During warm up, the thermostat remains closed so that the coolant within the engine heats quickly and aids the warming up process.

As the coolant temperature increases, the thermostat gradually opens, allowing a supply of lower temperature coolant (from the radiator) to enter the water pump and circulate through the engine.

WARNING: *A thermostat with an internal by-pass should never be removed as a countermeasure to overheating. Removing the thermostat actually makes the problem worse because more coolant bypasses the radiator, thereby reducing cooling even more.*

1. Drain the cooling system and save the coolant for reuse.

CAUTION: *When draining the coolant, keep in mind that cats and dogs are attracted by the ethylene glycol antifreeze, and are quite likely to drink any that is left in an uncovered container or in puddles on the ground. This will prove fatal in sufficient quantity. Always drain the coolant into a sealable container. Coolant should be reused unless it is contaminated or several years old.*

2. Remove the water inlet housing and remove the thermostat. Carefully observe the positioning of the thermostat within the housing.

3. Install the new thermostat in the housing, making sure it is in correctly. It is possible--and

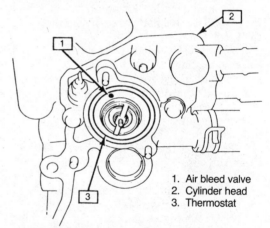

1. Air bleed valve
2. Cylinder head
3. Thermostat

Correct placement of the air bleed valve during thermostat replacement

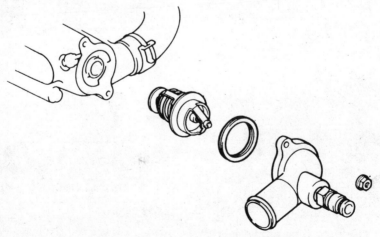

Thermostat assembly. Prizm shown, Nova similar

quite embarassing--to install it backwards. Additionally, make certain that the air bleed valve aligns with the protrusion on the water inlet housing. Failure to observe this placement can result in poor air bleeding and possible overheating.

4. Install the water inlet housing cover with a new gasket. Install the two hold down bolts and tighten them to 20 ft. lbs. Do not overtighten these bolts!

5. Refill the cooling system with coolant.

6. Start the engine. During the warm up period, observe the temperature gauge for normal behavior. Also during this period, check the water inlet housing area for any sign of leakage. Remeber to check for leaks under both cold and hot conditions.

Combination Manifolds
REMOVAL AND INSTALLATION

4A-LC

The intake and exhaust manifolds on the 4A-LC engine are a one-piece or combination design. They can not be separated from each other or removed individually.

1. Disconnect the negative battery cable.

2. Remove the air cleaner assembly.

3. Label and disconnect all vacuum hoses at the carburetor.

4. Disconnect the accelerator cable and, for automatic transmissions, the throttle cable.

5. Label and disconnect the electrical connections at the carburetor.

6. Disconnect the fuel line at the fuel pump.

7. Carefully loosen and remove the carburetor mounting bolts and remove the carburetor.

CAUTION: *The carburetor bowls contain gasoline which may spill or leak during removal. Observe no smoking/no open flame precautions. Have a Class B-C (dry powder) fire extinguisher within arm's reach at all times.*

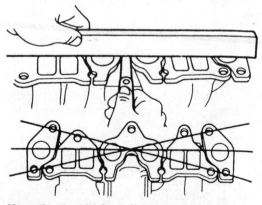

Measuring the 4A-LC manifold for warpage

NOTE: *Keep the carburetor level during removal and handling. As soon as it is off the car, wrap or cover it with a clean towel to keep dirt out.*

8. Remove the Early Fuel Evaporation (EFE) gasket.

9. Remove the vacuum line and dashpot bracket.

10. Carefully remove the heat shields on the manifold; don't break the bolts.

11. Safely elevate and support the vehicle on jackstands.

12. Disconnect the exhaust pipe at the manifold and exhaust bracket at the engine.

13. Remove the hose at the converter pipe.

14. Lower the car to the ground and remove or disconnect the vacuum hose to the brake booster.

15. Remove the bracket for the accelerator and throttle cables.

16. Evenly loosen and then remove the bolts and nuts holding the manifold to the engine. Remove the manifold and its gaskets.

17. Using a precision straight edge and a feeler gauge, check the mating surfaces of the manifold for warpage. If the warpage is greater than the maximum allowable specification, replace the manifold.

Maximum permitted warpage: Intake 0.2mm; Exhaust 0.3mm

18. When reinstalling, always use new gaskets and make sure they are properly positioned. Place the manifold in position and loosely install the nuts and bolts until all are just snug. Double check the placement of the manifold and in two passes tighten the retaining nuts and bolts to 18 ft .lbs.

19. Reinstall the bracket for the accelerator and throttle cables and connect the vacuum hose to the brake vacuum booster.

20. Elevate and safely support the car on jackstands.

21. Reconnect the hose at the converter pipe. Install the exhaust bracket at the engine and, using new gaskets, connect the exhaust pipe to the manifold.

22. Lower the vehicle to the ground. Install the heat shield onto the manifold.

23. Reinstall the vacuum line and the dashpot bracket.

24. Install the EFE gasket.

25. Reinstall the carburetor. Slowly and evenly tighten the mounting nuts and bolts to 8-10 ft. lbs. Connect the electrical connectors to the carburetor.

26. Connect and secure the fuel line to the fuel pump.

27. Attach the accelerator cable and throttle valve cable (automatic trans.).

28. Observing the labels made earlier, install

the vacuum lines. Be careful of the routing and make sure that each line fits snugly on its port. double check each line for crimps or twists.

29. Install the air cleaner assembly and connect the negative battery cable.

Intake Manifold
REMOVAL AND INSTALLATION
4A-GE

1. Disconnect the negative battery cable.
2. Drain the cooling system.

CAUTION: *When draining the coolant, keep in mind that cats and dogs are attracted by the ethylene glycol antifreeze, and are quite likely to drink any that is left in an uncovered container or in puddles on the ground. This will prove fatal in sufficient quantity. Always drain the coolant into a sealable container. Coolant should be reused unless it is contaminated or several years old.*

3. Remove the air cleaner assembly.
4. Remove the upper radiator hose at the engine.
5. Disconnect the accelerator cable and, on automatic transmissions, the throttle valve cable.
6. Label and disconnect vacuum hoses at the manifolds.
7. Disconnect and remove the fuel delivery pipe (fuel rail) and remove the injectors. During removal, be careful not to drop the injectors.

CAUTION: *The fuel system is under pressure. Release pressure slowly and contain spillage. Observe no smoking/no open flame precautions. Have a Class B-C (dry powder) fire extinguisher within arm's reach at all times.*

8. Disconnect the vacuum hose to the brake booster and remove the heat shield(s) from the manifold(s).
9. Safely raise the car and support it on jackstands.
10. Disconnect the wire for the water temper-

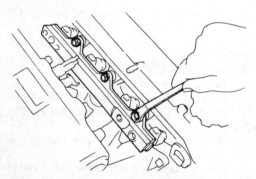

Removing the fuel rails and injectors on the 4A-GE engine

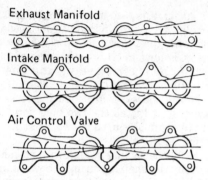

Check for warpage in three positions on 4A-GE manifolds and air control valve

ature sensor and remove the water outlet housing (thermostat housing) and the bypass pipe.

11. Remove the exhaust bracket and disconnect the exhaust pipe at the manifold. Remove the support bracket for the intake manifold.
12. Lower the vehicle to the ground.
13. Remove the intake manifold with the air control valve and gaskets and/or remove the exhaust manifold with its gaskets.
14. Using a precision straight edge and a feeler gauge, check the mating surfaces of the manifolds for warpage. If the warpage is greater than the maximum allowable specification, replace the manifold.

Maximum allowable warpage:
- Intake Manifold: 0.05mm
- Exhaust Manifold: 0.3mm
- Air Control Valve: 0.05mm.

15. When reinstalling, always use new gaskets and make sure they are properly positioned. Place the manifold(s) in position and loosely install the nuts and bolts until all are just snug. Double check the placement of the manifold(s) and in two passes tighten the retaining nuts and bolts. The exhaust manifold retaining bolts should be tightened to 18 ft. lbs. and the intake manifold bolts should be tightened to 20 ft. lbs. The bolts for the intake support bracket should also be tightened to 20 ft. lbs

16. With the manifold(s) in place, elevate and support the vehicle; install the support bracket for the intake manifold and connect the exhaust pipe to the exhaust manifold. Attach the exhaust bracket.

17. Install the bypass pipe, the water outlet housing and connect the wiring to the water temperature sensor.
18. Lower the car to the ground and install the heat shield(s) on the manifolds.
19. Connect the vacuum hose for the brake vacuum booster.
20. Install the fuel delivery pipe and the injectors. Tighten the mounting bolts to 13 ft. lbs.

21. Observing the labels made earlier, install the vacuum lines. Be careful of the routing and make sure that each line fits snugly on its port.

22. Double check each line for crimps or twists.

23. Connect the accelerator cable and throttle valve cable (automatic trans.)

24. Reconnect the upper radiator hose.

25. Install the air cleaner assembly.

26. Refill the coolant.

27. Connect the negative battery cable.

4A-FE

1. Disconnect the negative battery cable.

2. Drain the cooling system.

CAUTION: *When draining the coolant, keep in mind that cats and dogs are attracted by the ethylene glycol antifreeze, and are quite likely to drink any that is left in an uncovered container or in puddles on the ground. This will prove fatal in sufficient quantity. Always drain the coolant into a sealable container. Coolant should be reused unless it is contaminated or several years old.*

3. Remove the air cleaner assembly.

4. Label and disconnect the vacuum hoses at the manifold.

5. Label and disconnect the wiring to the throttle position sensor, the cold start injector, the injector connectors, the air control valve and the vacuum sensor.

6. Disconnect the cold start injector pipe.

CAUTION: *The fuel system is under pressure. Release pressure slowly and contain spillage. Observe no smoking/no open flame precautions. Have a Class B-C (dry powder) fire extinguisher within arm's reach at all times.*

7. Disconnect the water hose from the air valve.

8. Raise and safely support the car on jackstands.

9. Remove the intake manifold support bracket. Lower the car to the ground.

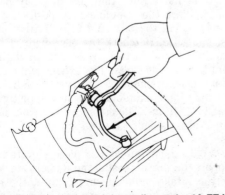

Removing the cold start injector line at the 4A-FE intake manifold

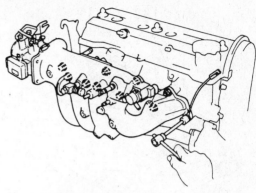

Prizm intake manifold assembly

10. Remove the seven bolts, two nuts and the ground cable. Remove the intake manifold and its gaskets.

11. Measure the intake manifold mating surface with a precision straight edge and a feeler gauge. If the warpage exceeds 0.2mm, the manifold must be replaced.

12. To reassemble, install the manifold with new gaskets in position. Attach the seven bolts, two nuts and the ground cable connector.

13. Raise and safely support the car; install the manifold support bracket and its bolts. Lower the car to the ground.

14. Tighten the manifold mounting nuts and bolts evenly to 14 ft. lbs.

15. Connect the water hose to the air valve.

16. Connect the fuel line to the cold-start injector.

17. Connect the wiring to the throttle position sensor, the cold start injector, the injector connectors, the air control valve and the vacuum sensor.

18. Observing the labels made earlier, install the vacuum lines. Be careful of the routing and make sure that each line fits snugly on its port. Double check each line for crimps or twists.

19. Connect the accelerator and throttle valve (automatic trans.) cables to their brackets.

20. Refill the coolant.

21. Install the air cleaner assembly and connect the negative battery cable.

Exhaust Manifold

REMOVAL AND INSTALLATION

4A-FE

1. Disconnect the negative battery cable.

2. Remove the five bolts and remove the upper heat shield (insulator) from the manifold.

3. Raise and safely support the vehicle on jackstands.

4. Disconnect the exhaust pipe from the exhaust manifold and remove the manifold support and its two bolts.

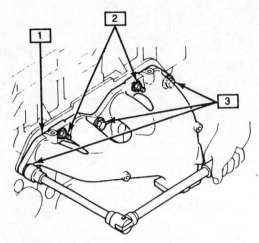

1. Exhaust manifold
2. Nut
3. Bolt

Location of attaching hardware, 4A-FE exhaust manifold

5. Lower the vehicle to the ground. Disconnect the oxygen sensor wire.

6. Remove the two nuts and three bolts holding the manifold to the engine. Remove the manifold and its gaskets. When the manifold is clear of the car, remove the lower heat shield.

7. Measure the exhaust manifold mating surface with a precision straight edge and a feeler gauge. If the warpage exceeds 0.28mm, the manifold must be replaced.

8. Before reinstalling, attach the lower heat shield to the manifold with the three bolts. Tighten the bolts to 18 ft. lbs.

9. Install the manifold with new gaskets and tighten its bolts and nuts to 18 ft. lbs.

10. Raise the car and safely support in on jackstands. Install the manifold support and tighten the bolts to 18 ft. lbs.

11. Connect the exhaust pipe to the manifold with new gaskets and tighten the bolts to 18 ft. lbs.

12. Lower the car to the ground. Install the upper heat shield on the manifold and tighten its five bolts to 18 ft. lbs.

13. Connect the wiring to the oxygen sensors.

14. Connect the negative battery cable.

4A-GE

1. Disconnect the negative battery cable.

2. Drain the cooling system.

CAUTION: *When draining the coolant, keep in mind that cats and dogs are attracted by the ethylene glycol antifreeze, and are quite likely to drink any that is left in an uncovered container or in puddles on the ground. This will prove fatal in sufficient quantity. Always*

drain the coolant into a sealable container. Coolant should be reused unless it is contaminated or several years old.

3. Remove the air cleaner assembly.

4. Remove the upper radiator hose at the engine.

5. Disconnect the accelerator cable and, on automatic transmissions, the throttle valve cable.

6. Label and disconnect vacuum hoses at the manifolds.

7. Disconnect and remove the fuel delivery pipe (fuel rail) and remove the injectors. During removal, be careful not to drop the injectors.

CAUTION: *The fuel system is under pressure. Release pressure slowly and contain spillage. Observe no smoking/no open flame precautions. Have a Class B-C (dry powder) fire extinguisher within arm's reach at all times.*

8. Disconnect the vacuum hose to the brake booster and remove the heat shield(s) from the manifold(s).

9. Safely raise the car and support it on jackstands.

10. Disconnect the wire for the water temperature sensor and remove the water outlet housing (thermostat housing) and the bypass pipe.

11. Remove the exhaust bracket and disconnect the exhaust pipe at the manifold. Remove the support bracket for the intake manifold.

12. Lower the vehicle to the ground.

13. Remove the intake manifold with the air control valve and gaskets and/or remove the exhaust manifold with its gaskets.

14. Using a precision straight edge and a feeler gauge, check the mating surfaces of the manifolds for warpage. If the warpage is greater than the maximum allowable specification, replace the manifold.

Maximum allowable warpage: Intake Manifold: 0.05mm; Exhaust Manifold: 0.3mm; Air Control Valve: 0.05mm.

15. When reinstalling, always use new gaskets and make sure they are properly positioned. Place the manifold(s) in position and loosely install the nuts and bolts until all are just snug. Double check the placement of the manifold(s) and in two passes tighten the retaining nuts and bolts. The exhaust manifold retaining bolts should be tightened to 18 ft. lbs. and the intake manifold bolts should be tightened to 20 ft. lbs. The bolts for the intake support bracket should also be tightened to 20 ft. lbs

16. With the manifold(s) in place, elevate and support the vehicle; install the support bracket for the intake manifold and connect the exhaust pipe to the exhaust manifold. Attach the exhaust bracket.

17. Install the bypass pipe, the water outlet housing and connect the wiring to the water temperature sensor.

18. Lower the car to the ground and install the heat shield(s) on the manifolds.

19. Connect the vacuum hose for the brake vacuum booster.

20. Install the fuel delivery pipe and the injectors. Tighten the mounting bolts to 13 ft. lbs.

21. Observing the labels made earlier, install the vacuum lines. Be careful of the routing and make sure that each line fits snugly on its port.

22. Double check each line for crimps or twists.

23. Connect the accelerator cable and throttle valve cable (automatic trans.)

24. Reconnect the upper radiator hose.

25. Install the air cleaner assembly.

26. Refill the coolant.

27. Connect the negative battery cable.

Air Conditioning Compressor

REMOVAL AND INSTALLATION

All Nova (4A-LC and 4A-GE)

CAUTION: *Please re-read the air conditioning section in chapter one so that the system may be discharged properly. Always wear eye protection and gloves when discharging the system. Observe no smoking/ no open flame rules.*

1. Disconnect the negative battery cable.

2. Remove the electrical connector to the compressor.

3. Safely discharge the system.

4. Remove the two hoses from the compressor fittings. Immediately cap the compressor ports and the hose ends to prevent dirt from entering.

5. Remove the fan shroud.

6. Loosen the compressor drive belt.

7. Remove the compressor mounting bolts and remove the compressor from the engine.

You are reminded that the compressor is a heavy component--support it securely when removing the bolts.

8. When reinstalling, attach the compressor mounting bolts and tighten them to 20 ft. lbs.

9. Install and tighten the drive belt to the correct tension. Make sure the belt is correctly seated on its pulleys.

10. Install the fan shroud.

11. Connect the hoses to the compressor and connect the electrical leads.

12. Connect the negative battery cable.

13. Evacuate and recharge the air conditioning system as explained in Chapter One.

Prizm (4A-FE)

CAUTION: *Please re-read the air conditioning section in chapter one so that the system may be discharged properly. Always wear eye protection and gloves when discharging the system. Observe no smoking/ no open flame rules.*

1. Disconnect the negative battery cable.

2. Remove the electrical connector to the compressor.

3. Safely discharge the system.

4. Remove the two hoses from the compressor fittings. Immediately cap the compressor ports and the hose ends to prevent dirt from entering.

5. Loosen or remove the compressor drive belt.

6. Elevate and safely support the vehicle on jackstands. Remove the splash shield under the engine.

7. Remove the compressor mounting bolts and remove the compressor from the engine. You are reminded that the compressor is a heavy component--support it securely when removing the bolts.

8. When reinstalling, support the compressor in place and install the retaining bolts. Tighten them to 18. ft. lbs.

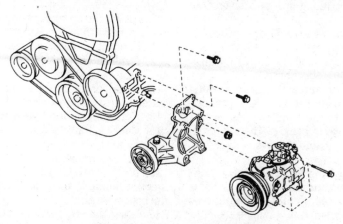

Prizm air conditioning compressor

9. With the vehicle safely supported by jackstands, reinstall the splash shields.

10. Lower the vehicle and install the drive belt. Adjust it to the proper tension.

11. Use new o-rings in the hose ends and connect the hoses to the compressor. tighten both lines only to 18 ft. lbs.

12. Install the wiring to the compressor.

13. Connect the negative battery cable.

14. Evacuate and recharge the air conditioning system as explained in Chapter One.

Radiator

REMOVAL AND INSTALLATION

Nova

1. Drain the coolant by opening the engine block and radiator drain cocks. Collect the coolant in a clean container and save for reuse.

CAUTION: *When draining the coolant, keep in mind that cats and dogs are attracted by the ethylene glycol antifreeze, and are quite likely to drink any that is left in an uncovered container or in puddles on the ground. This will prove fatal in sufficient quantity. Always drain the coolant into a sealable container. Coolant should be reused unless it is contaminated or several years old.*

2. Unplug the wiring to the cooling fan(s).

3. Remove the fan shroud, the four bolts on the top of the radiator tank and, if equipped with air conditioning, the two bolts on the bottom radiator tank.

4. If equipped with automatic transmission, disconnect the oil cooler lines running to the radiator. Use a clean container to collect the oil which runs out. Cap the lines immediately to prevent dirt form entering the system.

5. Disconnect the overflow hose at the radiator neck.

6. Disconnect the upper and lower radiator hoses from the radiator.

7. Remove the two radiator hold-down brackets and lift the radiator out of the engine compartment.

8. After reinstalling the radiator, attach the holddown brackets.

9. Connect the upper and lower radiator hoses and the coolant overflow hose.

10. If equipped with automatic transmission, remove the plugs from the lines and connect the oil cooler lines to the radiator.

11. Reinstall the four bolts at the top tank and, on automatics, install the two bolts at the lower tank.

12. Connect the wiring for the fan(s).

13. Confirm that the draincocks on the engine and radiator are closed. Refill the cooling system with the proper amount of engine coolant.

14. Add automatic transmission fluid in an amount equal to that lost from the oil cooler during removal.

15. Start the engine and check hose and line connections for leaks. Allow the engine to warm up to normal operating temperature. Check carefully for leaks under both cold and hot conditions.

16. Check the automatic transmission fluid and add if necessary.

Prizm

1. Disconnect the negative battery cable.

2. Drain the coolant by opening the engine block and radiator drain cocks. Collect the coolant in a clean container and save for reuse.

CAUTION: *When draining the coolant, keep in mind that cats and dogs are attracted by the ethylene glycol antifreeze, and are quite likely to drink any that is left in an uncovered container or in puddles on the ground. This will prove fatal in sufficient quantity. Always drain the coolant into a sealable container. Coolant should be reused unless it is contaminated or several years old.*

3. Remove the coolant overflow reservoir.

4. Disconnect the upper radiator hose from the radiator and the lower radiator hose from the thermostat housing.

5. If equipped with automatic transmission, disconnect the oil cooler lines running to the radiator.

6. Remove the upper radiator brackets.

7. Disconnect the wiring running to the fan(s).

8. Remove the radiator and fan assembly from the car. If the radiator is to be worked on or replaced, the fan and shroud assembly, the lower hose and the lower rubber mounts must be removed. Don't forget to install them on the new unit before installing it.

9. With the necessary parts mounted on the radiator, install the radiator in the car. Install the upper mounting brackets. Tighten them to 7.5 ft. lbs. (89 INCH lbs.)

10. Install the oil cooler hoses to the radiator if equipped with automatic transmission.

11. Connect the electrical lead(s) to the fan(s).

12. Replace the coolant overflow reservoir and connect the hose.

13. Install and secure the upper and lower radiator hoses. Use new clamps.

14. Connect the negative battery cable.

15. Confirm that the draincocks on the engine and radiator are closed. Refill the cooling system with the proper amount of engine coolant.

16. Add automatic transmission fluid in an amount equal to that lost from the oil cooler during removal.

17. Start the engine and check hose and line connections for leaks. Allow the engine to warm

up to normal operating temperature. Check carefully for leaks under both cold and hot conditions.

18. Check the automatic transmission fluid and add if necessary.

Condenser

REMOVAL AND INSTALLATION

Nova

CAUTION: *Please re-read the air conditioning section in chapter one so that the system may be discharged properly. Always wear eye protection and gloves when discharging the system. Observe no smoking/ no open flame rules.*

1. Safely discharge the air conditioning system.
2. Remove the grille and the hood lock brace.
3. Disconnect the flexible discharge hose from the condenser inlet fitting. Use two wrenches, one to counterhold the fitting and one to turn. Failure to counterhold the fitting may result in damage to the lines.
4. Disconnect the liquid line from the condenser outlet. Again, use two wrenches.
5. Cap the open lines immediately to prevent moisture from entering the system.
6. Remove the four bolts holding the condenser and remove the condenser. Take great care not to damage the fins on the condenser during removal.
7. When reinstalling, make sure the rubber cushions fit on the mounting flange correctly.
8. Install the four bolts holding the condenser.
9. Connect the liquid line to the condenser and tighten it to 10 ft. lbs.
10. Connect the flexible discharge hose and tighten it to 16 ft. lbs.

NOTE: *The lightweight fittings on the lines and hoses are easily damaged. Do not overtighten the threaded fittings.*

11. Install the front grille and hood lock brace.
12. If a different condenser was installed, add 1.4-1.7 oz. of compressor oil to the compressor.
13. Evacuate and recharge the system.

Prizm

CAUTION: *Please re-read the air conditioning section in chapter one so that the system may be discharged properly. Always wear eye protection and gloves when discharging the system. Observe no smoking/ no open flame rules.*

1. Safely discharge the system.
2. Disconnect the negative battery cable.
3. Remove the front grille, the hood lock and its brace.

4. Remove the front bumper.
5. Disconnect the liquid line and the discharge hose at the condenser. Use two wrenches, one to hold the assembly and one to turn the fitting. Failure to counterhold the lines may result in damage to the lines, hoses and fittings. Cap the open lines immediately to prevent moisture from entering the system.
6. Remove the four mounting bolts and remove the condenser.
7. When reinstalling, mount the condenser and install its four bolts.
8. Connect the liquid tube and the discharge hose to the condenser. Tighten the liquid tube to 10 ft. lbs. and the discharge hose to 18 ft. lbs.

NOTE: *The lightweight fittings on the lines and hoses are easily damaged. Do not overtighten the threaded fittings.*

9. Reinstall the front bumper.
10. Install the hood lock and center brace. Install the grille.
11. If the condenser has been replaced with a different unit, add 1.4-1.7 ounces of compressor oil to the compressor.
12. Connect the negative battery cable.
13. Evacuate and recharge the system.

Water Pump

REMOVAL AND INSTALLATION.

Nova (4A-LC and 4A-GE Engines)

1. Drain the engine coolant by opening the radiator and engine block draincocks. Collect the coolant in clean containers and save for reuse.

CAUTION: *When draining the coolant, keep in mind that cats and dogs are attracted by the ethylene glycol antifreeze, and are quite likely to drink any that is left in an uncovered container or in puddles on the ground. This will prove fatal in sufficient quantity. Always drain the coolant into a sealable container. Coolant should be reused unless it is contaminated or several years old.*

2. On the 4A-GE engine, remove the power steering drive belt.

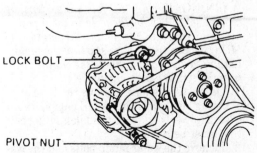

LOCK BOLT

PIVOT NUT

The alternator adjusting bolts must be loosened to remove the water pump belt

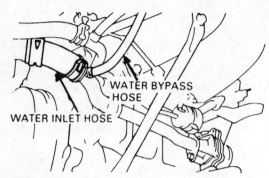

WATER BYPASS HOSE

WATER INLET HOSE

Remove these two hoses before removing the water inlet pipe

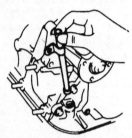

Removing the oil dipstick tube. Always use a new seal (o-ring) on the tube when reinstalling

3. Loosen the water pump pulley bolts.

4. Loosen the alternator locking bolt and the pivot nut.

5. Move the alternator to its loosest position and remove the belt.

6. On the 4A-LC engine, remove the power steering drive belt.

7. Remove the four bolts on the water pump pulley and remove the pulley.

8. Disconnect the water inlet and the water bypass hoses from the water inlet pipe.

9. Disconnect and remove the water inlet pipe by removing the two clamp bolts and the two nuts at the back of the pump. Remove the o-ring from the back of the pump.

10. Remove the mounting bolt for the dipstick tube; remove the tube and dipstick. Immediately plug the hole in block to prevent fluid from polluting the oil.

WARNING: *During the following steps, if coolant should get by the plug in the dipstick hole and run into the motor, the engine oil MUST be changed before starting the motor. Failure to do so can damage the engine bearings. Very noisy--very expensive.*

11. On 4A-LC engines, remove the No.1 (upper) timing belt cover. On 4A-GE engines, both the No. 2 (lower) and No. 3 (middle) timing belt covers must be removed.

12. Remove the water pump bolts and the water pump.

13. To reinstall, place the water pump gasket

(o-ring) on the block and install the pump. Tighten the mounting bolts to 11 ft. lbs.

14. Install the timing belt cover(s), making sure they are properly seated and not rubbing on the belt or other moving parts.

15. Install a new seal (o-ring) on the dipstick tube and lightly coat it with engine oil. Remove the plug and install the dipstick tube and dipstick; secure the mounting bolt.

16. Using a new o-ring, install the inlet pipe to the water pump.

17. Attach the clamps and bolts to hold the pipe in place.

18. Connect the water inlet and water bypass hoses to the inlet pipe.

19. Install the water pump pulley and tighten the four pulley bolts finger tight.

20. For 4A-LC engines, install the power steering drive belt.

21. Install the drive belts on all the pulleys and adjust all of them to the correct tension.

22. With the belts in place and adjusted, the water pump pulley will now resist turning. Tighten the pulley bolts to 16-18 ft. lbs.

23. For the 4A-GE engine, install the power steering belt and adjust to the proper tension.

24. Confirm that the draincocks are closed on the engine block and radiator. Refill the engine coolant.

25. Start the engine and check for leaks.

Prizm (4A-FE Engine)

1. Remove the radiator cap. Drain the engine coolant by opening the radiator and engine block draincocks. Collect the coolant in clean containers and save for reuse.

CAUTION: *When draining the coolant, keep in mind that cats and dogs are attracted by the ethylene glycol antifreeze, and are quite likely to drink any that is left in an uncovered container or in puddles on the ground. This will prove fatal in sufficient quantity. Always drain the coolant into a sealable container. Coolant should be reused unless it is contaminated or several years old.*

2. Raise and safely support the vehicle on jackstands.

3. Remove the two nuts for the rear motor mount.

4. Lower the vehicle to the ground.

5. Remove the windshield washer fluid container.

6. If so equipped, remove the cruise control bracket with the control module.

7. Remove the through bolt for the right motor mount.

8. Place a jack under the engine. Use a piece of wood between the engine and the jack.

9. Raise the engine slowly and carefully.

Keep a close watch on lines and cables. The engine need only be raised enough to gain access to various nuts and bolts.

10. Loosen the water pump pulley bolts, but leave them in place.

11. Loosen the alternator lock bolt and pivot nut; swing the alternator towards the engine and remove the drive belt.

12. Loosen the pivot bolts and the lock bolt for the power steering pump and move it towards the engine; remove the power steering belt.

13. With the belts removed, the water pump pulley may be removed from the pump.

14. Lower the jack, allowing the engine to return to place.

15. Remove the water inlet and water bypass hoses from the water inlet pipe.

16. Remove the clamp holding the water inlet pipe to the engine. Loosen and remove the two nuts holding the inlet pipe to the water pump. Remove the pipe and its o-ring.

17. Remove the mounting bolt for the dipstick tube; remove the tube and dipstick. Immediately plug the hole in block to prevent fluid from polluting the oil.

WARNING: *During the following steps, if coolant should get by the plug in the dipstick hole and run into the motor, the engine oil MUST be changed before starting the motor. Failure to do so can damage the engine bearings. Very noisy--very expensive.*

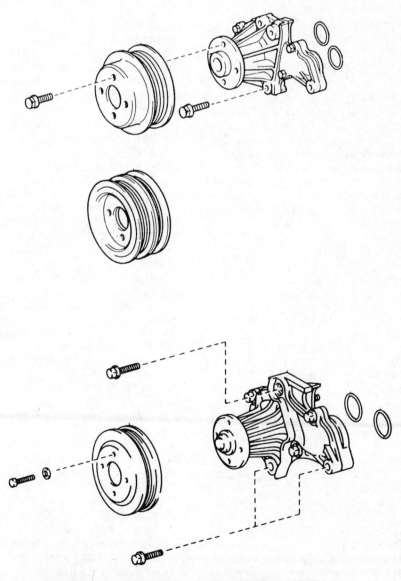

Water pump components: 4A-LC above, 4A-GE and 4A-FE below

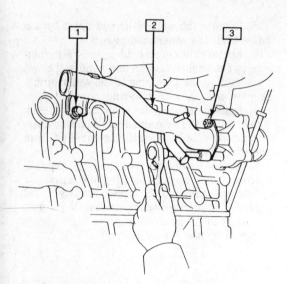

1. Pipe retaining brace
2. Water inlet pipe
3. Pipe retaining nuts

Removing the Prizm water inlet pipe

18. Remove the upper timing belt cover.

NOTE: *The timing belt is exposed with the cover(s) removed. Do not allow oil or coolant to contact the belt. This includes any fluid which may be accidentally transferred through rags, fingerprints, etc.*

19. Remove the three water pump bolts and remove the water pump.

20. When reinstalling, position a new o-ring

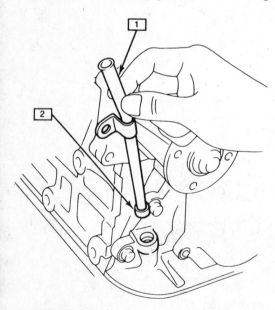

1. Oil dipstick tube
2. Tube o-ring

Removing the dipstick tube on the Prizm motor. Always plug the hole in the engine block when the tube is removed

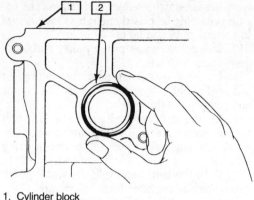

1. Cylinder block
2. Water pump o-ring

Always use a new gasket (o-ring) when installing a new water pump

on the engine and fit the water pump. Tighten the three bolts to 11 ft. lbs.

21. Install the upper timing belt cover.

22. Install a new o-ring on the dipstick tube.

23. Remove the plug in the engine and install the tube. Tighten the mounting bolt.

24. Using a new o-ring, install the water inlet pipe at the back of the water pump. Tighten the two nuts to 14. ft. lbs.

25. Connect the water inlet and water bypass hoses to the water inlet pipe.

26. Following the same jacking procedure as before, elevate the motor with the floor jack.

27. Install the water pump pulley and tighten the bolts finger tight. It will be easier to do the final tightening when the belts are installed.

28. Install the power steering belt and adjust its tension.

29. Install the alternator drive belt and adjust its tension.

30. Tighten the water pump pulley bolts to 17 ft. lbs.

31. Lower the jack, allowing the engine to return to its normal place.

32. Install the through bolt for the right motor mount. Tighten it to 64 ft. lbs.

33. Reinstall the cruise control module and the bracket, if so equipped.

34. Raise and safely support the vehicle on jackstands.

35. Install the two nuts for the rear mount and tighten them to 38 ft. lbs.

36. Lower the vehicle to the ground.

37. Replace the washer fluid container.

38. Confirm that the draincocks on the radiator and engine block are closed. Refill the cooling system with coolant.

39. Start the engine and check for leaks. Pay particular attention to any hose or fitting which was disassembled during the repair.

40. After the engine is shut off, double check

the drive belts for proper tension and adjust as necessary.

Cylinder Head

REMOVAL AND INSTALLATION

4A-LC Engine

NOTE: *All wires and hoses should be labled at the time of removal. The amount of time saved during reassembly makes the extra effort well worthwhile.*

1. Disconnect the negative battery cable.
2. Drain the cooling system and save the coolant in clean containers.

CAUTION: *When draining the coolant, keep in mind that cats and dogs are attracted by the ethylene glycol antifreeze, and are quite likely to drink any that is left in an uncovered container or in puddles on the ground. This will prove fatal in sufficient quantity. Always drain the coolant into a sealable container. Coolant should be reused unless it is contaminated or several years old.*

3. Remove the air cleaner assembly.
4. Elevate and safely support the vehicle on jackstands.
5. Drain the engine oil.

CAUTION: *Used motor oil may cause skin*

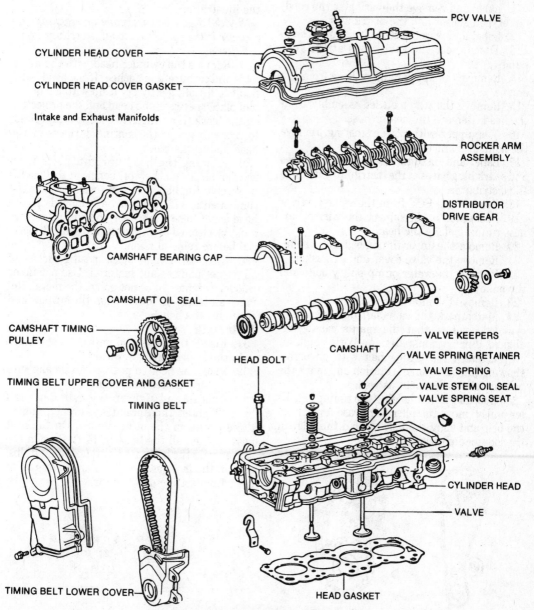

Exploded view of the 4A-LC cylinder head

cancer if repeatedly left in contact with the skin for prolonged periods. Although this is unlikely unless you handle oil on a daily basis, it is wise to thoroughly wash your hands with soap and water immediately after handling used motor oil.

6. Disconnect the exhaust pipe from the exhaust manifold and the exhaust bracket from the engine.

7. Disconnect the hose at the converter pipe.

8. If equipped with power steering, loosen the pivot bolt at the power steering pump.

9. Lower the vehicle to the ground.

10. Disconnect the accelerator and throttle control cables at the carburetor and bracket.

11. Label and remove the wiring at the cowl, the oxygen sensor and the distributor.

12. Label and disconnect the vacuum hoses.

13. Disconnect the fuel hoses at the fuel pump.

14. Remove the upper radiator hose from the engine.

15. Remove the water outlet assembly from the head. Remove the heater hose.

16. If equipped with power steering, remove the adjusting bracket.

17. Label and disconnect the vacuum hoses and spark plug wires at the distributor. Remove the distributor.

18. Remove the PCV from the valve cover.

19. Reposition or disconnect the wiring harness running along the head.

20. Remove the upper timing belt cover bolts.

21. Remove the valve cover and its gasket.

22. Remove the water pump pulley bolts and the pulley.

23. Remove the alternator belt.

24. Matchmark the camshaft pulley and the cylinder head so that the marks can be realigned during reinstallation. With chalk or crayon, mark the timing belt with an arrow showing the direction of rotation and mark the belt-to-pulley alignment as well.

25. Loosen the bolt holding the timing belt idler pulley; move the idler to release tension on the belt and snug the bolt to hold the idler in the loosened position.

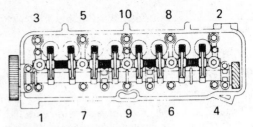

Cylinder head loosening sequence

26. Carefully pull or slide the timing belt off the cam pulley. Do not crimp the belt and do not force it off the pulley with tools.

27. Loosen and remove the head bolts gradually, in three passes and in the order shown in the illustration.

WARNING: *Head warpage or cracking can occur if the correct removal procedure is not followed.*

28. Remove the cylinder head with the manifolds and carburetor attached. If the head is difficult to lift off, gently pry it up with a suitable tool placed between the head and the projection on the block. If prying is needed, be careful not to score or gouge the mating surfaces of the head and/or the block.

29. Keeping the head upright, place it on wooden blocks on the workbench. If the head is to receive further work, the various external components will need to be removed. If the head is not to be worked on, the mating surface must be cleaned of all gasket and sealant material before reinstallation.

30. Clean the engine block mating surface of all gasket and sealant material. Use plastic or wooden scrapers so as not gouge the metal. Remove all traces of liquids from the surface and clean out the bolt holes.

To install:

31. Install the new head gasket on the block with the sealer facing upwards.

32. Place the head in position and make sure it is properly seated and aligned.

33. Install and tighten the cylinder head bolts. Tighten then gradually, evenly, and in three passes in the order shown. On the first pass, tighten all the bolts to 14 ft. lbs. On the second pass the bolts are tightened to 30 ft. lbs. and on the last pass the bolts are tightened to their final setting of 43 ft. lbs.

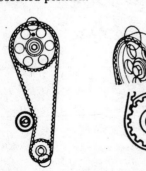

Mark the timing belt rotation before removal

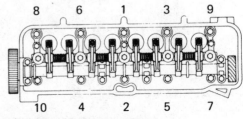

Cylinder head torque sequence

WARNING: *Failure to follow this procedure exactly may cause either premature gasket failure or head damage.*

34. Align the camshaft pulley mark(s) made during disassembly with the marks on the head and or block.

35. Install the timing belt onto the cam pulley, being careful not to allow the belt to become mispositioned on the lower (crank) pulley. Handle the belt carefully and avoid getting fluids or lubricants on the belt.

36. Loosen the holding bolt for the timing belt idler pulley and allow it to tension the belt.

37. Turn the crankshaft clockwise through at least two full revolutions; finish the rotation by aligning the timing marks at TDC. Double check that the small triangular mark on the cam pulley is at the top and pointing up.

38. Tighten the bolt for the timing belt idler pulley to 27 ft. lbs.

39. Using a belt tension gauge such as GM-23600-B or similar, check the timing belt tension. Correct tension is 0.6mm at 4.4 lbs.

40. If the head was disassembled during the repair, adjust the valves at this time. If the head was not disassembled, the valves need not be adjusted.

41. Install the valve cover and the upper timing cover.

42. Install the water pump pulley and bolts; install the alternator belt and adjust it to the correct tension.

43. Correctly position or reconnect the wiring harness running along the head.

44. Install the PCV valve in the valve cover.

45. Correctly install the distributor and connect the wiring, vacuum lines and spark plug wires.

46. Install the power steering adjusting bracket if so equipped.

47. Install the heater hose, the water outlet at the head and connect the upper radiator hose to the engine.

48. Connect the fuel lines to the fuel pump.

49. Observing the labels made earlier, connect the vacuum hoses to their ports. Make sure the hoses fit securely on the fittings and are not crimped or twisted.

50. Connect the wiring at the cowl, the oxygen sensor and the distributor.

51. Connect the accelerator and throttle control cables at the bracket and at the carburetor.

52. Safely raise and support the vehicle on jackstands.

53. If equipped with power steering, tighten the pivot bolt for the pump.

54. Connect the hose at the converter pipe.

55. Connect the exhaust bracket to the engine and connect the exhaust pipe to the manifold.

56. Lower the vehicle to the ground.

57. Install the air cleaner assembly.

58. Add the correct amount of fresh engine oil.

59. Confirm that the radiator and engine draincocks are closed and fill the cooling system with the correct amount of coolant. Install the radiator cap.

60. Double check all installation items, paying particular attention to loose hoses or hanging wires, untightened nuts, poor routing of hoses and wires (too tight or rubbing) and tools left in the engine area.

61. Connect the negative battery cable.

63. Start the engine; during the warm up period, check carefully for any signs of fluid leaks or engine overheating.

64. When the engine has reached normal operating temperature, check the ignition timing and adjust the idle speed as necessary.

4A-GE Engine

NOTE: *All wires and hoses should be labled at the time of removal. The amount of time saved during reassembly makes the extra effort well worthwhile.*

1. Disconnect the negative battery cable

2. Open the draincocks on the engine and radiator. Collect the coolant in clean containers.

CAUTION: *When draining the coolant, keep in mind that cats and dogs are attracted by the ethylene glycol antifreeze, and are quite likely to drink any that is left in an uncovered container or in puddles on the ground. This will prove fatal in sufficient quantity. Always drain the coolant into a sealable container. Coolant should be reused unless it is contaminated or several years old.*

3. Remove the air cleaner assembly.

4. Disconnect the cruise control cable if so equipped.

5. Disconnect the throttle cable from the throttle linkage.

6. Remove the heater hose from the cylinder head rear cover.

7. Label and remove the vacuum hoses from the throttle body.

8. If equipped with cruise control, remove the actuator and bracket assembly.

9. Remove the ignition coil.

10. Remove the upper radiator hose from the cylinder head and the radiator.

11. Remove the brake booster vacuum hose.

12. Remove the PCV hose.

13. Unbolt and remove as a unit the fuel pressure regulator.

14. Unbolt and remove the EGR valve with the lines attached.

15. Remove the cold start injector hose.

CAUTION: *The fuel system is under pressure. Release pressure slowly and contain*

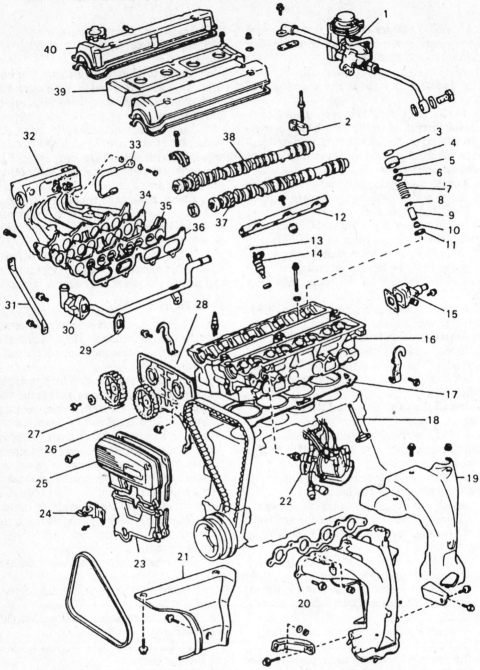

1. EGR valve
2. Camshaft bearing cap
3. Adjusting shim
4. Valve lifter
5. Valve keepers
6. Valve spring retainer
7. Valve spring
8. Snap ring
9. Valve guide bushing
10. Valve stem oil seal
11. Valve spring seal
12. Delivery pipe
13. O-ring
14. Injector

15. Cylinder head rear cover
16. Cylinder head
17. Cyllinder head gasket
18. Valve
19. Upper exhaust manifold insulator
20. Exhaust manifold
21. Lower exhaust manifold insulator
22. Distributor
23. No. 2 timing belt cover
24. Engine mounting bracket
25. No. 3 timing belt cover
26. Exhaust camshaft timing pulley
27. Intake camshaft timing pulley
28. No. 4 timing belt cover

29. Gasket
30. Water outlet
31. Intake manifold stay
32. Intake manifold
33. Cold start injection pipe
34. Gasket
35. Air control valve
36. Gasket
37. Exhaust valve camshaft
38. Intake valve camshaft
39. Cylinder head center cover
40. Cylinder head cover

Exploded view of the 4A-GE head

spillage. Observe no smoking/no open flame precautions. Have a Class B-C (dry powder) fire extinguisher within arm's reach at all times.

16. Remove the No. 1 fuel line.

17. Remove the first and second water bypass hoses from the auxilary air valve.

18. Remove the vacuum pipe and the cylinder head rear cover.

19. Remove, disconnect or reposition the wiring harness(es) around the head as necessary.

20. Remove the distributor.

21. Remove the exhaust manifold and its gaskets.

22. Remove the fuel delivery pipe and the injectors. DO NOT drop the injectors.

23. Remove the intake manifold support bracket; remove the intake manifold and the intake air control valve.

24. Remove the power steering drive belt.

25. Remove the upper timing belt cover and the valve covers.

26. Remove the water outlet fitting with the bypass pipe and the belt adjusting bar.

27. Remove the spark plugs.

28. Turn the crankshaft clockwise, stopping so that the groove in the crank pulley aligns with the idler pulley bolt. Additionally, check that the valve lifters on No. 1 cylinder are loose (the cam lobes are NOT depressing the lifters). If the valves are under tension, rotate the crank one full revolution and check again. The engine is now on TDC/compression.

29. Remove the right motor mount.

30. Remove the water pump pulley.

31. Remove the lower and middle (Nos. 2 and 3) timing belt covers.

WARNING: *The bolts are different lengths. Label or diagram the correct location of each bolt as it is removed. Improper placement during reassembly can cause engine damage.*

32. Place matchmarks on the timing belt and the belt pulleys. Make sure that you mark each pulley and the belt clearly. Additionally, mark an arrow on the belt showing the direction of rotation.

33. Carefully slide the timing belt off the camshaft pulleys. Do not pry on the belt with tools. Keep the belt under light upward tension so that the bottom (crankshaft) end doesn't shift position on its pulley.

34. Remove the camshaft pulleys. Use an adjustable wrench to counterhold the cams during removal. Look for the flats on the cam and fit the wrench to them.

35. With the pulleys removed, the end plate (otherwise called No. 4 timing cover) may be removed.

36. Loosen the head bolts in the order shown in the diagram. Make three complete passes, loosening them slowly, evenly and in order.

37. Remove the cylinder head. If it is difficult to remove, it may be pried up gently with a suitable tool. Be very careful not to scratch or gouge the mating surfaces when prying the head up.

38. Keeping the head upright, place it on wooden blocks on the workbench. If the head is to receive further work, the various components will need to be removed. If the head is not to be worked on, the mating surface must be cleaned of all gasket and sealant material before reinstallation.

39. Clean the engine block mating surface of all gasket and sealant material. Use plastic or wooden scrapers so as not gouge the metal. Remove all traces of liquids from the surface and clean out the bolt holes.

40. Install the new head gasket on the block. Make sure it is properly placed and that all the holes and passages in the block line up with the holes in the gasket.

41. Place the head in position and make sure it is properly seated and aligned.

42. Apply a light coat of oil to the threads of the cylinder head bolts.

43. Install the ten cylinder head bolts.

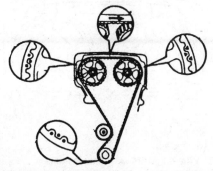

Examples of matchmarks on timing belt and pulleys. Don't forget an arrow showing the direction of rotation. The belt will break if put on backwards

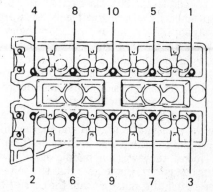

4A-GE engine: Remove the head bolts in this sequence

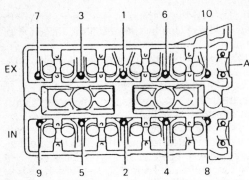

4A-GE engines: Tighten the head bolts in this sequence

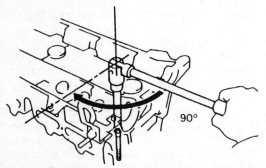

Apply a dot of paint to the front of each head bolt. Apply 90° of rotation in the correct sequence. After all are set, repeat the pattern, tightening each bolt through an additional 90°

NOTE: *The bolts for the exhaust side are 108mm long; the bolts for the intake side are 87.5mm long.*

44. Tighten the cylinder head bolts in three passes and in sequence. The first pass should tighten them to 8-10 ft. lbs., the second pass to 16. ft. lbs. and the third pass to 22 ft. lbs.

45. Mark the front (towards the front of the car) of each bolt with a dot of paint.

46. In the specified order, tighten each bolt through exactly 90° of rotation.

47. Repeat the procedure, tightening each bolt an additional 90°. Check that the paint marks on each bolt are now facing rearward.

48. Apply RTV sealer or similar to the cylinder head. Install new cam end seals and coat them lightly with multi-purpose grease.

49. Install the end plate or No.4 timing cover.

50. Install the right side engine mount bracket and tighten its bolts to 18 ft. lbs.

51. Install the camshaft pulleys. Be sure to align the camshaft knock pin and the camshaft pulley. Tighten the pulley bolts to 34 ft. lbs.

52. Install the lower and middle (nos 2 and 3) timing belt covers. Remember that the bolts are different lengths; make certain the correct bolt is in the correct location.

53. Install the water pump pulley.

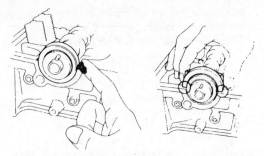

Sealant must be applied to the head before reinstalling the valve cover

54. Install the right engine mount. Tighten the through bolt to 58 ft. lbs.

55. Install the spark plugs. Correct tightness is 13 ft. lbs.

56. Reinstall the water outlet with the bypass pipe and the belt adjusting bar.

57. Install the valve covers.

58. Install the alternator and power steering drive belts. Adjust the belts to the correct tension.

59. Install the intake manifold and intake air control valve. Tighten the bolts to 20 ft. lbs

60. Install the bracket and support for the intake manifold.

61. Install the fuel delivery pipe and the injectors. Make sure the insulators and spacers have been placed properly. Make sure the injectors rotate smoothly in their seats.

62. Tighten the delivery pipe retaining bolts to 13. ft. lbs.

63. Install the exhaust manifold tighten its nuts and bolts to 18 ft. lbs.

64. Reinstall the distributor.

65. Attach, reposition or connect the wiring harness(es) around the head. Make sure that all retaining clips are used and are secure. Douuble check the wiring to eliminate any contact with moving parts.

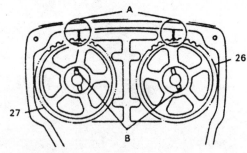

A   MATCHMARK
B   KNOCK PIN
26 EXHAUST CAMSHAFT TIMING PULLEY
27 INTAKE CAMSHAFT TIMING PULLEY

Align the cam pulleys before installing the timing belt

66. Install the vacuum pipe and the cylinder head rear cover with a new gasket.

67. Connect the first and second bypass hoses to the auxilary air valve.

68. Connect the No.1 fuel line.

69. Use new gaskets and connect the cold start injector line. Tighten the bolts to 13 ft. lbs.

70. Replace the EGR valve and use a new gasket.

71. Use a new o-ring and attach the fuel pressure regulator. Tighten the regulator bolts to 6.8 ft. lbs (82 INCH lbs.)

72. Install the PCV hose and the brake vacuum hose.

73. Install the radiator hose at the radiator and the cylinder head.

74. Install the ignition coil.

75. Install the cruise control actuator and bracket assembly if so equipped.

76. Observing the labels made earlier, connect the vacuum hose to the throttle body.

77. Attach the heater hose to the cylinder head rear cover.

78. Connect the throttle valve and accelerator cables.

79. Connect the cruise control cable, if so equipped.

80. Install the air cleaner assembly.

81. Confirm that the draincocks on the radiator and engine block are closed. Fill the cooling system with coolant.

82. Double check all installation items, paying particular attention to loose hoses or hanging wires, untightened nuts, poor routing of hoses and wires (too tight or rubbing) and tools left in the engine area.

83. Connect the negative battery cable.

84. Start the engine. During the warm up period, check for any sign of leakage or overheating. Check engine timing and adjust the idle speed if necessary.

85. After the engine is shut off, check the drive belts and adjust the tension if necessary.

4A-FE Engine

NOTE: *All wires and hoses should be labled at the time of removal. The amount of time saved during reassembly makes the extra effort well worthwhile.*

1. Disconnect the negative battery cable.

2. Open the draincocks on the engine and radiator. Collect the coolant in clean containers.

CAUTION: *When draining the coolant, keep in mind that cats and dogs are attracted by the ethylene glycol antifreeze, and are quite likely to drink any that is left in an uncovered container or in puddles on the ground. This will prove fatal in sufficient quantity. Always drain the coolant into a sealable container. Coolant should be reused unless it is contaminated or several years old.*

3. Raise the vehicle and safely support it on jackstands.

4. Remove the lower right splash (stone) shield.

5. Remove the two covers for the rear engine mount nuts and studs.

6. Remove the two rear transaxle mount-to-main crossmember mounting nuts.

7. Remove the two center mount-to-center crossmember nuts.

8. Lower the vehicle to the ground.

9. Remove the air cleaner assembly.

10. Disconnect or remove throttle cable, the transmission kick-down cable (automatic) and, if equipped, the cruise control actuator cable.

11. Label and disconnect the vacuum lines. Loosen, disconnect or reposition the wiring harnesses running to the head.

12. Disconnect the fuel inlet line.

CAUTION: *The fuel system is under pressure. Release pressure slowly and contain spillage. Observe no smoking/no open flame precautions. Have a Class B-C (dry powder) fire extinguisher within arm's reach at all times.*

13. Remove the cold start injector line.

14. Remove the coolant hoses by disconnecting their junctions at the head.

15. Disconnect the heater hoses.

16. Remove the water outlet housing and the water inlet housing.

17. Label and remove the spark plug wires.

18. Remove the PCV valve.

19. Loosen the air conditioning compressor, power steering pump and alternator brackets as necessary; remove the valve cover.

20. Remove the drive belts.

21. Remove the air conditioning idler pulley.

22. Disconnect the wiring at the cruise control actuator (if so equipped); remove the actuator and its bracket.

23. Remove the windshield washer reservoir.

24. Support the engine with a support fixture such as GM J 28467-A or a chain hoist. Alternatively, a floor jack may be placed below the engine; use a piece of wood on the jack to distribute the load.

25. Remove the right engine mount through bolt.

26. Raise the engine enough to gain access to the water pump pulley bolts.

27. Remove the water pump pulley.

28. Lower the engine back to its normal position. Remove the wiring harness from the upper timing belt cover.

29. Raise the vehicle and safely support it on jackstands.

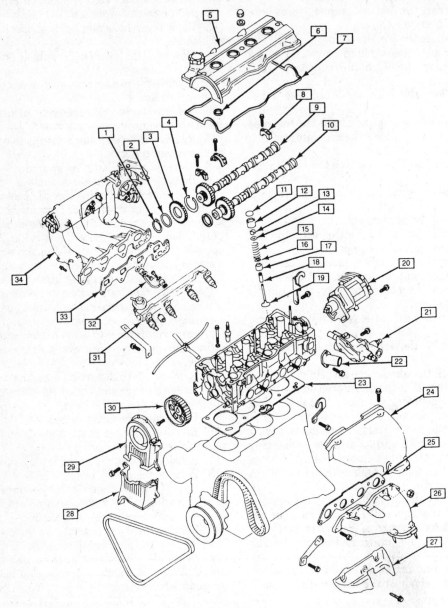

1. Camshaft snapring
2. Wave washer
3. Camshaft sub-gear
4. Camshaft gear spring
5. Valve cover (cylinder head cover)
6. Spark plug tube gasket
7. Valve cover gasket
8. Camshaft bearing cap
9. Instake camshaft
10. Exhaust camshaft
11. Adjusting shim
12. Valve lifter
13. Valve keepers
14. Valve spring retainer
15. Valve spring
16. Valve spring seat
17. Valve stem oil seal
18. Valve guide bushing
19. Valve
20. Distributor
21. Water inlet housing
22. Water outlet housing
23. Head gasket
24. Exhaust manifold upper insulator (heat shield)
25. Exhaust manifold gasket
26. Exhaust manifold
27. Exhaust manifold lower insulator (heat shield)
28. Center timing belt cover
29. Upper timing belt cover
30. Camshaft timing gear
31. Fuel rail
32. Cold-start injector pipe
33. Intake manifold gasket
34. Intake manifold

Exploded view of the 4A-FE head

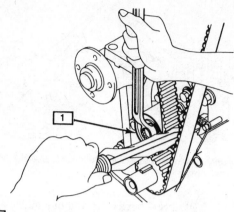

Loosen the idler pulley and move it to its loosest position

30. Remove the cylinder head-to-cylinder block bracket.

31. Remove the exhaust pipe support bracket and disconnect the exhaust pipe from the exhaust manifold.

32. Remove the upper timing belt cover and then the center timing belt cover.

NOTE: *The timing belt is exposed with the cover removed. Do not allow the belt to become contaminated with fluids or lubricants. This includes accidental contact by rags, fingerprints, etc.*

33. Remove the right engine mount bracket.

34. By turning the crankshaft clockwise, set the engine to TDC/compression. Align the timing mark at zero (on the crank) and check that the valve lifters for No. 1 cylinder are NOT under compression from the camshafts; the cam lobes should be pointed up. The small hole in the exhaust camshaft pulley should be aligned with the mark on the camshaft cap.

35. Remove the distributor.

36. Remove the plug from the lower timing belt cover.

37. Matchmark the timing belt and pulleys at the crankshaft and both camshafts. Mark an arrow on the belt showing the direction of rotation.

38. Loosen the idler pulley bolt and push the pulley into its loosest position. Tighten the bolt to hold the idler in this loosened position.

39. Holding the timing belt with a clean cloth, slide the belt off the camshaft pulleys. Keep light upward tension on the belt so that it does not change its position on the lower (crankshaft) pulley.

WARNING: *Do not pry on the belt with tools. Do not crease or crimp the belt. Be careful not to drop anything into the lower belt cover. Keep the timing belt clean and free of fluids and lubricants.*

40. Using a 10mm, 12-point deep socket wrench, loosen the cylinder head bolts in the proper sequence. It is recommended that the tension be released in two or even three passes.

WARNING: *Head warping or cracking can result from improper removal procedures.*

41. Remove the cylinder head with the manifolds attached. If the head is difficult to lift off, carefully pry with a suitable tool between the head and a projection on the block. Be careful not to scratch or gouge the mating surfaces of the head or block.

42. Place the head on wooden blocks on the workbench. If the head is to be disassembled, the external parts will need to be removed. If the head is to be reused intact, the mating surface must be cleaned of all gasket and sealant material. Clean the mating surface on the block of all traces of gasket material and fluids. Clean the bolt holes, removing all fluid and solid material.

43. When reassembling, place the new head gasket in position on the block. Make sure it is placed correctly and that all the holes line up.

44. Carefully install the cylinder head in position on the block. Make sure the head is seated over the guide dowels.

45. Apply a light coat of engine oil to the threads of the head bolts and under the caps of the bolts. Place the bolts in their holes.

46. Tighten the bolts in the proper sequence. Repeat the pattern three times, tightening the first pass to 14 ft. lbs., the second pass to 28 ft. lbs. and the third pass to the final setting of 44 ft. lbs.

47. If the camshafts have not been turned while the head was removed, double check their placement against the marks on the head. If the cams were moved, they must be turned into the TDC/compression position.

48. Double check that the crankshaft is still in

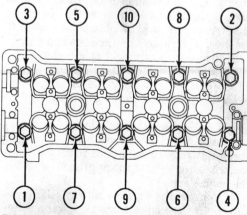

Remove the 4A-FE cylinder head bolts in this order

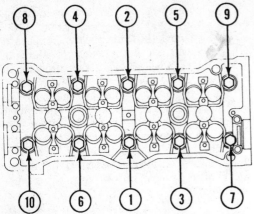

Install the cylinder head bolts for the 4A-FE in this order

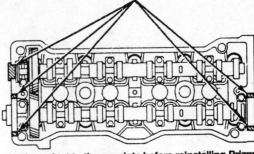

Apply sealant to these points before reinstalling Prizm valve cover

its TDC position. Carefully reinstall the timing belt over the cam pulleys, making sure the matchmarks align exactly. The slightest error in placement can greatly reduce engine performance and possibly damage the engine.

With the belt correctly installed, loosen the bolt holding the idler pulley in the loosened position. The pulley will spring against the belt, providing tension on it. Turn the crankshaft pulley clockwise two full revolutions (from TDC to TDC) and double check that all the components are properly aligned. Tighten the idler pulley bolt to 27 ft. lbs.

49. Reinstall the distributor.
50. Attach the right side engine mount bracket.
51. Install the air conditioning idler pulley.
52. Install the center timing belt cover and the upper timing belt cover.
53. Raise the vehicle and safely support it on jackstands.
54. Using new gaskets and bolts, connect the exhaust pipe to the exhaust mainfold. Tighten the bolts to 18 ft. lbs. Install the exhaust manifold support bracket.
55. Install the cylinder head-to-cylinder block bracket.
56. Lower the vehicle to the ground. Connect or reinstall the wiring harness to the upper timing belt cover.
57. Raise the engine enought to gain access to the water pump. Install the water pump pulley and lower the engine into its normal position.
58. Install the right engine mount through bolt and tighten it to 64 ft. lbs. When this bolt is secured, the engine lifting apparatus may be removed from the car.
59. Install the windshield washer reservoir.
60. If equipped with cruise control, reinstall the actuator and its bracket and connect the wiring to the actuator.

61. Install the drive belts and adjust them to the proper tension.
62. Place sealant on the valve cover in the proper locations and install the valve cover. Tighten the retaining nuts to 15 ft. lbs.
63. Install the PCV valve.
64. Install the spark plugs, and connect the water inlet housing and the water outlet housing.
65. Reinstall the heater hoses and the coolant hoses.
66. Install the fuel rail and injectors.
67. Connect the cold start injector pipe.
68. Connect the fuel inlet line.
69. Observing the labels made earlier, carefully connect the vacuum lines and electrical leads. Make sure the vacuum hoses are properly seated on their ports and are not kinked or twisted. Electrical connectors must be clean and firmly attached at all points. Double check the routing of lines and wires to avoid any contact with moving parts.
70. Depending on equipment, connect the transaxle kick-down cable (automatic), the cruise control actuator cable and/or the accelerator cable.
71. Install the air cleaner assembly.
72. Raise the vehicle and safely support it on jackstands. Attach the two rear mount-to-main crossmember nuts and tighten them to 45 ft. lbs. Install the two center mount-to-center crossmember nuts and tighten them to 45 ft. lbs. Install the covers on the nuts and studs.
73. Install the lower right splash shield.
74. Lower the vehicle to the ground.
75. Confirm that the radiator and engine block draincocks are closed and refill the cooling system.
76. Double check all installation items, paying particular attention to loose hoses or hanging wires, untightened nuts, poor routing of hoses and wires (too tight or rubbing) and tools left in the engine area.
77. Connect the negative battery cable.
78. Start the engine. During the warm up period, check for any sign of leakage or overheat-

ing. Check engine timing and adjust the idle speed if necessary.

79. After the engine is shut off, check the drive belts and adjust the tension if necessary.

CYLINDER HEAD CLEANING AND INSPECTION

4A-LC

1. With the head removed from the car, remove the carburetor, the fuel pump and the intake and exhaust manifolds.

2. Remove the rocker arm assembly, following procdures outlined earlier in this chapter.

3. Use a dial indicator to measure the camshaft end play (axial end play or thrust clearance). Standard play is 0.08–0.18mm. Maximum allowable free play is 0.25mm. Free play at or beyond the maximum requires replacement of the head.

4. Remove the camshaft, following procedures outlined later in this chapter.

5. Remove the valves, following procedures outlined later in this chapter.

6. Using a wire brush chucked into an electric drill, remove all the carbon from the combustion chambers in the head. Be careful not to scratch the head surface.

7. Use a gasket scraper and remove all material from the manifold and head surfaces, again being careful not to scratch the surface.

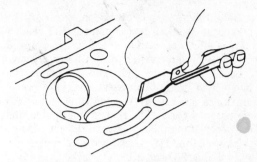

Do not scratch the head mating surface when removing old gasket material

8. Use a valve guide brush or a fine-bristled rifle bore brush with solvent to clean the valve guides.

9. Use a clean cloth and a stiff bristle brush with solvent to thoroughly clean the head assembly. Make sure that no material is washed into the bolt holes or passages. If possible, dry the head with compressed air to remove fluid and solid matter from all the passages.

WARNING: *Do not clean the head in a hot tank or chemical bath. Parts of the head will dissolve.*

10. With the head clean and dry, use a precision straight-edge and a feeler gauge to measure the head for warpage. Also measure the

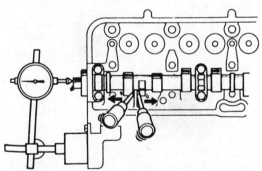

Checking the camshaft endplay on a 4A-LC engine. Use of a dial indicator is required

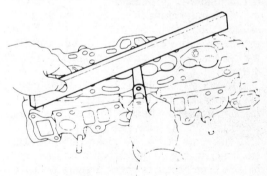

Checking the cylinder head for warpage

Maximum head surface warpage:
0.05 mm (0.0020 in.)
Maximum manifold surface warpage:
0.1 mm (0.004 in.)
Maximum reface: 0.1 mm (0.004 in.)

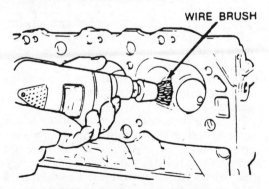

WIRE BRUSH

Removing combustion chamber carbon; make sure it is removed and not merely burnished

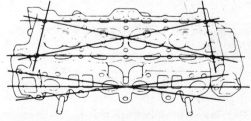

Cylinder head warpage clearances

manifold faces. Any warpage in excess of the maximum requires replacement of the head.

11. If all is well with the head to this point, it is highly recommended that it be taken to a professional facility such as a machine shop for sophisticated crack testing. The various procedures are much more reliable than simple examination by eye. The cost is reasonable and the peace of mind is well worth the cost. If any cracks are found, the head must be replaced.

12. While the head is being checked, carefully scrape the carbon from the tops of the pistons. Don't scratch the metal of the piston tops and don't damage the cylinder walls. Remove all the carbon and fluid from the cylinder.

13. If repairs are needed to the valves, camshaft or other components, follow the appropriate procedures outlined in this chapter.

4A-GE

1. With the head removed from the car, remove the camshafts following procedures outlined later in this chapter.

2. Remove the valve lifters and the adjusting shims following procedures outlined later in this chapter.

3. Remove any external fittings, brackets, cables, etc.

4. Remove the valves following procedures outlined later in this chapter.

5. Carefully scrape the carbon from the tops of the pistons. Don't scratch the metal of the piston tops and don't damage the cylinder walls. Remove all the carbon and fluid from the cylinder.

6. Clean all the gasket material from the block, manifold and head surfaces. If possible, use compressed air to blow the carbon and oil from the bolt holes and passages.

7. Using a wire brush chucked into an electric drill, remove all the carbon from the combustion chambers in the head. Be careful not to scratch the head surface.

8. Use a valve guide brush or a fine-bristled

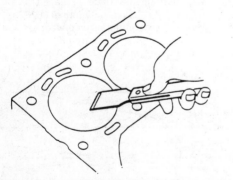

Removing carbon from the piston tops; do not scratch the pistons

rifle bore brush with solvent to clean the valve guides.

9. Use a clean cloth and a stiff bristle brush with solvent to thoroughly clean the head assembly. Make sure that no material is washed into the bolt holes or passages. If possible, dry the head with compressed air to remove fluid and solid matter from all the passages.

WARNING: *Do not clean the head in a hot tank or chemical bath. Parts of the head will dissolve.*

10. With the head clean and dry, use a precision straight-edge and a feeler gauge to measure the head for warpage. Also measure the manifold faces. Any warpage in excess of the maximum requires replacement of the head.

Maximum allowable warpage:
- Cylinder block face: 0.05mm
- Intake manifold face: 0.05mm
- Exhaust manifold face: 0.10mm

11. If all is well with the head to this point, it is highly recommended that it be taken to a professional facility such as a machine shop for sophisticated crack testing. The various procedures are much more reliable than simple examination by eye. The cost is reasonable and the peace of mind is well worth
the cost. If any cracks are found, the head must be replaced.

4A-FE

1. With the head removed from the engine, remove the intake and exhaust manifolds, following procedures outline earlier in this chapter.

2. Remove the camshafts, following procedures outlined later in this chapter.

3. Remove the valve lifters and the adjusting shims.

4. Remove the spark plug tubes.

5. Remove the engine hoist hooks.

6. Remove the valves, using procedures outlined later in this chapter.

7. Remove the half-circle plug at the end of the head.

8. Using a wire brush chucked into an electric drill, remove all the carbon from the combustion chambers in the head. Be careful not to scratch the head surface.

9. Use a valve guide brush or a fine-bristled rifle bore brush with solvent to clean the valve guides.

10. Use a clean cloth and a stiff bristle brush with solvent to thoroughly clean the head assembly. Make sure that no material is washed into the bolt holes or passages. If possible, dry the head with compressed air to remove fluid and solid matter from all the passages.

WARNING: *Do not clean the head in a hot*

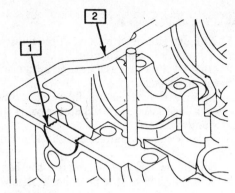

1. Half circle plug
2. Cylinder head

tank or chemical bath. Parts of the head will dissolve.

11. With the head clean and dry, use a precision straight-edge and a feeler gauge to measure the head for warpage. Also measure the manifold faces. Any warpage in excess of the maximum requires replacement of the head.
Maximum allowable warpage:
- Cylinder block face: 0.05mm
- Intake manifold face: 0.10mm
- Exhaust manifold face: 0.10mm

12. If all is well with the head to this point, it is highly recommended that it be taken to a professional facility such as a machine shop for sophisticated crack testing. The various procedures are much more reliable than simple examination by eye. The cost is reasonable and the peace of mind is well worth
the cost. If any cracks are found, the head must be replaced.

CYLINDER HEAD RESURFACING

The Nova and Prizm cylinder heads from all engines may be resurfaced by a reputable machine shop. Resurfacing is recommended if the engine suffered a massive overheating, such as from a failed head gasket.

The heads are manufactured to be as light as possible; consequently, there is not much excess metal on the face. Any machining must be minimal. If too much metal is removed, the head becomes unusable. A head which exceeds the maximum warpage specification CANNOT be resurfaced. The machine shop will have a list of minimum head thicknesses; at no time may this minimum be exceeded.

Valve Springs and Valves
REMOVAL AND INSTALLATION

NOTE: *This procedure requires the use of a valve stem compressor. This common tool is*

available at most auto supply stores. It may also be possible to rent one from supplier.

WARNING: *It is absolutely essential that all components be kept in order after removal. Old ice trays make excellent holders for small parts. The containers should be labeled so that the parts may be reinstalled in their original location. Keep the valves in numbered order in a holder such as an egg carton or an inverted box with holes punched in it. Label the container so that each valve may be replaced in its exact position. (Example: Exhaust #1, #2 etc.)*

4A-LC

1. Remove the head from the engine and remove the rocker arm and cam shafts, following procedures outlined in this chapter.
2. Using a valve spring compressor, compress the valve spring and remove the keeper at the top of the valve shaft.
3. Slowly release the tension on the compressor and remove it. Remove the spring retainer (upper cap), the valve spring, the valve stem oil seal and the lower spring seat.
4. The valve is then removed from the bottom of the head.
5. Repeat steps 2-5 for each valve in the head, keeping them labeled and in order.
6. Thoroughly clean and decarbon each valve. Inspect each valve and spring as outlined later in this chapter.
7. Lubricate the the valve stem and guide with engine oil. Install the valve in the cylinder head and position the lower spring seat.
8. Coat the valve face and seat with a light coat of valve grinding compound. Attach the suction cup end of the valve grinding tool to the head of the valve (it helps to moisten it first).
9. Rotate the tool between the palms, changing position and and lifting the tool often to prevent grooving. Lap in the until a smooth, evenly polished surface is evident on both the seat and face.

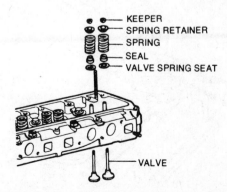

Typical valve and related components

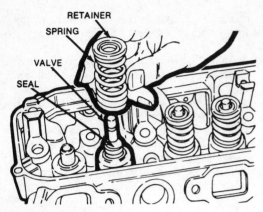

RETAINER
SPRING
VALVE
SEAL

Installing the valve

10. Remove the valve from the head. Wipe away all traces of grinding compound from the surfaces. Clean out the valve guide with a solvent-soaked rag. Make sure there are NO traces of compound in or on the head.

11. Proceed through the remaining valves, lapping them one at a time to their seats. Clean the area after each valve is done.

12. When all the valves have been lapped, thoroughly clean or wash the head with solvent. There must be NO trace of grinding compound present.

13. Lubricate the new valve stem seal with engine oil and install it onto the valve stem over the lower seat.

14. Install the valve spring and the upper seat, compress the spring and install the two keepers. Relax tension on the compressor and make sure everything is properly placed. Tap on the installed valve stem with a plastic mallet to ensure proper locking of the retainers.

15. Install the half-circle plug at the end of the head. Coat it with a silicone sealer before installation.

16. Complete the reassembly of the head by installing the camshafts and the manifolds.

Lapping a valve in by hand

4A-GE and 4A-FE Engines

1. Remove the head following procedures outlined earlier in this chapter.

2. On 4A-FE motors, remove the intake and exhaust manifolds.

3. Remove the camshafts following procedures outlined later in this chapter. Label the shafts and their retainers.

4. Remove the valve lifters and the adjusting shims.

5. On the 4A-GE engine, remove the bond cable and the right engine hoist hook. Remove the temperature sensor bracket and the left engine hoist hook.

For the 4A-FE, simply remove the hoist hooks.

6. Remove the spark plug tubes from the head.

7. Attach the spring compressor. For the 4A-GE use GM tool J-37134 or similar and for the 4A-FE use J-8062 with a J-37979 adaptor or similar tools.

8. Compress the valve spring and remove the keepers at the top of the valve shaft.

9. Slowly release the tension on the compressor and remove it. Remove the spring retainer (upper cap), the valve spring, the valve stem oil seal and the lower spring seat. The valve is then removed from the bottom of the head.

10. Repeat steps 2-5 for each valve in the head, keeping them labeled and in order. Remove the half-circle plug at the end of the head.

11. Thoroughly clean and decarbon each valve. Inspect each valve and spring as outlined later in this chapter.

12. Lubricate the the valve stem and guide with engine oil. Install the valve in the cylinder head.

13. Coat the valve face and seat with a light coat of valve grinding compound. Attach the suction cup end of the valve grinding tool to the head of the valve (it helps to moisten it first).

14. Rotate the tool between the palms, changing position and and lifting the tool often to prevent grooving. Lap in the until a smooth, evenly polished surface is evident on both the seat and face.

15. Remove the valve from the head. Wipe away all traces of grinding compound from the surfaces. Clean out the valve guide with a solvent-soaked rag. Make sure there are NO traces of compound in or on the head.

16. Proceed through the remaining valves, lapping them one at a time to their seats. Clean the area after each valve is done.

17. When all the valves have been lapped, thoroughly clean or wash the head with solvent. There must be NO trace of grinding compound present. Lubricate the new valve stem

seal with engine oil and install it onto the valve stem over the lower seat.

18. Install the valve spring and the upper seat, compress the spring and install the two keepers. Relax tension on the compressor and make sure everything is properly placed. Tap on the installed valve stem with a plastic mallet to ensure proper locking of the retainers.

19. On the 4A-GE, install the spark plug tubes, the engine hangers, the temperature sensor bracket and the bond cable.

For the 4A-FE, install the tubes and the hangers.

20. Install the valve lifters and the adjusting shims. Don't attempt to adjust the valves until after the head is bolted onto the engine.

21. Coat the half-circle plug with silicone sealant and install it in position.

22. Complete the reassembly of the head by installing the camshafts and the manifolds (4A-FE) following procedures outlined in this chapter.

INSPECTION AND MEASUREMENT

NOTE: *Accurate measuring equipment capable of reading to 0.0001 (ten thousandths) inch is necessary for this work. A micrometer and a hole (bore) gauge will be needed.*

Inspect the valve faces and seats for pits, burned spots, and other evidence of poor seating. If the valve face is in such poor shape that the head of the valve must be cut to true the contact face, discard the valve.

The correct angle for the valve face is given in the Valve Specifications Chart at the beginning of this chapter. It is recommended that any reaming or refacing be done by a reputable machine shop.

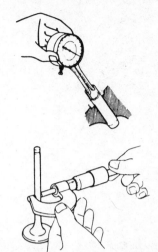

Measure the diameter of the valve guide and the valve stem. The difference is the stem clearance

Check the valve stem for scoring and/or burned spots. If the stem and head are in acceptable condition, clean the valve thoroughly with solvent to remove all gum and varnish.

Use the micrometer to measure the diameter of the valve stem. Use the hole gauge to measure the inside diameter of the valve guide for that valve. Subtract the stem diameter from the guide diameter and compare the difference to the chart. If not within specifications, determine the cause (worn valve or worn guide) and replace the worn part(s).

Using a steel square, check the valve spring for correct height and squareness. If the squareness is not within 2mm, replace the spring. If the free height of the spring is not within specification, replace the spring. The installed height of the spring must be measured with the spring under tension in the head. Assemble the valve and spring with the retainers and clips into the head; modify a small steel ruler to fit and record the distance from the bottom spring seat to the upper retainer. If not within specification, shim washers (one or more) any be added between the lower spring seat and the spring.

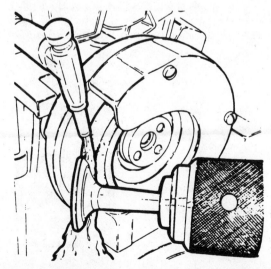

Valve refacings should be handled by a reputable machine shop

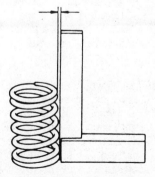

Checking the valve spring for squareness

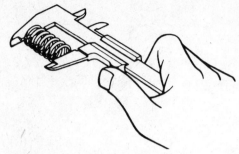

Checking the spring free height

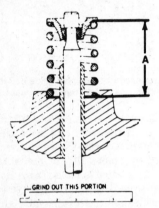

Measure the valve spring installed height (A) with a modified steel ruler

NOTE: *Use only washers designed for this purpose.*

Valve Seats

The valve seats for all Nova and Prizm engines are not replaceable. A failed seat (which cannot be recut) requires replacement of the head. Seat recutting is a precise art and is best performed by a machine shop. Seat concentricity should also be checked by a professional facility.

Valve Guides

INSPECTION

Valve guides should be cleaned as outlined earlier and checked when the stem-to-guide clearance is measured. As a general rule, if the engine admits oil through the guides (and the oil seals are in good condition), the guides are worn.

Valve guides which are not excessively worn or distorted may, in some cases, be knurled rather than replaced. Knurling is a process in which metal inside the valve guide is displaced and raised by a cutter, making a very fine cross-hatched pattern. This raised pattern reduces the clearance to the valve stem and provides excellent oil control. The possibility of knurling

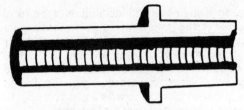

Cross-section of a knurled valve guide

rather than replacing the valve guides should be discussed with a machinist.

REMOVAL AND INSTALLATION

CAUTION: *Replacing the valve guides requires heating the head to high temperatures and the use of special tools. Do not attempt this repair if you are not equipped with the proper heating and handling equipment. Do not attempt this repair unless equipped with the correct valve guide tools and a reamer.*

When handling the heated head, always use heavy gloves and tongs.

4A-LC Engine

1. Heat the cylinder head evenly to 194°F.
2. Carefully remove the head from the heat source and support it upright on the workbench.
3. Using valve guide tool such as J-25367-1 or similar, and a hammer, drive the guide out of the head.
4. Reheat the head to 194°F (90°C) and support it on the workbench.
5. Use the guide tool and a hammer to drive in the new guide until it projects 14.5–15.0mm.
6. Allow the head and guide to air cool. Do not attempt to quick-cool the metal with any water or fluid.
7. Measure the inner diameter of the guide. Compare this to the stem diameter of the new valve. If the stem to guide clearance is insuffi-

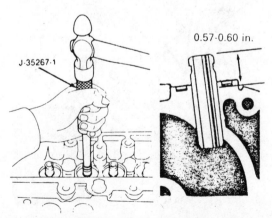

Correct installation of 4A-LC valve guides. GM special tool shown

cient, ream the new guide with a sharp 7mm reamer until the correct clearance is obtained.

4A-GE

1. Break off the upper part of the old bushing. Wrap an old valve stem in tape to prevent the stem from dropping too far into the guide. Pad the surrounding area with rags. Insert the old valve into the guide and strike the valve with a hammer.

WARNING: *Be careful not to damage the surrounding area in which the lifter sits.*

2. Heat the cylinder head gradually, in water, to 212°F.

3. Carefully remove the head from the water. Use tool J-37133 or similar and a hammer to drive out the guide.

4. With the guide removed, measure the bore (in the head) into which the guide fits. If the bore is greater than 10.9mm, have the bore ground to 11.05–11.08mm and install a 0.05mm oversize guide. If the bore is greater than 11.08mm, the head must be replaced.

5. Reheat the head in water to 212°F (100°C), then carefully remove it from the water.

6. Using the removal and installation tool (J-37133), drive in the new guide until the snap ring makes contact with the cylinder head.

7. Measure the inner diameter of the guide. Compare this to the stem diameter of the new valve. If the stem to guide clearance is insufficient, ream the new guide with a sharp 6mm reamer until the correct clearance is obtained.

4A-FE

1. Gradually heat the cylinder head to 212°F.

2. Carefully remove the head from the heat source.

3. Using tool J-37133 or similar and a hammer to drive out the guide.

4. With the guide removed, measure the bore (in the head) into which the guide fits. If the bore is greater than 10.9mm, have the bore ground to 11.05–11.08mm and install a

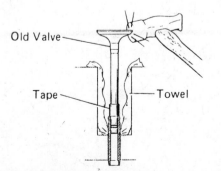

A quick an handy method for breaking off the tops of 4A-GE valve guides before removal

Old Valve

Tape — Towel

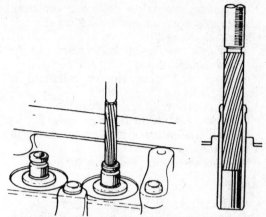

Use a precision reamer to enlarge new valve guides if necessary

0.05mm oversize guide. If the bore is greater than 11.08mm, the head must be replaced.

5. Reheat the head to 212°F (100°C) and then remove it from the heat.

6. Using the removal and installation tool (J-37133) and an adapter such as J 38277, drive in the new guide until it projects 12.5–13.0mm above the head.

7. Measure the inner diameter of the guide. Compare this to the stem diameter of the new valve. If the stem to guide clearance is insufficient, ream the new guide with a sharp 6mm reamer until the correct clearance is obtained.

Oil Pan

REMOVAL AND INSTALLATION

4A-LC

1. Disconnect the negative battery cable.

2. Safely raise and support the vehicle on jackstands.

3. Drain the engine oil and replace the drain plug when the pan is empty.

CAUTION: *Used motor oil may cause skin cancer if repeatedly left in contact with the skin for prolonged periods. Although this is unlikely unless you handle oil on a daily basis, it is wise to thoroughly wash your hands with soap and water immediately after handling used motor oil.*

4. Remove the right splash shield.

5. Remove the oil pan bolts.

6. Remove the oil pan. If the pan is difficult to remove, tap it gently with a rubber or plastic mallet. Do not use a pry bar to release it.

WARNING: *Do not bend or deform the edge (flange) of the oil pan during removal.*

7. Clean the pan thoroughly and remove all sludge and solid matter. Clean the mating surfaces of the pan and the engine, removing all traces of old gasket material and sealer. During

the cleaning, remove the drain bolt and clean the threads. Install a new gasket on the bolt and install the bolt in the pan.

8. Apply a new gasket and/or sealant to the pan and install the pan to the engine.

9. Install and tighten the pan bolts to 4 ft. lbs. (48 INCH lbs.)

10. Install the right splash shield.

11. Lower the vehicle to the ground.

12. Refill the engine oil and connect the negative battery cable.

13. Start the engine and check for leaks.

4A-GE

1. Disconnect the negative battery cable.

2. Safely raise and support the vehicle on jackstands.

3. Drain the engine oil and replace the drain plug when the pan is empty.

CAUTION: *Used motor oil may cause skin cancer if repeatedly left in contact with the skin for prolonged periods. Although this is unlikely unless you handle oil on a daily basis, it is wise to thoroughly wash your hands with soap and water immediately after handling used motor oil.*

4. Remove the right splash shield.

5. Remove the front exhaust pipe. Disconnect it at the manifold and the catalytic converter.

6. Remove the exhaust bracket.

7. Remove the oil pan bolts. Remove the oil pan. If the pan is difficult to remove, tap it gently with a rubber or plastic mallet. Do not use a pry bar to release it.

WARNING: *Do not bend or deform the edge (flange) of the oil pan during removal.*

8. Clean the pan thoroughly and remove all sludge and solid matter. Clean the mating surfaces of the pan and the engine, removing all traces of old gasket material and sealer. During the cleaning, remove the drain bolt and clean the threads. Install a new gasket on the bolt and install the bolt in the pan.

9. Apply a new gasket and/or sealant to the pan and install the pan to the engine.

10. Install and tighten the pan bolts to 4 ft. lbs. (48 INCH lbs.).

11. Install the front exhaust pipe and its bracket.

12. Install the right splash shield.

13. Lower the vehicle to the ground.

14. Refill the engine oil and connect the negative battery cable.

15. Start the engine and check for leaks.

4A-FE

1. Disconnect the negative battery cable.

2. Elevate and safely support the vehicle on jackstands.

3. Remove the right and left splash shields.

4. Drain the oil.

CAUTION: *Used motor oil may cause skin cancer if repeatedly left in contact with the skin for prolonged periods. Although this is unlikely unless you handle oil on a daily basis, it is wise to thoroughly wash your hands with soap and water immediately after handling used motor oil.*

5. Disconnect the sensor to the oxygen sensor.

6. Remove the front exhaust pipe. Disconnect the pipe at the catalytic converter and the exhaust manifold.

7. Remove the two nuts and the 19 bolts from the oil pan. Remove the oil pan from the engine.

WARNING: *Use caution when removing the oil pan. The oil pump at the front of the engine may be damaged during removal. Use caution not to damage the edge of the pan.*

8. Remove the two nuts and two bolts holding the oil pick-up and strainer to the engine. Remove the pick-up assembly and its gasket.

9. Clean the mating surfaces of the pan and cylinder block of all sealant and gasket material. Remove any traces of oil on these surfaces.

10. Thoroughly clean the pick-up and screen assembly and allow it to air dry.

11. Install the pick-up and strainer assembly with a new gasket. Tighten the nuts and bolts to 7.5 ft. lbs. (90 INCH lbs.).

12. Apply a continuous bead of GM Sealant 1050026 or similar to both sides of the new oil pan gasket and place the gasket in position on the pan.

13. Install the pan onto the engine with all the nuts and bolts finger tight.

14. Tighten the nuts and bolts to 3.6 ft. lbs. (44 INCH lbs.).

15. Connect the exhaust pipe to the catalytic converter and to the exhaust manifold.

16. Connect the wiring to the oxygen sensor.

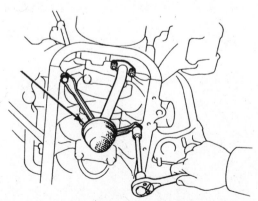

Arrow indicates the oil strainer and pick-up assembly on the 4A-FE engine

17. Install the left and right splash shields.
18. Lower the vehicle to the ground.
19. Refill the engine oil and connect the negative battery cable.
20. Start the engine and check for leaks.

Oil Pump

REMOVAL AND INSTALLATION

NOTE: *This procedure requires special-purpose tools which may not be in your everyday tool set. Snapring pliers (internal and external) and pulley removers of various sizes are available at most reputable tool outlets.*

1. Disconnect the negative battery cable.
2. Remove the oil pan as previoulsly outlined.
3. Drain the cooling system

CAUTION: *When draining the coolant, keep in mind that cats and dogs are attracted by the ethylene glycol antifreeze, and are quite likely to drink any that is left in an uncovered container or in puddles on the ground. This will prove fatal in sufficient quantity. Always drain the coolant into a sealable container. Coolant should be reused unless it is contaminated or several years old.*

4. Loosen the water pump pulley bolts.
5. Remove the alternator bolts.
6. If equipped with power steering, remove the drive belt.
7. If equipped with air conditioning, loosen the air conditioning idler pulley and the adjustor. Remove the drive belt and then remove the idler pulley and adjustor.
8. Remove the alternator bolts and remove the alternator; place it or suspend it out of the way.
9. Remove the water pump pulley.
10. Disconnect the upper radiator hose at the engine.
11. Label and disconnect the vacuum hoses running through the work area.
12. Remove the No.1 (upper) timing belt cover and its gasket.
13. Remove the No.3 (middle) timing belt cover and its gasket.
14. Rotate the crankshaft to the TDC/compression postion.
15. Elevate and safely support the vehicle on jackstands. Double check the placement of the stands and the stability of the car on the stands.
16. Remove the right splash shield.
17. Remove the flywheel cover.
18. Remove the crankshaft pulley. Block the flywheel to prevent the crank from turning.
19. Remove the No.2 (lower) timing belt cover.
20. Mark the position of the camshaft and

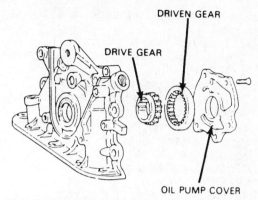

Exploded view of the oil pump

crankshaft timing pulleys on the timing belt and mark an arrow on the belt showing the direction of rotation.

21. Loosen the timing belt idler pulley bolt, move the pulley to release tension on the belt and tighten the bolt. This holds the pulley in the loosened position.
22. Slip the timing belt off the crankshaft timing pulley.
23. Remove the crankshaft timing pulley.
24. Remove the dipstick tube.
24. Remove the timing belt idler pulley.
25. Remove the bolts in the oil pump case and carefully remove the oil pump. It may require gentle tapping to loosen it; use only a plastic or rubber mallet.
26. When reinstalling, place the new gasket against the block and install the oil pump to the crankshaft with the spline teeth of the drive gear engaged with the large teeth of the crankshaft. Tighten the bolts to 18 ft. lbs.
27. Install the timing belt idler pulley.
28. Install the dipstick tube.
29. Install the crankshaft timing pulley.
30. Install the timing belt. (Refer to: Timing

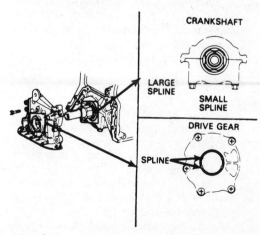

Aligning the oil pump drive gear with the crankshaft

Belt--Removal and Installation later in this chapter.).

31. Install the lower belt cover.

32. Install the crankshaft pulley and tighten it to 87 ft. lbs.

33. Install the flywheel cover.

34. Install the right splash guard and lower the vehicle to the ground.

35. Install the middle and upper timing belt covers with their gaskets.

36. Reconnect the vacuum hoses.

37. Attach the water pump pulley; leave the bolts finger tight.

38. Position and secure the alternator.

39. If so equipped, install the air conditioning adjusting bolt, idler pulley and belt. Install the belt and adjust it to the proper tension.

40. Install the power steering belt and adjust it if so equipped.

41. Tighten the water pump bolts.

42. With a new gasket, install the oil pick-up and strainer assembly. Tighten the nuts and bolts to 6.8 ft. lbs.

43. Refill the cooling system.

44. Install the oil pan following procedures outlined previously.

45. Start the engine and check for leaks. Allow the engine to warm up fully and check the work area carefully under warm and cold conditions.

4A-GE

1. Disconnect the negative battery cable.
2. Remove the oil pan as previously outlined.
3. Remove the oil pick-up and strainer.
4. Remove the oil pan baffle plate.
5. Drain the cooling system.
CAUTION: *When draining the coolant, keep in mind that cats and dogs are attracted by the ethylene glycol antifreeze, and are quite likely to drink any that is left in an uncovered container or in puddles on the ground. This will prove fatal in sufficient quantity. Always drain the coolant into a sealable container. Coolant should be reused unless it is contaminated or several years old.*

6. Disconnect the accelerator cable or linkage.
7. Remove the cruise control actuator if so equipped.
8. Remove the washer tank.
9. Remove the upper radiator hose at the engine block.
10. Remove the power steering and/or the air conditioning drive belt(s).
11. Loosen the bolts to the water pump pulley and then remove the alternator drive belt.
12. Remove the spark plugs.
13. Rotate the crankshaft and position the engine at TDC/compression. The crankshaft mark

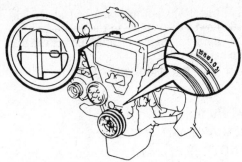

Aligning the 4A-GE motor at TDC/compression for No. 1 cylinder

aligns at zero and the camshaft, when viewed through the oil filler cap, has a small cavity pointing upward.

14. Use a floor jack and a piece of wood to slightly elevate the engine. Remove the right engine mount; then remove the three bolts and remove the right reinforcing plate for the engine mount.

15. Remove the water pump pulley.

16. Remove the crankshaft pulley. Counterhold the crankshaft or block the flywheel to prevent the crank from turning.

17. Remove the timing belt covers.
WARNING: *The timing belt cover bolts are different lengths and MUST be returned to the proper hole at reassembly. During removal, diagram or label each bolt and its correct position.*

18. Remove the timing belt guide.

19. Loosen the idler pulley bolt, push it all the way to the left and tighten the bolt. This removes tension from the belt.

20. Matchmark the belt and all the pulleys so that the belt may be reinstalled exactly as it was before. Mark an arrow on the belt showing direction of rotation.

21. Remove the timing belt from the lower pulley (crankshaft timing pulley). If you are careful, the belt may remain undisturbed on the camshaft pulleys.

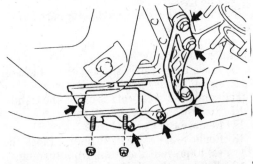

Arrows indicate the nuts and bolts holding the right engine mount and the reinforcing plate on a 4A-GE engine

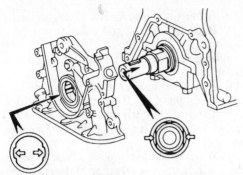

Correct positions for installation of the oil pump on 4A-GE and 4A-FE engines

22. Remove the idler pulley and spring.
23. Remove the crankshaft timing pulley.
24. Remove the PCV hose.
25. Remove the dipstick and tube.
26. Remove the seven bolts in the oil pump and carefully remove the pump. If it is difficult to remove, tap it lightly with a plastic or rubber mallet. Do not pry it off or strike it with a metal hammer.
27. When reinstalling, place a new gasket on the block. Install the oil pump to the crankshaft with the spline teeth to the drive gear engaged with the large teeth of the crankshaft.
28. Install the seven retaining bolts and tighten them to 16 ft. lbs.
29. Install the dipstick tube and dipstick.
30. Install the crankshaft timing pulley.
31. Install the timing belt idler pulley.
32. Install the timing belt. (Refer to Timing Belt--Removal and Installation procedures in this chapter.)
33. Install the timing belt guide. It should install with the cupped side facing outward.
34. Make sure the gaskets are properly seated in the timing belt covers and reinstall the covers. Make sure each bolt is in the correct hole.
35. Install the crankshaft pulley. Again using a counterholding device, tighten the bolt to 101 ft. lbs.
36. Install the water pump pulley and tighten the bolts finger tight. Install the valve covers.
37. Install the right side engine mount. Tighten the nut to 38 ft. lbs. and the through bolt to 64 ft. lbs.
38. Install the reinforcement for the right motor mount and tighten the bolts to 31 ft. lbs.
39. Install the spark plugs.
40. Install the alternator drive belt and tighten the water pump pulley bolts.
41. Install and adjust the power steering and/ or the air conditioner drive belts.
42. Connect the upper radiator hose.
43. Install the windshield washer reservoir.
44. If equipped with cruise control, reinstall the cruise control actuator.

45. Connect the accelerator cable or linkage.
46. Install the oil pan baffle plate. Clean the contact surfaces thoroughly, apply a bead of sealer to the baffle plate and press the baffle plate into position. Be very careful not to get any sealant into the oil passages.
47. Install the oil pick-up and strainer assembly. Install the PCV hose.
48. Install the oil pan, following procedures discussed in this chapter.
49. Using new gaskets, reconnect the exhaust pipe. Tighten the bolts to the catalytic converter to 32 ft. lbs. and the bolts to the exhaust manifold 46 ft. lbs.
50. Install the flywheel cover.
51. Install the stiffener plate and the center engine mount.
52. Refill the engine with oil.
53. Refill the coolant system.
54. Start the engine and check for leaks. Allow the engine to warm up to normal operating temperature and check the work area carefully for signs of seepage.
55. With the engine shut off, check the tension of the drive belts and adjust if necessary. Reinstall the splash guards under the car.

4A-FE

1. Disconnect the negative battery cable and elevate the vehicle. Safely support it on jackstands. Remove the splashshield(s).
2. Remove the protectors from the two center engine mount nuts and studs.
3. Remove the two center transaxle mount-to-center crossmember nuts.
4. Remove the two rear transaxle mount-to-main crossmember nuts.
5. Drain the engine oil
CAUTION: *Used motor oil may cause skin cancer if repeatedly left in contact with the skin for prolonged periods. Although this is unlikely unless you handle oil on a daily basis, it is wise to thoroughly wash your hands with soap and water immediately after handling used motor oil.*
6. Remove the oil pan. Remove the oil pick-up and strainer assembly.
7. Lower the vehicle to the ground.
8. Depending on equipment, loosen the air conditioning compressor bracket, the power steering pump bracket and the alternator bracket as applicable. Remove the drive belts.
9. Remove the alternator from its mounts and place it out of the way. The wiring may be left attached.
10. Lift out the windshield washer fluid reservoir.
11. Support the engine. This may be done from above with tool J 28467-A or a chain hoist or from below with a floor jack. Be very careful

of the jack placement (the oil pan is removed); use a piece of wood to distribute the load and protect the engine.

12. Remove the through bolt in the right engine mount.

13. Remove the water pump pulley.

14. Lower the engine to its normal position.

15. Remove the crankshaft pulley.

16. Remove the timing belt covers.

17. Remove the timing belt guide from the crank pulley.

18. Loosen the idler pulley bolt, push it all the way to the left and tighten the bolt. This removes tension from the belt.

19. Matchmark the belt and all the pulleys so that the belt may be reinstalled exactly as it was before. Mark an arrow on the belt showing direction of rotation.

20. Remove the timing belt from the lower pulley (crankshaft timing pulley). If you are careful, the belt may remain undisturbed on the camshaft pulleys.

21. Remove the idler pulley and spring.

22. Remove the dipstick and dipstick tube.

23. Remove the crankshaft timing pulley.

24. Raise the vehicle and safely support it on jackstands.

25. Remove the seven bolts holding the oil pump.

26. Remove the seven bolts in the oil pump and carefully remove the pump. If it is difficult to remove, tap it lightly with a plastic or rubber mallet. Do not pry it off or strike it with a metal hammer.

27. When reinstalling, place a new gasket on the block. Install the oil pump to the crankshaft with the spline teeth to the drive gear engaged with the large teeth of the crankshaft.

28. Install the seven retaining bolts and tighten them to 16 ft. lbs.

29. Lower the vehicle to the ground.

30. Install the timing belt idler pulley.

31. Install the dipstick tube and dipstick.

32. Install the timing belt. (Refer to Timing Belt--Removal and Installation procedures in this chapter.)

33. Install the timing belt guide. It should install with the cupped side facing outward.

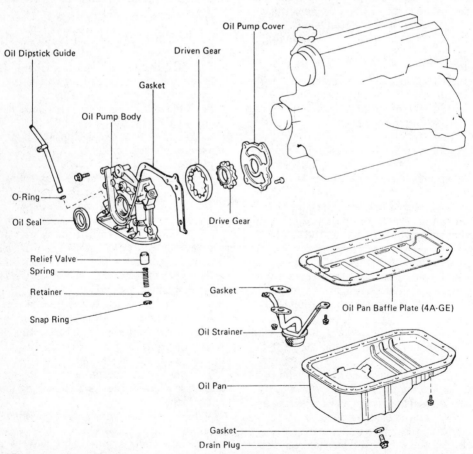

Detail of the oil pump system on 4A-GE. The 4A-FE is similar without the baffle plate. Any gasket shown should be replaced before reassembly

34. Make sure the gaskets are properly seated in the timing belt covers and reinstall the covers. Make sure each bolt is in the correct hole.

35. Install the crankshaft pulley. Tighten the bolt to 87 ft. lbs.

36. Elevate the motor to gain access to the water pump.

37. Install the water pump pulley.

38. Install the right engine mount through bolt. Tighten the through bolt to 64 ft. lbs. When the bolt is secure, the engine lifting apparatus may be removed.

39. Position and install the alternator.

40. Reinstall the drive belts for the alternator, power steering and air conditioning as applicable. Adjust the belts to the correct tension.

41. Raise the vehicle and safely support it on jackstands.

42. Install the oil pick-up and strainer assembly.

43. Apply a continuous bead of sealer (GM 1050026 or similar) to both sides of the new pan gasket.

44. Place the gasket on the pan and install the pan to the block. Tighten the bolts and nuts to 3.6 ft. lbs. (44 INCH lbs.)

45. Install the two rear transaxle mount-to-main crossmember nuts and tighten them to 45 ft. lbs. Install the two center transaxle mount-to-center crossmember nuts and tighten them to 45 ft. lbs.

46. Install the protectors over the nuts and studs for the mounts.

47. Lower the vehicle to the ground.

48. Install the windshield washer fluid reservoir.

49. Refill the engine with the correct amount of fresh oil.

50. Connect the negative battery cable.

51. Start the engine and check for leaks. Allow the engine to warm up to normal operating temperature and check the work area carefully for signs of seepage.

52. With the engine shut off, check the tension of the drive belts and adjust if necessary. Reinstall the splash guard(s) under the car.

Timing Belt Covers

REMOVAL AND INSTALLATION

4A-LC

1. Disconnect the negative battery cable.

2. Remove the right side splash shield under the engine.

3. Loosen the water pump pulley bolts and remove the alternator belt. Remove the power steering drive belt if so equipped.

4. Remove the bolts and remove the water pump pulley.

5. Loosen the air conditioning idler pulley mounting bolt. Loosen the adjusting nut and then remove the air conditioning drive belt if so equipped. Remove the idler pulley.

6. Rotate the crankshaft clockwise and set the engine to TDC/compression on No. 1 cylinder. Loosen the crankshaft pulley mounting bolt and remove the crank pulley.

NOTE: *Before removing the pulley, check that the rockers on the No. 1 cylinder are loose and that the timing marks on the crankshaft align at the zero setting. If the rockers are not loose, rotate the crankshaft one full revolution, stopping again at the zero point.*

7. Remove the mounting bolts and the No. 1 (upper) cover.

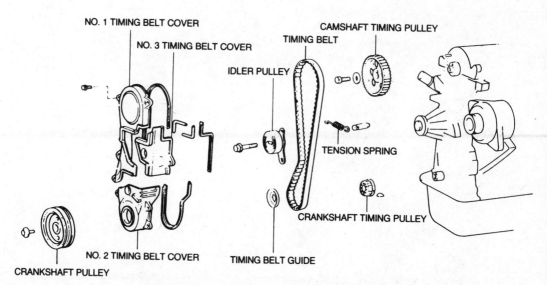

Timing belt and related components, 4A-LC engine

8. Remove the four bolts and remove the center engine mount.

9. Place a block of wood on a floor jack and position it under the motor. Raise the engine slightly, remove two bolts and then remove the right engine mount.

10. Lower the engine and then remove the No. 2 (lower) and the No. 3 (center) covers with their gaskets.

11. When reinstalling, make certain that the gaskets and their mating surfaces are clean and free from dirt and oil. The gasket itself must be free of cuts and deformations and must fit securely in the grooves of the covers.

12. Install the No.3 cover with its gasket, then install the No. 2 cover and its gasket. Before tightening the bolts fully, check that the gaskets have not fallen out of place.

13. Raise the engine slightly and install the right engine mount.

14. Lower the engine into place and install the center engine mount. Tighten the bolts to 29 ft. lbs.

15. Install the upper timing belt cover.

16. Install the crankshaft pulley; tighten the bolt to 87 ft. lbs.

17. Install the water pump pulley and tighten the bolts finger tight.

18. Reinstall the idler pulley for the air conditioning belt. Install the belt and adjust it by turning the adjustor into position.

19. Tighten the water pump pulley bolts.

20. Install the power steering drive belt if so equipped.

21. Install the splash shield.

22. Connect the negative battery cable.

4A-GE

1. Disconnect the negative battery cable.

2. Elevate the vehicle and safely support it on jackstands.

3. Remove the right front wheel.

4. Remove the splash shield from under the car.

5. Drain the coolant into clean containers. Close the draincocks when the system is empty.

CAUTION: *When draining the coolant, keep in mind that cats and dogs are attracted by the ethylene glycol antifreeze, and are quite likely to drink any that is left in an uncovered container or in puddles on the ground. This will prove fatal in sufficient quantity. Always*

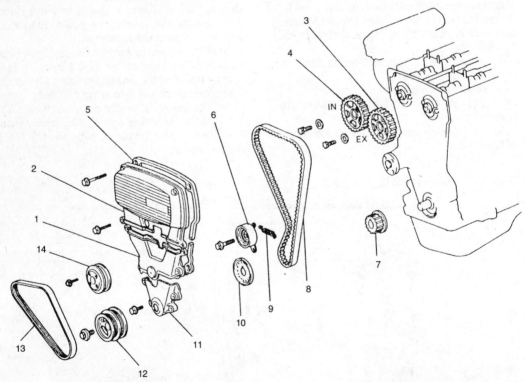

1. No.2 Timing belt cover	5. Gasket	10. Timing belt guide
2. No.3 timing belt cover	6. Idler pulley	11. No.1 timing belt cover
3. Exhaust camshaft timing pulley	7. Crankshaft timing pulley	12. Crankshaft pulley
	8. Timing belt	13. Drive belt
4. Intake camshaft pulley	9. Tension spring	14. Water pump pulley

4A-GE timing belt, cover and related components

drain the coolant into a sealable container. Coolant should be reused unless it is contaminated or several years old.

6. Lower the car to the ground. Disconnect the accelerator cable and, if equipped, the cruise control cable.

7. Remove the cruise control actuator if so equipped.

8. Carefully remove the ignition coil.

9. Disconnect the radiator hose at the water outlet.

10. Remove the power steering drive belt and the alternator drive belt.

11. Remove the spark plugs.

12. Rotate the crankshaft clockwise and set the engine to TDC/compression on No.1 cylinder. Align the crankshaft marks at zero; look through the oil filler hole and make sure the small hole in the end of the camshaft can be seen.

13. Raise and safely support the vehicle. Disconnect the center engine mount.

14. Lower the vehicle to the ground.

15. Support the engine either from above or below. Disconnect the right engine mount from the engine.

16. Raise the engine and remove the mount.

17. Remove the water pump pulley.

18. Remove the crankshaft pulley. The use of a counterholding tool such as J-8614-01 or similar is highly recommended.

19. Remove the ten bolts and remove the timing belt covers with their gaskets.

WARNING: *The bolts are different lengths; they must be returned to their correct location at reassembly. Label or diagram the bolts during removal.*

20. When reinstalling, make certain that the gaskets and their mating surfaces are clean and free from dirt and oil. The gasket itself must be free of cuts and deformations and must fit securely in the grooves of the covers.

21. Reinstall the covers and their gaskets and the 10 bolts in their proper positions.

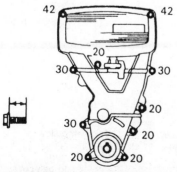

Timing cover bolts must be installed in the correct locations for 4A-GE engines. Bolt lengths shown are in millimeters (mm)

22. Install the crankshaft pulley, again using the counterholding tool. Tighten the bolt to 101 ft. lbs.

23. Install the water pump pulley.

24. Install the right engine mount. Tighten the through bolt to 58 ft. lbs.

25. Reinstall the spark plugs and their wires.

26. Install the alternator drive belt and the power steering drive belt. Adjust the belts to the correct tension.

27. Connect the radiator hose to the water outlet port.

28. Install the ignition coil.

29. Install the cruise control actuator and the cruise control cable if so equipped.

30. Connect the accelerator cable.

31. Refill the cooling system with the correct amount of anti-freeze and water.

32. Connect the negative battery cable.

33. Start the engine and check for leaks. Allow the engine to warm up and check the work areas carefully for seepage.

34. Install the splash shield under the car.

35. Install the right front wheel.

4A-FE

1. Disconnect the negative battery cable.

2. Elevate the vehicle and safely support it on jackstands.

3. Remove the right splash shield under the car.

4. Lower the vehicle. Remove the wiring harness from the upper timing belt cover.

5. Depending on equipment, loosen the air conditioner compressor, the power steering pump and the alternator on their adjusting bolts. Remove the drive belts.

6. Remove the crankshaft pulley. The use of a counterholding tool such as J 8614-01 or similar is highly recommended.

7. Remove the valve cover.

8. Remove the windshield washer reservoir.

9. Elevate and safely support the vehicle.

10. Support the engine either from above (Tool 28467-A or chain hoist) or below (floor jack and wood block) and remove the through bolt at the right engine mount.

11. Remove the protectors on the mount nuts and studs for the center and rear transaxle mounts.

12. Remove the two rear transaxle mount-to-main crossmember nuts. Remove the two center transaxle mount-to-center crossmember nuts.

13. Carefully elevate the engine enough to gain access to the water pump pulley.

14. Remove the water pump pulley. Lower the engine to its normal position.

15. Remove the four bolts and the lower tim-

ing cover. Remove the center timing cover and its bolt, then the upper cover with its four bolts.

16. If further work is to be done, the car may be lowered to the ground but the engine must remain supported until the mount(s) are reinstalled.

17. When reinstalling, make certain that the gaskets and their mating surfaces are clean and free from dirt and oil. The gasket itself must be free of cuts and deformations and must fit securely in the grooves of the covers.

18. Install the covers and the bolts; tighten the bolts to 3.6 ft. lbs. (44 INCH lbs.)

19. Elevate the engine and install the water pump pulley.

20. Lower the engine to its normal position. Install the through bolt in the right engine mount and tighten it to 64 ft. lbs. with the bolt secure, the engine lifting apparatus may be removed.

21. Install the valve cover.

22. Install the crankshaft pulley and tighten its bolt to 87 ft. lbs.

23. Reinstall the air conditioning compressor, the power steering pump and the alternator. Install their belts and adjust them to the correct tension.

24. Reconnect the wiring harness to the upper timing belt cover.

25. Raise the vehicle and safely support it on jackstands.

26. Install the two nuts on the center transaxle mount and the rear transaxle mount. Tighten all the nuts to 45 ft. lbs.

27. Install the protectors on the nuts and studs.

28. Install the splashshield under the car.

29. Lower the vehicle to the ground.

30. Install the windshield washer reservoir and connect the negative battery cable.

Timing Belt and Camshaft Sprocket
REMOVAL AND INSTALLATION

NOTE: *Timing belts must always be handled carefully and kept completely free of dirt, grease, fluids and lubricants. This includes any accidental contact from spillage, fingerprints, rags, etc. These same precautions apply to the pulleys and contact surfaces on which the belt rides.*

The belt must never be crimped, twisted or bent. Never use tools to pry or wedge the belt into place. Such actions will damage the

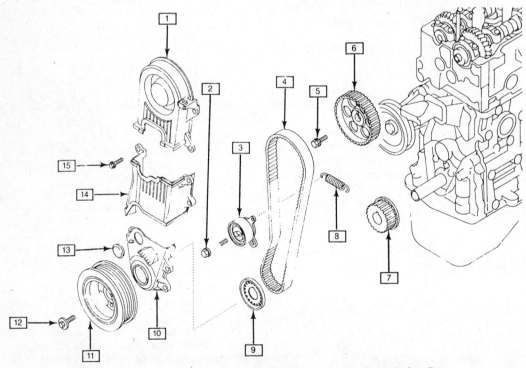

1. Upper timing belt cover	6. Camshaft timing pulley	11. Crankshaft pulley
2. Bolt	7. Crankshaft timing gear	12. Bolt
3. Idler pulley	8. Tension spring	13. Inspection plug
4. timing belt	9. Timing belt guide	14. Center timing belt cover
5. Bolt	10. Lower timing belt cover	15. Bolt

Timing covers, belt and related components in 4A-FE engine

structure of the belt and possibly cause breakage.

4A-LC

1. Remove the timing belt covers using procedures described earlier in this chapter.

2. If not done as part of the cover removal, rotate the crankshaft clockwise to the TDC/compression position for No. 1 cylinder. Insure that the crankshaft marks align at zero and that the rocker arms on No. 1 cylinder are loose.

3. Loosen the timing belt idler pulley to relieve the tension on the belt.

4. Make matchmarks on the belt and both pulleys showing the exact placement of the belt. Mark an arrow on the belt showing its direction of rotation.

5. Carefully slip the timing belt off the pulleys.

WARNING: *Do not disturb the position of the camshaft or the crankshaft during removal.*

6. Remove the idler pulley bolt, pulley and return spring.

7. Use an adjustable wrench mounted on the flats of the camshaft to hold the cam from moving. Loosen the center bolt in the camshaft pulley and remove the pulley.

8. Check the timing belt carefully for any signs of cracking or deterioration. Pay particular attention to the area where each tooth or cog attaches to the backing of the belt. If the belt shows signs of damage, check the contact faces of the pulleys for possible burrs or scratches.

9. Check the idler pulley by holding it in your hand and spinning it. It should rotate freely

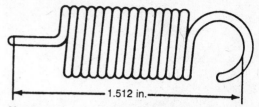

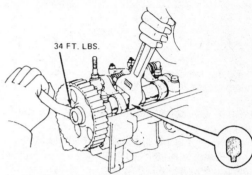

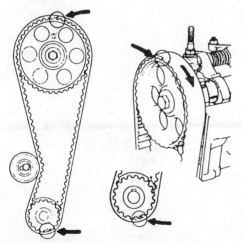

Always matchmark the belt and both pulleys before removing the timing belt. Mark an arrow on the belt showing direction of rotation

Always measure the free length of the idler pulley tensioning spring. For the 4A-LC, the correct length is 1.512 in

Make sure the cam is firmly held when removing the timing belt sprocket

and quietly. Any sign of grinding or abnormal noise indicates replacement of the pulley.

10. Check the free length of the tension spring. Correct length is 38.5mm measured at the inside faces of the hooks. A spring which has stretched during use will not apply the correct tension to the pulley; replace the spring.

11. If you can test the tension of the spring, look for 8.4 lbs. of tension at 50mm of length. If in doubt, replace the spring.

12. Reinstall the camshaft timing belt pulley, making sure the pulley fits properly on the shaft and that the timing marks align correctly. Tighten the center bolt to 34 ft. lbs.

13. Before reinstalling the belt, double check that the crank and camshafts are exactly in their correct positions. The alignment mark on the end of the camshaft bearing cap should show through the small hole in the camshaft pulley and the small mark on the crankshaft

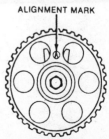

Make sure the camshaft alignment mark shows through the small hole in the pulley

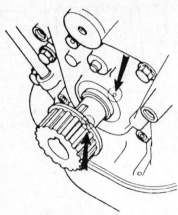

The crankshaft and oil pump marks must be aligned before reinstalling the timing belt

timing belt pulley should align with the mark on the oil pump.

14. Reinstall the timing belt idler pulley and the tension spring. Pry the pulley to the left as far as it will go and temporarily tighten the retaining bolt. This will hold the pulley in its loosest position.

15. Install the timing belt, observing the matchmarks made earlier. Make sure the belt is fully and squarely seated on the upper and lower pulleys.

16. Using the equipment installed during the removal of the timing covers, elevate the engine enough to gain access to the work area.

17. Loosen the retaining bolt for the timing belt idler pulley and allow it to tension the belt.

18. Temporarily install the crankshaft pulley bolt and turn the crank clockwise two full revolutions from TDC to TDC. Insure that each timing mark realigns exactly.

19. Tighten the timing belt idler pulley retaining bolt to 27 ft. lbs.

20. Measure the timing belt deflection (Tool 23600 B or similar), looking for 6–7mm of deflection at 4.4 pounds of pressure. If the deflec-

tion is not correct, readjust the idler pulley by repeating steps 15 through 18.

21. Remove the bolt from the end of the crankshaft.

22. Lower the engine into position and install the right engine mount.

23. Install the timing belt guide onto the crankshaft and install the lower timing belt cover.

24. Continue reassembly of the timing belt covers as outlined previously in this chapter.

4A-GE

1. Remove the timing belt covers following procedures explained previously in this chapter.

2. Remove the timing belt guide from the crankshaft pulley.

3. Loosen the timing belt idler pulley, move it to the left (to take tension off the belt) and tighten its bolt.

4. Make matchmarks on the belt and all pulleys showing the exact placement of the belt. Mark an arrow on the belt showing its direction of rotation.

5. Carefully slip the timing belt off the pulleys.
WARNING: *Do not disturb the position of the camshafts or the crankshaft during removal.*

6. Remove the idler pulley bolt, pulley and return spring.

7. Remove the PCV hose and the valve covers.

8. Use an adjustable wrench to counterhold the camshaft. Be careful not to damage the cylinder head. Loosen the center bolt in each camshaft pulley and remove the pulley. Label the pulleys and and keep them clean.

9. Check the timing belt carefully for any signs of cracking or deterioration. Pay particular attention to the area where each tooth or cog attaches to the backing of the belt. If the belt shows signs of damage, check the contact

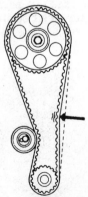

After the timing belt is reinstalled, always check for the correct tension. See text for correct procedure

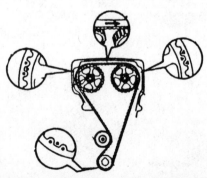

Examples of matchmarks on timing belt and pulleys. Don't forget an arrow showing the direction of rotation. The belt will break if put on backwards

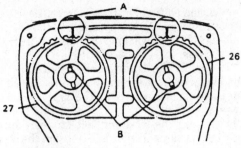

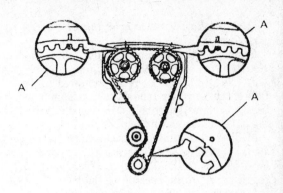

A   MATCHMARK
B   KNOCK PIN
26   EXHAUST CAMSHAFT TIMING PULLEY
27   INTAKE CAMSHAFT TIMING
       PULLEY

Align the cam pulleys before installing the timing belt

faces of the pulleys for possible burrs or scratches.

10. Check the idler pulley by holding it in your hand and spinning it. It should rotate freely and quietly. Any sign of grinding or abnormal noise indicates replacement of the pulley.

11. Check the free length of the tension spring. Correct length is 43.5mm measured at the inside faces of the hooks. A spring which has stretched during use will not apply the correct tension to the pulley; replace the spring.

12. If you can test the tension of the spring, look for 22 lbs. of tension at 50mm of length. If in doubt, replace the spring.

13. Align the camshaft knock pin and the pulley. Reinstall the camshaft timing belt pulleys, making sure the pulley fits properly on the shaft and that the timing marks align correctly. Tighten the center bolt on each pulley to 34 ft. lbs. Be careful not to damage the cylinder head during installation.

14. Before reinstalling the belt, double check that the crank and camshafts are exactly in their correct positions. The alignment marks on the pulleys should align with the cast marks on the head and oil pump.

15. Reinstall the valve covers and the PCV hose.

16. Install the timing belt idler pulley and its tensioning spring. Move the idler to the left and temporarily tighten its bolt.

17. Carefully observing the matchmarks made earlier, install the timing belt onto the pulleys.

18. Slowly release tension on the idler pulley bolt and allow the idler to take up tension on the timing belt. DO NOT allow the idler to slam into the belt; the belt may become damaged.

19. Temporarily install the crankshaft pulley bolt. Turn the engine clockwise through two complete revolutions, stopping at TDC. Check that each pulley aligns with its marks.

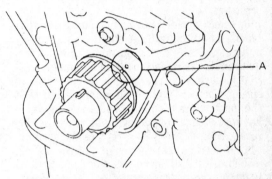

For the 4A-GE engine, make certain all the timing marks (A) are aligned before timing belt is installed

20. Using tool J 23600-B or similar, check the tension of the timing belt at a point halfway between the two camshaft sprockets. The correct deflection is 4mm at 4.4 lbs. pressure. If the belt tension is incorrect, readjust it by repeating steps 19 and 20. If the tension is correct, tighten the idler pulley bolt to 27 ft. lbs.

21. Remove the crankshaft pulley bolt.

22. Install the timing belt guide onto crankshaft timing pulley.

23. Reinstall the timing belt covers, following procedures outlined previously in this chapter.

4A-FE

1. Remove the timing belt covers using procedures described earlier in this chapter.

2. If not done as part of the cover removal, rotate the crankshaft clockwise to the TDC/compression position for No. 1 cylinder.

3. Loosen the timing belt idler pulley to relieve the tension on the belt, move the pulley away from the belt and temporarily tighten the bolt to hold it in the loose position.

4. Make matchmarks on the belt and both pulleys showing the exact placement of the belt. Mark an arrow on the belt showing its direction of rotation.

5. Carefully slip the timing belt off the pulleys.

WARNING: *Do not disturb the position of*

the camshafts or the crankshaft during removal.

6. Remove the idler pulley bolt, pulley and return spring.

7. Use an adjustable wrench mounted on the flats of the camshaft to hold the cam from moving. Loosen the center bolt in the camshaft timing pulley and remove the pulley.

8. Check the timing belt carefully for any signs of cracking or deterioration. Pay particular attention to the area where each tooth or cog attaches to the backing of the belt. If the belt shows signs of damage, check the contact faces of the pulleys for possible burrs or scratches.

9. Check the idler pulley by holding it in your hand and spinning it. It should rotate freely and quietly. Any sign of grinding or abnormal noise indicates replacement of the pulley.

10. Check the free length of the tension spring. Correct length is 38.5mm measured at the inside faces of the hooks. A spring which has stretched during use will not apply the correct tension to the pulley; replace the spring.

11. If you can test the tension of the spring, look for 8.4 lbs. of tension at 50mm of length. If in doubt, replace the spring.

12. Reinstall the camshaft timing belt pulley, making sure the pulley fits properly on the shaft and that the timing marks align correctly. Tighten the center bolt to 43 ft. lbs.

13. Before reinstalling the belt, double check that the crank and camshafts are exactly in their correct positions. The alignment mark on the end of the camshaft bearing cap should show through the small hole in the camshaft pulley and the small mark on the crankshaft timing belt pulley should align with the mark on the oil pump.

14. Reinstall the timing belt idler pulley and

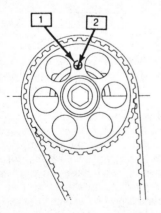

1. Camshaft gear hole
2. Exhaust camshaft cap mark

Correct alignment of the 4A-FE camshaft before reinstallation of the timing belt

the tension spring. Pry the pulley to the left as far as it will go and temporarily tighten the retaining bolt. This will hold the pulley in its loosest position.

15. Install the timing belt, observing the matchmarks made earlier. Make sure the belt is fully and squarely seated on the upper and lower pulleys.

16. Loosen the retaining bolt for the timing belt idler pulley and allow it to tension the belt.

17. Temporarily install the crankshaft pulley bolt and turn the crank clockwise two full revolutions from TDC to TDC. Insure that each timing mark realigns exactly.

18. Tighten the timing belt idler pulley retaining bolt to 27 ft. lbs.

19. Measure the timing belt deflection (Tool 23600 B or similar), looking for 5–6mm of deflection at 4.4 pounds of pressure. If the deflection is not correct, readjust the idler pulley by repeating steps 15 through 18.

20. Remove the bolt from the end of the crankshaft.

21. Install the timing belt guide onto the crankshaft and install the lower timing belt cover.

22. Continue reassembly of the timing belt covers as outlined previously in this chapter.

Camshaft and Bearings
REMOVAL AND INSTALLATION

NOTE: *Camshaft end play (thrust clearance) must be checked before the cam is removed. Please refer to the "Inspection" section for details of this check.*

4A-LC

1. Remove the valve cover.
2. Drain the cooling system.
CAUTION: *When draining the coolant, keep in mind that cats and dogs are attracted by the ethylene glycol antifreeze, and are quite likely to drink any that is left in an uncovered container or in puddles on the ground. This will prove fatal in sufficient quantity. Always drain the coolant into a sealable container. Coolant should be reused unless it is contaminated or several years old.*
3. Loosen the water pump pulley bolts.
4. Remove the alternator belt.
5. Raise the vehicle and safely support it on jackstands.
6. Remove the power steering pivot bolt, if so equipped.
7. Remove the bolt which goes through both the upper and lower timing belt covers.
8. Lower the vehicle to the ground. Remove the power steering pump belt if so equipped.
9. Remove the water pump pulley.

10. Disconnect the upper radiator hose at the engine water outlet.

11. Label and disconnect vacuum hoses.

12. Remove the upper timing belt cover and its gasket.

13. At the distributor, label and disconnect the spark plug wires, the vacuum hoses and the electrical connections. Remove the distributor.

14. Disconnct the hoses at the fuel pump and remove the fuel pump.

15. Remove the distributor gear bolt.

16. Remove the rocker arm assembly.

17. Rotate the crankshaft clockwise and set the engine to TDC/compression on No. 1 cylinder. Make sure the rockers for cylinder No.1 are loose. If not, rotate the crankshaft one full turn.

18. Matchmark and remove the timing belt from the camshaft pulley. Suppport the belt so that it doesn't change position on the crankshaft pulley.

19. Loosen the camshaft bearing cap bolts a little at a time and in the correct sequence. After removal, label each cap.

20. Remove the camshaft oil seal (at the pulley end) and then remove the camshaft by lifting it straight out of its bearings.

> WARNING: *Although reasonable in weight, the cam is brittle in nature. Handle it gently and do not allow it to fall or hit objects. It may break into pieces.*

21. When reinstalling, coat all the bearing journals with engine oil and place the camshaft in the cylinder head.

22. Place bearing caps Nos. 2,3 and 4 on each journal with the arrows pointing towards the front of the engine.

23. Apply multi-purpose grease to the inside of the oil seal. and apply liquid sealer on the outer circumference of the oil seal.

24. Install the seal in position, being very careful to get it straight. Do not allow the seal to cock or move out of place during installation.

25. Install the bearing cap for bearing No.1 and apply silicone sealant to the lower ends of the of the seal.

26. Tighten each bearing cap little at a time and in the correct sequence. Tighten the bolts to 9 ft. lbs.

27. Hold the camshaft with an adjustable wrench and tighten the drive gear to 22 ft. lbs.

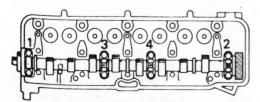

Loosen and remove 4A-LC bearing caps in this order

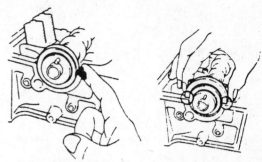

Apply sealant to these points before reinstalling the Nova 4A-LC valve cover

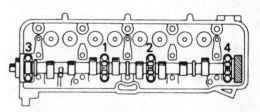

Tighten the bearing caps in this order

28. Install the timing belt as previously outlined.

29. Install the rocker arm assembly.

30. Install the fuel pump with a new gasket and connect the hoses.

31. Replace the distributor and connect its vacuum hoses, electrical connections and the spark plug wires.

32. Install the upper timing belt cover but don't install the bolt which holds both the upper and the lower covers yet.

33. Connect the vacuum hoses.

34. Connect the upper radiator hose to the water outlet.

35. Install the water pump pulley and tighten the bolts finger tight.

36. Install the power steering drive belt if so equipped.

37. Elevate the vehicle and safely support it on jackstands.

38. Install the bolt which connects the upper and lower timing belt covers.

39. Install the power steering pump pivot bolt and the belt; adjust the belt tension.

40. Lower the vehicle. Install the alternator belt and adjust it to the correct tension.

41. Tighten the water pump pulley bolts.

42. Refill the cooling system.

43. Install the valve cover with a new gasket.

4A-GE

1. Remove the valve covers and the timing belt cover following procedures outlined previously in this chapter.

2. Make certain the engine is set to TDC/compression on No. 1 cylinder. Remove the tim-

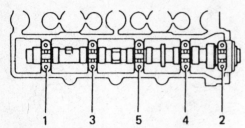

Remove the 4A-GE camshaft bearing caps in this order

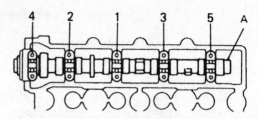

Tighten the 4A-GE bearing caps (intake and exhaust) in this order

ing belt following procedures outlined earlier in this chapter.

3. Remove the crankshaft pulley if so desired.

4. Remove the camshaft timing belt pulleys.

5. Loosen and remove the camshaft bearing caps in the proper sequence. It it recommended that the bolts be loosened in two or three passes.

6. With the bearing caps removed, the camshaft(s) may be lifted clear of the head. If both cams are to be removed, label them clearly-- they are not interchangable.

WARNING: *Although reasonable in weight, the cam is brittle in nature. Handle it gently and do not allow it to fall or hit objects. It may break into pieces.*

7. When reinstalling, place the camshaft(s) in position on the head. The exhaust cam has the distributor drive gear on it. Observe the markings on the bearing caps and place them according to their numbered positions. The arrow should point to the front of the engine.

8. Tighten the bearing cap bolts in the correct sequence and in three passes to a final tightness of 9 ft. lbs. (108 INCH lbs.).

9. Position the camshafts so that the guide pins (knock pins) are in the proper position. This step is critical to the correct valve timing of the engine.

10. Install the camshaft timing pulleys and tighten the bolts to 34 ft. lbs. Double check the positioning of the camshaft pulleys and the guide pin.

11. Double check the positioning of the camshaft pulleys and the guide pin.

12. Install the crankshaft pulley if it was removed. Tighten its bolt to 101 ft. lbs. and double check its position to be on TDC.

13. Install the timing belt and tensioner. Adjust the belt according to procedures outlined previously in this chapter.

14. Install the timing belt covers.

15. Install the valve covers.

4A-FE

1. Remove the valve cover.

2. Remove the timing belt covers.

3. Remove the timing belt and idler pulley following procedures outlined previously in this chapter.

4. Hold the exhaust camshaft with an adjustable wrench and remove the camshaft timing belt gear. Be careful not to damage the head or the camshaft during this work.

5. Gently turn the camshafts with an adjustable wrench until the service bolt hole in the intake camshaft end gear is straight up or in the "12 o'clock" position.

6. Alternately loosen the bearing cap bolts in

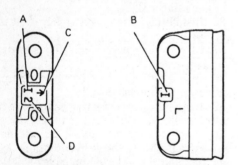

A   I = INTAKE   E = EXHAUST
B   I = INTAKE   E = EXHAUST
C   FRONT MARK
D   I.D. FOR BEARING
     NO. 2 THRU NO. 5

Examples of markings on camshaft bearing caps. Note that the bearing on the right is for position No. 1 only. 4A-GE caps shown, 4A-FE similar

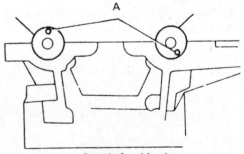

A. Camshaft guide pins
B. Exhaust camshaft
C. Intake camshaft

Correct position of guide pins, 4A-GE camshaft

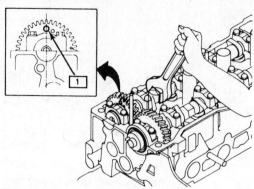

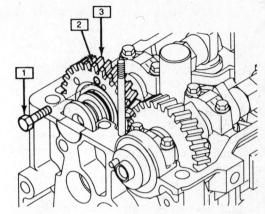

| 1 | SERVICE BOLT HOLE (INTAKE CAMSHAFT) |

Correct position of the service bolt hole before removal of the 4A-FE intake camshaft

1. Service bolt
2. Sub-gear
3. Main gear

Always install a service bolt to lock the intake cam gears together

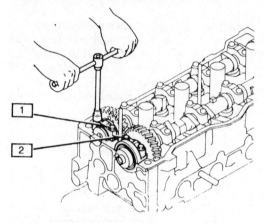

1. Intake bearing cap bolt
2. Exhaust bearing cap bolt

For the 4A-FE, alternately loosen the bolts for the No. 1 bearing cap on both the intake and exhaust camshafts

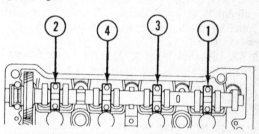

On the 4A-FE, remove the camshaft bearing caps in this order. Intake cam shown, exhaust cam uses identical order

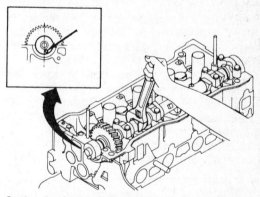

Setting the 4A-FE exhaust cam guide pin to the "just past 5 o'clock" position

the number one (closest to the pulleys) intake and exhaust bearing caps.

7. Attach the intake camshaft end gear to the sub gear with a service bolt. The service bolt should match the following specifications:

- Thread diameter: 6.0mm
- Thread pitch: 1.0mm
- Bolt length: 16-20mm

8. Uniformly loosen each intake camshaft bearing cap bolt a little at a time and in the correct sequence.

WARNING: *The camshaft must be held level while it is being removed. If the camshaft is not kept level, the portion of the cylinder head receiving the thrust may crack or become damaged. This in turn could cause the camshaft to bind or break.*

Before removing the intake camshaft, make sure the rotational force has been removed from the sub gear; that is, the gear should be in a neutral or "unloaded" state.

9. Remove the bearing caps and remove the intake camshaft.

NOTE: *If the camshaft cannot be removed straight and level, retighten the No.3 bearing cap. Alternately loosen the bolts on the bearing cap a little at a time while pulling upwards on the camshaft gear. DO NOT attempt to pry or force the cam loose with tools.*

10. With the intake camshaft removed, turn the exhaust camshaft approximately 105°, so

that the guide pin in the end is just past the "5 o'clock" position. This puts equal loadings on the camshaft, allowing easier and safer removal.

11. Loosen the exhaust camshaft bearing cap bolts a little at a time and in the correct sequence.

12. Remove the bearing caps and remove the exhaust camshaft.

NOTE: *If the camshaft cannot be removed straight and level, retighten the No.3 bearing cap. Alternately loosen the bolts on the bearing cap a little at a time while pulling upwards on the camshaft gear. DO NOT attempt to pry or force the cam loose with tools.*

13. When reinstalling, remember that the camshafts must be handled carefully and kept straight and level to avoid damage.

14. Place the exhaust camshaft on the cylinder head so that the cam lobes press evenly on the lifters for cylinders Nos. 1 and 3. This will put the guide pin in the "just past 5 o'clock" position.

15. Place the bearing caps in position according to the number cast into the cap. The arrow should point towards the pulley end of the motor.

16. Tighten the bearing cap bolts gradually and in the proper sequence to 9.5 ft. lbs. (115 INCH lbs.)

17. Apply multi-purpose grease, such as GM 1051344 or similar, to a new exhaust camshaft oil seal.

18. Install the exhaust camshaft oil seal using tool J 35403 or similar. Be very careful not to install the seal on a slant or allow it to tilt during installation.

19. Turn the exhaust cam until the cam lobes of No.4 cylinder press down on their lifters.

20. Hold the intake camshaft next to the exhaust camshaft and engage the gears by matching the alignment marks on each gear.

21. Keeping the gears engaged, roll the intake camshaft down and into its bearing journals.

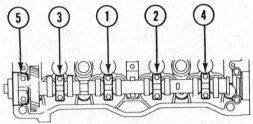

Tighten the 4A-FE camshaft bearing cap bolts in this order. Exhaust cam shown, intake uses identical order

This is tricky, but not hard to do. Take your time and pay close attention.

22. Place the bearing caps for Nos. 2,3,4 and 5 in position. Observe the numbers on each cap and make certain the arrows point to the pulley end of the motor.

23. Gradually tighten each bearing cap bolt in the same order as the exhaust camshaft bolts. Tighten each bolt to 9.5 ft. lbs. (115 INCH lbs.)

24. Remove any retaining pins or bolts in the intake camshaft gears.

25. Install the number one bearing cap for the intake camshaft.

NOTE: *If the No.1 bearing cap does not fit properly, gently push the cam gear towards the rear of the engine by levering between the gear and the head.*

26. Turn the exhaust camshaft one full revolution from TDC/compression on No.1 cylinder to the same position. Check that the mark on the exhaust camshaft gear matches exactly with the mark on the intake camshaft gear.

27. Counterhold the exhaust camshaft and install the timing belt pulley. Tighten the bolt to 43 ft. lbs.

28. Double check both the crankshaft and camshaft positions, insuring that they are both set to TDC/compression for No.1 cylinder.

29. Install the timing belt following procedures outlined previously in this chapter.

30. Install the timing belt covers and the valve cover.

INSPECTION AND MEASUREMENT

The end play or thrust clearance of the camshaft(s) must be measured with the camshaft installed in the head. It may be checked before removal or after reinstallation. To check the end play, mount a dial indicator accurate to ten one-thousandths (four decimal places) on the end of the block, so that the tip bears on the end of the camshaft. (The timing belt must be removed. On some motors, it will be necessary to remove the pulleys for unobstructed access to the camshaft.) Set the scale on the dial indicator to zero. Using a screwdriver or similar tool, gently lever the camshaft fore-and-aft in its mounts. Record the amount of deflection

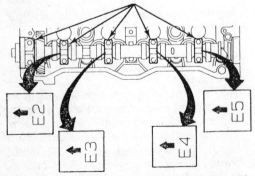

Examples of bearing cap markings and position. 4A-FE exhaust cam shown

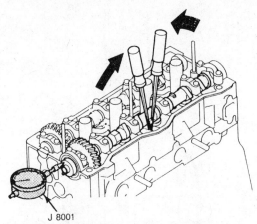

J 8001

Checking camshaft end play. GM tool number shown

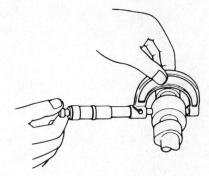

Use a micrometer to check the camshaft journal diameter

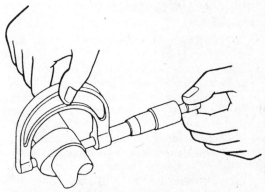

Measure the height of each camshaft lobe. Wear may be caused by infrequent oil changes

shown on the gauge and compare this number to the Camshaft Specifications Chart at the beginning of this chapter.

Excessive end-play may indicate either a worn camshaft or a worn head; the worn cam is most likely and much cheaper to replace. Chances are good that if the cam is worn in this dimension (axial), substantial wear will show up in other measurements.

Mount the cam in V-blocks and set the dial indicator up on the round center journal. Zero the dial and rotate the camshaft. The circular runout should not exceed 0.06mm on the 4A-LC or 0.04mm on the 4A-GE and 4A-FE motors. Excess runout means the cam must be replaced.

Using a micrometer or Vernier caliper, measure the diameter of all the journals and the height of all the lobes. Record the readings and compare them to the Camshaft Specifications Chart in the beginning of this chapter. Any measurement beyond the stated limits indicates wear and the camshaft must be replaced.

Lobe wear is generally accompanied by scoring or visible metal damage on the lobes. Overhead camshaft engines are very sensitive to proper lubrication with clean, fresh oil. A worn

cam may be your report card for poor maintenance intervals and late oil changes.

If a new cam is required on the 4A-LC engine, order new rockers to accompany it so that there are two new surfaces in contact. On the twin-cam motors, a new cam will require readjusting the valves, so new shims are in order. If, by coincidence, one valve measures out the same as before, replace the present shim with a new one to get two new surfaces in contact.

The clearance between the camshaft and its journals (bearings) must also be measured. Clean the camshaft, the journals and the bearing caps of any remaining oil and place the camshaft in position on the head. Lay a piece of compressable gauging material (Plastigage® or similar) on top of each journal on the cam.

Install the bearing caps in their correct order with the arrows pointing towards the front (pulley end) of the motor. Install the bearing cap bolts and tighten them in three passes to the correct tightness of 9 ft. lbs.

WARNING: *Do not turn the camshaft with the gauging material installed.*

Remove the bearing caps (in the correct order) and measure the gauging material at its widest point by comparing it to the scale provided with the package. Compare these measure-

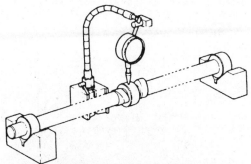

Use a dial indicator to check the run-out (eccentricity) of the center camshaft bearing

ments to the Camshaft Specifications Chart at the beginning of this chapter. Any measurement beyond specifications indicates wear. If you have already measured the cam (or replaced it) and determined it to be usable, excess bearing clearance indicates the need for a new head due to wear of the journals.

Remove the camshaft from the head and remove all traces of the gauging material. Check carefully for any small pieces clinging to contact faces.

Pistons and Connecting Rods

REMOVAL AND INSTALLATION--ALL ENGINES

NOTE: *These procedures may be performed with the engine in the car. If additional overhaul work is to be performed, it will be easier if the engine is removed and mounted on an engine stand. Most stands allow the block to be rotated, giving easy access to both the top and bottom.*

These procedures require certain hand tools which may not be in your tool box. A cylinder ridge reamer, a numbered punch set, piston ring expander, snap-ring tools and piston installation tool (ring compressor) are all necessary for correct piston and rod repair. These tools are commonly available from retail tool suppliers; you may be able to rent them from larger automotive supply houses.

1. Remove the cylinder head.
2. Elevate and safely support the vehicle on jackstands.
3. Drain the engine oil
CAUTION: *Used motor oil may cause skin cancer if repeatedly left in contact with the skin for prolonged periods. Although this is unlikely unless you handle oil on a daily basis, it is wise to thoroughly wash your hands with soap and water immediately after handling used motor oil.*
4. Remove any splash shield or rock guards which are in the way and remove the oil pan.
5. Using a numbered punch set, mark the cylinder number on each piston rod and bearing cap. Do this BEFORE loosening any bolts.
6. Loosen and remove the rod cap nuts and the rod caps. It will probably be necessary to tap the caps loose; do so with a small plastic mallet or other soft-faced tool. Keep the bearing insert with the cap when it is removed.
7. Use short pieces of hose to cover the bolt threads; this protects the bolt, the crankshaft and the cylinder walls during removal.
8. One piston will be at the lowest point in its cylinder. Cover the top of this piston with a rag.

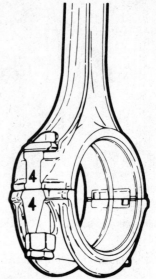

Use a numbered punch to identify both parts of each connecting rod with its cylinder number

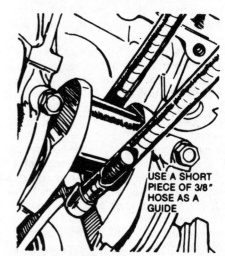

USE A SHORT PIECE OF 3/8" HOSE AS A GUIDE

Use lengths of vacuum hose or rubber tubing to protect the crankshaft journals and cylinder walls during piston installation

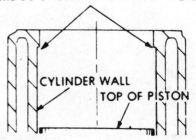

RIDGE CAUSED BY CYLINDER WEAR

CYLINDER WALL
TOP OF PISTON

Cylinder ridge

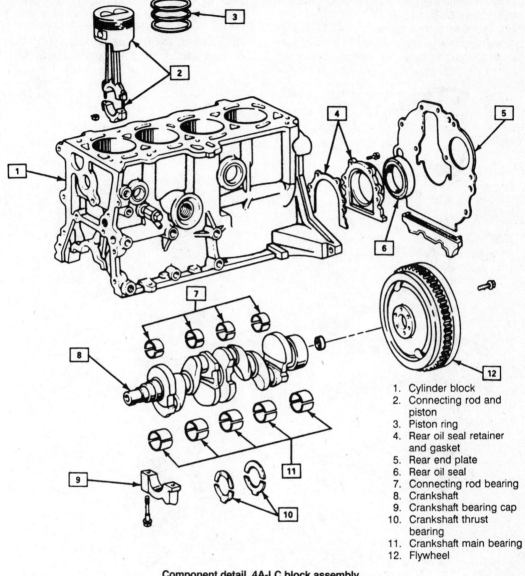

1. Cylinder block
2. Connecting rod and piston
3. Piston ring
4. Rear oil seal retainer and gasket
5. Rear end plate
6. Rear oil seal
7. Connecting rod bearing
8. Crankshaft
9. Crankshaft bearing cap
10. Crankshaft thrust bearing
11. Crankshaft main bearing
12. Flywheel

Component detail, 4A-LC block assembly

Push the piston out with a hammer handle

Examine the top area of the cylinder with your fingers, looking for a noticeable ridge around the cylinder. If any ridge is felt, it must be carefully removed by using the ridge reamer. Work with extreme care to avoid cutting too deeply.

When the ridge is removed, carefully remove the rag and ALL the shavings from the cylinder. No metal cuttings may remain in the cylinder or the wall will be damaged when the piston is removed. A small magnet can be helpful in removing the fine shavings.

9. After the cylinder is de-ridged, squirt a liberal coating of engine oil onto the cylinder walls until evenly coated. Carefully push the piston and rod assembly upwards from the bottom by

using a wooden hammer handle on the bottom of the connecting rod.

10. The next lowest piston should be gently pushed downwards from above. This will cause the crankshaft to turn and relocate the other pistons as well. When the piston is in its lowest position, repeat steps 8 and 9. Repeat the procedure for each of the remaining pistons.

11. When all the pistons are removed, clean the block and cylinder walls thoroughly with

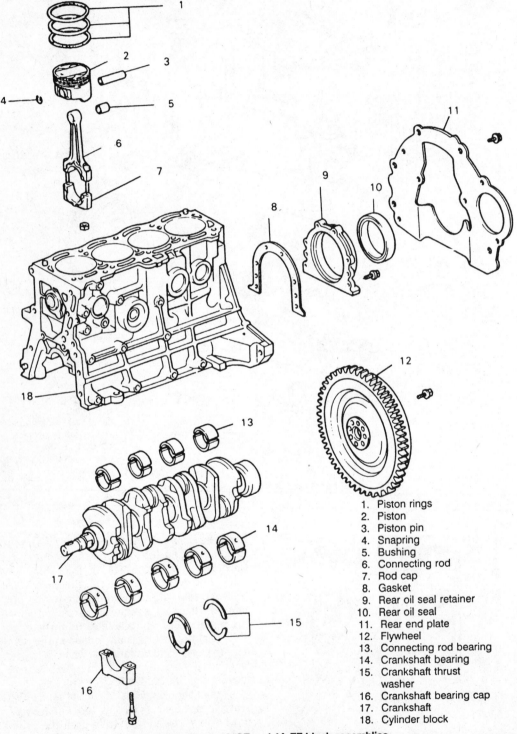

1. Piston rings
2. Piston
3. Piston pin
4. Snapring
5. Bushing
6. Connecting rod
7. Rod cap
8. Gasket
9. Rear oil seal retainer
10. Rear oil seal
11. Rear end plate
12. Flywheel
13. Connecting rod bearing
14. Crankshaft bearing
15. Crankshaft thrust washer
16. Crankshaft bearing cap
17. Crankshaft
18. Cylinder block

Component detail, 4A-GE and 4A-FE block assemblies

solvent. This makes a tremendous mess under the engine--use a large drain pan to collect the drippings.

12. When ready for reassembly, remember that all the pistons, rods and caps must be reinstalled in the correct cylinder. Make certain that all labels and stamped numbers are present and legible. Double check the piston rings; make certain that the ring gaps DO NOT line up, but are evenly spaced around the piston at about 120° intervals. Double check the bearing insert at the bottom of the rod for proper mounting. Reinstall the protective rubber hose pieces on the bolts.

13. Liberally coat the cylinder walls and the crankshaft journals with clean, fresh engine oil. Also apply oil to the bearing surfaces on the connecting rod and the cap.

14. Identify the "Front" mark on each piston and rod and position the piston loosely in its cylinder with the marks facing the front (pulley end) of the motor.

WARNING: *Failure to observe the "Front" marking and its correct placement can lead to sudden and catastrophic engine failure.*

15. Install the ring compressor (piston installation tool) around one piston and tighten it gently until the rings are compressed almost completely.

16. Gently push down on the piston top with a wooden hammer handle or similar soft-faced tool and drive the piston into the cylinder bore. Once all three rings are within the bore, the piston will move with some ease.

WARNING: *If any resistance or binding is encountered during the installation, DO NOT apply force. Tighten or adjust the ring compressor and/or reposition the piston. Brute force will break the ring(s) or damage the piston.*

17. From underneath, pull the connecting rod into place on the crankshaft. Remove the rubber hoses from the bolts. Check the rod cap to confirm that the bearing is present and correctly mounted, then install the rod cap (observing the correct number and position) and its nuts.

Leaving the nuts finger tight will make installation of the remaining pistons and rods easier.

18. Assemble the remaining pistons in the same fashion, repeating steps 15, 16 and 17.

19. With all the pistons installed and the bearing caps secured finger tight, the retaining nuts may be tightened to their final setting. For each pair of nuts, make three passes alternating between the two nuts on any given rod cap. The three tightening steps should be to 12, 24 and 36 ft. lbs. The intent is to draw each cap up to the crank straight and under even pressure at the nuts.

20. Turn the crankshaft through several clockwise rotations, making sure everything moves smoothly and there is no binding. With the piston rods connected, the crank may be stiff to turn--try to turn it in a smooth continuous motion so that any binding or stiff spots may be felt.

21. Reinstall the oil pan. Even if the engine is to remain apart for other repairs, install the oil pan to protect the bottom end and tighten the bolts to the correct specification--this eliminates one easily overlooked mistake during future reassembly.

22. If the engine is to remain apart for other repairs, pack the cylinders with crumpled newspaper or clean rags (to keep out dust and grit) and cover the top of the motor with a large rag. If the engine is on a stand, the whole block can be protected with a large plastic trash bag.

23. If no further work is to be performed, continue reassembly by installing the head, timing belt, etc.

24. When the engine is restarted after reassembly, the exhaust will be very smoky as the oil within the cylinders burns off. This is normal; the smoke should clear quickly during warm up. Depending on the condition of the spark plugs, it may be wise to check for any oil fouling after the engine is shut off.

CLEANING AND INSPECTION

Pistons

With the pistons removed from the engine, use a ring removing tool (ring expander) to remove the rings. Keep the rings labeled and

RING COMPRESSOR

Install the piston using a ring compresser

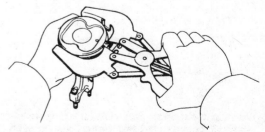

Removing the piston rings with a ring expander

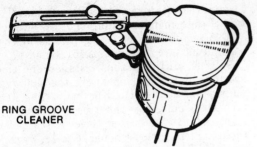

RING GROOVE
CLEANER

The ring grooves can be cleaned and de-carboned with a special tool

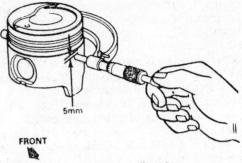

5mm

FRONT

Measuring the 4A-LC piston diameter

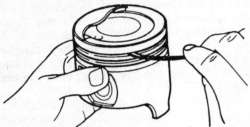

A piece of broken ring serves well to clean piston grooves

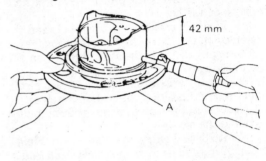

42 mm

A

A   MICROMETER
Measuring the 4A-GE piston diameter. 42mm = 1.65 in

stored by piston number. Clearly label the pistons by number so that they do not get interchanged.

Clean the carbon from the piston top and sides with a stiff bristle brush and cleaning solvent. Do not use a wire brush for cleaning.

CAUTION: *Wear goggles during this cleaning; the solvent is very strong and can cause eye damage.*

Clean the ring grooves (lands) either with a specially designed tool or with a piece of a broken piston ring. Remove all the carbon from the grooves and make sure that the groove shape (profile) is square all the way around the piston. When all the lands have been cleaned, again

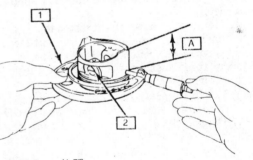

A. 38.5 mm (1.5″)
1. Micrometer
2. Piston hole center line
Measuring the piston diameter, 4A-FE

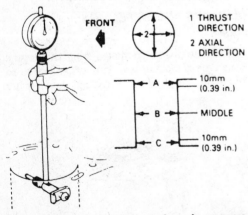

FRONT

1 THRUST
   DIRECTION
2 AXIAL
   DIRECTION

A — 10mm (0.39 in.)
B — MIDDLE
C — 10mm (0.39 in.)

Checking the cylinder bore requires six measurements—3 locations and two dimensions—in each cylinder

bathe the piston in solvent and clean the lands with the bristle brush.

Before any measurements are begun, visually examine the piston (a magnifying glass can be handy) for any signs of cracks--particularly in the skirt area--or scratches in the metal. Anything other than light surface scoring disqualifies the piston from further use. The metal will become unevenly heated and the piston may break apart during use.

Hold the piston and rod upright and attempt to move the piston back and forth along the piston pin (wrist pin). There should be NO motion in this axis. If there is, replace the piston and wrist pin.

Accurately measure the cylinder bore diameter in two dimensions (thrust and axial, or if you prefer, left-right and fore-aft) and in three locations (upper, middle and bottom) within the cylinder. That's six measurements in each bore; record them in order. Normal measurements for all Nova and Prizm engines are:

- New: 81.0–81.03mm
- Max Wear limit: 81.23mm

Having recorded the bore measurements, now measure the piston diameter. Do this with a micrometer at right angles to the piston pin. The location at which the piston is measured varies by engine type:

- 4A-LC: Measure at a point 5mm from lower edge of the oil ring groove.
- 4A-GE: Measure at a point 42mm from the longest part of the pison skirt.
- 4A-FE: Measure at a point 38.5mm from the longest part of the piston skirt.

Record each measurement for each piston.

The piston-to-cylinder wall clearance (sometimes called oil clearance) is determined by subtracting the piston diameter from the measured diameter of its respective cylinder. The difference will be in thousandths or ten-thousandths of an inch. Compare this number to the Piston and Ring Specifications Chart at the beginning of this chapter. Excess clearance may indicate the need for either new pistons or block reboring.

Connecting rods

The connecting rods must be free from wear, cracking and bending. Visually examine the rod, particularly at its upper and lower ends. Look for any sign of metal stretching or wear. The piston pin should fit cleanly and tightly through the upper end, allowing no sideplay or wobble. The bottom end should also be an exact ½ circle, with no deformity of shape. The bolts must be firmly mounted and parallel.

The rods may be taken to a machine shop for exact measurement of twist or bend. This is generally easier and cheaper than purchasing a seldom used rod-alignment tool.

PISTON PIN (WRIST PIN) REPLACEMENT

NOTE: *The piston and pin are a matched set and must be kept together. Label everything and store parts in identified containers.*

1. Remove the pistons from the engine and remove the rings from the pistons.
2. Remove the snapring at the ends of the piston pin. This may be done with either snapring pliers or needle-nosed pliers; don't try to lever it out with a screwdriver.
3. Support the piston and rod on its side in a press. Make certain the piston is square to the motion of the press and that the rod is com-

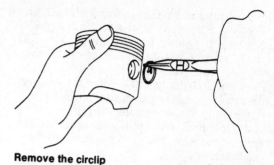

Remove the circlip

pletely supported with blocks. Leave open space below the piston for the pin to emerge.

4. Line up the press and insert a brass rod of the same or slightly smaller diameter as the piston pin. It is important that the rod press evenly on the entire face of the pin, but not on the piston itself.
5. Using smooth and controlled motion, press the pin free of the piston. Do not use sudden or jerky motions; the piston may crack.
6. When reassembling, identify the front of the piston by its small dot or cavity on the top. Identify the front of the piston rod by the small mark cast into one face of the rod. Make sure the marks on the piston and rod are both facing the same direction. Also insure that the correct piston pin is to be reinstalled--they are not interchangable.
7. For the 4A-LC and 4A-FE engines, install one snapring in the piston and insert the piston under the press with the snap-ring down. Position the rod and support it. Coat the piston pin with clean oil and press it into place, using the same press set-up as removal. The piston pin will bottom onto the snap-ring; don't force it beyond the stopping point. Install the other snapring to lock the pin in place.

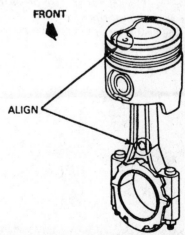

Align the piston and connecting rod "front" marks before reassembly

8. For the 4A-GE motor, install one snapring. Place the piston in water and gradually heat the water to the boiling point. DO NOT drop the piston into already hot water. The minimum required temperature is 176°F (80°C); a little hotter makes it a little easier. This will expand the piston so that the pin will fit smoothly. While the water is heating, apply a coat of clean oil to the piston pin and have the pin at hand when the piston is removed from the water.

CAUTION: *You are dealing with hot metal and boiling water. Tongs, thick heat-resistant gloves and towels are required.*

Remove the piston from the boiling water (carefully!) and hold it with gloves or several towels. Making sure the front marks align on the piston and connecting rod, hold the rod in position and press the piston pin into place with your thumb. The pin will bottom against the snapring. Allow the piston to air cool and when it is cool to the touch, install the other snapring. Check that the piston rocks freely on its pin without binding.

PISTON RING REPLACEMENT

NOTE: *Although a piston ring can be reused if in good condition and carefully removed, it is recommended that the rings be replaced with new ones any time they are removed from the pistons.*

A piston ring expander is necessary for removing piston rings without damaging them; any other method (screwdriver blades, pliers, etc.) usually results in the rings becoming bent, scratched or broken. When the rings are removed, clean the grooves thoroughly with a bristle brush and solvent. Make sure that all traces of carbon and varnish are removed.

WARNING: *Wear goggles during this cleaning; the solvent is very strong and can cause eye damage. Do not use a wire brush or a caustic solvent on the pistons.*

Check the piston condition and diameter fol-

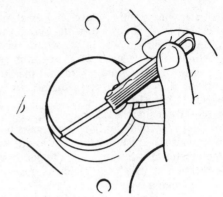

Checking the piston ring end gap

lowing procedures outlined earlier in this chapter. Piston ring end gap should be checked when the rings are removed from the pistons. Incorrect end gap indicates that the wrong size rings are being used; ring breakage could occur.

Squirt some clean oil into the cylinder so that the top two or three inches of the wall is covered. Gently compress one of the rings to be used and insert it into the cylinder. Use and upside-down piston and push the ring down about an inch below the top of the cylinder. Using the piston to push the ring keeps the ring square in the cylinder; if it gets crooked, the next measurement may be inaccurate.

Using a feeler gauge, measure the end gap in the ring and compare it to the Piston and Ring Specifications chart at the beginning of this chapter. If the gap is excessive, either the ring is incorrect or the cylinder walls are worn beyond acceptible limits. If the measurement is too tight, the ends of the ring may be filed to enlarge the gap after the ring is removed form the cylinder. If filing is needed, make certain that the ends are kept square and that a fine file is used.

Check the pistons to see that the ring grooves and oil return holes have been properly cleaned. Slide each piston ring into its groove and check the side clearance with a feeler gauge. Make sure you insert the feeler gauge between the ring and its lower edge; any wear that develops forms a step at the inner portion of the lower land. If the piston grooves have worn to the extent that fairly high steps exist on the lower land, the piston must be replaced. Rings are not sold in oversize thicknesses to compensate for ring groove wear.

Using the ring expander, install the rings on the piston, *lowest ring first.* There is a high risk of ring breakage or piston damage if the rings are installed by hand or without the expander. The correct spacing of the ring end gaps is critical to oil control. No two gaps should align, they should be evenly spaced around the piston with

The 4A-GE piston must be heated to install the piston pin. At 176°F, the pin should push in with thumb pressure

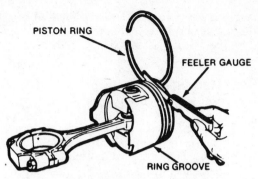

Checking the piston ring side clearance

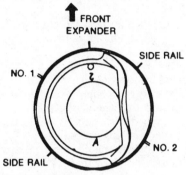

Piston ring positioning

the gap in the oil ring expander facing the front of the piston (aligned with the mark on the top of the piston). Once the rings are installed, the pistons must be handled carefully and protected from dirt and impact.

CONNECTING ROD BEARING REPLACEMENT

Connecting rod bearings on all Nova and Prizm engines consist of two halves or shells which are not interchangeable in the rod and cap. When the shells are in position, the ends extend slightly beyond the rod and cap surfaces so that when the bolts are tightened, the shells will be clamped tightly in place. This insures a positive seating and prevents turning. A small tang holds the shells in place within the cap and rod housings.

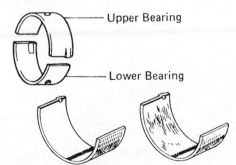

Examples of upper and lower bearing shells. Note the position of the oil hole

NOTE: *The ends of the bearing shells must never be filed flush with the mating surface of the rod or cap.*

If a rod becomes noisy or is worn so that its clearance on the crankshaft is sloppy, a new bearing of the correct undersize must be selected and installed. There is no provision for adjustment. Under no circumstances should the rod end or cap be filed to compensate for wear, nor should shims of any type be used.

Inspect the rod bearings while the rods are out of the engine. If the shells are scored or show flaking they should be replaced. ANY scoring or ridge on the crankshaft means the crankshaft must be replaced. Because of the metallurgy in the crankshaft, welding and/or regrinding the crankshaft is not recommended. The bearing faces of the crank may not be restored to their original condition causing premature bearing wear and possible failure.

Replacement bearings are available in three standard sizes marked either "1", "2" or "3" on the bearing shell and possibly on the rod cap. Do not confuse the mark on the bearing cap with the cylinder number. It is quite possible that No. 3 piston rod contains a number 1 size bearing. The rod cap may have a "1" marked on it. (You should have stamped a 3 or other identifying code on both halves of the rod before disassembly.)

Measuring the clearance between the connecting rod bearings and the crankshaft (oil clearance) is done with a plastic measuring material such as Plastigage® or similar product.

1. Remove the rod cap with the bearing shell. Completely clean the cap, bearing shells and the journal on the crankshaft. Blow any oil from the oil hole in the crank. The plastic measuring material is soluble in oil and will begin to dissolve if the area is not totally free of oil.

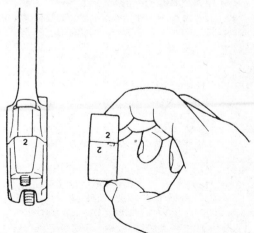

Look for the manufacturer's codes to identify standard bearing sizes. Don't confuse the number on the rod end cap with its position (cylinder) number

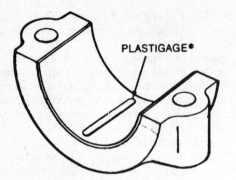

PLASTIGAGE®

Plastic measuring material installed on the lower bearing shell

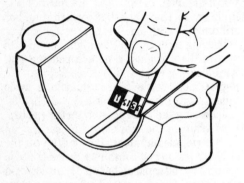

Measure the compressed plastic to determine the bearing clearance

2. Place a piece of the measuring material lengthwise along the bottom center of the lower bearing shell. Install the cap and shell and tighten the bolts in three passes to 36 ft. lbs.

NOTE: *Do not turn the crankshaft with the measuring material installed.*

3. Remove the bearing cap with the shell. The flattened plastic material will be found sticking to either the bearing shell or the crank journal. DO NOT remove it yet.

4. Use the scale printed on the packaging for the measuring material to measure the flattened plastic at its widest point. The number within the scale which is closest to the width of the plastic indicates the bearing clearance in thousandths of an inch.

5. Check the specifications chart in the beginning of this chapter for the proper clearance. If there is any measurement is approaching the maximum acceptible value, replace the bearing.

6. When the correct bearing is determined, clean off the gauging material, oil the bearing thoroughly on its working face and install it in the cap. Install the other half of the bearing into the rod end and attach the cap to the rod. Tighten the nuts evenly, in three passes to 36 ft. lbs.

7. With the proper bearing installed and the nuts properly tightened, it should be possible to move the connecting rod back and forth a bit on the crankshaft. If the rod cannot be moved, either the bearing is too small or the rod is misaligned.

Rear Main Seal

REMOVAL AND INSTALLATION.

Nova and Prizm

1. Remove the transaxle from the vehicle. Follow procedures outlined in Chapter 7.

2. If equipped with a manual transaxle, perform the following procedures:

  a. Matchmark the pressure plate and flywheel.

  b. Remove the pressure plate-to-flywheel bolts and the clutch assembly from the vehicle.

  c. Remove the flywheel-to-crankshaft bolts and the flywheel. The flywheel is a moderately heavy component. Handle it carefully and protect it on the workbench.

3. If equipped with an automatic transaxle, perform the following procedures:

  a. Matchmark the flywheel (flexplate or driveplate) and crankshaft.

  b. Remove the torque converter drive plate-to-crankshaft bolts and the torque converter drive plate.

4. Remove the bolts holding the rear end plate to the engine and the remove the rear end plate.

5. Remove the rear oil seal retainer-to-engine bolts, rear oil seal retainer to oil pan bolts and the rear oil seal retainer.

6. Using a small pry bar, pry the rear oil seal retainer from the mating surfaces.

7. Using a drive punch or a hammer and small screwdriver, drive the oil seal from the rear bearing retainer.

8. Using a putty knife, clean the gasket mounting surfaces. Make certain that the contact surfaces are completely free of oil and foreign matter.

NOTE: *When removing the rear oil seal, be*

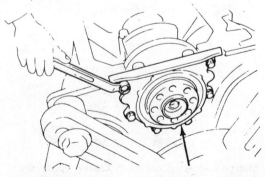

Removing the rear oil seal retainer

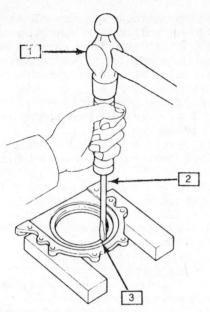

1. Hammer
2. Screwdriver
3. Rear main oil seal

Removing the rear main oil seal from the retainer. Note the supports under the housing

careful not to damage the seal mounting surface.

9. Clean the oil seal mounting surface.

10. Using multi-purpose grease, lubricate the new seal lips.

11. Using a seal installation tool such as J-35388 or similar, tap the seal straight into the bore of the retainer.

12. Position a new gasket on the retainer and coat it lightly with gasket sealer. Fit the seal retainer into place on the motor; be careful when installing the oil seal over the crankshaft.

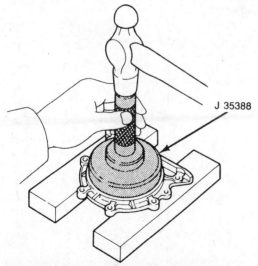

J 35388

Installing the new rear main seal using GM tool

13. Install the six retaining bolts and tighten them to 7 ft. lbs.(84 INCH lbs.)

14. Install the rear end plate. Tighten its bolts to 7.5 ft. lbs. (90 INCH lbs.).

15. Reinstall either the flexplate (automatic) or the flywheel (manual), carefully observing the matchmarks made earlier. Tighten the flexplate bolts to 58 ft. lbs. or the flywheel bolts to 61 ft. lbs.

16. Install wither the torque converter (automatic) or the clutch disc and pressure plate (manual).

17. Reinstall the transaxle, following procedures outlined in Chapter 7.

Crankshaft and Main Bearings
REMOVAL AND INSTALLATION

1. Remove the engine assembly from the car, following procedures outlined earlier in this chapter. Mount the engine securely on a stand which allows it to be rotated.

2. Remove the timing belt and tensioner assemblies.

3. Turn the engine upside down on the stand. Remove the oil pan and the oil strainer.

4. Remove the oil pump.

5. Remove either the clutch and pressure plate (manual transmission).

6. Remove either the flywheel (manual) or the drive plate (automatic).

7. Remove the rear end plate.

8. Remove the rear oil seal retainer.

9. Using a numbered punch set, mark each connecting rod cap with its correct cylinder number. Remove the rod caps and their bearings; keep the bearings with their respective caps.

10. Measure the crankshaft endplay (thrust clearance) before removing the crank. Attach a dial indicator, such as J 8001 or similar, to the end of the block and set the tip to bear on the front end of the crankshaft. With a screw driv-

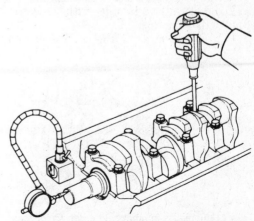

Use a dial indicator to measure crankshaft end play

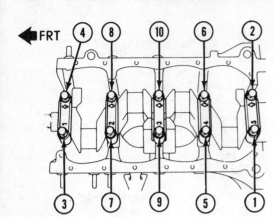

Remove the main bearing cap bolts in this order

er, gently move the crankshaft back and forth and record the reading shown on the dial.

- Standard Endplay, new: 0.02mm
- Acceptable Endplay
  4A-LC: 0.020–0.185mm
  All others: 0.02–0.22mm
- Maximum allowable: 0.3mm

If the end play is excessive, the thrust washers will need to be replaced as a set.

11. Gradually loosen and remove the main bearing cap bolts in three passes and in the correct order. Remove just the bolts, leaving the caps in place.

12. When all the bolts are removed, use two bolts placed in the No. 3 bearing cap to wiggle the cap back and forth. This will loosen the cap and allow it and the thrust washers to be removed. Note and/or label the thrust washers as to their placement and position. If they are to be reused, they must be reinstalled exactly as they were.

13. Remove the remaining caps. Keep the caps in order and keep the bearing shell with its respective cap.

14. Lift the crankshaft out of the block. The crankshaft is a moderately heavy component.

15. Remove the upper bearing shells from the block and place them in order with the corresponding bearing caps.

16. Check and measure the crankshaft and

bearings according to the procedures give in "Cleaning and Inspection" later in this section.

17. When reassembling, clean the bearing caps and journals in the block thoroughly. Coat the bearings with a liberal application of clean motor oil.

18. Fit the upper bearings halves into the block and position the lower bearing halves in the bearing caps.

19. Place the crankshaft into the engine block, making sure it fits exactly into its mounts.

20. Install the upper thrust washers on the center main bearing with the oil grooves facing outward.

21. Install the main bearing caps and the lower thrust washers in the proper sequence. Make sure the arrows on the caps point towards the front (pulley end) of the motor.

22. Tighten the cap bolts in three passes and in the correct sequence to 44 ft. lbs.

23. Double check the endplay of the crank by repeating step 10 of this procedure.

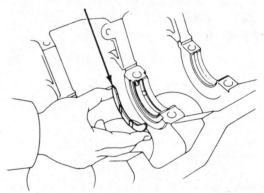

Correct position of the upper thrust washer when reinstalling

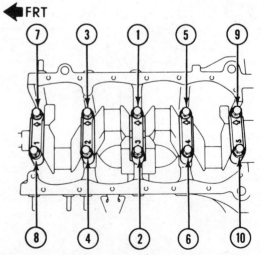

Install and tighten the main bearing cap bolts in this order

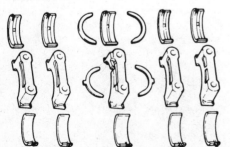

Keep all the pieces in numbered order. Exact reassembly is required

24. Turn the crankshaft through one or two full clockwise rotations, making sure that it turns smoothly and evenly with no binding.

25. Attach the piston rods, following procedures given earlier in this chapter. Remember that the rod caps must be reinstalled in their original positions.

26. Install a new rear main oil seal into the retainer and install the retainer onto the block. Tighten the bolts to 7.0 ft. lbs. (84 INCH lbs.).

27. Install the rear end plate on the engine.

28. Install either the driveplate (automatic) or the flywheel (manual), observing the matchmarks made during removal.

29. If equipped with a manual transmission, reinstall the clutch disc and pressure plate.

30. Install the oil pump.

31. Install the oil strainer and oil pan, using new gaskets.

32. Rotate the engine into its upright position and continue reassembly of the timing belt, idler pulley and covers.

33. Reinstall the engine in the car, following procedures outlined earlier in this chapter.

CLEANING AND INSPECTION

With the crankshaft removed from the engine, clean the crank, bearings and block areas thoroughly. Visually inspect each crankshaft section for any sign of wear or damage, paying close attention to the main bearing journals. ANY scoring or ridge on the crankshaft means the crankshaft must be replaced. Because of the metallurgy in the crankshaft, welding and/or regrinding the crankshaft is not recommended. The bearing faces of the crank may not be restored to their original condition causing premature bearing wear and possible failure.

Mount the crankshaft on V-blocks and set a dial indicator to bear on the center main journal. Slowly rotate the crank and record the circular runout as shown on the dial. Runout in excess of 0.06mm disqualifies the crankshaft from further use. It must be replaced.

Using a micrometer, measure the diameter of each journal on the crankshaft and record the measurements. The acceptable specifications

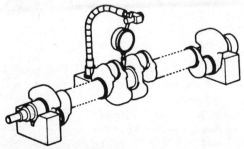

Measuring crankshaft run-out

Measure each journal at its outer points to determine taper

for both connecting rod and main journals are found in the Crankshaft and Connecting Rod specifications chart at the beginning of this chapter. If ANY journal is beyond the acceptable range, the crank must be replaced.

Additionally, each journal must be measured at both outer edges. When one measurement is subtracted from the other, the difference is the measurement of journal taper. Any taper beyond 0.2mm is a sign of excess wear on the journal; the crankshaft must be replaced.

BEARING REPLACEMENT

1. With the engine out of the car and inverted on a stand, remove the main bearing caps in the correct sequence, following procedures given earlier in this section.

2. Once the bearing caps are removed, the lower bearing shell may be inspected. Check closely for scoring or abrasion of the bearing surface. If this lower bearing is worn or damaged, both the upper and lower half should be replaced.

NOTE: *Always replace bearing shells in complete pairs.*

3. If the lower bearing half is in good condition, the upper shell may also be considered usable.

4. The bearing shells, the crank throws and the flat surface of the engine block (on the oil pan face) are stamped with numbers (1 through 5) indicating the standard bearing size. This size is determined during the initial manufacturing and assembly process; replacement bearings must be of the same code (thickness) if the correct clearances are to be maintained.

If the code on the bearing shell is unreadable, use the number on the block and the number on the crank throw to determine the bearing code. Refer to the proper selection chart to find the correct bearing for that position.

5. Lift the crankshaft from the engine block and remove the upper bearing shells. Clean the area thoroughly, allow the surfaces to air dry and coat all the journals with a liberal coating of clean engine oil.

6. Coat the new bearings to be installed with clean engine oil and install them in the block. Carefully place the crankshaft in position.

Cylinder Block

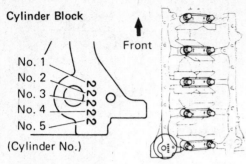

No. 1
No. 2
No. 3
No. 4
No. 5

(Cylinder No.)

Front

Crankshaft

Front

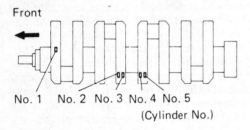

No. 1   No. 2   No. 3   No. 4   No. 5

(Cylinder No.)

Bearing

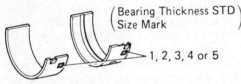

(Bearing Thickness STD)
Size Mark

1, 2, 3, 4 or 5

Location of main bearing codes

Cylinder Block No.	1	2	3	1	2	3	1	2	3
Crankshaft No.	0	0	0	1	1	1	2	2	2
Bearing No.	1	2	3	2	3	4	3	4	5

Example: Block mark "2", crankshaft mark "1" = bearing "3"

Main bearing selection table for 4A-LC and 4A-GE engines

Crankshaft Block Mark	1	2	3	1	2	3	1	2	3
Crankshaft Mark	0	0	0	1	1	1	2	2	2
Bearing Mark	1	2	3	3	2	4	3	4	5

Main bearing selection table for 4A-FE (Prizm) motors

7. Do not oil the lower bearing shells or the caps at this time. Install the bearing shells into the clean, dry caps.

8. Place a piece of plastic gauging material (such as Plastigage® or similar) lengthwise (fore-and-aft) across the full width of each of the five crankshaft main bearing journals. Remember that the measuring material is dissolved by oil. Keep the exposed part of the crank clean and dry.

9. Install the bearing caps with their bearing shells in their correct location and with the arrows pointing towards the front of the motor.

10. Install the bearing cap bolts and tighten them in three passes and in the correct sequence to 44 ft. lbs.

WARNING: *Do not rotate the crankshaft with the measuring plastic installed.*

11. Observing the correct removal sequence, gradually loosen and remove the bearing cap bolts. Carefully remove the bearing caps; the measuring media will be stuck to either the inside of the bearing shell or the face of the crankshaft.

12. Using the scale provided with the package of the measuring media, measure the gauging material at its widest point. This measurement represents the main bearing oil clearance and should be checked against the Crankshaft and Connecting Rod Specifications chart at the beginning of this chapter.

13. Remove every piece of the plastic gauging material from the crank and bearing caps. Coat the lower bearings (in the caps) with clean motor oil.

14. Install the main bearing caps and the lower thrust washers in the proper sequence. Make sure the arrows on the caps point towards the front (pulley end) of the motor.

15. Tighten the cap bolts in three passes and in the correct sequence to 44 ft. lbs.

16. Double check the endplay of the crank by repeating step 10 of this procedure.

17. Turn the crankshaft through one or two full clockwise rotations, making sure that it turns smoothly and evenly with no binding.

Cylinder Block

Most inspection and service work on the cylinder block should be handled by a machinist or professional engine rebuilding shop. Included in this work are bearing alignment checks, line boring, deck resurfacing, hot-tanking and cylinder block boring. Any or all of this work requires that the block be completely stripped of all components and transported to the shop. A block that has been checked and properly serviced will last much longer than one whose owner cut corners during a repair.

Cylinder de-glazing (honing) can be performed by the owner/mechanic who is careful and takes time to be accurate. The cylinder bores become glazed during normal operation of the engine as the rings ride up and down constantly. This shiny glaze must be removed in order for a new set of piston rings to seat properly.

Cylinder hones are available at most auto tool stores and parts jobbers. With the piston and rod assemblies removed from the block, cover the crankshaft completely with a rag to keep

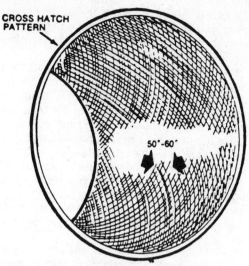

CROSS HATCH PATTERN

50°-60°

Cylinders should be honed to look like this

grit from collecting on it. Install the hone into the chuck of a variable speed drill (preferred in place of a constant speed drill) and insert the hone into the cylinder.

NOTE: *Make sure the drill and hone are kept square to the cylinder bore during the entire honing procedure.*

Start the hone and move it up and down in the cylinder at a rate which will produce approximately a 60° crosshatch pattern. DO NOT extend the hone below the bottom of the cylinder bore. After the crosshatched pattern is established, remove the hone and check the piston fit.

Remove the piston and wash the cylinder with a solution of detergent and water to remove the honing and cylinder grit. Wipe the bores out several times with a clean rag soaked in fresh engine oil. Remove the cover from the crankshaft and check closely to see that NO grit has found its way onto the crankshaft.

Flywheel and Ring Gear

REMOVAL AND INSTALLATION

NOTE: *This procedure may performed with the engine in the car, however, access will be cramped.*

1. Remove the transaxle, following procedures outlined in Chapter Seven.
2. For cars equipped with automatic transmissions:
   a. Matchmark the torque converter and the driveplate. Correct positioning will be required during reassembly.
   b. Remove the bolts holding the torque converter to the driveplate and remove the torque converter. DON'T drop it.

c. Matchmark the driveplate and the crankshaft.
   d. Loosen the retaining bolts a little at a time and in a criss-cross pattern. Support the driveplate as the last bolts are removed and then lift the driveplate away from the engine.
3. For manual transmission cars:
   a. Matchmark the pressure plate assembly and the flywheel.
   b. Loosen the pressure plate retaining bolts a little at a time and in a criss-cross pattern. Support the pressure plate and clutch assembly as the last bolt is removed and lift them away from the flywheel.

CAUTION: *The clutch disc contains asbestos, which has been determined to be a cancer causing agent. Never clean the clutch assembly with compressed air! Avoid inhaling dust from the clutch during disassembly. When cleaning components, use commercially available brake cleaning fluids.*

c. Matchmark the flywheel and crankshaft. Loosen the retaining bolts evenly and in a criss-cross pattern. Support the flywheel during removal of the last bolts and remove the flywheel.
4. Carefully inspect the teeth on the flywheel or driveplate for any signs of wearing or chipping. If anything beyond minimal contact wear is found, replace the unit.

NOTE: *Since the flywheel is driven by the starter gear, you would be wise to inspect the starter drive if any wear is found on the flywheel teeth. A worn starter can cause damage to the flywheel.*

5. When reassembling, place the flywheel or driveplate in position on the crankshaft and make sure the matchmarks align. Install the retaining bolts finger tight.
6. Tighten the bolts in a diagonal pattern and in three passes. Tighten the flywheel bolts (manual transmission) to 58 ft. lbs. or the driveplate bolts (automatic transmission) to 47 ft. lbs.
7. Install either the clutch and pressure plate assembly and tighten its mounting bolts to 14 ft. lbs. or the torque converter, tightening its mounting bolts to 20 ft. lbs. on Nova models and 31 ft. lbs. on Prizm models.

NOTE: *If the clutch appears worn or cracked in any way, replace it with a new disc, pressure plate and release bearing. The slight extra cost of the parts will prevent having to remove the transaxle again later.*

8. Reinstall the transaxle assembly.

RING GEAR REPLACEMENT

If the ring gear teeth on the driveplate or flywheel are damaged, the unit must be replaced.

The ring gear cannot be separated or reinstalled individually.

If a flywheel is replaced on a manual transmission car, the installation of a new clutch disc, pressure plate and release bearing is highly recommended.

EXHAUST SYSTEM

Safety Precautions

For a number of reasons, exhaust system work can be the most dangerous type of work you can do on your car. Always observe the following precautions:

• Support the car extra securely. Not only will you often be working directly under it, but you'll frequently be using a lot of force, say, heavy hammer blows, to dislodge rusted parts. This can cause a car that's improperly supported to shift and possibly fall.

• Wear goggles. Exhaust system parts are always rusty. Metal chips can be dislodged, even when you're only turning rusted bolts. Attempting to pry pipes apart with a chisel makes the chips fly even more frequently.

• If you're using a cutting torch, keep it a great distance from either the fuel tank or lines. Stop what you're doing and feel the temperature of the fuel bearing pipes on the tank frequently. Even slight heat can expand and/or vaporize fuel, resulting in accumulated vapor, or even a liquid leak, near your torch.

• Watch where your hammer blows fall and make sure you hit squarely. You could easily tap a brake or fuel line when you hit an exhaust system part with a glancing blow. Inspect all lines and hoses in the area where you've been working.

CAUTION: *Be very careful when working on or near the catalytic converter. External temperatures can reach 1,500°F (816°C) and more, causing severe burns. Removal or installation should be performed only on a cold exhaust system.*

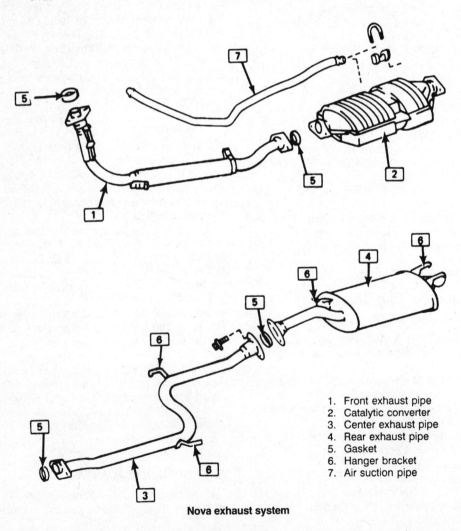

1. Front exhaust pipe
2. Catalytic converter
3. Center exhaust pipe
4. Rear exhaust pipe
5. Gasket
6. Hanger bracket
7. Air suction pipe

Nova exhaust system

Special Tools

A number of special exhaust system tools can be rented from auto supply houses or local stores that rent special equipment. A common one is a tail pipe expander, designed to enable you to join pipes of identical diameter.

It may also be quite helpful to use solvents designed to loosen rusted bolts or flanges. Soaking rusted parts the night before you do the job can speed the work of freeing rusted parts considerably. Remember that these solvents are often flammable. Apply only to parts after they are cool!

The exhaust system of the Nova and Prizm consists of four pieces. At the front of the car, the first section of pipe connects the exhaust manifold to the catalytic converter. On Prizm models, this pipe contains a section of flexible, braided pipe. The catalytic converter is a sealed, non-servicable unit which can be easily unbolted from the system and replaced if necessary.

An intermediate or center pipe containing a built-in resonator (pre-muffler) runs from the catalytic converter to the muffler at the rear of the car. Should the resonator fail, the entire pipe must be replaced. The muffler and tailpipe at the rear should always be replaced as a unit.

The exhaust system is attached to the body by several welded hooks and flexible rubber hangers; these hangers absorb exhaust vibrations and isolate the system from the body of the car. A series of metal heat shields runs along the exhaust piping, protecting the underbody from excess heat.

When inspecting or replacing exhaust system parts, make sure there is adequate clearance from all points on the body to avoid possible overheating fo the floorpan. Check the complete system for broken damaged, missing or poorly positioned parts. Rattles and vibrations in the exhaust system are usually caused by misalignment of parts. When aligning the system, leave all the nuts and bolts loose until everything is in its proper place, then tighten the hardware working from the front to the rear. Remember that what appears to be proper clearance during repair may change as the car moves down the road. The motion of the engine, body and suspension must be considered when replacing parts.

COMPONENT REMOVAL AND INSTALLATION

CAUTION: *DO NOT perform exhaust repairs with the engine or exhaust hot. Allow the system to cool completely before attempting any work.*

Also, exhaust systems are noted for sharp edges, flaking metal and rusted bolts. Gloves

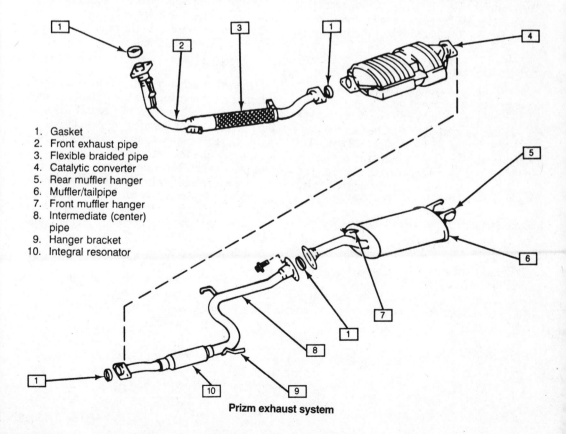

1. Gasket
2. Front exhaust pipe
3. Flexible braided pipe
4. Catalytic converter
5. Rear muffler hanger
6. Muffler/tailpipe
7. Front muffler hanger
8. Intermediate (center) pipe
9. Hanger bracket
10. Integral resonator

Prizm exhaust system

and eye protection are required. A healthy supply of penetrating oil and rags is highly recommended.

NOTE: *ALWAYS use a new gasket at each pipe joint whenever the joint is disassembled. Use new nuts and bolts to hold the joint properly. These two low-cost items will serve to prevent future leaks as the system ages.*

Front Pipe

1. Elevate and safely support the vehicle on jackstands.
2. Disconnect the oxygen sensor.
3. Remove the two bolts holding the pipe to the exhaust manifold.
4. Remove the two bolts holding the pipe to the catalytic converter.
5. Remove the bolts from the crossmember bracket and remove the pipe from under the car.
6. Attach the new pipe to the crossmember bracket. Install the bolts at both the manifold and the catalyst ends, leaving them finger tight until the pipe is correctly positioned. Make certain the gaskets are in place and straight.
7. Tighten the pipe-to-manifold bolts to 46 ft. lbs.
8. Tighten the bolts at the converter to 32 ft. lbs.
9. Reconnect the oxygen sensor.
10. Lower the vehicle to the ground, start the system and check for leaks. Small exhaust leaks will be most easily heard when the system is cold.

Catalytic Converter

With the car safely supported on jackstands, the converter is removed simply by removing the two bolts at either end. The Nova models have an air suction pipe attached to the converter which must be disconnected (2 bolts) before removal. When reinstalling the converter, install it with new gaskets and tighten the end bolts to 32 ft. lbs. Reconnect the air suction pipe (Nova) and lower the car to the ground.

Intermediate Pipe (Resonator Pipe)

1. Elevate and safely support the vehicle on jackstands.
2. Remove the two bolts holding the pipe to the catalytic converter.
3. Remove the bolts holding the intermediate pipe to the muffler inlet pipe.

4. Disconnect the rubber hangers and remove the pipe.
5. Install the new pipe by suspending it in place on the rubber hangers. Install the gaskets at each end and install the bolts finger tight.
6. Double check the placement of the pipe and insure proper clearance to all body and suspension components.
7. Tighten the bolts holding the pipe to the catalytic converter to 32 ft. lbs., then tighten the bolts to the muffler inlet pipe to 32 ft. lbs.
8. Lower the car to the ground. Start the engine and check for leaks.

Muffler and Tailpipe Assembly

1. Elevate and safely support the vehicle on jackstands.
2. Remove the two bolts holding the muffler inlet pipe to the intermediate pipe.
3. Disconnect the forward bracket on the muffler.
4. Disconnect the rear muffler bracket (three bolts) and remove the muffler from under the car.
5. When reinstalling, suspend the muffler from its front and rear hangers and check it for correct positioning under the body. If the old muffler had been rattling or hitting the body it is possible that the hangers and brackets have become bent from a light impact.
6. Attach the inlet pipe to the intermediate pipe and tighten the bolts to 32 ft. lbs.
7. Lower the vehicle to the ground, start the engine and check for leaks.

Complete System

If the entire exhaust system is to be replaced, it is much easier to remove the system as a unit than remove each individual piece. Disconnect the first pipe at the manifold joint and work towards the rear removing brackets and hangers as you go. Don't forget to disconnect the air suction pipe on the Nova catalytic converter. Remove the rear muffler bracket and slide the entire exhaust system out form under the car. The new system can then be bolted up on the workbench and easily checked for proper tightness and gasket integrity.

When installing the new assembly, suspend it from the flexible hangers first, then attach the fixed (solid) brackets. Check the clearance to the body and suspension and install the manifold joint bolts, tightening them to 46 ft. lbs.

Emission Controls

EMISSION CONTROLS

Component location and vacuum routing diagrams are located at the end of this chapter. Please refer to them before beginning any disassembly or testing.

There are three sources of automotive pollutants; crankcase fumes, exhaust gases, and gasoline evaporation. The pollutants formed from these substances fall into three categories: unburnt hydrocarbons (HC), carbon monoxide (CO), and oxides of nitrogen (NOx). The equipment used to limit these pollutants is called emission control equipment.

Due to varying state, federal, and provincial regulations, specific emission control equipment may vary by area of sale. The U.S. emission equipment is divided into two categories: California and 49 State. In this section, the term "California" applies only to cars originally built to be sold in California. Some California emissions equipment is not shared with equipment installed on cars built to be sold in the other 49 states. Models built to be sold in Canada also have specific emissions equipment, although in many cases the 49 State and Canadian equipment is the same.

Both carbureted and fuel injected cars require an assortment of systems and devices to control emissions. Newer cars rely more heavily on computer (ECM) management of many of the engine controls. This eliminates the many of the vacuum hoses and linkages around the engine. In the lists that follow, remember that not every component is found on every car.

ECM CONTROLLED SYSTEMS
- Fuel Evaporative Control (EVAP)
- Carburetor Feedback System
- Deceleration Fuel Cutoff
- Three-Way Oxidation Catalyst (TWC-OC or TWC)
- Cold Mixture Heater (CMH)

NON-ECM CONTROLLED SYSTEMS

- Positive Crankcase Ventilation (PCV)
- Throttle Positioner (TP)
- Exhaust Gas Recirculation (EGR)
- Air Suction (AS)
- High Altitude Compensation (HAC)
- Automatic Hot Air Intake (HAI)
- Hot Idle Compensation (HIC)
- Automatic Choke
- Choke Breaker (CB)
- Choker Opener
- Auxiliary Accelerator Pump (AAP)
- Heat Control Valve

Positive Crankcase Ventilation (PCV) System

SYSTEM OPERATION

A closed positive crankcase ventilation system is used on all Nova and Prizm models. This system cycles incompletely burned fuel which works its way past the piston rings back into the intake manifold for reburning with the fuel/air mixture. The oil filler cap is sealed and the air is drawn from the top of the crankcase into the intake manifold through a valve with a variable orifice.

This valve (commonly known as the PCV valve) regulates the flow of air into the manifold according to the amount of manifold vacuum. When the throttle plates are open fairly wide, the valve fully. However, at idle speed, when the manifold vacuum is at maximum, the PCV valve reduces the flow in order not to unnecessarily affect the small volume of mixture passing into the engine.

During most driving conditions, manifold vacuum is high and all of the vapor from the crankcase, plus a small amount of excess air, is drawn into the manifold via the PCV valve. At full throttle, the increase in the volume of blowby and the decrease in manifold vacuum make the flow via the PCV valve inadequate. Under these conditions, excess vapors are drawn into

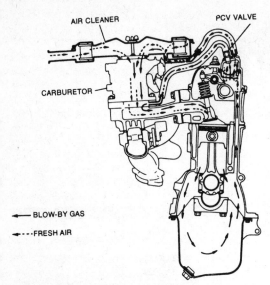

Typical positive crankcase ventilation system

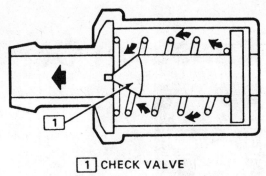

1 CHECK VALVE

Cross section of typical PCV valve. The valve should rattle when shaken

the air cleaner and pass into the engine along with the fresh air.

A plugged valve or hose may cause a rough idle, stalling or low idle speed, oil leaks in the engine and/or sludging and oil deposits within the engine and air cleaner. A leaking valve or hose could cause an erratic idle or stalling.

TESTING AND TROUBLESHOOTING

The PCV is easily checked with the engine running at normal idle speed (warmed up). Remove the PCV valve from the valve cover or intake manifold, but leave it connected to its hose. Place your thumb over the end of the valve to check for vacuum. If there is no vacuum, check for plugged hoses or ports. If these are open, the valve is faulty. With the engine off, remove the PCV valve completely. Shake it end to end, listening for the rattle of the needle inside the valve. If no rattle is heard, the needle is jammed (probably with oil sludge) and the valve should be replaced.

An engine which is operated without crankcase ventilation can be damaged very quickly. It is important to check and change the PCV valve at regular maintenance intervals.

REMOVAL AND INSTALLATION

Remove the PCV valve from the cylinder head cover or intake manifold. Remove the hose from the valve. Take note of which end of the valve was in the manifold. This one-way valve must be reinstalled correctly or it will not function. While the valve is removed, the hoses should be checked for splits, kinks and blockages. Check the vacuum port (that the hoses connect to) for any clogging.

Remember that the correct function of the

PCV system is based on a sealed engine--an air leak at the oil filler cap and/or around the oil pan can defeat the design of the system.

Evaporative Emission Control System (EVAP or EECS)
OPERATION

This system reduces hydrocarbon emissions by storing and routing evaporated fuel from the fuel tank and the carburetor's float chamber (carbureted Nova--4A-LC only) through the charcoal canister to the intake manifold for combustion in the cylinders at the proper time.

When the ignition is OFF, hydrocarbons from the carburetor float chamber pass through the control valve into the canister. Fuel vapors from the fuel tank pass into the charcoal canister through a check valve located on the canister.

When the ignition is switch ON, but the engine is NOT running, the control valve is energized blocking the movement of fuel vapor from the carburetor's float chamber. Vapors from the fuel tank can still flow and be stored in the charcoal canister.

With the engine running above 1500 rpm, the fuel vapors are purged from the canister into the intake manifold. If deceleration occurs, the throttle position switch opens (disconnects) and the ECM detects the change. The control valve is de-energized and the purging of vapor is stopped. This eliminates the delivery of excess fuel vapor during periods of poor or reduced combustion.

When there is pressure in the fuel tank (such as from summer heat or long periods of driving) the canister valve opens, allowing vapor to enter the canister and be stored for future delivery to the engine.

TESTING AND CHECKING

Before embarking on component removal or extensive diagnosis, perform a complete visual check of the system. Every vacuum line and vapor line (including the lines running to the tank) should be inspected for cracking, loose clamps, kinks and obstructions. Additionally, check the tank for any signs of deformation or crushing. Each vacuum port on the engine or manifold should be checked for restriction by dirt or sludge.

The evaporative control system is generally not prone to component failure in normal circumstances; most problems can be tracked to the causes listed above.

Fuel Filler Cap

Check that the filler cap seals effectively. Remove the filler cap and pull the safety valve outward to check for smooth operation. Replace the filler cap if the seal is defective or if it is not operating properly.

Charcoal Canister

1. Label and disconnect the lines running to the canister. Remove the charcoal canister from the vehicle.

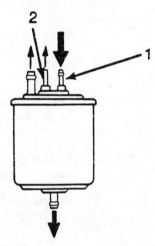

1. TANK PIPE
2. PURGE PIPE
Checking the charcoal canister

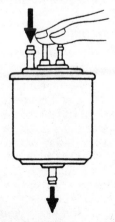

Cleaning the charcoal canister

2. Visually check the charcoal canister for cracks or damage.

3. Check for a clogged filter and stuck check valve. Using low pressure compressed air, blow into the tank pipe and check that the air flows without resistance from the other pipes. If this does not test positive replace the canister.

4. Clean the filter in the canister by blowing no more than 43 psi of compressed air into the pipe to the outer vent control valve while holding the other upper canister pipes closed.

> NOTE: *Do not attempt to wash the charcoal canister. Also be sure that no activated carbon comes out of the canister during the cleaning process.*

5. Replace or reinstall the canister as needed.

Outer Vent Control Valve

1. Label and disconnect the hoses from the control valve but leave the wiring for the valve connected.

2. Check that the valve is open by blowing air through it when the ignition switch is in the OFF position.

3. Check that the valve is closed when the ignition switch is in the ON position.

4. Reconnect the hoses to the proper locations. If the valve doesn't operate correctly, double check the fuse and wiring before replacing the valve.

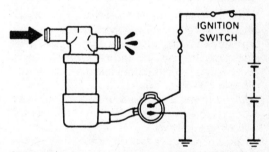

Check the outer vent control valve with the ignition OFF and ON. Note that there should be no flow with the ignition on

Thermo Switch (Nova)

1. Drain the coolant from the radiator into a clean container.

> CAUTION: *When draining the coolant, keep in mind that cats and dogs are attracted by the ethylene glycol antifreeze, and are quite likely to drink any that is left in an uncovered container or in puddles on the ground. This will prove fatal in sufficient quantity. Always drain the coolant into a sealable container. Coolant should be reused unless it is contaminated or several years old.*

2. Remove the thermoswitch from the intake manifold. The switch is located behind the TVSV (thermo vacuum switching valve).

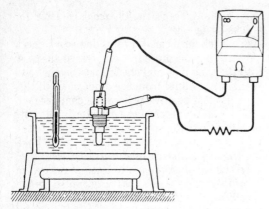

The Nova thermoswitch should have continuity if cooled below 109°F

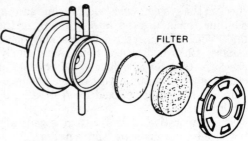

The EGR vacuum modulator filter

3. Cool the thermo switch off until the temperature is below 109°F (43°C). Check that there is continuity through the switch by the use of an ohmmeter.

4. Using hot water, bring the temperature of the switch to above 131°F (55°C). Check that there is no continuity when the switch is in water above this temperature.

5. Apply sealer to the threads of the switch and reinstall it in the manifold.

6. Refill the radiator with coolant.

REMOVAL AND INSTALLATION

Removal and installation of the various evaporative emission control system components consists of labeling and unfastening hoses, loosening retaining screws, and removing the part which is to be replaced from its mounting point.

NOTE: *When replacing any EVAP system hoses, always use hoses that are fuel-resistant or are marked EVAP. Use of hose which is not fuel-resistant will lead to premature hose failure.*

Exhaust Gas Recirculation (EGR) System

OPERATION

The EGR system reduces oxides of nitrogen. This is accomplished by recirculating some of the exhaust gases through the EGR valve to the intake manifold, lowering peak combustion temperatures.

Whenever the engine coolant is below 122°F (50°C), the thermostatic vacuum switching valve (TVSV) connects manifold vacuum to the EGR vacuum modulator and at the same time to the EGR valve.

The EGR vacuum modulator controls the EGR valve by modulating the vacuum signal with an atmospheric bleed. This bleed is controlled by the amount of exhaust pressure acting on the bottom of the EGR vacuum modulator (diaphragm).

Since recirculation of exhaust gas is undesirable at low rpm or idle, the system limits itself by sensing the exhaust flow. Under low load conditions, such as low speed driving, the exhaust pressure is low. In this state, the diaphragm in the modulator is pushed down by spring force and the modulator valve opens to allow outside air into the vacuum passage. The vacuum in the line is reduced, the EGR valve does not open as far, and the amount of recirculation is reduced.

Under high load conditions or high rpm driving, the exhaust pressure is increased. This pushes the modulator diaphragm upwards and closes the bleed valve. A full vacuum signal is transmitted to the EGR valve; it opens completely and allows full recirculation. The slight reduction in combustion temperature (and therefore power) is not noticed at highway speeds or under hard acceleration.

Prizm vehicles also control the EGR with a vacuum solenoid valve (VSV). This device allows the ECM to further control the EGR under certain conditions. The ECM will electrically close the VSV if the engine is not warmed up, the throttle valve is in the idle position or if the engine is under very hard acceleration. Aside from these conditions, the Prizm EGR operates in accordance with the normal vacuum modulator function.

TESTING AND SERVICING

Carbureted Nova w/4A-LC Engine

EGR SYSTEM OPERATION

1. Check and clean the filter in the EGR vacuum modulator. Use compressed air (if possible) to blow the dirt out of the filters and check the filters for contamination or damage.

2. Using a tee (3-way connector), connect a vacuum gauge to the hose between the EGR valve and the vacuum pipe.

3. Check the seating of the EGR valve by starting the engine and seeing that it runs at a smooth idle. If the valve is not completely closed, the idle will be rough.

4. With the engine coolant temperature below 122°F (50°C), the vacuum gauge should read zero at 2000 rpm. This indicates that the thermostatic vacuum control valve (TVCV) is functioning correctly at this temperature range.

5. Warm the engine to normal operating temperature. Check the vacuum gauge and confirm low vacuum at 2000 rpm. This indicates the TVSV and the EGR vacuum modulator are working correctly in this temperature range.

6. Disconnect the vacuum hose from the **R** port on the EGR vacuum modulator and, using another piece of hose, connect the **R** port directly to the intake manifold. Check that the vacuum gauge indicates high vacuum at 2,000 rpm.

NOTE: *As a large amount of exhaust gas enters, the engine will misfire slightly at this time.*

7. Disconnect the vacuum gauge and reconnect the vacuum hoses to their proper locations.

8. Check the EGR valve by applying vacuum directly to the valve with the engine at idle. (This may be accomplished wither by bridging vacuum directly from the intake manifold or by using a hand-held vacuum pump.) The engine should falter and die as the full load of recirculated gasses enters the engine.

9. If no problem is found with this inspection, the system is OK; otherwise inspect each part.

THERMOSTATIC VACUUM SWITCHING VALVE

1. Drain the cooling system.
CAUTION: *When draining the coolant, keep in mind that cats and dogs are attracted by the ethylene glycol antifreeze, and are quite likely to drink any that is left in an uncovered container or in puddles on the ground. This will prove fatal in sufficient quantity. Always drain the coolant into a sealable container. Coolant should be reused unless it is contaminated or several years old.*

2. Remove the thermostatic vacuum switching valve.

3. Cool the thermostatic vacuum switching valve to below 45°F (7°C).

4. Check that air flows from pipe **J** to pipes **M** and **L**, and flows from pipe **K** to pipe **N**.

5. Heat the thermostatic vacuum switching valve to 63-122°F (17-50°C) generally room temperature).

6. Check that air flows from pipe **K** to pipes **N** and **L** and flows from pipe **J** to pipe **M**.

7. Heat the TVSV to above 154°F (68°C).

8. Check that air flows from the pipe **K** to

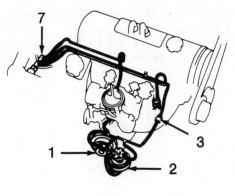

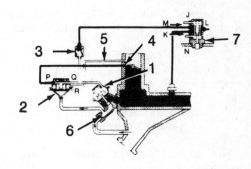

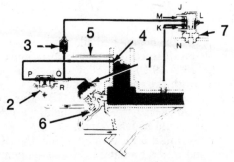

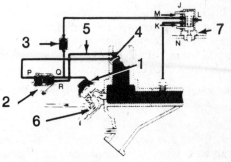

1. E.G.R. valve
2. E.G.R. vacuum modulator
3. Check valve
4. E.G.R. port
5. E.G.R. "R" port
6. Pressure chamber
7. Thermostatic vacuum switching valve

EGR system components

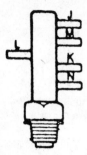

Port identification for testing the TVSV. Make sure you label each hose during disassembly

pipes **M** and **L**, and does **NOT** flow from pipe **J** to any other pipes.

9. Apply liquid sealer to the threads of the TVSV and reinstall.

10. Refill the cooling system.

11. If a problem is found with any of the above procedures, replace the valve

EGR VALVE

1. Remove the EGR valve.

2. Check the valve for sticking and heavy carbon deposits. If a problem is found, replace the valve.

3. Reinstall the EGR valve with a new gasket.

EGR VACUUM MODULATOR

1. Label and disconnect the vacuum hoses from ports **P**, **Q**, and **R** of the EGR vacuum modulator.

2. Plug the **Q** and **R** ports with your fingers.

3. Blow air into port **P**. Check that the air passes freely through the sides of the air filter side.

4. Start the engine and maintain 2,000 rpm.

5. Repeat the test above. Check that there is a strong resistance to air flow.

6. Reconnect the vacuum hoses to the proper locations.

CHECK VALVE

Inspect the check valve (one-way valve) by gently blowing air into each end of the valve or hose. Air should flow from the orange pipe to the black pipe but SHOULD NOT flow from the black pipe to the orange pipe.

Fuel Injected Nova (4A-GE) and Prizm (4A-FE)

EGR SYSTEM OPERATION
4A-GE

1. Check and clean the filter in the EGR vacuum modulator. Use compressed air (if possible) to blow the dirt out of the filters and check the filters for contamination or damage.

2. Using a tee (3-way connector), connect a vacuum gauge to the hose between the EGR valve and the vacuum pipe.

3. Check the seating of the EGR valve by starting the engine and seeing that it runs at a smooth idle. If the valve is not completely closed, the idle will be rough.

4. With the engine coolant temperature below 95°F (35°C), the vacuum gauge should read zero at 3500 rpm. This indicates that the bi-metal vacuum switching valve (BVSV) is functioning correctly at this temperature range.

5. Warm the engine to normal operating temperature. Check the vacuum gauge and confirm low vacuum at 3500 rpm. This indicates the BVSV and the EGR vacuum modulator are working correctly in this temperature range.

6. Disconnect the vacuum hose from the **R** port on the EGR vacuum modulator and, using another piece of hose, connect the **R** port directly to the intake manifold. Check that the vacuum gauge indicates high vacuum at 3500 rpm.

NOTE: *As a large amount of exhaust gas enters, the engine will misfire slightly at this time.*

7. Disconnect the vacuum gauge and reconnect the vacuum hoses to their proper locations.

8. Check the EGR valve by applying vacuum directly to the valve with the engine at idle. (This may be accomplished either by bridging vacuum directly from the intake manifold or by using a hand-held vacuum pump.) The engine should falter and die as the full load of recirculated gasses enters the engine.

9. If no problem is found with this inspection, the system is OK; otherwise inspect each part.

EGR VALVE

1. Remove the EGR valve.

2. Check the valve for sticking and heavy carbon deposits. If a problem is found, replace the valve.

3. Reinstall the EGR valve with a new gasket.

EGR VALVE
4A-FE

1. Start the engine and allow it to warm up completely. The coolant temperature must be above 120°F (49°C). The following tests are performed with the engine running.

2. Place a finger on the EGR valve diaphragm. Accelerate the engine slightly; the diaphragm should be felt to move.

3. Disconnect a vacuum hose from the EGR valve and connect a hand held vacuum pump.

4. Apply 10 inches of vacuum to the valve. The diaphragm should move (check again with your finger) and the engine may momentarily run rough or stall.

5. An EGR valve failing either of these quick

tests should be replaced. The valves cannot be cleaned or adjusted.

EGR VACUUM MODULATOR
4A-CE

1. Label and disconnect the vacuum hoses from ports **P**, **Q**, and **R** of the EGR vacuum modulator.
2. Plug the **P** and **R** ports with your fingers.
3. Blow air into port **Q**. Check that the air passes freely through the sides of the air filter.
4. Start the engine and maintain 3500 rpm.
5. Repeat the test above. Check that there is a strong resistance to air flow.
6. Reconnect the vacuum hoses to the proper locations.

Vacuum Switching Valve (Nova)

1. The vacuum switching valve is located on the left strut tower. The vacuum switching circuit is checked by blowing air into the pipe under the following conditions:

　a. Connect the vacuum switching valve terminals to the battery.

　b. Blow into the tube and check that the VSV switch is open.

　c. Disconnect the positive battery terminal.

　d. Blow into the tube and check that the VSV switch is closed (no flow).

2. Check for a short circuit within the valve. Using an ohmmeter, check that there is no continuity between the positive terminal and the VSV body. If there is continuity, replace the VSV.

3. Check for an open circuit. Using an ohmmeter, measure the resistance (ohms) between the two terminals of the valve. The resistance should be 38-44Ω at 68°F (20°C). If the resistance is not within specifications, replace the VSV.

NOTE: *The resistance--ohmmage--will vary slightly with temperature. It will decrease in cooler temperatures and increase with heat. Use common sense; slight variations due to*

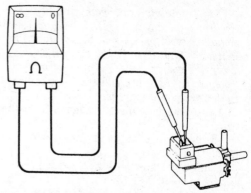

Checking the resistance on the vacuum suction valve

temperature range are not necessarily a sign of a failed valve.

Bi-metal Vacuum Switching Valve (BVSV)
4A-GE and 4A-FE Engines

Despite the impressive name, this valve does nothing more than allow vacuum to flow through the system depending on engine coolant temperature. The bi-metallic element within the switch reacts to temperature changes, opening or closing the valve at a pre-determined level. To test the valve:

1. Drain the coolant from the radiator into a suitable container.

CAUTION: *When draining the coolant, keep in mind that cats and dogs are attracted by*

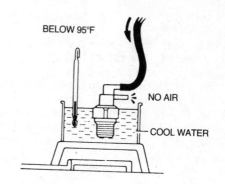

BELOW 95°F

NO AIR

COOL WATER

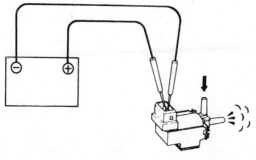

VACUUM SWITCHING VALVE

The vacuum switching valve allows air to pass when electricity is applied

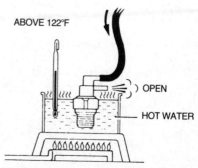

ABOVE 122°F

OPEN

HOT WATER

Testing the BVSV for correct function

the ethylene glycol antifreeze, and are quite likely to drink any that is left in an uncovered container or in puddles on the ground. This will prove fatal in sufficient quantity. Always drain the coolant into a sealable container. Coolant should be reused unless it is contaminated or several years old.

2. Label and disconnect the hoses from the BVSV.

3. Remove the valve from the intake manifold.

4. Using cool water, cool the threaded part of the valve to below 95°F (35°C). Blow air into the upper (center) port; there should be NO air passage through the valve. It does not allow vacuum to pass until the engine warms up.

5. Using warm water, heat the threaded part of the valve to above 122°F (50°C) and blow into the port again. The valve should allow the air to pass through.

If a problem is found with either the "on" or "off" functions of the valve, replace it with a new one.

6. Using an ohmmeter, measure the resistance between the terminal on the VSV. Resistance should be 33-39Ω at 68°F (20°C).

7. Apply liquid sealer to the threads of the BVSV and reinstall it. Connect the vacuum lines.

8. Refill the radiator with coolant.

EGR VACUUM MODULATOR
4A-FE

1. Label and remove the three hoses from the modulator.

2. Place your fingers over ports **P** and **R**; blow into port **Q**. Air should flow freely from the sides of the air filter on the modulator.

3. Connect a vacuum pump to port **S** (on the bottom of the unit) and plug tubes **P** and **R** with your fingers. Blow air into tube **Q** and attempt to draw a vacuum with the pump. You SHOULD NOT be able to develop a vacuum within the system.

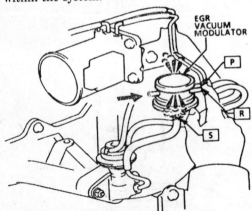

Port designations for Prizm EGR vacuum modulator

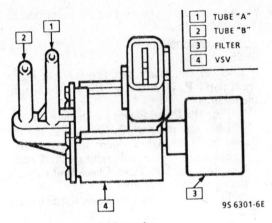

1	TUBE "A"
2	TUBE "B"
3	FILTER
4	VSV

9S 6301-6E

Prizm vacuum switching valve

4. If the modulator fails any of these tests, it must be replaced.

VACUUM SWITCHING VALVE (VSV)
4A-FE

1. Label and disconnect the two hoses from the VSV.

2. With the ignition OFF, disconnect the connector at the VSV.

3. Check the resistance between the two terminals on the VSV. Look for 33-39Ω resistance. If the resistance is incorrect, replace the unit. If the resistance is proper, proceed with the next step.

4. Gently blow air into port **A**. Air should come out through the filter but SHOULD NOT come out through port **B**.

5. Reconnect the electrical connector.

6. Turn the ignition switch ON (but don't start the motor) and ground the Diagnosis Switch Terminal. This is found in the diagnostic connector near the air cleaner assembly and is labeled as terminal **T**. Use a jumper wire with clips to ground the terminal.

WARNING: *Be careful not to ground other terminals in the connector (even accidentally)--severe electrical damage may result!*

7. Blow air into port **A**; the air should exit through port **B**.

8. If the VSV fails either of the air flow tests, it should be replaced.

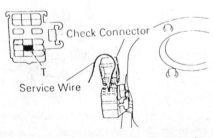

Location of terminal T in the check connector

REMOVAL AND INSTALLATION OF COMPONENTS

Exhaust emission control equipment is generally simple to work on and easy to get to on the motor. The air cleaner assembly will need to be removed. Always label each vacuum hose before removing it--they must be replaced in the correct position.

Most of the valves and solenoids are made of plastic, particularly at the vacuum ports. Be very careful during removal not to break or crack the ports; you have almost no chance of regluing a broken fitting. Remember that the plastic has been in a hostile environment (heat and vibration); the fittings become brittle and less resistant to abuse or accidental impact.

EGR valves are generally held in place by two bolts. The bolts can be difficult to remove due to corrosion. Once the EGR is off the engine, clean the bolts and the bolt holes of any rust or debris. Always replace the gasket any time the EGR valve is removed.

Oxygen Sensor

The oxygen (O_2) sensor is located on the exhaust manifold to detect the concentration of oxygen in the exhaust gas. Using highly refined metals (zirconia and platinum), the sensor uses changes in the oxygen content to generate an electrical signal which is transmitted to the ECM. The computer in turn reacts to the signal by adjusting the fuel metering at the injectors or at the carburetor. More or less fuel is delivered into the cylinders and the correct oxygen level is maintained.

4A-LC ENGINE

1. Warm up the engine to normal operating temperature.
2. Connect the voltmeter to the service connector. This round, green connector is located behind the right shock tower. Connect the positive probe to the OX terminal and the negative probe to the **E** terminal.
3. Run the engine at 2500 rpm for 90 seconds or more. This allows the sensor to achieve a stable temperature and the exhaust flow to stabilize.
4. Maintain the engine at 2500 rpm and check the meter. The meter needle should fluctuate at least 8 times in 10 seconds in the 0-6 volt range. This indicates that the sensor is working properly.
5. If the sensor fails the test, perform a careful inspection of all the wiring and connectors in the system. A loose connection can cause the sensor to fail this test. Repeat the voltage test after the inspection.

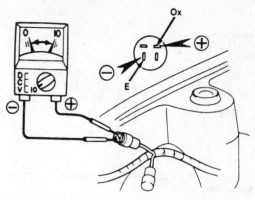

Testing hook-up for 4A-LC oxygen sensor

4A-GE

1. Warm up the engine to normal operating temperature.
2. Connect the voltmeter to the check connector. Hook the negative probe to terminal **VF** and the positive probe to terminal **E1**.
3. Run the engine at 2500 rpm for at least 90 seconds.
4. With the engine speed being maintained at 2500 rpm, use a jumper wire to connect terminals **T** and **E1** at the check connector.
5. Watch the voltmeter and note the number of times the needle fluctuates in 10 seconds. If it moves eight times or more, the sensor is working properly.

   a. If the needle moves less than eight times but more than zero, disconnect the terminal **T-to-E1** jumper. Still maintaining 2500 rpm, measure the voltage between terminals **E1** and **VF**. If the voltage is above zero, replace the oxygen sensor. If the voltage is zero, read and record the diagnostic codes (refer to "Check Engine Light and Diagnostic Codes" later in this chapter) and repair the necessary items.

   b. If the needle does not move at all (zero), read and record the trouble codes and repair the affected system.

NOTE: *Perform a careful inspection of all*

Voltmeter

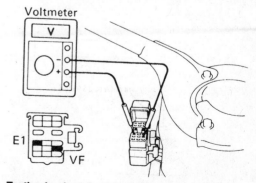

Testing hook-up for the 4A-GE oxygen sensor

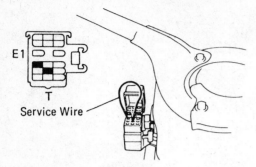

Location of terminal E1 and T on Prizm check engine connector

the wiring and connectors in the system. A loose connection can cause the sensor to fail these tests. Repeat the voltage test after the inspection. (Refer to "Check Engine Light and Diagnostic Codes" later in this chapter.)

4A-FE

WARNING: *Use only a 10MΩ digital voltmeter. Use of any other type of equipment may damage the ECM or other components.*

1. Warm the car up to normal operating temperature.

2. Run the engine above 1200 rpm for at least two minutes.

3. Trace the wiring from the sensor to the first connector. Clean the wiring so that the blue and white wires are easily seen as well as the black and brown wires entering the connector from the other side.

4. With the engine running at 1200 rpm, place the positive probe of the meter into the back of the connector at the black wire. Connect the negative probe of the meter to a known good ground.

5. The meter should vary between 0 and 1 volt. If this is true, the sensor is working properly.

6. If the voltage does not vary from 0 to 1 volt, disconnect the oxygen sensor at the connector. Using a jumper wire, connect the black

wire to ground. The voltmeter should display voltage less than 0.2v (200 mV) with the engine running. If the displayed voltage is at or less than 0.2v, either the sensor or the sensor connection has failed.

7. If the voltage is above 0.2v in the previous test, remove the jumper wire. Turn the engine off, then turn the ignition to the ON position without starting the motor. Recheck the voltage in the black wire:

    a. Voltage of 0.3-0.6v shows that the ECM is faulty.

    b. Voltage over 0.6 volts indicates a possibly faulty ECM, a bad connection or an open (break) in the brown wire.

    c. Voltage less than 0.3 volts indicates a possibly faulty ECM, a bad connection or an open (break) in the black wire.

REMOVAL AND INSTALLATION

WARNING: *Care should be used during the removal of the oxygen sensor. Both the sensor and its wire can be easily damaged.*

1. The best condition in which to remove the sensor is with the engine in a "mid-warm" state. This is generally achieved after two to five minutes (depending on outside temperature) of running after a cold start. The exhaust manifold has developed enough heat to expand and make the removal easier but is not so hot that it has become untouchable.

Wearing heat resistant gloves is highly recommended during this repair.

2. With the ignition OFF, disconnect the wiring for the sensor.

3. Unscrew the oxygen sensor from the manifold.

NOTE: *Special wrenches, either socket or open-end, are available from reputable retail outlets for removing the oxygen sensor. These tools make the job much easier and often prevent un-necessary damage.*

4. During and after the removal, use great care to protect the tip of the sensor if it is to be reused. Do not allow it to come in contact with

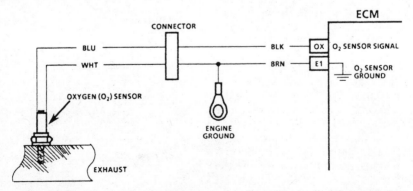

Wiring for Prizm oxygen sensor. Connect test probes at the back of the connector

fluids or dirt. Do not attempt to clean it or wash it.

5. When re-installing, apply a coat of anti-seize compound to the threads but DO NOT allow any to get on the tip of the sensor. This includes any accidental or momentary contact from rags, etc.

Some replacement sensors come with the compound already on the threads. Do not remove it or try to clean it.

6. Install the sensor in the manifold. Tighten it to 30 ft. lbs.

7. Reconnect the electrical connector and insure a clean, tight connection.

3-Way and Oxidation Catalyst (TWC-OC) System

OPERATION

The catalytic converter is a muffler-like container built into the exhaust system to aid in the reduction of HC, CO and NOx emissions by changing them into nitrogen, carbon dioxide and water vapor through the action of the catalyst upon the exhaust gas.

The 3-way catalytic convertor is the best type to use since it can change all three types of emissions into non-polluting gases. In this type of converter nitrous oxides are chemically reduced by the catalyst and reformed into the molecules of oxygen and nitrogen. The oxygen formed by the reduction reaction is then used to oxidize carbon monoxide and the hydrocarbons, forming carbon dioxide and water vapor.

For the catalytic converter to work most efficiently, the following conditions must be met:
- Operating temperature must be over 500°F (260°C).
- Air/fuel ratio must be held closely at 14.7:1.

PRECAUTIONS

- Use only unleaded fuel.
- Avoid prolonged idling; the engine should run no longer than 20 minutes at curb idle, nor longer than 10 minutes at fast idle.
- Reduce the fast idle speed, by quickly depressing and releasing the accelerator pedal, as soon as the coolant temperature reaches 120°F (49°C).
- DO NOT disconnect any spark plug leads while the engine is running.
- Always make engine compression checks as quickly as possible. Excess fuel can be pumped through the motor and build up in the converter.
- DO NOT dispose of the catalyst in a place where anything coated with grease, gas, or oil is present; spontaneous combustion could result.
- Since the inside of the catalyst must reach 500°F (260°C) to work efficiently, the outside of the converter will also become very hot. Always be aware of what may be under the car when you park. Parking a hot exhaust system over dry grass, leaves or other flammable items may lead to a fire.

Feedback Carburetor System

OPERATION

The Carburetor Feedback system is designed to keep the air/fuel ratio at an optimum 14.7:1 during normal operation; excluding warm-up and acceleration.

This is a rather simple system. The carburetor is designed to run richer than it normally should. This sets up a rich limit of system operation. When a leaner operation is desired, the computer (ECM) commands air to bleed into the carburetor's main metering system and

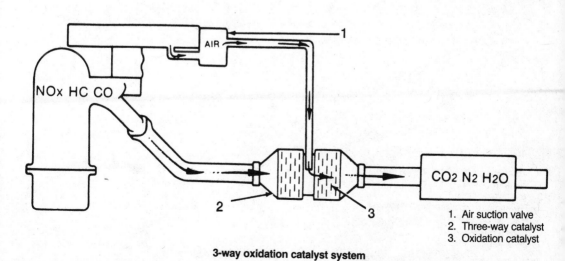

1. Air suction valve
2. Three-way catalyst
3. Oxidation catalyst

3-way oxidation catalyst system

into the carburetor's primary bore. A lean operating condition is therefore easy to obtain.

The computer (ECM) receives information from the oxygen sensor, two vacuum switches and the distributor.

The output of the computer is a signal to the electric air bleed control valve (EBCV). When the EBCV is energized, it bleeds air into the main air bleed circuit and into the slow air bleed port of the carburetor. This additional air leans the fuel mixture. When the EBCV is not energized, the air/fuel ratio moves towards the rich limit.

With the engine running and the coolant temperature below 45°F (7°C), the thermostatic vacuum switch valve (TVSV) applies atmospheric pressure to vacuum switch **B** by connecting ports **J** to **L** (of the TVSV). With these conditions, vacuum switch **B** is de-energized, the electric bleed control valve (EBCV) is off (de-energized) and both air bleeds are off. The carburetor is therefore operating toward its rich limits, desirable on a cold motor. The computer will not be controlling or influencing air/fuel ratio while the engine is cold.

When the coolant temperature rises above 60°F (16°C), with the engine operating between 1500 and 4200 rpm, the thermostatic vacuum switching valve (TVSV) applies vacuum to vacuum switch **B** by connecting ports **K** to **L** of the TVSV.

Vacuum switch **B** closes, signaling the ECM. Vacuum switch **A** is closed (opens at high vacuum) also signaling the ECM. With these two switches closed, if the oxygen sensor senses a rich condition in the exhaust (high voltage-1.0v), the ECM commands the electric bleed control valve to be energized, bleeding air into the main metering system of the carburetor and the intake manifold. This action results in the air/fuel ratio becoming leaner.

Once the air/fuel ratio is detected as being too lean by the oxygen sensor (low voltage-0.1v), the ECM will de-energize the EBCV and close both bleed ports. By shutting off the air, the mixture begins moving back towards the rich limit. The system is operating in the "closed loop" mode, during which it will adjust itself and then react to the adjustments. It should be noted that to energize the electric bleed control valve (EBCV) the ECM completes its electrical circuit on its ground side.

TESTING

Checking the Carburetor Feedback System

1. Check the TVSV with the engine cold. The coolant temperature must be below 45°F (7°C).

2. Disconnect the vacuum hose from the vacuum switch **B**. Start the engine and check no vacuum is felt in the disconnected vacuum hose.

3. Reconnect the vacuum hose and check the EBCV with the engine warmed up to normal operating temperature.

4. Disconnect the EBCV connector. Maintain an engine speed of approximately 2,500 rpm.

5. Reconnect the connector and check that the engine speed drops by about 300 rpm momentarily.

6. With the engine at idle, repeat the disconnect/reconnect test on the EBCV connnector. Check that the engine speed does NOT change.

7. Disconnect the hose from the vacuum switch **B**. Repeat steps 4 and 5 above. Check that the engine speed does not change.

8. If no problems are found with this inspection, the system is operating properly; otherwise inspect each component part.

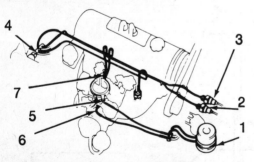

1. Electronic air bleed control valve (EBCV)
2. Vacuum switch "A"
3. Vacuum switch "B"
4. Thermostatic vacuum switching valve
5. Main air bleed port
6. Slow air bleed port
7. Throttle positioner port

Feedback carburetor component location

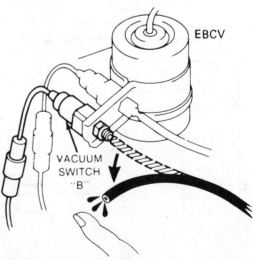

EBCV and Vacuum switch

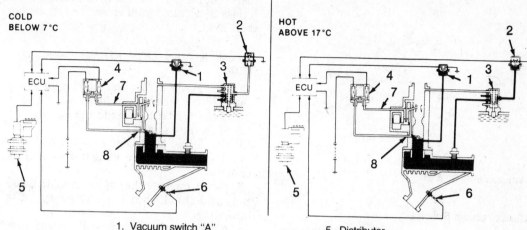

1. Vacuum switch "A"
2. Vacuum switch "B"
3. Thermostatic vacuum switching valve
4. Electronic air bleed control valve
5. Distributor
6. Oxygen sensor
7. Main air bleed port
8. Slow air bleed port

Feedback carburetor system operation

Checking the Air Bleed Control Valve (EBCV)

1. Check for a short circuit. Using an ohmmeter, check that there is no continuity between the positive (+) terminal (the terminal closest to the lock tab) and the EBCV body. If there is continuity, replace the EBCV.

2. Check for an open circuit. Using an ohmmeter, measure the resistance between the positive (+) terminal and the other terminal. The resistance should be between 11-13Ω at 68°F (20°C). If the resistance is not within specification, replace the EBCV. Remember that the resistance will vary slightly with temperature. Resistance (ohms) will decrease as the temperature drops. Use common sense here--a reading of 16 ohms on a hot day does not necessarily indicate a failed valve.

Checking Vacuum Switch A

1. Using an ohmmeter, check that there is continuity between the switch terminal and the switch body.

2. Start the engine and run it until normal operating temperature is reached.

3. Using an ohmmeter, check that there is NO continuity between the switch terminal and the switch body.

4. If either test is failed, replace the switch.

By means of a signal from the Ox sensor, carburetor primary side main air bleed and slow air bleed volume are controlled to maintain optimum air-fuel mixture in accordance with existing driving conditions, thereby cleaning HC, CO and NOx. In addition, driveability and fuel economy are improved.

Coolant Temp.	TVSV	Condition	Engine rpm	Vacuum S/W		Air Fuel Ratio in the Exhaust Manifold	Ox Sensor Signal	Computer	EBCV	Air Bleed
				A	B					
Below 7°C (45°F)	OPEN (J-L)	—	—	—	OFF	—	—	OFF	CLOSED	OFF
Above 17°C (63°F)	OPEN (K-L)	Idling	Below 1,300 rpm	—	—	—	—	OFF	CLOSED	OFF
		Cruising	Between 1,500 and 4,200	ON	ON	RICH	RICH	ON	OPEN	Feedback air bleed
						LEAN	LEAN	OFF	CLOSED	
			Above 4,400 rpm	—	—	—	—	OFF	CLOSED	OFF
		Heavy loads*	—	ON	OFF	—	—	OFF	CLOSED	OFF
		Deceleration	Above 1,500 rpm	OFF	ON	—	—	ON	OPEN	ON

Remark: *Intake vacuum: below 85 mmHg (3.35 in.Hg, 11.3 kPa)

Feedback carburetor system operation

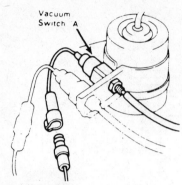

Vacuum switch "A"

Check Vacuum Switch B

1. Using an ohmmeter, check that there is NO continuity between the switch terminal and the switch body.
2. Start the engine and run until normal operating temperature is reached.
3. Using an ohmmeter, check that there is continuity between the switch terminal and the body.
4. If either test is failed, replace the switch.

Deceleration Fuel Cut-Off System

OPERATION

This system cuts off part of the fuel flow to the idle (or slow) circuit of the carburetor to prevent overheating and afterburning in the exhaust system. The first fuel cut solenoid is kept energized by the ECM whenever the engine is running. The only exception is if the vacuum signal is above 8.46 in.Hg with the rpm above 2290. (This combination will be sensed by the ECM when the vacuum switch A de-energizes with a vacuum signal above its calibrated value.) With the first fuel cut-off solenoid valve de-energized, the carburetor's slow (or idle) circuit

fuel is cut off. This will occur whenever the vehicle is decelerated from an engine rpm higher than 2290.

CHECKING THE OPERATION OF THE FUEL CUT-OFF SYSTEM

NOTE: *Perform this test quickly to avoid overheating the catalytic converter.*
1. Connect a tachometer to the engine.
2. Start the engine.
3. Check that the engine runs normally.
4. Disconnect the vacuum switch **A** connector.
5. Slowly increase the engine speed to 2,300 rpm, and check that the engine speed is fluctuating.
6. Reconnect the vacuum switch connector. Again slowly increase the engine speed to 2,300 rpm and check that the engine operation returns to normal.
7. If no problem is found with this test, the system is working properly. If any problem is found, inspect each component part.

CHECKING THE FIRST FUEL CUT-OFF SOLENOID VALVE

1. Remove the two-wire solenoid valve from the carburetor.
CAUTION: *Gasoline may run from the carburetor. Observe no smoking/no open flame precautions. Have a dry powder (Type B-C) fire extinguisher within reach at all times.*
2. Apply 12v to one of the solenoid wires while grounding the other.
3. You should be able to feel a distinct click within the solenoid as the circuit is completed and released. This shows that the solenoid is engaging and disengaging properly.
4. Check the O-ring for damage.
5. Reinstall the valve and connect the wiring connector.

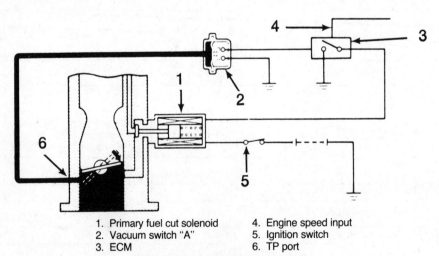

1. Primary fuel cut solenoid
2. Vacuum switch "A"
3. ECM
4. Engine speed input
5. Ignition switch
6. TP port

Deceleration fuel cut-off components

This system cuts off part of the fuel in the slow circuit of the carburetor to prevent overheating and afterburning in the exhaust system.

Engine RPM	Vacuum in the Vacuum S/W	Vacuum S/W (A)	Computer	1st Fuel Cut Solenoid Valve	Slow Circuit in Carburetor
Below 1,900 rpm	—	—	ON	ON	OPEN
Above 2,290 rpm	Below 180 mm Hg 7.09 in. Hg 24.0 kPa	ON	ON	ON	OPEN
	Above 215 mm Hg 8.46 in. Hg 28.7 kPa	OFF	OFF	OFF	CLOSED

Deceleration fuel cut-off system operation

Cold Mixture Heater (CMH)

OPERATION

The cold-mixture heater (CMH) system reduces cold engine emissions and improves driveability during engine warm-up. The intake manifold is heated during cold engine warm-up to accelerate vaporization of the liquid fuel.

The computer looks at alternator terminal **L** to determine if the engine is running and also watches the engine's coolant temperature. If the engine is running and the coolant temperature is below 109°F (43°C), the computer energizes the cold mixture heater relay, which in turn applies battery voltage to the cold mixture heater. The CMH is a multi-element heater ring that is mounted between the carburetor base and the intake manifold. Once the coolant temperature exceeds 131°F (55°C) the CMH relay is de-energized and the heater elements turn off.

TESTING

Checking the Cold Mixture System Operation

1. Start the engine. The coolant temperature must be below 109°F (43°C).
2. Using a voltmeter, check that there is voltage between the positive (+) terminal (white/red wire) and the ground.
WARNING: *The voltmeter probe should be inserted from the rear side of the connector.*
3. Allow the engine to warm up and check the CHM with the engine warm. The coolant temperature should be above 131°F (55°C).
4. Using a voltmeter, check that there is NO voltage. If no problem is found with this inspection, the system is working properly.

Checking the Mixture Heater

1. Unplug the wiring connector.
2. Using an ohmmeter, check the resistance between the heater terminals. The resistance

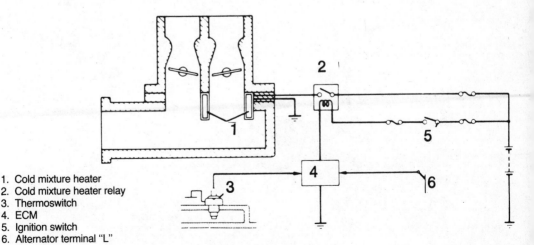

1. Cold mixture heater
2. Cold mixture heater relay
3. Thermoswitch
4. ECM
5. Ignition switch
6. Alternator terminal "L"

Cold mixture heater system

To reduce cold engine emission and improve driveability, the intake manifold is heated during cold engine operation to accelerate vaporization of the liquid fuel.

IG S/W	Engine	Coolant Temp.	Thermo S/W	ECM	CMH Relay	CMH
OFF	Not running	—	—	—	OFF	OFF
ON	Not running	—	—	OFF	OFF	OFF
	Running	Below 43°C (109°F)	ON	ON	ON	ON (Heated)
		Above 55°C (131°F)	OFF	OFF	OFF	OFF

Cold mixture heater operation chart

should be 0.5-2.0Ω. Readings outside this range require replacement of the heater element.

3. Replug the wiring connector.

Checking the Cold Mixture Heater Relay

1. Check that there is continuity between the No. 1 and 2 terminals. Check that there is NO continuity between the No. 3 and 4 terminals.

NOTE: *The relay is located under the air intake hose behind the battery.*

2. Apply battery voltage to terminal No. 1 and ground terminal No. 2. Use the ohmmeter to check for continuity between terminals 3 and 4.

Throttle Positioner System
OPERATION

To reduce HC and CO emissions, the throttle positioner (TP) opens the throttle valve to slightly more than the idle position when decelerating. This keeps the air/fuel ratio from becoming excessively rich when the throttle valve is quickly closed. In addition, the TP is used to increase idle rpm when power steering fluid pressure exceeds a calibrated value and/or when a large electrical load is placed on the electrical system (headlights, rear defogger etc).

With the engine idling and an electrical load energized, the vacuum switching valve (VSV) is energized. This directs atmospheric pressure through the VSV to the rear TP diaphragm (A). The action of the spring on the diaphragm is transmitted to the push rod. This causes the throttle valve to open slightly and increase engine rpm. If all of the heavy electrical loads are off, the VSV is off, maintaining vacuum on the diaphragm and preventing the push rod from moving.

Vacuum from the **TP** port of the carburetor acts on a second diaphragm (B), closing the throttle valve. With the vehicle cruising, the

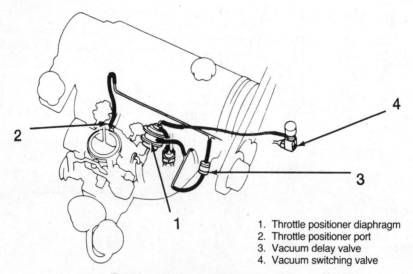

1. Throttle positioner diaphragm
2. Throttle positioner port
3. Vacuum delay valve
4. Vacuum switching valve

Throttle positioner component location

vacuum signal in both chambers is low which maintains the **TP** in its high speed (open) position. However, when the vehicle is decelerated, vacuum on diaphragm A increases quickly which closes the throttle valve somewhat.

The delay action of the vacuum transmitting valve makes the vacuum increase on diaphragm **B** occur slowly which allows the throttle valve to close at a controlled rate. This slow closing prevents the radical change in emissions caused by the throttle valve slamming shut as the driver suddenly lifts completely off the accelerator, such as when going down a steep hill or preparing to use the brakes.

In the event that power steering pressure exceeds a calibrated value, (such as in a full-lock turn while parking) atmospheric pressure is pulled into chamber A causing diaphragm A to move, increasing rpm. This compensates for the power steering system dragging down the idle speed as it delivers needed fluid pressure.

TESTING

Checking the Throttle Positioner System Operation

1. Start the engine and warm up to normal operating temperature.

2. Check the idle speed and adjust if necessary.

3. Disconnect the hose from the TVSV **M** port and plug the **M** port. This will shut off the choke opener and EGR system.

4. Disconnect the vacuum hose from **TP** diaphragm **A**. Check that the **TP** is set at the first step (electrical load idle up). Throttle Positioner at the first setting speed:

- Manual Trans: 800 rpm
- Auto. Trans: 900 rpm

If not at the specified speed, adjust the speed with the adjusting screw.

NOTE: *The adjustment should be made with the cooling fan (at the radiator) OFF.*

5. Disconnect the vacuum hose from the throttle positioner diaphragm **B** and plug the end of the hose.

6. Check that the throttle positioner is set at the second step. The setting speed with the throttle positioner on the second step should be as follows:

- Manual Trans: 1,300 ± 200 rpm
- Auto. Trans: 1,400 ± 200 rpm

7. Reconnect the vacuum hose to the throttle positioner diaphragm **B** and check that the engine returns to the first step setting speed within 2-6 seconds.

8. Reconnect the vacuum hose to diaphragm **A**.

9. Reconnect the hose to the TVSV **M** port.

Checking the Vacuum Delay Valve

1. Check that air flows without resistance from **B** to **A**.

2. Check that air flows with difficulty from **A** to **B**.

3. If a problem is found, replace the vacuum delay valve.

NOTE: *When replacing the vacuum delay valve, side **A** should face the throttle positioner.*

Checking the Vacuum Switching Valve

With the engine at idling at normal operating temperature, turn on the high beam headlights.

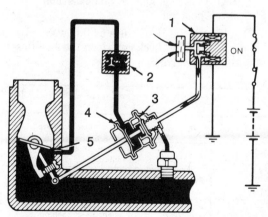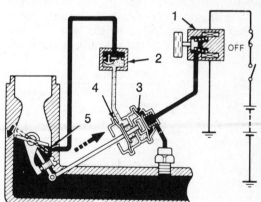

1. Vacuum switching valve
2. Vacuum delay valve
3. Diaphragm A
4. Diaphragm B
5. Throttle positioner port

Throttle positioner operation

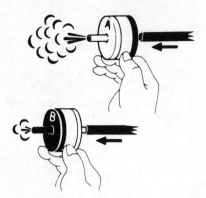

Checking the vacuum delay valve

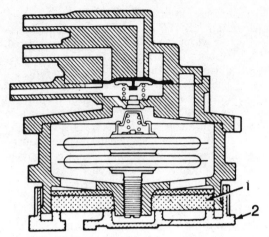

1. Air filter
2. Cover

High altitude compensation valve

The throttle positioner should move to the first step positions and the idle should increase slightly.

Checking the Power Steering Idle-Up Switch

With the engine at idling at normal operating temperature, turn the steering wheel until the wheels are against their stops. Hold the wheels against the stops and check that the throttle positioner moves to the first position. The idle should increase slightly.

High Altitude Compensation (HAC)
OPERATION

As altitude increases, air density decreases so that the air/fuel mixture becomes richer. (The same amount of fuel is mixing with less air so the percentage of fuel is higher.) The high altitude compensation (HAC) system insures a proper air/fuel mixture by supplying additional air to the primary low and high speed circuits of the carburetor and advancing the ignition timing to improve driveability at altitudes above 3930 feet. Above 3930 feet, the bellows in the high altitude compensation valve is expanded which closes Port **A**.

With Port **A** closed, the manifold vacuum is allowed to act on the HAC diaphragm. The diaphragm opens Port **B** to the atmosphere (through the HAC valve), allowing air to enter the carburetor's primary low and high speed fuel circuits. This same vacuum signal acts on the distributor sub-diaphragm adding 8 degrees of timing advance.

At altitudes below 2,570 feet, the HAC bellows are contracted opening Port **A**. This vacuum signal with air reduces the vacuum to the distributor's sub-diaphragm (no timing advance). With vacuum strength reduced, port **B** is closed allowing no air bleed into the carburetor's low and high speed circuits.

TESTING

Checking the High Altitude Compensation System Operation

1. Check the HAC valve as follows:
    a. Visually check and clean the air filter in the HAC valve.

Condition	VSV for electrical load	TP Port Vacuum	Diaphragm A	Diaphragm B	Throttle Valve
					To reduce HC and CO emissions, the throttle positioner opens the throttle valve slightly more than at idle when decelerating. This causes the air-fuel mixture to burn completely.
Idling	ON	—	Pushed out by diaphragm spring	—	slightly opens (Idle up)
	OFF	Intake manifold vacuum	—	Pulled by intake manifold vacuum	Idle speed position
Cruising	—	Nearly atmospheric pressure	—	Pushed out by diaphragm spring	High speed position
Deceleration	—	Intake manifold vacuum	—	*Pulled by intake manifold vacuum	Slightly opens and *slowly closes to the idling position
Remarks: *This action is delayed by the VTV.					

Throttle positioner operation chart

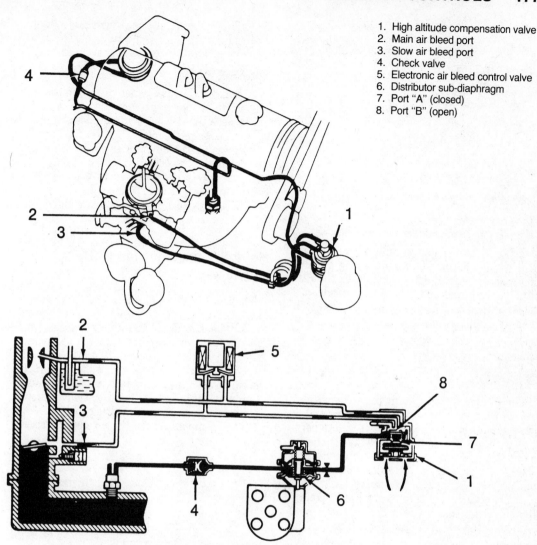

1. High altitude compensation valve
2. Main air bleed port
3. Slow air bleed port
4. Check valve
5. Electronic air bleed control valve
6. Distributor sub-diaphragm
7. Port "A" (closed)
8. Port "B" (open)

High altitude compensation system components

b. At high altitude (above 3930 ft), blow into any one of the two ports on top of the HAC valve with the engine idling and check that the HAC valve is open to the atmosphere.

c. At low altitude (below 2570 ft), blow into any one of the two ports on top of the HAC valve with the engine idling and check that the HAC valve is closed.

2. Check the ignition timing as follows:

a. Disconnect the vacuum hose with the check valve from the distributor sub-dia-phragm and plug the end of the hose.

b. Check the ignition timing. It should be a maximum of 5° BTDC at 950 rpm.

c. Reconnect the hose to the distributor sub-diaphragm.

d. Check the ignition timing. It should be about 13° BTDC at 950 rpm.

3. Disconnect the vacuum hose from the check valve at the back side and plug the end of the hose. Check that the ignition timing remains stable for more than one minute.

4. Stop the engine and reconnect the hoses to their proper locations.

5. Disconnect the two hoses on the top of the HAC valve. Blow air into each hose and check that the air flows into the carburetor.

6. Reconnect the hoses to their proper locations.

7. Any component not opening or closing properly should be replaced.

Checking the Check Valve

1. Check the valve by blowing air into each pipe:

2. Check that air flows from the orange pipe to the black pipe.

3. Check that air does not flow from the black pipe to the orange pipe.

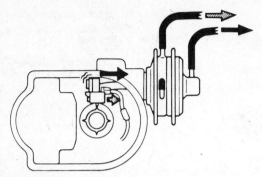

Distributor vacuum advance

Checking the Distributor Vacuum Advance

Remove the distributor cap and rotor. Plug one port of the sub-diaphragm. Using a hand-held vacuum pump, apply vacuum to the diaphragm, checking that the vacuum advance moves when the vacuum is applied. Reinstall the rotor and distributor cap.

Hot Air Intake (HAI)
OPERATION

This system directs hot air to the carburetor in cold weather to improve driveability and to prevent carburetor icing. With the air temperature in the air cleaner below 72°F (22°C), the atmospheric port in the hot idle compensation valve is closed, sending the full manifold vacuum signal to the hot air intake (HAI) diaphragm. The HAI diaphragm moves, opening the air control valve which directs the heated air (from the exhaust manifold) into the air cleaner.

Once the air cleaner temperature exceeds 84°F (29°C), the HIC atmospheric port is open allowing atmospheric pressure to act on the hot air intake diaphragm. This keeps the air control valve closed, allowing the intake air to come directly down the air cleaner's snorkel from outside the car. This air is always cooler than the air from around the exhaust manifold.

TESTING

1. Remove the air cleaner cover and cool the HIC valve by blowing compressed air on it.
2. Check that the air control valve closes the cool air passages at idle.
3. Reinstall the air cleaner cover and warm up the engine.
4. Check that the air control valve opens the cool air passage at idle.
5. Visually check the hoses and connections for cracks, leaks or damage.

Hot Idle Compensation (HIC)
OPERATION

The Hot Idle Compensation (HIC) System allows the air controlled by the HIC valve to enter the intake manifold, maintaining proper air/fuel mixture during idle at high temperatures. When the air cleaner temperature is below 72°F (22°C), the HIC valve's atmospheric port is closed. This allows supplies intake manifold vacuum to the hot air intake (HAI) valve, allowing heated air to enter the air cleaner.

As the temperature in the air cleaner rises,

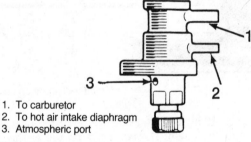

1. To carburetor
2. To hot air intake diaphragm
3. Atmospheric port

HIC valve

As altitude increases, the air-fuel mixture becomes richer. This system insures proper air-fuel mixture by supplying additional air to the primary low and high speed circuit of the carburetor and advances the ignition timing to improve driveability at high altitude above 1,198 m (3,930 ft).

Altitude	Bellows in HAC Valve	Port A in HAC Valve	Port B in HAC Valve	Distributor Sub-diaphragm	Air from HAC Valve	Vacuum Ignition Timing
High Above 1,198 m (3,930 ft.)	Expanded	CLOSED	OPEN	Pulled (Always)	Led into primary low and high speed circuit	Advanced (+ 8°) (Always)
Low Below 783 m (2,570 ft)	Contracted	OPEN	CLOSED	*Not pulled	Stopped	*Not advanced

Remarks: * However, because of an orifice in the distributor sub-diaphragm pipe leading to the HAC valve, the sub-diaphragm is pulled only during high vacuum such as when idling.

High altitude compensation (HAC) system operation

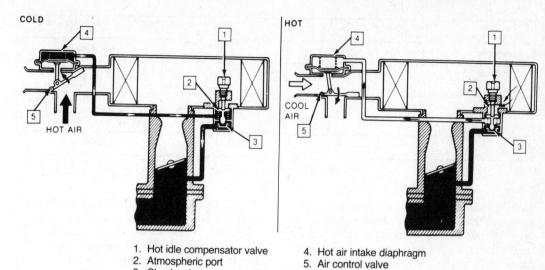

1. Hot idle compensator valve
2. Atmospheric port
3. Check valve
4. Hot air intake diaphragm
5. Air control valve

Hot air intake system components

This system leads a hot air supply to the carburetor in cold weather to improve driveability and to prevent the carburetor from icing in extremely cold weather.

Temperature in Air Cleaner	HIC Valve	Air Control Valve	Intake Air
Cold Below 22°C (72°F)	Atmospheric port is CLOSED	Hot air passage OPEN	HOT
Hot Above 29°C (84°F)	Atmospheric port is OPEN	Cool air passage OPEN	COOL

Hot air intake system operation chart

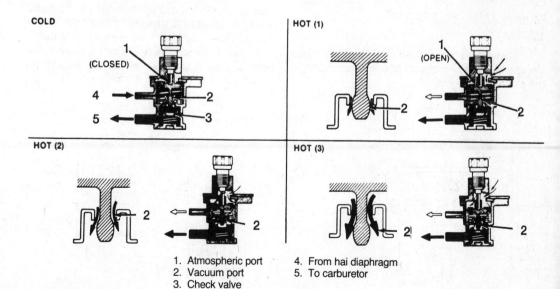

1. Atmospheric port
2. Vacuum port
3. Check valve
4. From hai diaphragm
5. To carburetor

HIC system operation

Temperature in Air Cleaner	HIC Valve Atmospheric Port	HIC Valve Vacuum Port Opening	HIC System
This system allows the air controlled by the HIC valve to enter the intake manifold to maintain proper air-fuel mixture during high temperatures at idle.			
HOT (1) Between 29°C (84°F) and 52°C (126°F)	OPEN	MINIMUM	OFF
HOT (2) Between 59°C (138°F) and 82°C (180°F)	OPEN	PARTIAL	ON Air volume is controlled by HIC valve
HOT (3) Above 89°C (192°F)	OPEN	MAXIMUM	ON

HIC system operation chart

the HIC valve will increase its opening to the atmosphere which, in turn, increases pressure on the diaphragm. As the pressure increases the HAC valve will close more, pulling cooler (more dense) air into the carburetor.

When air cleaner temperatures are between 84°F (29°C) and 126°F (52°C), the HIC valve's atmospheric port opens slightly. This begins to increase the pressure on the HAI diaphragm and its air control valve begins to close.

When intake air temperatures reach 138°F (59°C), both the atmospheric port and the vacuum port of the HIC valve open further. This action steadily increases the pressure on HAI diaphragm and continues to close the air control valve, pulling more cool air into the carburetor. At the same time, the opening of the vacuum port allows outside air to bleed into the intake manifold to maintain the proper air/fuel mixture during high temperature at idle.

Finally at temperatures above 192°F (89°C), the HIC valve's atmospheric and vacuum ports open fully, applying maximum pressure to the HAI diaphragm and closing the air control valve completely. This allows the coolest possible air to enter the carburetor.

TESTING

1. Check that air flows from the HAI diaphragm side to the carburetor side while closing the atmospheric port.

2. Check that air does not flow from the carburetor side to the HAI diaphragm side.

3. Below 72°F (22°C), check that air does NOT flow from the HAI diaphragm side to the atmosphere port while closing the intake manifold side.

4. Heat the HIC valve to above 84°F (29°C).

5. Check that air flows from the HAI diaphragm side to the atmospheric port while closing the carburetor side.

Automatic Choke
OPERATION

The automatic choke system temporarily supplies a rich air/fuel mixture to the engine by closing the choke valve (plate) when the engine is cold. At cold temperatures with the ignition switch ON but the engine not running, there is no voltage supplied from the alternator's L terminal at the choke heater. The bi-metal choke spring is contracted, closing the choke valve.

As soon as the engine is running, the L terminal supplies voltage to the choke heater. The heat generated is transferred to the bi-metal spring causing it to unwind-opening the choke valve. This helps provide a relatively quick transition between the rich (cold) setting to the normally open position when the engine no longer requires the rich air/fuel mixture.

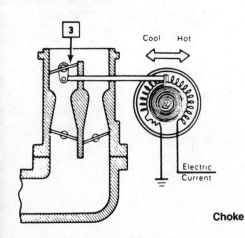

Choke system components

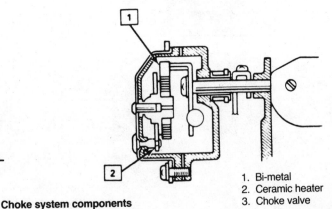

1. Bi-metal
2. Ceramic heater
3. Choke valve

This system temporarily supplies a rich mixture to the engine by closing the choke valve when the engine is cold.

IG S/W	Engine	Current from L Terminal to Heater	Bimetal	Choke Valve
OFF	Not running	Not flowing	Expanded	CLOSED
ON	Not running	*Not flowing	Expanded	CLOSED
	Running	Flowing	Heated and contracted	OPEN

Remarks: *On alternators with IC regulator, slight voltage will occur when the ignition switch is turned ON, but not sufficient current to warm up the heater.

Choke system operation chart

TESTING

Checking the Automatic Choke

1. Allow the choke valve to close.
2. Start the engine.
3. Check that the choke valve begins to open and the choke housing is heated.

Checking the Heating Coil

1. Unplug the wire connector.
2. Measure the resistance with an ohmmeter. The resistance should read: 19-24 ohms 68°F (20°C). Allow for slight variations due to temperature differences.

Choke Opener System

OPERATION

The choke opener system, after warm-up, forcibly holds the choke valve open to prevent an over-rich mixture and releases the fast idle cam to the 3rd (lowest) step to lower the engine rpm.

When engine coolant temperature is below 122°F (50°C), the thermostatic vacuum switching valve connects port **J** to port **M** which places atmospheric pressure on the choke valve. Through the choke opener linkage, the fast idle cam is set at the first (high idle) or second step.

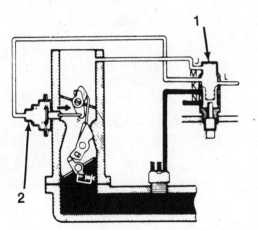
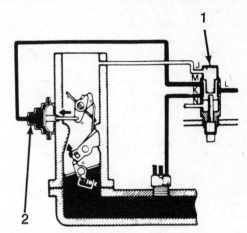

1. Thermostatic vacuum switching valve
2. Choke opener diaphragm

Choke opener system operation

After warm up, this system forcibly holds the choke valve open to prevent an over-rich mixture and releases the fast idle to the 3rd step to lower engine rpm.

Coolant Temp.	TVSV	Diaphragm	Choke Valve	Fast Idle Cam	Engine RPM
Below 50°C (122°F)	OPEN (J-M)	Released by spring tension	Closed by automatic choke	Set at 1st or 2nd step	HIGH
Above 68°C (154°F)	OPEN (K-M)	Pulled by manifold vacuum	OPEN	Released to 3rd step	LOW

Choke opener system operation

When the coolant temperature exceeds 154°F (68°C), the TVSV connects Port **K** to Port **M** which now applies manifold vacuum to the choke opener diaphragm. This action opens the choke valve further and releases the fast idle cam to the third step and idle speed decreases.

TESTING

Check the choke Opener System Operation

1. Disconnect the vacuum hose from the choke opener diaphragm. With the coolant temperature below 122°F (50°C), step down on the accelerator pedal and release it.

2. Start the engine.

3. Reconnect the vacuum hose and check that the choke linkage does not move.

4. Warm the engine to normal operating temperature and shut it off.

5. Disconnect the vacuum hose from the choke opener diaphragm.

6. Set the fast idle cam. While holding the throttle slightly open, push the choke plate closed and hold it closed as you release the throttle.

7. Turn the key and start the motor but DO NOT touch the accelerator pedal.

8. Reconnect the vacuum hose. The choke linkage should move and the fast idle cam should release to the third step (lowest rpm).

Checking the TVSV

For testing procedures for the TVSV please refer to the EGR system testing procedures earlier in this chapter.

Checking the Diaphragm

Check that the choke linkage moves in accordance with the amount of vacuum applied. If a problem is found, replace the diaphragm.

Auxiliary Acceleration Pump (AAP)
OPERATION

When accelerating with a cold engine, the main acceleration pump's capacity is insufficient to provide enough fuel for good acceleration. The auxiliary acceleration pump system compensates for this by forcing more fuel into the acceleration nozzle to obtain better cold engine performance.

When engine coolant temperature is below 122°F (50°C), the thermostatic vacuum switching valve connects port **K** to port **N** which connects manifold vacuum to the AAP diaphragm. When engine rpm is relatively steady, the diaphragm moves against its spring causing its fuel chamber to fill. Whenever the engine is accelerated, the vacuum signal to the AAP diaphragm diminishes quickly. The diaphragm is pushed by its spring, forcing its fuel into the main acceleration circuit and out its nozzle.

After coolant temperature exceeds 154°F (68°C), the TVSV blocks Port **K** and Port **N** stopping the operation of the auxiliary acceleration pump system. The additional fuel requirement for warm engine acceleration is adequately handled by the main acceleration pump (carburetor) circuit.

TESTING

Checking the Auxiliary Acceleration Pump System

1. Check that the coolant temperature is below 122°F (50°C). Remove the cover from the air cleaner and start the engine.

2. Pinch the AAP hose, and shut off the engine.

3. Release the hose. Check that gasoline spurts out from the accelerator nozzle in the

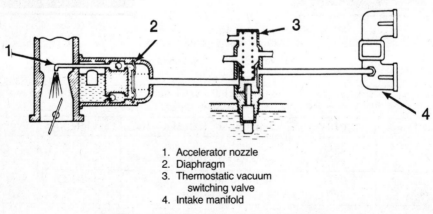

1. Accelerator nozzle
2. Diaphragm
3. Thermostatic vacuum
   switching valve
4. Intake manifold

Auxiliary acceleration pump system components

When accelerating with a cold engine, the main acceleration pump capacity is insufficient to provide good acceleration. The AAP system compensates for this by forcing more fuel into the acceleration nozzle to obtain better cold engine performance.

Coolant Temp	TVSV	Engine	Intake Vacuum	Diaphragm in AAP	Fuel
Below 50°C (122°F)	OPEN (K-N)	Constant RPM	HIGH	Pulled by vacuum	Drawn into AAP chamber
		Acceleration	LOW	Returned by spring tension	Forced into acceleration nozzle
Above 68°C (154°F)	CLOSED (K-N)	—	—	No operation	—

Auxiliary acceleration pump system chart

carburetor. Don't perform this test too often--you may flood the motor.

3. Restart the engine and warm it to normal operating temperature. Repeat steps 2 and 3 above. Check that gasoline DOES NOT spurt out from the accelerator nozzle.

4. Reinstall the air cleaner cover.

Checking the Auxiliary Acceleration Pump Diaphragm

1. Start the engine.
2. Disconnect the hose from the AAP diaphragm.
3. Apply vacuum directly to the AAP diaphragm (at idle) with a hand held vacuum pump.

4. Check that the engine rpm changes as the vacuum is released from the system.
5. Reconnect the AAP hose.

Heat Control Valve
OPERATION

When the engine is cold, the heat control valve improves fuel vaporization for better driveability by quickly heating the intake manifold. Once the engine has warmed up, it helps keep the intake manifold at proper temperature.

With the engine cold, the bi-metal spring positions the heat control valve to direct some of the engine's hot exhaust gases under the intake

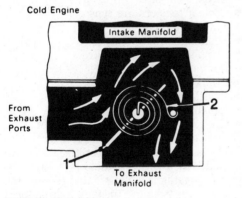

Cold Engine

Intake Manifold

From Exhaust Ports

To Exhaust Manifold

1. Heat control valve
2. Bi-metal

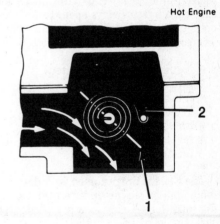

Hot Engine

Heat control valve operation

When cold, this device improves fuel vaporization for better driveability by quickly heating the intake manifold. After warm-up, it keeps the intake manifold at the proper temperature.

Engine	Bimetal	Exhaust Gas Passage	Intake Manifold
COLD	EXPANDED	Above the heat control valve	Heated quickly
HOT	CONTRACTED	Under the heat control valve	Heated to a suitable temperature

Heat control valve operation chart

manifold which quickly bring it to the proper operating temperature.

When the engine is hot, the bi-metal spring contracts, moving the position of the heat control valve to direct most of the exhaust under the valve and away from direct contact with the intake manifold.

TESTING

The valve within the exhaust system has a counterweight on the outside of the pipe. This counterweight is viewed most easily from under the car. With the engine cold, check that the counterweight is in the upper position. After the engine has been warmed up, check that the weight has moved to the lower position.

Check Engine Light and Diagnostic Codes.

OPERATION

4A-GE

The *Check Engine* light is the device providing communication between the Electronic Control Module (ECM) and the driver. The ECM controls the electronic fuel injection, the electronic spark control, the diagnostic function and the fail-safe or default function.

The ECM receives signals from various sensors indicating changing engine operating conditions. These signals are utilized by the ECM to determine the injection duration (amount of time each injector stays open) to maintain the optimum air/fuel ratio under all conditions. The conditions affecting the injector duration are:

- Exhaust gas oxygen content
- Intake air mass
- Intake air temperature
- Coolant temperature
- Engine rpm
- Acceleration/deceleration
- Electrical load
- Air conditioning on/off

The ECM is programmed with data for optimum ignition timing under any and all operating conditions. Using data provide by the sensors, the ECM triggers the spark within each cylinder at precisely the right instant for the existing conditions.

The ECM detects any malfunctions or abnormalities in the sensor network and lights the *Check Engine* light on the dash panel. At the same time the trouble is identified by circuit and a diagnostic code is recorded within the ECM. This diagnostic code can be read by the number of blinks of the instrument light when both check engine terminals are shorted under the hood. For the 4A-GE engine in 49-state

trim, there are 13 different codes; California cars produce 14 codes.

In the event of an internal computer malfunction, the ECM is programmed with back-up or default values. This allows the car to run on a fixed set of "rules" for engine operation. Driveability may suffer since the driving conditions cannot be dealt with by the faulty computer. This back-up programming allows the computer to fail with out stranding the car, hence the nickname fail-safe. No computer is safe from failure, but a back-up system helps make the best of the situation.

With the exception of the oxygen sensor (discussed earlier in this chapter) the testing and replacement of the various sensors is discussed in Chapter 5.

4A-FE

The ECM is a precision unit consisting of a one-chip micro computer, and analog/digital converter, an input/output unit, a read-only memory (ROM) and a random access memory (RAM). It is an essential part of the electronic control system, controlling many engine functions as well as possessing a self-diagnostic capability and a fail-safe or default memory.

The ECM receives information from many sensors on the engine. Based on the constantly changing data, it controls the fuel delivery and spark timing. The sensors communicating with the ECM are:

- Oxygen sensor
- Coolant temperature sensor
- Throttle switch
- Mainfold air temperature
- Manifold absolute pressure
- Ignition signal
- Crank angle sensor
- Vehicle speed sensor
- Exhaust gas recirculation system
- Central processing unit of the ECM

If the system is free of any faults after the engine starts, the warning light on the dashboard turns off. When the ECM detects a fault, the *Check Engine* light is illuminated to alert the driver. At the same time, the fault code is stored in the ECM for future reading. The code is stored in the memory even if the fault is momentary or self-corrects. The code is not erased from the memory until the power is removed from the ECM for 20 seconds or more.

Should the ECM detect a fault in any system for which it cannot compensate or develop its own internal fault, it will engage its back-up program. This program is a set of fixed values which allows the car to keep running under adverse circumstances. Because the fixed values in the memory may not correspond to the actual conditions, driveability may suffer when the system is in this default mode. The systems controlled by this back-up memory are:

- Oxygen sensor
- Coolant temperature sensor
- Throttle switch
- Vehicle speed sensor
- Manifold air temperature sensor
- Manifold absolute pressure sensor
- Central processing unit in the ECM

By maintaining the function of these critical sensors, the car is not disabled during the occurrence of an electrical fault in the main system.

With the exception of the oxygen sensor (discussed earlier in this chapter) the testing and replacement of the various sensors is discussed in Chapter 5.

FAULT CODES AND THEIR MEANING

4A-GE

To read the code(s) from the ECM:

1. The following initial conditions must be met or the code will not be transmitted from the ECM:

    a. Battery voltage above 11 volts

    b. Throttle plate fully closed--keep your foot off the accelerator

    c. Transmission selector in neutral

    d. All accessory switches off

2. Turn the ignition switch ON, but DO NOT start the engine.

3. Use a service (jumper) wire to short both terminals of the engine check connector, located under the hood near the wiper motor.

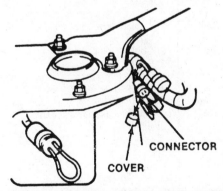

Location of Nova check engine connector (4A-GE)

4. The diagnosis code(s) will be indicated by the number of flashes of the *Check Engine* light.

If the system is normal, the light will blink repeatedly every ½ second. This indication is displayed when no codes are stored in the ECM. It serves as a confirmation the the ECM has nothing to tell you--all is well.

If a fault code is stored, its two digit code will be indicated in the pattern of the flashing. For example, code 21 would be indicated by two flashes, a pause, and one flash. There will be a 1½ second pause between the first and second digit of a code. If more than one code is stored, the next will be transmitted after a 2½ second pause. Once all the codes have been flashed, the system will wait 4½ seconds and repeat the entire series. It will continue sending the fault codes as long as the initial conditions are met and the engine check connector is shorted across terminal **T** and **E1**.

NOTE: *If more than one code is stored, they will be delivered in numerical order from the lowest to the highest, regardless of which code occurred first. The order of the codes DOES NOT indicate the order of occurrence.*

5. After the code(s) have been read and recorded, turn the ignition switch to OFF and disconnect the jumper wire.

WARNING: *Disconnecting the wire with the ignition ON may cause severe damage to the ECM.*

4A-FE

To read the codes from the ECM:

1. With the ignition OFF, use a service (jumper) wire to ground the diagnostic switch in the connector under the hood.

2. Without touching the accelerator pedal, turn the ignition to ON but DO NOT start the motor.

3. The codes will be displayed through the flashing of the *Check Engine* light. Count the number of flashes to determine the numerical code.

If the system is normal and has no codes stored, the lamp will flash on and off several times rhythmically. If this signal is received, no further codes will be transmitted from the ECM.

Stored fault codes will be displayed in numerical order from lowest to highest without regard to which code occurred first. All codes are two digit and will be displayed with a one second pause between digits. (Example: Code

CODE NO. 13   CODE NO. 21   CODE NO. 13

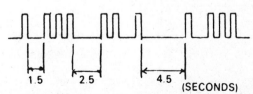

1.5   2.5   4.5
(SECONDS)

Examples of multiple code display on 4A-GE system

Code No.	Number of CHECK ENGINE blinks	System	Trouble area
–	_⊓⊓⊓⊓⊓⊓⊓_ ON OFF	Normal	–
12	_⊓⊓⊓_	RPM signal	1. Distributor circuit 2. Distributor 3. Igniter circuit 4. Igniter 5. Starter signal circuit 6. ECM
13	_⊓⊓⊓⊓_	RPM signal	1. Distributor circuit 2. Distributor 3. ECM
14	_⊓⊓⊓⊓⊓_	Ignition signal	1. Igniter and ignition coil circuit 2 Igniter and ignition coil 3. ECM
21	_⊓⊓⊓_	Exhaust oxygen sensor signal	1. Exhaust oxygen sensor circuit 2. Exhaust oxygen sensor 3. ECM
		Exhaust oxygen sensor heater	1. Exhaust oxygen sensor heater circuit 2. Exhaust oxygen sensor heater 3. ECM
22	_⊓⊓⊓⊓_	Coolant temp. sensor signal	1. Coolant temp. sensor circuit 2. Coolant temp. sensor 3. ECM
24	_⊓⊓⊓⊓⊓_	Manifold air temp. sensor signal	1. Manifold air temp. sensor circuit 2. Manifold air temp. sensor 3. ECM
25	_⊓⊓⊓⊓⊓⊓_	Air-fuel ratio lean malfunction	1. Injector circuit 2. Injector 3. Fuel line pressure 4. Ignition system 5. Mass air flow sensor 6. Exhaust oxygen sensor circuit 7. Exhaust oxygen sensor 8. ECM 9. Air intake system

Trouble codes for 4A-GE (Nova) ECM

.Code No.	Number of CHECK ENGINE blinks	System	Trouble area
26		Air-fuel ratio Rich malfunction	1. Injector circuit 2. Injector 3. Fuel line pressure 4. Cold start injector 5. Mass air flow sensor 6. ECM 7. Exhaust oxygen sensor circuit 8. Exhaust oxygen sensor
31		Mass air flow sensor signal	1. Mass air flow sensor circuit 2. Air flow meter 3. ECM
41		Throttle position sensor signal	1. Throttle position sensor circuit 2. Throttle position sensor 3. ECM
42		Vehicle speed sensor signal	1. Vehicle speed sensor circuit 2. Vehicle speed sensor 3. ECM
43		Starter signal	1. Starter relay circuit 2. IG switch, main relay circuit 3. ECM
51		Switch signal	1. A/C switch 2. Throttle position sensor circuit 3. Throttle position sensor 4. ECM 5. A/C switch circuit 6. A/C switch amplifier
* 71		EGR system malfunction	1. EGR system (EGR vale, EGR hose, etc.) 2. EGR gas temp. sensor circuit 3. EGR gas temp. sensor 4. VSV for EGR 5. VSV for EGR circuit 6. ECM

* For California

Trouble codes for 4A-GE (Nova) ECM

EXAMPLE: OXYGEN SENSOR SIGNAL (CODE 21)

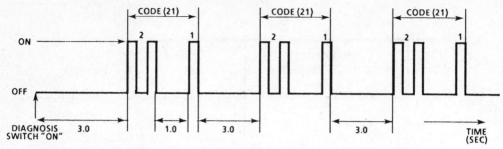

DIAGNOSTIC CODE		DIAGNOSTIC AREA
NO.	MODE	
--	ON / OFF	NORMAL
12		RPM SIGNAL
13		RPM SIGNAL
14		IGNITION SIGNAL
21		OXYGEN SENSOR
22		COOLANT TEMPERATURE SENSOR
24		MANIFOLD AIR TEMPERATURE SENSOR
25		LEAN AIR/FUEL RATIO
26		RICH AIR/FUEL RATIO
31		MANIFOLD ABSOLUTE PRESSURE SENSOR
41		THROTTLE POSITION SENSOR
42		VEHICLE SPEED SENSOR
43		STARTER SIGNAL
51		SWITCH SIGNAL
71		EGR MALFUNCTION

Code display and table for 4A-FE (Prizm)

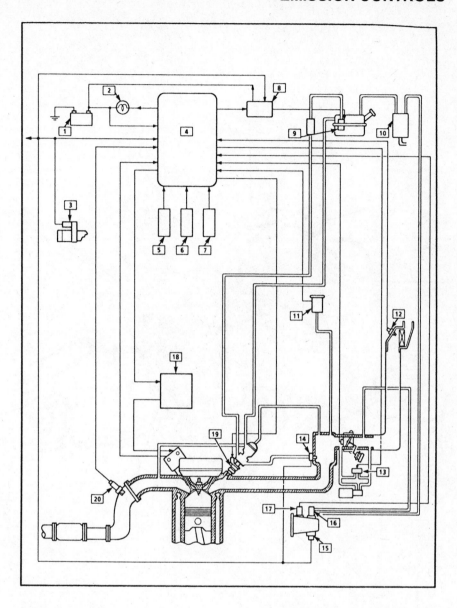

1 BATTERY

2 CHECK ENGINE WARNING LIGHT

3 STARTER MOTOR

4 ELECTRONIC CONTROL MODULE (ECM)

5 A/C INPUT

6 PARK/NEUTRAL (P/N) INPUT

7 VEHICLE SPEED SENSOR (VSS) INPUT

8 CIRCUIT OPENING RELAY

9 FUEL PUMP

10 FUEL VAPOR CANISTER

11 MANIFOLD ABSOLUTE PRESSURE (MAP) SENSOR

12 MANIFOLD AIR TEMPERATURE (MAT) SENSOR

13 AIR CONDITIONING/VACUUM SWITCHING VALVE (A/C VSV) (IF EQUIPPED)

14 COLD START INJECTOR VALVE

15 COLD START INJECTOR VALVE SWITCH

16 BIMETAL VACUUM SWITCHING VALVE (BVSV)

17 COOLANT TEMPERATURE SENSOR (CTS)

18 IGNITER

19 FUEL INJECTOR

20 OXYGEN (O$_2$) SENSOR

Vacuum and wiring diagram, 89–90 Prizm (4A-FE) 49 St. and Canada

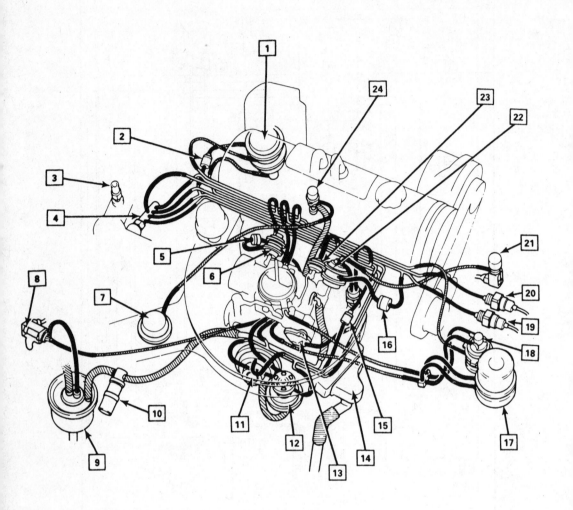

1. DISTRIBUTOR
2. CHECK VALVE
3. THERMO SWITCH
4. THERMOSTATIC VACUUM SWITCHING VALVE
5. JET
6. CHOKE BREAKER
7. HOT AIR INTAKE DIAPHRAGM
8. VACUUM SWITCHING VALVE
9. CHARCOAL CANISTER
10. OUTER VENT CONTROL VALVE
11. EGR VALVE
12. EGR VACUUM MODULATOR
13. AUXILIARY ACCELERATION PUMP
14. AIR SUCTION VALVE
15. CHECK VALVE
16. DELAY VALVE
17. ELECTRIC AIR BLEED CONTROL VALVE
18. HIGH ALTITUDE COMPENSATION VALVE
19. VACUUM SWITCH (A)
20. VACUUM SWITCH (B)
21. VACUUM SWITCHING VALVE
22. THROTTLE POSITIONER
23. CHOKE OPENER
24. HOT IDLE COMPENSATOR

Component location, 85–86 Nova (4A-LC) 49 St. and Canada

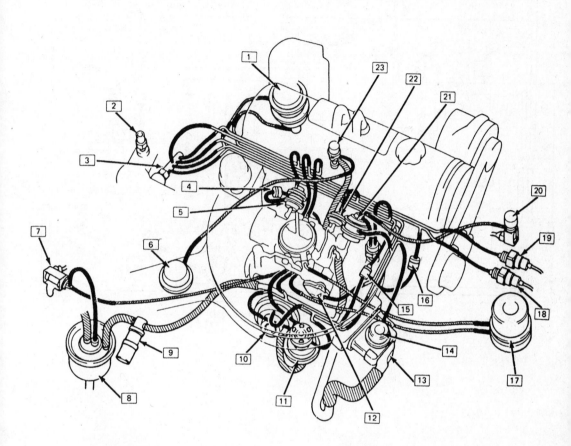

1. DISTRIBUTOR
2. THERMO SWITCH
3. THERMOSTATIC VACUUM SWITCHING VALVE
4. JET
5. CHOKE BREAKER
6. HOT AIR INTAKE DIAPHRAGM
7. VACUUM SWITCHING VALVE
8. CHARCOAL CANISTER
9. OUTER VENT CONTROL VALVE
10. EGR VALVE
11. EGR VACUUM MODULATOR
12. AUXILIARY ACCELERATION PUMP
13. AIR SUCTION VALVE (REED VALVE)
14. AIR SUCTION VALVE (SHUT OFF VALVE)
15. CHECK VALVE
16. DELAY VALVE
17. ELECTRIC AIR BLEED CONTROL VALVE
18. VACUUM SWITCH (A)
19. VACUUM SWITCH (B)
20. VACUUM SWITCHING VALVE
21. THROTTLE POSITIONER
22. CHOKE OPENER
23. HOT IDLE COMPENSATOR

Component location, 85–86 Nova (4A-LC) California

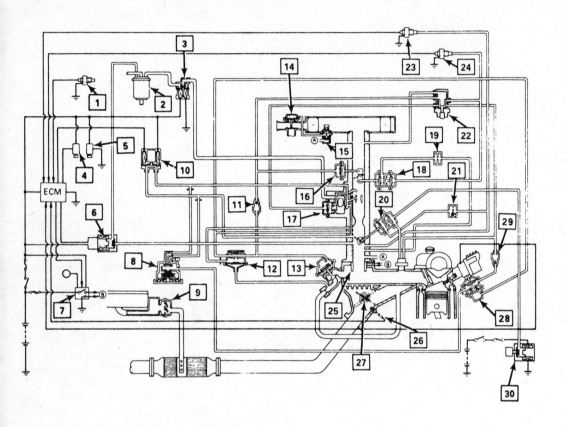

1. THERMO SWITCH
2. CHARCOAL CANISTER
3. OUTER VENT CONTROL VALVE
4. PRIMARY FUEL CUT SOLENOID
5. SECONDARY FUEL CUT SOLENOID
6. VACUUM SWITCHING VALVE
7. COLD MIXTURE HEATER RELAY
8. HIGH ALTITUDE COMPENSATOR VALVE
9. AIR SUCTION VALVE
10. ELECTRIC AIR BLEED CONTROL VALVE
11. CHECK VALVE
12. EGR VACUUM MODULATOR
13. EGR VALVE
14. HOT AIR INTAKE DIAPHRAGM
15. HOT IDLE COMPENSATOR VALVE
16. CHOKE OPENER
17. AUXILIARY ACCELERATOR PUMP
18. CHOKE BREAKER
19. JET
20. THROTTLE POSITIONER
21. DELAY VALVE
22. THERMOSTATIC VACUUM SWITCHING VALVE
23. VACUUM SWITCH (A)
24. VACUUM SWITCH (B)
25. COLD MIXTURE HEATER
26. OXYGEN SENSOR
27. HEAT CONTROL VALVE
28. DISTRIBUTOR
29. CHECK VALVE
30. VACUUM SWITCHING VALVE

Vacuum and wiring diagram, 85–86 Nova (4A-LC) 49 St. and Canada

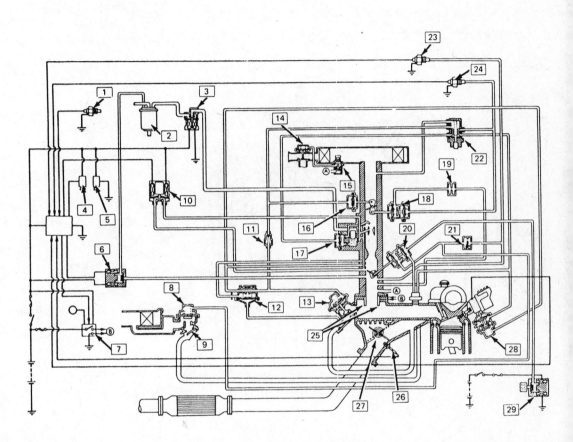

1. THERMO SWITCH
2. CHARCOAL CANISTER
3. OUTER VENT CONTROL VALVE
4. PRIMARY FUEL CUT SOLENOID
5. SECONDARY FUEL CUT SOLENOID
6. VACUUM SWITCHING VALVE
7. COLD MIXTURE HEATER RELAY
8. AIR SUCTION VALVE (SHUT OFF VALVE)
9. AIR SUCTION VALVE (REED VALVE)
10. ELECTRIC AIR BLEED CONTROL VALVE
11. CHECK VALVE
12. EGR VACUUM MODULATOR
13. EGR VALVE
14. HOT AIR INTAKE DIAPHRAGM
15. HOT IDLE COMPENSATOR VALVE
16. CHOKE OPENER

17. AUXILIARY ACCELERATOR PUMP
18. CHOKE BREAKER
19. JET
20. THROTTLE POSITIONER
21. DELAY VALVE
22. THERMOSTATIC VACUUM SWITCHING VALVE
23. VACUUM SWITCH (A)
24. VACUUM SWITCH (B)
25. COLD MIXTURE HEATER
26. OXYGEN SENSOR
27. HEAT CONTROL VALVE
28. DISTRIBUTOR
29. VACUUM SWITCHING VALVE

Vacuum and wiring diagram, 85–86 Nova (4A-LC) California

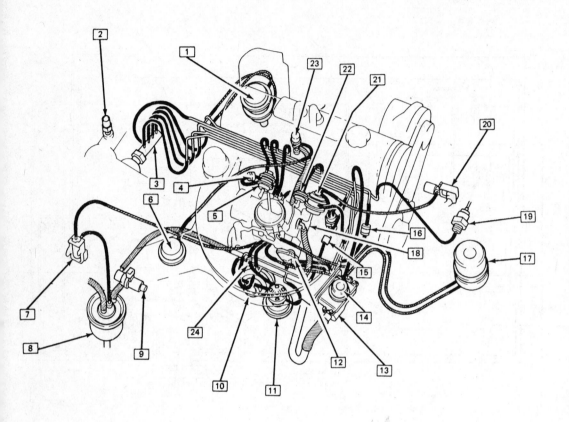

1. DISTRIBUTOR
2. THERMO SWITCH
3. THERMOSTATIC VACUUM SWITCHING VALVE
4. JET
5. CHOKE BREAKER
6. HOT AIR INTAKE DIAPHRAGM
7. VACUUM SWITCHING VALVE
8. CHARCOAL CANISTER
9. OUTER VENT CONTROL VALVE
10. EGR VALVE
11. EGR VACUUM MODULATOR
12. AUXILIARY ACCELERATION PUMP
13. AIR SUCTION VALVE (REED VALVE)
14. AIR SUCTION VALVE (SHUT OFF VALVE)
15. CHECK VALVE
16. DELAY VALVE
17. ELECTRIC AIR BLEED CONTROL VALVE
18. THROTTLE POSITION SWITCH
19. VACUUM SWITCH
20. VACUUM SWITCHING VALVE
21. THROTTLE POSITIONER
22. CHOKE OPENER
23. HOT IDLE COMPENSATOR
24. JET

Component location, 87 Nova (4A-LC) California

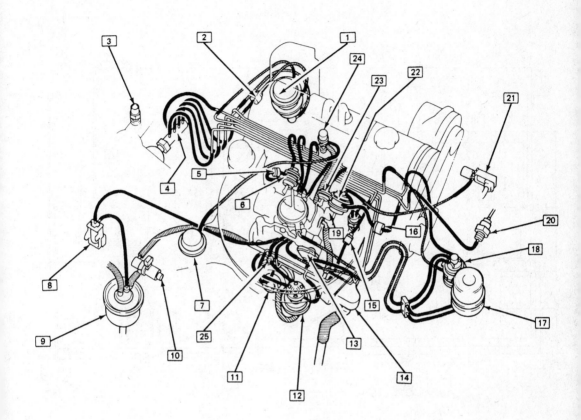

1. DISTRIBUTOR
2. CHECK VALVE
3. THERMO SWITCH
4. THERMOSTATIC VACUUM SWITCHING VALVE
5. JET
6. CHOKE BREAKER
7. HOT AIR INTAKE DIAPHRAGM
8. VACUUM SWITCHING VALVE
9. CHARCOAL CANISTER
10. OUTER VENT CONTROL VALVE
11. EGR VALVE
12. EGR VACUUM MODULATOR

13. AUXILIARY ACCELERATION PUMP
14. AIR SUCTION VALVE
15. CHECK VALVE
16. DELAY VALVE
17. ELECTRIC AIR BLEED CONROL VALVE
18. HIGH ALTITUDE COMPENSATION VALVE
19. THROTTLE POSITION SWITCH
20. VACUUM SWITCH
21. VACUUM SWITCHING VALVE
22. THROTTLE POSITIONER
23. CHOKE OPENER
24. HOT IDLE COMPENSATOR
25. JET

Component location, 87 Nova (4A-LC) 49 St. and Canada

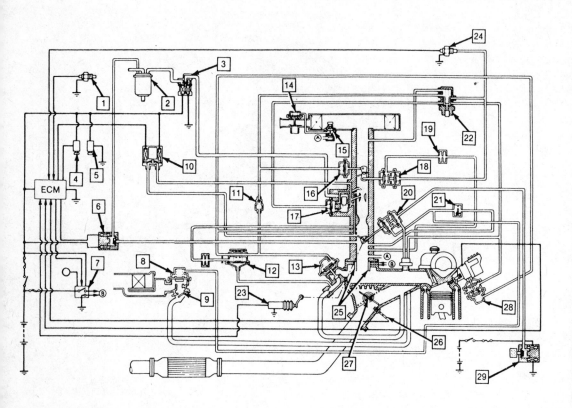

1. THERMO SWITCH
2. CHARCOAL CANISTER
3. OUTER VENT CONTROL VALVE
4. PRIMARY FUEL CUT SOLENOID
5. SECONDARY FUEL CUT SOLENOID
6. VACUUM SWITCHING VALVE
7. COLD MIXTURE HEATER RELAY
8. AIR SUCTION VALVE (SHUT OFF VALVE)
9. AIR SUCTION VALVE (REED VALVE)
10. ELECTRIC AIR BLEED CONTROL VALVE
11. CHECK VALVE
12. EGR VACUUM MODULATOR
13. EGR VALVE
14. HOT AIR INTAKE DIAPHRAGM
15. HOT IDLE COMPENSATOR VALVE

16. CHOKE OPENER
17. AUXILIARY ACCELERATOR PUMP
18. CHOKE BREAKER
19. JET
20. THROTTLE POSITIONER
21. DELAY VALVE
22. THERMOSTATIC VACUUM SWITCHING VALVE
23. THROTTLE POSITION SWITCH
24. VACUUM SWITCH
25. COLD MIXTURE HEATER
26. OXYGEN SENSOR
27. HEAT CONTROL VALVE
28. DISTRIBUTOR
29. VACUUM SWITCHING VALVE
30. JET

Vacuum and wiring diagram, 87 Nova (4A-LC) California

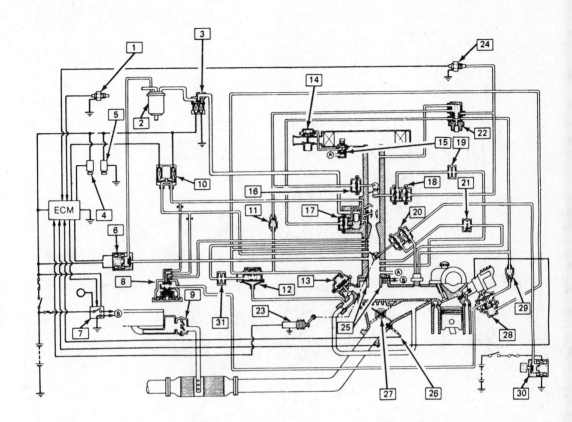

1. THERMO SWITCH
2. CHARCOAL CANISTER
3. OUTER VENT CONTROL VALVE
4. PRIMARY FUEL CUT SOLENOID
5. SECONDARY FUEL CUT SOLENOID
6. VACUUM SWITCHING VALVE
7. COLD MIXTURE HEATER RELAY
8. HIGH ALTITUDE COMPENSATOR VALVE
9. AIR SUCTION VALVE
10. ELECTRIC AIR BLEED CONTROL VALVE
11. CHECK VALVE
12. EGR VACUUM MODULATOR
13. EGR VALVE
14. HOT AIR INTAKE DIAPHRAGM
15. HOT IDLE COMPENSATOR VALVE
16. CHOKE OPENER
17. AUXILIARY ACCELERATOR PUMP
18. CHOKE BREAKER
19. JET
20. THROTTLE POSITIONER
21. DELAY VALVE
22. THERMOSTATIC VACUUM SWITCHING VALVE
23. THROTTLE POSITION SWITCH
24. VACUUM SWITCH
25. COLD MIXTURE HEATER
26. OXYGEN SENSOR
27. HEAT CONTROL VALVE
28. DISTRIBUTOR
29. CHECK VALVE
30. VACUUM SWITCHING VALVE
31. JET

Vacuum and wiring diagram, 87 Nova (4A-LC) 49 St. and Canada

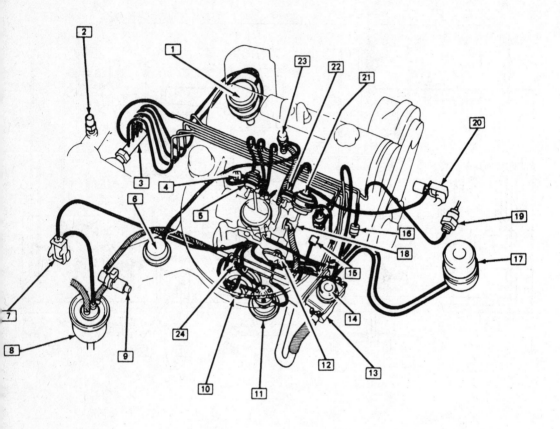

1	DISTRIBUTOR	13	AIR SUCTION VALVE (REED VALVE)
2	THERMO SWITCH	14	AIR SUCTION VALVE (SHUT OFF VALVE)
3	THERMOSTATIC VACUUM SWITCHING VALVE	15	CHECK VALVE
4	JET	16	DELAY VALVE
5	CHOKE BREAKER	17	ELECTRIC AIR BLEED CONTROL VALVE
6	HOT AIR INTAKE DIAPHRAGM	18	THROTTLE POSITION SWITCH
7	VACUUM SWITCHING VALVE	19	VACUUM SWITCH
8	FUEL VAPOR CANISTER	20	VACUUM SWITCHING VALVE
9	OUTER VENT CONTROL VALVE	21	THROTTLE POSITIONER
10	EGR VALVE	22	CHOKE OPENER
11	EGR VACUUM MODULATOR	23	HOT IDLE COMPENSATOR
12	AUXILIARY ACCELERATION PUMP	24	JET

Component location, 88 Nova (4A-LC) California with manual trans

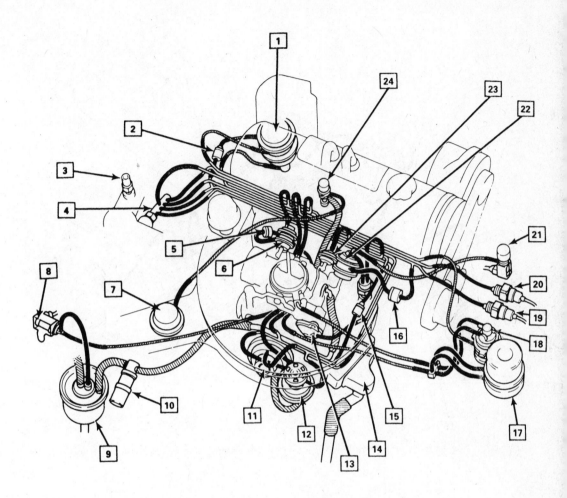

1. DISTRIBUTOR
2. CHECK VALVE
3. THERMO SWITCH
4. THERMOSTATIC VACUUM SWITCHING VALVE
5. JET
6. CHOKE BREAKER
7. HOT AIR INTAKE DIAPHRAGM
8. VACUUM SWITCHING VALVE
9. CHARCOAL CANISTER
10. OUTER VENT CONTROL VALVE
11. EGR VALVE
12. EGR VACUUM MODULATOR
13. AUXILIARY ACCELERATION PUMP
14. AIR SUCTION VALVE
15. CHECK VALVE
16. DELAY VALVE
17. ELECTRIC AIR BLEED CONTROL VALVE
18. HIGH ALTITUDE COMPENSATION VALVE
19. VACUUM SWITCH (A)
20. VACUUM SWITCH (B)
21. VACUUM SWITCHING VALVE
22. THROTTLE POSITIONER
23. CHOKE OPENER
24. HOT IDLE COMPENSATOR

Component location, 88 Nova (4A-LC) 49 St. and Canada with manual trans

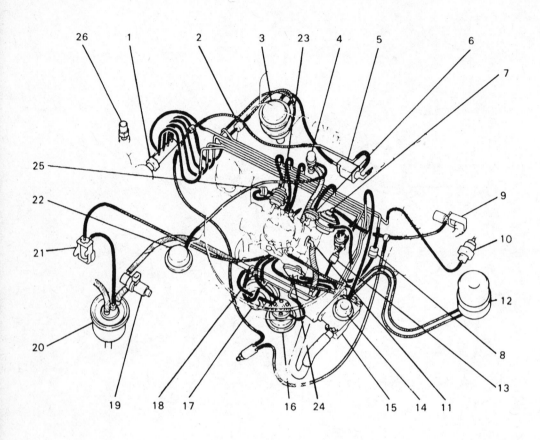

1	TVSV	14	AS SHUT-OFF VALVE
2	CHECK VALVE	15	AS READ VALVE
3	DISTRIBUTOR	16	EGR VACUUM MODULATOR
4	HIC VALVE	17	EGR VALVE
5	VSV	18	JET
6	CHOKE OPENER	19	OUTER VENT CONTROL VALVE
7	TP	20	FUEL VAPOR CANISTER
8	VTV	21	VSV
9	VSV	22	HAI DIAPHRAGM
10	VACUUM SWITCH	23	CB
11	THROTTLE POSITION SWITCH	24	AAP
12	EBCV	25	JET
13	CHECK VALVE	26	THERMO SWITCH

Component location, 88 Nova (4A-LC) California with automatic trans

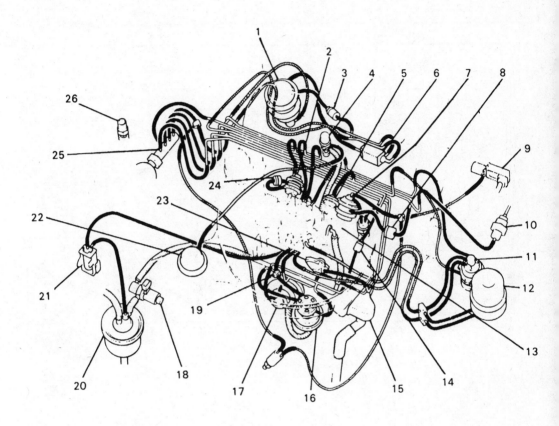

1	DISTRIBUTOR	14	CHECK VALVE
2	CB	15	AS READ VALVE
3	CHECK VALVE	16	EGR VACUUM MODULATOR
4	HIC VALVE	17	EGR VALVE
5	CHOKE OPENER	18	OUTER VENT CONTROL VALVE
6	VSV	19	JET
7	TP	20	FUEL VAPOR CANISTER
8	VTV	21	VSV
9	VSV	22	HAI DIAPHRAGM
10	VACUUM SWITCH	23	AAP
11	HAC VALVE	24	JET
12	EBCV	25	TVSV
13	THROTTLE POSITION SWITCH	26	THERMO SWITCH

Component location, 88 Nova (4A-LC) 49 St. and Canada with automatic trans

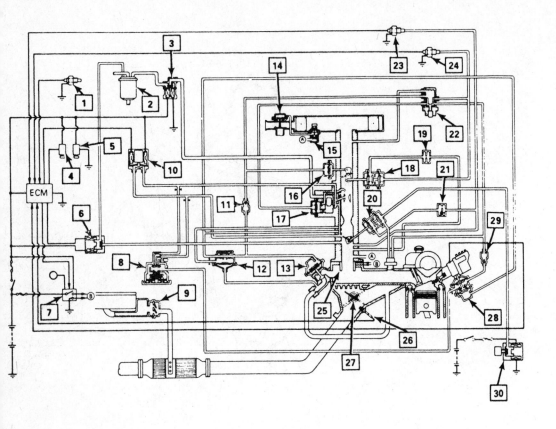

1. THERMO SWITCH
2. CHARCOAL CANISTER
3. OUTER VENT CONTROL VALVE
4. PRIMARY FUEL CUT SOLENOID
5. SECONDARY FUEL CUT SOLENOID
6. VACUUM SWITCHING VALVE
7. COLD MIXTURE HEATER RELAY
8. HIGH ALTITUDE COMPENSATOR VALVE
9. AIR SUCTION VALVE
10. ELECTRIC AIR BLEED CONTROL VALVE
11. CHECK VALVE
12. EGR VACUUM MODULATOR
13. EGR VALVE
14. HOT AIR INTAKE DIAPHRAGM
15. HOT IDLE COMPENSATOR VALVE
16. CHOKE OPENER

17. AUXILIARY ACCELERATOR PUMP
18. CHOKE BREAKER
19. JET
20. THROTTLE POSITIONER
21. DELAY VALVE
22. THERMOSTATIC VACUUM SWITCHING VALVE
23. VACUUM SWITCH (A)
24. VACUUM SWITCH (B)
25. COLD MIXTURE HEATER
26. OXYGEN SENSOR
27. HEAT CONTROL VALVE
28. DISTRIBUTOR
29. CHECK VALVE
30. VACUUM SWITCHING VALVE

Vacuum and wiring diagram, 88 Nova (4A-LC) 49 St. and Canada with manual trans

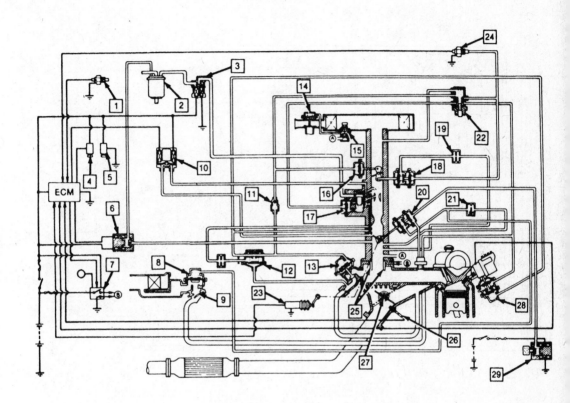

1. THERMO SWITCH
2. CHARCOAL CANISTER
3. OUTER VENT CONTROL VALVE
4. PRIMARY FUEL CUT SOLENOID
5. SECONDARY FUEL CUT SOLENOID
6. VACUUM SWITCHING VALVE
7. COLD MIXTURE HEATER RELAY
8. AIR SUCTION VALVE (SHUT OFF VALVE)
9. AIR SUCTION VALVE (REED VALVE)
10. ELECTRIC AIR BLEED CONTROL VALVE
11. CHECK VALVE
12. EGR VACUUM MODULATOR
13. EGR VALVE
14. HOT AIR INTAKE DIAPHRAGM
15. HOT IDLE COMPENSATOR VALVE

16. CHOKE OPENER
17. AUXILIARY ACCELERATOR PUMP
18. CHOKE BREAKER
19. JET
20. THROTTLE POSITIONER
21. DELAY VALVE
22. THERMOSTATIC VACUUM SWITCHING VALVE
23. THROTTLE POSITION SWITCH
24. VACUUM SWITCH
25. COLD MIXTURE HEATER
26. OXYGEN SENSOR
27. HEAT CONTROL VALVE
28. DISTRIBUTOR
29. VACUUM SWITCHING VALVE
30. JET

Vacuum and wiring diagram, 88 Nova (4A-LC) California with manual trans

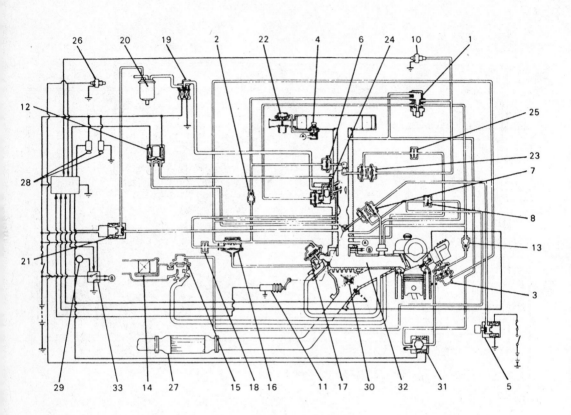

1	TVSV	17	EGR VALVE
2	CHECK VALVE	18	JET
3	DISTRIBUTOR	19	OUTER VENT CONTROL VALVE
4	HIC VALVE	20	FUEL VAPOR CANISTER
5	VSV	21	VSV
6	CHOKE OPENER	22	HAI DIAPHRAGM
7	TP	23	CB
8	VTV	24	AAP
9	VSV	25	JET
10	VACUUM SWITCH	26	THERMO SWITCH
11	THROTTLE POSITION SWITCH	27	TWC
12	EBCV	28	SOLENOID VALVE
13	CHECK VALVE	29	CHC RELAY
14	AS SHUT-OFF VALVE	30	HEAT CONTROL VALVE
15	AS READ VALVE	31	DSD
16	EGR VACUUM MODULATOR	32	CMH
		33	CMH RELAY

Vacuum and wiring diagram, 88 Nova (4A-LC) California with automatic trans

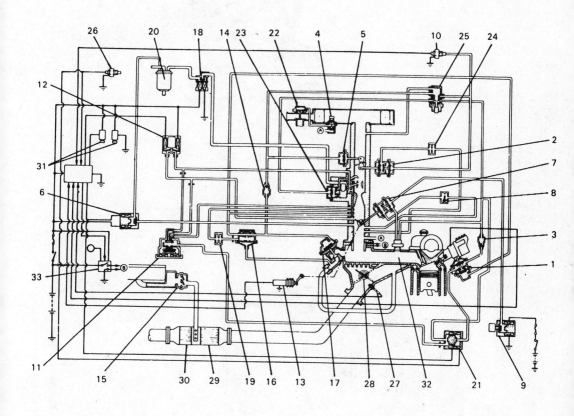

1	DISTRIBUTOR	17	EGR VALVE
2	CB	18	OUTER VENT CONTROL VALVE
3	CHECK VALVE	19	JET
4	HIC VALVE	20	FUEL VAPOR CANISTER
5	CHOKE OPENER	21	VSV
6	VSV	22	HAI DIAPHRAGM
7	TP	23	AAP
8	VTV	24	JET
9	VSV	25	TVSV
10	VACUUM SWITCH	26	THERMO SWITCH
11	HAC VALVE	27	OXYGEN SENSOR
12	EBCV	28	HEAT CONTROL VALVE
13	THROTTLE POSITION SWITCH	29	TWC
14	CHECK VALVE	30	OC
15	AS READ VALVE	31	SOLENOID VALVE
16	EGR VACUUM MODULATOR	32	CMH
		33	CMH RELAY

Vacuum and wiring diagram, 88 Nova (4A-LC) 49 St. and Canada with automatic trans

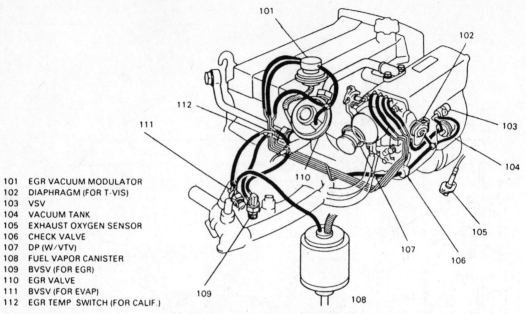

101   EGR VACUUM MODULATOR
102   DIAPHRAGM (FOR T-VIS)
103   VSV
104   VACUUM TANK
105   EXHAUST OXYGEN SENSOR
106   CHECK VALVE
107   DP (W/VTV)
108   FUEL VAPOR CANISTER
109   BVSV (FOR EGR)
110   EGR VALVE
111   BVSV (FOR EVAP)
112   EGR TEMP SWITCH (FOR CALIF.)

Component location, 88 Nova (4A-GE)

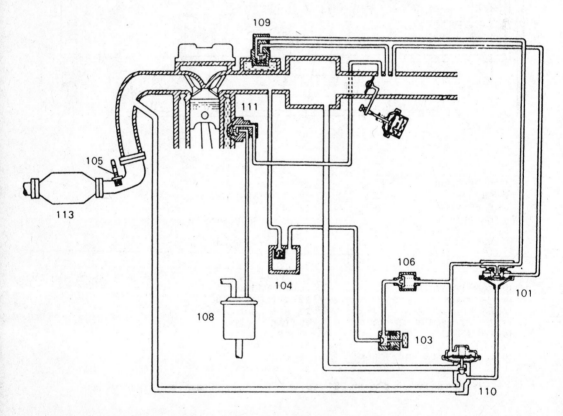

101	EGR VACUUM MODULATOR	108	FUEL VAPOR CANISTER
103	VSV	109	BVSV (FOR EGR)
104	VACUUM TANK	110	EGR VALVE
105	EXHAUST OXYGEN SENSOR	111	BVSV (FOR EVAP)
106	CHECK VALVE	113	TWC

Vacuum routing, 88 Nova (4A-GE)

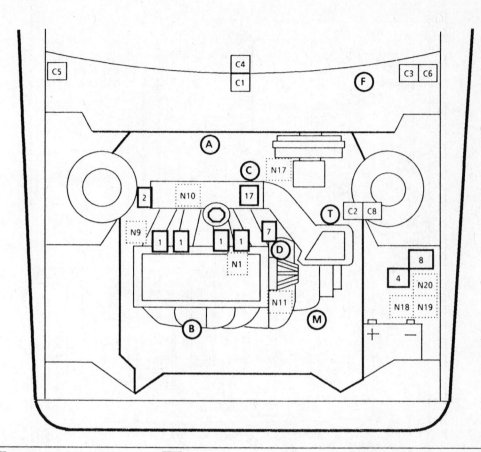

COMPUTER HARNESS
C1 Electronic Control Module (ECM)
C2 Check Connector
C3 "Check Engine" Light
C4 Circuit Opening Relay
C5 ECM Harness Grounds
C6 Fuse Panel
C8 Fuel Pump Test Connector
    (Part of C2)

NOT ECM CONNECTED
N1 Crankcase Vent Valve (PCV)
N9 Fuel Pressure Regulator Valve
N10 Cold Start Injector
N11 Cold Start Injector Valve Switch
N17 Fuel Vapor Canister
N18 A/C Fan Relay #1
N19 A/C Fan Relay #2
N20 A/C Compressor Relay

Exhaust Gas Recirculation (EGR) Valve

CONTROLLED DEVICES
1   Fuel Injectors
2   Idle Vacuum Switching Valve (VSV)
4   EFI Main Relay
7 *EGR Vacuum Switching Valve (VSV)
8   Cooling Fan Relay
17 Throttle Body

INFORMATION SENSORS
A   Manifold Absolute Pressure (MAP)
    Sensor
B   Oxygen (O_2) Sensor
C   Throttle Switch (TS)
D   Coolant Temperature Sensor (CTS)
F   Vehicle Speed Sensor (VSS)
M   Park/Neutral (P/N) Switch
T   Manifold Air Temperature (MAT)
    Sensor

* California Only

Component location, 89–90 Prizm (4A-FE)

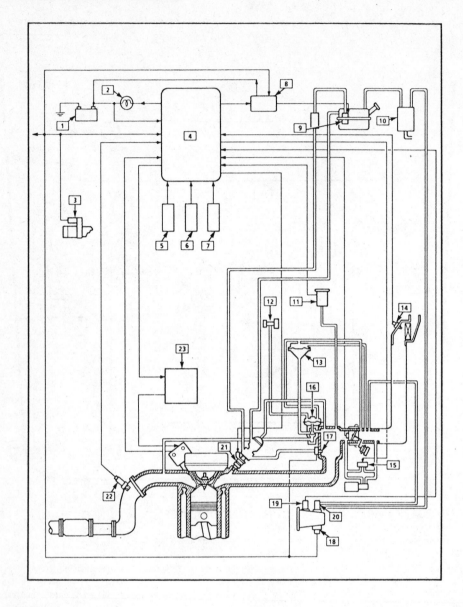

1	BATTERY	**12**	VSV (EGR)
2	CHECK ENGINE WARNING LIGHT	**13**	EGR VACUUM MODULATOR
3	STARTER MOTOR	**14**	MANIFOLD AIR TEMPERATURE (MAT) SENSOR
4	ELECTRONIC CONTROL MODULE (ECM)	**15**	AIR CONDITIONING VACUUM SWITCHING VALVE (A/C VSV) (IF EQUIPPED)
5	A/C INPUT		
6	PARK/NEUTRAL (P/N) SWITCH INPUT	**16**	EXHUAST GAS RECIRCULATION (EGR) VALVE
7	VEHICLE SPEED SENSOR (VSS) INPUT	**17**	COLD START INJECTOR
8	CIRCUIT OPENING RELAY	**18**	COOLANT TEMPERATURE SENSOR (CTS)
9	FUEL PUMP	**19**	BIMETAL VACUUM SWITCHING VALVE (BVSV)
10	FUEL VAPER CANISTER	**20**	FUEL INJECTOR
11	MANIFOLD ABSOLUTE PRESSURE (MAP) SENSOR	**21**	OXYGEN (O_2) SENSOR
		22	IGNITER

Vacuum and wiring diagram, 89–90 Prizm (4A-FE) California

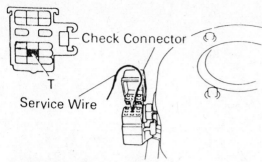

Ground the diagnostic switch terminal (T) to read Prizm ECM codes

21 will show two flashes, a one second pause and then one flash.) Each code will be displayed three times in a row with a three second pause between each code. After any one code has been flashed three times, the next stored code will be displayed three times and so on.

4. After the code(s) have been read and recorded, turn the ignition switch to OFF and disconnect the jumper wire.

WARNING: *Disconnecting the wire with the ignition ON may cause severe damage to the ECM.*

RESETTING THE CHECK ENGINE LIGHT

Once the codes have been read and recorded, the memory on the ECM may be cleared of any stored codes by removing the power to the ECM for at least 20 (4A-GE) or 30 (4A-FE) seconds.

This is most easily done by removing the STOP fuse from the fusebox for the necessary period of time.

WARNING: *The ignition MUST be OFF when the fuse is removed and reinstalled. Serious and disabling damage may occur if this precaution is not followed.*

Remember that the codes are there to indicate a problem area. Don't clear the code just to get the dashboard light off--find the problem and fix it for keeps. If you erase the code and ignore the problem, the code will reset (when the engine is restarted) if the problem is still present.

The necessary time to clear the computer increases as the temperature drops. To be safe, remove the fuse for a full minute under all conditions. The system can also be cleared by disconnecting the negative battery cable, but this will require resetting other memory devices such as the clock and/or radio. If for any reason the memory does not clear, any stored codes will be retained. Any time the ECM is cleared, the car should be driven and then re-checked to confirm a "normal" signal from the ECM.

NOTE: *In the event of any mechanical work requiring the disconnection of the negative battery cable, the ECM should be interrogated for stored codes before removing the cable. Once the cable is removed, the codes will be lost almost immediately. Always check for stored codes before beginning any other diagnostic work.*

Fuel System

CARBURETED FUEL SYSTEM

Mechanical Fuel Pump
REMOVAL AND INSTALLATION

Since the position of the fuel tank is lower than the carburetor, fuel cannot flow to the carburetor under its own power. The mechanical fuel pump is a diaphragm type with built in check valves in the pump chambers. These valves open only in the direction of fuel flow.

The pump is located at the side of the cylinder head intake manifold. To remove the fuel pump:

1. With the engine cold and the key removed from the ignition, label and disconnect the fuel hoses from the fuel pump. Plug the lines as soon as they are removed.
CAUTION: *The fuel system contains gasoline. Wear eye protection and contain spillage. Observe no smoking/no open flame precautions. Have a Class B-C (dry powder) fire extinguisher within arm's reach at all times.*
2. Remove the mounting bolts holding the pump.
3. Remove the fuel pump and the heat insulator assembly.
4. Cover the fuel pump mounting face on the cylinder head to prevent oil leakage.

Troubleshooting Basic Fuel System Problems

Problem	Cause	Solution
Engine cranks, but won't start (or is hard to start) when cold	• Empty fuel tank • Incorrect starting procedure • Defective fuel pump • No fuel in carburetor • Clogged fuel filter • Engine flooded • Defective choke	• Check for fuel in tank • Follow correct procedure • Check pump output • Check for fuel in the carburetor • Replace fuel filter • Wait 15 minutes; try again • Check choke plate
Engine cranks, but is hard to start (or does not start) when hot— (presence of fuel is assumed)	• Defective choke	• Check choke plate
Rough idle or engine runs rough	• Dirt or moisture in fuel • Clogged air filter • Faulty fuel pump	• Replace fuel filter • Replace air filter • Check fuel pump output
Engine stalls or hesitates on acceleration	• Dirt or moisture in the fuel • Dirty carburetor • Defective fuel pump • Incorrect float level, defective accelerator pump	• Replace fuel filter • Clean the carburetor • Check fuel pump output • Check carburetor
Poor gas mileage	• Clogged air filter • Dirty carburetor • Defective choke, faulty carburetor adjustment	• Replace air filter • Clean carburetor • Check carburetor
Engine is flooded (won't start accompanied by smell of raw fuel)	• Improperly adjusted choke or carburetor	• Wait 15 minutes and try again, without pumping gas pedal • If it won't start, check carburetor

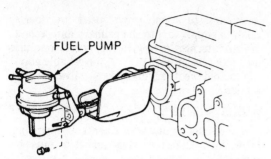

Location of mechanical fuel pump on 4A-LC engine

5. When reinstalling, always use a new gasket. Place the pump and heat insulator in position and install the two bolts.

6. Connect the hoses to the fuel pump.

7. Start the engine and check for leaks.

TESTING

Before performing any checks on the fuel pump, two conditions must be met. First, the pump must be internally "wet". Run a small amount of fuel into the pump so that the check valves will seal properly when tested. Dry valves may not seal and will yield false test results.

Hold the pump without blocking either pipe and operate the pump lever, noting the amount of force needed to move it. This is the reference point for all the tests. Do not apply more than this amount of force to the lever during the testing. Excessive force can damage an otherwise usable pump.

1. To check the inlet valve, block off the outlet and return pipes with your fingers. Operate the lever. There should be an increase in the free play and the arm should move freely.

2. Check the outlet valve by blocking the inlet port with your finger and operating the lever. The arm should lock when the normal amount of force is applied.

3. The diaphragm is checked by blocking the inlet and outlet pipes. When normal force is applied to the lever, the lever should lock and not move. Any lever motion indicates a ruptured diaphragm. This is a common cause of poor fuel mileage and poor acceleration since the correct

amount of fuel is not being delivered to the carburetor.

> NOTE: *The fuel pump must pass all three of these tests to be considered usable. If the pump fails one or more tests, it must be replaced.*

4. Check the oil seal within the pump. Block off the vent hole in the lower part of the pump housing. The lever arm should lock when normal force is applied.

Carburetor

The carburetor is the most complex part of the fuel system. Carburetors vary greatly in construction, but they all operate the same

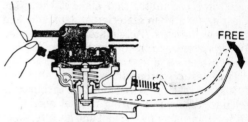

Checking the inlet valve

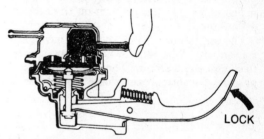

Checking the outlet valve

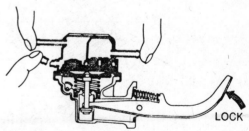

Checking the fuel pump diaphragm

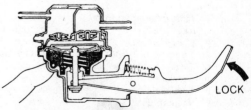

Checking the fuel pump oil seal

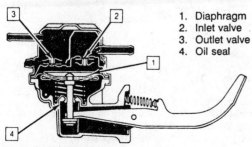

1. Diaphragm
2. Inlet valve
3. Outlet valve
4. Oil seal

Fuel pump components

way; their job is to supply the correct mixture of fuel and air to the engine in response to varying conditions.

Despite their complexity, carburetors function on a simple physical principle known as the venturi principle. Air is drawn into the engine by the pumping action of the pistons. As the air enters the top of the carburetor, it passes through a venturi or restriction in the throttle bore. The air speeds up as it passes through the venturi, causing a slight drop in pressure. This pressure drop pulls fuel from the float bowl through a nozzle in the throttle bore. The air and fuel mix to form a fine mist, which is distributed to the cylinders through the intake manifold.

There are six different systems (fuel/air circuits) in a carburetor that make it work; the Float system, Main Metering system, Idle and Low Speed system, Accelerator Pump system, Power system, and the Choke System. The way these systems are arranged in the carburetor determines the carburetor's size and shape.

It's important to remember that carburetors seldom give trouble during normal operation. Other than changing the fuel and air filters and making sure the idle speed and mixture are proper at every tune-up, there's not much maintenance you can perform on the average carburetor.

The carburetor used on the Nova model is a conventional 2-barrel, downdraft type similar to domestic carburetors. The main circuits are: primary, for normal operational requirements; secondary, to supply high speed fuel needs; float, to supply fuel to the primary and secondary circuits; accelerator, to supply fuel for quick and safe acceleration; choke, for reliable starting in cold weather; and power valve, for fuel economy.

ADJUSTMENTS

Before making any adjustments to the carburetor, ALL of the following conditions must be met:

- All accessories switched off
- Ignition timing correctly set
- Transmission in neutral, parking brake set, wheels blocked front and rear.
- Fuel level (float level) correctly set; view the fuel level in the small window on the right side of the carburetor.
- Tachometer correctly connected. Please refer to Chapter Two for detailed instructions.

When adjusting the carburetor, please resist the temptation to randomly turn screws hoping for the best. The many adjustments on a carburetor interrelate; if you change one setting you may affect three other things. A detailed, reasoned approach to driveability problems will yield much better (and quicker) results than guessing and groping.

Curb Idle (Warm Idle)

The curb idle is adjusted by turning the idle adjusting screw located on the rear of the carburetor. The knob has a knurled plastic head to make grasping easier. Turn it clockwise to in-

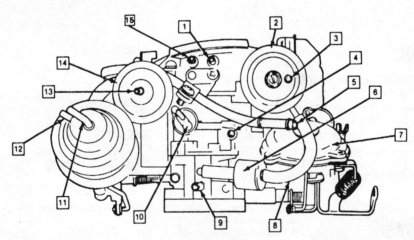

1. Atmosphere port to port J of TVSV
2. Choke breaker
3. To port L of TVSV
4. TP port to throttle positioner
5. Fuel inlet line
6. Vacuum delay valve
7. Secondary throttle vacuum actuator
8. Manifold vacuum to choke breaker
9. Manifold vacuum to HIC valve at the air cleaner
10. No. 2 secondary fuel cut relay
11. To VSV
12. Manifold vacuum (on intake manifold)
13. To M port of TVSV
14. Choke opener
15. Secondary air bleed port to high altitude compensator (HAC)

Front view of the Nova carburetor

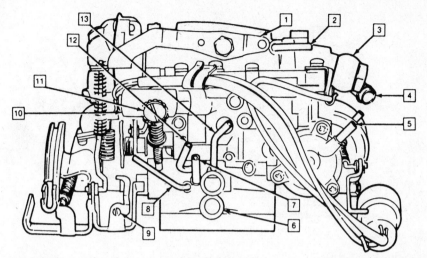

1. Main acceleration pump lever arm
2. Main air bleed port to EBCV
3. Fuel inlet union
4. Bowl vent to charcoal canister
5. Aux.accelerator pump-- vacuum from TVSV
6. Idle mixture adjustment screw plug
7. EGR port to port P of EGR vacuum modulator
8. Charcoal canister purge port from VSV
9. Fast idle adjusting screw
10. No.1 slow cut fuel solenoid
11. Idle speed adjustment screw
12. EGR R port to R port of EGR vacuum modulator
13. Slow air bleed port to EBCV

Rear view of the Nova carburetor

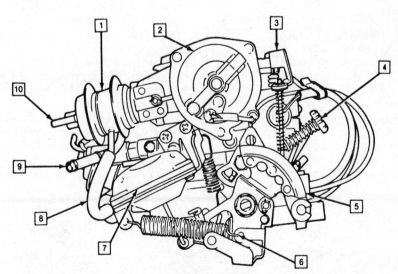

1. Choke breaker
2. Electric choke
3. Accelerator pump lever arm
4. Idle speed adjustment screw
5. Primary throttle lever
6. Throttle return spring
7. Secondary throttle vacuum actuator
8. Manifold vacuum
9. Fuel inlet line
10. From port L of TVSV

Left side view of the Nova carburetor

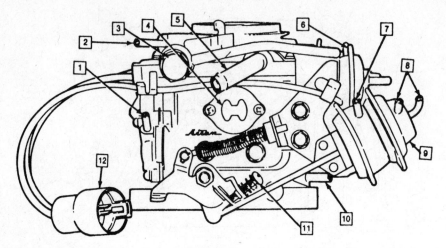

1. Vacuum signal from TVSV to aux. acceleration pump
2. Main air bleed from EBCV
3. Union--fuel line
4. Float bowl window
5. Bowl vent to charcoal canister
6. Choke opener
7. Ported vacuum signal from throttle port
8. Manifold vacuum to VSV
9. Throttle positioner diaphragm
10. Manifold vacuum to HIC valve at the air cleaner
11. Throttle positioner adjustment screw
12. Connector for electric choke and fuel cut solenoids 1 and 2

Right side view of the Nova carburetor

crease idle speed. Correct idle speed for the carbureted Nova is 650 rpm w/manual transmission and 750 rpm w/automatic transmission.

Fast Idle

1. Stop the engine and remove the air cleaner housing.

2. Disconnect and plug the hot idle compensator hose to prevent rough idling.

3. Disconnect the hose from the Thermovacuum Switching Valve (TVSV) port M and plug the port. This will shut off the choke opener and EGR systems.

4. Hold the throttle slightly open, (either move the linkage on the carb or pull lightly on the throttle cable.) push the choke plate closed and hold it closed as you release the throttle.

The carburetor is now "fooled" into thinking it is performing a cold start--the choke is set

and the various external controls are not functioning. These conditions duplicate cold start conditions.

5. Start the engine but DO NOT touch the accelerator pedal or cable. (If you do, the choke will release and step 4 will be needed again.)

CAUTION: *The engine will be running; be careful of moving parts and belts! Keep loose fitting clothes and long hair well away from the engine area!*

6. The correct fast idle speed is 3000 rpm. If adjustment is necessary, turn the fast idle adjusting screw at the lower rear of the carburetor.

WARNING: *Do not allow the engine to run on fast idle any longer than necessary. Once the correct fast idle is achieved, release the fast idle by depressing the accelerator and releasing it. Allow the engine to run at curb idle*

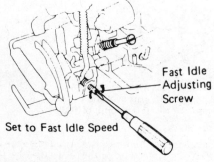

Fast Idle Adjusting Screw

Set to Fast Idle Speed

Adjusting the fast idle screw

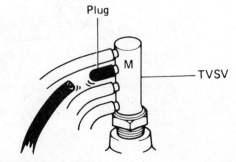

Plug

M

TVSV

"M" port on the TVSV

for about 30 seconds and switch the engine off.

7. Remove the plug and reconnect the hose to the M port of the TVSV.

Throttle Positioner

1. Disconnect the hose from the Thermovacuum Switching Valve (TVSV) port **M** and plug the port. Disconnect the vacuum hose from throttle positioner (TP) diaphragm **A**.

2. Check that the TP is set at the first step; correct engine speed is:
- Manual transmission: 800 rpm
- Automatic transmission: 900 rpm

If necessary, adjust the speed with the adjusting screw.

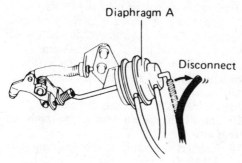

Diaphragm A

Disconnect

Vacuum hose at diaphragm "A"

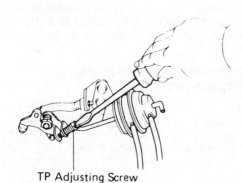

TP Adjusting Screw

Throttle positioner adjusting screw

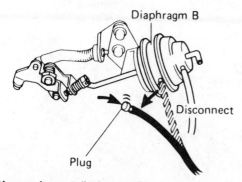

Diaphragm B

Disconnect

Plug

Vacuum hose at diaphragm "B"

NOTE: *Make the adjustment with the cooling (radiator) fan OFF.*

3. Reconnect the vacuum hose to diaphragm **A**.

4. Disconnect the hose from diaphragm **B** and plug the hose end.

5. Check that the TP is set at the second step. The correct engine speed in this position is:
- Manual transmission: 1400 ± 200 rpm
- Automatic transmission: 1500 ± 200 rpm

6. Reconnect the vacuum hose to diaphragm **B** and check that the engine returns to normal idle within 2–6 seconds.

7. Remove the plug and reconnect the vacuum hose to TVSV port **M**.

Float and Fuel Level

The float level is not externally adjustable. Removal of the air horn assembly or top of the carburetor is required. The engine should be cold during this procedure. All work is performed with the engine off.

The float in the carburetor controls the entry of fuel into the bowl of the carburetor. (The bowl is simply a reservoir which keeps fuel available at all times.) The function of the float is to react to the level of fuel in the bowl and open or close a valve, thus maintaining the correct amount of fuel. The principle is identical to the float in a toilet tank; when the correct level is reached, the flow is shut off.

The position of the float (and therefore the amount of fuel available) is critical to the proper operation of the engine. If too little fuel is in the bowl, the engine may starve on sharp corners or on hills; too much fuel can literally lead to overflowing and flooding of the engine. To adjust the float level:

1. Remove the air cleaner assembly and disconnect the choke linkage.

2. Disconnect the acclerator pump connecting rod.

3. Remove the pump arm pivot screw and the pump arm.

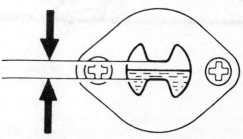

CORRECT LEVEL

No float level adjustment is necessary when the fuel level falls between the line on the carburetor sight glass

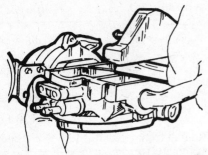

Checking the float level with the float in resting on the needle valve

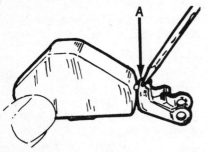

Float adjustment at point (A) while in the resting position

Measuring the float in the raised position

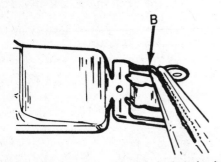

Float adjustment at point (b) while in the raised position

4. Remove the fuel hose and union.

5. Remove the eight air horn screws. Be careful to identify and collect the external parts attached to the screws, such as wire clamps, brackets and the steel number plate.

6. Disconnect the choke link.

7. Lift the air horn with its gasket from the body of the carburetor.

8. Disconnect the wires at the connector.

9. Remove the gasket from the air horn assembly. Invert the air horn so that the float hangs down by its own weight. Check the clearance between the float tip and the air horn. The correct clearance is 7.0mm. If necessary, adjust the float lip by bending it gently into position.

10. Lift up the float and check the clearance between the needle valve plunger and the float lip. Correct clearance is 1.6–2.0mm. If necessary, adjust the clearance by bending the outer part of the float lip.

NOTE: *If the float has become misadjusted, it may be due to the float filling with gasoline. Give the float a gentle shake and listen for any liquid within. If fuel is inside the float, replace the float and reset the levels.*

11. Install a new gasket onto the air horn.

12. Place the air horn in position on the carburetor body and install the choke link.

13. Install the eight screws. Make certain the brackets, clips and steel tag are reinstalled as well.

14. Connect the fuel hose and union.

15. Install the pump arm pivot screw and pump arm.

16. Connect the pump arm connecting rod.

17. Attach the choke linkage.

18. Install the air cleaner. Start the engine and check carefully for fuel and/or vacuum leaks. The engine may be difficult to start; once it is running smoothly, recheck the fuel level in the sight glass.

CARBURETOR REMOVAL AND INSTALLATION

NOTE: *Each fuel and vacuum line must be tagged or labeled individually during disassembly.*

1. Remove the air cleaner assembly.

2. Disconnect the accelerator cable from the carburetor.

3. If equipped with automatic transmission, disconnect the throttle position cable.

4. Unplug the wiring connector.

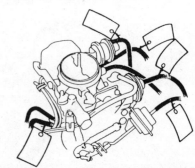

Tag and label every hose during disassembly

5. Label and disconnect the:
   a. carburetor vacuum hoses
   b. fuel inlet hoses
   c. charcoal canister hose

CAUTION: *The carburetor contains gasoline. Wear eye protection and contain spillage. Observe no smoking/no open flame precautions. Have a Class B-C (dry powder) fire extinguisher within arm's reach at all times.*

6. Remove the carburetor mounting nuts.

7. Remove the cold mixture heater wire clamp and lift out the EGR vacuum modulator bracket.

8. Lift the carburetor off the engine and place it on a clean cloth on the workbench. If desired, the insulator (base gasket) may also be removed.

9. Cover the inlet area of the manifold with clean rags. This will prevent the entry of dust, dirt and loose parts.

10. When reinstalling, place the insulator on the manifold, making sure it is correctly positioned.

11. Install the carburetor onto the manifold.

12. Install the EGR vacuum modulator bracket. Clamp the cold mixture heater wire into place.

13. Tighten the carburetor mounting nuts.

14. Reconnect the fuel inlet hose, the charcoal canister hose and the vacuum hoses.

15. Connect the wiring connector.

16. connect the accelerator cable; connect the throttle position cable if equipped with automatic transmission.

17. Reinstall the air cleaner.

CARBURETOR OVERHAUL

Efficient carburetion depends greatly on careful cleaning and inspection during overhaul since dirt, gum, water, or varnish in or on the carburetor parts are often responsible for poor performance.

Overhaul your carburetor in a clean, dustfree area. Carefully disassemble the carburetor, referring often to the exploded views. Keep all similar and look-alike parts segregated during disassembly and cleaning to avoid accidental interchange during assembly. Make a note of all jet sizes.

When the carburetor is disassembled, wash all parts (except diaphragms, electric choke units, pump plunger, and any other plastic, leather, fiber, or rubber parts) in clean carburetor solvent. Do not leave parts in the solvent any longer than necessary to sufficiently loosen the deposits. Excessive cleaning may remove the special finish from the float bowl and check valve bodies leaving these parts unfit for service. Rinse all parts in clean solvent and blow them dry with compressed air or allow them to air dry. Wipe clean all cork, plastic, and fiber parts with clean, lint-free cloth.

Blow out all passages and jets with compressed air and be sure that there are no restrictions or blockages. Never use wire or similar tools to clean jets, fuel passages, or air bleeds. Clean all jets and valves separately to avoid accidental interchange.

Check all parts for wear or damage. If wear or damage is found, replace the defective parts. Pay special attention to the following areas:

1. Check the float needle and seat for wear. If wear is found, replace the complete assembly.

2. Check the float hinge pin for wear and the float(s) for dents or distortion. Replace the float if fuel has leaked into it.

3. Check the throttle and choke shaft bores for wear or an out-of-round condition. Damage or wear to the throttle arm, shaft or shaft bore will often require the replacement of the throttle body. These parts require a close tolerance of fit; wear may allow air leakage, which could affect starting and idling.

NOTE: *Throttle shafts and bushings are not included in overhaul kits. They may be available separately.*

4. Inspect the idle mixture adjusting needles for burrs or grooves. Any such condition requires replacement of the needle, since you will not be able to obtain a satisfactory idle.

5. Test the accelerator pump check valves. They should pass air one way but not the other. Replace the valve if necessary. If the valve is satisfactory, wash the valve again to remove breath moisture.

6. Check the bowl cover for warped surfaces with a straightedge.

7. Closely inspect the valves and seats for wear and damage, replacing as necessary.

8. After the carburetor is assembled, check the choke valve (plate) for freedom of operation.

Carburetor overhaul kits are recommended for each overhaul. These kits contain all the gaskets and new parts to replace those that deteriorate most rapidly. Failure to replace all parts supplied with the kit (especially gaskets) can result in poor performance later.

Some carburetor manufacturers supply overhaul kits of 3 basic types: minor repair; major repair; and gasket kits. Generally, they contain the following:

Minor Repair
- All gaskets
- Float needle valve
- Volume control screw
- All diaphragms
- Spring for the pump diaphragm
- All gaskets

Major Repair Kits:
- All jets and gaskets

- All diaphragms
- Float needle valve
- Volume control screw
- Pump ball valve
- Float(s)
- All gaskets

Gasket Kits:

- All gaskets

After cleaning and checking all components, reassemble the carburetor, using new parts and referring to the exploded view. When reassembling, make sure that all screws and jets are tight in their seats, but do not overtighten, as the tips will be distorted. Tighten all screws gradually, in rotation. Do not tighten the needle valve(s) into their seats; uneven jetting will result. Always use new gaskets. Be sure to adjust the float level when reassembling.

NOTE: *The following instructions are organized so that only one component group is being worked on at a time. This helps avoid confusion and interchange of parts. To make reassembly easier, always arrange disassembled parts in order on the workbench. Be very careful not to mix up or lose small pieces such as balls, clips or springs.*

Reassembly and adjustment of the carburetor requires accurate measuring equipment capable of checking clearances to the $\frac{1}{1000}$mm. These specialized carburetor clearance guages are available at reputable tool retailers but may be difficult to find.

1. Remove the carburetor as outlined previously.

2. To remove the AIR HORN assembly, disconnect the choke link and the pump connecting rod.

3. Remove the pump arm pivot screw and the pump arm.

4. Remove the fuel hose and union.

5. Remove the eight air horn screws. Be careful to identify and collect the external parts attached to the screws, such as wire clamps, brackets and the steel number plate.

6. Disconnect the choke link.

7. Lift the air horn with its gasket from the body of the carburetor.

8. Disconnect the wires at the connector.

9. Remove the first and second solenoids from the carburetor body.

10. Remove the float pivot pin, float and needle valve assembly.

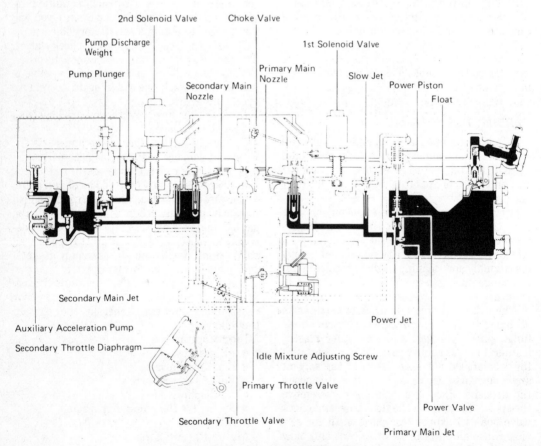

Nova's carburetor component location

11. Remove the air horn gasket.

12. Remove the needle valve seat and gasket.

13. Remove the power piston retainer, power piston and spring.

14. Pull out the pump plunger and remove the boot.

15. Begin disassembly of the BODY by removing the throttle positioner. Disconnect the link and remove the two bolts.

16. Remove the stopper gasket, the pump discharge weight, the long spring and the large discharge ball.

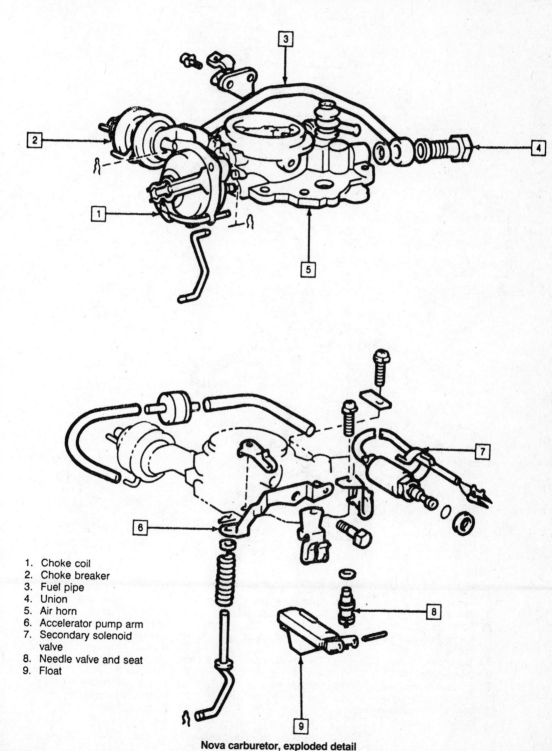

1. Choke coil
2. Choke breaker
3. Fuel pipe
4. Union
5. Air horn
6. Accelerator pump arm
7. Secondary solenoid valve
8. Needle valve and seat
9. Float

Nova carburetor, exploded detail

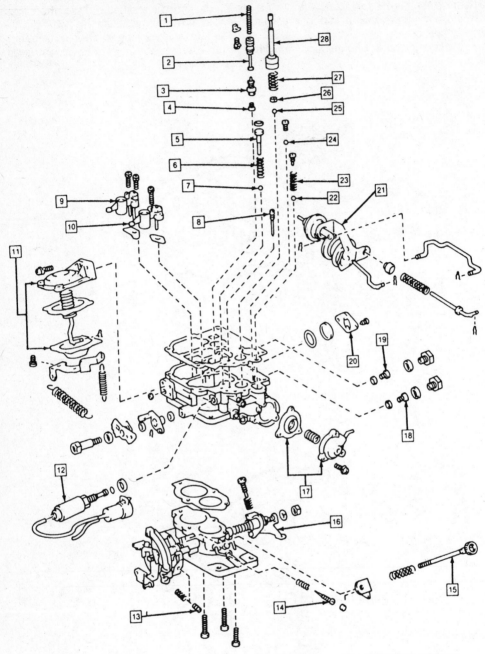

1. Power piston spring
2. Power piston
3. Power valve
4. Power jet
5. Pump discharge weight
6. Spring
7. Steel ball
8. Slow jet (idle jet)
9. Secondary small venturi
10. Primary small venturi
11. Secondary throttle valve actuator assembly
12. Primary solenoid valve
13. Fast idle adjusting screw
14. Idle mixture adjusting screw
15. Idle speed adjusting screw
16. Throttle positioner lever
17. Aux. accelerator pump
18. Primary main jet
19. Secondary main jet
20. Sight glass retainer
21. Choke breaker and throttle positioner diaphragm
22. Steel ball
23. Spring
24. Steel ball
25. Steel ball
26. Check ball retainer
27. Pump damping spring
28. Pump plunger

Exploded view of the Nova carburetor

CHILTON'S
FUEL ECONOMY
& TUNE-UP TIPS

Tune-up • Spark Plug Diagnosis • Emission Controls

Fuel System • Cooling System • Tires and Wheels

General Maintenance

CHILTON'S FUEL ECONOMY & TUNE-UP TIPS

Fuel economy is important to everyone, no matter what kind of vehicle you drive. The maintenance-minded motorist can save both money and fuel using these tips and the periodic maintenance and tune-up procedures in this Repair and Tune-Up Guide.

There are more than 130,000,000 cars and trucks registered for private use in the United States. Each travels an average of 10-12,000 miles per year, and, and in total they consume close to 70 billion gallons of fuel each year. This represents nearly ⅔ of the oil imported by the United States each year. The Federal government's goal is to reduce consumption 10% by 1985. A variety of methods are either already in use or under serious consideration, and they all affect you driving and the cars you will drive. In addition to "down-sizing", the auto industry is using or investigating the use of electronic fuel delivery, electronic engine controls and alternative engines for use in smaller and lighter vehicles, among other alternatives to meet the federally mandated Corporate Average Fuel Economy (CAFE) of 27.5 mpg by 1985. The government, for its part, is considering rationing, mandatory driving curtailments and tax increases on motor vehicle fuel in an effort to reduce consumption. The government's goal of a 10% reduction could be realized — and further government regulation avoided — if every private vehicle could use just 1 less gallon of fuel per week.

How Much Can You Save?

Tests have proven that almost anyone can make at least a 10% reduction in fuel consumption through regular maintenance and tune-ups. When a major manufacturer of spark plugs sur-

TUNE-UP

1. Check the cylinder compression to be sure the engine will really benefit from a tune-up and that it is capable of producing good fuel economy. A tune-up will be wasted on an engine in poor mechanical condition.

2. Replace spark plugs regularly. New spark plugs alone can increase fuel economy 3%.

3. Be sure the spark plugs are the correct type (heat range) for your vehicle. See the Tune-Up Specifications.

Heat range refers to the spark plug's ability to conduct heat away from the firing end. It must conduct the heat away in an even pattern to avoid becoming a source of pre-ignition, yet it must also operate hot enough to burn off conductive deposits that could cause misfiring.

The heat range is usually indicated by a number on the spark plug, part of the manufacturer's designation for each individual spark plug. The numbers in bold-face indicate the heat range in each manufacturer's identification system.

Manufacturer	Typical Designation
AC	R **45** TS
Bosch (old)	WA **145** T30
Bosch (new)	HR **8** Y
Champion	RBL **15** Y
Fram/Autolite	**4**15
Mopar	P-**62** PR
Motorcraft	BRF-**42**
NGK	BP **5** ES-15
Nippondenso	W **16** EP
Prestolite	14GR **5** 2A

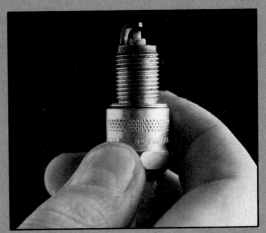

Periodically, check the spark plugs to be sure they are firing efficiently. They are excellent indicators of the internal condition of your engine.

On AC, Bosch (new), Champion, Fram/Autolite, Mopar, Motorcraft and Prestolite, a higher number indicates a hotter plug. On Bosch (old), NGK and Nippondenso, a higher number indicates a colder plug.

4. Make sure the spark plugs are properly gapped. See the Tune-Up Specifications in this book.

5. Be sure the spark plugs are firing efficiently. The illustrations on the next 2 pages show you how to "read" the firing end of the spark plug.

6. Check the ignition timing and set it to specifications. Tests show that almost all cars have incorrect ignition timing by more than 2°.

veyed over 6,000 cars nationwide, they found that a tune-up, on cars that needed one, increased fuel economy over 11%. Replacing worn plugs alone, accounted for a 3% increase. The same test also revealed that 8 out of every 10 vehicles will have some maintenance deficiency that will directly affect fuel economy, emissions or performance. Most of this mileage-robbing neglect could be prevented with regular maintenance.

Modern engines require that all of the functioning systems operate properly for maximum efficiency. A malfunction anywhere wastes fuel. You can keep your vehicle running as efficiently and economically as possible, by being aware of your vehicle's operating and performance characteristics. If your vehicle suddenly develops performance or fuel economy problems it could be due to one or more of the following:

PROBLEM	POSSIBLE CAUSE
Engine Idles Rough	Ignition timing, idle mixture, vacuum leak or something amiss in the emission control system.
Hesitates on Acceleration	Dirty carburetor or fuel filter, improper accelerator pump setting, ignition timing or fouled spark plugs.
Starts Hard or Fails to Start	Worn spark plugs, improperly set automatic choke, ice (or water) in fuel system.
Stalls Frequently	Automatic choke improperly adjusted and possible dirty air filter or fuel filter.
Performs Sluggishly	Worn spark plugs, dirty fuel or air filter, ignition timing or automatic choke out of adjustment.

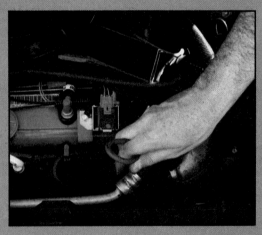

Check spark plug wires on conventional point type ignition for cracks by bending them in a loop around your finger.

Be sure that spark plug wires leading to adjacent cylinders do not run too close together. (Photo courtesy Champion Spark Plug Co.)

7. If your vehicle does not have electronic ignition, check the points, rotor and cap as specified.

8. Check the spark plug wires (used with conventional point-type ignitions) for cracks and burned or broken insulation by bending them in a loop around your finger. Cracked wires decrease fuel efficiency by failing to deliver full voltage to the spark plugs. One misfiring spark plug can cost you as much as 2 mpg.

9. Check the routing of the plug wires. Misfiring can be the result of spark plug leads to adjacent cylinders running parallel to each other and too close together. One wire tends to pick up voltage from the other causing it to fire "out of time".

10. Check all electrical and ignition circuits for voltage drop and resistance.

11. Check the distributor mechanical and/or vacuum advance mechanisms for proper functioning. The vacuum advance can be checked by twisting the distributor plate in the opposite direction of rotation. It should spring back when released.

12. Check and adjust the valve clearance on engines with mechanical lifters. The clearance should be slightly loose rather than too tight.

SPARK PLUG DIAGNOSIS

Normal

APPEARANCE: This plug is typical of one operating normally. The insulator nose varies from a light tan to grayish color with slight electrode wear. The presence of slight deposits is normal on used plugs and will have no adverse effect on engine performance. The spark plug heat range is correct for the engine and the engine is running normally.

CAUSE: Properly running engine.

RECOMMENDATION: Before reinstalling this plug, the electrodes should be cleaned and filed square. Set the gap to specifications. If the plug has been in service for more than 10-12,000 miles, the entire set should probably be replaced with a fresh set of the same heat range.

Oil Deposits

APPEARANCE: The firing end of the plug is covered with a wet, oily coating.

CAUSE: The problem is poor oil control. On high mileage engines, oil is leaking past the rings or valve guides into the combustion chamber. A common cause is also a plugged PCV valve, and a ruptured fuel pump diaphragm can also cause this condition. Oil fouled plugs such as these are often found in new or recently overhauled engines, before normal oil control is achieved, and can be cleaned and reinstalled.

RECOMMENDATION: A hotter spark plug may temporarily relieve the problem, but the engine is probably in need of work.

Incorrect Heat Range

APPEARANCE: The effects of high temperature on a spark plug are indicated by clean white, often blistered insulator. This can also be accompanied by excessive wear of the electrode, and the absence of deposits.

CAUSE: Check for the correct spark plug heat range. A plug which is too hot for the engine can result in overheating. A car operated mostly at high speeds can require a colder plug. Also check ignition timing, cooling system level, fuel mixture and leaking intake manifold.

RECOMMENDATION: If all ignition and engine adjustments are known to be correct, and no other malfunction exists, install spark plugs one heat range colder.

Carbon Deposits

APPEARANCE: Carbon fouling is easily identified by the presence of dry, soft, black, sooty deposits.

CAUSE: Changing the heat range can often lead to carbon fouling, as can prolonged slow, stop-and-start driving. If the heat range is correct, carbon fouling can be attributed to a rich fuel mixture, sticking choke, clogged air cleaner, worn breaker points, retarded timing or low compression. If only one or two plugs are carbon fouled, check for corroded or cracked wires on the affected plugs. Also look for cracks in the distributor cap between the towers of affected cylinders.

RECOMMENDATION: After the problem is corrected, these plugs can be cleaned and reinstalled if not worn severely.

MMT Fouled

APPEARANCE: Spark plugs fouled by MMT (Methycyclopentadienyl Maganese Tricarbonyl) have reddish, rusty appearance on the insulator and side electrode.

CAUSE: MMT is an anti-knock additive in gasoline used to replace lead. During the combustion process, the MMT leaves a reddish deposit on the insulator and side electrode.

RECOMMENDATION: No engine malfunction is indicated and the deposits will not affect plug performance any more than lead deposits (see Ash Deposits). MMT fouled plugs can be cleaned, regapped and reinstalled.

High Speed Glazing

APPEARANCE: Glazing appears as shiny coating on the plug, either yellow or tan in color.

CAUSE: During hard, fast acceleration, plug temperatures rise suddenly. Deposits from normal combustion have no chance to fluff-off; instead, they melt on the insulator forming an electrically conductive coating which causes misfiring.

RECOMMENDATION: Glazed plugs are not easily cleaned. They should be replaced with a fresh set of plugs of the correct heat range. If the condition recurs, using plugs with a heat range one step colder may cure the problem.

Ash (Lead) Deposits

APPEARANCE: Ash deposits are characterized by light brown or white colored deposits crusted on the side or center electrodes. In some cases it may give the plug a rusty appearance.

CAUSE: Ash deposits are normally derived from oil or fuel additives burned during normal combustion. Normally they are harmless, though excessive amounts can cause misfiring. If deposits are excessive in short mileage, the valve guides may be worn.

RECOMMENDATION: Ash-fouled plugs can be cleaned, gapped and reinstalled.

Detonation

APPEARANCE: Detonation is usually characterized by a broken plug insulator.

CAUSE: A portion of the fuel charge will begin to burn spontaneously, from the increased heat following ignition. The explosion that results applies extreme pressure to engine components, frequently damaging spark plugs and pistons.

Detonation can result by over-advanced ignition timing, inferior gasoline (low octane) lean air/fuel mixture, poor carburetion, engine lugging or an increase in compression ratio due to combustion chamber deposits or engine modification.

RECOMMENDATION: Replace the plugs after correcting the problem.

Photos Courtesy Champion Spark Plug Co.

EMISSION CONTROLS

13. Be aware of the general condition of the emission control system. It contributes to reduced pollution and should be serviced regularly to maintain efficient engine operation.

14. Check all vacuum lines for dried, cracked or brittle conditions. Something as simple as a leaking vacuum hose can cause poor performance and loss of economy.

15. Avoid tampering with the emission control system. Attempting to improve fuel econ-

FUEL SYSTEM

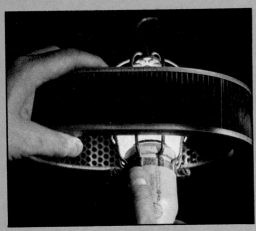

Check the air filter with a light behind it. If you can see light through the filter it can be reused.

Extremely clogged filters should be discarded and replaced with a new one.

18. Replace the air filter regularly. A dirty air filter richens the air/fuel mixture and can increase fuel consumption as much as 10%. Tests show that 1/3 of all vehicles have air filters in need of replacement.

19. Replace the fuel filter at least as often as recommended.

20. Set the idle speed and carburetor mixture to specifications.

21. Check the automatic choke. A sticking or malfunctioning choke wastes gas.

22. During the summer months, adjust the automatic choke for a leaner mixture which will produce faster engine warm-ups.

COOLING SYSTEM

29. Be sure all accessory drive belts are in good condition. Check for cracks or wear.

30. Adjust all accessory drive belts to proper tension.

31. Check all hoses for swollen areas, worn spots, or loose clamps.

32. Check coolant level in the radiator or ex-pansion tank.

33. Be sure the thermostat is operating properly. A stuck thermostat delays engine warm-up and a cold engine uses nearly twice as much fuel as a warm engine.

34. Drain and replace the engine coolant at least as often as recommended. Rust and scale

TIRES & WHEELS

38. Check the tire pressure often with a pencil type gauge. Tests by a major tire manufacturer show that 90% of all vehicles have at least 1 tire improperly inflated. Better mileage can be achieved by over-inflating tires, but never exceed the maximum inflation pressure on the side of the tire.

39. If possible, install radial tires. Radial tires deliver as much as 1/2 mpg more than bias belted tires.

40. Avoid installing super-wide tires. They only create extra rolling resistance and decrease fuel mileage. Stick to the manufacturer's recommendations.

41. Have the wheels properly balanced.

omy by tampering with emission controls is more likely to worsen fuel economy than improve it. Emission control changes on modern engines are not readily reversible.

16. Clean (or replace) the EGR valve and lines as recommended.

17. Be sure that all vacuum lines and hoses are reconnected properly after working under the hood. An unconnected or misrouted vacuum line can wreak havoc with engine performance.

23. Check for fuel leaks at the carburetor, fuel pump, fuel lines and fuel tank. Be sure all lines and connections are tight.

24. Periodically check the tightness of the carburetor and intake manifold attaching nuts and bolts. These are a common place for vacuum leaks to occur.

25. Clean the carburetor periodically and lubricate the linkage.

26. The condition of the tailpipe can be an excellent indicator of proper engine combustion. After a long drive at highway speeds, the inside of the tailpipe should be a light grey in color. Black or soot on the insides indicates an overly rich mixture.

27. Check the fuel pump pressure. The fuel pump may be supplying more fuel than the engine needs.

28. Use the proper grade of gasoline for your engine. Don't try to compensate for knocking or "pinging" by advancing the ignition timing. This practice will only increase plug temperature and the chances of detonation or pre-ignition with relatively little performance gain.

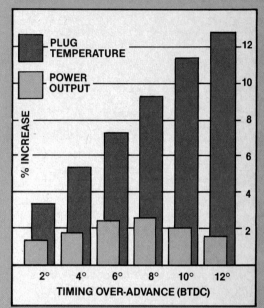

Increasing ignition timing past the specified setting results in a drastic increase in spark plug temperature with increased chance of detonation or preignition. Performance increase is considerably less. (Photo courtesy Champion Spark Plug Co.)

that form in the engine should be flushed out to allow the engine to operate at peak efficiency.

35. Clean the radiator of debris that can decrease cooling efficiency.

36. Install a flex-type or electric cooling fan, if you don't have a clutch type fan. Flex fans use curved plastic blades to push more air at low speeds when more cooling is needed; at high speeds the blades flatten out for less resistance. Electric fans only run when the engine temperature reaches a predetermined level.

37. Check the radiator cap for a worn or cracked gasket. If the cap does not seal properly, the cooling system will not function properly.

42. Be sure the front end is correctly aligned. A misaligned front end actually has wheels going in differed directions. The increased drag can reduce fuel economy by .3 mpg.

43. Correctly adjust the wheel bearings. Wheel bearings that are adjusted too tight increase rolling resistance.

Check tire pressures regularly with a reliable pocket type gauge. Be sure to check the pressure on a cold tire.

GENERAL MAINTENANCE

Check the fluid levels (particularly engine oil) on a regular basis. Be sure to check the oil for grit, water or other contamination.

A vacuum gauge is another excellent indicator of internal engine condition and can also be installed in the dash as a mileage indicator.

44. Periodically check the fluid levels in the engine, power steering pump, master cylinder, automatic transmission and drive axle.

45. Change the oil at the recommended interval and change the filter at every oil change. Dirty oil is thick and causes extra friction between moving parts, cutting efficiency and increasing wear. A worn engine requires more frequent tune-ups and gets progressively worse fuel economy. In general, use the lightest viscosity oil for the driving conditions you will encounter.

46. Use the recommended viscosity fluids in the transmission and axle.

47. Be sure the battery is fully charged for fast starts. A slow starting engine wastes fuel.

48. Be sure battery terminals are clean and tight.

49. Check the battery electrolyte level and add distilled water if necessary.

50. Check the exhaust system for crushed pipes, blockages and leaks.

51. Adjust the brakes. Dragging brakes or brakes that are not releasing create increased drag on the engine.

52. Install a vacuum gauge or miles-per-gallon gauge. These gauges visually indicate engine vacuum in the intake manifold. High vacuum = good mileage and low vacuum = poorer mileage. The gauge can also be an excellent indicator of internal engine conditions.

53. Be sure the clutch is properly adjusted. A slipping clutch wastes fuel.

54. Check and periodically lubricate the heat control valve in the exhaust manifold. A sticking or inoperative valve prevents engine warm-up and wastes gas.

55. Keep accurate records to check fuel economy over a period of time. A sudden drop in fuel economy may signal a need for tune-up or other maintenance.

17. Using a pair of tweezers, remove the plunger retainer and the small ball.
18. Remove the slow jet from the body.
19. Remove the power valve with the jet.
20. Disassemble the power valve and jet.
21. Remove the throttle positioner levers. Re-

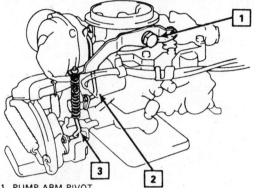

1. PUMP ARM PIVOT
2. CHOKE LINK
3. PUMP ROD

Carburetor pump linkage

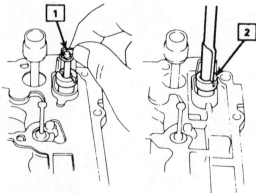

1. NEEDLE VALVE
2. SEAT

Needle valve removal

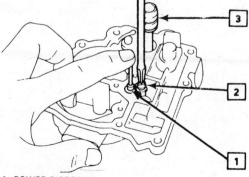

1. POWER PISTON
2. POWER PISTON RETAINER
3. PUMP PLUNGER

Removing the power piston

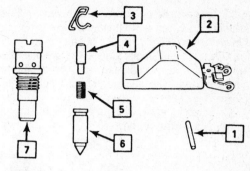

1. PIVOT PIN   5. SPRING
2. FLOAT   6. NEEDLE VALVE
3. PIN CLIP   7. STRAINER
4. PLUNGER

Float and needle valve components

move the primary main passage plug, primary main jet and the gasket.
22. Remove the auxilary accelerator pump (AAP) housing, spring and diaphragm.
23. Remove the inlet plug and the small ball for the AAP.
24. Remove the outlet plug, short spring and the small ball.
25. Remove the primary and secondary venturies.
26. Remove the sight glass retainer, the glass and its O-ring.
27. Remove the throttle return spring and the throttle back spring.
28. Remove the nut and the throttle lever.
29. Remove the bolt and the fast idle cam.
30. Remove the secondary throttle valve diaphragm by disconnecting the linkage and removing the assembly with its gasket.
31. Remove the three bolts and the vacuum passage bolt. Separate the carburetor body from the carburetor flange.
32. Clean all the disassembled parts before inspecting them. Wash and clean the cast metal parts with a soft brush in carburetor cleaner. Clean off the carbon around the throttle plates. Wash the other parts thoroughly in cleaner.

Blow all dirt and other foreign matter from the jets, fuel passages and restrictions within the body.

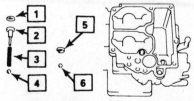

1. STOPPER GASKET
2. PUMP DISCHARGE WEIGHT   5. PLUNGER RETAINER
3. SPRING   6. CHECK BALL (SMALL)
4. DISCHARGE BALL (LARGE)

Accelerator pump check balls and components

33. Inspect the float and needle valve. Check the pivot pin for scratches and excessive wear. Inspect the float for breaks in the lip and wear in the pivot pin holes. Check the needle valve plunger for wear or damage and the spring for deformation. The strainer should be checked for rust or breaks.

34. Make certain the power piston moves smoothly within its bore.

35. Check the power valve for proper air flow. In its normal (expanded) condition, no air should pass through it. When compressed at one end, air hould enter the end and exit through the side vent.

36. Inspect the fuel cut solenoids. Connect the solenoid leads to the battery terminals (the solenoid with only one lead requires a jumper

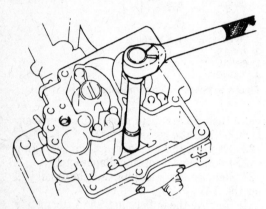

Removing the power valve

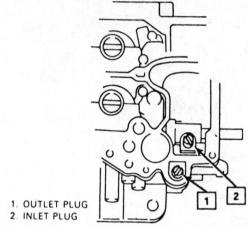

1. OUTLET PLUG
2. INLET PLUG

Removing the auxillary accelerator pump check ball plugs

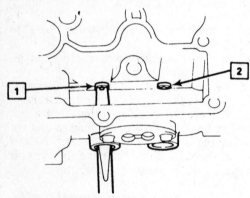

1. PRIMARY JET
2. SECONDARY JET

Removing the main jets

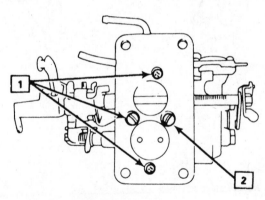

1. RETAINING SCREWS
2. SPECIAL PASSAGE SCREW

Body and flange retaining screws. Note that one screw contains a vacuum passage

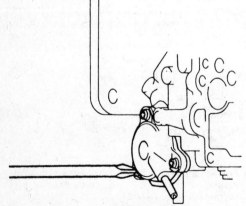

Removing the auxillary accelerator pump

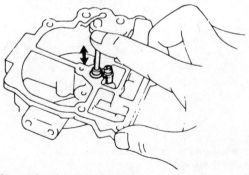

Inspecting the power piston

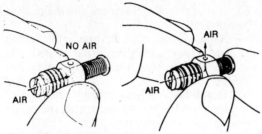

Inspecting the power valve

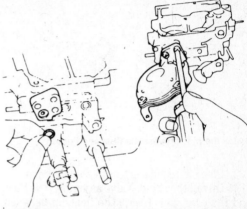

Installing the secondary throttle valve diaphragm

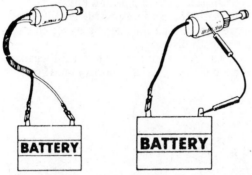

Testing the primary (left) and secondary fuel cut solenoids

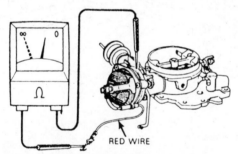

RED WIRE

Checking the resistance of the choke heater

between the case and the battery) and check that the solenoid clicks as the last connection is made. The solenoid should click each time the battery is connected or disconnected. If a solenoid is not operating correctly, replace it.

37. Install new O-rings on the solenoids.

38. Inspect the choke heater by using an ohmmeter to measure its resistance. Corrrect resistance is 18Ω. If a problem is found, the air horn assembly must be repalced.

39. Reassembly begins by placing a new gasket and the carburetor body onto the flange.

40. Install the vacuum passage bolt, then install the three retaining bolts.

41. Assemble the secondary throttle diaphragm, position the gasket and install the assembly. Connect the linkage.

42. Install the fast idle cam with the bolt.

43. Install the throttle lever with its nut.

44. Install the throttle back spring and the throttle return spring.

45. Install the sight glass with its O-ring and retainer.

46. Install the primary and secondary small ventures over new gaskets. Install the O-ring on the primary small ventures.

47. Install the auxilary accelerator pump by first installing the outer plug, the short spring and the small ball. Install the inlet plug and the small ball, followed by the AAP housing, spring and diaphragm.

48. Install the primary main jet and passage plug with a new gasket.

49. Install the secondary main jet and passage plug with a new gasket.

50. Instll the throttle lever.

51. Install the slow jet.

52. Assemble the power valve and jet and install them in position.

53. Install the discharge large ball, the long spring, the pump discharge weight and the stopper gasket.

54. Use tweezers to insert the plunger small ball and the retainer.

55. Reinstall the throttle positioner and connect its linkage.

56. On the air horn, install the valve seat over the gasket into the fuel inlet.

57. Install the needle valve, spring, and plunger onto the seat.

58. Install the float and pivot pin.

59. Measure and adjust the float clearances (level) by following procedures and specifications outlined earlier in this chapter.

60. After adjusting the float level, remove the float, plunger, spring and needle valve. Assemble the pin clip onto the needle valve.

61. Install the power piston spring and piston into its bore and install the retainer.

62. Install the acceleration pump plunger and its boot.

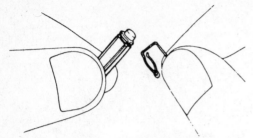

Install the pin clip after the float is adjusted

63. Place a new gasket onto the air horn.
64. Install the needle valve assembly, the float and the pivot pin. Insert the float lip between the plunger and the clip when installing the float.

65. Install the solenoid valves into the body of the carburetor.
66. Assemble the air horn and body. Install the eight screws, paying particular attention to the various brackets, wire clamps and steel number plate.
67. Install the accelerator pump arm. Install the pump arm to the air horn with the pump plunger hole and lever aligned.
68. Connect the choke link and the pump connecting link.
69. Install the fuel pipe and union.
70. With the carburetor still on the bench, move the various linkages by hand, checking for smooth operation.
71. Check the throttle plate for full opening. It should move 90° from horizontal. If needed,

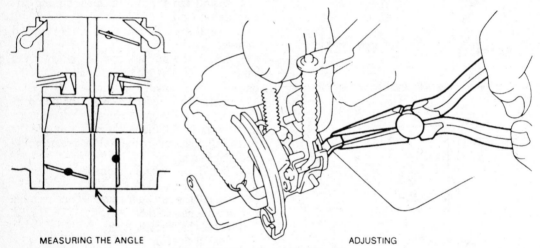

MEASURING THE ANGLE   ADJUSTING

Adjusting the primary throttle plate

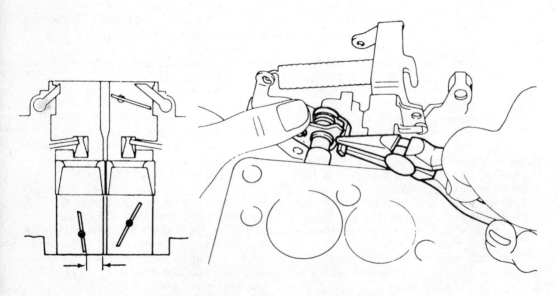

MEASURING THE CLEARANCE   ADJUSTING

Adjusting the secondary throttle plate clearance

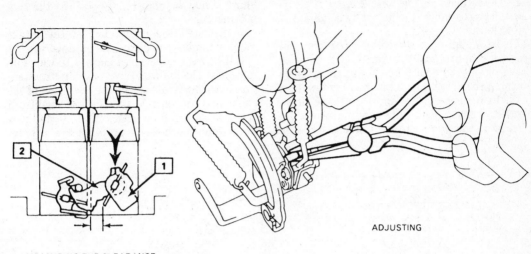

MEASURING THE CLEARANCE

1. PRIMARY KICK LEVER
2. SECONDARY KICK LEVER

Measuring and adjusting the secondary touch

adjust its travel by bending the first throttle lever stopper.

72. Check the clearance of the secondary throttle plate. When wide open, the secondary throttle plate should have 13mm clearance to the body of the bore. Adjust this clearance by bending the secondary throttle lever stopper.

73. Check the clearance for the secondary touch. This is the point at which the secondary throttle begins to open under acceleration. Move the primary throttle plate open, watching for the point at which the first kick lever just touches the second kick lever. At this point, the primary throttle plate should have 0.230 in. clearance.

74. Set the throttle lever to the first step of the fast idle cam. With the choke plate fully closed, check the clearance of the primary throttle plate. The correct clearance is 1.15mm; the clearance may be adjusted by turning the fast idle adjusting screw.

75. The choke unloader is adjusted by bending the fast idle lever as necessary. Open the primary throttle plate fully (with the choke plate closed, from the previous step) and check that the choke plate has 3mm of clearance.

76. Check the choke breaker. Hold the throttle slightly open, push the choke closed and hold it closed as your release the throttle. Apply vacuum to the choke breaker 1st diaphragm.

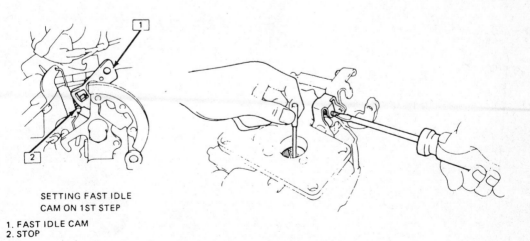

SETTING FAST IDLE
CAM ON 1ST STEP

1. FAST IDLE CAM
2. STOP

ADJUSTING

Adjusting the fast idle setting

The choke plate should have 2.5mm of clearance. The clearance is adjusted by bending the relief lever.

77. Now apply vacuum to both the first and second diaphragms. Clearance at the choke plate should become 6mm. Adjustment is by turning the diaphragm adjustment screw.

78. Release the choke and throttle settings. With the choke plate fully open, measure the length of the pump stroke. Correct stroke is 2mm; it may be adjusted by bending the connecting link.

79. Reinstall the carburetor on the intake manifold, following directions outlined earlier.

80. Start the engine and allow it to warm up normally. During this time, pay careful attention to the high idle speed, the operation of the choke and its controls and the idle quality. If you worked carefully and accurately, and performed the bench set-up properly, the carbure-

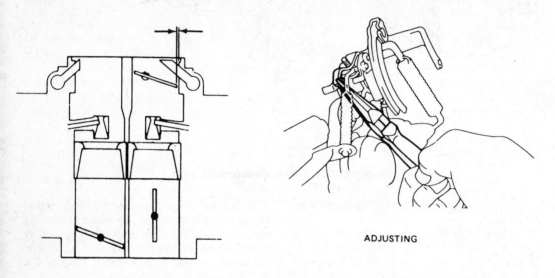

MEASURING THE CLEARANCE

ADJUSTING

Adjusting the choke unloader

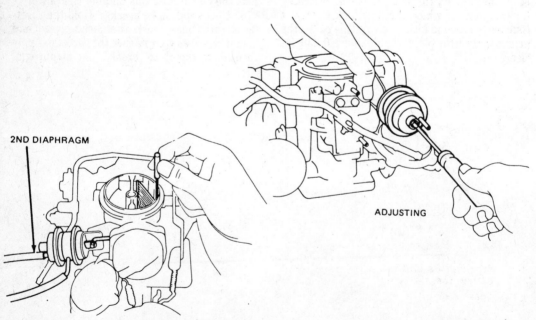

2ND DIAPHRAGM

ADJUSTING

Adjusting the choke breaker in two steps. Remember to apply vacuum to both diaphragms during the second step

tor should need very little fussing after it's reinstalled.

FUEL INJECTION SYSTEM

NOTE: *This book contains testing and service procedures for your car's fuel injection system. More comprehensive testing and diagnosis procedures may be found in* CHILTON'S GUIDE TO FUEL INJECTION AND FEEDBACK CARBURETORS, *book number 7488, available at your local retailer.*

Electric Fuel Pump
REMOVAL AND INSTALLATION

The electric fuel pump used on fuel injected Nova and Prizm cars is contained within the fuel tank. It cannot be removed without removing the tank from the car.

NOTE: *Before removing fuel system parts, clean them with a spray-type engine cleaner. Follow the instructions on the cleaner. Do not soak fuel system parts in liquid cleaning solvent.*

CAUTION: *The fuel injection system is under pressure. Release pressure slowly and contain spillage. Observe no smoking/no open flame precautions. Have a Class B-C (dry powder) fire extinguisher within arm's reach at all times.*

1. Remove the filler cap.
2. Using a siphon or pump, drain the fuel from the tank and store it in a proper metal container with a tight cap.
3. Remove the rear seat cushion to gain access to the electrical wiring.
4. Disconnect the fuel pump and sending unit wiring at the connector.
5. Raise the vehicle and safely support it on jackstands.
6. Loosen the clamp and remove the filler neck and overflow pipe from the tank.
7. Remove the supply hose from the tank. Wrap a rag around the fitting to collect escaping fuel. Disconnect the breather hose from the tank, again using a rag to control spillage.
8. Cover or plug the end of each disconnected line to keep dirt out and fuel in.
9. Support the fuel tank with a floor jack or transmission jack. Use a broad piece of wood to distribute the load. Be careful not to deform the bottom of the tank.
10. Remove the fuel tank support strap bolts.
11. Swing the straps away from the tank and lower the jack. Balance the tank with your other hand or have a helper assist you. The tank is bulky and may have some fuel left in it. If its balance changes suddenly, the tank may fall.
12. Remove the fuel filler pipe extension, the breather pipe assembly and the sending unit assembly. Keep these items in a clean, protected area away from the car.
13. To remove the electric fuel pump:
    a. Disconnect the two pump-to-harness wires.
    b. Loosen the pump outlet hose clamp at the bracket pipe.

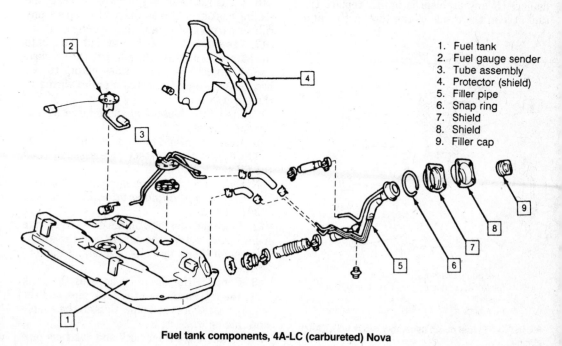

1. Fuel tank
2. Fuel gauge sender
3. Tube assembly
4. Protector (shield)
5. Filler pipe
6. Snap ring
7. Shield
8. Shield
9. Filler cap

Fuel tank components, 4A-LC (carbureted) Nova

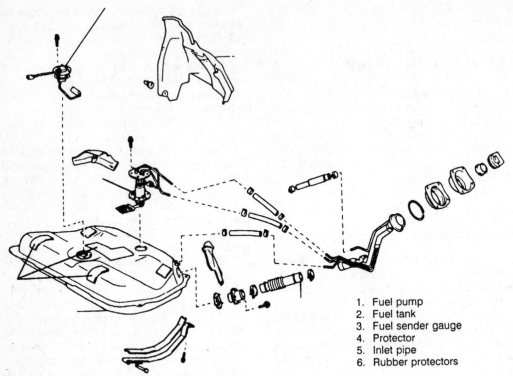

1. Fuel pump
2. Fuel tank
3. Fuel sender gauge
4. Protector
5. Inlet pipe
6. Rubber protectors

Fuel tank components, 4A-GE (fuel injected Nova). Prizm similar

c. Remove the pump from the bracket and the outlet hose from the bracket pipe.

d. Separate the outlet hose and the filter from the pump.

14. While the tank is out and disassembled, inspect it for any signs of rust, leakage or metal damage. If any problem is found, replace the tank. Clean the inside of the tank with water

1. Fuel pump bracket
2. Electrical connector
3. Gasket
4. Fuel hose
5. Pump
6. Fuel pump filter
7. Clip
8. Rubber cushion

Prizm (4A-FE) fuel pump assembly. Nova with 4A-GE similar

and a light detergent and rinse the tank thoroughly several times.

15. Inspect all of the lines, hoses and fittings for any sign of corrosion, wear or damage to the surfaces. Check the pump outlet hose and the filter for restrictions.

16. When reassembling, ALWAYS replace the sealing gaskets with new ones. Also replace any rubber parts showing any sign of deterioration.

17. Assemble the outlet hose and filter onto the pump; then attach the pump to the bracket.

18. Connect the outlet hose clamp to the bracket pipe and connect the pump wiring to the harness wire.

19. Install the fuel pump and bracket assembly onto the tank.

20. Install the sending unit assembly.

21. Connect the breather pipe assembly and the filler pipe extension.

NOTE: *Tighten the breather pipe screw to 17 INCH lbs. and all other attaching screws to 30 INCH lbs.*

22. Place the fuel tank on the jack and elevate it into place within the car. Attach the straps and install the strap bolts, tightening them to 29 ft. lbs.

23. Connect the breather hose to the tank pipe, the return hose to the tank pipe and the supply hose to its tank pipe. tighten the supply hose fitting to 21 ft. lbs.

24. Connect the filler neck and overflow pipe

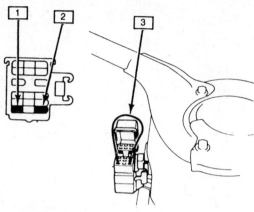

1. FP terminal
2. Battery positive (+) terminal
3. Jumper wire

Checking the electric fuel pump at the check connector

to the tank. Make sure the clamps are properly seated and secure.

25. Lower the vehicle to the ground.

26. Connect the pump and sending unit electrical connectors to the harness.

27. Install the rear seat cushion.

28. Using a funnel, pour the fuel that was drained from its container into the fuel filler.

29. Install the fuel filler cap.

30. Start the engine and check carefully for any sign of leakage around the tank and lines.

TESTING

Since the fuel pump is concealed within the tank, it is difficult to test directly at the pump. It is possible to test the pump from under the hood, listening for pump function and feeling the fuel delivery lines for the build-up of pressure.

1. Turn the ignition switch ON, but do not start the motor.

2. Using a jumper wire, short both terminals of the fuel pump check connector. The check connector is located under the hood near the wiper motor. Connect the terminals labled **FP** and **+B**.

3. Check that there is pressure in the hose running to the delivery pipe. You should hear fuel pressure noise and possibly hear the pump at the rear of the car.

4. Remove the jumper wire.

5. Turn the ignition to OFF. If the fuel pump failed to function, it may indicate a faulty pump, but before removing the tank and pump, check the following items within the pump system:

    a. the fusible link

    b. fuses (EFI/15amp and IGN/7.5amp)

    c. fuel injection main relay

    d. fuel pump circuit opening relay

    e. all wiring connections and grounds.

Fuel injectors

The injectors--electrically triggered valves--deliver a measured quantity of fuel into the intake manifold according to signals from the ECM. As driving condtions change, the computer signals each injector to stay open a longer or shorter period of time, thus controlling the amount of fuel introduced into the engine. An injector, being an electric component, is either on or off (open or closed); there is no variable control for an injector other than duration.

Cleanliness equals sucess when working on a fuel injected system. Every component must be treated with the greatest care and be protected from dust, grime and impact damage. The miniaturized and solid state circuitry is easily damaged by a jolt. Additionally, care must be used in dealing with electrical connectors. Look for and release any locking mechanisms on the connector befor separating the connectors. When

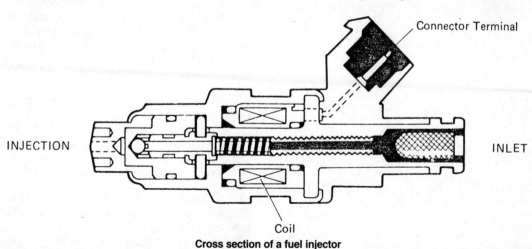

Cross section of a fuel injector

reattaching, make sure each pin is properly lined up and seated before pushing the connector closed.

REMOVAL AND INSTALLATION

4A-GE

CAUTION: *The fuel system is under pressure. Release pressure slowly and contain spillage. Observe no smoking/no open flame precautions. Have a Class B-C (dry powder) fire extinguisher within arm's reach at all times.*

1. Disconnect the negative battery cable.

NOTE: *If you are diagnosing a driveability problem, check the ECM for any stored trouble codes BEFORE disconnecting the cable. The codes will be lost after the battery is disconnected.*

2. Disconnect the PCV hose from the valve cover.

3. Remove the vacuum sensing hose from the pressure regulator.

4. Disconnect the fuel return hose from the pressure regulator.

5. Place a towel or container under the cold start injector pipe. Loosen the two union bolts at the fuel line and remove the pipe with its gaskets.

6. Remove the fuel inlet pipe mounting bolt and disconnect the fuel inlet hose by removing the fuel union bolt, the two gaskets and the hose.

7. Disconnect the injector electrical connections.

8. At the fuel delivery pipe (rail), remove the three bolts. Lift the delivery pipe and the injectors free of the engine. DON'T drop the injectors!

9. Remove the four insulators and three collars from the cylinder head.

10. Pull the injectors free of the delivery pipe.

11. Before installing the injectors back into the fuel rail, install a NEW O-ring on each injector.

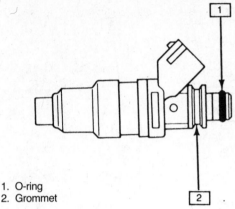

1. O-ring
2. Grommet

Injector with seals

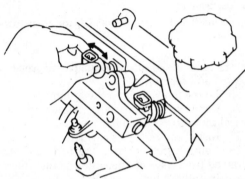

Make certain the injector can be rotated in place after installation

12. Coat each O-ring with a light coat of gasoline (NEVER use oil of any sort)and install the injectors into the delivery pipe. Make certain each injector can be smoothly rotated. If they do not rotate smoothly, the O-ring is not in its correct position.

13. Install the insulators into each injector hole. Place the three spacers on the delivery pipe mounting holes in the cylinder head.

14. Place the delivery pipe and injectors on the cylinder head and again check that the injectors rotate smoothly. Install the three bolts and tighten them to 13 ft. lbs.

15. Connect the electrical connectors to each injector.

16. Install two new gaskets and attach the inlet pipe and fuel union bolt. Tighten the bolt to 22 ft. lbs. Install the mounting bolt.

17. Install new gaskets and connect the cold start injector pipe to the delivery pipe and cold start injector. Install the fuel line union bolts and tighten them to 13 ft. lbs.

18. Connect the fuel return hose and the vacuum sensing hose to the pressure regulator. Attach the PCV hose to the valve cover.

19. Connect the battery cable to the negative

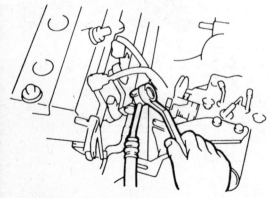

Removing fuel delivery pipe hose

battery terminal. Start the engine and check for leaks.

CAUTION: *If there is a leak at any fitting, the line will be under pressure and the fuel may spray in a fine mist. This mist is extremely explosive. Shut the engine off immediately if any leakage is detected. Use rags to wrap the leaking fitting until the pressure diminishes and wipe up any fuel from the engine area.*

4A-FE

1. Disconnect the negative battery cable.
2. Disconnect the PCV hoses from the valve cover and the vacuum sensing hose from the fuel pressure regulator.
3. Disconnect the fuel return hose from the fuel pressure regulator.
4. Remove the wiring connectors from the injectors.
5. Remove the pressure regulator by loosening the two bolts and pulling the regulator from the delivery pipe.
6. Label and remove the four vacuum hoses running to the EGR vacuum modulator. Remove the nut and bracket with the modulator.

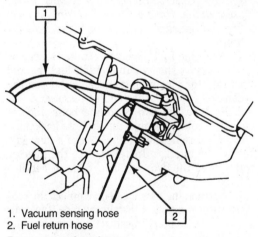

1. Vacuum sensing hose
2. Fuel return hose

Pressure regulator hoses

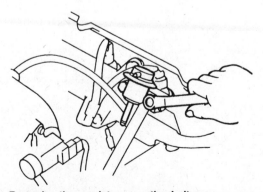

Removing the regulator mounting bolts

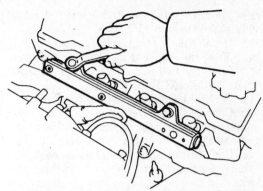

Removing the fuel delivery pipe. Prizm shown, Nova similar, but with three retaining bolts

7. Disconnect the fuel union bolt at the inlet pipe. Remove the pipe and the two gaskets.
8. Remove the two bolts holding the delivery pipe and then remove the delivery pipe and the injectors. Don't drop the injectors!
9. Remove the two spacers and the four insulators from the cylinder head.
10. Pull the injectors free of the delivery pipe.
11. Before installing the injectors back into the fuel rail, install a NEW O-ring on each injector.
12. Coat each O-ring with a light coat of gasoline (NEVER use oil of any sort)and install the injectors into the delivery pipe. Make certain each injector can be smoothly rotated. If they do not rotate smoothly, the O-ring is not in its correct position.
13. Install the four insulators and two spacers in place.
14. Place the delivery pipe and injectors on the cylinder head and again check that the injectors rotate smoothly. Install the two bolts and tighten them to 11 ft. lbs.
15. Install two new gaskets and attach the inlet pipe and fuel union bolt. Tighten the bolt to 22 ft. lbs.
16. Install the EGR vacuum modulator with its bracket and nut. Connect the four vacuum hoses to their proper ports.
17. Install new gaskets and connect the cold start injector pipe to the delivery pipe and cold

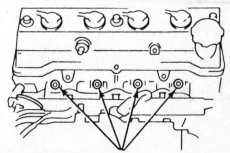

Placement of injector insulators

start injector. Install the fuel line union bolts and tighten them to 13 ft. lbs.

18. Install a new O-ring on the pressure regulator. Push the regulator into the delivery pipe and install the two bolts. Tighten the bolts to 5.5 ft. lbs. (65 INCH lbs.)

19. Connect the injector wiring connectors.

20. Connect the fuel return hose and the vacuum sensing hose to the pressure regulator. Attach the PCV hoses to the valve cover.

21. Connect the battery cable to the negative battery terminal. Start the engine and check for leaks.

> CAUTION: *If there is a leak at any fitting, the line will be under pressure and the fuel may spray in a fine mist. This mist is extremely explosive. Shut the engine off immediately if any leakage is detected. Use rags to wrap the leaking fitting until the pressure diminishes and wipe up any fuel from the engine area.*

TESTING

The simplest way to test the injectors is simply to listen to them with the engine running. Use either a stethoscope-type tool or the blade of a long screw driver to touch each injector while the engine is idling. You should hear a distinct clicking as each injector opens and closes.

Additionally, the resistance of the injector can be easily checked. Disconnect the negative battery cable and remove the electrical connector from the injector to be tested. Use an ohmeter to check the resistance across the terminals of the injector. Correct ohmmage is approximately 13.8Ω at 68°F; slight variations are acceptable due to temperature conditions.

Bench testing of the injectors can only be done using expensive special equipment. Generally this equipment can be found at a dealership and sometimes at a well-equipped machine shop or performance shop. There is no provision for field testing the injectors by the owner/mechanic. DO NOT attempt to test the injector

by removing it from the engine and making it spray into a jar.

Never attempt to check a removed injector by hooking it directly to the battery. The injector runs on a much smaller voltage and the 12 volts from the battery will destroy it internally. Since this happens at the speed of electricity, you don't get a second chance.

FUEL INJECTION SENSORS AND CONTROLS

4A-GE

COLD START INJECTOR

1. Test the resistance of the cold start injector before removing it. Disconnect its electrical lead and use an ohmmeter to measure resistance between the terminals. Correct rsistance is 3–5Ω; allow for slight variations due to temperature.

2. If the injector must be replaced, disconnect the negative battery cable.

3. Remove the wiring connector at the injector if not already done for testing purposes.

> CAUTION: *The fuel system is under pressure. Release pressure slowly and contain spillage. Observe no smoking/no open flame precautions. Have a Class B-C (dry powder) fire extinguisher within arm's reach at all times.*

4. Wrap the fuel pipe connection in a rag or towel. Remove the two union bolts and the cold start injector pipe with its gaskets. Loosen the union bolts at the other end as necessary.

5. Remove the two retaining bolts and remove the cold start injector with its gaskets.

6. When reinstalling, always use a new gasket for the injector. Install it with the injector and tighten the two mounting bolts to 7 ft. lbs. (84 INCH lbs.).

7. Again using new gaskets, connect the cold start injector pipe to the delivery pipe (fuel rail) and to the cold start injector. Tighten the bolts to 13 ft. lbs.

8. Install the wiring to the cold start injector.

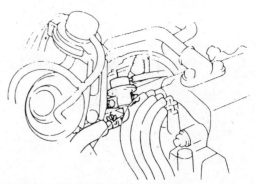

Testing injector resistance

Location of fuel pressure regulator

9. Connect the negative battery cable.

10. Start the engine and check for leaks.

FUEL PRESSURE REGULATOR

1. Remove the vacuum sensing hose from the fuel pressure regulator.

CAUTION: *The fuel system is under pressure. Release pressure slowly and contain spillage. Observe no smoking/no open flame precautions. Have a Class B-C (dry powder) fire extinguisher within arm's reach at all times.*

2. Remove the fuel hose from the regulator.

3. Remove the two retaining bolts and pull the regulator out of the fuel rail.

4. When reinstalling, the two retaining bolts are tightened to 5.5 ft. lbs. (65 INCH lbs) Connect the two hoses (fuel and vacuum).

5. Start the engine and check carefully for leaks.

MASS AIR FLOW SENSOR

The mass air flow sensor communicates with the ECM about the amount of air being taken

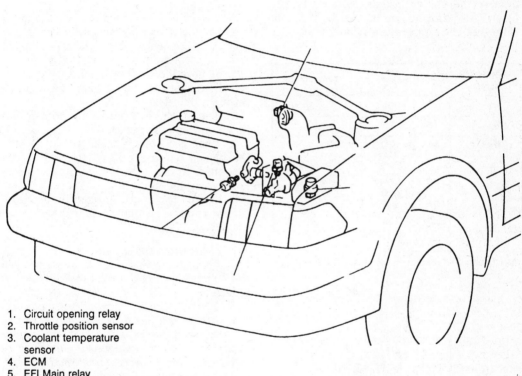

1. Circuit opening relay
2. Throttle position sensor
3. Coolant temperature sensor
4. ECM
5. EFI Main relay
6. Start injector time switch

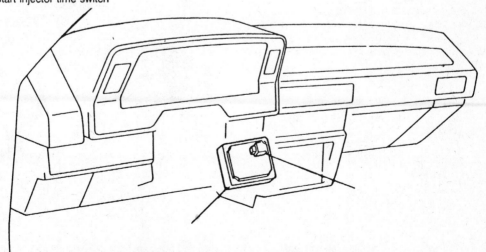

Location of electronic components, Nova with 4A-GE engine

into the engine. The intake air flow moves a trap door which is connected to a potentiometer. This variable load switch controls the amount of electricity sent to the ECM. Depending on the signal received, the ECM governs the fuel injectors to deliver the proportionally correct amount of fuel into the engine. The air box must be handled carefully during testing and/or replacement.

1. Unplug the wiring connector at the mass air flow sensor.

2. Using an ohmmeter and the chart, measure the resistance between the terminals as indicated. The sensor must pass ALL tests; if any one is failed, the air sensor must be replaced. Note that the temperature related reading is

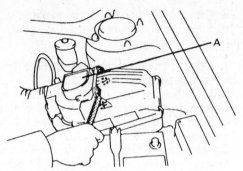

Removing the mass air flow sensor (A)

Between terminals	Resistance	Temperature
$V_S - E_2$	20 – 3,000 Ω	–
$V_C - E_2$	100 – 300 Ω	–
$V_B - E_2$	200 – 400 Ω	–
$THA - E_2$	10 – 20 kΩ	– 20°C (–4°F)
	4 – 7 kΩ	0°C (32°F)
	2 – 3 kΩ	20°C (68°F)
	0.9 – 1.3 kΩ	40°C (104°F)
	0.4 – 0.7 kΩ	60°C (204°F)
$F_C - E_1$	Infinity	–

Resistance chart for testing the mass air flow sensor

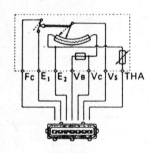

Fc E_1 E_2 V_B V_C V_S THA

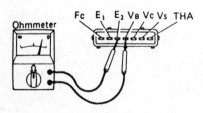

Mass air flow sensor schematic (above) and terminal identification

measured in "kΩ" or kilo-ohms. Don't forget to reset the meter to a higher scale.

3. If replacement is needed, label and disconnect the vacuum lines running to the sensor.

4. Remove the air cleaner hose.

5. Disconnect the wiring connector if not already done for testing purposes.

6. Remove the four nuts and the mass air flow sensor and its gasket.

7. When reinstalling, make absolutely sure that the air sensor and its gasket are correctly postioned. No air leaks are acceptable. Install and tighten the four nuts.

8. Install the wiring connector, the air cleaner hose and the vacuum hoses.

THROTTLE BODY

1. Either drain the coolant from the throttle body by disconnecting a coolant hose or open the engine draincock until the fluid level is reduced.

WARNING: *Housepets and small animals are attracted to the odor and taste of engine coolant (antifreeze). It is a highly poisonous mixture of chemicals; special care must be taken to protect open containers and spillage.*

2. Disconnect the throttle return spring.

3. Disconnect the throttle cable.

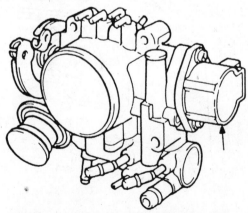

Throttle body assembly. Arrow indicates throttle position sensor

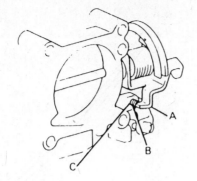

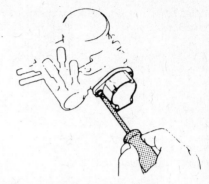

Adjusting the throttle position sensor

A   THROTTLE LEVER
B   NO CLEARANCE
C   THROTTLE STOP SCREW
Checking the throttle valve

4. Label and disconnect the vacuum hoses.

5. Carefully remove the throttle postion sensor wiring connector.

6. Remove the air cleaner hose.

7. Remove the water hoses from the air valve.

8. Remove the two bolts and two nuts and the throttle body with its gasket.

9. Wash and clean the cast metal parts with a soft brush and carburetor cleaner. Use compressed air to blow through all the passages and openings.

10. Check the throttle valve to see that there is NO clearance between the stop screw and the throttle lever when the throttle plate is fully closed.

11. Check the throttle position sensor (TPS). Insert a 0.47mm feeler gauge between the throttle stop screw and the lever. Connect an ohmmeter between terminal **IDL** and E_2. Loosen the two screws holding the TPS and gradually turn the TPS clockwise until the ohmmeter deflects, but no more. Secure the TPS screws at this point. Double check the clearance at the lever and stop screw.

Additional resistance tests may be made on the TPS using the chart.

12. To reinstall, place a new gasket in position and install the throttle body with its two nuts and two bolts. Make certain everything is properly positioned before securing the unit. Tighten the bolts to 16 ft. lbs.

13. Connect the water hoses to the air valve.

14. Install the air cleaner hose and the vacuum hoses.

15. Connect the wiring to the throttle position sensor.

16. Connect the accelerator cable and its return spring.

17. Refill the coolant to the proper level.

ELECTRONIC FUEL INJECTION (EFI) MAIN RELAY

1. The relay is located under the hood, behind the left headlight area. Turn the ignition ON without starting the engine and listen for a noise from the relay.

2. Turn the ignition off and remove the connector from the relay. Using the ohmmeter, check for continuity between terminals **1** and **3**.

3. Check that there is NO continuity between terminals **2** and **4**.

4. Check that there is NO continuity between terminals **3** and **4**.

5. If the relay fails ANY of these tests, replace it.

CIRCUIT OPENING RELAY

1. The relay is located behind the lower center of the dashboard, adjacent to the ECM.

Clearance between lever and stop screw	Between terminals	Resistance
0 mm (0 in.)	VTA -- E_2	0.2 – 0.8 kΩ
0.35 mm (0.0138 in.)	IDL – E_2	Less than 2.3 kΩ
0.59 mm (0.0232 in.)	IDL – E_2	Infinity
Throttle valve fully opened position	VTA – E_2	3.3 – 10 kΩ
–	Vcc – E_2	3 – 7 kΩ

Throttle position sensor resistance check

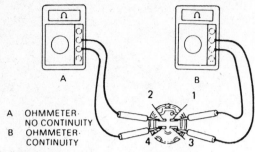

A OHMMETER·
    NO CONTINUITY
B OHMMETER·
    CONTINUITY

Testing the EFI main relay—4A-GE

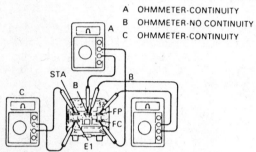

A OHMMETER·CONTINUITY
B OHMMETER·NO CONTINUITY
C OHMMETER·CONTINUITY

Checking continuity on the circuit opening relay

With the ignition off, unplug the connector and use an ohmmeter to check for continuity between terminals **STA** and **E**.

2. Check that there is continuity between terminals **B** and **Fc**.

3. Check that there is NO continuity between terminals **B** and **Fp**.

4. If the relay fails any test, it must be replaced.

START INJECTOR TIME SWITCH

1. Remove the connector at the switch.

2. Use an ohmmeter to measure the resistance between terminals **STA** and **STJ**. Refer to the chart for the proper values.

3. If the time switch is to be replaced, drain the coolant from the system.

WARNING: *Housepets and small animals are attracted to the odor and taste of engine coolant (antifreeze). It is a highly poisonous mixture of chemicals; special care must be taken to protect open containers and spillage.*

4. Remove the switch and its gasket.

5. Install the new switch with a new gasket and tighten it to 25 ft. lbs.

6. Refill the coolant and attach the wiring connector to the switch.

Between terminals	Resistance (Ω)	Coolant temp.
STA – STJ	20 – 40	Below 30°C (95°F)
	40 – 60	Above 40°C (95°F)
STA – Ground	20 – 80	—

Resistance chart for checking the start injector time switch sensor

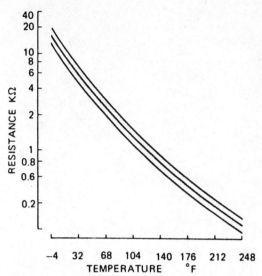

Resistance chart for testing the water temperature sensor

COOLANT TEMPERATURE SENSOR

1. Disconnect the wiring to the sensor.

2. Using an ohmmeter, measure the resistance across the terminals of the sensor. Refer to the chart for the correct resistance values. Note that the resistance will change as a function of the coolant temperature, not the air temperature.

3. If the sensor must be changed, the coolant must be drained. Do this only with the engine cold.

WARNING: *Housepets and small animals are attracted to the odor and taste of engine coolant (antifreeze). It is a highly poisonous mixture of chemicals; special care must be taken to protect open containers and spillage.*

4. Using the correct size wrench, remove the sensor by unscrewing it. Install the new sensor and tighten it.

5. Refill the coolant to the proper level.

6. Connect the wiring to the sensor.

4A-FE

COLD START INJECTOR

1. Disconnect the negaytive battery cable.

2. Disconect the wiring at the injector.

3. Loosen and remove the fuel line at the injector.

The fuel system is under pressure. Release pressure slowly and contain spillage. Observe no smoking/no open flame precautions. Have a Class B-C (dry powder) fire extinguisher within arm's reach at all times.

4. Remove the two retaining bolts and remove the injector.

5. When reinstalling, position the new injec-

tor in the intake manifold, install the retaining bolts and tighten them to 7 ft. lbs. (84 INCH lbs.)

6. Connect the fuel line, then connect the wiring harness to the injector.

7. Connect the negative battery cable.

FUEL PRESSURE REGULATOR

1. Disconnect the negative battery cable.

2. Disconnect the vacuum hose from the regulator.

3. Disconnect the fuel return line from the regulator.

CAUTION: *The fuel system is under pressure. Release pressure slowly and contain spillage. Observe no smoking/no open flame precautions. Have a Class B-C (dry powder) fire extinguisher within arm's reach at all times.*

4. Remove the two retaining bolts and remove the fuel pressure regulator.

5. When reinstalling, place the new regulator on the fuel rail, install the bolts and tighten them to 7 ft. lbs. (84 INCH lbs.).

6. Connect the fuel return line, making sure the clamp is properly placed and secure.

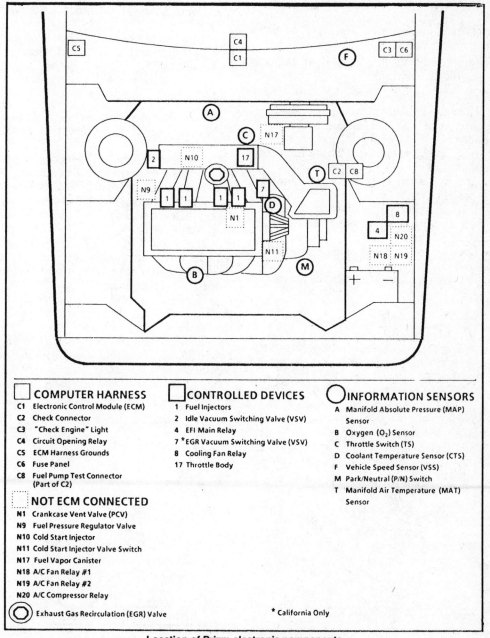

COMPUTER HARNESS
- C1 Electronic Control Module (ECM)
- C2 Check Connector
- C3 "Check Engine" Light
- C4 Circuit Opening Relay
- C5 ECM Harness Grounds
- C6 Fuse Panel
- C8 Fuel Pump Test Connector (Part of C2)

NOT ECM CONNECTED
- N1 Crankcase Vent Valve (PCV)
- N9 Fuel Pressure Regulator Valve
- N10 Cold Start Injector
- N11 Cold Start Injector Valve Switch
- N17 Fuel Vapor Canister
- N18 A/C Fan Relay #1
- N19 A/C Fan Relay #2
- N20 A/C Compressor Relay

CONTROLLED DEVICES
- 1 Fuel Injectors
- 2 Idle Vacuum Switching Valve (VSV)
- 4 EFI Main Relay
- 7 *EGR Vacuum Switching Valve (VSV)
- 8 Cooling Fan Relay
- 17 Throttle Body

INFORMATION SENSORS
- A Manifold Absolute Pressure (MAP) Sensor
- B Oxygen (O$_2$) Sensor
- C Throttle Switch (TS)
- D Coolant Temperature Sensor (CTS)
- F Vehicle Speed Sensor (VSS)
- M Park/Neutral (P/N) Switch
- T Manifold Air Temperature (MAT) Sensor

 Exhaust Gas Recirculation (EGR) Valve   * California Only

Location of Prizm electronic components

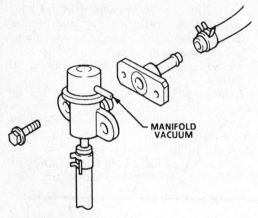

MANIFOLD VACUUM

Prizm fuel pressure regulator

7. Connect the vacuum hose, then connect the negative battery cable.

THROTTLE BODY

1. Disconnect the negative battery cable.
2. Remove the air cleaner and intake duct assembly.
3. Disconnect the electrical wiring from the throttle switch.
4. Remove the two bolts holding the throttle cable bracket.
5. If so equipped, remove the transaxle shift cable (automatic transmission) and/or the cruise control cable.
6. Label and remove the vacuum hoses to the throttle body.
7. Remove the vacuum hose to the air valve.

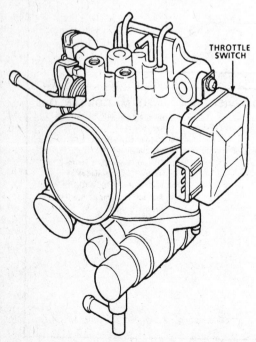

THROTTLE SWITCH

8. Remove the four bolts holding the throttle body and carefully remove the throttle body.
9. When reinstalling, always use a new gasket between the throttle body and the intake. Do not use sealants of any kind on the gasket. Place the throttle body in position, install the four bolts and tighten them to 16 ft. lbs. Make very certain that the throttle body is properly placed before tightening the bolts; no air leaks are acceptable.
10. Install the throttle cable and its bracket.
11. If so equipped, reattach the transaxle cable and/or the cruise control cable.
12. Connect the vacuum hose to the air valve.
13. Connect the vacuum hoses to the throttle body.
14. Connect the electrical connector to the throttle switch and install the air cleaner and duct assembly.
15. Connect the negative battery cable.

THROTTLE SWITCH ADJUSTMENT

NOTE: *This procedure may be performed on the car; removal of the throttle body is not required.*

1. With the ignition OFF, remove the electrical connector from the throttle switch.
2. Loosen the two small bolts holding the switch to the throttle body. Loosen them just enough to allow the switch to be moved if necessary, but no more.
3. Insert a 0.0276 in (0.70mm) feeler gauge between the throttle stop screw and the throttle lever. Connect an ohmmeter between terminals IDL and E2 on the switch.
4. Gradually turn the switch clockwise until the meter deflects, showing continuity; secure the sensor with the two screws.
5. Remove the feeler gauge and insert another of 0.80mm. The ohmmeter should show NO continuity with the larger gauge inserted.
6. Adjust the switch as necessary to gain the correct function for each feeler gauge. Tighten

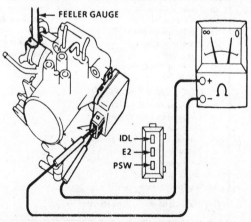

FEELER GAUGE

IDL
E2
PSW

Throttle body assembly with throttle switch, 4A-FE   **Adjusting the Prizm throttle switch**

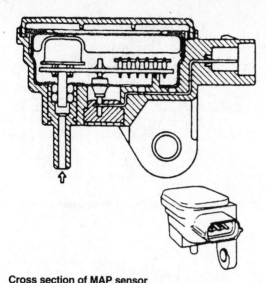

Cross section of MAP sensor

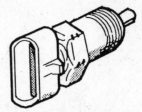

Coolant temperature sensor. Remember to coat the threads with sealant before reassembly

the screws when the correct position is achieved.

7. Connect the wiring harness to the throttle switch

MANIFOLD ABSOLUTE PRESSURE (MAP) SENSOR

Located on the firewall, this sensor advises the ECM of pressure changes in the intake manifold. It consists of a semi-conductor pressure converting element which converts a pressure change into an electrical signal. The ECM sends a 5 volt reference signal to the MAP sensor; the change in air pressure changes the resistance within the sensor. The ECM reads the change from its reference voltage and signals the injectors to react accordingly.

Replacing the MAP sensor simply requires disconnecting the vacuum hose and the electrical connector, and unbolting the sensor from the firewall. Inspect the vacuum hose over its entire length for any signs of cracking or splitting. The slightest leak can cause false messages to be send to the ECM.

MANIFOLD AIR TEMPERATURE (MAT) SENSOR

The MAT sensor advises the ECM of changes in intake air temperature (and therefore air density). As air temperature of the intake varies, the ECM, by monitoring the voltage change, adjusts the amount of fuel injection according to the air temperature.

To replace the MAT sensor:

1. Remove the air cleaner cover.

2. With the ignition OFF, disconnect the electrical connector.

3. Push the MAT sensor out from inside the air cleaner housing.

4. Install the new sensor, making sure it is properly placed and secure.

5. Connect the wiring harness, and replace the air cleaner cover.

COOLANT TEMPERATURE SENSOR

The coolant temperature sensor is located under the air cleaner assembly and behind the distributor. Its function is to advise the ECM of changes in engine temperature by monitoring the changes in coolant temperature. The sensor must be handled carefully during removal. It can be damaged (thereby affecting engine performance) by impact.

The sensor may be tested following the procedures listed previously for the 4A-GE engine. The temperature and resistance chart is the same. If the sensor must be replaced:

WARNING: *Perform this procedure only on a cold engine.*

1. Relieve the pressure within the cooling system. It may be helpful to partially drain the block to lower the coolant level.

WARNING: *Housepets and small animals are attracted to the odor and taste of engine coolant (antifreeze). It is a highly poisonous mixture of chemicals; special care must be taken to protect open containers and spillage.*

2. Remove the air cleaner assembly.

3. With the ignition OFF, disconnect the electrical connector to the coolant temperature sensor.

4. Using the proper sized wrench, carefully unscrew the sensor from the engine.

5. Before reinstalling, coat the threads of the sensor with a sealant. Install the sensor and tighten it to 18 ft. lbs.

6. Reconnect the electrical connector. Install the air cleaner assembly.

7. Refill the coolant to the proper level.

ELECTRONIC FUEL INJECTION (EFI) MAIN RELAY

1. The EFI relay is located on the fuse block (juction block) under the hood behind the left headlight. Test the function of the relay by turning the ignition ON and listening or feeling the relay. An operation noise should be heard (or felt) from the relay.

2. Turn the ignition OFF. Disconnect the connetor from the relay and use an ohmmeter to check for continuity between relay terminals 3 and 4.

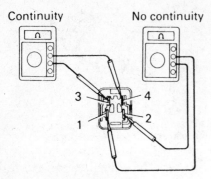

Continuity   No continuity

Continuity check, Prizm EFI relay

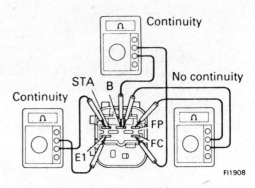

Continuity

STA   B   No continuity

Continuity

E1

FI1908

Checking continuity of Prizm circuit opening relay

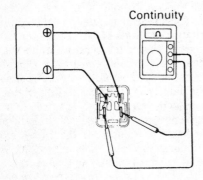

Continuity

Function check, Prizm EFI relay

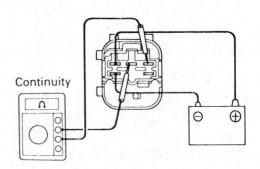

Continuity

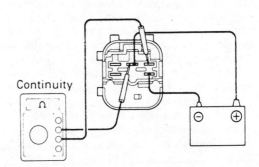

Continuity

Checking the function of the Prizm circuit opening relay

3. There should be NO continuity between terminals 1 and 2. If the relay fails either of these tests, replace it.

4. Using jumper wires, connect battery voltage across terminals 3 and 4 (Connect the battery positive (+) to terminal 4) and check terminals 1 and 2 for continuity. With 12 volts applied, continuity should be present.

5. Reinstall the relay in place.

CIRCUIT OPENING RELAY

1. Remove the ECM cover under the center console. Remove the circuit opening relay and its wiring.

2. With the ignition OFF, disconnect the relay.

3. Using an ohmmeter, check that there is continuity between terminals STA and E1.

4. Check that there is continuity between terminals B and FC.

5. Check that there is NO continuity between terminals B and FP. If the relay fails any of these checks, it must be replaced.

6. Using jumper wires, connect the battery positive (+) terminal to terminal STA and the battery negative terminal to terminal E1. Use the ohmmeter to check that there is now continuity between terminals B and FP.

7. Change the jumper wires so that the positive terminal connects to terminal B and the negative connects to terminal FC. Check that

there is now continuity between terminals B and FP.

8. If the relay fails either of these funtional tests, it must be replaced.

FUEL TANK

REMOVAL AND INSTALLATION

NOTE: *Before removing fuel system parts, clean them with a spray-type engine cleaner. Follow the instructions on the cleaner. Do not soak fuel system parts in liquid cleaning solvent.*

CAUTION: *The fuel injection system is under pressure. Release pressure slowly and contain spillage. Observe no smoking/no open flame precautions. Have a Class B-C (dry powder) fire extinguisher within arm's reach at all times.*

1. Remove the filler cap.

2. Using a siphon or pump, drain the fuel from the tank and store it in a proper metal container with a tight cap.

3. Remove the rear seat cushion to gain access to the electrical wiring.

4. Disconnect the fuel pump and sending unit wiring at the connector.

5. Raise the vehicle and safely support it on jackstands.

6. Loosen the clamp and remove the filler neck and overflow pipe from the tank.

7. Remove the supply hose from the tank. Wrap a rag around the fitting to collect escaping fuel. Disconnect the breather hose from the tank, again using a rag to control spillage.

8. Cover or plug the end of each disconnected line to keep dirt out and fuel in.

9. Support the fuel tank with a floor jack or transmission jack. Use a broad piece of wood to distribute the load. Be careful not to deform the bottom of the tank.

10. Remove the fuel tank support strap bolts.

11. Swing the straps away from the tank and lower the jack. Balance the tank with your other hand or have a helper assist you. The tank is bulky and may have some fuel left in it. If its balance changes suddenly, the tank may fall.

12. Remove the fuel filler pipe extension, the breather pipe assembly and the sending unit assembly. Keep these items in a clean, protected area away from the car.

13. While the tank is out and disassembled, inspect it for any signs of rust, leakage or metal damage. If any problem is found, replace the tank. Clean the inside of the tank with water and a light detergent and rinse the tank thoroughly several times.

14. Inspect all of the lines, hoses and fittings for any sign of corrosion, wear or damage to the surfaces. Check the pump outlet hose and the filter for restrictions.

15. When reassembling, ALWAYS replace the sealing gaskets with new ones. Also replace any rubber parts showing any sign of deterioration.

16. Connect the breather pipe assembly and the filler pipe extension.

NOTE: *Tighten the breather pipe screw to 17 INCH lbs. and all other attaching screws to 30 INCH lbs.*

17. Place the fuel tank on the jack and elevate it into place within the car. Attach the straps and install the strap bolts, tightening them to 29 ft. lbs.

18. Connect the breather hose to the tank pipe, the return hose to the tank pipe and the supply hose to its tank pipe. tighten the supply hose fitting to 21 ft. lbs.

19. Connect the filler neck and overflow pipe to the tank. Make sure the clamps are properly seated and secure.

20. Lower the vehicle to the ground.

21. Connect the pump and sending unit electrical connectors to the harness.

22. Install the rear seat cushion.

23. Using a funnel, pour the fuel that was drained from its container into the fuel filler.

24. Install the fuel filler cap.

25. Start the engine and check carefully for any sign of leakage around the tank and lines.

Chassis Electrical

6

UNDERSTANDING AND TROUBLESHOOTING ELECTRICAL SYSTEMS

At the rate which both import and domestic manufacturers are incorporating electronic control systems into their production lines, it won't be long before every new vehicle is equipped with one or more on-board computer. These electronic components (with no moving parts) should theoretically last the life of the vehicle, provided nothing external happens to damage the circuits or memory chips.

While it is true that electronic components should never wear out, in the real world malfunctions do occur. It is also true that any computer-based system is extremely sensitive to electrical voltages and cannot tolerate careless or haphazard testing or service procedures. An inexperienced individual can literally do major damage looking for a minor problem by using the wrong kind of test equipment or connecting test leads or connectors with the ignition switch ON. When selecting test equipment, make sure the manufacturers instructions state that the tester is compatible with whatever type of electronic control system is being serviced. Read all instructions carefully and double check all test points before installing probes or making any test connections.

The following section outlines basic diagnosis techniques for dealing with computerized automotive control systems. Along with a general explanation of the various types of test equipment available to aid in servicing modern electronic automotive systems, basic repair techniques for wiring harnesses and connectors is given. Read the basic information before attempting any repairs or testing on any computerized system, to provide the background of information necessary to avoid the most common and obvious mistakes that can cost both time and money. Although the replacement and testing procedures are simple in themselves, the systems are not, and unless one has a thorough understanding of all components and their function within a particular computerized control system, the logical test sequence that these systems demand cannot be followed. Minor malfunctions can make a big difference, so it is important to know how each component affects the operation of the overall electronic system to find the ultimate cause of a problem without replacing good components unnecessarily. It is not enough to use the correct test equipment; the test equipment must be used correctly.

Safety Precautions

CAUTION: *Whenever working on or around any computer based microprocessor control system, always observe these general precautions to prevent the possibility of personal injury or damage to electronic components.*

● Never install or remove battery cables with the key ON or the engine running. Jumper cables should be connected with the key OFF to avoid power surges that can damage electronic control units. Engines equipped with computer controlled systems should avoid both giving and getting jump starts due to the possibility of serious damage to components from arcing in the engine compartment when connections are made with the ignition ON.

● Always remove the battery cables before charging the battery. Never use a high output charger on an installed battery or attempt to use any type of "hot shot" (24 volt) starting aid.

● Exercise care when inserting test probes into connectors to insure good connections without damaging the connector or spreading the pins. Always probe connectors from the rear (wire) side, NOT the pin side, to avoid accidental shorting of terminals during test procedures.

• Never remove or attach wiring harness connectors with the ignition switch ON, especially to an electronic control unit.

• Do not drop any components during service procedures and never apply 12 volts directly to any component (like a solenoid or relay) unless instructed specifically to do so. Some component electrical windings are designed to safely handle only 4 or 5 volts and can be destroyed in seconds if 12 volts are applied directly to the connector.

• Remove the electronic control unit if the vehicle is to be placed in an environment where temperatures exceed approximately 176°F (80°C), such as a paint spray booth or when arc or gas welding near the control unit location in the car.

ORGANIZED TROUBLESHOOTING

When diagnosing a specific problem, organized troubleshooting is a must. The complexity of a modern automobile demands that you approach any problem in a logical, organized manner. There are certain troubleshooting techniques that are standard:

1. Establish when the problem occurs. Does the problem appear only under certain conditions? Were there any noises, odors, or other unusual symptoms?

2. Isolate the problem area. To do this, make some simple tests and observations; then eliminate the systems that are working properly. Check for obvious problems such as broken wires, dirty connections or split or disconnected vacuum hoses. Always check the obvious before assuming something complicated is the cause.

3. Test for problems systematically to determine the cause once the problem area is isolated. Are all the components functioning properly? Is there power going to electrical switches and motors? Is there vacuum at vacuum switches and/or actuators? Is there a mechanical problem such as bent linkage or loose mounting screws? Doing careful, systematic checks will often turn up most causes on the first inspection without wasting time checking components that have little or no relationship to the problem.

4. Test all repairs after the work is done to make sure that the problem is fixed. Some causes can be traced to more than one component, so a careful verification of repair work is important to pick up additional malfunctions that may cause a problem to reappear or a different problem to arise. A blown fuse, for example, is a simple problem that may require more than another fuse to repair. If you don't look for a problem that caused a fuse to blow, for example, a shorted wire may go undetected.

Experience has shown that most problems tend to be the result of a fairly simple and obvious cause, such as loose or corroded connectors or air leaks in the intake system; making careful inspection of components during testing essential to quick and accurate troubleshooting. Special, hand held computerized testers designed specifically for diagnosing a system are available from a variety of aftermarket sources, as well as from the vehicle manufacturer, but care should be taken that any test equipment being used is designed to diagnose that particular computer controlled system accurately without damaging the control unit (ECU) or components being tested.

NOTE: *Pinpointing the exact cause of trouble in an electrical system can sometimes only be accomplished by the use of special test equipment. The following describes commonly used test equipment and explains how to put it to best use in diagnosis. In addition to the information covered below, the manufacturer's instructions booklet provided with the tester should be read and clearly understood before attempting any test procedures.*

TEST EQUIPMENT

Jumper Wires

Jumper wires are simple, yet extremely valuable, pieces of test equipment. Jumper wires are merely wires that are used to bypass sections of a circuit. The simplest type of jumper wire is merely a length of multi-strand wire with an alligator clip at each end. Jumper wires are usually fabricated from lengths of standard automotive wire and whatever type of connector (alligator clip, spade connector or pin connector) that is required for the particular vehicle being tested. The well equipped tool box will have several different styles of jumper wires in several different lengths. Some jumper wires are made with three or more terminals coming from a common splice for special purpose testing. In cramped, hard-to-reach areas it is advisable to have insulated boots over the jumper wire terminals in order to prevent accidental grounding, sparks, and possible fire, especially when testing fuel system components.

Jumper wires are used primarily to locate open electrical circuits, on either the ground (–) side of the circuit or on the hot (+) side. If an electrical component fails to operate, connect the jumper wire between the component and a good ground. If the component operates only with the jumper installed, the ground circuit is open. If the ground circuit is good, but the component does not operate, the circuit between the power feed and component is open. You can sometimes connect the jumper wire directly from the battery to the hot terminal of the component, but first make sure the component uses 12 volts in operation. Some electrical components, such as fuel injectors, are designed to operate on about 4 volts and running 12 volts directly to the injector terminals can burn out the wiring. By inserting an inline fuseholder between a set of test leads, a fused jumper wire can be used for bypassing open circuits. Use a 5 amp fuse to provide protection against voltage spikes. When in doubt, use a voltmeter to check the voltage input to the component and measure how much voltage is being applied normally. By moving the jumper wire successively back from the lamp toward the power source, you can isolate the area of the circuit where the open is located. When the component stops functioning, or the power is cut off, the open is in the segment of wire between the jumper and the point previously tested.

CAUTION: *Never use jumpers made from wire that is of lighter gauge than used in the circuit under test. If the jumper wire is of too small gauge, it may overheat and possibly melt. Never use jumpers to bypass high resistance loads (such as motors) in a circuit. Bypassing resistances, in effect, creates a short circuit which may, in turn, cause damage and fire. Never use a jumper for anything other than temporary bypassing of components in a circuit.*

12 Volt Test Light

The 12 volt test light is used to check circuits and components while electrical current is flowing through them. It is used for voltage and ground tests. Twelve volt test lights come in different styles but all have three main parts; a ground clip, a probe, and a light. The most commonly used 12 volt test lights have pick-type probes. To use a 12 volt test light, connect the ground clip to a good ground and probe wherever necessary with the pick. The pick should be sharp so that it can penetrate wire insulation to make contact with the wire, without making a large hole in the insulation. The wrap-around light is handy in hard to reach areas or where it is difficult to support a wire to push a probe pick into it. To use the wrap around light, hook the wire to probed with the hook and pull the trigger. A small pick will be forced through the wire insulation into the wire core.

CAUTION: *Do not use a test light to probe electronic ignition spark plug or coil wires. Never use a pick-type test light to probe wiring on computer controlled systems unless specifically instructed to do so. Any wire insulation that is pierced by the test light probe should be taped and sealed with silicone after testing.*

Like the jumper wire, the 12 volt test light is used to isolate opens in circuits. But, whereas the jumper wire is used to bypass the open to operate the load, the 12 volt test light is used to locate the presence of voltage in a circuit. If the test light glows, you know that there is power up to that point; if the 12 volt test light does not glow when its probe is inserted into the wire or connector, you know that there is an open circuit (no power). Move the test light in successive steps back toward the power source until the light in the handle does glow. When it does glow, the open is between the probe and point previously probed.

NOTE: *The test light does not detect that 12 volts (or any particular amount of voltage) is present; it only detects that some voltage is present. It is advisable before using the test light to touch its terminals across the battery posts to make sure the light is operating properly.*

Self-Powered Test Light

The self-powered test light usually contains a 1.5 volt penlight battery. One type of self-powered test light is similar in design to the 12 volt test light. This type has both the battery and the light in the handle and pick-type probe tip. The second type has the light toward the open tip, so that the light illuminates the contact point. The self-powered test light is dual purpose piece of test equipment. It can be used to test for either open or short circuits when power is isolated from the circuit (continuity test). A powered test light should not be used on any computer controlled system or component unless specifically instructed to do so. Many engine sensors can be destroyed by even this small amount of voltage applied directly to the terminals.

Open Circuit Testing

To use the self-powered test light to check for open circuits, first isolate the circuit from the vehicle's 12 volt power source by disconnecting the battery or wiring harness connector. Connect the test light ground clip to a good ground and probe sections of the circuit sequentially with the test light. (start from either end of the circuit). If the light is out, the open is between the probe and the circuit ground. If the light is on, the open is between the probe and end of the circuit toward the power source.

Short Circuit Testing

By isolating the circuit both from power and from ground, and using a self-powered test light, you can check for shorts to ground in the circuit. Isolate the circuit from power and ground. Connect the test light ground clip to a good ground and probe any easy-to-reach test point in the circuit. If the light comes on, there is a short somewhere in the circuit. To isolate the short, probe a test point at either end of the isolated circuit (the light should be on). Leave the test light probe connected and open connectors, switches, remove parts, etc., sequentially, until the light goes out. When the light goes out, the short is between the last circuit component opened and the previous circuit opened.

NOTE: *The 1.5 volt battery in the test light does not provide much current. A weak battery may not provide enough power to illuminate the test light even when a complete circuit is made (especially if there are high resistances in the circuit). Always make sure that the test battery is strong. To check the battery, briefly touch the ground clip to the probe; if the light glows brightly the battery is strong enough for testing. Never use a self-powered test light to perform checks for opens or shorts when power is applied to the electrical system under test. The 12 volt vehicle power will quickly burn out the 1.5 volt light bulb in the test light.*

Voltmeter

A voltmeter is used to measure voltage at any point in a circuit, or to measure the voltage drop across any part of a circuit. It can also be used to check continuity in a wire or circuit by indicating current flow from one end to the other. Voltmeters usually have various scales on the meter dial and a selector switch to allow the selection of different voltages. The voltmeter has a positive and a negative lead. To avoid damage to the meter, always connect the negative lead to the negative (–) side of the circuit (to ground or nearest the ground side of the circuit) and connect the positive lead to the positive (+) side of the circuit (to the power source or the nearest power source). Note that the negative voltmeter lead will always be black and that the positive voltmeter will always be some color other than black (usually red). Depending on how the voltmeter is connected into the circuit, it has several uses.

A voltmeter can be connected either in parallel or in series with a circuit and it has a very high resistance to current flow. When connected in parallel, only a small amount of current will flow through the voltmeter current path; the rest will flow through the normal circuit current path and the circuit will work normally. When the voltmeter is connected in series with a circuit, only a small amount of current can flow through the circuit. The circuit will not work properly, but the voltmeter reading will show if the circuit is complete or not.

Available Voltage Measurement

Set the voltmeter selector switch to the 20V position and connect the meter negative lead to the negative (–) post of the battery. Connect the positive meter lead to the positive (+) post of the battery and turn the ignition switch ON to provide a load. Read the voltage on the meter or digital display. A well charged battery should register over 12 volts. If the meter reads below 11.5 volts, the battery power may be insufficient to operate the electrical system properly. This test determines voltage available from the battery and should be the first step in any electrical trouble diagnosis procedure. Many electrical problems, especially on computer controlled systems, can be caused by a low state of charge in the battery. Excessive corrosion at the battery cable terminals can cause a poor contact that will prevent proper charging and full battery current flow.

Normal battery voltage is 12 volts when fully charged. When the battery is supplying current to one or more circuits it is said to be "under load". When everything is off the electrical system is under a "no-load" condition. A fully charged battery may show about 12.5 volts at no load; will drop to 12 volts under medium load; and will drop even lower under heavy load. If the battery is partially discharged the voltage decrease under heavy load may be excessive, even though the battery shows 12 volts or more at no load. When allowed to discharge further, the battery's available voltage under load will decrease more severely. For this reason, it is important that the battery be fully charged during all testing procedures to avoid errors in diagnosis and incorrect test results.

Voltage Drop

When current flows through a resistance, the voltage beyond the resistance is reduced (the larger the current, the greater the reduction in voltage). When no current is flowing, there is no voltage drop because there is no current flow. All points in the circuit which are connected to the power source are at the same voltage as the power source. The total voltage drop always equals the total source voltage. In a long circuit with many connectors, a series of small, unwanted voltage drops due to corrosion at the connectors can add up to a total loss of voltage which impairs the operation of the normal loads in the circuit.

INDIRECT COMPUTATION OF VOLTAGE DROPS

1. Set the voltmeter selector switch to the 20 volt position.
2. Connect the meter negative lead to a good ground.

3. Probe all resistances in the circuit with the positive meter lead.

4. Operate the circuit in all modes and observe the voltage readings.

DIRECT MEASUREMENT OF VOLTAGE DROPS

1. Set the voltmeter switch to the 20 volt position.

2. Connect the voltmeter negative lead to the ground side of the resistance load to be measured.

3. Connect the positive lead to the positive side of the resistance or load to be measured.

4. Read the voltage drop directly on the 20 volt scale.

Too high a voltage indicates too high a resistance. If, for example, a blower motor runs too slowly, you can determine if there is too high a resistance in the resistor pack. By taking voltage drop readings in all parts of the circuit, you can isolate the problem. Too low a voltage drop indicates too low a resistance. If, for example, a blower motor runs too fast in the MED and/or LOW position, the problem can be isolated in the resistor pack by taking voltage drop readings in all parts of the circuit to locate a possibly shorted resistor. The maximum allowable voltage drop under load is critical, especially if there is more than one high resistance problem in a circuit because all voltage drops are cumulative. A small drop is normal due to the resistance of the conductors.

HIGH RESISTANCE TESTING

1. Set the voltmeter selector switch to the 4 volt position.

2. Connect the voltmeter positive lead to the positive (+) post of the battery.

3. Turn on the headlights and heater blower to provide a load.

4. Probe various points in the circuit with the negative voltmeter lead.

5. Read the voltage drop on the 4 volt scale. Some average maximum allowable voltage drops are:

FUSE PANEL – 7 volts
IGNITION SWITCH – 5volts
HEADLIGHT SWITCH – 7 volts
IGNITION COIL (+) – 5 volts
ANY OTHER LOAD – 1.3 volts
NOTE: *Voltage drops are all measured while a load is operating; without current flow, there will be no voltage drop.*

Ohmmeter

The ohmmeter is designed to read resistance (ohms) in a circuit or component. Although there are several different styles of ohmmeters, all will usually have a selector switch which permits the measurement of different ranges of resistance (usually the selector switch allows the multiplication of the meter reading by 10, 100, 1000, and 10,000). A calibration knob allows the meter to be set at zero for accurate measurement. Since all ohmmeters are powered by an internal battery (usually 9 volts), the ohmmeter can be used as a self-powered test light. When the ohmmeter is connected, current from the ohmmeter flows through the circuit or component being tested. Since the ohmmeter's internal resistance and voltage are known values, the amount of current flow through the meter depends on the resistance of the circuit or component being tested.

The ohmmeter can be used to perform continuity test for opens or shorts (either by observation of the meter needle or as a self-powered test light), and to read actual resistance in a circuit. It should be noted that the ohmmeter is used to check the resistance of a component or wire while there is no voltage applied to the circuit. Current flow from an outside voltage source (such as the vehicle battery) can damage the ohmmeter, so the circuit or component should be isolated from the vehicle electrical system before any testing is done. Since the ohmmeter uses its own voltage source, either lead can be connected to any test point.

NOTE: *When checking diodes or other solid state components, the ohmmeter leads can only be connected one way in order to measure current flow in a single direction. Make sure the positive (+) and negative (–) terminal connections are as described in the test procedures to verify the one-way diode operation.*

In using the meter for making continuity checks, do not be concerned with the actual resistance readings. Zero resistance, or any resistance readings, indicate continuity in the circuit. Infinite resistance indicates an open in the circuit. A high resistance reading where there should be none indicates a problem in the circuit. Checks for short circuits are made in the same manner as checks for open circuits except that the circuit must be isolated from both power and normal ground. Infinite resistance indicates no continuity to ground, while zero resistance indicates a dead short to ground.

RESISTANCE MEASUREMENT

The batteries in an ohmmeter will weaken with age and temperature, so the ohmmeter must be calibrated or "zeroed" before taking measurements. To zero the meter, place the selector switch in its lowest range and touch the two ohmmeter leads together. Turn the calibration knob until the meter needle is exactly on zero.

NOTE: *All analog (needle) type ohmmeters*

must be zeroed before use, but some digital ohmmeter models are automatically calibrated when the switch is turned on. Self-calibrating digital ohmmeters do not have an adjusting knob, but its a good idea to check for a zero readout before use by touching the leads together. All computer controlled systems require the use of a digital ohmmeter with at least 10 megohms impedance for testing. Before any test procedures are attempted, make sure the ohmmeter used is compatible with the electrical system or damage to the onboard computer could result.

To measure resistance, first isolate the circuit from the vehicle power source by disconnecting the battery cables or the harness connector. Make sure the key is OFF when disconnecting any components or the battery. Where necessary, also isolate at least one side of the circuit to be checked to avoid reading parallel resistances. Parallel circuit resistances will always give a lower reading than the actual resistance of either of the branches. When measuring the resistance of parallel circuits, the total resistance will always be lower than the smallest resistance in the circuit. Connect the meter leads to both sides of the circuit (wire or component) and read the actual measured ohms on the meter scale. Make sure the selector switch is set to the proper ohm scale for the circuit being tested to avoid misreading the ohmmeter test value.

CAUTION: *Never use an ohmmeter with power applied to the circuit. Like the self-powered test light, the ohmmeter is designed to operate on its own power supply. The normal 12 volt automotive electrical system current could damage the meter.*

Ammeters

An ammeter measures the amount of current flowing through a circuit in units called amperes or amps. Amperes are units of electron flow which indicate how fast the electrons are flowing through the circuit. Since Ohms Law dictates that current flow in a circuit is equal to the circuit voltage divided by the total circuit resistance, increasing voltage also increases the current level (amps). Likewise, any decrease in resistance will increase the amount of amps in a circuit. At normal operating voltage, most circuits have a characteristic amount of amperes, called "current draw" which can be measured using an ammeter. By referring to a specified current draw rating, measuring the amperes, and comparing the two values, one can determine what is happening within the circuit to aid in diagnosis. An open circuit, for example, will not allow any current to flow so the ammeter reading will be zero. More current flows

through a heavily loaded circuit or when the charging system is operating.

An ammeter is always connected in series with the circuit being tested. All of the current that normally flows through the circuit must also flow through the ammeter; if there is any other path for the current to follow, the ammeter reading will not be accurate. The ammeter itself has very little resistance to current flow and therefore will not affect the circuit, but it will measure current draw only when the circuit is closed and electricity is flowing. Excessive current draw can blow fuses and drain the battery, while a reduced current draw can cause motors to run slowly, lights to dim and other components to not operate properly. The ammeter can help diagnose these conditions by locating the cause of the high or low reading.

Multimeters

Different combinations of test meters can be built into a single unit designed for specific tests. Some of the more common combination test devices are known as Volt/Amp testers, Tach/Dwell meters, or Digital Multimeters. The Volt/Amp tester is used for charging system, starting system or battery tests and consists of a voltmeter, an ammeter and a variable resistance carbon pile. The voltmeter will usually have at least two ranges for use with 6, 12 and 24 volt systems. The ammeter also has more than one range for testing various levels of battery loads and starter current draw and the carbon pile can be adjusted to offer different amounts of resistance. The Volt/Amp tester has heavy leads to carry large amounts of current and many later models have an inductive ammeter pickup that clamps around the wire to simplify test connections. On some models, the ammeter also has a zero-center scale to allow testing of charging and starting systems without switching leads or polarity. A digital multimeter is a voltmeter, ammeter and ohmmeter combined in an instrument which gives a digital readout. These are often used when testing solid state circuits because of their high input impedance (usually 10 megohms or more).

The tach/dwell meter combines a tachometer and a dwell (cam angle) meter and is a specialized kind of voltmeter. The tachometer scale is marked to show engine speed in rpm and the dwell scale is marked to show degrees of distributor shaft rotation. In most electronic ignition systems, dwell is determined by the control unit, but the dwell meter can also be used to check the duty cycle (operation) of some electronic engine control systems. Some tach/dwell meters are powered by an internal battery, while others take their power from the car battery in use. The battery powered testers usually require calibration much like an ohmmeter before testing.

Special Test Equipment

A variety of diagnostic tools are available to help troubleshoot and repair computerized engine control systems. The most sophisticated of these devices are the console type engine analyzers that usually occupy a garage service bay, but there are several types of aftermarket electronic testers available that will allow quick circuit tests of the engine control system by plugging directly into a special connector located in the engine compartment or under the dashboard. Several tool and equipment manufacturers offer simple, hand held testers that measure various circuit voltage levels on command to check all system components for proper operation. Although these testers usually cost about $300–500, consider that the average computer control unit (or ECM) can cost just as much and the money saved by not replacing perfectly good sensors or components in an attempt to correct a problem could justify the purchase price of a special diagnostic tester the first time it's used.

These computerized testers can allow quick and easy test measurements while the engine is operating or while the car is being driven. In addition, the on-board computer memory can be read to access any stored trouble codes; in effect allowing the computer to tell you where it hurts and aid trouble diagnosis by pinpointing exactly which circuit or component is malfunctioning. In the same manner, repairs can be tested to make sure the problem has been corrected. The biggest advantage these special testers have is their relatively easy hookups that minimize or eliminate the chances of making the wrong connections and getting false voltage readings or damaging the computer accidentally.

NOTE: *It should be remembered that these testers check voltage levels in circuits; they don't detect mechanical problems or failed components if the circuit voltage falls within the preprogrammed limits stored in the tester PROM unit. Also, most of the hand held testes are designed to work only on one or two systems made by a specific manufacturer.*

A variety of aftermarket testers are available to help diagnose different computerized control systems. Owatonna Tool Company (OTC), for example, markets a device called the OTC Monitor which plugs directly into the assembly line diagnostic link (ALDL). The OTC tester makes diagnosis a simple matter of pressing the correct buttons and, by changing the internal PROM or inserting a different diagnosis cartridge, it will work on any model from full size to subcompact, over a wide range of years. An adapter is supplied with the tester to allow connection to all types of ALDL links, regardless of the number of pin terminals used. By inserting an updated PROM into the OTC tester, it can be easily updated to diagnose any new modifications of computerized control systems.

Wiring Harnesses

The average automobile contains about ½ mile of wiring, with hundreds of individual connections. To protect the many wires from damage and to keep them from becoming a confusing tangle, they are organized into bundles, enclosed in plastic or taped together and called wire harnesses. Different wiring harnesses serve different parts of the vehicle. Individual wires are color coded to help trace them through a harness where sections are hidden from view.

A loose or corroded connection or a replacement wire that is too small for the circuit will add extra resistance and an additional voltage drop to the circuit. A ten percent voltage drop can result in slow or erratic motor operation, for example, even though the circuit is complete. Automotive wiring or circuit conductors can be in any one of three forms:

1. Single strand wire
2. Multi-strand wire
3. Printed circuitry

Single strand wire has a solid metal core and is usually used inside such components as alternators, motors, relays and other devices. Multi-strand wire has a core made of many small strands of wire twisted together into a single conductor. Most of the wiring in an automotive electrical system is made up of multi-strand wire, either as a single conductor or grouped together in a harness. All wiring is color coded on the insulator, either as a solid color or as a colored wire with an identification stripe. A printed circuit is a thin film of copper or other conductor that is printed on an insulator backing. Occasionally, a printed circuit is sandwiched between two sheets of plastic for more protection and flexibility. A complete printed circuit, consisting of conductors, insulating material and connectors for lamps or other components is called a printed circuit board. Printed circuitry is used in place of individual wires or harnesses in places where space is limited, such as behind instrument panels.

Wire Gauge

Since computer controlled automotive electrical systems are very sensitive to changes in resistance, the selection of properly sized wires is critical when systems are repaired. The wire gauge number is an expression of the cross section area of the conductor. The most common system for expressing wire size is the American Wire Gauge (AWG) system.

Wire cross section area is measured in circular mils. A mil is $\frac{1}{1000}$ in. (0.001 in.); a circular mil is the area of a circle one mil in diameter. For example, a conductor ¼ in. in diameter is 0.250 in. or 250 mils. The circular mil cross section area of the wire is 250 squared (250^2)or 62,500 circular mils. Imported car models usually use metric wire gauge designations, which is simply the cross section area of the conductor in square millimeters (mm^2).

Gauge numbers are assigned to conductors of various cross section areas. As gauge number increases, area decreases and the conductor becomes smaller. A 5 gauge conductor is smaller than a 1 gauge conductor and a 10 gauge is smaller than a 5 gauge. As the cross section area of a conductor decreases, resistance increases and so does the gauge number. A conductor with a higher gauge number will carry less current than a conductor with a lower gauge number.

NOTE: *Gauge wire size refers to the size of the conductor, not the size of the complete wire. It is possible to have two wires of the same gauge with different diameters because one may have thicker insulation than the other.*

12 volt automotive electrical systems generally use 10, 12, 14, 16 and 18 gauge wire. Main power distribution circuits and larger accessories usually use 10 and 12 gauge wire. Battery cables are usually 4 or 6 gauge, although 1 and 2 gauge wires are occasionally used. Wire length must also be considered when making repairs to a circuit. As conductor length increases, so does resistance. An 18 gauge wire, for example, can carry a 10 amp load for 10 feet without excessive voltage drop; however if a 15 foot wire is required for the same 10 amp load, it must be a 16 gauge wire.

An electrical schematic shows the electrical current paths when a circuit is operating properly. It is essential to understand how a circuit works before trying to figure out why it doesn't. Schematics break the entire electrical system down into individual circuits and show only one particular circuit. In a schematic, no attempt is made to represent wiring and components as they physically appear on the vehicle; switches and other components are shown as simply as possible. Face views of harness connectors show the cavity or terminal locations in all multi-pin connectors to help locate test points.

If you need to backprobe a connector while it is on the component, the order of the terminals must be mentally reversed. The wire color code can help in this situation, as well as a keyway, lock tab or other reference mark.

NOTE: *Wiring diagrams are not included in this book. As cars and trucks have become more complex and available with longer option lists, wiring diagrams have grown in size and complexity. It has become almost impossible to provide a readable reproduction of a wiring diagram in a book this size. Information on ordering wiring diagrams from the vehicle manufacturer can be found in the owner's manual.*

WIRING REPAIR

Soldering is a quick, efficient method of joining metals permanently. Everyone who has the occasion to make wiring repairs should know how to solder. Electrical connections that are soldered are far less likely to come apart and will conduct electricity much better than connections that are only "pig-tailed" together. The most popular (and preferred) method of soldering is with an electrical soldering gun. Soldering irons are available in many sizes and wattage ratings. Irons with higher wattage ratings deliver higher temperatures and recover lost heat faster. A small soldering iron rated for no more than 50 watts is recommended, especially on electrical systems where excess heat can damage the components being soldered.

There are three ingredients necessary for successful soldering; proper flux, good solder and sufficient heat. A soldering flux is necessary to clean the metal of tarnish, prepare it for soldering and to enable the solder to spread into tiny crevices. When soldering, always use a resin flux or resin core solder which is non-corrosive and will not attract moisture once the job is finished. Other types of flux (acid core) will leave a residue that will attract moisture and cause the wires to corrode. Tin is a unique metal with a low melting point. In a molten state, it dissolves and alloys easily with many metals. Solder is made by mixing tin with lead. The most common proportions are 40/60, 50/50 and 60/40, with the percentage of tin listed first. Low priced solders usually contain less tin, making them very difficult for a beginner to use because more heat is required to melt the solder. A common solder is 40/60 which is well suited for all-around general use, but 60/40 melts easier, has more tin for a better joint and is preferred for electrical work.

Soldering Techniques

Successful soldering requires that the metals to be joined be heated to a temperature that will melt the solder – usually 360–460°F (182–238°C). Contrary to popular belief, the purpose of the soldering iron is not to melt the solder itself, but to heat the parts being soldered to a temperature high enough to melt the solder when it is touched to the work. Melting flux-cored solder on the soldering iron will usually destroy the effectiveness of the flux.

NOTE: *Soldering tips are made of copper for good heat conductivity, but must be "tinned" regularly for quick transference of heat to the project and to prevent the solder from sticking to the iron. To "tin" the iron, simply heat it and touch the flux-cored solder to the tip; the solder will flow over the hot tip. Wipe the excess off with a clean rag, but be careful as the iron will be hot.*

After some use, the tip may become pitted. If so, simply dress the tip smooth with a smooth file and "tin" the tip again. An old saying holds that "metals well cleaned are half soldered." Flux-cored solder will remove oxides, but rust, bits of insulation and oil or grease must be removed with a wire brush or emery cloth. For maximum strength in soldered parts, the joint must start off clean and tight. Weak joints will result in gaps too wide for the solder to bridge.

If a separate soldering flux is used, it should be brushed or swabbed on only those areas that are to be soldered. Most solders contain a core of flux and separate fluxing is unnecessary. Hold the work to be soldered firmly. It is best to solder on a wooden board, because a metal vise will only rob the piece to be soldered of heat and make it difficult to melt the solder. Hold the soldering tip with the broadest face against the work to be soldered. Apply solder under the tip close to the work, using enough solder to give a heavy film between the iron and the piece being soldered, while moving slowly and making sure the solder melts properly. Keep the work level or the solder will run to the lowest part and favor the thicker parts, because these require more heat to melt the solder. If the soldering tip overheats (the solder coating on the face of the tip burns up), it should be retinned. Once the soldering is completed, let the soldered joint stand until cool. Tape and seal all soldered wire splices after the repair has cooled.

Wire Harness and Connectors

The on-board computer (ECM) wire harness electrically connects the control unit to the various solenoids, switches and sensors used by the control system. Most connectors in the engine compartment or otherwise exposed to the elements are protected against moisture and dirt which could create oxidation and deposits on the terminals. This protection is important because of the very low voltage and current levels used by the computer and sensors. All connectors have a lock which secures the male and female terminals together, with a secondary lock holding the seal and terminal into the connector. Both terminal locks must be released when disconnecting ECM connectors.

These special connectors are weather-proof and all repairs require the use of a special terminal and the tool required to service it. This tool is used to remove the pin and sleeve terminals. If removal is attempted with an ordinary pick, there is a good chance that the terminal will be bent or deformed. Unlike standard blade type terminals, these terminals cannot be straightened once they are bent. Make certain that the connectors are properly seated and all of the sealing rings in place when connecting leads. On some models, a hinge-type flap provides a backup or secondary locking feature for the terminals. Most secondary locks are used to improve the connector reliability by retaining the terminals if the small terminal lock tangs are not positioned properly.

Molded-on connectors require complete replacement of the connection. This means splicing a new connector assembly into the harness. All splices in on-board computer systems should be soldered to insure proper contact. Use care when probing the connections or replacing terminals in them as it is possible to short between opposite terminals. If this happens to the wrong terminal pair, it is possible to damage certain components. Always use jumper wires between connectors for circuit checking and never probe through weatherproof seals.

Open circuits are often difficult to locate by sight because corrosion or terminal misalignment are hidden by the connectors. Merely wiggling a connector on a sensor or in the wiring harness may correct the open circuit condition. This should always be considered when an open circuit or a failed sensor is indicated. Intermittent problems may also be caused by oxidized or loose connections. When using a circuit tester for diagnosis, always probe connections from the wire side. Be careful not to damage sealed connectors with test probes.

All wiring harnesses should be replaced with identical parts, using the same gauge wire and connectors. When signal wires are spliced into a harness, use wire with high temperature insulation only. With the low voltage and current levels found in the system, it is important that the best possible connection at all wire splices be made by soldering the splices together. It is seldom necessary to replace a complete harness. If replacement is necessary, pay close attention to insure proper harness routing. Secure the harness with suitable plastic wire clamps to prevent vibrations from causing the harness to wear in spots or contact any hot components.

NOTE: *Weatherproof connectors cannot be replaced with standard connectors. Instruc-*

tions are provided with replacement connector and terminal packages. Some wire harnesses have mounting indicators (usually pieces of colored tape) to mark where the harness is to be secured.

In making wiring repairs, it's important that you always replace damaged wires with wires that are the same gauge as the wire being replaced. The heavier the wire, the smaller the gauge number. Wires are color-coded to aid in identification and whenever possible the same color coded wire should be used for replacement. A wire stripping and crimping tool is necessary to install solderless terminal connectors. Test all crimps by pulling on the wires; it should not be possible to pull the wires out of a good crimp.

Wires which are open, exposed or otherwise damaged are repaired by simple splicing. Where possible, if the wiring harness is accessible and the damaged place in the wire can be located, it is best to open the harness and check for all possible damage. In an inaccessible harness, the wire must be bypassed with a new insert, usually taped to the outside of the old harness.

When replacing fusible links, be sure to use fusible link wire, NOT ordinary automotive wire. Make sure the fusible segment is of the same gauge and construction as the one being replaced and double the stripped end when crimping the terminal connector for a good contact. The melted (open) fusible link segment of the wiring harness should be cut off as close to the harness as possible, then a new segment spliced in as described. In the case of a damaged fusible link that feeds two harness wires, the harness connections should be replaced with two fusible link wires so that each circuit will have its own separate protection.

NOTE: *Most of the problems caused in the wiring harness are due to bad ground connections. Always check all vehicle ground connections for corrosion or looseness before performing any power feed checks to eliminate the chance of a bad ground affecting the circuit.*

Repairing Hard Shell Connectors

Unlike molded connectors, the terminal contacts in hard shell connectors can be replaced. Weatherproof hard-shell connectors with the leads molded into the shell have non-replacable terminal ends. Replacement usually involves the use of a special terminal removal tool that depress the locking tangs (barbs) on the connector terminal and allow the connector to be removed from the rear of the shell. The connector shell should be replaced if it shows any evidence of burning, melting, cracks, or breaks. Replace

individual terminals that are burnt, corroded, distorted or loose.

NOTE: *The insulation crimp must be tight to prevent the insulation from sliding back on the wire when the wire is pulled. The insulation must be visibly compressed under the crimp tabs, and the ends of the crimp should be turned in for a firm grip on the insulation.*

The wire crimp must be made with all wire strands inside the crimp. The terminal must be fully compressed on the wire strands with the ends of the crimp tabs turned in to make a firm grip on the wire. Check all connections with an ohmmeter to insure a good contact. There should be no measurable resistance between the wire and the terminal when connected.

Mechanical Test Equipment

Vacuum Gauge

Most gauges are graduated in inches of mercury (in.Hg), although a device called a manometer reads vacuum in inches of water (in. H_2O). The normal vacuum reading usually varies between 18 and 22 in.Hg at sea level. To test engine vacuum, the vacuum gauge must be connected to a source of manifold vacuum. Many engines have a plug in the intake manifold which can be removed and replaced with an adapter fitting. Connect the vacuum gauge to the fitting with a suitable rubber hose or, if no manifold plug is available, connect the vacuum gauge to any device using manifold vacuum, such as EGR valves, etc. The vacuum gauge can be used to determine if enough vacuum is reaching a component to allow its actuation.

Hand Vacuum Pump

Small, hand-held vacuum pumps come in a variety of designs. Most have a built-in vacuum gauge and allow the component to be tested without removing it from the vehicle. Operate the pump lever or plunger to apply the correct amount of vacuum required for the test specified in the diagnosis routines. The level of vacuum in inches of Mercury (in.Hg) is indicated on the pump gauge. For some testing, an additional vacuum gauge may be necessary.

Intake manifold vacuum is used to operate various systems and devices on late model vehicles. To correctly diagnose and solve problems in vacuum control systems, a vacuum source is necessary for testing. In some cases, vacuum can be taken from the intake manifold when the engine is running, but vacuum is normally provided by a hand vacuum pump. These hand vacuum pumps have a built-in vacuum gauge that allow testing while the device is still attached to the component. For some tests, an additional vacuum gauge may be necessary.

HEATING AND AIR CONDITIONING

Blower Motor (Fan Motor)

The blower motor is located under the dashboard on the far right side of the car. It is accessible from under the dashboard without removing the dash. The blower motor turns the fan, which circulates the heated, cooled or fresh air within the car. Aside from common electrical problems, the blower motor may need to be removed to clean out leaves or debris which have been sucked into the casing.

NOTE: *The blower motor may be removed without disconnecting heater hoses. If the car is equipped with air conditioning, the air conditioning system must be discharged and the evaporator unit removed. Please refer to "Evaporator--Removal and Installation" later in this chapter. Once the unit is removed, the blower motor can be removed following the procedures below.*

REMOVAL AND INSTALLATION

Nova

1. Remove the three screws attaching the retainer.
2. Remove the glove box assembly.
3. Remove the air duct between the heater case and blower assembly.
4. Disconnect the blower motor wire connector at the motor case.
5. Disconnect the air source selector control cable at the blower assembly.
6. Loosen the two nuts and the bolt attaching the blower assembly, then remove the blower.
7. With the blower removed, check the case for any debris or signs of fan contact. Inspect the fan for wear spots, cracked blades or hub, loose retaining nut or poor alignment.
8. To reinstall, place the blower in position, making sure it is properly aligned within the case. Install the two bolts and the nut and tighten them.
9. Connect the selector control cable at the blower assembly.
10. Connect the wire harness to the motor and install the ductwork between the heater case and the blower assembly.
11. Install the glove box assembly and install the retainer with its three screws.

Prizm

1. Disconnect the negative battery cable.
2. Remove the rubber duct running between the heater case and the blower.
3. Disconnect the wiring from the motor.
4. Remove the three screws holding the motor and remove the blower motor.

5. With the blower removed, check the case for any debris or signs of fan contact. Inspect the fan for wear spots, cracked blades or hub, loose retaining nut or poor alignment.
6. To reinstall, place the blower in position, making sure it is properly aligned within the case. Install the three screws and tighten them.
7. Connect the wiring to the motor.
8. Install the rubber air duct and connect the negative battery cable.

Heater Core

The heater core is simply a small heat exchanger (radiator) within the car. If the driver selects heat on the control panel, a water valve is opened allowing engine coolant to circulate through the heater core. The blower fan circulates air through the fins, picking up the heat from the engine coolant. The heated air is ducted into the car and the coolant is routed back to the engine. Moving the control to a cooler setting reduces the amount of hot water flowing into the core, thus reducing the amount of heat.

REMOVAL AND INSTALLATION

Nova

1. Disconnect the negative battery cable and then drain the cooling system.

CAUTION: *When draining the coolant, keep in mind that cats and dogs are attracted by the ethylene glycol antifreeze, and are quite likely to drink any that is left in an uncovered container or in puddles on the ground. This will prove fatal in sufficient quantity. Always drain the coolant into a sealable container. Coolant should be reused unless it is contaminated or several years old.*

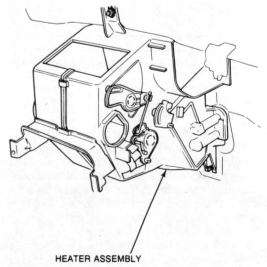

HEATER ASSEMBLY

Nova heater assembly

2. Disconnect the heater hose from the core in the engine compartment.

3. Remove the six clips from the lower part of the heater case, then remove the lower part of the case.

4. Carefully pry open the lower part of the heater case.

5. Remove the core assembly from the heater case. Handle the core carefully and do not allow the fins to be crushed or deformed.

6. When reinstalling, position the core properly and install the lower part of the case.

7. Install the six clips, making sure each is properly secured.

8. Connect the heater hoses. Check them for any signs of weakness or fraying and use new clamps if necessary.

9. Refill the coolant to the proper level.

10. Connect the negative battery cable.

Prizm

NOTE: *The heater case and core are located directly behind the center console. Access to the heater case requires removal of the entire console as well as most of the dashboard assembly. Please refer to the proper sub-topics for removal procedures. Instrument Cluster, Instrument Panel, Console and Radio Removal are explained later in this chapter. Steering Wheel Removal and Installation is discussed in Chapter 8.*

1. Disconnect the negative battery cable.

2. Remove the steering wheel.

3. Remove the trim bezel from the instrument cluster.

4. Remove the cup holder from the console.

5. Remove the radio.

6. Remove the instrument panel (dashboard) assembly and the instrument cluster. Label and carefully disconnect all of the dash wiring harnesses. Remember to release the locking mechanism on each connector first.

7. Remove the center console and all the console trim. Work carefully and don't break the plastic pieces.

8. Remove the lower dash trim and the side window air deflectors.

9. Drain the coolant from the cooling system. CAUTION: *When draining the coolant, keep in mind that cats and dogs are attracted by the ethylene glycol antifreeze, and are quite likely to drink any that is left in an uncovered container or in puddles on the ground. This will prove fatal in sufficient quantity. Always drain the coolant into a sealable container. Coolant should be reused unless it is contaminated or several years old.*

10. Disconnect the control cables from the heater case. Don't lose any of the small clips.

11. Disconnect the ductwork from the heater case.

1. BLOWER ASSEMBLY
2. DUCT
3. HEATER ASSEMBLY

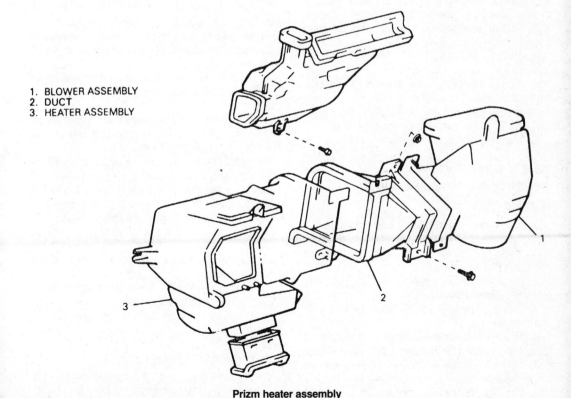

Prizm heater assembly

12. Disconnect the blower switch wiring harness and heater control assembly.

13. Remove the two center console support braces.

14. Loosen the clamps and remove the heater hoses from the case. Remove the grommet from the cowling.

15. Remove the mounting nuts and bolts holding the heater core and the air distribution case to the firewall.

16. Remove the heater case and air distribution case from the car as a unit.

17. Remove the screws and clips from the case halves and separate the case.

18. Remove the heater core from the case.

19. Install the heater core into the case, position the case halves and secure the retaining screws and clips.

20. Install the case assembly in the car and secure it with the mounting nuts and bolts.

21. Connect the heater hoses (use new clamps if necessary) and attach the grommet to the cowl.

22. Connect the air ducts to the case and connect the control cables.

23. Install the two center console support braces.

24. Install the blower wiring harness and the heater control assembly.

25. Place the dashboard in position within the car. When it is loosely in place, connect the wiring harness connectors, making sure each is firmly seated and the wiring properly secured.

26. Install the center console and its trim pieces.

27. Install the radio.

28. Install the cup holder.

29. Install the trim bezel around the instrument cluster.

30. Install the steering wheel.

31. Refill the coolant to the proper level.

32. Connect the negative battery cable.

Heater Control Panel

REMOVAL AND INSTALLATION

Nova and Prizm

1. Disconnect the negative battery cable.

2. Remove the steering wheel.

3. Remove the two screws holding the hood release lever assembly.

4. Remove the four screws holding the left lower dashboard panel.

5. Remove the upper and lower steering column covers.

6. Use a small screwdriver or similar tool to gently pry the switches from the lower dash trim panel. Disconnect the wiring and remove the switches.

7. Remove the two screws under the panel

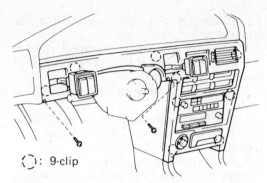

○ : 9-clip

Location of screws and clips holding the dashboard trim panel

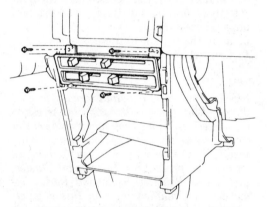

With the dash trim removed, the heater control panel bolts can be easily removed

and pull out the center cluster finish panel. It is also secured by spring clips behind the dash--pull straight out away from the dash so as not to break the plastic.

8. Remove the four screws holding the heater control panel and slide the panel out of the dash.

9. When reinstalling, place the control panel in the dash, make sure it is straight and install the four retaining screws.

10. Place the finish panel in place and push it into the dash so that each spring clip engages. Install the two lower screws.

11. Connect the wiring to the switches and press the switches firmly into place.

12. Install the upper and lower steering wheel covers.

13. Install the lower left dash cover and its four screws.

14. Install the hood release lever assembly.

15. Install the steering wheel.

16. Connect the negative battery cable.

Evaporator

REMOVAL AND INSTALLATION

CAUTION: *PLEASE RE-READ THE AIR CONDITIONING SECTION IN CHAPTER*

ONE SO THAT THE SYSTEM MAY BE DISCHARGED PROPERLY! ALWAYS WEAR EYE PROTECTION AND GLOVES WHEN DISCHARGING THE SYSTEM! OBSERVE NO SMOKING/NO OPEN FLAME RULES!

Nova

1. Disconnect the negative battery cable.
2. Safely discharge the air conditioning system.
3. Disconnect the suction tube from the evaporator assembly, then disconnect the liquid line from the assembly. Cap the open fittings immediately to prevent the entry of dirt and moisture.
4. Remove the grommets from the inlet and outlet fittings.
5. Remove the glove box.
6. Remove the lower cover from under the dashboard.
7. Disconnect the air conditioning switch connector.
8. Disconnect the vehicle wiring harness at the connector.
9. Remove the four nuts and three bolts securing the cooling assembly and remove the evaporator assembly from the car.
10. Remove the air conditioning amplifier.
11. Remove the air conditioning wiring harness from the case.
12. Remove the five clamps and two screws and remove the lower casing.
13. Remove the two screws holding the upper casing and remove the casing.
14. Remove the heat insulator and clamp from the outlet tube.
15. Disconnect the liquid line tube from the inlet fitting of the expansion valve.
16. Disconnect the expansion valve from the inlet fitting of the evaporator.

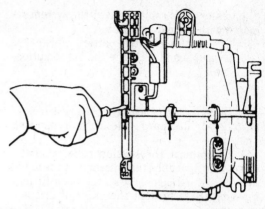

Separating the Nova evaporator case halves

17. Remove the pressure switch if necessary.
18. Inspect the evaporator fins for blockage. Check all the fittings for cracks or scratches.
19. To reassemble, connect the expansion valve to the inlet fitting of the evaporator and tighten the nut to 17 ft. lbs.
20. Connect the liquid line tube to the inlet fitting of the expansion valve.
21. Install the pressure switch, if removed, and tighten it to 10 ft. lbs.
22. Install the clamp and heat insulator to the outlet tube.
23. Assemble the upper and lower cases onto the evaporator unit.
24. Reinstall the thermistor if it was removed.
25. Install the air conditioning wire harness onto the evaporator unit.
26. Install the air conditioning amplifier.
27. Place the assembled unit in place inside the car and install the retaining nuts and bolts.
    WARNING: *Be careful not to pinch the wiring harness(es) during installation.*
28. Connect the air conditioning switch.
29. Connect the vehicle wiring harness to the connector.
30. Install the glove box and the under-dash cover.
31. Install the grommets on the inlet and outlet fittings.
32. Connect the liquid line to the evaporator inlet fitting and tighten it to 10 ft. lbs. Make sure the rubber washer (O-ring) is present inside the line and make certain the joint is correctly threaded before tightening it. Do not overtighten the joint.
33. Connect the suction tube to the evaporator unit outlet fitting and tighten it to 24 ft. lbs. Again, make sure the rubber washer (O-ring) is present inside the line and make certain the joint is correctly threaded before tightening it. Do not overtighten the joint.
34. If the evaporator was replaced with a NEW unit, add 1.5 oz. of compressor oil to the

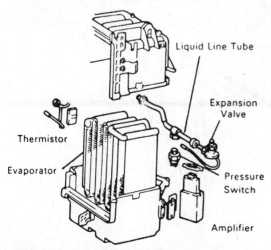

Liquid Line Tube

Expansion Valve

Thermistor

Evaporator

Pressure Switch

Amplifier

Exploded view of Nova evaporator assembly

compressor. This replaces oil in the system removed with the old evaporator.

35. Connect the negative battery cable.
36. Evacuate and recharge the air conditioning system.

Prizm

1. Disconnect the negative battery cable.
2. Safely discharge the air conditioning system.
3. Disconnect the suction tube from the evaporator assembly, then disconnect the liquid line from the assembly. Cap the open fittings immediately to prevent the entry of dirt and moisture.
4. Remove the grommets from the inlet and outlet fittings.
5. Remove the glove box.
6. Disconnect the wiring harness connectors.
7. Remove the four nuts and four screws holding the evaporator unit. Remove the unit through the front of the instrument panel.
8. Remove the connectors and the wiring harness from the case.
9. Remove the four clips and four screws; remove the upper casing and then the lower casing.
10. Disconnect the liquid tube from the inlet fitting of the expansion tube.
11. Remove the packing and the heat sensing tube from the suction tube of the evaporator.
   NOTE: *Cap the open lines and fittings immediately to prevent the entry of dirt and moisture.*
12. Remove the expansion valve.
13. Inspect the evaporator fins for blockage. Check all the fittings for cracks or scratches. Never use water to clean the evaporator.
14. When reinstalling, assemble the expansion valve to the inlet fitting of the evaporator and tighten the nut to 17 ft. lbs.
15. Install the heat sensing tube and its packing to the suction tube of the evaporator.
16. Connect the liquid tube to the inlet fitting of the expansion valve and tighten it to 10 ft. lbs.
17. Assemble the lower casing and the upper casing and secure them with the four clips and the four screws.
18. Connect the wiring harness connectors.

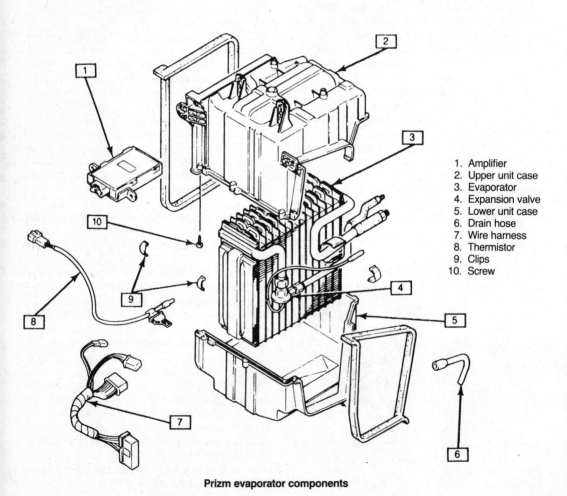

1. Amplifier
2. Upper unit case
3. Evaporator
4. Expansion valve
5. Lower unit case
6. Drain hose
7. Wire harness
8. Thermistor
9. Clips
10. Screw

Prizm evaporator components

Removing the Prizm expansion valve. Note the use of two wrenches to counterhold the fittings

19. Place the assembled unit in place within the car and secure its four mounting bolts and four nuts.
20. Install the wiring connectors onto the evaporator case.
21. Install the glove box.
22. Install the grommets on the inlet and outlet fittings.
23. Connect the liquid tube to the inlet fitting. Make sure the O-ring is in place and that the joint is correctly threaded. Tighten the joint to 10 ft. lbs. Do not overtighten.
24. Install the suction tube to the case inlet fitting. Make sure the O-ring is in place and that the joint is correctly threaded. Tighten the joint to 24 ft. lbs. Do not overtighten.
25. If the evaporator was replaced with a NEW unit, add 1.5 oz. of compressor oil to the compressor. This replaces oil in the system removed with the old evaporator.
26. Connect the negative battery cable.
27. Evacuate and recharge the air conditioning system.

RADIO

REMOVAL AND INSTALLATION

Nova

1. Disconnect the negative battery cable.
2. Remove the steering wheel and then the upper and lower steering column covers.
3. Use a small screwdriver or similar tool to gently pry the switches from the lower dash trim panel. Disconnect the wiring and remove the switches.
4. Remove the two screws under the panel and pull out the center cluster finish panel. It is also secured by spring clips behind the dash-- pull straight out away from the dash so as not to break the plastic.

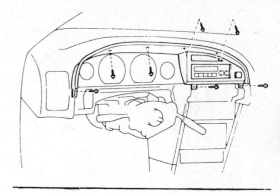

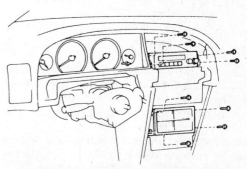

Removing the Nova upper trim panel and the radio with its accessories

5. Remove the seven screws holding the upper trim panel.
6. Remove the eight screws holding the radio and its accessories trim cover.
7. Slide the radio out of the dash. Disconnect the antenna lead and the wiring connector.
8. When reinstalling, connect the wiring and antenna leads and place the radio in the dash. Make sure the wiring is not crushed or pinched.
9. Install the eight screws, making sure the radio is straight and in position.
10. Install the upper trim panel.
11. Route the switch cables through the openings in the center trim panel. Install the center cluster finish panel, making sure all the clips engage properly. Install the two screws.
12. Connect the switches to the wiring harnesses and push the switches firmly into place in the trim panel.
13. Install the upper and lower steering column covers and reinstall the steering wheel.
14. Connect the negative battery cable.

Prizm

1. Remove the seven screws from the steering column covers and remove the covers.
2. Remove the two attaching screws from the lower part of the trim panel.
3. Remove the trim panel, being careful of the concealed spring clips behind the panel.
4. Disconnect the wiring from the switches mounted in the trim panel.

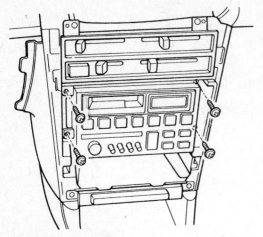

Prizm radio mounting screws

5. Remove the four mounting screws from the radio.

6. Remove the radio from the dash until the wiring connectors are exposed.

7. Disconnect the two electrical connectors and the antenna cable from the body of the radio and remove the radio from the car.

8. When reinstalling, connect all the wiring and antenna cable first, then place the radio in position within the dash.

9. Install the four attaching screws.

10. Reconnect the wiring harnesses to the switches in the trim panel and make sure the switches are secure in the panel.

11. Install the trim panel (make sure all the spring clips engage) and install the two screws.

12. Install the steering column covers and the seven screws.

13. Install the steering wheel.

WINDSHIELD WIPERS

Blade and Arm

REMOVAL AND INSTALLATION

Nova

1. To remove the wiper blades lift up on the spring release tab on the wiper blade-to-wiper arm connector.

2. Pull the blade assembly off the wiper arm.

3. Press the old wiper blade insert down, away from the blade assembly, to free it from the retaining clips on the blade ends. Slide the insert out of the blade. Slide the new insert into the blade assembly and bend the insert upward slightly to engage the retaining clips.

4. To replace a wiper arm, unscrew the acorn nut which secures it to the pivot and carefully pull the arm upward and off the pivot. Install the arm by placing it on the pivot and tighten-

ing the nut. Remember that the arm must be reinstalled in its exact previous position or it will not cover the correct area during use.

Prizm

The wiper blade can be removed by detaching the blade tip from the first wiper arm notch, then sliding the blade off the wiper arm. The new blade is installed by sliding the blade groove through the wiper arm notches.

The wiper arm is removed by lifting up the cap at the bottom of the arm, removing the locknut and lifting the arm free of the pivot. When reinstalling, make sure the arm is installed in its exact previous position before tightening the nut.

CHILTON TIP: *If one wiper arm does not move when turned on or only moves a little bit, check the retaining nut at the bottom of the arm. The extra effort of moving wet snow or leaves off the glass can cause the nut to come loose--the pivot will turn without moving the arm.*

Windshield wiper motor
REMOVAL AND INSTALLATION
Front wipers

1. Disconnect the negative battery terminal.

2. Disconnect the electrical connector from the wiper motor.

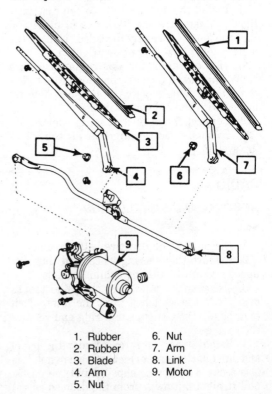

1. Rubber	6. Nut
2. Rubber	7. Arm
3. Blade	8. Link
4. Arm	9. Motor
5. Nut	

Nova wiper motor and linkage

1. Wiper arm cap
2. Wiper linkage cover
3. Attaching nut
4. Wiper arm
5. Wiper linkage
6. Wiper motor

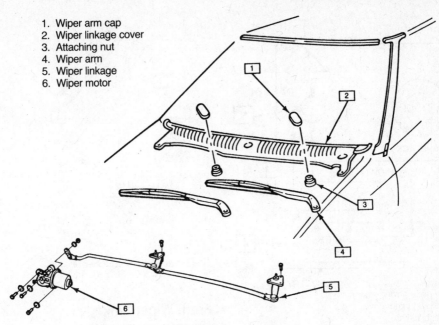

Prizm front wiper components

3. Remove the mounting bolts and remove the motor from the firewall.

4. Remove the wiper linkage from the wiper motor assembly.

5. Installation is the reverse of removal.

Rear Wiper

1. Remove the wiper arm from the pivot and remove the spacer and washer on the pivot.

2. Remove the cover (trim) panel on the inside of the hatch lid.

3. Remove the plastic cover on the wiper motor and disconnect the wiring connector from the motor.

4. Remove the mounting nuts and bolts and remove the wiper motor.

5. When reinstalling, position the motor and secure it in the hatch lid.

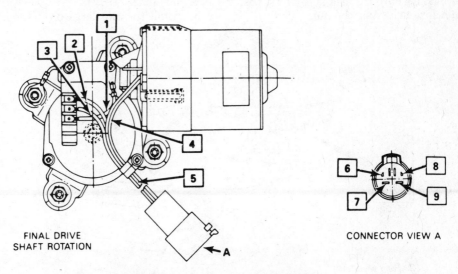

FINAL DRIVE
SHAFT ROTATION

CONNECTOR VIEW A

1. Black lead
2. Green lead
3. Green/brown lead
4. Red lead
5. Blue lead

6. Low spd/red lead
7. 12v/green lead
8. High spd/blue lead
9. Park sw/green-brown lead

Wiring diagram, Nova wiper motor

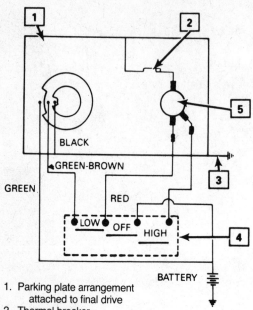

BLACK

GREEN-BROWN

GREEN

RED

LOW OFF HIGH

BATTERY

1. Parking plate arrangement
   attached to final drive
2. Thermal breaker
3. Ground (motor)
4. Wiper switch
5. Commutator

Nova wiper motor circuit schematic

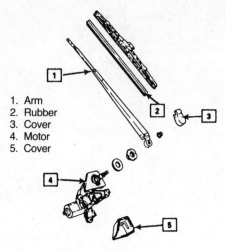

1. Arm
2. Rubber
3. Cover
4. Motor
5. Cover

Nova rear wiper components

6. Connect the wiring harness and install the plastic cover.

7. Install the inner trim panel on the hatch lid.

8. Install the wiper arm with its washer and spacer, making sure the arm is correctly positioned before tightening the nut.

Front Wiper Linkage

REMOVAL AND INSTALLATION

1. Remove the windshield wiper motor as previously outlined.

2. Loosen the wiper arm retaining nuts and remove the arms.

3. Unfasten the large wiper pivot retaining nuts and remove the linkage assembly through the access hole.

4. When reinstalling, place the linkage through the access hole and line up the pivots in their holes. This can be like trying to put an octopus into a paper bag; keep your temper and take your time.

5. Install the two large pivot retaing nuts

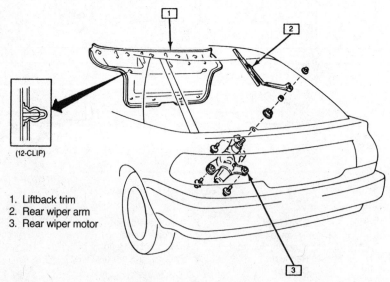

(12-CLIP)

1. Liftback trim
2. Rear wiper arm
3. Rear wiper motor

Prizm rear wiper components

onto the pivots. Before final tightening, make sure the linkage is aligned in all its holes.

6. Reinstall the wiper motor.

INSTRUMENTS AND SWITCHES

Instrument Cluster

REMOVAL AND INSTALLATION

Nova

1. Disconnect the negative battery cable.
2. Remove the steering wheel.
3. Remove the left side speaker grille. The

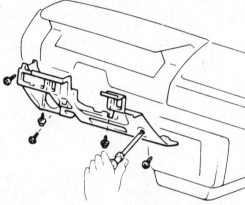

Removing the Nova lower steering column cover

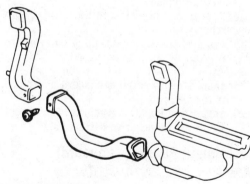

Nova heater ducts

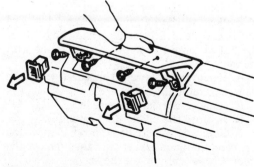

Removing the Nova instrument hood

grille may be attached with a clip (which must be pulled loose to remove the grille) or with a screw.

4. Remove the lower trim cover from the steering column.
5. Remove the hood release lever.
6. Remove the heater duct assembly.
7. Remove the instrument hood. Remove the air conditioner outlet register, then remove the four screws and remove the hood.
8. Remove the six screws from the instrument cluster, and disconnect the speedometer cable and the wiring connectors. Remove the meter assembly from the instrument panel.
9. To reinstall, connect the wiring harnesses and the speedometer cable to the cluster. Place the cluster in the dash and secure the six screws. Make certain the wiring is properly placed so as not to become pinched or crushed.
10. Install the air conditioning outlet then install the hood and its screws. .
11. Install the heater duct assembly.
12. Install the hood release lever and the lower steering column trim.
13. Reinstall the speaker grille.
14. Install the steering wheel and connect the negative battery cable.

Prizm

NOTE: *Removing the steering wheel is not required, but may make the job easier.*

1. Disconnect the negative battery cable.
2. Remove the hood release lever.
3. Remove the four screws from the lower left dash trim and pull the trim out.
4. Disconnect the wiring from the radio speaker.
5. If equipped with air conditioning, remove the ductwork from the lower air outlet.
6. Remove the trim panel from the car.
7. Remove the upper and lower steering column covers.
8. Remove the two screws from the trim panel (bezel).
9. Pull the panel out, releasing the spring clips behind the dash. With the panel loose, disconnect the wiring to the dash switches.
10. Remove the switches from the panel.
11. Remove the two electrical connectors and the cigarette lighter from the trim bezel and remove the bezel from the car.
12. Remove the four screws holding the instrument cluster trim.
13. Disconnect the wiring from the hazard (4-way) flasher and dimmer switches.
14. Remove the cluster trim panel.
15. Remove the four attaching screws holding the cluster, move it away from the dash and disconnect the wiring harnesses and the speedometer cable.

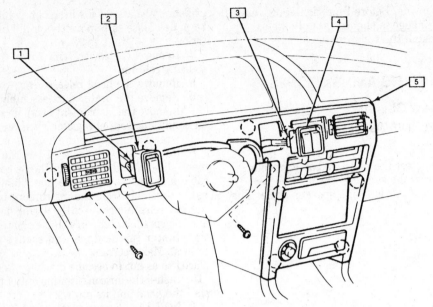

1. Electrical connector
2. Rear wiper-washer switch
3. Electrical connector
4. Cruise control/defogger switch
5. Trim bezel

Prizm lower dash panel (bezel)

16. Remove the instrument cluster from the car.

17. When reinstalling, connect the speedometer and electrical cables to the cluster. Install the cluster and the four retaining screws.

18. Attach the wiring connectors for the hazard flasher and the dimmer switches.

19. Install the cluster trim bezel.

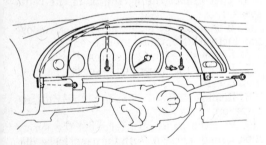

Prizm instrument cluster trim panel

Removing the Prizm instrument cluster

20. Place the dash switches in place on the lower trim bezel and connect the wiring to the switches.

21. Install the lower trim bezel, making sure all the clips engage.

22. Install the steering column upper and lower covers.

23. Connect the air conditioning ductwork to the lower air outlet if so equipped.

24. Attach the wiring to the radio speaker.

25. Install the lower left dashboard trim panel and its four screws.

26. Install the hood release lever.

27. Connect the negative battery cable.

Instrument Panel (Dashboard)

REMOVAL AND INSTALLATION

Nova

1. Disconnect the negative battery cable.

2. Remove the steering wheel.

3. Remove the left side speaker grille. The grille may be attached with a clip (which must be pulled loose to remove the grille) or with screws.

4. Remove the lower trim cover from the steering column.

5. Remove the hood release lever.

6. Remove the heater duct assembly.

7. Remove the instrument hood. Remove the air conditioner outlet register, then remove the four screws and remove the hood.

8. Remove the six screws from the instru-

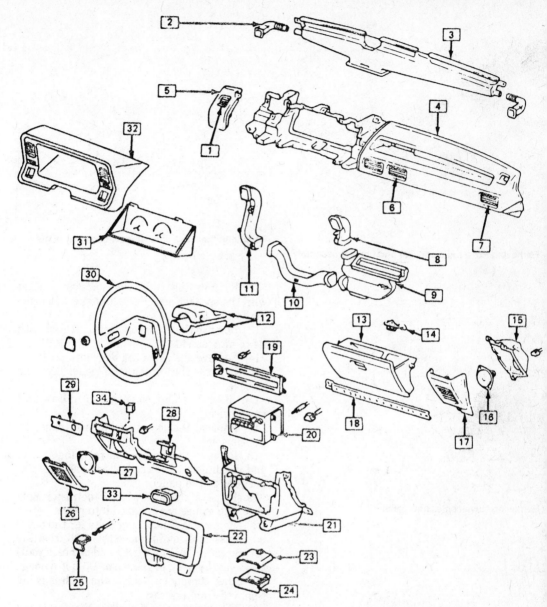

1. Side defroster nozzle
2. Side defroster duct
3. Defroster nozzle
4. Dashboard
5. End trim panel
6. Center register
7. Side register
8. No. 3 heater duct
9. Duct
10. No. 2 heater duct
11. No. 1 heater duct
12. Column covers
13. Glove compartment door
14. Door lock striker
15. Speaker bracket
16. Speaker
17. No. 2 speaker panel
18. Glove door reinforcement
19. Heater control panel
20. Radio
21. Lower center cluster finish panel
22. Center cluster finish panel
23. Retainer
24. Ash tray
25. Hood release lever
26. No. 1 speaker panel
27. Speaker
28. Lower finish panel
29. Finish panel
30. Steering wheel
31. Combination meter
32. Meter hood
33. Lower register
34. ECT indicator (A/T)

Nova dashboard components

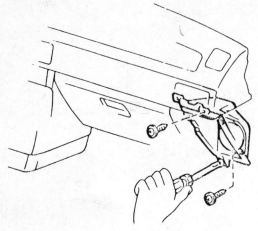

Removing Nova radio speaker and bracket assembly

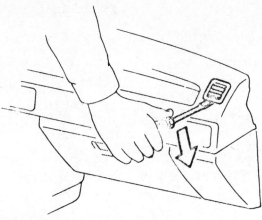

Removing the Nova side window defroster ducts

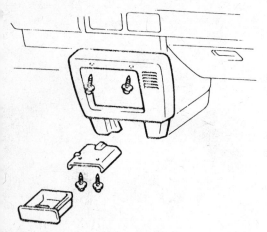

Removing Nova center trim panel

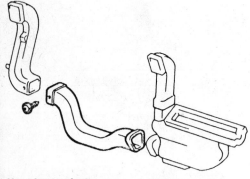

Nova heater ducts

12. Remove the right side speaker bracket with the speaker attached. Disconnect the wiring to the speaker.

13. Remove the glove compartment door with its reinforcement.

14. Femove the glove box door lock striker.

15. Remove the center trim panel over the console.

16. Remove the radio equipment and accessories.

17. Remove the lower center trim panel on the console.

18. Remove the heater control panel. Label and disconnect the electrical and vacuum connections to the panel.

19. Remove the side-window defroster nozzles. The grilles are snapped into place.

20. Remove the mounting bolts for the dashboard assembly and remove the dash from the car. Be careful of any wiring and/or hoses routed along the back of the dash. Do not damage any other components while the dash is being removed from the car.

21. When reinstalling, position the dashboard in the car. Attach any wiring harnesses to the inside of the dash before securing the mounting bolts.

22. Install the side defroster nozzles.

23. Install the heater control panel and connect its wiring and vacuum lines. Install the trim panel on the lower console.

24. Install the radio and accessory equipment and install its trim panel.

25. Install the glove box door lock striker.

26. Install the glove box door with the door reinforcement.

27. Install the right side speaker bracket and speaker. Connect the wiring to the speaker.

28. Install the speaker grille.

29. Install the end trim panel.

30. Install the heater ducts to the dash vents.

ment cluster, and disconnect the speedometer cable and the wiring connectors. Remove the meter assembly from the instrument panel.

9. Disconnect the heating ducts to the dash vents.

10. Remove the finish panel on the end of the dash.

11. Remove the right side speaker grille.

Make sure they are properly connected and will not come loose.

31. Install the instrument assembly, connecting the speedometer cable and the wiring connectors.

32. Install the hood for the instrument cluster and then install the air outlet grilles.

33. Connect the air ductwork to the grilles.

34. Install the hood release lever.

35. Install the steering column trim covers.

36. Install the left side speaker grille.

37. Install the steeing wheel

38. Connect the negative battery cable.

Prizm

1. Disconnect the negative battery cable.

2. Remove the hood release lever.

3. Remove the four screws from the lower left dash trim and pull the trim out.

4. Disconnect the wiring from the radio speaker.

5. If equipped with air conditioning, remove the ductwork from the lower air outlet and remove the trim panel from the car.

6. Remove the steering wheel.

7. Remove the upper and lower steering column covers.

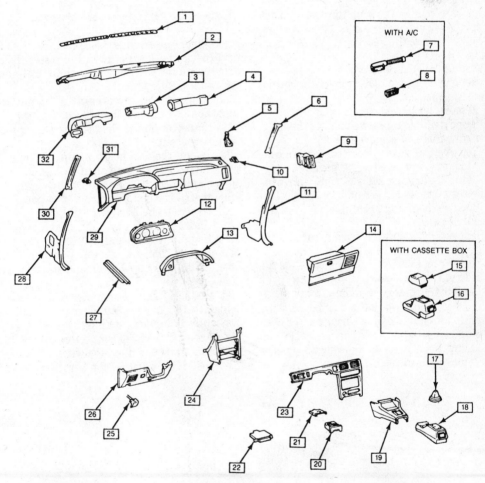

1. Defroster grille	12. Instrument cluster	23. Trim bezel
2. Defroster duct	13. Cluster bezel	24. Center console triim
3. Center ventilation duct	14. Gove box and trim assembly	25. Hood release lever
4. Right ventilation duct	15. Cassette box	26. Left lower dash trim
5. Brace	16. Rear console	27. Scuff plate
6. "A" pillar trim	17. Shift lever boot (M/T)	28. Cowl side trim
7. A/C duct	18. Rear console	29. Instrument panel
8. Lower A/C deflector	19. Front console	30. "A" pillar trim
9. Right ventilation deflector	20. Ashtray	31. Left window deflector
10. Right window deflector	21. Retainer	32. Left ventilation duct
11. Cowl side trim	22. Cup holder	

Prizm dashboard components

8. Remove the two screws from the trim panel (bezel).

9. Pull the panel out, releasing the spring clips behind the dash. With the panel loose, disconnect the wiring to the dash switches.

10. Remove the switches from the panel.

11. Remove the two electrical connectors and the cigarette lighter from the trim bezel and remove the bezel from the car.

12. Remove the four screws holding the instrument cluster trim.

13. Disconnect the wiring from the hazard (4-way) flasher and dimmer switches.

14. Remove the cluster trim panel.

15. Remove the four attaching screws holding the cluster, move it away from the dash and disconnect the wiring harnesses and the speedometer cable. Remove the instrument cluster from the car.

16. Remove the cup holder.

17. Remove the radio. Disconnect the wiring and antenna cables.

18. Remove the glove box and trim assembly.

19. Remove the four screws holding the heater control panel and remove the panel.

20. Remove the screws from the center console trim panel and remove the panel.

21. Carefully pry the left and right side-window defroster vents loose from the dash.

22. Remove the five attaching bolts from the instrument panel.

23. Disconnect the three wiring connectors and the relay unit on the left side of the dash.

24. Disconnect the electrical connector on the right side of the dashboard.

25. Detach the defroster duct retainers behind the dash and remove the dashboard from the vehicle. Be careful of any wiring and/or hoses routed along the back of the dash. Do not damage any other components while the dash is being removed from the car.

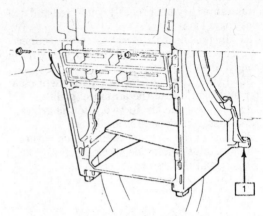

Removing the Prizm center dash trim panel

26. When reinstalling, place the dash in position inside the car. Be careful to insert the defroster duct retainers into their bulkhead (firewall) clips.

27. Connect the three electrical connectors and the relay unit on the left side and the harness connector on the right side to their proper wire harnesses.

28. Install the dashboard mounting bolts.

29. Install the left and right side-window defroster outlets.

30. Install the center console trim panel.

31. Reinstall the heater control panel.

32. Install the glove box and trim assembly.

33. Install the radio and connect the electrical and antenna cables.

34. Install the cup holder and its attaching screws.

35. Connect the speedometer and electrical cables to the instrument cluster. Install the cluster and the four retaining screws.

36. Attach the wiring connectors for the hazard flasher and the dimmer switches.

37. Install the cluster trim bezel.

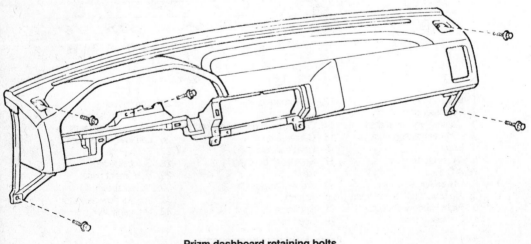

Prizm dashboard retaining bolts

38. Place the dash switches in place on the lower trim bezel and connect the wiring to the switches.

39. Install the lower trim bezel, making sure all the clips engage.

40. Install the steering column upper and lower covers.

41. Connect the air conditioning ductwork to the lower air outlet if so equipped.

42. Attach the wiring to the radio speaker.

43. Install the lower left dashboard trim panel and its four screws.

44. Install the hood release lever.

45. Install the steering wheel.

46. Connect the negative battery cable.

Console

REMOVAL AND INSTALLATION

The consoles in the Nova and Prizm are simply removed by detaching the mounting screws. On the Nova models, many of these screws are concealed by plastic covers which may be popped off with a small screwdriver or similar tool. The consoles can be lifted over the shifter handle and removed from the car. Be very careful not to lose any small parts between the floor pan and carpet while the console is out.

Once the console is removed, take an extra moment to clean it thoroughly and apply a vinyl protectant. You can now get all the crevices that have been blocked by the seats and hidden by the carpet. When the console is reinstalled, make sure that any wires in the area are not pinched by the console or pierced by the mounting screws.

Combination Switch (Windshield Wiper and Headlight Switch)

REMOVAL AND INSTALLATION

1. Remove the steering wheel.

2. Remove the lower left dashboard trim panel.

3. Disconnect the air duct from the vent in the lower panel.

4. Remove the upper and lower steering column covers.

5. Disconnect the wiring from the combination switch to the dashboard wiring harness.

6. Remove the mounting bolts and remove the combination switch.

7. When reinstalling, position the switch carefully onto the column and secure the mounting screws.

8. Connect the wiring harness(es) from the switch to the dashboard harness.

9. Install the upper and lower column covers.

10. Install the air duct to the lower trim panel and install the panel.

11. Install the steering wheel.

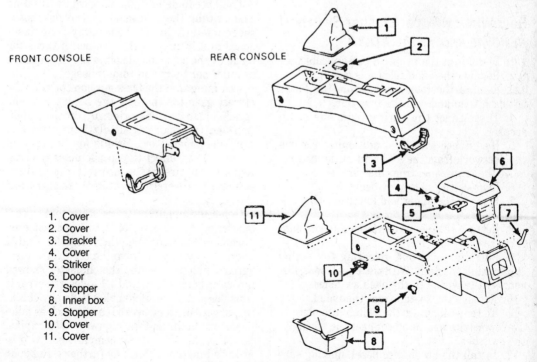

FRONT CONSOLE   REAR CONSOLE

1. Cover
2. Cover
3. Bracket
4. Cover
5. Striker
6. Door
7. Stopper
8. Inner box
9. Stopper
10. Cover
11. Cover

Nova console components

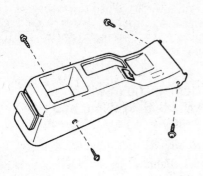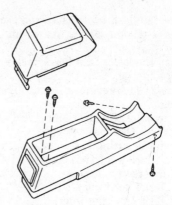

Prizm console (left) and console with cassette box

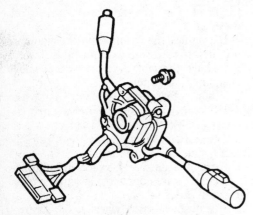

Combination switch—Nova shown, Prizm similar

Rear Window Wiper/Washer Switch

REMOVAL AND INSTALLATION

1. Disconnect the negative battery cable.
2. Remove the hood release lever.
3. Remove the four screws from the lower left dash trim and pull the trim out.
4. Disconnect the wiring from the radio speaker.
5. If equipped with air conditioning, remove the ductwork from the lower air outlet and remove the trim panel from the car.
6. Remove the steering wheel.
7. Remove the upper and lower steering column covers.
8. Remove the two screws from the trim panel (bezel).
9. Pull the panel out, releasing the spring clips behind the dash. With the panel loose, disconnect the wiring to the dash switches.
10. Remove the switch from the panel.
11. To reinstall, press the switch into place in the lower trim bezel and connect the wiring to the switches.
12. Install the lower trim bezel, making sure all the clips engage.

13. Install the steering column upper and lower covers.
14. Connect the air conditioning ductwork to the lower air outlet if so equipped.
15. Attach the wiring to the radio speaker.
16. Install the lower left dashboard trim panel and its four screws.
17. Install the hood release lever.
18. Install the steering wheel.
19. Connect the negative battery cable.

Headlight Switch

Please refer to "Combination Switch" outlined earlier in this chapter.

Speedometer Cable

The speedometer cable connects a rotating gear within the transaxle to the dashboard speedometer/odometer assembly. The dashboard unit interprets the number of turns the made by the cable and displays the information as miles per hour and total mileage.

Assuming that the transmission contains the correct gear for the car, the accuracy of the speedometer depends primarily on tire condition and tire diameter. Badly worn tires (too small in diameter) or overinflation (too large in diameter) can affect the speedometer reading. Replacement tires of the incorrect overall diameter (such as oversize snow tires) can also affect the readings.

Generally, manufacturers state that speedometer/odometer error of ±10% is considered normal due to wear and other variables. Stated another way, if you drove the car over a measured 1 mile course and the odometer showed anything between 0.9 and 1.1 miles, the error is considered normal. If you plan to do any checking, always use a measured course such as mileposts on an Interstate highway or turnpike. Never use another car for comparison--the other car's inherent error may further cloud your readings.

The speedometer cable can become dry or develop a kink within its case. As it turns, the ticking or light knocking noise it makes can easily lead an owner to chase engine related problems in error. If such a noise is heard, carefully watch the speedometer needle during the speed range in which the noise is heard. Generally, the needle will jump or deflect each time the cable binds. The needle motion may be very small and hard to notice; a helper in the back seat should look over the driver's shoulder at the speedometer while the driver concentrates on driving.

CHILTON TIP: *The slightest bind in the speedometer cable can cause unpredicatable behavior in the cruise control system. If the cruise control exhibits intermittent surging or loss of set speed symptoms, check the speedometer cable first.*

To replace the speedometer cable:

1. Follow the appropriate procedure given previously for removal of the instrument cluster. the cluster need not be fully removed, but only loosened to the point of being able to disconnect the speedometer cable.

2. Disconnect the speedometer cable and check that any retaining clamps or clips between the dash and the firewall are released.

3. Safely elevate the car and support it on jackstands.

NOTE: *Depending on the length of your arm, you may be able to reach the cable connection at the transaxle without raising the car, but it's much easier with the car elevated.*

4. Disconnect the cable fitting at the transaxle and lift the cable and case away from the transaxle.

5. Follow the cable back to the firewall, releasing any clips or retainers.

6. From inside the car, work the speedometer cable through the grommet in the firewall into the engine compartment. It may be necessary to pop the grommet out of the firewall and transfer it to the new cable.

7. When reinstalling, track the new cable into position, remembering to attach the grommet to the firewall securely. Make absolutely certain that the cable is not kinked, or routed near hot or moving parts. All curves in the cable should be very gentle and not located near the ends.

8. Attach any retaining clips, brackets or retainers, beginning from the middle of the cable and working towards each end.

9. Attach the cable to the transaxle. Remember that the cable has a formed, square end on it; this shaped end must fit into a matching hole in the transaxle mount. Don't try to force the cable collar (screw fitting) into place if the cable isn't seated properly.

10. Inside the car, hold the other end of the cable with your fingers or a pair of tapered-nose pliers. Gently attempt to turn the cable; if it's properly seated at the other end, the cable will NOT turn more than about ¼ turn. If the cable turns freely, the other end is not correctly seated.

11. Lower the car to the ground.

12. Attach the speedometer cable to the instrument cluster, again paying close attention to the fit of the square-cut end into the square hole. Don't force the cable retainer--you'll break the clips.

13. Reinstall the instrument cluster following procedures outlined previously.

LIGHTING

Headlights

REMOVAL AND INSTALLATION

Sealed beam

1. Remove the headlight bezel (trim) and/or the radiator grille, as necessary.

2. The sealed beam is held in place by a retainer and either 2 or 4 small screws. Identify these screws before applying any tools.

WARNING: *DO NOT confuse the small retaining screws with the larger aiming screws! There will be two aiming screws or adjustors for each lamp. (One adjustor controls the up/down motion and the other controls the left/right motion.) Identify the adjustors and avoid them during removal. If they are not disturbed, the new headlamp will be in identical aim to the old one.*

3. Using a small screwdriver (preferably magnetic) and a pair of taper-nose pliers if necessary, remove the small screws in the headlamp retainer. DON'T drop the screws; they vanish into unknown locations.

CHILTON TIP: *A good kitchen or household magnet placed on the shank of the screwdriver will provide enough grip to hold the screw during removal.*

4. Remove the retainer and the headlamp may be gently pulled free from its mounts. Detach the connector from the back of the sealed beam unit and remove the unit from the car.

CAUTION: *The retainers can have very sharp edges. Wear gloves.*

5. Place the new headlamp in position and connect the wiring harness. Remember to install the rubber boot on the back of the new lamp--its a water seal. Make sure the headlight is right-side up.

6. Have an assistant turn on the headlights and check the new lamp for proper function,

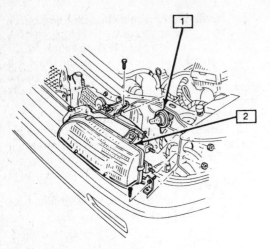

1. Headlamp bulb
2. Headlamp assembly

Replacing a headlight bulb—Prizm and Nova

checking both high and low beams before final assembly.

7. Install the retainer and the small screws that hold it.

8. Reinstall the headlight bezel and/or grille

Replaceable Bulb/Fixed Lens

NOTE: *This type of light is replace from behind the unit. The lens is not removed or loosened.*

1. Open and support the hood.

2. Remove the wiring connector from the back the lamp. Be careful to release the locking tab completely before removal.

3. Grasp the base of the bulb holder and collar, twist it counterclockwise (as viewed from the engine compartment) and carefully remove the bulb holder and bulb from the housing.

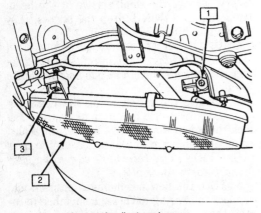

1. Right-left adjustment screw
2. Headlamp assembly
3. Up-down adjustment screw

Adjustor locations for replaceable bulb headlamp assemblies

4. Using gloves or a rag, hold the bulb and release the clip on the holder. Remove the bulb.

5. Install the new bulb in the holder and make sure the clip engages firmly.

WARNING: *Hold the new bulb with a clean cloth or a piece of paper. DO NOT touch or grasp the bulb with your fingers. The oils from your skin will produce a hot spot on the glass envelope, shortening bulb life by up to 50%. If the bulb is touched accidentally, clean it with alcohol and a clean rag before installation.*

6. Install the holder and bulb into the housing. Note that the holder has guides which must align with the housing. When the holder is correctly seated, turn the collar clockwise to lock the holder in place.

7. Connect the wiring harness. Turn on the headlights and check the function of the new bulb on both high and low beam.

Signal and Marker Lights
REMOVAL AND INSTALLATION
Front Turn Signals

NOTE: *This can be done with the car on the ground. Access is improved if the car is safely supported on jackstands.*

1. From behind the bumper, disconnect the electrical connector.

2. Remove the two nuts from the housing.

3. Remove the turn signal lamp housing.

NOTE: *If only the bulb is to be changed, the lens may be removed from the front.*

4. Reassemble the housing in reverse order of disassembly.

Side Marker Lights (Parking Lights)
FRONT

1. Remove the retaining screws. On Nova models, the screws are visible at the rear corner of the lens. On the Prizm, the screw is under the hood.

2. Gently remove the lighting assembly from the body of the car.

3. Disconnect the bulb and socket(s) from the housing.

4. Reassemble in reverse order.

REAR

1. Only the Nova models have separate rear sidemarker lights. The Prizm incorporates the sidelights into the taillight assemblies. For the Nova, remove the two screws in the sidemarker lens.

2. Remove the lighting assembly from the bodywork.

3. Disconnect the bulb and socket from the lighting assembly.

4. Reassemble in reverse order.

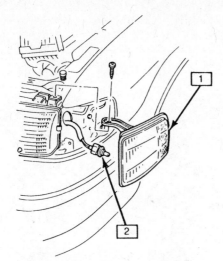

1. Front parking/sidemarker lamp housing
2. Front parking lamp

Prizm front parking lamp assembly

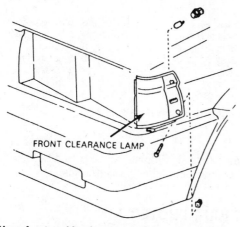

FRONT CLEARANCE LAMP

Nova front parking lamp assembly

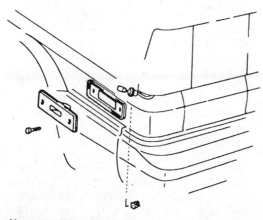

Nova rear sidemarker lamp

Rear Turn Signal, Brake and Parking Lights

1. Raise the trunk lid and remove or fold back the trunk carpeting.

2. Disconnect the wiring from the bulb holder(s).

3. If a bulb is to be changed, remove the bulb holder from the housing by pressing the tab and lifting out the holder. Replace the bulb and re-insert the housing.

4. Remove the nuts holding the taillight assembly in place. Some may be difficult to reach; a swivel or "wobble" fitting for your socket set can be a valuable asset for this job.

5. Remove the lens assembly from the outside of the car.

6. When reinstalling the lens assembly, pay close attention to the placement of the gasket. It must be correctly positioned and evenly crushed to prevent water from entering the trunk. Double check the holes through which the threaded studs pass; caulk them if needed.

7. Install the retaining nuts and tighten them evenly. Do not overtighten them or the lens may crack.

8. Install the electrical connectors. Have a helper operate the lights while you check the function at the rear of the car.

9. Replace the trunk carpet.

TRAILER WIRING

Wiring the car for towing is fairly easy. There are a number of good wiring kits available and these should be used, rather than trying to design your own. All trailers will need brake lights and turn signals as well as tail lights and side marker lights. Most states require extra marker lights for overly wide trailers. Also, most states have recently required back-up lights for trailers, and most trailer manufacturers have been building trailers with back-up lights for several years.

Additionally, some trailers have electric brakes. Others can be fitted with them as an option, depending on the weight to be carried.

Add to this an accessories wire, to operate trailer internal equipment or to charge the trailer's battery, and you can have as many as seven wires in the harness.

Determine the equipment on your trailer and buy the wiring kit necessary. The kit will contain all the wires needed, plus a plug adapter set which includes the female plug, mounted on the bumper or hitch, and the male plug to be wired into the trailer harness.

When installing the kit, follow the manufacturer's instructions. The color coding of the wires is standard throughout the industry.

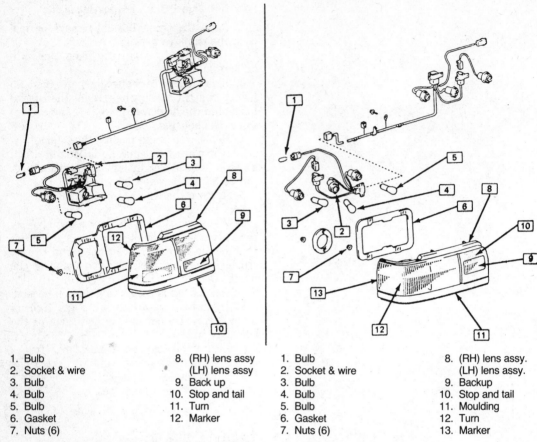

1. Bulb	8. (RH) lens assy	1. Bulb	8. (RH) lens assy.
2. Socket & wire	(LH) lens assy	2. Socket & wire	(LH) lens assy.
3. Bulb	9. Back up	3. Bulb	9. Backup
4. Bulb	10. Stop and tail	4. Bulb	10. Stop and tail
5. Bulb	11. Turn	5. Bulb	11. Moulding
6. Gasket	12. Marker	6. Gasket	12. Turn
7. Nuts (6)		7. Nuts (6)	13. Marker

Tail light assemblies (sedan, left; hatchback, right). Nova shown, Prizm similar

One point to note: some domestic vehicles, and most imported vehicles, have separate turn signals at the rear. On most domestic vehicles, the brake lights and rear turn signals operate with the same bulb. For those vehicles with separate turn signals, you can purchase an isolation unit so that the brake lights won't blink whenever the turn signals are operated.

You can also go to your local electronics supply house and buy four diodes to wire in series with the brake and turn signal bulbs. Diodes will isolate the brake and turn signals. The choice is yours. The isolation units are simple and quick to install, but far more expensive than the diodes. The diodes, however, require more work to install properly, since they require the cutting of each bulb's wire and soldering the diode into place.

The best wiring kits are those with a spring loaded cover on the vehicle mounted socket. This cover prevents dirt and moisture from corroding the terminals. Never let the vehicle socket hang loosely. Always mount it securely to the bumper or hitch. If you don't get a connector with a cover, at least put a piece of tape over the end of the connector when not in use. Most trailer lighting failures can be traced to corroded connectors and/or poor grounds.

CIRCUIT PROTECTION

Fuses

REPLACEMENT

Both the Nova and the Prizm have fuses found in two locations. One fuse box is located within the cabin of the car, just under the extreme left side of the dashboard. This fuse box generally contains the fuses for body and cabin electrical circuits such as the wipers, rear defogger, ignition, cigarette lighter, etc. In addition, various relays and circuit breakers for cabin equipment are also mounted on or around this fuse box.

The second fuse block is found under the hood on the forward part of the left wheelhouse. The Nova uses a combination fuse block and relay board while the Prizm has an additional relay board next to the fusebox. The fuses and relays generally control the engine and major electrical systems on the car, such as

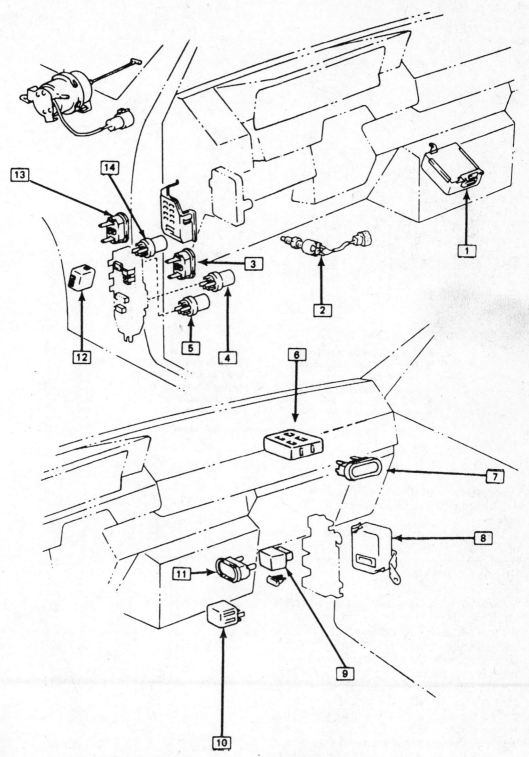

1. Emission computer
2. Clutch switch (M/T)
3. Circuit breaker (for defogger)
4. Defogger relay
5. Taillight relay
6. Seat belt relay
7. Circuit breaker (for door lock)
8. Cruise computer
9. Clutch start relay (M/T)
10. Heater relay
11. Circuit breaker (for heater)
12. Flasher
13. Circuit breaker (for power window)
14. Power window relay

Nova passenger compartment relay location

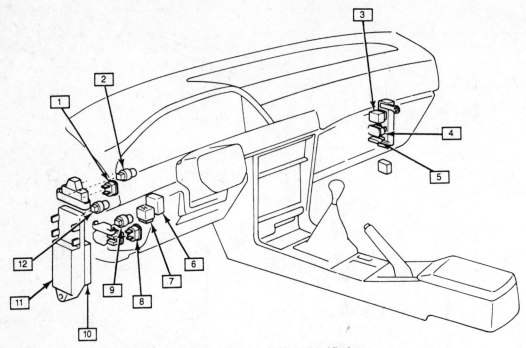

1. Defogger circuit breaker (30A)
2. Rear window defogger relay
3. Heater main relay
4. Heater circuit breaker (30A)
5. A/C fuse (7.5A)
6. Door lock control relay
7. Turn signal flasher
8. Power window circuit breaker (30A)
9. Power window main relay
10. Number 1 fuse and relay block
11. Integration relay
12. Taillamp control relay

Prizm passenger compartment relay location

headlights (separate fuses for left and right), air conditioning, horns, fuel injection, ECM, and fans.

Both the Nova and the Prizm have an additional small panel below the right side dash board containing a fuse (air conditioner) and a relay and circuit breaker for the heater system.

Each fuse location is labled on the fuseblock identifying its primary circuit, but designations such as "Engine", "CDS Fan" or "ECU-B" may not tell you what you need to know. A fuse can control more than one circuit, so check related fuses. As an example, you'll find the Prizm cruise control drawing its power through the fuse labled "ECM-IG". (This sharing of fuses is necessary to conserve space and wiring; if each circuit had its own fuse, the fuse box would be the size of the trunk lid.)

The individual fuses are of the plastic or "slip-fuse" type. They connect into the fusebox with two small blades, similar to a household wall plug. Removing the fuse with the fingers can be difficult; there isn't a lot to grab onto. For this reason, the fusebox contains a small plastic fuse remover which can be clipped over

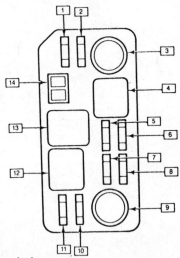

fuses and relays
1. "left head" (10A)
2. "Right head" (10A)
3. "Fan relay #1"
4. "Engine main" relay
5. "EFI" (15A)
6. "Hazard-horn" (15A)
7. "Dome" (10A)
8. Not used
9. "Horn" relay
10. "Fan-I/up" (75A)
11. "Charge" (75A)
12. "Headlight control" relay
13. "EFI" relay
14. "Fan" (30A)

Prizm under-hood fuse block

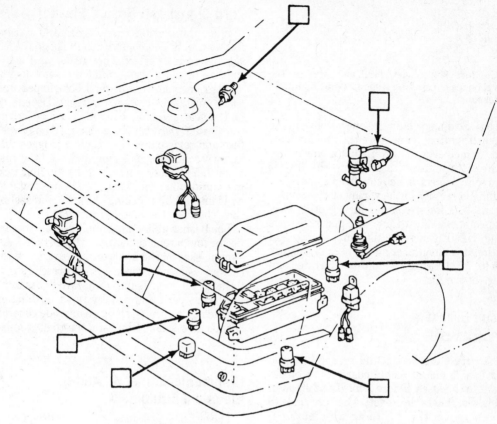

1. Neutral start switch (A/T)
2. Washer valve
3. Headlight relay (in relay block)
4. Fan relay (in relay block)

5. A/C relay (in relay block)
6. A/C relay (in relay block)
7. Main relay (in relay block)

Nova engine compartment switches and relays

the back of the fuse and used as a handle to pull it free.

Once the fuse is out, view the fusible element through the clear plastic of the fuse case. An intact fuse will show a continuous horseshoe-shaped wire within the plastic. This element simply connects one blade with the other; if it's intact, power can pass. If the fuse is blown, the link inside the fuse will show a break, possibly accompanied by a small black mark. This shows that the link broke when the electrical current exceeded the wires ability to carry it.

It is possible for the link to become weakened (from age or vibration) without breaking. In this case, the fuse will look good but fail to pass the proper amount of current, causing some electrical item to not work.

Once removed, any fuse may be checked for continuity with an ohmmeter. A reliable general rule is to always replace a suspect fuse with a

fuse and relays
1. A/C clutch relay
2. A/C fan relay #2
3. CDS fan (30A)
4. A/C fan relay #3

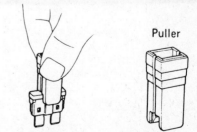

Puller

Prizm under-hood relay board

Use the fuse puller to remove a fuse. Do not twist the fuse when removing

A blown fuse (left) compared with an intact fuse. The fuse cannot be inspected without removing it from the fusebox

new one. So doing eliminates one variable in the diagnostic path and may cure the problem outright. Rememeber, however, that a blown fuse is rarely the cause of a problem; the fuse is opening to protect the circuit from some other malfunction either in the wiring or the component itself. Always replace a fuse or other electrical component with one of equal amperage rating; NEVER increase the ampere rating of the circuit. The number on the back of the fuse body (5, 7.5, 10, 15 ,etc.) indicates the rated amperage of the fuse.

Circuit Breakers
REPLACEMENT

The circuit breakers found on the fuse and relay boards mount to the boards with blades similar to the fuses. Before removing a breaker, always disconnect the negative battery cable to prevent potentially damaging electrical "spikes" within the system. Simply remove the breaker by pulling straight out from the relay board. Do not twist the relay; damage may occur to the connectors inside the housing.

NOTE: *Some circuit breakers on the Nova and Prizm do not reset automatically. Once tripped, they must be reset by hand. Use a small screwdriver or similar tool; insert it in the hole in the back of the breaker and push gently. Once the breaker is reset, either check it for continuity with an ohmmeter or reinstall it and check the circuit for function.*

Reinstall the circuit breaker by pressing it straight in to its mount. Make certain the blades line up correctly and that the circuit breaker is fully seated. Reconnect the negative battery cable and check the circuit for function.

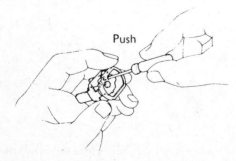

Push

Resetting a circuit breaker

Turn Signal and Hazard Flasher

The combination turn signal and hazard flasher unit is located under the dash on the left side near the fuse box. The flasher unit is not the classic round "can" found on many domestic cars; instead, it is a small box-shaped unit easily mistaken for another relay. Depending on the year and model of your Nova or Prizm, the flasher may be plugged directly into the fuse and relay panel or it may be plugged into its own connector and mounted near the fuse panel. The flasher unit emits the familiar ticking sound when the signals are in use and may be identified by touching the case and feeling the "click" as the system functions.

The flasher unit simply unplugs from its connector and a replacement may be installed. Assuming that all the bulbs on the exterior of the car are working properly, the correct rate of flash for the turn signals or hazard lights is 60-75 flashes per minute. Very rapid flashing on one side only or no flashing on one side generally indicates a failed bulb rather than a failed flasher.

Communication and "Add-on" Electrical Equipment

The elecrical system in your car is designed to perform under reasonable operating conditions without interference between components. Before any additional electrical equipment is installed, it is recommended that you consult your Chevrolet or Geo dealer or a reputable repair facility familiar with the vehicle and its systems.

If the vehicle is equipped with mobile radio equipment (CB, HAM, Business radio and/or mobile telephone) it may have an effect upon the operation of the ECM. Radio frequency interference (RFI) from the communications system can be picked up by the car's wiring harnesses and conducted into the ECM, giving it the wrong messages at the wrong time. Although well shielded against RFI, the ECM should be further protected through the following steps:

1. Install the antenna as far as possible from the ECM. Since the ECM is located behind the center console, the antenna should be mounted at the rear of the car.

2. Keep the antenna wiring a minimum of eight inches away from any wiring running to the ECM and from the ECM itself. NEVER wind the antenna wire around any other wiring.

3. Mount the equipment as far from the ECM as possible. Be very careful during installation not to drill through any wires or short a

wire harness with a mounting screw.

4. Insure that the electrical feed wire(s) to the equipment are properly and tightly connected. Loose connectors can cause interference.

5. Make certain that the equipment is properly grounded to the car. Poor grounding can damage expensive equipment.

6. Make sure the antenna is "trimmed" or adjusted for optimum function.

Troubleshooting Basic Lighting Problems

Problem	Cause	Solution
Lights		
One or more lights don't work, but others do	• Defective bulb(s) • Blown fuse(s) • Dirty fuse clips or light sockets • Poor ground circuit	• Replace bulb(s) • Replace fuse(s) • Clean connections • Run ground wire from light socket housing to car frame
Lights burn out quickly	• Incorrect voltage regulator setting or defective regulator • Poor battery/alternator connections	• Replace voltage regulator • Check battery/alternator connections
Lights go dim	• Low/discharged battery • Alternator not charging • Corroded sockets or connections • Low voltage output	• Check battery • Check drive belt tension; repair or replace alternator • Clean bulb and socket contacts and connections • Replace voltage regulator
Lights flicker	• Loose connection • Poor ground • Circuit breaker operating (short circuit)	• Tighten all connections • Run ground wire from light housing to car frame • Check connections and look for bare wires
Lights "flare"—Some flare is normal on acceleration—if excessive, see "Lights Burn Out Quickly"	• High voltage setting	• Replace voltage regulator
Lights glare—approaching drivers are blinded	• Lights adjusted too high • Rear springs or shocks sagging • Rear tires soft	• Have headlights aimed • Check rear springs/shocks • Check/correct rear tire pressure
Turn Signals		
Turn signals don't work in either direction	• Blown fuse • Defective flasher • Loose connection	• Replace fuse • Replace flasher • Check/tighten all connections
Right (or left) turn signal only won't work	• Bulb burned out • Right (or left) indicator bulb burned out • Short circuit	• Replace bulb • Check/replace indicator bulb • Check/repair wiring
Flasher rate too slow or too fast	• Incorrect wattage bulb • Incorrect flasher	• Flasher bulb • Replace flasher (use a variable load flasher if you pull a trailer)
Indicator lights do not flash (burn steadily)	• Burned out bulb • Defective flasher	• Replace bulb • Replace flasher
Indicator lights do not light at all	• Burned out indicator bulb • Defective flasher	• Replace indicator bulb • Replace flasher

Troubleshooting Basic Turn Signal and Flasher Problems

Most problems in the turn signals or flasher system, can be reduced to defective flashers or bulbs, which are easily replaced. Occasionally, problems in the turn signals are traced to the switch in the steering column, which will require professional service.

F = Front   R = Rear   ● = Lights off   o = Lights on

Problem		Solution
Turn signals light, but do not flash		• Replace the flasher
No turn signals light on either side		• Check the fuse. Replace if defective. • Check the flasher by substitution • Check for open circuit, short circuit or poor ground
Both turn signals on one side don't work		• Check for bad bulbs • Check for bad ground in both housings
One turn signal light on one side doesn't work		• Check and/or replace bulb • Check for corrosion in socket. Clean contacts. • Check for poor ground at socket
Turn signal flashes too fast or too slow		• Check any bulb on the side flashing too fast. A heavy-duty bulb is probably installed in place of a regular bulb. • Check the bulb flashing too slow. A standard bulb was probably installed in place of a heavy-duty bulb. • Check for loose connections or corrosion at the bulb socket
Indicator lights don't work in either direction		• Check if the turn signals are working • Check the dash indicator lights • Check the flasher by substitution

One indicator light doesn't light	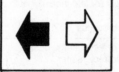	• On systems with 1 dash indicator: See if the lights work on the same side. Often the filaments have been reversed in systems combining stoplights with taillights and turn signals.
		    Check the flasher by substitution
		• On systems with 2 indicators: Check the bulbs on the same side
		    Check the indicator light bulb
		    Check the flasher by substitution

Troubleshooting Basic Dash Gauge Problems

Problem	Cause	Solution
Coolant Temperature Gauge		
Gauge reads erratically or not at all	• Loose or dirty connections • Defective sending unit	• Clean/tighten connections • Bi-metal gauge: remove the wire from the sending unit. Ground the wire for an instant. If the gauge registers, replace the sending unit.
	• Defective gauge	• Magnetic gauge: disconnect the wire at the sending unit. With ignition ON gauge should register COLD. Ground the wire; gauge should register HOT.
Ammeter Gauge—Turn Headlights ON (do not start engine). Note reaction		
Ammeter shows charge Ammeter shows discharge Ammeter does not move	• Connections reversed on gauge • Ammeter is OK • Loose connections or faulty wiring • Defective gauge	• Reinstall connections • Nothing • Check/correct wiring • Replace gauge
Oil Pressure Gauge		
Gauge does not register or is inaccurate	• On mechanical gauge, Bourdon tube may be bent or kinked	• Check tube for kinks or bends preventing oil from reaching the gauge
	• Low oil pressure	• Remove sending unit. Idle the engine briefly. If no oil flows from sending unit hole, problem is in engine.
	• Defective gauge	• Remove the wire from the sending unit and ground it for an instant with the ignition ON. A good gauge will go to the top of the scale.
	• Defective wiring	• Check the wiring to the gauge. If it's OK and the gauge doesn't register when grounded, replace the gauge.
	• Defective sending unit	• If the wiring is OK and the gauge functions when grounded, replace the sending unit
All Gauges		
All gauges do not operate	• Blown fuse • Defective instrument regulator	• Replace fuse • Replace instrument voltage regulator
All gauges read low or erratically	• Defective or dirty instrument voltage regulator	• Clean contacts or replace
All gauges pegged	• Loss of ground between instrument voltage regulator and car • Defective instrument regulator	• Check ground • Replace regulator
Warning Lights		
Light(s) do not come on when ignition is ON, but engine is not started	• Defective bulb • Defective wire	• Replace bulb • Check wire from light to sending unit
	• Defective sending unit	• Disconnect the wire from the sending unit and ground it. Replace the sending unit if the light comes on with the ignition ON.
Light comes on with engine running	• Problem in individual system • Defective sending unit	• Check system • Check sending unit (see above)

Troubleshooting the Heater

Problem	Cause	Solution
Blower motor will not turn at any speed	• Blown fuse • Loose connection • Defective ground • Faulty switch • Faulty motor • Faulty resistor	• Replace fuse • Inspect and tighten • Clean and tighten • Replace switch • Replace motor • Replace resistor
Blower motor turns at one speed only	• Faulty switch • Faulty resistor	• Replace switch • Replace resistor
Blower motor turns but does not circulate air	• Intake blocked • Fan not secured to the motor shaft	• Clean intake • Tighten security
Heater will not heat	• Coolant does not reach proper temperature • Heater core blocked internally • Heater core air-bound • Blend-air door not in proper position	• Check and replace thermostat if necessary • Flush or replace core if necessary • Purge air from core • Adjust cable
Heater will not defrost	• Control cable adjustment incorrect • Defroster hose damaged	• Adjust control cable • Replace defroster hose

Troubleshooting Basic Windshield Wiper Problems

Problem	Cause	Solution
Electric Wipers		
Wipers do not operate— Wiper motor heats up or hums	• Internal motor defect • Bent or damaged linkage • Arms improperly installed on linking pivots	• Replace motor • Repair or replace linkage • Position linkage in park and reinstall wiper arms
Wipers do not operate— No current to motor	• Fuse or circuit breaker blown • Loose, open or broken wiring • Defective switch • Defective or corroded terminals • No ground circuit for motor or switch	• Replace fuse or circuit breaker • Repair wiring and connections • Replace switch • Replace or clean terminals • Repair ground circuits
Wipers do not operate— Motor runs	• Linkage disconnected or broken	• Connect wiper linkage or replace broken linkage
Vacuum Wipers		
Wipers do not operate	• Control switch or cable inoperative • Loss of engine vacuum to wiper motor (broken hoses, low engine vacuum, defective vacuum/fuel pump) • Linkage broken or disconnected • Defective wiper motor	• Repair or replace switch or cable • Check vacuum lines, engine vacuum and fuel pump • Repair linkage • Replace wiper motor
Wipers stop on engine acceleration	• Leaking vacuum hoses • Dry windshield • Oversize wiper blades • Defective vacuum/fuel pump	• Repair or replace hoses • Wet windshield with washers • Replace with proper size wiper blades • Replace pump

MANUAL TRANSMISSION

Understanding the Manual Transmission and Clutch

Because of the way an internal combustion engine breathes, it can produce torque, or twisting force, only within a narrow speed range. Most modern engines must turn at about 2,500–3,000 rpm to produce their peak torque. By 4,500 rpm they are producing so little torque that continued increases in engine speed produce no power increases.

The manual transmission and clutch are employed to vary the relationship between engine speed and the speed of the wheels so that adequate engine power can be produced under all circumstances. The clutch allows engine torque to be applied to the transmission input shaft gradually, due to mechanical slippage. The car can then be started smoothly from a full stop.

The transmission changes the ratio between the rotating speeds of the engine and the wheels by the use of gears. 4-speed or 5-speed transmissions are most common. The lower gears allow full engine power to be applied to the rear wheels during acceleration at low speeds.

The clutch drive plate is a thin fiber disc, the center of which is splined to the transmission input shaft. Both sides of the disc are covered with a layer of material which is similar to brake lining and is capable of allowing slippage without roughness or excessive noise.

The clutch cover or pressure plate is bolted to the engine flywheel and incorporates a diaphragm spring which provides the pressure to engage the clutch. The driven disc is sandwiched between the pressure plate and the smooth surface of the flywheel when the clutch pedal is released, thus forcing it to turn at the same speed as the engine crankshaft.

The mainshaft passes all the way through the transmission, from the clutch to the driveshaft. This shaft is separated at one point, so that front and rear portions can turn at different speeds.

Power is transmitted by a countershaft in the lower gears and reverse. The gears of the countershaft mesh with gears on the mainshaft, allowing power to be carried from one to the other. All the countershaft gears are integral with that shaft, while several of the mainshaft gears can either rotate independently of the shaft or be locked to it. Shifting from one gear to the next causes one of the gears to be freed from rotating with the shaft and locks another to it. Gears are locked and unlocked by internal dog clutches which slide between the center of the gear and the shaft. The forward gears usually employ synchronizers — friction members which smoothly bring gear and shaft to the same speed before the toothed dog clutches are engaged.

The clutch is operating properly if:

1. It will stall the engine when released with the vehicle held stationary.

2. The shift lever can be moved freely between first and reverse gears when the vehicle is stationary and the clutch disengaged and the engine running at normal idle speed.

Clutch pedal free-play adjustment is important. There should be a small but noticeable amount of play in the clutch pedal before it begins to release the clutch. This play or looseness should be easily felt at the top of the pedal travel. (As you begin to push the clutch pedal towards the floor, the first inch or so of travel should have no effect on the clutch engagement). Inadequate free-play wears all parts of the clutch releasing mechanisms and may cause slippage. Excessive free-play may cause inadequate release and hard shifting of gears.

Some clutches use a hydraulic system in place of mechanical linkage. In these systems, moving the clutch pedal develops pressure in a column of fluid rather than pulling on a cable. If the clutch fails to release, fill the clutch master cylinder with fluid to the proper level and pump the clutch pedal to fill the system with fluid. Bleed the system in the same way as a brake system. If leaks are located, tighten loose connections or overhaul the master or slave cylinder as necessary.

Manual transmissions used in Nova/Prizm cars are mated to their engine families. For example, the gearboxes used with the 4A-LC engine remain the same year to year, but will be internally different from transmissions used with the 4A-GE or 4A-FE engines.

Adjustments

SHIFT LEVER FREE PLAY

Nova

The shift lever free play is adjusted through the use of a replaceable shim installed at the bottom of the lower shift lever seat. Select a shim of a thickness that allows about $\frac{1}{10}$ lb. preload at the top of the lever and install it in the shift lever seat.

SHIFT CABLES

The shift control cables are precisely adjusted at the factory during assembly and cannot be accurately adjusted in the field. Should either of the cables become stretched and therefore out of adjustment, the individual cable must be replaced. Any attempt to adjust the shift cables can cause poor shifting and/or transmission damage. If the shift cable(s) must be replaced, proceed as follows:

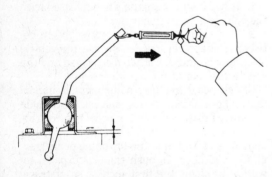

SHIM THICKNESS			
mm	in.	mm	in.
0.3	(0.012)	0.8	(0.031)
0.4	(0.016)	0.9	(0.035)
0.5	(0.020)	1.0	(0.039)
0.6	(0.024)	1.1	(0.043)
0.7	(0.028)	1.2	(0.047)

Checking Nova shift lever free play

Nova

1. Disconnect the negative battery cable.
2. Disconnect the shift cable(s) and retaining clips at the transaxle.
3. Remove the center console and shifter boot.
4. Disconnect the shift cable(s) from the shifter assembly.
5. Remove the left front sill plate and lift or pull the carpet back to gain access to the cables.
6. Remove the retaining screws at the floor pan and remove the shift cable(s) from the car.
7. Position the new cable(s) and install the retaining screws.
8. Reposition the carpet and install the sill plate.
9. Route the cable(s) to the transaxle. This is easier if the car is elevated and safely supported. Lower the car after the cables are in position.
10. Position the cable(s) and install the retaining clips at the transaxle.
11. Connect the cable(s) to the shifter assembly.
12. Install the center console and shifter boot.
13. Connect the negative battery cable.

Prizm

1. Disconnect the negative battery cable.
2. Remove the shift lever knob and the shifter boot.
3. Remove the front and rear center console halves.
4. Remove the center air duct.
5. Remove the ECM mounting nuts and remove the ECM from under the dashboard.
6. Remove the cable hold-down brackets.
7. Remove the four shifter assembly mounting bolts.
8. Remove the shift cable retainer and end clips from the shifter assembly.
9. Remove the shifter control assembly.
10. Disconnect the cable retainers at the transaxle.
11. Remove the shift cables by pulling them from the outside of the firewall.
12. Install the new cables by going through the firewall from the outside.
13. Position the cables in their brackets at the transaxle and install the retaining clips.
14. Connect the cables to their transaxle mounts and install the clips.
15. Connect the cables and install the clips at the shifter assembly.
16. Install the shifter assembly and its four bolts. Tighten the bolts to 15 ft. lbs.
17. Install the cable hold-down brackets.
18. Reinstall the ECM and the center air duct.
19. Install the front and rear halves of the console.

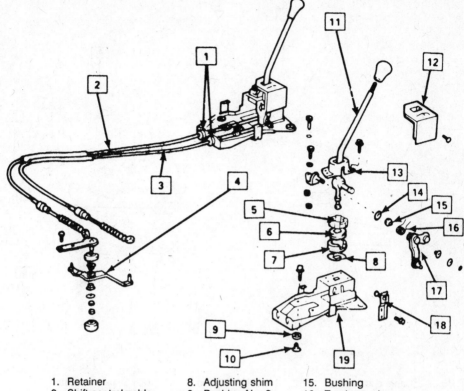

1. Retainer
2. Shift control cable
3. Select control cable
4. Selecting bellcrank
5. Spacer
6. Upper seat
7. Lower seat

8. Adjusting shim
9. Bushing No. 2
10. Bushing No. 1
11. Shift lever
12. Shift lever cover
13. Shift lever cap
14. Washer

15. Bushing
16. Torsion spring
17. Selecting bellcrank
18. Spring holder
19. Shift lever retainer

Nova shifter and cable assembly

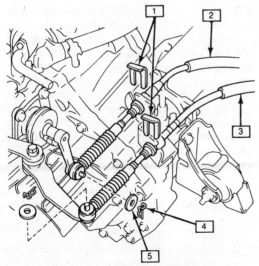

1. Cable retainer
2. Shift control cable
3. Shift select cable
4. Cable end clip
5. Cable end washer

Prizm shift cables at transaxle

20. Install the shift lever boot and knob.
21. Connect the negative battery cable.

Back-up Light Switch
REMOVAL AND INSTALLATION

The reverse light switch is mounted on the side of the transaxle housing. Its removal and replacement is easily accomplished by disconnecting the wiring connector from the switch and unscrewing the switch from the case. A specially sized socket such as GM Tool J-35451 or its equivalent is necessary. Because of the placement of the switch, it is extremely difficult to reach the switch with any other type of tool. Install the new switch and tighten it to 15 ft. lbs. for the Nova or 30 ft. lbs. for the Prizm. Reinstall the electrical connector.

TRANSAXLE

Before attempting to repair the clutch or transaxle for reasons beyond obvious failure,

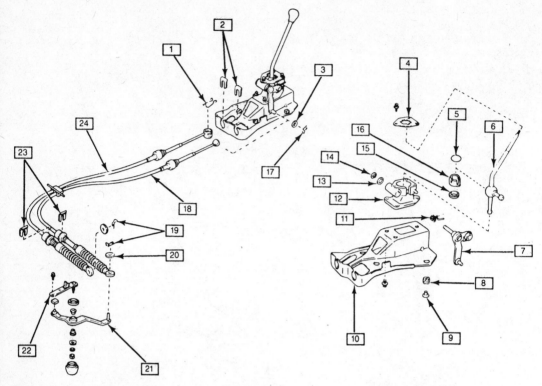

1. Cable end clips
2. Retainer clips
3. Plate washer
4. Shift lever cover
5. Snap ring
6. Shift lever
7. Selecting bellcrank
8. Bushing No. 2
9. Bushing No.1
10. Control shift lever
    retainer plate
11. Torsion spring
12. Shift lever housing
13. Plate washer
14. E-clip
15. shift lever seat bushing
16. Shift lever ball seat
17. Clip
18. Shift select cable
19. Clips
20. Plate washer
21. Selecting bellcrank
22. Selecting bellcrank
    support
23. Retainer clips
24. Shift control cable

Prizm shifter and cable assembly

the problem and probable cause should be identified. A great percentage of manual transaxle and clutch problems are accompanied by shifting difficulties such as gear clash, grinding or refusal to engage gears. When any of these

J 35451

Installing reverse light switch; GM tool shown.

problems occur, a careful analysis should be performed to determine cause.

Driveline noises can become baffling, but don't be too quick to assign fault to the transaxle. The noise may actually be coming from other sources such as tires, road surfaces, wheel bearings, engine or exhaust system. Noises will also vary by vehicle size, engine type and amount of insulation within the body. Remember also that the transaxle, like any mechanical device, is not totally quiet in its operation and will exhibit some normal operating noise.

When checking for driveline noises, follow these guide lines:

1. Select a smooth , level asphalt road to reduce tire and body noises. Check and set the tire pressures before beginning.

2. Drive the vehicle far enough to thoroughly warm up all the lubricants; this may require driving as much as 10 or 12 miles before testing.

3. Note the speed at which the noise occurs and in which gear(s).

4. Check for noises with the vehicle stopped and the engine running.

5. Does the noise change when the clutch pedal is pushed in or released?

6. Determine the throttle condition(s) at which the noise occurs:

    a. Drive (leading throttle)--the engine is under load and the car is accelerating at some rate.

    b. Float (neutral throttle)--the engine is maintaining a constant speed at light throttle on a level road.

    c. Coast (trailing throttle)--the engine is not driving the car, the throttle is closed with the car in gear and in motion. An example is a long downhill grade.

    d. Some combination of the above.

7. Does the noise change as the car corners or changes direction? Is the change in the noise different on left and right turns? Does the noise change as the car rises and falls on its suspension over bumps and dips?

8. Identify the noise by type (whine, click, knock, grinding, buzzing, etc.) and think through possible causes such as loose components, something rubbing, poor lubrication, or worn parts.

9. Check all other causes first. Its much easier to check the wheel bearings and the exhaust system than to remove the transaxle. Modern manual transmissions are extremely reliable and rarely fail if given reasonable maintenance and freedom from outright abuse. Assume that the noise is not in the transaxle until diagnosed otherwise.

REMOVAL AND INSTALLATION

Nova

1. Disconnect the negative battery terminal.

2. Remove the air cleaner and inlet duct.

3. From the transaxle, disconnect the back-up light switch connector, the speedometer cable, the thermostat housing and the ground wire.

4. Remove the four shift cable-to-transaxle clips, the clutch slave cylinder-to-transaxle bolts and the slave cylinder.

5. Remove the (2) upper transaxle-to-engine bolts and the upper transaxle mount bolt.

6. Attach an engine support tool or equivalent, and support the engine. Raise and support the front of the vehicle on jackstands.

7. Remove the left wheel. From under the vehicle, remove the left, right and center splash shields. Remove the center beam-to-chassis bolts and the center beam.

8. Remove the flywheel cover-to-engine bolts and the cover.

9. Disconnect the lower control arms from the steering knuckles.

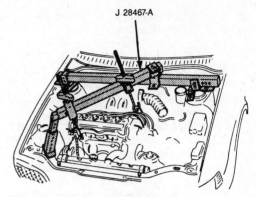

J 28467-A

GM engine support apparatus

10. Disconnect both halfshafts from the transaxle.

11. Disconnect the battery cable and ignition switch wire from the starter. Remove the starter-to-engine bolts and the starter.

12. Support the transaxle with a floor jack.

13. Remove the transaxle-to-engine bolts and the lower the transaxle from the vehicle.

14. To install, make sure the input shaft splines align with the clutch disc splines. Elevate the transaxle and slide it into position. Do not remove the jack until the retaining bolts are installed; the transaxle may be damaged if left hanging on the input shaft.

15. Install the lower bellhousing bolts and the bolts at the back side of the transmission. Tighten the 12mm bolts to 47 ft. lbs. and the 10mm bolts to 34 ft. lbs.

16. Install the starter and the starter retaining bolts. The jack may be removed from under the transaxle when these bolts are secured.

17. Connect the driveshafts to the transaxle and tighten the bolts to 27 ft. lbs.

18. Reconnect the left and right control arms at the steering knuckles.

19. Reinstall the flywheel inspection cover.

20. Install the center beam and tighten its bolts to 29 ft. lbs.

21. Install the splash shields and the left front wheel.

22. Lower the vehicle from the stands. Install the two upper bellhousing bolts and the transaxle mount upper bolt. The engine support devices may be removed from the engine.

23. Connect the backup light switch.

24. Reinstall the shift cables and their clips. Install the clutch slave cylinder.

25. Connect the ground wire to the transmission and attach the wiring to the starter.

26. Connect the thermostat housing and the speedometer cable to the transaxle.

27. Install the air cleaner and intake duct.

28. Connect the negative battery cable.

29. Check the level of the fluid in the transaxle and fill or top off as needed.

Prizm

1. Install an engine support and tension it to support the engine without raising it.
2. Remove the battery hold-down, the battery and tray.
3. Disconnect the electrical connector to the reverse lights and disconnect the ground strap running to the transaxle.
4. Remove the two actuator mounting bolts and the actuator line bracket.
5. Remove the shift cable retainers and end clips.
6. Remove the shift cables from their brackets and place the cables out of the way.
7. Remove the cover and brace from the left transaxle mount.
8. Remove the throught bolt from the mount.
9. Remove the two upper transaxle to engine bolts.
10. Remove the upper starter bolt and remove the speedometer cable.
11. Raise the vehicle and safely support it.
CAUTION: *The engine hoist is in place and under tension. Use care when repositioning the vehicle and make necessary adjustments to the engine support.*
12. Remove the splash shields. Drain the transaxle oil.
13. Disconnect the electrical connections at the starter.
14. Remove the bottom starter bolt and the starter.

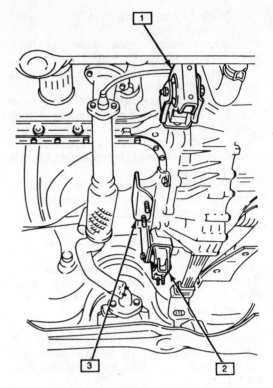

1. Front transaxle mount
2. Rear transaxle mount
3. Center transaxle mount

Location of transaxle mounts

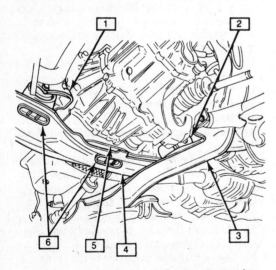

1. Front transaxle mount
2. Rear transaxle mount
3. Main crossmember
4. Center crossmember
5. Center transaxle mount
6. Mount bolt shields

Location of mounts and crossmembers. Prizm shown, Nova similar.

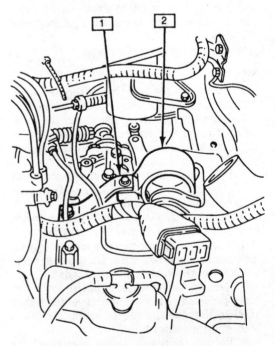

1. Transaxle mount brace
2. Left transaxle mount

Detail of left transaxle mount assembly

15. Remove the drive axles.

16. Remove the three bolts holding the center crossmember to the radiator support.

17. Remove the covers from the front and center mount bolts.

18. Remove the two front mount bolts, then the center mount bolts and then the two rear mount bolts.

19. Remove the two bolts holding the center crossmember to the main crossmember.

20. Remove the three exhaust hanger bracket nuts and the exhaust hanger.

21. Use a floor jack and a wide piece of wood to support the main crossmember.

22. Remove the eight bolts holding the main crossmember to the body.

23. Remove the two bolts holding the lower control arm brackets to the body.

CAUTION: *The crossmembers are loose and free to fall. Make sure they are properly supported.*

24. Slowly lower the main crossmember while holding onto the center crossmember.

25. At the front transaxle mount, remove the through bolt and mount.

26. Remove the front mounting bracket from the transaxle.

27. Remove the center mount from the transaxle with its two bolts.

28. Remove the inspection cover bolt.

29. Remove the two lower transaxle bracket to transaxle mount bolts.

30. Lower the vehicle to the ground.

CAUTION: *The engine hoist is in place and under tension. Use care when repositioning the vehicle and make necessary adjustments to the engine support.*

31. Remove the remaining transaxle mount to transaxle bracket bolt.

32. Slowly lower the engine support device to gain clearance for the removal of the transaxle.

33. Remove the transaxle mount.

34. Safely elevate and support the vehicle on stands.

CAUTION: *The engine hoist is in place and under tension. Use care when repositioning the vehicle and make necessary adjustments to the engine support.*

35. Support the transaxle with a floor jack, making sure it is properly placed and balanced.

36. Remove the lower front and rear bolts holding the transaxle to the engine.

37. Remove the transaxle assembly from the engine and lower it slowly on the floor jack.

To install:

38. Elevate the transaxle into position, making sure the input shaft aligns with the cluch splines.

39. Install the lower front and rear bolts holding the transaxle to the engine.

40. Remove the floor jack from under the transaxle.

41. Attach the electrical wiring to the starter.

42. Install the lower starter bolt snugly.

43. Lower the vehicle to the ground

CAUTION: *The engine hoist is in place and under tension. Use care when repositioning the vehicle and make necessary adjustments to the engine support.*

44. Install the left transaxle mount upper bolt and two lower bolts snugly.

45. Take tension on the engine support device and raise the transaxle. Install the through bolt loosely in the mount.

46. Tighten the through bolt to 69 ft. lbs. Tighten the upper transaxle mount bolt to 45 ft. lbs.

47. Install the mount cover and bracket. Tighten the cover bolts to 45ft. lbs.

48. Install the two upper transaxle to engine bolts and tighten them to 34 ft. lbs.

49. Install the upper starter bolt and tighten it to 29 ft. lbs.

50. Connect the speedometer cable.

51. Position the shift cables into the brackets and connect the cable retainers and end clips.

52. Install the two actuator mounting bolts snugly, then install the actuator line bracket and bolt. Tighten the actuator line and mounting bolts to 15 ft. lbs.

53. Connect the ground strap and the electrical connector for the reverse lights.

54. Install the air cleaner assembly.

55. Elevate and safely support the vehicle.

CAUTION: *The engine hoist is in place and under tension. Use care when repositioning the vehicle and make necessary adjustments to the engine support.*

56. Tighten the two remaining lower transaxle mount bolts to 45 ft. lbs. (These are the bolts installed in step 39.).

57. Tighten the lower starter bolt to 29 ft. lbs.

58. Install the center mount and its two bolts and tighten them to 45 ft. lbs. Install the inspection cover bolt and tighten it to 45 ft. lbs.

59. Install the front mount bracket on the transaxle.

60. Install the front mount and through bolt loosely.

NOTE: *When installing the front mount, the weight on the mount must go twoard the transaxle for proper mount alignment.*

61. Position the center crossmember over the center and rear transaxle mount studs; start two nuts on the center mount.

62. Loosely install the three bolts holding the center crossmember to the radiator support.

63. Loosely install the two front mount bolts.

64. Raise the main crossmember into position over the rear mount studs and slign all under-

body bolts. Install the two rear mount nuts loosely.

65. Install the eight main crossmember to underbody bolts loosely.

66. Install the two lower control arm bracket bolts loosely.

67. Loosely install the two bolts holding the center crossmember to the main crossmember.

68. Install the exhaust hanger bracket and its three nuts. The crossmembers, mounts, through bolts and brackets should now all be in place and held loosely by their nuts and bolts. If any repositioning is necessary, do so now.

69. Tighten the components below in the order listed to the correct torque specification:

    a. Main crossmember to underbody bolts: 152 ft. lbs.

    b. Lower control arm bolts: 94 ft. lbs.

    c. Center crossmember to radiator support bolts: 45 ft. lbs.

    d. Front, center and rear mount bolts: 45 ft. lbs.

    e. Exhaust hanger bracket nuts: 9.5 ft. lbs. (115 INCH lbs.)

    f. Front mount through bolt: 69 ft. lbs.

70. Install the covers on the front and center mount bolts.

71. Reinstall the drive axles.

72. Fill the transaxle with the correct amount of oil.

73. Install the splash shields.

74. Lower the vehicle to the ground. Remove the engine support apparatus.

75. Install the battery tray, battery and holddown clamp.

Overhaul

WARNING: *The use of the correct special tools or their equivalent is REQUIRED for this procedure.*

Before servicing the transaxle, it is important to insure cleanliness. The outside of the case should be thoroughly cleaned with solvent or spray cleaner. Any dirt entering the unit may damage moving parts. The work area and workbench should be cleaned before the work is begun and maintained in clean condition during the repair. If the repair must be abandoned for more than a few minutes, cover the work area and components with a large cloth or sheet.

All disassembled parts should be cleaned with solvent and dried with compressed air if possible. Do not use solvent on Neoprene seals. Lubricate the seals with clean transaxle oil and use petroleum jelly to hold thrust washers in place during assembly. This eases installation and does not leave harmful residue in the system.

Before installing bolts into aluminum parts, dip the threads in clean oil or coat them with an anti-seize compound to prevent galling or seizing. Always use a torque wrench to avoid overtightening fittings. Aluminum parts are very susceptible to damage and must be handled carefully. Certain internal parts are made of very soft metals and must be protected from impacts which could cause damage or cracks. While a certain amount of force is needed to separate or assemble parts, the force should be applied smoothly and evenly; sharp impact will damage components. Reusing snaprings and circlips is not recommended; they lose their tension during the removal process.

TRANSAXLE DISASSEMBLY

1. Remove the transaxle from the car, following procedures outlined previously. Secure the transaxle to a work stand.

2. Remove the clutch release fork, the clutch release bearing and the speedometer driven gear.

3. Remove the clutch release cylinder-to-transaxle bolts and the release cylinder.

4. Using the back-up light switch socket or equivalent, remove the back-up light switch.

5. Remove the transaxle case cover bolts and the cover.

6. Using a dial indicator, measure the 5th gear thrust clearance. The clearance must be 0.10–0.66mm; if not, the selective snapring will need to be replaced during reassembly.

7. Remove the shift selector bellcrank, the set bolt, the shift and selecting lever.

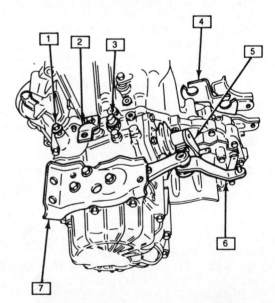

1. Ground wire bolt	5. Shift control bellcrank
2. Left mount brace	6. Shift select bellcrank
3. Backup switch	7. Left mount bracket
4. Shift cable bracket	

Transaxle assembly removed from vehicle

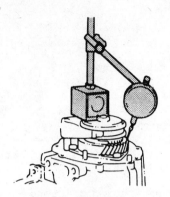

MARK	THICKNESS
A	2.25 mm (0.0886")
B	2.31 mm (0.0909")
C	2.37 mm (0.0933")
D	2.47 mm (0.0957")
E	2.49 mm (0.0980")
F	2.55 mm (0.1004")
G	2.61 mm (0.1028")

Measuring 5th gear thrust clearance with a dial indicator. Use the chart to select a replacement snapring if needed.

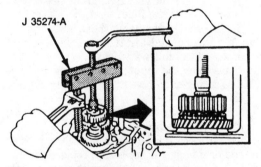

Removing 5th gear; GM tool shown.

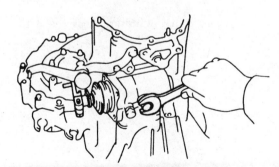

Removing the set bolt

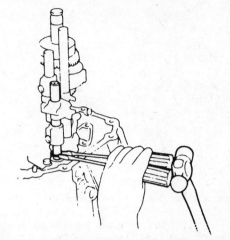

The two screwdriver trick for removing snaprings. Note the blades positioned vertically.

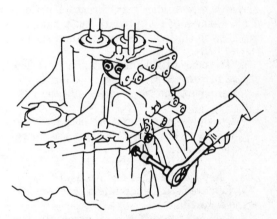

Removing the plugs and lockbolt assemblies

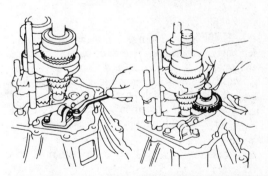

Removing the reverse shaft arm bracket and idler.

8. Engage the gears, remove the 5th gear locknut and disengage the gears.

9. Remove the bolt with the lockwasher from the No. 3 shift fork.

10. Using a pair of small prybars or screwdrivers and a hammer, tap the 5th gear snapring from the shaft.

11. Remove the 5th gear hub sleeve and driven gear. Using a gear puller or equivalent, press the 5th drive gear from the shaft.

12. Remove the rear bearing retainer and both bearing snaprings. Remove the reverse idler gear shaft bolt and the No. 2 shift fork shaft snapring.

13. Using a No. 40 Torx® bit or equivalent, remove the 3 plug, seal, spring, ball and lockball assemblies. If necessary, use a magnet to remove the seats, springs and balls.

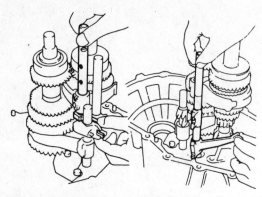

Removing the shift forks and shafts

14. Remove the transaxle case-to-bellhousing case bolts and tap the cases apart with a plastic hammer.

15. Remove the reverse shift arm bracket. Remove the reverse idler gear, thrust washer and shaft. Using a pair of prybars and a hammer, tap out the shift shaft snaprings and remove the set bolts.

16. To remove the shift forks and shift fork shafts, perform the following procedures:

　a. Remove the No. 2 fork shaft and shift head.

　b. Using a magnet, remove both balls.

　c. Remove the No. 3 fork shaft and the reverse shift fork.

　d. Pull out the No. 1 fork shaft.

　e. Remove the No. 1 and No. 2 shift forks.

17. Remove both the input and output shafts at the same time.

18. Remove the differential assembly, the magnet and the oil receiver.

Input shaft

1. Using a feeler gauge, measure the 3rd and 4th thrust clearance. Standard clearances are: 3rd gear, 0.10–0.35mm and 4th gear, 0.10–0.55mm. Maximum allowable clearances: 3rd gear, 0.40mm and 4th gear, 0.60mm.

If the 3rd gear clearance is exceeded, 3rd and 4th gears must be replaced. If the 4th gear

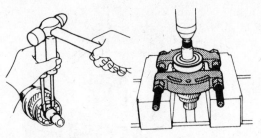

Use a split-plate and a press to remove 4th gear, bearing and synchro.

clearance is exceeded, 4th and 5th gears must be replaced.

2. Using a small pair of prybars and a hammer, tap the snaprings from the input shaft.

3. Using a press and a split plate tool, press the radial ball bearing and 4th gear from the input shaft. Remove the needle roller bearings and the synchronizer ring.

4. Using a pair of snapring pliers, remove the snapring from the input shaft. Use a press and a split plate tool to press the No. 2 sleeve, 3rd gear, the synchronizer ring and the needle roller bearing from the input shaft.

5. Clean all components thoroughly and dry with compressed air if possible. Inspect compenents as follows:

　a. Check the input shaft bearing surfaces for scoring and/or wear; if necessary, replace the shaft.

　b. Check the input shaft splines for wear; if necessary, replace the shaft.

　c. Inspect the bearings for scoring, wear and/or damage; if necessary, replace them.

　d. Check the gears and synchronizer parts for damage and/or excessively worn teeth; if necessary, replace them.

　e. Using a dial indicator, check the shaft

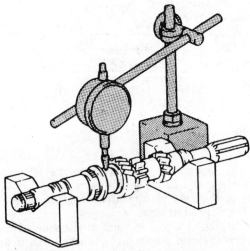

Use V-blocks and a dial indicator to measure run-out.

3RD GEAR　　　　　　　4TH GEAR

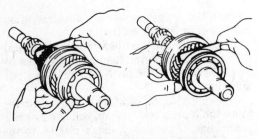

Measuring 3rd and 4th gear thrust clearances

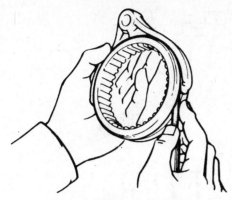

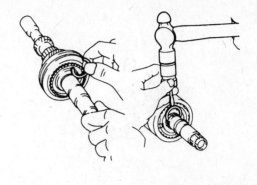

Measuring shift fork clearance to hub sleeve.

MARK	THICKNESS
0	2.30 mm (0.0906")
1	2.36 mm (0.0929")
2	2.42 mm (0.0953")
3	2.48 mm (0.0976")
4	2.54 mm (0.1000")
5	2.60 mm (0.1034")

Use the chart to select the correct snapring for 3rd gear and 4th gear retention.

runout; if runout exceeds 0.50mm, replace the shaft.

f. Using a feeler gauge, measure the clearance between the shift forks and the hub sleeves. If the clearance is less than 0.60mm, replace the synchronizer.

6. Using multi-purpose grease, lubricate the needle roller bearings.

7. Place the synchronizer ring onto the 3rd gear, align the ring slots with the shifting keys. Using a shop press and a split plate tool, press the 3rd gear/No. 2 hub sleeve onto the input shaft.

8. Select a snapring which will allow minimum axial play and install it onto the input shaft.

9. Using a feeler gauge, measure the 3rd gear thrust clearance; it should be 0.10–0.35mm.

10. Using multi-purpose grease, lubricate the needle roller bearings.

11. Place the synchronizer ring onto the 4th gear and align the ring slots with the shifting keys.

12. Using a shop press, press the radial ball bearing onto the input shaft.

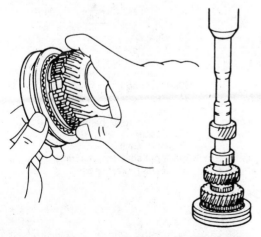

3rd gear bearing, synchronizer ring and No. 2 hub

13. Select a snapring which will allow minimum axial play and install it onto the shaft.

14. Using a feeler gauge, measure the 4th gear thrust clearance; it should be 0.10–0.55mm.

Output Shaft

1. Using a feeler gauge, measure the 1st and 2nd gear thrust clearance on the output shaft. Standard clearances are: 1st gear, 0.10-40mm and 2nd gear, 0.10–0.45mm. Maximum allowable clearances are: 1st gear, 0.45mm and 2nd gear, 0.50mm. If 1st gear clearance is incorrect, 1st and 2nd gears must be replaced. If 2nd gear clearance is incorrect, replace 2nd and 3rd gears.

2. Using a press and a split plate tool, press the radial ball bearing, the 4th driven gear and spacer from the output shaft.

3. Using a shop press and a split plate tool, press the 3rd driven gear, 2nd gear, the needle roller bearing, the spacer and the synchronizer ring from the output shaft. Remove the needle roller bearings and the synchronizer ring.

4. Remove the snapring.

5. Now press the No. 1 hub sleeve, the 1st gear/synchronizer ring, the needle roller bearing, the thrust washer and locking ball from the output shaft. Remove the needle roller bearings and the synchronizer ring.

6. Clean all components thoroughly and dry with compressed air if possible. Inspect compenents as follows:

a. Check the input shaft bearing surfaces for scoring and/or wear; if necessary, replace the shaft.

b. Check the input shaft splines for wear; if necessary, replace the shaft.

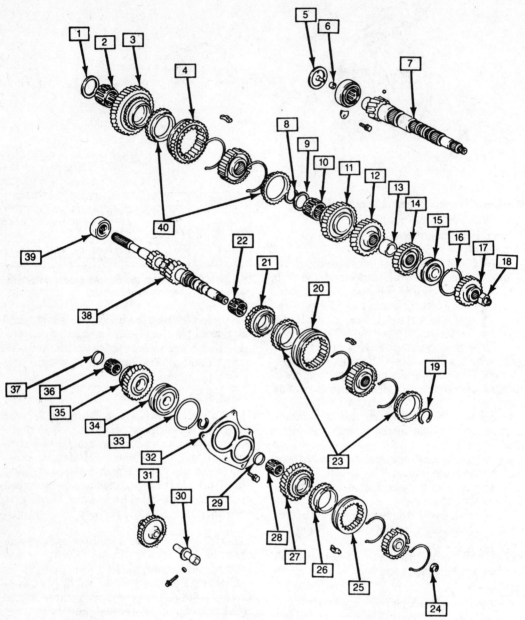

1. Thrust washer	15. Rear bearing	29. Spacer
2. Needle roller bearing	16. Snapring	30. Idler gear shaft
3. 1st gear	17. 5th driven gear	31. Reverse idler gear
4. No. 1 hub sleeve	18. Lock nut	32. Rear bearing retainer
5. Output shaft cover	19. Snapring	33. Snapring
6. Slotted spring pin	20. No. 2 hub sleeve	34. Rear bearing
7. Output shaft	21. 3rd gear	35. 4th gear
8. Snapring	22. Needle roller bearing	36. Needle roller bearing
9. Spacer	23. Synchronizer rings	37. Spacer
10. Needle roller bearing	24. Snapring	38. Input shaft
11. 2nd gear	25. No. 3 hub sleeve	39. Input shaft front bearing
12. 3rd driven gear	26. Synchronizer rings	40. Synchronizer rings
13. Output gear spacer	27. 5th gear	
14. 4th driven gear	28. Needle roller bearing	

Input and output shaft components

1ST GEAR 2ND GEAR

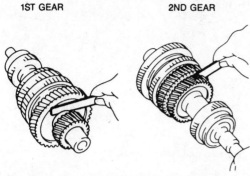

Measuring 1st and 2nd gear thrust clearances.

c. Inspect the bearings for scoring, wear and/or damage; if necessary, replace them.

d. Check the gears and synchronizer parts for damage and/or excessively worn teeth; if necessary, replace them.

e. Using a dial indicator, check the shaft runout; if runout exceeds 0.50mm, replace the shaft.

f. Using a feeler gauge, measure the clearance between the shift forks and the hub sleeves.

7. Install the locking ball into the output shaft. Install the thrust washer onto the shaft by positioning it's groove securely over the locking ball.

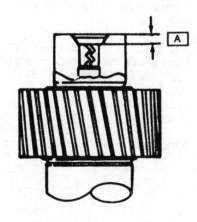

A 6.0 mm (0.236")

Slotted spring pin

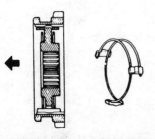

Hub sleeve assembly; arrow points to engine side.

NOTE: *If the output shaft was replaced, drive a slotted spring pin into the output shaft to a depth of 6.0mm.*

8. Using multi-purpose grease, lubricate the needle roller bearing.

9. Place the synchronizer ring onto the 1st gear and align the ring slots with the shifting keys.

10. Press the 1st gear/No. 1 hub sleeve assembly onto the output shaft.

11. Select a snapring which will allow minimum axial play and install it onto the shaft.

12. Using a feeler gauge, measure the 1st gear thrust clearance; is should be 0.10–0.40mm.

13. Install the spacer. Position the synchronizer ring onto the gear and align the ring slots with the shifting keys.

14. Using multi-purpose grease, lubricate the needle roller bearings and install the 2nd gear.

15. Using a shop press and a split plate tool, press the 3rd driven gear onto the output shaft.

16. Using a feeler gauge, measure the 2nd gear thrust clearance; is should be 0.10–0.45mm.

17. Install the spacer. Use a press and a split plate to press the 4th driven gear and bearing onto the output shaft.

Synchronizers

The transaxle is equipped with 3 synchronizers: 1st–2nd, 3rd–4th and 5th speeds.

1. From each synchronizer, remove both key springs.

2. Noting the relative positions, separate the hub, sleeve and keys; be sure to scribe the hub-to-sleeve location.

3. Clean, inspect and/or replace any worn or damaged parts.

4. Using a feeler gauge, measure the syn-

MARK	THICKNESS
A	2.50 mm (0.0984")
B	2.56 mm (0.1008")
C	2.62 mm (0.1031")
D	2.68 mm (0.1055")
E	2.74 mm (0.1074")
F	2.80 mm (0.1102")

Chart for selecting 1st gear snaprings

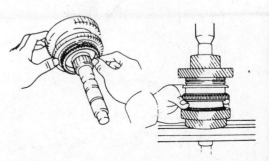

Second gear and 3rd driven gear assembled on shaft

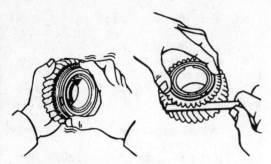

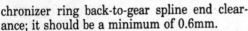

Checking synchronizer function and clearance.

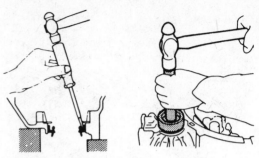

Removing and installing seals

chronizer ring back-to-gear spline end clearance; it should be a minimum of 0.6mm.

5. Align the scribe marks and assemble the hub to the sleeve; the extruded hub lip should be directed away from the sleeve's shift fork groove.

6. Install a retaining ring. Carefully pry the ring back and insert the keys (one at a time); be sure to position the ring so it is locked in place by the keys.

7. Install the other retaining ring; be sure the ring's open segment is out of phase with the open segment of the other ring. The open areas should NOT align.

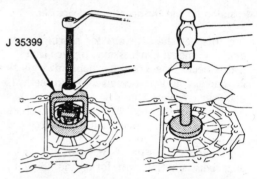

J 35399

Removing and installing case bearings. GM tool shown.

FRONT CASE

1. Use an input shaft bearing removal tool (or equivalent) and a slide hammer/puller to press the input shaft's front bearing from the case.

2. Remove the bolt and bearing lockplate. Using an output shaft bearing removal tool or equivalent, and a slide hammer/puller, press the output shaft's front bearing from the case.

3. Using a small prybar, pry the input shaft front oil seal and the right hand differential oil seal from the case.

4. Using the differential side bearing cup removal tool or equivalent, and a hammer, drive the right hand differential outer race from the case.

5. Check and clean the case.

6. Using a scraper or gasket cleaning tool, remove the sealant from the mating surfaces; be careful not to gouge or damage the aluminum surfaces.

7. Use the input shaft seal installation tool, drive the new oil seal into the case until it seats.

8. Drive the input shaft bearing into the case with the correct size bearing driver.

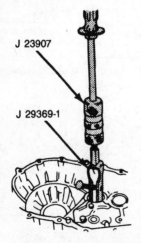

J 23907

J 29369-1

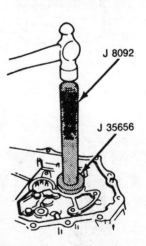

J 8092

J 35656

Removal (left) and installation of input shaft front bearing. GM tools shown.

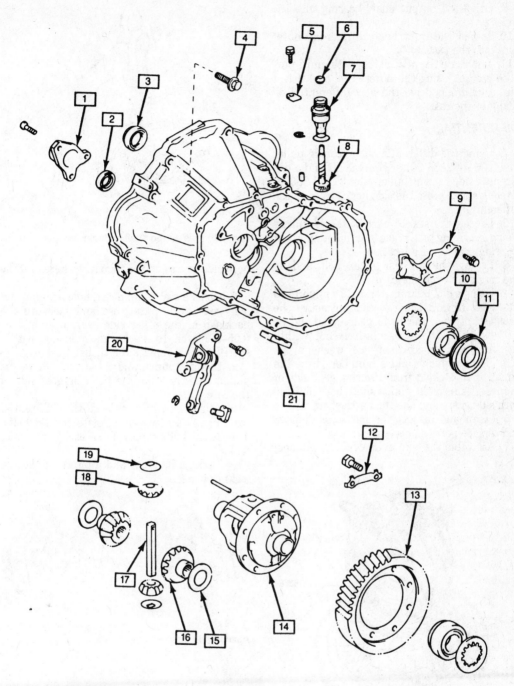

1. Front bearing retainer
2. Retainer seal
3. Axle seal
4. Transaxle mounting bolt
5. Speedometer housing hold-down
6. Speedometer gear seal
7. Speedometer housing
8. Speedometer driven gear
9. Oil receiver
10. Side bearing
11. Speedometer drive gear
12. Bolt lock plate
13. Ring gear
14. Differential case
15. Thrust washer
16. Side gear
17. Pinion Shaft
18. Pinion gear
19. Thrust washer
20. Reverse shift arm
21. Magnet

Differential components

9. Drive the output shaft bearing into the case.

10. Install the right hand differential outer race into the case.

11. Lubricate the new oil seal with multi-purpose grease. Using the differential seal driver and a hammer, drive the new differential oil seal into the case.

DIFFERENTIAL

1. Using the differential side bearing puller tool (GM J-22888-20) or equivalent, and a differential side bearing puller pilot (GM J-35378) or equivalent, press the side bearings from the differential case.

2. Loosen the staked part of the lockplate. Using a scribing tool, make alignment marks at the ring gear-to-case location.

3. Remove the ring gear-to-case bolts and tap the ring gear from the case.

4. Using a dial micrometer, hold a pinion and side gear toward the case and measure the backlash of the other side gear; it should be 0.05–0.20mm. If the backlash is not within specifications, replace the thrust washer.

5. Using a punch and a hammer, drive the pinion shaft lockpin from the ring gear side of the case. Remove the pinion shaft, both pinions, both side gears and the thrust washers.

6. Clean and inspect the parts for damage and replace parts as necessary.

7. Assemble the pinion shaft, both pinions,

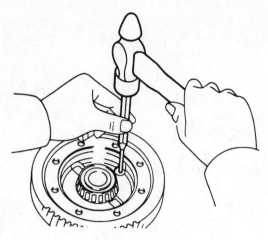

Removing the pinion shaft lock pin

both side gears and the thrust washers into the case.

8. Using a dial micrometer, hold a pinion and side gear toward the case and measure the backlash of the other side gear; it should be 0.05–0.20mm. If the backlash is not within specifications, replace the thrust washer.

9. Using a punch and a hammer, drive the pinion shaft lockpin into the ring gear side of the case.

10. Align the ring gear with the differential case, install a new locking plate and set bolts. Torque the bolts evenly, in several steps, to 71 ft. lbs.

11. Using a hammer and a punch, stake the locking plates.

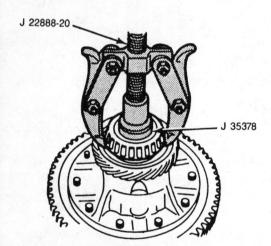

Removing side bearing; GM tools shown.

THRUST WASHER	THICKNESS
0.95 mm	(0.0374")
1.00 mm	(0.0394")
1.05 mm	(0.0413")
1.10 mm	(0.0433")
1.15 mm	(0.0453")
1.20 mm	(0.0472")

Measuring pinion gear backlash; use the chart to select replacement thrust washers.

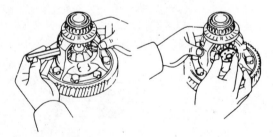

Assembling pinion and side gears

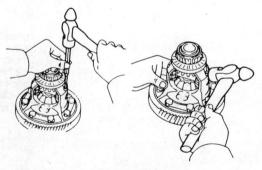

Installing pinion shaft locking pin.

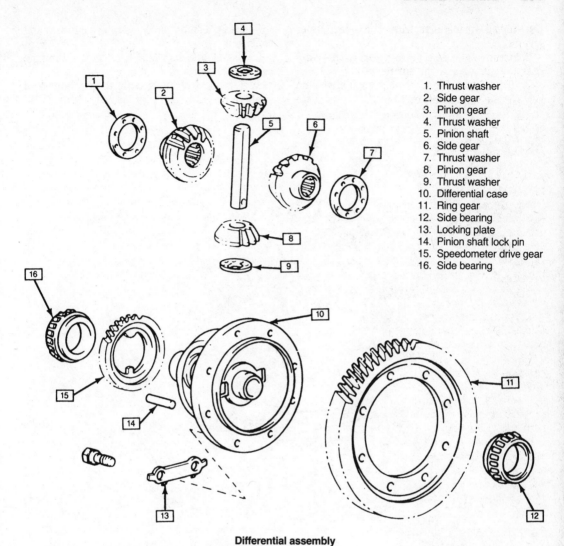

1. Thrust washer
2. Side gear
3. Pinion gear
4. Thrust washer
5. Pinion shaft
6. Side gear
7. Thrust washer
8. Pinion gear
9. Thrust washer
10. Differential case
11. Ring gear
12. Side bearing
13. Locking plate
14. Pinion shaft lock pin
15. Speedometer drive gear
16. Side bearing

Differential assembly

NOTE: *Stake a claw flush with the flat surface of the nut. For the claw contacting the protruding portion of the nut, stake only ½ on the tightening side.*

12. Using a press and the differential side bearing installer tool, press the differential side bearings onto the differential case.

SHIFT AND SELECT LEVER

1. Remove the shift/select lever assembly from the case.
2. Remove the E-ring and compression ring.
3. Using a pin punch and a hammer, drive the slotted spring pins from the No. 1 and No. 2 inner shift levers.
4. Remove the No. 2 shift inner lever, the No. 1 shift inner lever and the shift interlock plate.
5. Using a pin punch and a hammer, drive

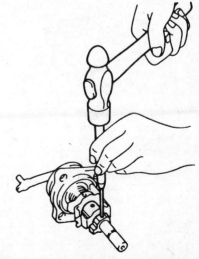

Removing No. 1 and No. 2 shift inner lever.

the slotted spring pins from the select inner lever.

6. Remove the select inner lever, the compression spring and the spring seat.

7. Tap the snapring from the lever shaft and remove the lever shaft and boot.

8. Using a small prybar, pry the out seal and replace it.

9. Clean and inspect the parts for damage; replace the parts, if necessary.

10. Grease the shaft, install the boot and shaft to the control shaft cover.

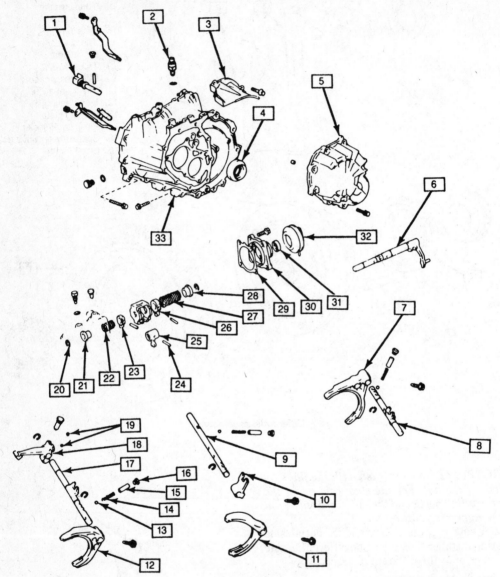

1. Reverse restrict pin
2. Reverse light switch
3. Protector
4. Drive axle seal
5. Transmission case cover
6. Shift and select lever shaft
7. No. 1 shift fork
8. No. 1 shift fork shaft
9. No. 2 shift fork shaft
10. Shift head
11. No. 2 shift fork
12. No. 3 shift fork
13. Ball
14. Spring
15. Seat
16. Plug
17. No. 3 shift fork shaft
18. Reverse shift fork
19. Fork lock balls
20. E-clip
21. No. 2 select spring seat
22. Spring
23. No.2 shift inner lever
24. Slotted spring pin
25. No.1 shift inner lever
26. Select inner lever
27. Spring
28. Select spring seat
29. Gasket
30. Control shaft cover
31. Oil seal
32. Boot
33. Transaxle case

Shift forks and shaft assemblies

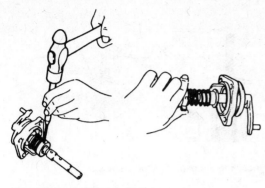

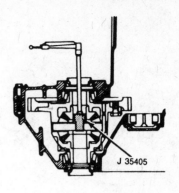

Removing select inner shaft

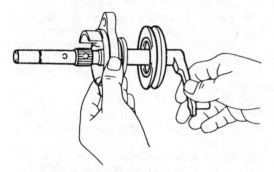

Lever shaft and boot assembly

MARK	THICKNESS
A	2.10 mm (0.00827")
B	2.15 mm (0.0846")
C	2.20 mm (0.0866")
D	2.25 mm (0.0886")
E	2.30 mm (0.0906")
F	2.35 mm (0.0925")
G	2.40 mm (0.0945")
H	2.45 mm (0.0965")
J	2.50 mm (0.0984")
K	2.55 mm (0.1004")
L	2.60 mm (0.1024")
M	2.65 mm (0.1043")
N	2.70 mm (0.1063")
P	2.75 mm (0.1083")
Q	2.80 mm (0.1102")
R	2.85 mm (0.1122")
S	2.90 mm (0.1142")
T	2.95 mm (0.1162")
U	3.00 mm (0.1182")

Checking the differential preload with GM tool. Use the chart to select the correct adjusting shims.

NOTE: *When installing the boot, be sure to position the boot's air bleed downward.*

11. Install the snapring, the spring seat, the compression spring and the select inner lever.

12. Using a pin punch and a hammer, drive in the slotted spring pin.

13. Align the interlock plate to the No. 1 inner shift lever and install it.

14. Install the No. 2 inner shift lever.

15. Using a pin punch and a hammer, drive in the slotted spring pins.

16. Install the compression spring, seat and E-ring.

TRANSAXLE RE-ASSEMBLY

1. Install the magnet into the bottom of the case.

2. Install the oil receiver and the differential into the case.

3. To adjust the differential side bearing preload, perform the following procedures:

  a. Install the thinnest side bearing shim into the transaxle case.

  b. Install the differential into the transaxle case.

  c. Install the transaxle case and tighten the bolts to 22 ft. lbs.

  d. Using the differential preload wrench and a torque wrench, measure the bearing preload; the new bearings should be 7–14 INCH lbs. or old bearings should be 4–9 INCH lbs.

NOTE: *The preload will change about 2.6–3.5 inch lbs. with each shim thickness.*

  e. If the preload is not correct, use the differential side bearing cup remover to remove the transaxle case side outer side bearing race. Select and install a different side bearing shim, install the side bearing outer race and the case. Torque the case bolts and check the preload.

  f. After the preload has been adjusted, remove the transaxle case.

4. Install the input and output shaft assemblies.

5. Install the shift forks and shift fork shafts by positioning the No. 1 and No. 2 shift forks into the No. 1 and No. 2 hub sleeve grooves. Insert the No. 1 fork shaft into the No. 1 shift fork hole.

6. Insert both interlock balls into the reverse shift fork hole. Install the No. 3 fork shaft and the reverse shift fork.

7. Install the No. 2 fork shaft, the shift head and the bolts; tighten the bolts to 12 ft. lbs.

8. Install the snaprings.

9. Place the reverse shift fork pivot into the

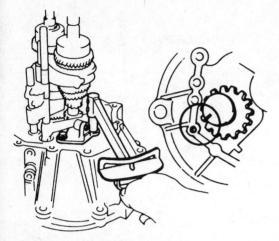

Reverse shaft and idler gear alignment.

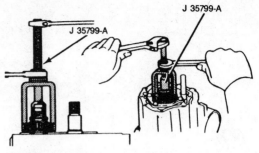

Installing 5th gear; GM tools shown

reverse shift arm and install the reverse shift arm into the transaxle case; the bolts should be tightened to 13 ft. lbs.

10. Install the reverse idler gear and shaft; align the gear mark with the case hole.

11. Apply Loctite® sealant No. 518 or equivalent to the front and main transaxle case mounting surfaces and assemble the cases. Tighten the main case-to-front case bolts to 22 ft. lbs.

12. Install the balls, springs and seats into the lockball assembly holes. Apply sealant to the plugs and lockball assembly. Tighten the plugs to 18 ft. lbs. and the lockball assembly to 29 ft. lbs.

13. Install the reverse idler gear shaft and torque the lockbolt to 18 ft. lbs.

14. Install both bearing snaprings and the No. 2 fork shaft snapring.

15. Install the rear bearing retainer; tighten the bolts to 14 ft. lbs.

16. Use the proper installation tool and a hammer to drive the 5th driven gear onto the shaft.

17. Install the spacer, the needle bearing, the 5th gear and the synchronizer ring.

18. Install the clutch hub, the shifting keys and the key springs onto the hub sleeve

NOTE: *When installing the shifting springs, position them under the shifting keys and position them so their gaps do not align with each other.*

19. Using the gear installation tool, drive the No. 3 hub sleeve, with the No. 3 shifting fork, and align the synchronizer ring slots with the shifting keys.

20. Using a dial indicator, measure the 5th gear thrust clearance; it should be 0.10–0.57mm.

21. Select and install a snapring which will allow minimum axial play, onto the output shaft.

22. Engage the 5th gear and install the locknut; tighten it to 87 ft. lbs. After installation, disengage the gear and stake the locknut.

23. Install the shifting fork bolt and tighten it to 12 ft. lbs.

24. Position a new gasket on the control shaft cover, install the shift/select lever and torque the bolts to 14 ft. lbs.

25. Install the bellcrank to the transaxle case and tighten the bolt to 22 ft. lbs.

26. Apply Loctite® No. 518 (or its equivalent) to the transaxle case, install the case cover and tighten the retaining bolts to 13 ft. lbs.

27. Install the front bearing retainer and tighten the bolts to 8 ft. lbs.

28. Apply lithium grease to the inside groove of the release bearing hub, the input shaft spline and the release fork contact surface. Install the release fork and the bearing.

29. Using the proper size socket, install and tighten the back-up light switch to 30 ft. lbs.

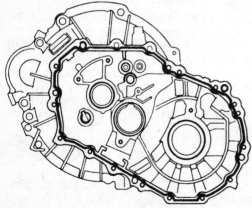

Apply sealant to mating surface of the front and main cases.

MARK	THICKNESS
A	2.25 mm (0.0886")
B	2.31 mm (0.0909")
C	2.37 mm (0.0933")
D	2.43 mm (0.0957")
E	2.49 mm (0.0980")
F	2.55 mm (0.1004")
G	2.61 mm (0.1028")

Selection chart for 5th gear snaprings

30. Install the speedometer driven gear.

31. Shift the transaxle and check it for smooth operation.

Halfshafts

REMOVAL AND INSTALLATION

Nova with 4A-LC engine and Prizm

1. Remove the wheel cover.

2. Remove the cotter pin, hub nut cap, hub nut and washer.

3. Loosen the wheel nuts.

4. Elevate and safely support the car.

5. Remove the front wheel.

6. Remove the lower control arm to ball joint attaching nuts and bolts.

7. Use a ball joint separator such as GM J-24319-01 or equivalent to remove the tie rod ball joint from the knuckle.

8. Remove the bolts holding the brake caliper bracket to the steering knuckle. Use stiff wire to suspend the caliper out of the way; do not let the caliper hang by its hose. Remove the brake disc.

9. Using a puller such as GM J-25287 or equivalent, push the axle from the hub.

NOTE: *The Prizm axle can be separated from the hub using a brass or plastic hammer. Nova requires the use of the puller.*

10. Use a slide hammer and appropriate end fitting (GM J-2619-01 and J 35762 or equivalents) to pull the driveshaft from the transaxle. Remove the shaft from the car.

11. When reinstalling, install shaft into transaxle. If necessary, use a long brass drift and a hammer to drive the housing ribs onto the inner joint.

12. Install the shaft into the wheel hub.

13. Install the lower control arm to the lower ball joint. Tighten the nuts and bolts to 59 ft. lbs.

14. Install the tie rod end to the steering knuckle and tighten the nut to 36 ft. lbs.

15. Install the brake disc; install the brake caliper and tighten the bolts to 65 ft. lbs.

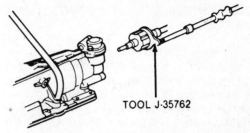

TOOL J-35762

Using a slide hammer and adaptor to remove 4A-LC driveshaft from 4A-LC transaxle.

16. Install the wheel.

17. Install the hub nut and washer.

18. Lower the vehicle to the ground.

19. Tighten the wheel lugs to 76 ft. lbs. Tighten the hub nut to 137 ft. lbs.

20. Install the nut, cap, cotter pin and washer. Install the wheel cover.

Nova with 4A-GE engine

1. Raise the front of the vehicle and support it with jackstands. Remove the tires.

2. Remove the cotter pin and locknut cap.

3. Have an assistant step on the brake pedal and at the same time, loosen and remove the bearing locknut.

4. While the assistant is still depressing the brake pedal, loosen and remove the six nuts which connect the halfshaft to the differential side gear shaft.

5. Remove the brake caliper and position it out of the way. Remove the brake disc.

6. Remove the two retaining nuts and then disconnect the lower arm from the steering knuckle.

7. Use a two-armed puller and remove the axle hub from the outer end of the halfshaft.

8. Remove the halfshaft.

9. To reinstall, place the outboard side of the shaft into the axle hub and then insert the inner end into the differential. Finger tighten the six nuts.

WARNING: *Be careful not to damage the boots during installation.*

10. Install the lower arm to the steering knuckle and tighten the bolts to 47 ft. lbs.

11. Install the disc and reinstall the caliper and bracket. tighten the bolts to 65 ft. lbs.

12. While an assistant depresses the brake pedal, tighten the six nuts holding the axle to the side gear shaft to 27 ft. lbs.

13. Install the hub nut and washer.

14. Install the wheel.

15. Lower the vehicle to the ground.

16. Tighten the wheel lugs to 76 ft. lbs. Tighten the hub nut to 137 ft. lbs.

17. Install the nut, cap, cotter pin and washer. Install the wheel cover.

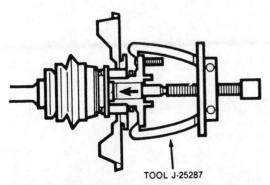

TOOL J-25287

Using GM tool to remove axle from 4A-LC hub

CONSTANT VELOCITY (CV) JOINT OVERHAUL

The drive axle assembly is a flexible unit consisting of an inner and outer constant velocity (cv) joint joined by an axle shaft. The inner joint, because of its "tri-pot" design, is completely flexible and allows the joint to flex left/right, up/down and compress/extend while the shaft is turning. This range of motion is neces-sary to allow the car to accelerate during all possible positions of the front wheels.

Because of the inner joint's flexibility, care must be taken not to over-extend the joint during repairs or handling. When either end of the shaft is disconnected from the car, any over-extension could result in separation of the internal components and possible joint failure.

The outer joint, being fixed into the hub, does not require the extreme flexibility of the inner

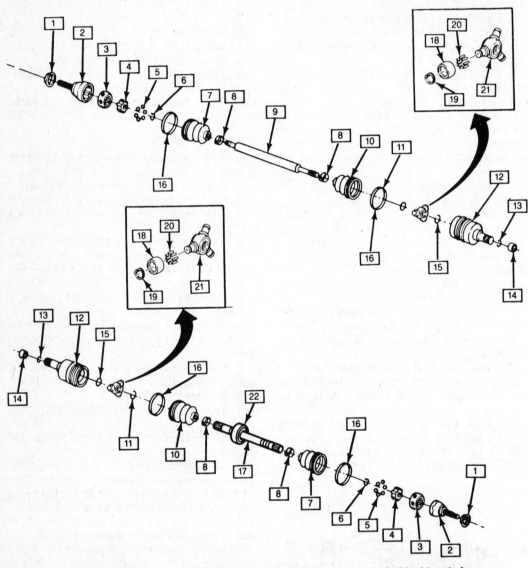

1. Deflector ring	9. Right side drive shaft	17. Left side drive shaft
2. CV joint outer race	10. Tri-pot (inboard) boot	18. Tri-pot joint ball
3. Case	11. Axle shaft retaining ring	19. Joint ball and bearing
4. CV joint inner race	12. Tri-pot joint housing	retainer
5. Balls	13. Axle shaft retaining pins	20. Needle bearings
6. Axle shaft snap ring	14. Drive axle dust cover	21. Joint spider
7. Outboard boot	15. Axle shaft snapring	22. Drive axle damper
8. Small boot clamp	16. Large boot clamps	

Driveshaft components—Prizm and Nova with 4A-LC engine

joint. The outer joint is a Rzeppa design (named for its inventor) and allows left/right motion while the axle is turning.

CV joints are protected by rubber boots or seals, designed to keep the high-temperature grease in and the road grime and water out. The most common cause of joint failure is a ripped boot which allows the lubricant to leave the joint, thus causing heavy wear. The boots are exposed to road hazards all the time and should be inspected frequently. Any time a boot is found to be damaged or slit, it should be replaced immediately. This is another very good example of maintenance being cheaper than repair; replacement boot kits are generally under $25 while a new joint can range close to $150 on some cars.

NOTE: *Whenever the driveshaft is held in a vise, use pieces of wood in the jaws to protect the components from damage or deformation.*

Nova with 4A-LC engine and Prizm

1. Remove the axle and mount in a vise so that the outer joint may be worked on.

2. Remove the boot retaining clamps. Slide the boot out of the way, exposing the joint.

3. Use snapring pliers to release the race retaining ring. Pull the shaft from the cage.

4. Using a brass drift, gently tap on the bottom of the cage until it tilts enough to all the first ball to be removed at the top.

5. Continue removing other balls is a similar fashion.

6. Rotate the cage and inner race 90° and remove the cage and inner race.

7. Clean and inspect all parts. The slightest imperfection on either the balls or the race will require replacement of the components. Look for any scratches, cracks or galling of the metal.

8. Position the driveshaft in the vise so that the inner joint may be worked on.

9. Remove the boot clamps. Slide the boot back, exposing the joint.

10. Remove the tri-pot housing from the axle shaft.

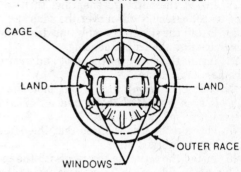

PIVOT CAGE AND INNER RACE AT 90°
TO CENTER LINE OF OUTER RACE
WITH CAGE WINDOWS ALIGNED
WITH LANDS OF OUTER RACE,
LIFT OUT CAGE AND INNER RACE.

CAGE — LAND — LAND — OUTER RACE — WINDOWS

Removing the cage and inner race

11. Remove the spacer ring with snapring pliers.

12. Use a brass drift and hammer to gently tap the joint assembly towards the center of the axle.

13. Remove the outer driveshaft snapring.

14. Remove the spider assembly from the axle by tapping it off with a brass punch and hammer. Apply force evenly around spider.

NOTE: *The spider assembly and axle should have factory alignment marks showing. Also note the marks on axle shaft and tri-pot housing. If no marks are present, make matchmarks before disassembly.*

15. Remove the boot.

16. Disassemble the spider assembly into its component parts of retainer, ball, needle bearing and spider.

17. Clean all parts thoroughly and inspect for wear, damage or corrosion. Replace any component which is not in virtually perfect condition.

18. Reassemble the spider assembly

19. Apply molybdenum grease liberally to tri-pot housing and spider.

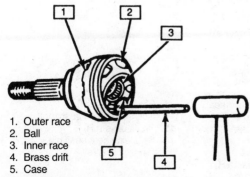

1. Outer race
2. Ball
3. Inner race
4. Brass drift
5. Case

Removing ball bearing assembly

SHAFT RETAINING RING
REMOVE FROM AXLE SHAFT
THEN SLIDE SPIDER
ASSEMBLY OFF AXLE

SNAP RING PLIERS

SPIDER ASSEMBLY

SPACER RING

SPACER RING
SLIDE RING BACK ON
AXLE SHAFT

NOTICE: BE SURE
SPACER RING IS SEATED IN
GROOVE AT REASSEMBLY

Removing the spider assembly from the shaft

20. Install the new boot onto the axle shaft and install a new small clamp.

21. Using the brass drift and hammer, install the spider assembly onto the shaft.

22. Install the outboard snapring, then tap the tri-pot assembly down over the snapring.

23. Install the spider assembly and drive axle assembly into the tri-pot housing.

24. Install the boot over the joint and secure the new large clamp.

NOTE: *Boot clamp pliers and installing tools such as GM J-35556 and J-34773-A make this job much easier.*

25. Position the axle shaft so that the outer joint may be worked on.

26. Install the cage into the race with the retaining ring side of the inner race facing the transaxle side of the shaft.

27. Pack the joint liberally with molybdenum grease and install the cage and inner race at 90° into the outer race.

28. Tip the race and install the six balls.

29. Install a new boot onto the shaft.

30. Install the race retaining ring on the shaft.

31. Insert the shaft into the inner race and make sure that the retaining ring is properly seated.

32. Fit the boot over the joint and install new boot clamps.

33. Check both joints for freedom of motion and lack of binding.

Nova with 4A-GE engine.

1. Remove the boot retaining clamps.

2. Using paint or a scribing tool, place matchmarks on the tri-pod housing and driveshaft. Do not punch the marks into the metal.

3. Remove the tri-pot housing from the driveshaft.

4. Use snapring pliers to remove the shaft retaining ring.

5. Use a punch and hammer to matchmark the driveshaft and spider.

6. Remove the spider assembly from the drive shaft with a brass punch and hammer.

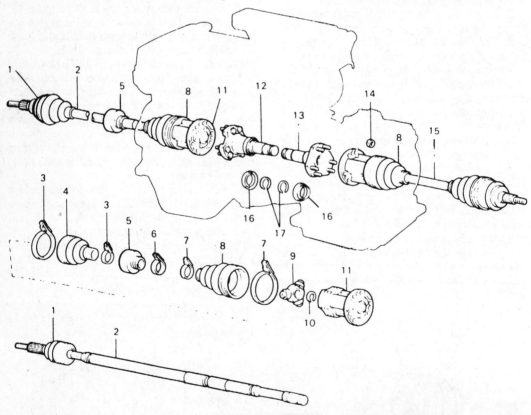

1. Joint, outer CV	7. Clamp, tri-pot joint seal ret.	13. Shaft, side gear (LH)
2. Shaft, drive (RH)	8. Seal, tri-pot joint	14. Nut, axle to side gear shaft
3. Clamp, outer CV joint seal ret.	9. Spider tri pot joint	15. Shaft, drive (LH)
4. Seal, outer CV joint	10. Ring, shaft ret.	16. Seal, side gear shaft oil
5. Damper, drive shaft	11. Housing, tri pot	17. Ring, oil seal ret
6. Clamp, damper ret.	12. Shaft, side gear (RH)	

Driveshaft components—Nova with 4A-GE engine

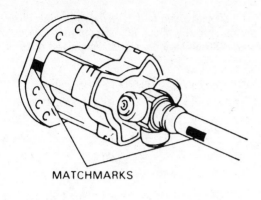

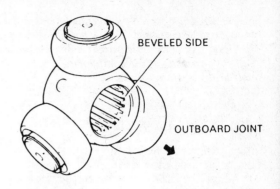

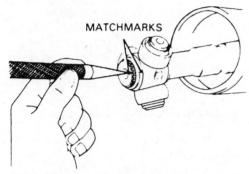

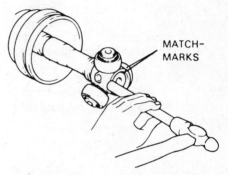

Correct placement of matchmarks before disassembly

Observe the matchmarks when installing the spider onto the shaft.

7. Remove the boot from the inner joint.

8. If working on the right axle, remove the driveshaft damper.

9. If working on the right axle, remove the outer joint boot.

10. Check the inside and outside of the seals for damage.

11. Clean all parts thoroughly and inspect for wear, damage or corrosion. Replace any component which is not in virtually perfect condition.

12. Reassemble the spider assembly.

13. If working on the right axle, temporarily install a new boot and new clamp to the outer joint.

14. If working on the right axle, install the drive shaft damper with a new clamp. Place the clamp in line with the groove of the driveshaft.

15. Temporarily install a new inner joint boot and new clamp to the driveshaft.

NOTE: *The boot and clamp for the inner joint are larger than those for the outer joint.*

16. Position the beveled side of the spider splines toward the outer CV joint. Align the matchmarks made earlier and tap the spider onto the driveshaft with a brass punch and hammer.

17. Install a NEW shaft retaining ring.

18. If working on the right axle, pack the outer joint boot with molybdenum grease. (Capacity is 0.25–0.30 lbs).

19. Install the boot over the joint.

20. Pack the tri-pot joint and boot with molybdenum grease. Correct capacites are: Manual transmission, 0.35–0.40 lbs. and Automatic transmission, 0.40–0.50 lbs.

21. Align the matchmarks made earlier and install the tri-pot housing onto the drive shaft.

22. Install the boot over the joint.

23. Be sure each boot in on the shaft groove. Bend each boot clamp into place and secure it.

24. Check both joints for freedom of motion and lack of binding.

25. Check that the boots are not stretched or compressed when the axle is in a normal or "at rest" position.

CLUTCH

CAUTION: *The clutch driven disc contains asbestos which has been determined to be a*

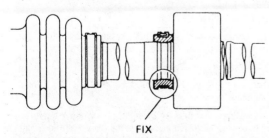
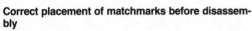

FIX

Right side axle, Nova with 4A-GE engine—make certain the damper retaining ring is in the groove.

cancer causing agent. Never clean clutch surfaces with compressed air. Avoid inhaling any dust from any clutch area! When cleaning clutch surfaces, use commercially available brake cleaning fluids.

Adjustments

PEDAL HEIGHT AND FREEPLAY

Adjust the pedal height to specification, by rotating the pedal stop (nut).

1. Adjust the clearance between the master cylinder piston and the pushrod to 1-5mm (Nova) or 5-15mm (Prizm). Loosen the pushrod locknut and rotate the pushrod while depressing the clutch pedal lightly with your finger.

2. Tighten the locknut when finished with the adjustment.

3. Adjust the release cylinder free-play by loosening the release cylinder pushrod locknut and rotating the pushrod until the specification is obtained.

4. Measure the clutch pedal free-play after performing the above adjustments. If it is not within specifications, repeat Steps 1–3 until it is.

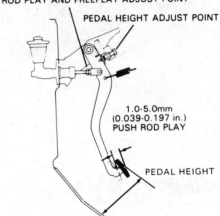

Clutch pedal height and freeplay adjustment

Troubleshooting Basic Clutch Problems

Problem	Cause
Excessive clutch noise	Throwout bearing noises are more audible at the lower end of pedal travel. The usual causes are: • Riding the clutch • Too little pedal free-play • Lack of bearing lubrication A bad clutch shaft pilot bearing will make a high pitched squeal, when the clutch is disengaged and the transmission is in gear or within the first 2" of pedal travel. The bearing must be replaced. Noise from the clutch linkage is a clicking or snapping that can be heard or felt as the pedal is moved completely up or down. This usually requires lubrication. Transmitted engine noises are amplified by the clutch housing and heard in the passenger compartment. They are usually the result of insufficient pedal free-play and can be changed by manipulating the clutch pedal.
Clutch slips (the car does not move as it should when the clutch is engaged)	This is usually most noticeable when pulling away from a standing start. A severe test is to start the engine, apply the brakes, shift into high gear and SLOWLY release the clutch pedal. A healthy clutch will stall the engine. If it slips it may be due to: • A worn pressure plate or clutch plate • Oil soaked clutch plate • Insufficient pedal free-play
Clutch drags or fails to release	The clutch disc and some transmission gears spin briefly after clutch disengagement. Under normal conditions in average temperatures, 3 seconds is maximum spin-time. Failure to release properly can be caused by: • Too light transmission lubricant or low lubricant level • Improperly adjusted clutch linkage
Low clutch life	Low clutch life is usually a result of poor driving habits or heavy duty use. Riding the clutch, pulling heavy loads, holding the car on a grade with the clutch instead of the brakes and rapid clutch engagement all contribute to low clutch life.

6. Punch matchmarks on the clutch cover (pressure plate) and flywheel so that the pressure plate can be returned to its original position during installation.

7. Slowly unfasten the screws which attach the retracting springs. Loosen each screw one turn at a time until the tension is released.

CAUTION: *If the screws are released too quickly, the clutch assembly will fly apart, causing possible injury!*

8. Separate the pressure plate from the clutch cover/spring assembly.

9. Inspect the parts for wear or deterioration. It is strongly recommended that all three components of the clutch system–disc, pressure plate and bearing–be replaced as a unit if any part is worn. The slight additional cost of the parts is more than offset by not having to disassemble it again later on to replace another component.

10. Inspect the flywheel for any signs of cracking, bluing in the steel (a sign of extreme heat) or scoring. Any bluing or cracks which are found require replacement of the flywheel. While the flywheel will not be perfectly smooth, it should be free of all but the slightest ridges and valleys or scores. Any gouging deep enough to catch your fingernail during inspection requires replacement. A scored flywheel will immediately attack a new clutch disc, causing slippage and vibration.

If the flywheel must be replaced, please refer to Chapter Three for further directions.

11. When reassembling, apply a thin coating of multipurpose grease to the release bearing

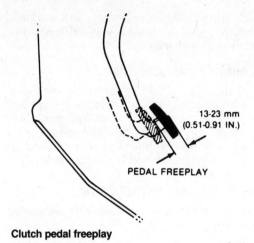

Clutch pedal freeplay

Disc and Pressure Plate
REMOVAL AND INSTALLATION

NOTE: *Do not allow grease or oil to get on any of the disc, pressure plate, or flywheel surfaces.*

1. Remove the transaxle from the car as previously detailed.

2. Remove the clutch cover and disc from the bellhousing.

3. Unfasten the release fork bearing clips. Withdraw the release bearing hub, complete with the release bearing.

4. Remove the tension spring from the clutch linkage.

5. Remove the release fork and support.

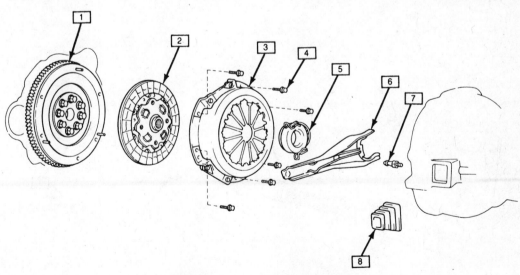

1. Flywheel
2. Clutch disc
3. Clutch cover
4. Clutch cover bolts
5. Release bearing
6. Clutch fork
7. Clutch fork pilot stand
8. Fork boot

Principal clutch components. Prizm shown, Nova similar.

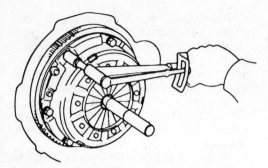

Always use a pilot tool when installing the clutch assembly.

hub and release fork contact points. Also, pack the groove inside the clutch hub with multipurpose grease and lubricate the pivot points of the release fork.

12. Align the matchmarks on the clutch cover and flywheel which were made during disassembly. Install the clutch and pressure plate assembly and tighten the retaining bolts just finger tight.

13. Center the clutch disc by using a clutch pilot tool or an old input shaft. (Pilot tools are available at most automotive parts stores.) Insert the pilot into the end of the input shaft front bearing, wiggle it gently to align the clutch disc and pressure plate and tighten the retaining bolts. The bolts should be tightened in two or three steps, gradually and evenly. Final bolt torque is 14 ft. lbs.

14. Install the release bearing, fork and boot.

15. Reinstall the transaxle as outlined previously in this chapter.

Clutch Master Cylinder

CHILTON TIP: *When inspecting the clutch hydraulic system for leakage or impaired function, check the inside of the firewall (under the carpet) below the clutch master cylinder. A master cylinder leak may not show up under the cylinder on the engine side of the firewall.*

REMOVAL AND INSTALLATION

1. Drain or siphon the fluid from the master cylinder.

2. Disconnect the hydraulic line to the clutch from the master cylinder.

WARNING: *Do not spill brake fluid on the painted surfaced of the vehicle.*

3. Inside the car, remove the underdash panel and the air duct.

4. Remove the pedal return spring.

5. Remove the spring clip and clevis pin.

6. Unfasten the bolts which secure the master cylinder to the firewall. Withdraw the assembly from the firewall side.

7. Install the master cylinder with its retaining nuts to the firewall.

8. Connect the line from the clutch to the master cylinder.

9. Connect the clevis and install the clevis pin and spring clip.

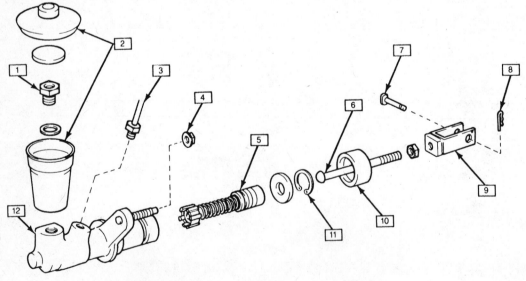

1. Reservoir tank bolt	5. Piston	9. Clevis
2. Reservoir tank	6. Pushrod	10. Boot
3. Clutch line	7. Clevis pin	11. Snap ring
4. Mounting nut	8. Spring clip	12. Master cylinder

Clutch master cylinder components

10. Install the pedal return spring.

11. Fill the reservoir with clean, fresh brake fluid and bleed the system.

12. Check the cylinder and the hose connection for leaks.

13. Adjust the clutch pedal.

14. Reinstall the air duct and underdash cover panel.

OVERHAUL

1. Clamp the master cylinder body in a vise with protected jaws.

2. Separate the reservoir assembly from the master cylinder.

3. Remove the snapring and remove the pushrod/piston assembly.

4. Inspect the master cylinder bore for scoring, grooving or corrosion. If any of these conditions are observed, replace the cylinder. Inspect piston, spring, push rod and boot for damage or wear replace any parts which are worn or defective.

5. Before reassembly, coat all parts with clean brake fluid.

6. Install the piston assembly in the cylinder bore.

7. Fit the pushrod over the washer and secure them with the snapring.

8. Install the reservoir and tighten the nut to 18 ft. lbs.

Clutch Slave Cylinder

REMOVAL AND INSTALLATION

WARNING: *Do not spill brake fluid on the painted surface of the vehicle.*

1. Raise the front of the car and support it with jackstands. Be sure that is is supported securely.

2. If necessary, remove the rear splash shield to gain access to the release cylinder.

3. Remove the clutch fork return spring.

4. Unfasten the hydraulic line from the release cylinder by removing its retaining nut.

5. Remove the release cylinder retaining nuts and remove the cylinder.

6. Reinstall the cylinder to the clutch housing and tighten the bolts to 9 ft. lbs. (108 INCH lbs).

7. Connect the hydraulic line and tighten it to 11 ft. lbs.

8. Install the clutch release spring.

9. Bleed the system and remember to top up the fluid in the master cylinder when finished.

10. Install the splash shield if it was removed.

11. Lower the car to the ground.

OVERHAUL

1. Remove the pushrod assembly and the rubber boot.

2. Withdraw the piston, complete with its cup; don't remove the cup unless it is being replaced.

3. Wash all the parts in brake fluid.

4. Replace any worn or damaged parts. Inspect the cylinder bore carefully for any sign of damage, wear or corrosion.

5. Before reassembly, coat all the parts in clean brake fluid. Insert the spring and piston into the cylinder.

6. Install the boot and insert the pushrod.

BLEEDING

1. Fill the master cylinder reservoir with brake fluid.

WARNING: *Do not spill brake fluid on the painted surface of the vehicle!*

2. Fit a tube over the bleeder plug and place

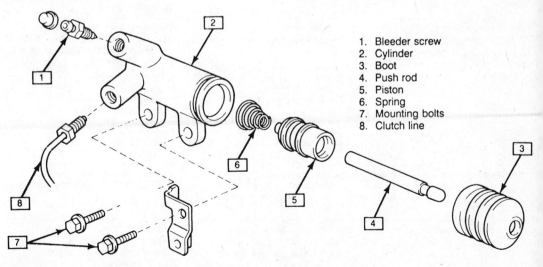

1. Bleeder screw
2. Cylinder
3. Boot
4. Push rod
5. Piston
6. Spring
7. Mounting bolts
8. Clutch line

Clutch slave (actuator) cylinder components

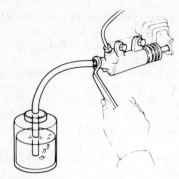

Slave cylinder bleeding

Pump the clutch pedal slowly to evacuate all the air from the system

the other end into a clean jar half-filled with brake fluid.

3. Depress the clutch pedal, loosen the bleeder plug with a wrench, and allow the fluid to flow into the jar.

4. Tighten the plug and then release the clutch pedal.

5. Repeat these steps until no air bubbles are visible in the bleeder tube.

6. When there are no more air bubbles, tight-en the plug while keeping the clutch pedal fully depressed.

7. Top off the fluid in the master cylinder reservoir.

8. Check the system for leaks.

AUTOMATIC TRANSMISSION

The Nova/Prizm family is found with two automatic transaxles, selected by the manufactur-

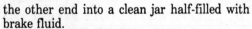

Troubleshooting Basic Automatic Transmission Problems

Problem	Cause	Solution
Fluid leakage	• Defective pan gasket	• Replace gasket or tighten pan bolts
	• Loose filler tube	• Tighten tube nut
	• Loose extension housing to transmission case	• Tighten bolts
	• Converter housing area leakage	• Have transmission checked professionally
Fluid flows out the oil filler tube	• High fluid level	• Check and correct fluid level
	• Breather vent clogged	• Open breather vent
	• Clogged oil filter or screen	• Replace filter or clean screen (change fluid also)
	• Internal fluid leakage	• Have transmission checked professionally
Transmission overheats (this is usually accompanied by a strong burned odor to the fluid)	• Low fluid level	• Check and correct fluid level
	• Fluid cooler lines clogged	• Drain and refill transmission. If this doesn't cure the problem, have cooler lines cleared or replaced.
	• Heavy pulling or hauling with insufficient cooling	• Install a transmission oil cooler
	• Faulty oil pump, internal slippage	• Have transmission checked professionally
Buzzing or whining noise	• Low fluid level	• Check and correct fluid level
	• Defective torque converter, scored gears	• Have transmission checked professionally
No forward or reverse gears or slippage in one or more gears	• Low fluid level	• Check and correct fluid level
	• Defective vacuum or linkage controls, internal clutch or band failure	• Have unit checked professionally
Delayed or erratic shift	• Low fluid level	• Check and correct fluid level
	• Broken vacuum lines	• Repair or replace lines
	• Internal malfunction	• Have transmission checked professionally

Lockup Torque Converter Service Diagnosis

Problem	Cause	Solution

No lockup	• Faulty oil pump
	• Sticking governor valve
	• Valve body malfunction
	    (a) Stuck switch valve
	    (b) Stuck lockup valve
	    (c) Stuck fail-safe valve
	• Failed locking clutch
	• Leaking turbine hub seal
	• Faulty input shaft or seal ring
		• Replace oil pump
		• Repair or replace as necessary
		• Repair or replace valve body or its
		   internal components as neces-
		   sary
		
		• Replace torque converter
		• Replace torque converter
		• Repair or replace as necessary

Will not unlock	• Sticking governor valve
	• Valve body malfunction
	    (a) Stuck switch valve
	    (b) Stuck lockup valve
	    (c) Stuck fail-safe valve
		• Repair or replace as necessary
		• Repair or replace valve body or its
		   internal components as neces-
		   sary

Stays locked up at too low a speed
  in direct
	• Sticking governor valve
	• Valve body malfunction
	    (a) Stuck switch valve
	    (b) Stuck lockup valve
	    (c) Stuck fail-safe valve
		• Repair or replace as necessary
		• Repair or replace valve body or its
		   internal components as neces-
		   sary

Locks up or drags in low or second	• Faulty oil pump
	• Valve body malfunction
	    (a) Stuck switch valve
	    (b) Stuck fail-safe valve
		• Replace oil pump
		• Repair or replace valve body or its
		   internal components as neces-
		   sary

Sluggish or stalls in reverse	• Faulty oil pump
	• Plugged cooler, cooler lines or
	  fittings
	• Valve body malfunction
	    (a) Stuck switch valve
	    (b) Faulty input shaft or seal
	       ring
		• Replace oil pump as necessary
		• Flush or replace cooler and flush
		  lines and fittings
		• Repair or replace valve body or its
		   internal components as neces-
		   sary

Loud chatter during lockup engage- ment (cold)	• Faulty torque converter • Failed locking clutch • Leaking turbine hub seal	• Replace torque converter • Replace torque converter • Replace torque converter

Vibration or shudder during lockup
  engagement
	• Faulty oil pump
	
	• Valve body malfunction
	
	• Faulty torque converter
	• Engine needs tune-up
		• Repair or replace oil pump as nec-
		  essary
		• Repair or replace valve body or its
		   internal components as neces-
		   sary
		• Replace torque converter
		• Tune engine

Vibration after lockup engagement	• Faulty torque converter • Exhaust system strikes underbody • Engine needs tune-up • Throttle linkage misadjusted	• Replace torque converter • Align exhaust system • Tune engine • Adjust throttle linkage

Vibration when revved in neutral
Overheating: oil blows out of dip
  stick tube or pump seal
	• Torque converter out of balance
	• Plugged cooler, cooler lines or fit-
	  tings
	• Stuck switch valve
		• Replace torque converter
		• Flush or replace cooler and flush
		  lines and fittings
		• Repair switch valve in valve body
		  or replace valve body

Shudder after lockup engagement	• Faulty oil pump
	• Plugged cooler, cooler lines or
	  fittings
	• Valve body malfunction
	
	• Faulty torque converter
	• Fail locking clutch
	• Exhaust system strikes underbody
	• Engine needs tune-up
	• Throttle linkage misadjusted
		• Replace oil pump
		• Flush or replace cooler and flush
		  lines and fittings
		• Repair or replace valve body or its
		   internal components as neces-
		   sary
		• Replace torque converter
		• Replace torque converter
		• Align exhaust system
		• Tune engine
		• Adjust throttle linkage

er for the best match of power transmission characteristics and engine performance. The Nova with 4A-LC engine and the Prizm (with 4A-FE engine) contain the A131L automatic transaxle while the Nova with 4A-GE engine contains the A240E transaxle.

The A131L transaxle is a three-speed automatic, developed specifically for transversly mounted engines. The wide gear ratios and efficient torque converter combine with the built-in locking clutches to operate quietly and efficiently.

The A240E four-speed transaxle may also be referred to as an ECT type or Electronically Controlled Transaxle. Is is controlled by a microcomputer, allowing the driver to select either the Normal or Power mode. The system function is overseen by an electronic control module (ECM); shift behavior and timing are triggered by the computer rather than by internal oil pressures. Should the system malfunction, the ECM will select a gear which allows the car to be driven, although performance will be greatly reduced.

Troubles occuring with the automatic transaxle can be caused by either the engine, the electronics or the transaxle itself. These areas should be distinctly isolated during troubleshooting. Begin with the simplest of possibilities (low fluid, loose wires, etc.) and eliminate all the external causes before committing to transaxle removal and repair.

Fluid Pan and Filter

REMOVAL AND INSTALLATION

1. Raise and safely support the vehicle.
2. Drain the transmission fluid.
3. Carefully loosen and remove the bolts holding the oil pan. Tap around the pan lightly with a plastic mallet, breaking the gasket tension by vibration. Do not pry the pan down with a screwdriver or similar tool; the pan is light-weight metal and will deform, causing leaks.
4. Remove all traces of gasket material from the pan and the transmission mating faces. Clean then carefully with a plastic or wooden scraper. Do not gouge the metal.
5. Clean the pan thoroughly of all oil and sediment.
6. Remove the bolts holding the screen (filter) and remove it from the car. Note that the bolts holding the filter may be different lengths; they must be replaced in the correct positions at reassembly.
7. Install the filter and tighten the bolts to 7 ft. lbs. (84 INCH lbs.).
8. Install a new gasket on the pan and bolt the pan into place. Snug the bolts in a criss-cross pattern, working from the center out. Tighten the pan bolts to 48 INCH lbs.

NOTE: *If the mating surfaces of the oil pan and transaxle are clean and straight, there is no need for gasket sealer during reassembly.*

Transmission Fluid Indications

The appearance and odor of the transmission fluid can give valuable clues to the overall condition of the transmission. Always note the appearance of the fluid when you check the fluid level or change the fluid. Rub a small amount of fluid between your fingers to feel for grit and smell the fluid on the dipstick.

If the fluid appears:	It indicates:
Clear and red colored	• Normal operation
Discolored (extremely dark red or brownish) or smells burned	• Band or clutch pack failure, usually caused by an overheated transmission. Hauling very heavy loads with insufficient power or failure to change the fluid, often result in overheating. Do not confuse this appearance with newer fluids that have a darker red color and a strong odor (though not a burned odor).
Foamy or aerated (light in color and full of bubbles)	• The level is too high (gear train is churning oil) • An internal air leak (air is mixing with the fluid). Have the transmission checked professionally.
Solid residue in the fluid	• Defective bands, clutch pack or bearings. Bits of band material or metal abrasives are clinging to the dipstick. Have the transmission checked professionally.
Varnish coating on the dipstick	• The transmission fluid is overheating

The use of sealer is generally not recommended on these transmissions.

9. Lower the vehicle to the ground and refill the automatic transmission fluid.

Adjustments

THROTTLE VALVE (TV) CABLE

1. With the ignition **OFF**, depress the accelerator pedal all the way. On carbureted vehicles, check that the throttle plates are fully open. If they are not, adjust the throttle linkage.

2. Peel the rubber dust boot back from the throttle valve cable.

3. Loosen the adjustment nuts on the throttle cable bracket (rocker cover) just enough to allow cable housing movement.

4. Have an assistant depress the accelerator pedal fully.

5. Adjust the cable housing so that the distance between its end and the cable stop collar is 0–1.0mm.

6. Tighten the adjustment nuts. Make sure that the adjustment hasn't changed. Install the dust boot.

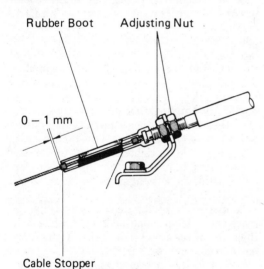

Throttle linkage adjustment—0–0.04 in (0–1mm)

NEUTRAL SAFETY SWITCH

1. Locate the neutral safety switch on the side of the transmission and loosen the switch retaining bolts.

2. Move the gear selector to the **NEUTRAL** position.

3. Disconnect the neutral safety switch connector and connect an ohmmeter between the two adjacent terminals on the switch lead.

4. Adjust the switch to the point where there is continuity between the two terminals. Tighten the retaining bolts.

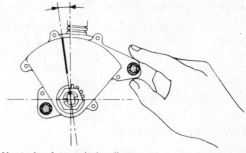

Neutral safety switch adjustment

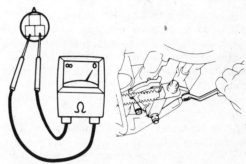

Connect an ohmmeter between the terminals as shown-

5. Move the shift selector to **PARK** and check that continuity is present. Move the selector to any of the other positions and check that there is no continuity when the car is in gear.

6. Reconnect the wiring to the switch.

SHIFT LINKAGE ADJUSTMENT

1. Loosen the adjusting nut on the linkage and check the linkage for freedom of movement.

2. Push the manual lever fully toward the right side of the car as far as it will go.

3. Return the lever two notches to the **NEUTRAL** position.

4. Set the gear selector to **NEUTRAL**. While holding the selector slightly to the right, have someone tighten the adjusting nut on the manual lever.

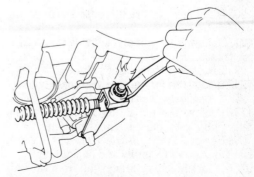

Adjusting the shift linkage-

REVERSE LIGHT SWITCH

The reverse light function is controlled by the neutral/start switch. When the switch is properly adjusted, the white lamps at the rear will only come on when the car is in reverse. Should it be necessary to replace the switch, simply unplug it and unbolt it.

Automatic Transaxle

REMOVAL AND INSTALLATION

Nova with 4A-LC Engine and A131L Transaxle

1. Disconnect the negative battery cable
2. Remove the air intake tube.
3. Disconnect the speedometer cable and neutral start wiring connector at the transmission. Loosen the lug nuts on the left front wheel.
4. Disconnect the thermostat housing at the transmission.
5. Disconnect the ground cable at the transmission.
6. Remove one upper mount to bracket bolt.
7. Label and disconnect any interfering wiring in the area of the transmission case.
8. Disconnect the throttle valve cable at the carburetor.
9. Remove two upper bellhousing bolts.
10. Support the engine using either GM tool J-28467-A or equivalent.
11. Raise the vehicle and support it safely on stands.
12. Remove the left front wheel.
13. Remove the splash shields under the car.
14. Remove the center beam.
15. Disconnect the shift cable at the transmission.
16. Remove the shift cable bracket.
17. Remove the cooler bracket and disconnect the cooler lines at the transaxle. Plug the lines to prevent leakage.
18. Remove the inspection cover on the bell housing and remove the torque converter bolts through the inspection hole.
19. Disconnect the left control arm at the ball joint.
20. Disconnect the right control arm at the ball joint.
21. Remove the right and left axle shafts from the transaxle.
22. Disconnect the starter bolts
23. Remove the three rear transaxle bolts.
24. Support the transaxle with a floor jack.
25. Remove the remaining mount bolts and remove the remaining bellhousing bolts.
26. Remove the transaxle from the vehicle. Handle the unit carefully and do not allow it to tip; the torque converter may fall from the unit and become damaged.

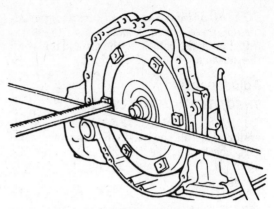

Measuring converter to case clearance

27. Before reinstallation, install the torque converter in the transmission. If the converter has been drained, refill it with 2.3 US qts. of Dexron® II ATF.
28. Check the torque converter installation. Use a straightedge and calipers to check the distance between the face of the converter and the surface of the transaxle housing. Correct free space is more than 20mm.
29. Apply multi-purpose grease to the contact points of the torque converter and the crankshaft.
30. Place the transaxle on the jack and lift into position. Align the guide pin with one of the holes in the driveplate (flywheel) and align the two pins on the block with the converter housing holes. Temporarily install one bolt to hold everything together.
31. Install all of the transmission housing bolts and tighten them. The larger bolts (12mm) should be tightened to 47 ft. lbs. and the smaller (10mm) bolts tightened to 34 ft. lbs.
32. Install the left engine mount and tighten the bolts to 38 ft, lbs.
33. Install the six torque converter bolts. Remove the guide pin and install the white bolt, then install the five yellow bolts. Tighten the bolts evenly and to 13 ft. lbs.
34. Install the inspection plate (engine rear cover plate).
35. Reinstall the starter.
36. Connect the drive shafts to the transaxle.
37. Install the center engine support and tighten the bolts to 29 ft. lbs.
38. Install the front and rear mounts, tightening the four bolts to 29 ft. lbs.
39. Connect the left and right control arms to the ball joints.
40. Reinstall the thermostat housing.
41. Connect the oil cooler lines to the transaxle.
42. Connect and adjust the shift control cable.
43. Install the speedometer cable.
44. Install and adjust the throttle valve cable.

45. Connect the neutral start switch connector. Connect or reposition any wiring which was moved to gain access during removal.

46. Install the air cleaner.

47. Fill the transaxle with the correct amount of Derxron® II ATF. If the transaxle has been disassembled and drained, install 5.8 US qts. If the transaxle was not disassembled and still contains fluid, add 2.4 US qts.

48. Double check all installation items, paying particular attention to loose hoses or hanging wires, untightened nuts, poor routing of hoses and wires (too tight or rubbing) and tools left in the engine area.

49. Install the splash shields below the engine. Install the left front wheel and lower the vehicle to the ground.

50. Connect the negative battery cable.

51. Start the engine and allow it to idle. With the wheels blocked front and rear and your foot on the brake, engage each gear and check that the transxle engages properly. Check that the car will not roll in **PARK**.

52. Allow the engine to idle with the transaxle in **PARK**; check the fluid level on the dipstick. Check all assembly points for any sign of leakage.

Nova with 4A-GE Engine and A240E Transaxle

1. Disconnect the negative battery cable.
2. Remove the air cleaner assembly.
3. Disconnect the neutral start switch.
4. Disconnect the solenoid valve wiring connector.
5. Disconnect the speed sensor.
6. Disconnect the speedometer cable.
7. Remove the water inlet assembly.
8. Remove the throttle cable from the throttle linkage.
9. Remove the transaxle dipstick tube.
10. Disconnect the battery ground cable from the transaxle housing.
11. Loosen, but do not remove the lug nuts on the left front wheel. Raise the vehicle and safely support it.
12. Drain the transaxle oil.
13. Remove the splash shields from under the engine.
14. Remove the shift control cable and brackets.
15. Disconnect the oil cooler lines at the transaxle. Plug the lines to prevent leakage.
16. Remove the front and rear engine mount bolts.
17. Remove the center engine mount member.
18. Carefully disconnect the oxygen sensor connector and remove the front exhaust pipe.
19. Disconnect and remove the left and right driveshafts from the transaxle.

20. Remove the left front wheel.
21. Remove the cotter pin, lock nut cap, lock nut and washer.
22. Remove the brake caliper assembly and support it with stiff wire out of the way. Do not disconnect the hose. Do not allow the caliper to hang by the hose.

CAUTION: *Brake pads and shoes contain asbestos, which has been determined to be a cancer causing agent. Never clean the brake surfaces with compressed air! Avoid inhaling any dust from brake surfaces! When cleaning brakes, use commercially available brake cleaning fluids.*

23. Remove the brake disc.
24. Remove the steering knuckle from the lower control arm.
25. Remove the left driveshaft.
26. Remove the starter motor and the bracket (stiffener plate).
27. Remove the engine rear cover plate (inspection plate).
28. Remove the torque converter mounting bolts.
29. Lower the vehicle to the ground.
30. Support the engine using GM tool J-28467 or equivalent.
31. Remove the three bolts from the rear engine mount.
32. Raise and safely support the vehicle. Remember that the engine support is in place; make necessary adjustments during jacking.
33. Support the transaxle with a jack. Remove the transaxle, keeping it level.
34. Remove the torque converter.
35. Before reinstallation, install the torque converter in the transmission. If the converter has been drained, refill it with 2.3 US qts. of Dexron® II ATF.
36 Check the torque converter installation. Use a straightedge and calipers to check the distance between the face of the converter and the surface of the transaxle housing. Correct free space is more than 20mm.
37. Apply multi-purpose grease to the contact points of the torque converter and the crankshaft.
38. Place the transaxle on the jack and lift into position. Use a guide pin to align the holes in the driveplate (flywheel) and align the two pins on the block with the converter housing holes. Temporarily install one bolt to hold everything together.
39. Install all of the transmission housing bolts and tighten them. The larger bolts (12mm) should be tightened to 47 ft. lbs. and the smaller (10mm) bolts tightened to 34 ft. lbs.
40. Install the three engine rear mount bolts and tighten them to 38 ft. lbs.
41. Install the six torque converter bolts. Re-

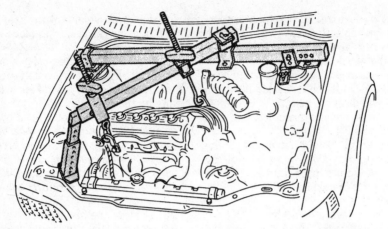

Using tool J-28467 to support the engine. An external hoist may be used but raising and lowering the car becomes difficult.

move the guide pin and install the white bolt, then install the five yellow bolts. Tighten the bolts evenly and to 20 ft. lbs.

42. Install the inspection plate (engine rear cover plate).

43. Reinstall the stiffener plate and the starter.

44. Install the left driveshaft with its washer, lock nut, lock nut cap and cotter pin.

45. Reconnect the steering knuckle to the lower control arm.

46. Install the brake disc. Install the caliper and tighten the mounting bolts to 18 ft. lbs.

47. Install the left front wheel; tighten the wheel nuts to 76 ft. lbs.

48. Connect both driveshafts to the transaxle.

49. Reinstall the front exhaust pipe using new gaskets. Connect the wiring to the oxygen sensor.

50. Install the engine center mounting member. Tighten the bolts to 29 ft. lbs.

51. Install the bolts for the front and rear engine mounts. Correct torque is 29 ft. lbs. When the mount bolts are secure, the engine support apparatus may be removed.

52. Connect the oil cooler lines to the transaxle.

53. Install the shift control cable and brackets.

54. Replace the splash shields under the engine.

55. Lower the vehicle to the ground.

56. Connect the ground strap to the transaxle housing.

57. Install the transaxle dipstick tube.

58. Install the water inlet assembly.

59. Attach the throttle cable to the linkage and adjust as necessary.

60. Install the speedometer cable and the speed sensor.

61. Connect the wiring to the solenoid valve.

62. Connect the wiring to the neutral start switch.

63. Install the air cleaner.

64. Fill the transaxle with the correct amount of Derxron® II ATF. If the transaxle has been disassembled and drained, install 7.6 US qts. If the transaxle was not disassembled and still contains fluid, add 3.1 US qts.

65. Double check all installation items, paying particular attention to loose hoses or hanging wires, untightened nuts, poor routing of hoses and wires (too tight or rubbing) and tools left in the engine area.

66. Connect the negative battery cable.

67. Start the engine and allow it to idle. With the wheels blocked front and rear and your foot on the brake, engage each gear and check that the transxle engages properly. Check that the car will not roll in **PARK**.

68. Allow the engine to idle with the transaxle in **PARK**; check the fluid level on the dipstick. Check all assembly points for any sign of leakage.

Prizm with 4A-FE engine and A131L Transaxle

1. Support the engine with GM tool J–28467–A or equivalent.

2. Remove the battery hold-down, battery and tray.

3. Remove the air cleaner assembly

4. Disconnect the connector at the neutral start switch.

5. Disconnect the ground strap from the transaxle case.

6. Remove the throttle cable from the throttle body.

7. Disconnect the cooling lines at the transaxle and plug the lines to prevent leakage.

8. Remove the shift cable retainer and end clip.

9. Remove the shift cable from its brackets and place the cable out of the way.

10. Remove the upper shift cable bracket from the transaxle housing.

11. Remove the left transaxle mount brace.

12. Remove the through bolt in the mount.

13. Remove the two upper transaxle-to-engine bolts.

14. Remove the upper starter bolts.

15. Disconnect the speedometer cable.

16. Raise the vehicle and safely support it.

17. Remove the splash shields from below the car.

18. Drain the transaxle oil.

19. Disconnect the electrical connections to the starter. Remove the bottom starter bolt and remove the starter.

20. Remove the driveshafts from the transaxle.

21. Remove the three bolts holding the center crossmember to the radiator support.

22. Remove the covers from the front and center mount bolts; remove the two front mount bolts, then the two center mount bolts.

23. Remove the two nuts from the rear mount.

24. Remove the two bolts holding the center crossmember to the main crossmember.

25. Remove the three nuts holding the exhaust hanger bracket and remove the bracket.

26. Use a floor jack to support the main crossmember. Check its placement carefully so that the crossmember will be balanced during removal.

27. Remove the eight bolts holding the main crossmember to the underbody.

28. On the left and right sides, remove the two bolts holding the control arm bracket to the underbody.

CAUTION: *Lower the main crossmember slowly while holding onto the center crossmember. The center crossmember is free to fall at this point and could cause serious injury or damage.*

29. At the front mount, remove the through bolt and the the mount.

30. Remove the front mount bracket from the transaxle.

31. Remove the center mount from the transaxle with its two bolts.

32. Remove the torque converter bolt shield and remove the bolts holding the torque converter to the flywheel.

33. Remove the two bolts holding the lower transaxle mount to the bracket.

34. Lower the vehicle to the ground.

35. Remove the remaining transaxle mount-to-bracket bolt.

36. Adjust the engine support apparatus to lower the transaxle and gain clearance for removal.

37. Disconnect the transaxle mount.

38. Raise and safely support the vehicle.

WARNING: *The engine support apparatus has been repositioned and the crossmembers are removed. Be very careful when raising the car.*

39. Use a floor jack to support the transaxle. Make sure it is properly positioned.

40. Remove the front and rear lower bolts holding the transaxle to the engine.

41. Carefully remove the transaxle, keeping it as level as possible. Remove the torque converter.

42. Before installing the transaxle, make sure that the torque converter is all the way into the pump and bushing. Use a straightedge across the front of the transaxle case and measure the inset to the converter. Clearance must be at least 20mm.

43. Lightly coat the converter to flywheel contact point with multi-purpose grease.

44. Support the transaxle on the floor jack and move it into place. Install the transaxle and hold it in place with the front and rear lower transaxle-to- engine bolts. Tighten the bolts snugly; they will be final tightened later.

45. Remove the jack from under the transaxle.

46. Install the starter and its lower bolt snugly. Connect the starter wiring.

47. Lower the vehicle to the ground.

WARNING: *The engine support apparatus has been repositioned and the crossmembers are removed. Be very careful when moving the car.*

48. Install the left transaxle mount.

49. Install the bolt for the upper mount bracket and the two bolts for the lower bracket snugly.

50. Adjust the engine support apparatus to raise the transaxle into position.

51. Install the through bolt for the transaxle mount and tighten it to 64 ft. lbs. Tighten the upper transaxle mounting bracket bolt to 45 ft. lbs.

52. Install the brace at the mount and tighten the bolts to 13 ft. lbs.

53. Install the two upper transaxle-to-engine bolts snugly.

54. Install the upper starter bolt snugly.

55. Tighten all the transaxle-to-engine bolts to 34 ft. lbs.

56. Tighten the upper starter bolt to 29 ft. lbs.

57. Install the speedometer cable.

58. Install the upper shift cable bracket, position the shift cable into the bracket and install the cable retainer and end clips.

59. Install the oil cooling lines.

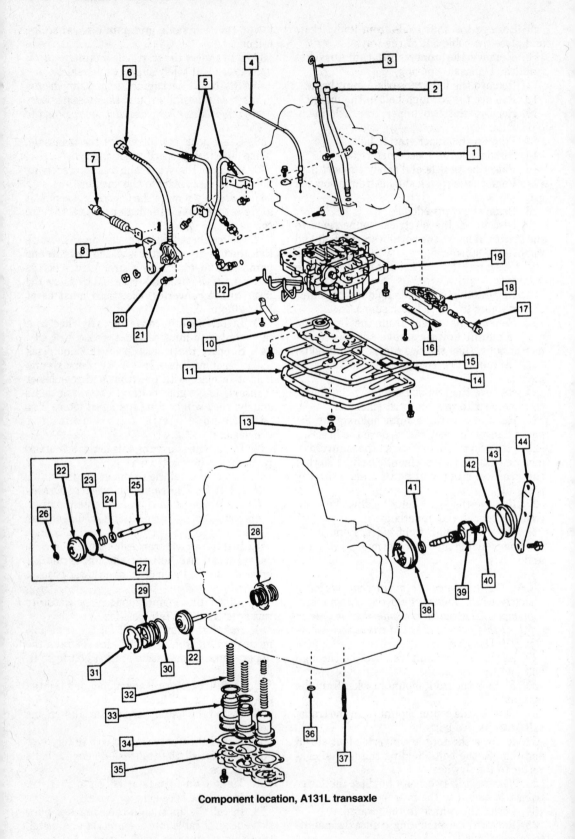

Component location, A131L transaxle

60. Connect the threttle cable at the throttle body.

61. Install the ground strap to the transaxle case.

62. Install the connector to the neutral start switch.

63. Install the air cleaner assembly.

64. Raise and safely support the vehicle.

65. Tighten the two lower transaxle mount bolts to 45 ft. lbs.

66. Tighten the lower starter bolt to 29 ft. lbs.

67. Install the torque converter to flywheel bolts and tighten them to 31 ft. lbs.

68. Install the converter bolt shield.

69. Install the center mount with two bolts to the transaxle; tighten the bolts to 45 ft. lbs.

70. Install the front mount bracket on the transaxle and tighten the bolts to 13 ft. lbs.

71. Install the front mount. Loosely install the through bolt.

NOTE: *As the front mount is installed, the weight on the mount must go towards the transaxle; this allows the mount to align properly.*

72. Position the center crossmember over the center and rear transaxle mount studs. Start two nuts on the center mount.

73. Loosely install the three bolts which hold the center crossmember to the radiator support.

74. Loosely install the two front mount bolts.

75. Raise the main crossmember into position over the rear mounting studs.

76. Align all the under body bolts and bolt holes.

77. Install the two rear mount nuts loosely.

78. Loosely install the eight bolts to hold the main crossmember to the underbody.

79. On each side, loosely install the two bolts holding the control arm brackets to the underbody.

80. Loosely install the two bolts holding the center crossmember to the main crossmember.

81. Install the exhaust hanger bracket and its three nuts. The crossmembers, mounts, through bolts and brackets should now all be in place and held loosely by their nuts and bolts. If any repositioning is necessary, do so now.

82. Tighten the components below in the order listed to the correct torque specification:

    a. Main crossmember to underbody bolts: 152 ft. lbs.

    b. Lower control arm bolts: 94 ft. lbs.

    c. Center crossmember to radiator support bolts: 45 ft. lbs.

    d. Front, center and rear mount bolts: 45 ft. lbs.

    e. Exhaust hanger bracket nuts: 9.5 ft. lbs. (115 INCH lbs.)

    f. Front mount through bolt: 64 ft. lbs.

83. Install the covers on the front and center mount bolts.

84. Reinstall the drive axles.

85. Fill the transaxle with the correct amount of Derxron® II ATF. If the transaxle has been disassembled and drained, install 5.8 US qts. If the transaxle was not disassembled and still contains fluid, add 2.4 US qts.

86. Double check all installation items, paying particular attention to loose hoses or hanging wires, untightened nuts, poor routing of hoses and wires (too tight or rubbing) and tools left in the engine area.

87. Install the splash shields below the engine. Install the left front wheel and lower the vehicle to the ground.

88. Remove the engine support apparatus.

89. Install the battery tray, battery and hold-down.

90. Start the engine and allow it to idle. With the wheels blocked front and rear and your foot on the brake, engage each gear and check that the transaxle engages properly. Check that the car will not roll in **PARK**.

91. Allow the engine to idle with the transaxle in **PARK**; check the fluid level on the dipstick. Check all assembly points for any sign of leakage.

1. Transaxle case	15. Magnet	30. O-ring
2. Oil filler tube	16. Detent spring	31. Snap ring
3. Transaxle dipstick	17. Manual valve	32. Spring
4. Throttle cable	18. Manual valve body	33. Piston
5. Oil cooler line	19. Valve body	34. Gasket
6. Neutral start switch	20. Nut (5 ft. lbs.)	35. Cover
7. Transmission control cable	21. Bolt (4 ft. lbs.)	36. Governor apply gasket
8. Shift lever	22. 2nd coast brake piston	37. Governor oil strainer
9. Oil tube bracket	23. Inner return spring	38. Governor body adaptor
10. Oil strainer (filter)	24. Washer	39. Governor body
11. Oil pan	25. Rod	40. Thrust washer
12. Oil tube	26. Snap ring	41. Plate washer
13. Drain plug	27. O-ring	42. O-ring
14. Oil pan gasket	28. Outer return spring	43. Cover
	29. Cover	44. Bracket

Component location, A131L transaxle

Suspension and Steering

8

FRONT SUSPENSION

The front suspension system is MacPherson strut design. The struts used on either side are a combination spring and shock absorber with the outer casing of the shock actually supporting the bottom of the spring. This arrangement saves space, weight and allows the spring and shock absorber to work on the same axis of compression.

The wheel hub is attached to the bottom of the strut. A strut mounting bearing at the top and a ball joint at the bottom allow the entire strut to rotate during cornering. The strut assembly, steering arm and steering knuckle are all combined in one assembly; there is no upper

Troubleshooting Basic Steering and Suspension Problems

Problem	Cause	Solution
Hard steering (steering wheel is hard to turn)	• Low or uneven tire pressure • Loose power steering pump drive belt • Low or incorrect power steering fluid • Incorrect front end alignment • Defective power steering pump • Bent or poorly lubricated front end parts	• Inflate tires to correct pressure • Adjust belt • Add fluid as necessary • Have front end alignment checked/ adjusted • Check pump • Lubricate and/or replace defective parts
Loose steering (too much play in the steering wheel)	• Loose wheel bearings • Loose or worn steering linkage • Faulty shocks • Worn ball joints	• Adjust wheel bearings • Replace worn parts • Replace shocks • Replace ball joints
Car veers or wanders (car pulls to one side with hands off the steering wheel)	• Incorrect tire pressure • Improper front end alignment • Loose wheel bearings • Loose or bent front end components • Faulty shocks	• Inflate tires to correct pressure • Have front end alignment checked/ adjusted • Adjust wheel bearings • Replace worn components • Replace shocks
Wheel oscillation or vibration transmitted through steering wheel	• Improper tire pressures • Tires out of balance • Loose wheel bearings • Improper front end alignment • Worn or bent front end components	• Inflate tires to correct pressure • Have tires balanced • Adjust wheel bearings • Have front end alignment checked/ adjusted • Replace worn parts
Uneven tire wear	• Incorrect tire pressure • Front end out of alignment • Tires out of balance	• Inflate tires to correct pressure • Have front end alignment checked/ adjusted • Have tires balanced

control arm. A rubber-bushed transverse link (control arm) connects the lower portion of the strut to the front crossmember via the ball joint; the link thus allows for vertical movement of the suspension. Novas with the 4A-GE engine have a front stabilizer bar (sway bar) connected between the control arms; this bar serves to reduce body roll during cornering.

The strut assembly provides rigidity and actually positions the wheel and driveshaft relative to the car, thus affecting alignment. In general, components are non-adjustable. If any component of the suspension is found to be bent or damaged, it must be replaced with an identical part. Do not substitute parts of lesser quality or different design. Torque values must be observed during reassembly to assure proper retention of the parts.

CAUTION: *Exercise great caution when working with the front suspension. Coil springs and other suspension components are under extreme tension and result in severe injury if released improperly. Never remove the nut on the top of the shock absorber piston without using the proper spring compressor tool.*

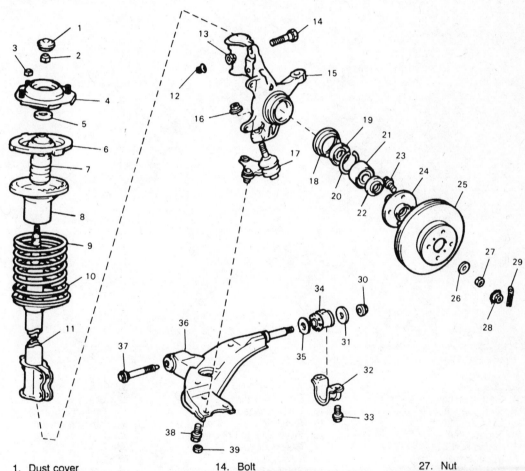

1. Dust cover	14. Bolt	27. Nut
2. Strut shaft nut	15. Steering knuckle	28. Cap
3. Strut support nut	16. Ball joint nut	29. Cotter pin
4. Strut support	17. Lower ball joint	30. Control arm nut
5. Spring seal	18. Dust deflector	31. Bushing retainer
6. Spring seat	19. Inner grease seal	32. Bushing bracket
7. Spring bumper	20. Snapring	33. Bolt
8. Upper insulator	21. Front axle hub bearing	34. Bushing
9. Coil spring	22. Outer grease seal	35. Bushing retainer
10. Lower insulator	23. Wheel stud	36. Lower control arm
11. Shock absorber/strut	24. Front axle hub	37. Bolt
12. Nut	25. Brake disc	38. Bolt
13. Camber adjustment cam	26. Hub washer	39. Nut

Front suspension components, Nova with 4A-LC engine

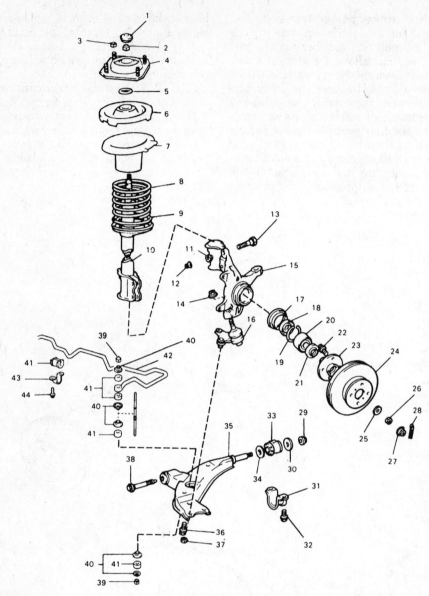

1. Dust cover	16. Lower ball joint	31. Bushing bracket
2. Strut shaft nut	17. Dust deflector	32. Bolt
3. Strut support nut	18. Inner grease seal	33. Control arm bushing
4. Strut support	19. Snapring	34. Bushing retainer
5. Support seal	20. Front axle hub bearing	35. Lower control arm
6. Spring seat	21. Outer hub seal	36. Bolt
7. Upper insulator	22. Wheel stud	37. Nut
8. Coil spring	23. Front axle hub	38. Bolt
9. Lower insulator	24. Brake disc	39. Nut
10. Shock absorber/strut	25. Hub washer	40. Stabilizer bar retainer
11. Camber adjustment cam	26. Nut	41. Insulator
12. Nut	27. Cap	42. Stabilizer bar
13. Bolt	28. Cotter pin	43. Bracket
14. Nut	29. Nut	44. Bolt
15. Steering knuckle	30. Bushing retainer	

Front suspension components, Nova wth 4A-GE engine

Spring and Shock Absorbers/Mac-Pherson Strut

TESTING

Shock Absorbers

The purpose of the shock absorber is simply to limit the motion of the spring during compression (bump) and rebound cycles. If the car were not equipped with these motion dampers, the up and down motion of the springs would multiply until the vehicle was alternately trying to leap off the ground and to pound itself into the pavement.

Contrary to popular rumor, the shocks do not affect the ride height of the car nor do they affect the ride quality except for limiting the pitch or bounce of the car. These factors are controlled by other suspension components such as springs and tires. Worn shock absorbers can affect handling; if the front of the car is rising or

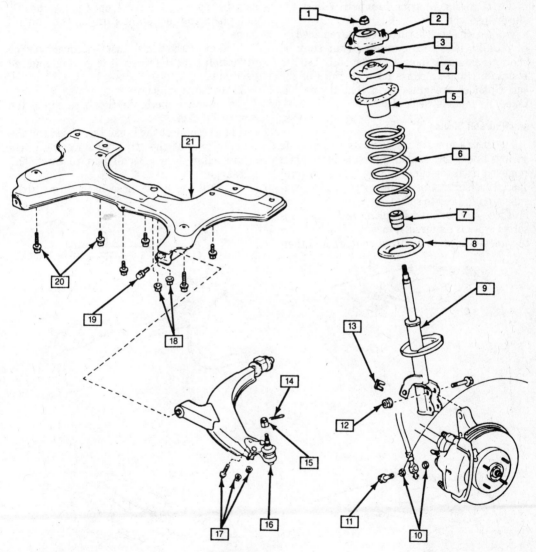

1. Strut rod piston nut
2. Suspension support
3. Dust seal
4. Spring seat
5. Upper insulator
6. Coil spring
7. Spring bumper
8. Lower insulator
9. Shock absorber
10. Brake line gaskets
11. Brake line to caliper bolt
12. Nut and bolt
13. Brake hose clip
14. Cotter pin
15. Ball joint castle nut
16. Ball joint
17. Nuts and bolt
18. Crossmember mounting nuts
19. Bolt
20. Crossmember mounting bolts
21. Suspension crossmember

Front suspension components, Prizm

falling excessively, the "footprint" of the tires changes on the pavement and steering response is affected. The simplest test of the shock absorbers is simply to push down on one corner of the unladen car and release it.

Observe the motion of the body as it is released. In most cases, it will come up beyond its original rest position, dip back below it and settle quickly to rest. This shows that the damper is slowing and controlling the spring action. Any tendency to excessive pitch (up-and-down) motion or failure to return to rest within 2–3 cycles is a sign of poor function within the shock absorber.

While each shock absorber can be replaced individually, it is recommended that they be changed as a pair (both front or both rear) to maintain equal response on both sides of the car. Chances are quite good that if one has failed, its mate is weak also.

MacPherson Struts

The struts are precise parts and retain the springs under tremendous pressure even when removed from the car. For this reason, several special tools and substantial specialized knowledge are required to safely and effectively work on these components. If spring and shock absorber work is required, it may not be a bad idea to remove the strut involved yourself and then consider taking it to a repair facility which is fully equipped and familiar with the car.

REMOVAL

1. Under the hood, remove the 3 or 4 (4A-GE) small nuts holding the top of the strut to the shock tower. DO NOT loosen the larger center nut.

2. Loosen the wheel lug nuts at the appropriate wheel.

3. Raise the vehicle and safely support it. It need not be any higher than the distance necessary to separate the tire from the ground. Do not place the jackstands under the control arms.

4. Remove the wheel. Install a cover over the driveshaft boot to protect it from fluid and impact damage.

5. On Nova vehicles:

   a. Remove the brake flex hose clip at the strut bracket.

   b. Disconnect the brake flex hose from the brake pipe at the strut. Remove the brake hose clips. Use a small pan to catch any leakage.

   c. Pull the brake hose back through the

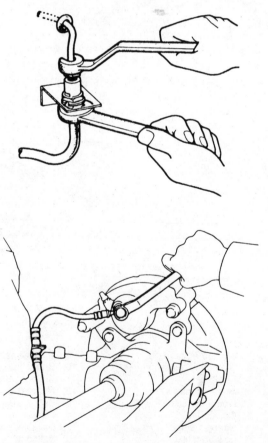

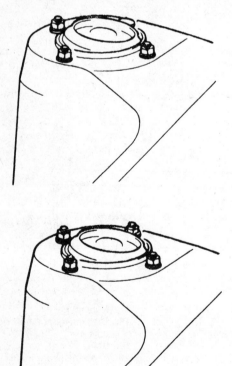

Upper strut retaining nuts. Nova with 4A-GE has four, all others have 3 per strut.

Use care in disconnecting the brake lines. Nova above, Prizm below

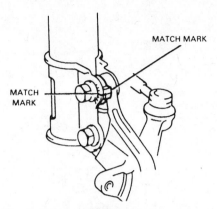

MATCH MARK

MATCH MARK

Marking the Nova camber shim before removal

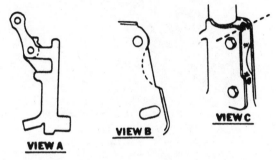

VIEW A

VIEW B

VIEW C

Marking the Prizm steering knuckle before disassembly

opening in the strut bracket. Plug the lines to prevent any dirt form entering.

d. Remove the 2 brake caliper mounting bolts and remove the caliper. Hang it out of the way with a piece of wire. Do not allow it to hang by the flex hose and do not disconnect the hose from the caliper.

e. Mark the position of the adjusting cam for reassembly.

6. On Prizm vehicles:

a. Disconnect the brake hose from the brake caliper and drain the fluid into a small pan.

b. Remove the clip from the brake hose and remove the hose from the bracket.

c. Use a sharp instrument or scribing tool to make matchmarks in all three dimensions on the steering knuckle. The strut must be reinstalled in its exact previous position.

7. Remove the 2 bolts which attach the shock absorber to the steering knuckle. The steering knuckle bolt holes have collars that extend about 5mm. Be careful to clear them when separating the steering knuckle from the strut assembly.

NOTE: *Press down on the lower suspension arm in order to remove the strut assembly. This must be done to clear the collars on the*

steering knuckle bolt holes when removing the strut assembly.

8. Remove the strut assembly. Remember that the spring is still under tension. It will stay in place as long as the top nut on the shock piston shaft is not loosened. Handle the strut carefully and do not allow the coating on the spring to become damaged.

DISASSEMBLY

CAUTION: *This procedure requires the use of a spring compressor; it cannot be performed without one. If you do not have access to this special tool, do not attempt to disassemble the strut. The coil springs are retained under considerable pressure. They can exert enough force to cause serious injury. Exercise extreme caution when disassembling the strut.*

1. Place the strut assembly in a pipe vise or strut vise.

WARNING: *Do not attempt to clamp the strut assembly in a flat jaw vise as this will result in damage to the strut tube.*

2. Attach a spring compressor and compress the spring until the upper spring retainer is free of any spring tension. Do not over-compress the spring.

3. Use a spring seat holder to hold the upper support and then remove the nut on the end of the shock piston rod.

4. Remove the bearing plate, the support and the upper spring retainer. Slowly and cautiously unscrew the spring compressor until all spring tension is relieved. Remove the spring and the dust cover.

NOTE: *Do not allow the piston rod to retract into the shock absorber. If it falls, screw a nut onto the rod and pull the rod out by the nut. Do not use pliers to grip the rod as they will damage its surface, resulting in leaks, uneven operation or seal damage. Be extremely careful not to stress or hit the rod.*

INSPECTION

Check the shock absorber by moving the piston shaft through its full range of travel. It should move smoothly and evenly throughout its entire travel without any trace of binding or notching. Use a small straightedge to check the piston shaft for any bending or deformation. If a Prizm shock absorber is replaced, the old one should be drilled at the bottom to vent the internal gas. Wear safety goggles and drill a small hole (2-3mm) into the base of the shock absorber. The gas within the strut is colorless, odorless and non-toxic, but should be vented to make the unit safe for disposal.

Inspect the spring for any sign of deterioration or cracking. The waterproof coating on the

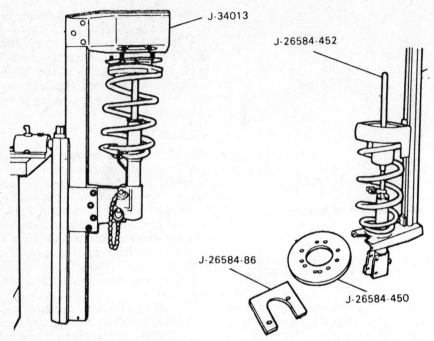

GM tools for compressing the spring and disassembling the strut. Equivalent tools may be rented from a reputable supply house.

coils should be intact to prevent rusting. A quick check for a cracked spring is to hit the spring sharply with a small metal mallet or wrench handle. An intact spring will resonate, similar to a distant gong; a cracked spring will have much less resonance and a distinctly different sound.

Check the upper strut mount assembly for any abnormal noise, binding or restricted motion. Lubricate the upper bearing with multipurpose grease before reinstallation.

ASSEMBLY AND INSTALLATION

WARNING: *Never reuse a self-locking nut. Always replace self-locking nuts with new hardware.*

1. Loosely assemble all components onto the the strut assembly. Make sure the mark on the upper spring seat is facing the outside of the vehicle.

2. Compress the spring, carefully aligning the shaft guide rod with the hole in the upper mount. Align the lower spring seat. Do not over-compress the spring; compress it just enough to allow installation of the shaft nut.

3. Install the shaft nut and tighten it until the strut shaft begins to rotate.

4. Double check that the spring is correctly seated in the upper and lower mounts and reposition it as needed. Slowly release the tension on the spring compressor and remove it from the strut assembly.

5. Tighten the shaft nut to 34 ft. lbs.

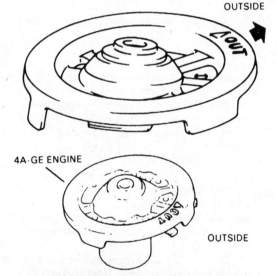

Make sure the upper strut seat marks face to the outside during reassembly.

6. On Nova vehicles, install the camber adjusting cam into the knuckle, observing the matchmarks made during disassembly.

7. Place the strut assembly in position and install the strut to knuckle attaching bolts. Tighten the bolts to the correct torque:
- Nova with 4A-LC engine: 105 ft. lbs.
- Nova with 4A-GE engine: 166 ft. lbs.
- Prism with 4A-FE engine: 194 ft. lbs.

8. Using a floor jack and a piece of wood,

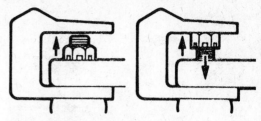

Using the balljoint separator

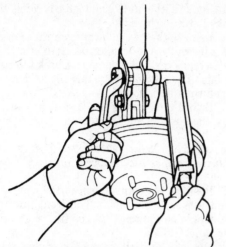

The strut to knuckle bolts must be set to the correct tightness.

gently elevate the control arm to the point that the upper mount can be aligned with the holes in the shock tower. Insert the bolts into the upper holes and install the nuts. Tighten the nuts to 23 ft. lbs. (Nova with 4A-LC) or 29 ft. lbs. (Nova with 4A-GE and Prizm).

9. Pack the shaft nut area with grease and install the dust cover.

10. On Nova vehicles, install the brake caliper and tighten the bolts to 65 ft. lbs. Pull the brake hose through the strut bracket opening and connect the fitting. Tighten the fitting to 11 ft. lbs. Install the flex hose clip at the strut bracket.

11. On Prizm vehicles, install the brake hose in the bracket and install the clip. Connect the hose to the caliper and tighten the fitting to 22 ft. lbs.

12. Install the wheel and install the lug nuts snugly.

13. Lower the vehicle to the ground. Tighten the wheel lug nuts to 76 ft. lbs.

14. Bleed the brake system and top up the brake fluid level. Please refer to Chapter 9 for complete directions.

Lower Ball Joint

INSPECTION

Raise the front of the vehicle and safely support it on stands. Do not place stands under the control arms; the arms must hang free. Grasp the tire at the top and bottom and move the top of the tire through an in-and-out motion. Look for any horizontal motion in the steering knuckle relative to the control arm. Such motion is an indication of looseness within the ball joint. If the joint is checked while disconnected from the knuckle, it should have minimal or no freeplay and should not twist in its socket un-

der finger pressure. Replace any joint showing looseness or free play.

REMOVAL AND INSTALLATION

NOTE: *The use of the correct tools is RE-QUIRED for this procedure. A ball joint separator is a commonly available tool which prevents damage to the joint and knuckle. Do not attempt to separate the joint with hammers, prybars or similar tools.*

1. Elevate and safely support the front of the vehicle. Do not place the stands under the control arms; they must hang free.

NOTE: *Do not allow the driveshaft joints to over-extend. The CV joints can become disconnected under extreme extension.*

2. Install a protective cover over the CV boot.

3. Remove the wheel.

4. Remove the cotter pin from the ball joint nut.

5. Loosen the castle nut but do not remove it. Unscrew it just to the top of the threads and install the ball joint separator. (GM Tool 34754 or equivalent) Use the nut to bear on the tool; this protects the threaded shaft from damage during removal.

6. Use the separator to loosen the ball joint from the steering knuckle.

7. Remove the nuts and bolt holding the ball joint to the control arm.

8. Remove the ball joint from the control arm and steering knuckle.

9. When reinstalling, attach the ball joint to the control arm and tighten the 2 bolts and 1 nut to 105 ft. lbs. (Prizm) or 59 ft. lbs. (Nova).

10. Carefully install the ball joint to the steering knuckle. Use a new castle nut and tighten it to 94 ft. lbs. (Prizm) or 82 ft. lbs. (Nova).

11. Install the cotter pin through the castle nut and stud.

12. Remove the protector from the CV boot.

13. Install the wheel.

14. Lower the vehicle to the ground.

Stabilizer Bar or Sway Bar
Nova with 4A-GE engine only

REMOVAL AND INSTALLATION

1. Disconnect the sway bar links from the lower control arms.

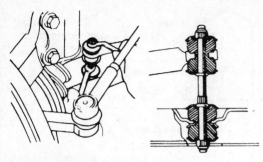

Front stabilizer bar link and bushings

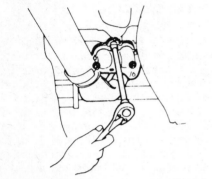

Disconnecting the exhaust system to allow stabilizer bar removal

2. Disconnect the sway bar brackets from the body.

CHILTON TIP: *Check the bushings inside the brackets for wear or deformation. A worn bushing can cause a distinct bang or "thunk" as the bar twists during cornering.*

3. Disconnect the exhaust pipe from the exhaust manifold.

4. Remove the sway bar from the car. Examine the insulators (bushings) carefully for any sign of wear and replace them if necessary.

5. To reinstall, place the bar in position and reconnect the exhaust system using new nuts. Tighten the nuts to 46 ft. lbs.

6. Install both stabilizer bar brackets and tighten the bolts to 14 ft. lbs.

7. Connect the sway bar links to the control arms with the bolts, insulators and new nuts. Tighten the nuts to 13 ft. lbs.

Lower Control Arm

REMOVAL AND INSTALLATION

Nova

1. Raise and safely support the vehicle. Do not place the stands under the control arms.

2. Remove the nuts and bolts holding the ball joint to the lower control arm.

3. On vehicles with the 4A-GE engine, remove the nut holding the sway bar link to the control arm and disconnect the link and bar from the control arm.

4. Remove the nuts and bolts holding the control arm to the body.

5. Remove the control arm from the car and check it carefully for cracks, bends or crimps in the metal or corrosion damage. Check the rubber bushing and replace it if any sign of damage or deformation is found.

6. Before reinstalling the arm, install or replace the bushing and tighten its retaining nut to 76 ft. lbs.

WARNING: *Never reuse a self-locking nut; always replace the removed nut with a new one.*

7. Position the control arm to the body and install the nuts and bolts. The front nut and bolt should be tightened to 105 ft. lbs. and the rear to 72 ft. lbs.

8. On vehicles with the 4A-GE engine, reinstall the sway bar and link; tighten the nut to 13 ft. lbs.

9. Install the ball joint attaching nuts and bolts and tighten them to 59 ft. lbs.

10. Have the wheel alignment checked by a reputable facility.

Prizm

NOTE: *Both lower control arms and the suspension crossmember must be removed as a unit even if only 1 arm is damaged.*

1. Raise and safely support the vehicle. Do not place the stands under the control arms or the suspension crossmember.

2. Remove the nuts and bolts holding the ball joints to the lower control arms.

3. Remove the nut and bolt holding the control arm rear brackets to the crossmember.

4. Place a floor jack under the suspension crossmember. Use a broad piece of wood between the jack and crossmember to evenly distribute the loading.

5. Remove the 6 bolts and 2 nuts holding the suspension crossmember. Carefully lower the crossmember (with the control arms attached) and remove from the car.

6. Remove the mounting bolt holding the control arm to the crossmember and remove the arm. Inspect the arm and bushing for damage, deformation or corrosion damage.

7. Install the control arm(s) to the crossmember and partially tighten the bolts. They should be tight enough to hold firmly, yet still be able to pivot when moderate force is applied.

8. Install the suspension crossmember and control arms to the body of the car and tighten the 6 nuts and 2 nuts.

9. Install the bolts holding the rear control arm brackets and partially tighten them.

10. Connect the ball joints to each arm and tighten the bolts to 105 ft. lbs.

11. Lower the vehicle to the ground. Bounce

the front end up and down several times to stabilize the suspension. The partially tightened joints will flex and seek a "normal" position.

12. With the vehicle on the ground (don't raise it or the suspension position will be lost), tighten the bolt holding the arm to the crossmember to 152 ft. lbs. Tighten the nut and bolt holding the rear bracket to the crossmember to 14 ft. lbs. and the rear bracket bolts to 94 ft. lbs.

13. Have the alignment checked by a reputable facility.

Knuckle, Hub and Wheel Bearing
REMOVAL, DISASSEMBLY AND INSTALLATION

WARNING: *The use of the correct tools is required for this repair. These procedures require the use of assorted joint separators, slide hammers, bearing pullers, seal extractors/drivers and snapring pliers which may not be in your tool box. Do not attempt repairs or disassembly if the correct tools are not available; damage and/or injury may result.*

Nova

1. Loosen the wheel nuts and the center axle nut.

2. Raise the vehicle and safely support it.

3. Remove the wheel.

4. Remove the brake hose retaining clip at the strut.

5. Disconnect the brake flex hose from the metal brake line. Use a small pan to collect spillage and plug the lines as soon as possible.

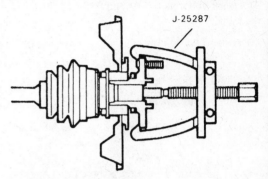

Removing the Nova driving axle.

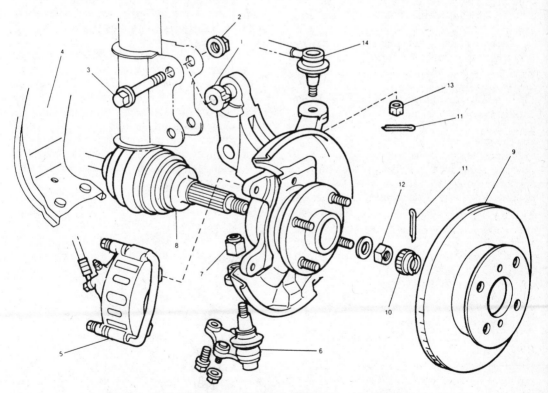

1. Camber adjustment cam	6. Lower ball joint	11. Cotter pin
2. Nut	7. Ball joint nut	12. Nut
3. Bolt	8. Drive axle	13. Tie rod ball joint nut
4. Lower control arm	9. Brake disc	14. Steering joint (tie rod
5. Brake caliper	10. Lock nut cap	joint)

Nova front hub and knuckle assembly

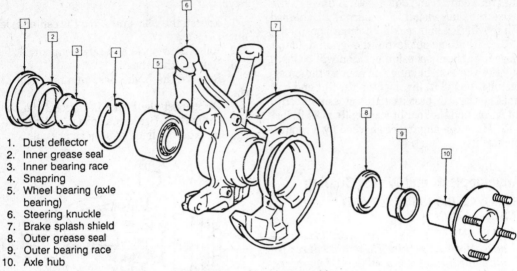

1. Dust deflector
2. Inner grease seal
3. Inner bearing race
4. Snapring
5. Wheel bearing (axle bearing)
6. Steering knuckle
7. Brake splash shield
8. Outer grease seal
9. Outer bearing race
10. Axle hub

Nova hub and bearing asembly

6. Remove the bolts holding the brake caliper to the knuckle; support the caliper with a piece of stiff wire out of the way.

7. Remove the brake disc.

8. Remove the drive axle nut. Use GM Tool J-25287 or equivalent to push out the drive axle.

9. Remove the cotter pin and the tie rod (steering rod) nut at the knuckle. Use a tie rod separator (GM Tool J-24329-01 or equivalent) to separate the joint.

10. Remove the nuts and bolt holding the ball joint to the control arm.

11. Matchmark the camber adjusting cam and the strut.

12. Remove the 2 bolts holding the knuckle to the strut. Remove the knuckle. The ball joint may be removed from the knuckle if desired.

13. Mount the knuckle securely in a vise. Use a screwdriver to remove the outer dust cover.

14. Using a slide hammer and puller (GM J-26941 or equivalent), remove the inner grease seal from the knuckle.

15. Remove the inner bearing snapring.

16. Remove the brake splash shield.

17. Remove the hub using an extractor such as GM Tools J-25287 and J-35378 or equivalent.

WARNING: *Whenever the hub is removed, the inner and outer grease seals MUST be replaced with new seals. The seals are not reusable.*

18. Use the same extractor to remove the outer bearing race from the hub.

19. Remove the outer grease seal with the slide hammer and puller.

20. Using a bearing driver of the correct size

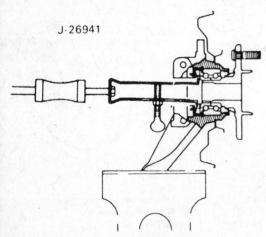

J-26941

Removing the Nova inner grease seal

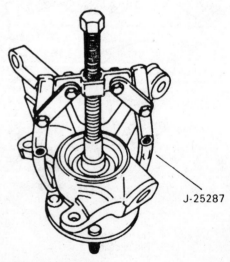

J-25287

Removing the Nova hub

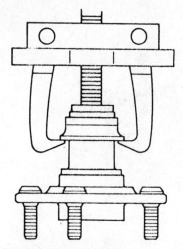

Removing the Nova outer bearing race

J-35737

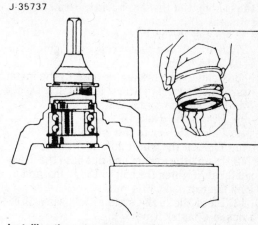

Installing the outer grease seal

(GM Tools J-35399 and J-35379 or equivalent), remove the bearing assembly.

21. Clean and inspect all parts but do not wash or clean the wheel bearing; it cannot be repacked. If the bearing is damaged or noisy, it must be replaced.

22. Using a bearing driver of the correct size (GM J-8092 and J-35411 or eqivalent), install the bearing into the hub.

23. Use a seal driver to install a new outer grease seal. (GM J-35737-1 or equivalent)

24. Apply sealer to the brake splash shield and install it to the knuckle.

25. Apply a layer of multi-purpose grease to the seal lip, seal and bearing. Install the hub with GM Tools J-8092 and J-35399 or equivalent.

26. Install the snapring.

27. Install a new inner grease seal using the correct size driver. (GM J-35737-2 or equivalent).

28. Install the outer dust cover (open end down) with GM Tool J-35379 or equivalent.

29. Install the lower ball joint to the control arm and tighten the nuts and bolt to 59 ft. lbs.

30. If the ball joint was removed from the knuckle, reinstall it. Install a new nut and temporarily tighten it to 14 ft. lbs. Back off the nut until clear of the knuckle and then retighten it to 82 ft. lbs.

31. Install the camber adjusting cam into the knuckle. Connect the knuckle to the strut lower bracket.

32. Insert the bolts from rear to front and align the matchmarks of the camber adjusting cam and the strut. Tighten the nuts to 105 ft. lbs. (4A-LC engine) or 166 ft. lbs. (4A-GE engines).

33. Connect the tie rod to the knuckle. Install the nut and tighten to 36 ft. lbs. Install the cotter pin.

34. Install the driveshaft into the hub.

35. Double check the nuts and bolt holding

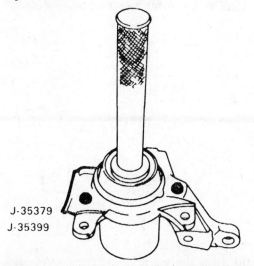

J-35379
J-35399

Removing the Nova wheel bearing

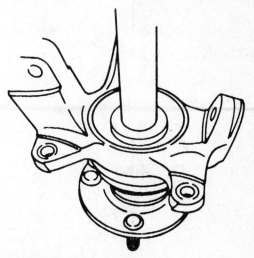

Installation of the Nova hub

the ball joint to the lower control arm. Correct torque is 59 ft. lbs.

36. Install the brake disc.

37. Reinstall the brake caliper. Tighten the bolts to 65 ft. lbs.

38. Connect the brake flex hose to the metal brake line. Correct tightness is 11 ft. lbs. Do not over-tighten this connection.

39. Install the wheel

40. Lower the car to the ground.

41. Tighten the wheel nuts to 76 ft. lbs.

42. Install the washer and nut onto the drive-shaft end. Tighten the bolt to 137 ft. lbs. and in-stall the cap and cotter pin.

43. Bleed the brake system, following direc-tions in Chapter Nine.

44. Have the alignment checked at a reputa-ble facility.

Prizm

1. Loosen the wheel nuts and the center axle nut.

2. Raise the vehicle and safely support it.

3. Remove the wheel.

4. Remove the center axle nut.

5. Remove the brake caliper and hang it out of the way on a piece of stiff wire. Do not discon-nect the brake line; do not allow the caliper to hang by the hose.

6. Remove the brake disc.

7. Remove the cotter pin and nut from the tie rod end.

8. Remove the tie rod end from the knuckle using a joint separator (GM Tool J-6627-A or equivalent).

9. Remove the bolt and 2 nuts holding the bottom of the ball joint to the control arm and remove the arm from the knuckle.

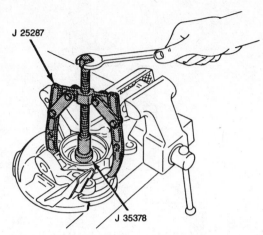

J 25287

J 35378

Prizm axle hub removal

10. Remove the 2 nuts from the steering knuckle. Place a protective cover or shield over the CV boot on the driveshaft.

11. Using a plastic mallet, tap the driveshaft free of the hub assembly.

12. Remove the 2 bolts and remove the axle hub assembly.

13. Clamp the knuckle in a vise with protect-ed jaws.

14. Remove the dust deflector. Loosen the nut holding the ball joint to the knuckle. Use a ball joint separator (GM Tool J-35413 or equiva-lent) to loosen and remove the joint

15. Use a slide hammer/extractor (GM Tool J-26941 or equivalent) to remove the outer oil seal.

16. Remove the snapring.

17. Using a hub puller and pilot (GM Tools J-25287 and J-35378 or equivalents), pull the axle hub from the knuckle.

18. Remove the brake splash shield (3 bolts).

19. Use a split plate bearing remover, puller

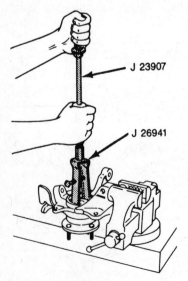

J 23907

J 26941

Removing Prizm oil seal

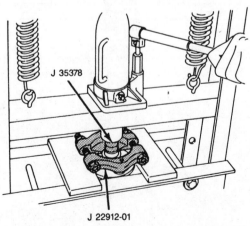

J 35378

J 22912-01

Using split plate tool to remove Prizm outer bearing race.

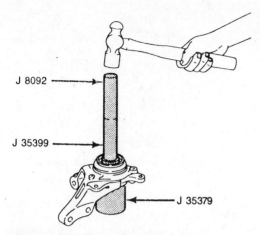

Removing Prizm inner bearing race

pilot and a shop press, remove the inner bearing race from the hub.

20. Remove the inner oil seal with the same tools used to remove the outer seal.

21. Place the inner race in the bearing. Support the knuckle and use an axle hub remover (GM Tool J-35399) with a plastic mallet to drive out the bearing.

22. Clean and inspect all parts but do not wash or clean the wheel bearing; it cannot be repacked. If the bearing is damaged or noisy, it must be replaced.

23. Press a new bearing race into the steering knuckle using a bearing driver of the correct size (GM J-8092 and J-37777 or equivalent).

24. Place a new bearing inner race on the hub bearing.

25. Insert the side lip of a new oil seal into the seal installer (GM J-35737-01 or equivalent) and drive the oil seal into the steering knuckle.

26. Apply multi-purpose grease to the oil seal lip.

27. Apply sealer to the brake splash shield and install the shield.

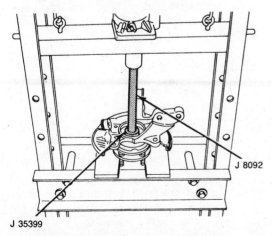

J 35399

Installing Prizm axle hub into steering knuckle

28. Use a hub installer (GM J-35399) to press the hub into the steering knuckle.

29. Install a new snapring into the hub.

30. Using a seal installer of the correct size, install a new outer oil seal into the steering knuckle.

31. Apply multi-purpose grease to the seal surfaces which will contact the driveshaft.

32. Support the knuckle and drive in a new dust deflector.

33. Install the ball joint into the knuckle and tighten the nut to 94 ft. lbs.

34. Temporarily install the hub assembly to the lower control arm and fit the driveaxle into the hub.

35. Install the knuckle to strut bolts, then install the tie rod end to the knuckle.

36. Tighten the strut bracket nuts to 194 ft. lbs. and tighten the tie rod end nut to 36 ft. lbs. Install the cotter pin.

37. Remove the old nut from the lower ball joint and install a new castle nut. Tighten the nut to 94 ft. lbs. and install a new cotter pin. (The old nut was used to draw the joint into the knuckle; the new nut assures retention.)

38. Connect the ball joint to the lower control arm and tighten the nuts to 105 ft. lbs.

39. Install the brake disc.

40. Install the brake caliper and tighten the bolts to 65 ft. lbs.

41. Install the center nut and washer on the drive axle.

42. Install the wheel

43. Lower the car to the ground.

44. Tighten the wheel nuts to 76 ft. lbs. and the axle bolt to 137 ft. lbs. Install the cap and cotter pin.

45. Remove the protective cover from the CV boot.

46. Have the alignment checked at a reputable facility.

Front End Alignment

Alignment of the front wheels is essential if your car is to go, stop and turn as designed. Alignment can be altered by collision, overloading, poor repair or bent components.

If you are diagnosing bizarre handling and/or poor road manners, the first place to look is the tires. Although the tires may wear as a result of an alignment problem, worn or poorly inflated tires can make you chase alignment problems which don't exist.

Once you have eliminated all other causes, unload everything from the trunk except the spare tire, set the tire pressures to the correct level and take the car to a reputable alignment facility. Since the alignment settings are measured in very small increments, it is almost impossible for the home mechanic to accurately determine the settings. The explanations that follow will help you understand the three dimensions of alignment: caster, camber and toe.

CASTER

Caster is the tilting of the steering axis either forward or backward from the vertical, when viewed from the side of the vehicle. A backward tilt is said to be positive and a forward tilt is said to be negative. Changes in caster affect the straight line tendency of the vehicle and the "return to center" of the steering after a turn. If the camber is radically different between the left and right wheels (such as after hitting a major pothole or curb), the car will exhibit a nasty pull to one side.

Caster is not adjustable on either the Nova or Prizm. The camber angle is fixed by the proper location of all the suspension components. If caster is found to be incorrect, the cause must be determined through examination of the suspension and body parts. Bent, loose or worn components must be replaced. Recent body work must also be considered as a cause; if the shock tower is not correctly located, the camber will not be correct.

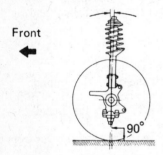

Front

Caster angle affects the tracking of the steering.

CAMBER

Camber is the tilting of the wheels from the vertical (leaning in or out) when viewed from

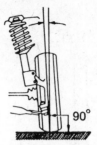

Camber is the inward or outward tilt of the wheel on the road.

the front of the vehicle. When the wheels tilt outward at the top, the camber is said to be positive. When the wheels tilt inward at the top the camber is said to be negative. The amount of tilt is measured in degrees from the vertical. This measurement is called camber angle.

Camber affects the position of the tire on the road surface during vertical suspension movement and cornering. Changes in camber affect the handling and ride qualities of the car as well as tire wear. Many tire wear patterns indicate camber related problems from misalignment, overloading or poor driving habits.

Camber is adjustable on the Nova and Prizm by turning the adjusting cam on each front strut. Anytime camber is adjusted, toe must be checked and reset if necessary.

TOE

Toe is the turning in or out (parallelism) of the wheels. The actual amount of toe setting is normally only a fraction of an inch. The purpose of toe-in (or out) specification is to ensure parallel rolling of the wheels. Toe-in also serves to offset the small deflections of the steering support system which occur when the vehicle is rolling forward or under braking.

Changing the toe setting will radically affect the overall "feel" of the steering, the behavior of the car under braking, tire wear and even fuel economy. Excessive toe (in or out) causes excessive drag or scrubbing on the tires.

Front Wheel Alignment Specifications

Years	Model	Caster (deg.)		Camber (deg.)		Toe-in (in.)
		Range	Pref.	Range	Pref.	
1985–88	Nova (4A-LC)	0.13P to 1.63P	0.88P	0.75N to 0.25P	0.5N	0.039
1988	Nova (4A-GE)	0 to 1.48P	0.74P	0.75N to 0.25P	0.5N	0.039
1989–90	Prizm (AT)	0.67P to 2.17P	1.42P	⁹⁄₁₀P to 1½P	⁹⁄₁₀P	0.039
1989–90	Prizm (MT)	0.58P to 2.08P	1.33P	½P to 1½P	¾P	0.039

Rear Wheel Alignment

| Years | Model | Camber (deg.) | | Toe-in (in.) |
		Range	Pref.	
85–88	Nova (All)	1.25N to 0.25P°	0.50N	0.15
89–90	Prizm (AT)	0.17N to 1.30P	0.57P	0.15
89–90	Prizm (MT)	0.08N to 1.40P	0.66P	0.15

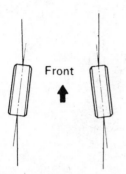

Toe in (or out) can affect tire wear and fuel economy.

Toe is adjustable on all Novas and Prizms and is generally measured either in fractional inches or degrees. It is adjusted by loosening the locknut on each tierod end and turning the rod until the correct reading is achieved. The rods left and right must remain equal in length during all adjustments.

REAR SUSPENSION

Spring and Shock Absorber/Mac-Pherson Struts

REMOVAL

Nova

1. Working inside the car, remove the shock absorber cover and rear window shelf. On some models it is necessary to remove the quarter window trim panel and the rear shelf to gain access to the shock mounts. Remove the speakers and/or speaker grilles as needed.
2. Raise the rear of the vehicle and support it with jackstands. Remove the wheel.
3. Disconnect the brake line from the flexible hose at the mounting bracket on the strut tube. Disconnect the flexible hose from the strut. Reconnect the 2 brake lines to each other but not to the strut. This will prevent excessive leakage.
4. Remove the 2 lower bolts holding the strut to the axle carrier.

5. Remove the 3 upper strut mounting nuts and carefully remove the strut assembly.
WARNING: *Do not loosen the center nut on the top of the shock absorber piston.*

DISASSEMBLY

CAUTION: *This procedure requires the use of a spring compressor; it cannot be performed without one. If you do not have access to this special tool, do not attempt to disassemble the strut. The coil springs are retained under considerable pressure. They can exert enough force to cause serious injury! Exercise extreme caution when disassembling the strut.*
1. Place the strut assembly in a pipe vise or strut vise.
WARNING: *Do not attempt to clamp the strut assembly in a flat jaw vise as this will result in damage to the strut tube.*
2. Attach a spring compressor and compress the spring until the upper suspension support is free of any spring tension. Do not over-compress the spring.
3. Hold the upper support and then remove the nut on the end of the shock piston rod.
4. Remove the support, coil spring, insulator and bumper.

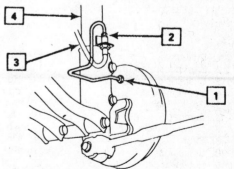

1. BRAKE LINE FITTING AT WHEEL CYLINDER
2. FITTING AT FLEXIBLE HOSE
3. FLEXIBLE HOSE
4. STRUT ASSEMBLY

Nova brake lines and strut bracket

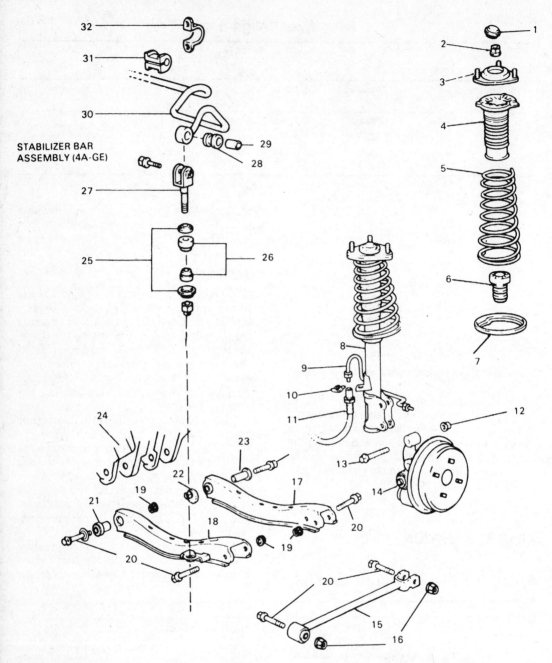

STABILIZER BAR
ASSEMBLY (4A-GE)

1. Dust cover	12. Nut	22. Toe-in adjusting cam nut
2. Strut piston rod nut	13. Bolt	23. Toe-in indicator
3. Suspension support	14. Hub carrier and brake	24. Body
4. Upper insulator	drum assembly	25. Retainer
5. Coil spring	15. Strut rod	26. Cushion
6. Bumper	16. Nut	27. Sway bar link
7. Lower insulator	17. No. 2 arm (rearward)	28. Bushing
8. Strut	18. No. 1 arm (forward)	29. Collar
9. Brake line	19. Nut	30. Sway bar
10. Retaining clip	20. Bolt	31. Bushing
11. Flexible brake hose	21. Bushing	32. Bracket

Nova rear suspension components

INSPECTION

Check the shock absorber by moving the piston shaft through its full range of travel. It should move smoothly and evenly throughout its entire travel without any trace of binding or notching. Use a small straightedge to check the piston shaft for any bending or deformation. If a shock absorber is replaced, the old one should be drilled at the bottom to vent the internal gas. Wear safety goggles and drill a small hole (2-3mm) into the base of the shock absorber. The

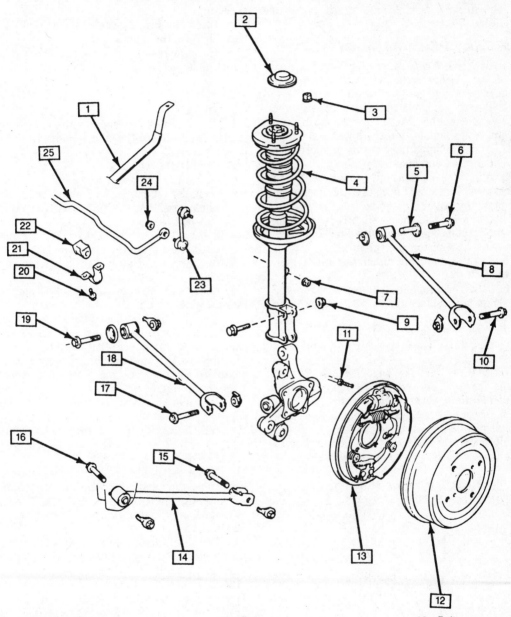

1. Fuel tank retaining strap	10. Bolt	19. Bolt
2. Tower cover	11. Brake line	20. Bolt
3. Strut piston rod nut	12. Brake drum	21. Bracket
4. Strut	13. Brake assembly	22. Bushing
5. Toe-in adjusting bolt	14. Strut rod	23. Sway bar link
6. Bolt	15. Bolt	24. Sway bar link nut
7. Nut	16. Bolt	25. Sway bar
8. No.2 arm (rearward)	17. Bolt	
9. Nut	18. No.1 arm (forward)	

Prizm rear suspension components

gas within the strut is colorless, odorless and non-toxic, but should be vented to make the unit safe for disposal.

Inspect the spring for any sign of deterioration or cracking. The waterproof coating on the coils should be intact to prevent rusting.

CAUTION: *Do not turn the piston rod within the cylinder if the piston rod is fully extended!*

ASSEMBLY AND INSTALLATION

WARNING: *Never reuse a self-locking nut! Always replace self-locking nuts with new hardware.*

1. Loosely assemble all components onto the the strut assembly. Make sure the spring end aligns with the hollow in the lower seat.

2. Align the upper suspension support with the piston rod and install the support.

3. Align the suspension support with the strut lower bracket. This assures the spring will be properly seated top and bottom.

4. Compress the spring slightly by pushing on the suspension support with one hand to expose the strut piston rod threads.

5. Install a new strut piston nut and tighten it to 36 ft. lbs.

6. Place the complete strut assembly into the lower mount and pin it in position with the bolts.

7. Use a floor jack to gently raise the suspension and guide the upper strut mount into position.

CAUTION: *The car is on jackstands. Elevate the floor jack only enough to swing the strut into position; do not raise the car!*

8. Disconnect the flexible brake line and the metal pipe. Connect the flexible hose to the strut, then reconnect the metal brake line to the flexible hose.

1. SUSPENSION SUPPORT
2. STRUT LOWER BRACKET

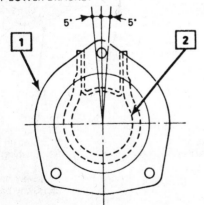

Correct relationship of upper and lower mounts when reassembling Nova rear strut.

9. Tighten the lower strut retaining nuts and bolts to 105 ft. lbs.

10. Tighten the 3 upper retaining bolts to 17 ft. lbs.

11. Install the wheel.

12. Lower the vehicle to the ground.

13. Reinstall the interior components as necessary.

14. Bleed the brake system. Please refer to Chapter Nine for complete directions.

15. Have the rear wheel alignment checked at a reputable facility.

Prizm

1. Elevate and safely support the vehicle on stands. Do not place the stands under the suspension arms.

2. Remove the wheel.

3. Disconnect the metal brake line from the wheel cylinder (at the backing plate) and from the flexible hose. Plug the lines as soon as possible to prevent leakage.

4. Remove the clip from the brake hose and remove the hose from the strut bracket.

5. Disconnect the sway bar link from the strut.

6. Remove the strut mounting bolts from the rear knuckle.

7. Remove the seat back side cushion (Sedan) or the rear sill side panel (Hatchback) to gain access to the upper strut mount.

8. Remove the 3 nuts holding the upper strut mount to the body. Do not loosen the center strut piston nut.

9. Remove the strut assembly from the vehicle.

NOTE: *Inspection and disassembly of the strut is the same as Nova, discussed previously.*

10. When reinstalling, place the assembled strut in position and install the 3 upper retaining nuts, tightening them to 29 ft. lbs.

11. Reinstall the seat back side cushion or the rear sill side panel.

12. Install the strut into the rear knuckle assembly; install the bolts and nuts and tighten them to 105 ft. lbs.

13. Reconnect the sway bar link to the strut. Tighten the bolts to 26 ft. lbs.

14. Connect the flexible brake hose into the bracket and install the clip.

15. Connect the metal line at the flexible hose and at the wheel cylinder. Make certain the fittings are properly threaded before tightening them.

16. Bleed the brake system. Please refer to Chapter Nine for complete instructions.

17. Reinstall the wheel.

18. Lower the car to the ground.

19. Have the rear alignment checked at a reputable repair facility.

Control Arms

REMOVAL

Nova and Prizm vehicles use two control arms on each rear wheel. To avoid the obvious confusion of referring to a "front rear control arm", they are referred to as No. 1 and No. 2, with arm No.1 being the closest to the front of the car.

No. 1 Arm

1. Raise and safely support the vehicle.
2. Disconnect the sway bar link if so equipped.
3. Remove the bolt holding the arm to the body.
4. Remove the bolt holding the arm to the suspension knuckle.
5. Remove the arm.

No. 2 Arm

1. Raise and safely support the vehicle.
2. Observe and matchmark the position of the adjusting cam at the body mount.
3. Disconnect the bolt holding the arm to the suspension knuckle.
4. Disconnect the bolt holding the arm to the body.
5. Remove the arm.
6. Inspect the arms for any bending or cracking. If the arm is not true in all dimensions, it must be replaced. Any attempt to straighten a bent arm will damage it. Also check the bushings within the ends of the arms and replace any which are deformed or too spongy. If a bushing must be replaced, do not grease it before installation.

INSTALLATION

1. Place the arm in position, install the arm to body bolts and partially tighten them. If installing arm No. 2, make sure the matchmarks for the adjusting cam are aligned.
2. Install the arm to the knuckle and partially tighten the bolts.
3. Reconnect the sway bar link if it was removed. Use a new nut and tighten it to 11 ft. lbs.
4. Install the wheel.
5. Lower the car to the ground. Bounce the car rear and front several times to position the suspension.
6. Tighten the retaining bolts at the body and the knuckle: Nova, 64 ft. lbs. and Prizm, 87 ft. lbs.
7. Have the alignment checked at a reputable facility.

Stabilizer Bar (Sway Bar)
REMOVAL AND INSTALLATION
Nova

1. Raise and safely support the vehicle
2. Remove the rear wheels.
3. Remove the nuts, retainers and cushions holding the sway bar links to the control arm.
4. Remove the bolts holding the stabilizer to the body.
5. Remove the bar with the links attached.
6. Remove and discard the bolts holding the links to the sway bar.
7. When reassembling, install new bolts to hold the links to the sway bar but do not tighten the bolts.
8. Place the bar in position and install but do not tighten the bolts holding the brackets to the body.
9. Connect the sway bar links to the control arms. Use new nuts and tighten them to 11 ft. lbs.
10. Tighten the bracket bolts to 9 ft. lbs. and then tighten the bolts holding the sway bar to the links to 22 ft. lbs.
11. Install the rear wheels.
12. Lower the car to the ground.

Prizm

1. Using either a transmission jack or a floor jack with a broad piece of wood, support the fuel tank from below. Use care not to dent or deform the tank.
2. Remove the fuel tank retaining straps.
3. Disconnect the stabilizer links from the strut assemblies.
4. Disconnect the stabilizer bar bracket bolts.
5. Remove the bar.
6. When reinstalling, place the bar in position, attach the body retaining brackets and then connect the links to the strut on each side.
7. Tighten the body bracket bolts to 14 ft. lbs. and the link bolts (both ends) to 26 ft. lbs.

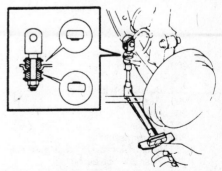

Note the position of bushings when reassembling the Nova rear stabilizer bar.

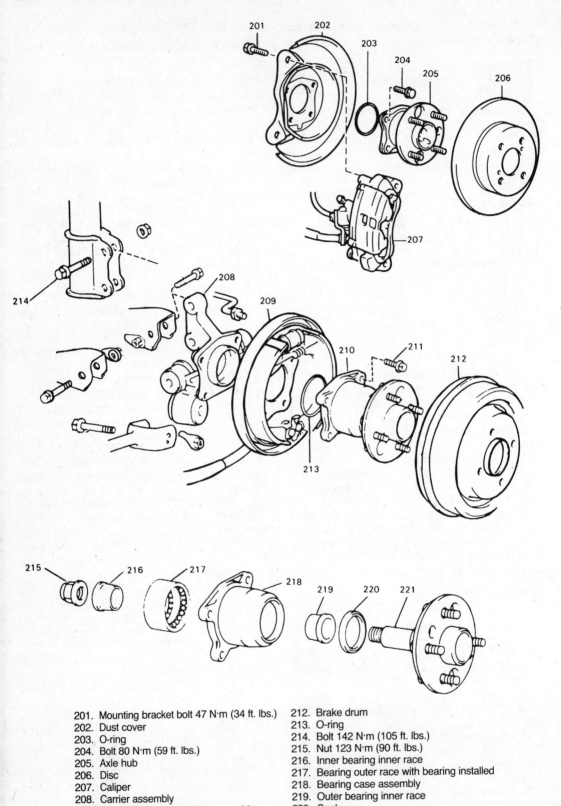

201. Mounting bracket bolt 47 N·m (34 ft. lbs.)	212. Brake drum
202. Dust cover	213. O-ring
203. O-ring	214. Bolt 142 N·m (105 ft. lbs.)
204. Bolt 80 N·m (59 ft. lbs.)	215. Nut 123 N·m (90 ft. lbs.)
205. Axle hub	216. Inner bearing inner race
206. Disc	217. Bearing outer race with bearing installed
207. Caliper	218. Bearing case assembly
208. Carrier assembly	219. Outer bearing inner race
209. Rear brake backing plate assembly	220. Seal
210. Rear axle hub assembly	221. Axle hub
211. Bolt 80 N·m (59 ft. lbs.)	

Nova rear hub and bearing components

8. Reinstall the fuel tank straps and tighten the bolts to 29 ft. lbs.

9. Remove the tank support jack.

Rear Wheel Bearing and Rear Axle Hub

REMOVAL AND INSTALLATION

WARNING: *The use of the correct tools is required for this repair. These procedures require the use of assorted bearing pullers, seal extractors/drivers and slide hammers which may not be in your tool box. Do not attempt repairs or disassembly if the correct tools are not available; damage and/or injury may result.*

Nova

1. Raise and safely support the vehicle.

2. Remove the wheel.

3. Remove the brake drum (4A-LC) or brake caliper and brake disc (4A-GE). If the caliper is removed, suspend it out of the way with a piece of stiff wire; do not let it hang by the hose.

CAUTION: *Brake pads and shoes contain asbestos, which has been determined to be a cancer causing agent. Never clean the brake surfaces with compressed air! Avoid inhaling any dust from brake surfaces! When cleaning brakes, use commercially available brake cleaning fluids.*

4. On 4A-LC, disconnect the brake line from the wheel cylinder.

5. Remove the 4 bolts holding the axle hub/ bearing assembly to the axle carrier and remove the hub and bearing assembly.

6. Remove the splash shield (4A-GE) or the rear brake shoes (4A-LC), then remove the O-ring. It must be replaced at reassembly.

7. Place the hub/bearing assembly in a vise with protected jaws. Do not clamp the hub any tighter than needed to hold it securely.

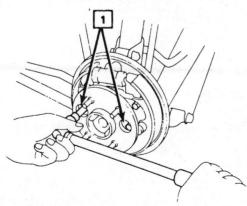

1. AXLE HUB BOLT ACCESS HOLES

Removing the axle hub from the brake backing plate.

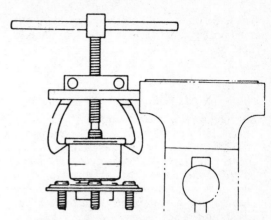

Removing the Nova bearing case from the hub. Note that the tool is clamped in the vise, not the hub. The outboard bearing inner race is removed in the same fashion.

8. Remove the hub nut.

9. Using an extractor such as GM Tool J-25287 or equivalent, remove the bearing case from the axle hub.

10. Remove the inner race, the inboard bearing and the outboard bearing.

11. Use the extractor again to remove the inner race from the outboard bearing.

12. Remove the seal from the axle hub.

13. To remove the outer bearing race, install the outboard bearing inner race so that it pushes against the outer race. Use Tool J-35440 or similar to press the race free.

NOTE: *Whenever the bearing assembly is removed, it must be replaced with a new bearing assembly. Reuse of the bearing after disassembly is NOT recommended.*

14. To reassemble, apply grease around the bearing outer race.

15. Press the new bearing outer race into the bearing case with Tool J-35400 or equivalent.

16. Install new bearings (inner and outer) and the inner races into the bearing case.

17. Lightly coat a new bearing seal with multi-purpose grease and install with a seal driver such as GM Tool J-35736 or equivalent.

18. Install the bearing case onto the hub with GM Tool J-35440 or equivalent.

19. Tighten the rear nut to 90 ft. lbs. and stake the nut with a chisel.

20. Install a new O-ring to the axle carrier.

21. Assemble the hub to either the brake backing plate (4A-LC) or the splash shield (4A-GE) and install. Tighten the bolts to 59 ft. lbs.

22. On 4A-LC cars, reinstall the rear brake shoes and connect the brake line to the wheel cylinder.

23. Reinstall either the rear brake drum or the brake disc and caliper.

24. Install the wheel and lower the car to the ground.

25. Refill the master cylinder and bleed the brake system, following instructions in Chapter Nine.

Prizm

1. Raise and safely support the vehicle.
2. Remove the wheel.
3. Remove the brake drum.

CAUTION: *Brake pads and shoes contain asbestos, which has been determined to be a cancer causing agent. Never clean the brake surfaces with compressed air! Avoid inhaling any dust from brake surfaces! When cleaning brakes, use commercially available brake cleaning fluids.*

4. Remove the 4 bolts holding the axle hub/ bearing assembly to the axle carrier and remove the hub and bearing assembly.
5. Remove the O-ring from the backing plate.
6. Mount the hub/bearing assembly in a vise with protected jaws.
7. Use a hammer and chisel (not a screwdriver) to unstake the wheel bearing lock nut.
8. Remove the lock nut.
9. Using a split plate bearing remover, a race puller pilot and an axle shaft puller (GM Tools J-22912, J-38278 and J-8433 respectively), separate the axle shaft from the hub.
10. Using the same tools, remove the inner bearing race.
11. Use a slide hammer and seal puller to remove the oil seal from the axle shaft.
12. Press the inner race off with a bearing race remover such as GM Tool J-35400 or equivalent.
13. Clean all components thoroughly and examine for any signs of cracking, abrasion or corrosion. Whenever the wheel bearings are re-

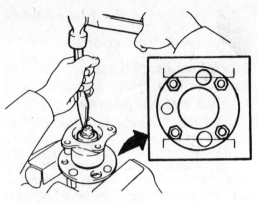

Unstaking the Prizm locknut

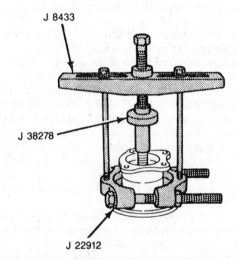

Removing the Prizm axle shaft from the hub. The inner race is separated from the axle shaft with the same tools.

1. Wheel bearing locknut
2. Bearing inner race
3. Bearing outer race
4. Axle shaft
5. Hub bolt
6. Oil seal
7. Axle hub
8. Bearing

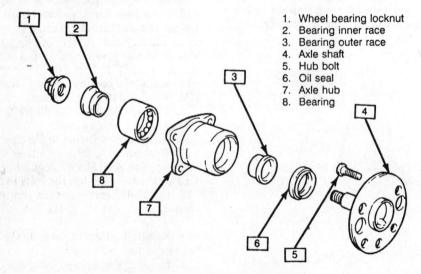

Prizm hub and bearing components

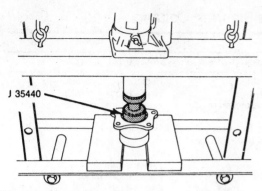

J 35440

Pressing the Prizm bearing race into the axle hub

moved or disassembled, they must be replaced with new bearings. Reuse of the old bearings is NOT recommended.

14. To reassemble, apply multi-purpose grease around the outer race of a new bearing and install the bearing into the inner race.

15. Using a seal installer and slide hammer, install a new oil seal onto the axle shaft.

16. Using the proper size installation tool, press the bearing and bearing outer race into the axle hub.

17. Press the bearing inner race into the axle hub.

18. Press the outer race onto the axle shaft.

19. Install a new wheel bearing lock nut and tighten it to 90 ft. lbs. Use a hammer and chisel the stake the nut in place.

20. Install a new O-ring onto the knuckle.

21. Place the axle hub/bearing assembly in position, install the bolts and tighten them to 59 ft. lbs.

22. Reinstall the brake drum.

23. Install the wheel and lower the car to the ground.

24. Although this repair should not have affected the rear alignment, it is recommended that the alignment be checked and adjusted if necessary.

Rear Wheel Alignment

The proper alignment of the rear wheels is as important as the alignment of the front wheels and should be checked periodically. The rear wheels are adjustable for both camber and toe. If the rear wheels are misaligned – particularly a toe-in error on one side – the car will exhibit unpredictable handling characteristics. The usual symptoms include a different turning responses into left and right corners and difficulty in maintaining a straight path, both due to the rear wheels attempting to steer the car. This "rear steer" behavior is particularly hazardous on slick surfaces; the back wheels of the car may attempt to go in directions unrelated to the front during braking or turning maneuvers.

STEERING

Steering Wheel
REMOVAL AND INSTALLATION

CAUTION: *Do not attempt to remove or install the steering wheel by hammering on it. Damage to the energy-absorbing steering column could result.*

1. Disconnect the negative battery cable.

2. Loosen the trim pad retaining screws from the back side of the steering wheel.

3. Lift the trim pad and horn button assembly(ies) from the wheel.

4. Remove the steering wheel hub retaining nut and washer.

5. Scratch matchmarks on the hub and shaft to aid in correct installation.

6. Use a steering wheel puller to remove the steering wheel.

7. Installation is performed in the reverse order of removal. Tighten the wheel retaining nut to 25 ft. lb.

Removing the steering wheel pad

Using a steering wheel puller to remove the steering wheel

Troubleshooting the Steering Column

Problem	Cause	Solution
Will not lock	• Lockbolt spring broken or defective	• Replace lock bolt spring
High effort (required to turn ignition key and lock cylinder)	• Lock cylinder defective	• Replace lock cylinder
	• Ignition switch defective	• Replace ignition switch
	• Rack preload spring broken or deformed	• Replace preload spring
	• Burr on lock sector, lock rack, housing, support or remote rod coupling	• Remove burr
	• Bent sector shaft	• Replace shaft
	• Defective lock rack	• Replace lock rack
	• Remote rod bent, deformed	• Replace rod
	• Ignition switch mounting bracket bent	• Straighten or replace
	• Distorted coupling slot in lock rack (tilt column)	• Replace lock rack
Will stick in "start"	• Remote rod deformed	• Straighten or replace
	• Ignition switch mounting bracket bent	• Straighten or replace
Key cannot be removed in "off-lock"	• Ignition switch is not adjusted correctly	• Adjust switch
	• Defective lock cylinder	• Replace lock cylinder
Lock cylinder can be removed without depressing retainer	• Lock cylinder with defective retainer	• Replace lock cylinder
	• Burr over retainer slot in housing cover or on cylinder retainer	• Remove burr
High effort on lock cylinder between "off" and "off-lock"	• Distorted lock rack	• Replace lock rack
	• Burr on tang of shift gate (automatic column)	• Remove burr
	• Gearshift linkage not adjusted	• Adjust linkage
Noise in column	• One click when in "off-lock" position and the steering wheel is moved (all except automatic column)	• Normal—lock bolt is seating
	• Coupling bolts not tightened	• Tighten pinch bolts
	• Lack of grease on bearings or bearing surfaces	• Lubricate with chassis grease
	• Upper shaft bearing worn or broken	• Replace bearing assembly
	• Lower shaft bearing worn or broken	• Replace bearing. Check shaft and replace if scored.
	• Column not correctly aligned	• Align column
	• Coupling pulled apart	• Replace coupling
	• Broken coupling lower joint	• Repair or replace joint and align column
	• Steering shaft snap ring not seated	• Replace ring. Check for proper seating in groove.
	• Shroud loose on shift bowl. Housing loose on jacket—will be noticed with ignition in "off-lock" and when torque is applied to steering wheel.	• Position shroud over lugs on shift bowl. Tighten mounting screws.
High steering shaft effort	• Column misaligned	• Align column
	• Defective upper or lower bearing	• Replace as required
	• Tight steering shaft universal joint	• Repair or replace
	• Flash on I.D. of shift tube at plastic joint (tilt column only)	• Replace shift tube
	• Upper or lower bearing seized	• Replace bearings
Lash in mounted column assembly	• Column mounting bracket bolts loose	• Tighten bolts
	• Broken weld nuts on column jacket	• Replace column jacket
	• Column capsule bracket sheared	• Replace bracket assembly

Troubleshooting the Steering Column (cont.)

Problem	Cause	Solution
Lash in mounted column assembly (cont.)	• Column bracket to column jacket mounting bolts loose	• Tighten to specified torque
	• Loose lock shoes in housing (tilt column only)	• Replace shoes
	• Loose pivot pins (tilt column only)	• Replace pivot pins and support
	• Loose lock shoe pin (tilt column only)	• Replace pin and housing
	• Loose support screws (tilt column only)	• Tighten screws
Housing loose (tilt column only)	• Excessive clearance between holes in support or housing and pivot pin diameters	• Replace pivot pins and support
	• Housing support-screws loose	• Tighten screws
Steering wheel loose—every other tilt position (tilt column only)	• Loose fit between lock shoe and lock shoe pivot pin	• Replace lock shoes and pivot pin
Steering column not locking in any tilt position (tilt column only)	• Lock shoe seized on pivot pin	• Replace lock shoes and pin
	• Lock shoe grooves have burrs or are filled with foreign material	• Clean or replace lock shoes
	• Lock shoe springs weak or broken	• Replace springs
Noise when tilting column (tilt column only)	• Upper tilt bumpers worn	• Replace tilt bumper
	• Tilt spring rubbing in housing	• Lubricate with chassis grease
One click when in "off-lock" position and the steering wheel is moved	• Seating of lock bolt	• None. Click is normal characteristic sound produced by lock bolt as it seats.
High shift effort (automatic and tilt column only)	• Column not correctly aligned	• Align column
	• Lower bearing not aligned correctly	• Assemble correctly
	• Lack of grease on seal or lower bearing areas	• Lubricate with chassis grease
Improper transmission shifting—automatic and tilt column only	• Sheared shift tube joint	• Replace shift tube
	• Improper transmission gearshift linkage adjustment	• Adjust linkage
	• Loose lower shift lever	• Replace shift tube

Troubleshooting the Ignition Switch

Problem	Cause	Solution
Ignition switch electrically inoperative	• Loose or defective switch connector	• Tighten or replace connector
	• Feed wire open (fusible link)	• Repair or replace
	• Defective ignition switch	• Replace ignition switch
Engine will not crank	• Ignition switch not adjusted properly	• Adjust switch
Ignition switch wil not actuate mechanically	• Defective ignition switch	• Replace switch
	• Defective lock sector	• Replace lock sector
	• Defective remote rod	• Replace remote rod
Ignition switch cannot be adjusted correctly	• Remote rod deformed	• Repair, straighten or replace

Troubleshooting the Turn Signal Switch

Problem	Cause	Solution
Turn signal will not cancel	• Loose switch mounting screws • Switch or anchor bosses broken • Broken, missing or out of position detent, or cancelling spring	• Tighten screws • Replace switch • Reposition springs or replace switch as required
Turn signal difficult to operate	• Turn signal lever loose • Switch yoke broken or distorted • Loose or misplaced springs • Foreign parts and/or materials in switch • Switch mounted loosely	• Tighten mounting screws • Replace switch • Reposition springs or replace switch • Remove foreign parts and/or material • Tighten mounting screws
Turn signal will not indicate lane change	• Broken lane change pressure pad or spring hanger • Broken, missing or misplaced lane change spring • Jammed wires	• Replace switch • Replace or reposition as required • Loosen mounting screws, reposition wires and retighten screws
Turn signal will not stay in turn position	• Foreign material or loose parts impeding movement of switch yoke • Defective switch	• Remove material and/or parts • Replace switch
Hazard switch cannot be pulled out	• Foreign material between hazard support cancelling leg and yoke	• Remove foreign material. No foreign material impeding function of hazard switch—replace turn signal switch.
No turn signal lights	• Inoperative turn signal flasher • Defective or blown fuse • Loose chassis to column harness connector • Disconnect column to chassis connector. Connect new switch to chassis and operate switch by hand. If vehicle lights now operate normally, signal switch is inoperative • If vehicle lights do not operate, check chassis wiring for opens, grounds, etc.	• Replace turn signal flasher • Replace fuse • Connect securely • Replace signal switch • Repair chassis wiring as required
Instrument panel turn indicator lights on but not flashing	• Burned out or damaged front or rear turn signal bulb • If vehicle lights do not operate, check light sockets for high resistance connections, the chassis wiring for opens, grounds, etc. • Inoperative flasher • Loose chassis to column harness connection • Inoperative turn signal switch • To determine if turn signal switch is defective, substitute new switch into circuit and operate switch by hand. If the vehicle's lights operate normally, signal switch is inoperative.	• Replace bulb • Repair chassis wiring as required • Replace flasher • Connect securely • Replace turn signal switch • Replace turn signal switch
Stop light not on when turn indicated	• Loose column to chassis connection • Disconnect column to chassis connector. Connect new switch into system without removing old.	• Connect securely • Replace signal switch

Troubleshooting the Turn Signal Switch (cont.)

Problem	Cause	Solution
Stop light not on when turn indicated (cont.)	Operate switch by hand. If brake lights work with switch in the turn position, signal switch is defective.	
	• If brake lights do not work, check connector to stop light sockets for grounds, opens, etc.	• Repair connector to stop light circuits using service manual as guide
Turn indicator panel lights not flashing	• Burned out bulbs	• Replace bulbs
	• High resistance to ground at bulb socket	• Replace socket
	• Opens, ground in wiring harness from front turn signal bulb socket to indicator lights	• Locate and repair as required
Turn signal lights flash very slowly	• High resistance ground at light sockets	• Repair high resistance grounds at light sockets
	• Incorrect capacity turn signal flasher or bulb	• Replace turn signal flasher or bulb
	• If flashing rate is still extremely slow, check chassis wiring harness from the connector to light sockets for high resistance	• Locate and repair as required
	• Loose chassis to column harness connection	• Connect securely
	• Disconnect column to chassis connector. Connect new switch into system without removing old. Operate switch by hand. If flashing occurs at normal rate, the signal switch is defective.	• Replace turn signal switch
Hazard signal lights will not flash—turn signal functions normally	• Blow fuse	• Replace fuse
	• Inoperative hazard warning flasher	• Replace hazard warning flasher in fuse panel
	• Loose chassis-to-column harness connection	• Conect securely
	• Disconnect column to chassis connector. Connect new switch into system without removing old. Depress the hazard warning lights. If they now work normally, turn signal switch is defective.	• Replace turn signal switch
	• If lights do not flash, check wiring harness "K" lead for open between hazard flasher and connector. If open, fuse block is defective	• Repair or replace brown wire or connector as required

Combination Switch
REMOVAL AND INSTALLATION

1. Disconnect the negative battery cable.
2. Remove the lower dash cover and the air duct.
3. On Prizm vehicles, remove the upper and lower steering column covers. On Nova vehicles, remove the lower column cover; the upper cover will come off with the switch.
4. Remove the steering wheel.
5. Disconnect the wiring at the connector.
6. Unscrew the mounting screws and remove the switch. The Nova switch will come off with the upper column cover.

7. When reinstalling, place the switch in position and tighten the bolts.
8. Connect the wiring harness and reinstall the steering wheel.
9. Reinstall the column cover(s).
10. Install the lower dash trim panel.
11. Connect the negative battery cable.

Ignition Switch/Ignition Lock
REMOVAL AND INSTALLATION

1. Disconnect the negative battery cable.
2. Unscrew the retaining screws and remove the upper and lower steering column covers.

3. Remove the 2 retaining screws and remove the steering column trim.

4. Turn the ignition key to the **ACC** position.

5. Push the lock cylinder stop in with a small, round object (cotter pin, punch, etc.) and pull out the ignition key and the lock cylinder.

NOTE: *You may find that removing the steering wheel and the combination switch makes the job easier.*

6. Loosen the mounting screw and withdraw the ignition switch from the lock housing.

7. When reinstalling, position the switch so

Troubleshooting the Manual Steering Gear

Problem	Cause	Solution
Hard or erratic steering	• Incorrect tire pressure	• Inflate tires to recommended pressures
	• Insufficient or incorrect lubrication	• Lubricate as required (refer to Maintenance Section)
	• Suspension, or steering linkage parts damaged or misaligned	• Repair or replace parts as necessary
	• Improper front wheel alignment	• Adjust incorrect wheel alignment angles
	• Incorrect steering gear adjustment	• Adjust steering gear
	• Sagging springs	• Replace springs
Play or looseness in steering	• Steering wheel loose	• Inspect shaft spines and repair as necessary. Tighten attaching nut and stake in place.
	• Steering linkage or attaching parts loose or worn	• Tighten, adjust, or replace faulty components
	• Pitman arm loose	• Inspect shaft splines and repair as necessary. Tighten attaching nut and stake in place
	• Steering gear attaching bolts loose	• Tighten bolts
	• Loose or worn wheel bearings	• Adjust or replace bearings
	• Steering gear adjustment incorrect or parts badly worn	• Adjust gear or replace defective parts
Wheel shimmy or tramp	• Improper tire pressure	• Inflate tires to recommended pressures
	• Wheels, tires, or brake rotors out-of-balance or out-of-round	• Inspect and replace or balance parts
	• Inoperative, worn, or loose shock absorbers or mounting parts	• Repair or replace shocks or mountings
	• Loose or worn steering or suspension parts	• Tighten or replace as necessary
	• Loose or worn wheel bearings	• Adjust or replace bearings
	• Incorrect steering gear adjustments	• Adjust steering gear
	• Incorrect front wheel alignment	• Correct front wheel alignment
Tire wear	• Improper tire pressure	• Inflate tires to recommended pressures
	• Failure to rotate tires	• Rotate tires
	• Brakes grabbing	• Adjust or repair brakes
	• Incorrect front wheel alignment	• Align incorrect angles
	• Broken or damaged steering and suspension parts	• Repair or replace defective parts
	• Wheel runout	• Replace faulty wheel
	• Excessive speed on turns	• Make driver aware of conditions
Vehicle leads to one side	• Improper tire pressures	• Inflate tires to recommended pressures
	• Front tires with uneven tread depth, wear pattern, or different cord design (i.e., one bias ply and one belted or radial tire on front wheels)	• Install tires of same cord construction and reasonably even tread depth, design, and wear pattern
	• Incorrect front wheel alignment	• Align incorrect angles
	• Brakes dragging	• Adjust or repair brakes
	• Pulling due to uneven tire construction	• Replace faulty tire

Troubleshooting the Power Steering Gear

Problem	Cause	Solution
Hissing noise in steering gear	• There is some noise in all power steering systems. One of the most common is a hissing sound most evident at standstill parking. There is no relationship between this noise and performance of the steering. Hiss may be expected when steering wheel is at end of travel or when slowly turning at standstill.	• Slight hiss is normal and in no way affects steering. Do not replace valve unless hiss is extremely objectionable. A replacement valve will also exhibit slight noise and is not always a cure. Investigate clearance around flexible coupling rivets. Be sure steering shaft and gear are aligned so flexible coupling rotates in a flat plane and is not distorted as shaft rotates. Any metal-to-metal contacts through flexible coupling will transmit valve hiss into passenger compartment through the steering column.
Rattle or chuckle noise in steering gear	• Gear loose on frame	• Check gear-to-frame mounting screws. Tighten screws to 88 N·m (65 foot pounds) torque.
	• Steering linkage looseness	• Check linkage pivot points for wear. Replace if necessary.
	• Pressure hose touching other parts of car	• Adjust hose position. Do not bend tubing by hand.
	• Loose pitman shaft over center adjustment	• Adjust to specifications
	NOTE: A slight rattle may occur on turns because of increased clearance off the "high point." This is normal and clearance must not be reduced below specified limits to eliminate this slight rattle.	
	• Loose pitman arm	• Tighten pitman arm nut to specifications
Squawk noise in steering gear when turning or recovering from a turn	• Damper O-ring on valve spool cut	• Replace damper O-ring
Poor return of steering wheel to center	• Tires not properly inflated	• Inflate to specified pressure
	• Lack of lubrication in linkage and ball joints	• Lube linkage and ball joints
	• Lower coupling flange rubbing against steering gear adjuster plug	• Loosen pinch bolt and assemble properly
	• Steering gear to column misalignment	• Align steering column
	• Improper front wheel alignment	• Check and adjust as necessary
	• Steering linkage binding	• Replace pivots
	• Ball joints binding	• Replace ball joints
	• Steering wheel rubbing against housing	• Align housing
	• Tight or frozen steering shaft bearings	• Replace bearings
	• Sticking or plugged valve spool	• Remove and clean or replace valve
	• Steering gear adjustments over specifications	• Check adjustment with gear out of car. Adjust as required.
	• Kink in return hose	• Replace hose
Car leads to one side or the other (keep in mind road condition and wind. Test car in both directions on flat road)	• Front end misaligned	• Adjust to specifications
	• Unbalanced steering gear valve	• Replace valve
	NOTE: If this is cause, steering effort will be very light in direction of lead and normal or heavier in opposite direction	

Troubleshooting the Power Steering Gear (cont.)

Problem	Cause	Solution
Momentary increase in effort when turning wheel fast to right or left	• Low oil level • Pump belt slipping • High internal leakage	• Add power steering fluid as required • Tighten or replace belt • Check pump pressure. (See pressure test)
Steering wheel surges or jerks when turning with engine running especially during parking	• Low oil level • Loose pump belt • Steering linkage hitting engine oil pan at full turn • Insufficient pump pressure • Pump flow control valve sticking	• Fill as required • Adjust tension to specification • Correct clearance • Check pump pressure. (See pressure test). Replace relief valve if defective. • Inspect for varnish or damage, replace if necessary
Excessive wheel kickback or loose steering	• Air in system • Steering gear loose on frame • Steering linkage joints worn enough to be loose • Worn poppet valve • Loose thrust bearing preload adjustment • Excessive overcenter lash	• Add oil to pump reservoir and bleed by operating steering. Check hose connectors for proper torque and adjust as required. • Tighten attaching screws to specified torque • Replace loose pivots • Replace poppet valve • Adjust to specification with gear out of vehicle • Adjust to specification with gear out of car
Hard steering or lack of assist	• Loose pump belt • Low oil level **NOTE:** Low oil level will also result in excessive pump noise • Steering gear to column misalignment • Lower coupling flange rubbing against steering gear adjuster plug • Tires not properly inflated	• Adjust belt tension to specification • Fill to proper level. If excessively low, check all lines and joints for evidence of external leakage. Tighten loose connectors. • Align steering column • Loosen pinch bolt and assemble properly • Inflate to recommended pressure
Foamy milky power steering fluid, low fluid level and possible low pressure	• Air in the fluid, and loss of fluid due to internal pump leakage causing overflow	• Check for leak and correct. Bleed system. Extremely cold temperatures will cause system aeriation should the oil level be low. If oil level is correct and pump still foams, remove pump from vehicle and separate reservoir from housing. Check welsh plug and housing for cracks. If plug is loose or housing is cracked, replace housing.
Low pressure due to steering pump	• Flow control valve stuck or inoperative • Pressure plate not flat against cam ring	• Remove burrs or dirt or replace. Flush system. • Correct
Low pressure due to steering gear	• Pressure loss in cylinder due to worn piston ring or badly worn housing bore • Leakage at valve rings, valve body-to-worm seal	• Remove gear from car for disassembly and inspection of ring and housing bore • Remove gear from car for disassembly and replace seals

Troubleshooting the Power Steering Pump

Problem	Cause	Solution
Chirp noise in steering pump	• Loose belt	• Adjust belt tension to specification
Belt squeal (particularly noticeable at full wheel travel and stand still parking)	• Loose belt	• Adjust belt tension to specification
Growl noise in steering pump	• Excessive back pressure in hoses or steering gear caused by restriction	• Locate restriction and correct. Replace part if necessary.
Growl noise in steering pump (particularly noticeable at stand still parking)	• Scored pressure plates, thrust plate or rotor • Extreme wear of cam ring	• Replace parts and flush system • Replace parts
Groan noise in steering pump	• Low oil level • Air in the oil. Poor pressure hose connection.	• Fill reservoir to proper level • Tighten connector to specified torque. Bleed system by operating steering from right to left—full turn.
Rattle noise in steering pump	• Vanes not installed properly • Vanes sticking in rotor slots	• Install properly • Free up by removing burrs, varnish, or dirt
Swish noise in steering pump	• Defective flow control valve	• Replace part
Whine noise in steering pump	• Pump shaft bearing scored	• Replace housing and shaft. Flush system.
Hard steering or lack of assist	• Loose pump belt • Low oil level in reservoir **NOTE:** Low oil level will also result in excessive pump noise • Steering gear to column misalignment • Lower coupling flange rubbing against steering gear adjuster plug • Tires not properly inflated	• Adjust belt tension to specification • Fill to proper level. If excessively low, check all lines and joints for evidence of external leakage. Tighten loose connectors. • Align steering column • Loosen pinch bolt and assemble properly • Inflate to recommended pressure
Foaming milky power steering fluid, low fluid level and possible low pressure	• Air in the fluid, and loss of fluid due to internal pump leakage causing overflow	• Check for leaks and correct. Bleed system. Extremely cold temperatures will cause system aeration should the oil level be low. If oil level is correct and pump still foams, remove pump from vehicle and separate reservoir from body. Check welsh plug and body for cracks. If plug is loose or body is cracked, replace body.
Low pump pressure	• Flow control valve stuck or inoperative • Pressure plate not flat against cam ring	• Remove burrs or dirt or replace. Flush system. • Correct
Momentary increase in effort when turning wheel fast to right or left	• Low oil level in pump • Pump belt slipping • High internal leakage	• Add power steering fluid as required • Tighten or replace belt • Check pump pressure. (See pressure test)
Steering wheel surges or jerks when turning with engine running especially during parking	• Low oil level • Loose pump belt • Steering linkage hitting engine oil pan at full turn • Insufficient pump pressure	• Fill as required • Adjust tension to specification • Correct clearance • Check pump pressure. (See pressure test). Replace flow control valve if defective.

Troubleshooting the Power Steering Pump (cont.)

Problem	Cause	Solution
Steering wheel surges or jerks when turning with engine running especially during parking (cont.)	• Sticking flow control valve	• Inspect for varnish or damage, replace if necessary
Excessive wheel kickback or loose steering	• Air in system	• Add oil to pump reservoir and bleed by operating steering. Check hose connectors for proper torque and adjust as required.
Low pump pressure	• Extreme wear of cam ring • Scored pressure plate, thrust plate, or rotor • Vanes not installed properly • Vanes sticking in rotor slots • Cracked or broken thrust or pressure plate	• Replace parts. Flush system. • Replace parts. Flush system. • Install properly • Freeup by removing burrs, varnish, or dirt • Replace part

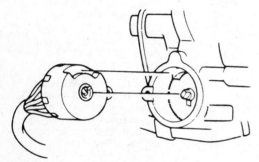

Align the switch before Installation

that the recess and the bracket tab are properly aligned. Install the retaining screw.

8. Make sure that both the lock cylinder and the column lock are in the ACC position. Slide the cylinder into the lock housing until the stop tab engages the hole in the lock.

9. Make certain the stop tab is firmly seated in the slot. Turn the key to each switch position, checking for smoothness of motions and a positive feel. Remove and insert the key a few times, each time turning the key to each switch position.

10. Reinstall the combination switch and the steering wheel if they were removed.

11. Install the steering column trim and the upper and lower column covers.

12. Connect the negative battery cable.

Steering Column

REMOVAL AND INSTALLATION

Nova

1. Remove the steering wheel.
2. Remove the combination switch.
3. Loosen the hole cover clamp screw.
4. Remove the pinch bolt from the yoke.

5. Remove the yoke from the steering gear.
6. Remove the bolts holding the lower column mounting brackets.
7. Remove the bolts holding the upper column to the instrument panel.
8. Remove the column from the car.
9. When reinstalling, place the column assembly into position and install the upper and lower bracket nuts and bolts finger tight.
10. Position the column assembly so the end of the lower support holes touch the mounting bolts.
11. Tighten the upper and lower support nuts and bolts to 19 ft. lbs.
12. Install the yoke and tighten the pinch bolt to 26 ft. lbs.
13. Install the hole cover clamp.
14. Install the combination switch.
15. Install the steering wheel.

Prizm

NOTE: *While it is possible to remove the column with the steering wheel attached, it is much easier if the wheel is removed.*

1. Disconnect the negative battery cable
2. Remove the left side lower dash trim panel; let it rest on the floor.
3. Remove the upper and lower column covers.
4. Disconnect the wiring harnesses to the combination switch and the ignition switch.
5. Disconnect the park/lock cable from the lock cylinder housing. (automatic transmission only)
6. Remove the air filter assembly to gain access to the steering gear.
7. Disconnect the yoke from the steering gear.
8. Remove the lower column mounting bolts.

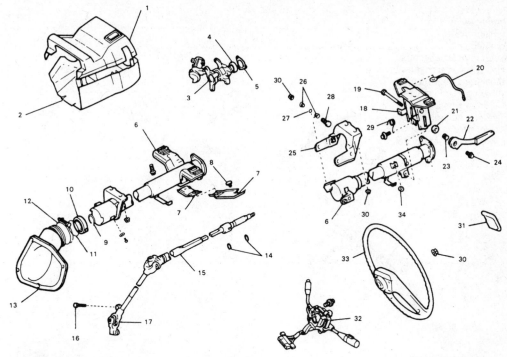

1. Column upper housing
2. Column lower housing
3. Upper bracket assembly
4. Main shaft bearing
5. Bearing retainer
6. Tube assembly
7. Column protector
8. Protector cushion
9. Main shaft bearing
   snapring
10. Shaft thrust stopper
11. O-ring
12. Hole cover clamp
13. Hole cover
14. Shaft snapring
15. Main shaft assembly
16. Pinch bolt
17. Sliding yoke
18. Break away bracket (Tilt)
19. Tilt lever lock bolt (Tilt)
20. Column ground cable
    (Tilt)
21. Plate washer (Tilt)
22. Tilt lever (Tilt)
23. Adjusting nut (Tilt)
24. Adjusting lever bolt (Tilt)
25. Lower support (Tilt)
26. Support tube bushing
    (Tilt)
27. O-ring (Tilt)
28. Pawl set bolt (Tilt)
29. Torsion spring (Tilt)
30. Nut
31. Wheel pad
32. Combination switch
33. Steering wheel
34. Return spring grommet.

Nova steering column components

9. Remove the upper column mounting bolts.

10. Remove the steering column from the car.

11. When reinstalling, place the column in position and tighten the upper and lower mounting bolts to 19 ft. lbs.

12. Connect the shaft yoke to the steering gear and tighten the bolt to 26 ft. lbs.

13. Install the air filter assembly.

14. Connect the wiring harnesses to the combination switch and the ignition switch.

15. Connect the park/lock cable to the lock cylinder housing. Make certain the clip is firmly seated.

16. Install the upper and lower column covers.

17. Reinstall the left side lower dash trim panel.

18. Connect the negative battery cable.

Tie Rod Ends

REMOVAL AND INSTALLATION

1. Raise the front of the vehicle and support it safely. Remove the wheel.

2. Remove the cotter pin and nut holding the tie rod to the steering knuckle.

3. Using a tie rod separator, press the tie rod out of the knuckle.

NOTE: *Use only the correct tool to separate the tie rod joint. Replace the joint if the rubber boot is cracked or ripped.*

4. Matchmark the inner end of the tie rod to the end of the steering rack.

5. Loosen the locknut and remove the tie rod from the steering rack.

6. Install the tie rod ends onto the rack ends and align the matchmarks made earlier.

7. Tighten the locknuts to 35 ft. lbs.

1. Hole cover
2. Intermediate shaft
3. Ignition harness connector
4. Lock cylinder assembly
5. Upper column cover
6. Multi-function switch
7. Wheel pad
8. Steering wheel
9. Steering column tube
10. Lower column cover
11. Lower instrument panel trim.

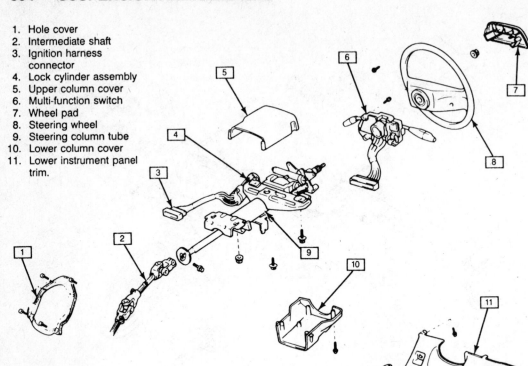

Prizm steering column components

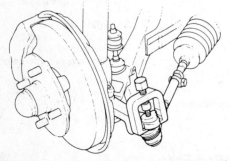

Removing the tie-rod end from the steering rack

8. Connect the tie rod joint to the knuckle. Tighten the nut to 36 ft. lbs. and install a new cotter pin.

9. Install the wheel and lower the vehicle to the ground.

10. Have the alignment checked at a reputable repair facility. The toe adjustment may have to be reset.

Manual Steering/Rack and Pinion

REMOVAL AND INSTALLATION

Nova

1. Remove the cover from the intermediate shaft.

2. Loosen the upper pinch bolt. Remove the lower pinch bolt at the pinion shaft.

3. Loosen the wheel lug nuts.

4. Elevate and safely support the vehicle.

5. Remove both front wheels.

6. Remove the cotter pins from both ball joints and remove the nuts.

7. Using a tie rod separator, remove both tie rod joints from the knuckles.

8. Remove the nuts and bolts attaching the steering rack to the body.

9. Remove the rack through the access hole.

10. Install the rack through the access hole. Secure it with the retaining bolts and nuts and tighten them to 43 ft. lbs.

11. Connect the tie rods to each knuckle. Tighten the nuts to 36 ft. lbs. and install new cotter pins.

12. Install the front wheels.

13. Lower the car to the ground.

14. Install the lower pinch bolt at the pinion shaft. Tighten the upper and lower bolts to 26 ft. lbs.

15. Install the cover on the intermediate shaft.

Prizm

1. Remove the cover from the intermediate shaft.

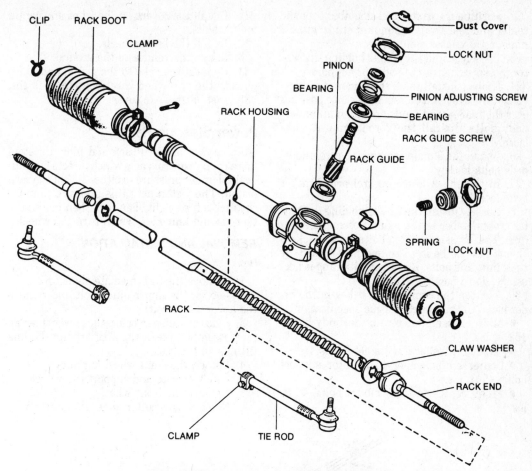

CLIP   RACK BOOT
CLAMP
Dust Cover
LOCK NUT
PINION
BEARING
PINION ADJUSTING SCREW
RACK HOUSING
BEARING
RACK GUIDE SCREW
RACK GUIDE
SPRING   LOCK NUT
RACK
CLAW WASHER
RACK END
CLAMP   TIE ROD

Exploded view of the rack and pinion steering gear

2. Loosen the upper pinch bolt. Remove the lower pinch bolt at the pinion shaft.

3. Loosen the wheel lug nuts.

4. Elevate and safely support the vehicle.

5. Remove both front wheels.

6. Install an engine support and tension it to support the engine without raising it.

CAUTION: *The engine hoist is in place and under tension. Use care when repositioning the vehicle and make necessary adjustments to the engine support.*

7. Remove the 3 bolts holding the center crossmember to the radiator support.

8. Remove the covers from the front and center mount bolts.

9. Remove the 2 front mount bolts, then the center mount bolts.

10. Support the crossmember and remove the 2 rear mount bolts.

11. Remove the 2 bolts holding the center crossmember to the main crossmember.

12. Use a floor jack and a wide piece of wood to support the main crossmember.

13. Remove the 8 bolts holding the main crossmember to the body.

14. Remove the 2 bolts holding the lower control arm brackets to the body.

CAUTION: *The crossmembers are loose and free to fall. Make sure they are properly supported.*

15. Slowly lower the main crossmember while holding onto the center crossmember.

16. Remove the cotter pins from both ball joints and remove the nuts.

17. Using a tie rod separator, remove both tie rod joints from the knuckles.

18. Remove the nuts and bolts attaching the steering rack to the body.

19. Remove the rack through the right side wheel well.

20. To reinstall the rack, place it in position through the right wheel well and tighten the bracket bolts to 45 ft. lbs.

21. Attach the tie rods to the knuckles. Tighten the nuts to 36 ft. lbs. and install new cotter pins.

22. Position the center crossmember over the center and rear transaxle mount studs; start 2 nuts on the center mount.

23. Loosely install the 3 bolts holding the center crossmember to the radiator support.

24. Loosely install the 2 front mount bolts.

25. Raise the main crossmember into position over the rear mount studs and align all underbody bolts. Install the 2 rear mount nuts loosely.

26. Install the 8 main crossmember to underbody bolts loosely.

27. Install the 2 lower control arm bracket bolts loosely.

28. Loosely install the 2 bolts holding the center crossmember to the main crossmember.

29. The crossmembers, bolts and brackets should now all be in place and held loosely by their nuts and bolts. If any repositioning is necessary, do so now.

30. Tighten the components below in the order listed to the correct torque specification:
• Main crossmember to underbody bolts: 152 ft. lbs.
• Lower control arm bolts: 94 ft. lbs.
• Center crossmember to radiator support bolts: 45 ft. lbs.
• Front, center and rear mount bolts: 45 ft. lbs.

31. Install the covers on the front and center mount bolts.

32. Install the front wheels.

33. Lower the vehicle to the ground.

34. Connect the yoke to the pinion and tighten both the upper and lower bolts to 26 ft. lbs.

35. Install the yoke cover.

Power Steering Rack

The power assisted rack and pinion system has a rotary control valve which directs hydraulic fluid under pressure to either side of the rack piston. The piston uses this pressure to move the rack left or right. The rack then moves the tie rods and knuckles, which turn the wheels.

REMOVAL AND INSTALLATION

Nova

1. Remove the intermediate shaft cover.

2. Loosen the upper pinch bolt and remove the lower pinch bolt.

3. Place a drain pan below the power steering rack assembly. Clean the area around the line fittings on the rack.

4. Loosen the front wheel lug nuts.

5. Safely elevate and support the vehicle.

6. Remove the front wheels.

7. Remove the cotter pins and nuts from

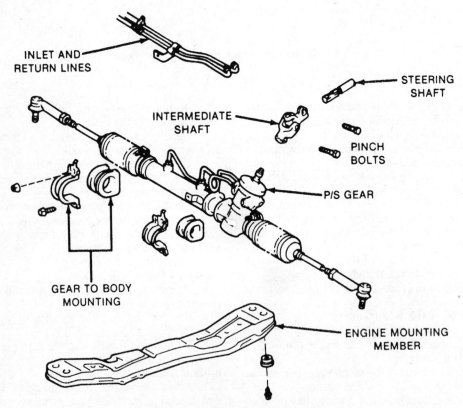

Nova power steering rack components

both tie rod joints. Separate the joints from the knuckle using a tie rod joint separator.

8. Support the transaxle with a jack.

9. Remove the rear bolts holding the engine crossmember to the body.

10. Remove the nut and bolt holding the rear engine mount to the mount bracket.

11. Label and disconnect the fluid pressure and return lines at the rack.

12. Remove the 4 bolts and nuts holding the rack brackets to the body. It will be necessary to slightly raise and lower the rear of the transaxle to gain access to the bolts.

13. Remove the rack through the access hole.

14. When reinstalling, place the rack in position through the access hole and install the retaining brackets to the body. Tighten the nuts and bolts to 39 ft. lbs.

15. Connect the fluid lines to the rack.

16. Install the nut and bolt holding the rear engine mount to the mount bracket. Tighten the nut and bolt to 29 ft. lbs.

17. Reinstall the engine crossmember bolts and tighten them to 29 ft. lbs.

18. Remove the jack from the transaxle.

19. Connect the tie rod ends to the knuckles. Tighten the nuts to 36 ft. lbs. and install new cotter pins.

20. Install the wheels and lower the vehicle to the ground.

21. Connect the intermediate shaft to the steering rack. Install the lower bolt; tighten both the upper and lower bolts to 26. ft. lbs. Install the intermediate shaft cover.

22. Add fluid and bleed the system.

23. Have the alignment checked and adjusted at a reliable repair facility.

Prizm

1. Place a drain pan under the steering rack.

2. Remove the cover from the intermediate shaft.

3. Loosen the upper pinch bolt. Remove the lower pinch bolt at the pinion shaft.

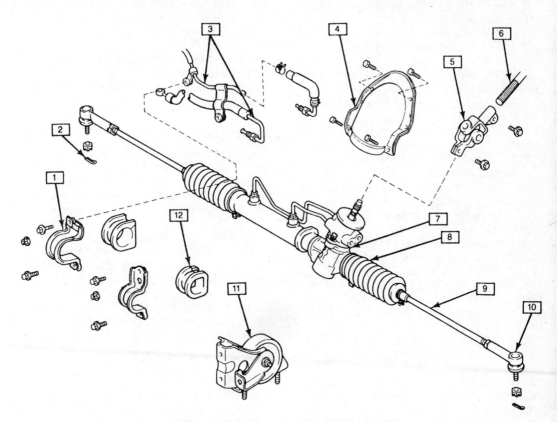

1. Mounting bracket
2. Cotter pin
3. Pressure and return lines
4. Column hole cover
5. Universal joint (yoke)
6. Intermediate shaft
7. Steering gear housing
8. Boot
9. Tie rod
10. Tie rod end
11. Engine mount
12. Grommet

Prizm power steering rack components

4. Loosen the wheel lug nuts.

5. Elevate and safely support the vehicle.

6. Remove both front wheels.

7. Install an engine support and tension it to support the engine without raising it.

CAUTION: *The engine hoist is now in place and under tension. Use care when repositioning the vehicle and make necessary adjustments to the engine support.*

8. Remove the 3 bolts holding the center crossmember to the radiator support.

9. Remove the covers from the front and center mount bolts.

10. Remove the 2 front mount bolts, then the center mount bolts and then the 2 rear mount bolts.

11. Remove the 2 bolts holding the center crossmember to the main crossmember.

12. Use a floor jack and a wide piece of wood to support the main crossmember.

13. Remove the 8 bolts holding the main crossmember to the body.

14. Remove the 2 bolts holding the lower control arm brackets to the body.

CAUTION: *The crossmembers are loose and free to fall. Make sure they are properly supported.*

15. Slowly lower the main crossmember while holding onto the center crossmember.

16. Remove the cotter pins from both tie rod ball joints and remove the nuts.

17. Using a tie rod separator, remove both tie rod joints from the knuckles.

18. Label and disconnect the fluid pressure and return lines from the rack.

19. Remove the nuts and bolts attaching the steering rack to the body.

20. Remove the rack through the right side wheel well.

21. To reinstall the rack, place it in position through the right wheel well and tighten the bracket bolts to 43 ft. lbs.

22. Connect the fluid lines to the rack and tighten the fittings to 33 ft. lbs. Make certain the fittings are correctly threaded before tightening them.

23. Attach the tie rods to the knuckles. Tighten the nuts to 36 ft. lbs. and install new cotter pins.

24. Position the center crossmember over the center and rear transaxle mount studs; start 2 nuts on the center mount.

25. Loosely install the 3 bolts holding the center crossmember to the radiator support.

26. Loosely install the 2 front mount bolts.

27. Raise the main crossmember into position over the rear mount studs and align all underbody bolts. Install the 2 rear mount nuts loosely.

28. Install the 8 main crossmember to underbody bolts loosely.

29. Install the 2 lower control arm bracket bolts loosely.

30. Loosely install the 2 bolts holding the center crossmember to the main crossmember.

31. The crossmembers, bolts and brackets should now all be in place and held loosely by their nuts and bolts. If any repositioning is necessary, do so now.

32. Tighten the components below in the order listed to the correct torque specification:

• Main crossmember to underbody bolts: 152 ft. lbs.

• Lower control arm bolts: 94 ft. lbs.

• Center crossmember to radiator support bolts: 45 ft. lbs.

• Front, center and rear mount bolts: 45 ft. lbs.

33. Install the covers on the front and center mount bolts.

34. Install the front wheels.

35. Lower the vehicle to the ground.

36. Connect the yoke to the pinion and tighten both the upper and lower bolts to 26 ft. lbs.

37. Install the yoke cover.

38. Add power steering fluid to the reservoir and bleed the system.

39. Have the alignment checked at a reliable repair facility.

Power Steering Pump

Both the Nova and Prizm use a 10-vane hydraulic pump to pressurize the system. The pump is driven by a multi-ribbed belt. The pump employs a flow control valve which is sensitive to engine rpm. As the engine speed increases, the valve reduces the pressure flow to the steering gear. When the engine is at low rpm or at idle, the valve delivers higher pressure to the rack, offsetting the higher resistance of a slow moving tire. This "variable ratio" power steering offers a combination of high power assist at low speeds, thus making parking and turning easier, as well as firmer, less sensitive steering reactions at highway speeds.

REMOVAL AND INSTALLATION

Nova with 4A-LC engine

1. Place a drain pan below the pump.

2. Remove the air cleaner assembly

3. Remove the clamp from the fluid return hose. Disconnect the pressure and return hoses at the pump. Plug the hoses and suspend them with the ends upward to prevent leakage.

4. Loosen the pump pulley nut. Push down on the belt to keep the pulley from turning.

5. Remove the adjusting bolt.

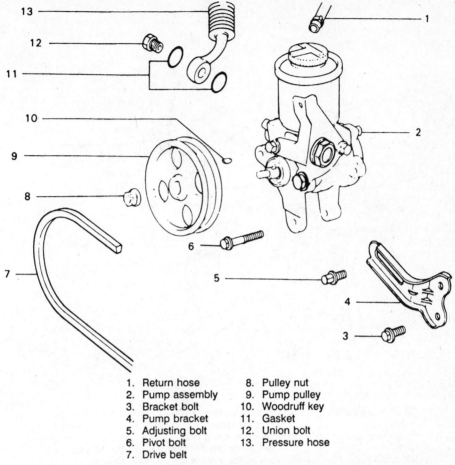

1. Return hose
2. Pump assembly
3. Bracket bolt
4. Pump bracket
5. Adjusting bolt
6. Pivot bolt
7. Drive belt
8. Pulley nut
9. Pump pulley
10. Woodruff key
11. Gasket
12. Union bolt
13. Pressure hose

Nova with 4A-LC engine—power steering pump components

6. Remove the pivot bolt and remove the drive belt.

7. Remove the pump assembly.

8. Remove the pump bracket.

9. Remove the pulley. Be careful not to lose the small woodruff key between the pulley and the shaft.

10. To reinstall, place the pump in position and temporarily install the 2 mounting bolts.

11. Install the pump bracket and tighten the bolts to 29 ft. lbs.

12. Install the pump pulley and the woodruff key. Tighten the pulley nut to 32 ft. lbs.

13. Install the drive belt, making certain that all the grooves of the belt are engaged on the pulley. Adjust the belt to the proper tension.

14. Connect the pressure and return lines to the pump. Tighten the fittings to 33 ft. lbs. Install the clamp on the return hose.

15. Install the air cleaner assembly.

16. Fill the reservoir to the proper level with power steering fluid and bleed the system.

17. After the car has been driven for about an hour, double check the belt adjustment.

Nova with 4A-GE engine

1. Place a drain pan below the pump.

2. Remove the air cleaner assembly.

3. Disconnect the return hose from the pump, then disconnect the pressure hose. Plug the lines immediately to prevent fluid loss and contamination.

4. Remove the splash shield under the engine.

5. Remove the pulley nut. Push down on the drive belt to prevent the pulley from turning.

6. Loosen the idler pulley nut and loosen the adjusting bolt.

7. Remove the drive belt.

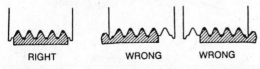

RIGHT   WRONG   WRONG

There is only 1 correct way to install the drive belt.

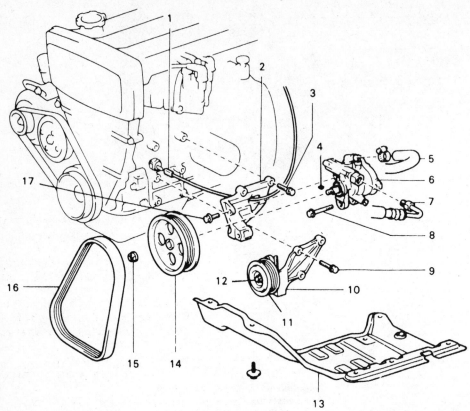

1. Oil pressure switch connector
2. Pump bracket
3. Bolt
4. Woodruff key
5. Return hose
6. Pump assembly
7. Pressure hose
8. Lower mounting bolt
9. Idler pulley bracket bolt
10. Idler pulley bracket
11. Idler pulley
12. Idler pulley nut
13. Splash shield
14. Pump pulley
15. Pump pulley nut
16. Drive belt
17. Upper mounting bolt

Nova with 4A-GE engine—power steering pump components

8. Loosen the pump pulley and woodruff key. Don't lose the woodruff key.

9. Remove the upper mounting bolt.

10. Loosen the lower mounting bolt and pivot the pump downward.

11. Disconnect the oil pressure switch connector.

12. Remove the pump bracket mounting bolts; remove the pump from the engine with the bracket attached.

13. Remove the pulley from the pump and the pump from the bracket.

14. Remove the idler pulley bracket.

15. When reinstalling, mount the pump on the bracket and loosely install the lower mounting bolt.

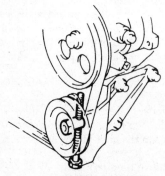

4A-GE idler pulley and adjusting bolt

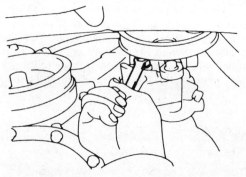

Removing the 4A-GE upper pump mounting bolt.

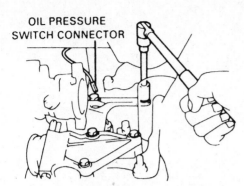

Location of 4A-GE oil pressure switch connector

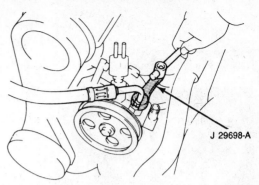

Removing the Prizm pressure hose. The GM tool shown makes the job easier.

16. Temporarily insert the pulley onto the pump shaft without the woodruff key. The pulley cannot be installed after the pump is installed on the engine.

17. Install the pump and bracket onto the engine. Tighten the upper mounting bolts to 29 ft. lbs.

18. Connect the oil pressure switch connector.

19. Install the idler pulley bracket; tighten the 3 mounting bolts to 29 ft. lbs.

20. Tighten the lower mounting bolts to 29 ft. lbs.

21. Install the woodruff key into the pulley and install the drive belt. Make certain the ribs of the belt are properly placed on all the pulleys.

22. Tighten the pulley nuts on the pump and idler to 28 ft. lbs.

23. Connect the pressure hose and tighten its fitting to 33 ft. lbs.

24. Connect the return hose.

25. Install the air cleaner and install the lower splash shield.

26. Adjust the belt to the proper tension.

27. Fill the reservoir to the proper level with power steering fluid and bleed the system.

28. After the car has been driven for about an hour, double check the belt adjustment.

Prizm

1. Place a drain pan below the pump.

2. Elevate and safely support the vehicle.

3. Remove the right front wheel.

4. Place a floor jack under the engine block and support it. Use a broad piece of wood to spread the load evenly and prevent damage.

5. Remove the bolt from the right side engine mount and lower the engine about 50mm to gain access to the lower power steering pump through-bolt.

6. Working through the right wheel well, remove the lower pump through-bolt.

7. Disconnect the fluid lines from the pump and plug them immediately.

8. Remove the upper mounting bolt from the pump and remove the pump.

9. When reinstalling, place the pump in position and install the mounting bolts. Tighten them to 29 ft. lbs.

10. Raise the engine to its normal position and install the engine mount bolt, tightening it to 69 ft. lbs.

11. Connect the fluid lines to the pump and tighten the pressure hose fitting to 34 ft. lbs.

12. Install the belt and adjust it to the proper tension.

13. Install the right front wheel.

14. Remove the jack and drain pan from under the engine.

15. Lower the vehicle to the ground.

16. Fill the reservoir to the proper level with power steering fluid and bleed the system.

17. After the car has been driven for about an hour, double check the belt adjustment.

BLEEDING THE POWER STEERING SYSTEM

Any time the power steering system has been opened or disassembled, the system must be bled to remove any air which may be trapped in the lines. Air will prevent the system from providing the correct pressures to the rack. The correct fluid level reading will not be obtained if the system is not bled.

1. With the engine running, turn the wheel all the way to the left and shut off the engine.

2. Add power steering fluid to the **COLD** mark on the indicator.

3. Start the engine and run at fast idle for about 15 seconds. Stop the engine and recheck the fluid level. Add to the **COLD** mark as needed.

4. Start the engine and bleed the system by turning the wheels from left to right 3 or 4 times.

5. Stop the engine and check the fluid level and condition. Fluid with air in it is a light tan color. This air must be eliminated from the system before normal operation can be obtained. Repeat Steps 3 and 4 until the correct fluid color and fluid level is obtained.

Brakes

9

BRAKE SYSTEM

Understanding the Brakes

HYDRAULIC SYSTEM

Hydraulic systems are used to actuate the brakes of all modern automobiles. A hydraulic system rather than a mechanical system is used for two reasons. First, fluid under pressure can be carried to all parts of an automobile by small hoses – some of which are flexible – without taking up a significant amount of room or posing routing problems. Second, a great mechanical advantage can be given to the brake pedal, and the foot pressure required to actuate the brakes can be reduced by making the surface area of the master cylinder pistons smaller than that of any of the pistons in the wheel cylinders or calipers.

The master cylinder consists of a fluid reservoir and a single or double cylinder and piston assembly. Double type master cylinders are designed to separate the front and rear braking systems hydraulically in case of a leak. The master cylinder coverts mechanical motion from the pedal into hydraulic pressure within the lines. This pressure is translated back into mechanical motion at the wheels by either the wheel cylinder (drum brakes) or the caliper (disc brakes). Since these components receive the pressure from the master cylinder, they are generically classed as slave cylinders in the system.

Steel lines carry the brake fluid to a point on the vehicle's frame near each of the vehicle's wheels. The fluid is then carried to the slave cylinders by flexible tubes in order to allow for suspension and steering movements.

Each wheel cylinder contains two pistons, one at either end, which push outward in opposite directions and force the brake shoe into contact with the drum. In disc brake systems, the slave cylinders are part of the calipers. One or four cylinders are used to force the brake pads against the disc, but all cylinders contain one piston only. All slave cylinder pistons employ some type of seal, usually made of rubber, to minimize the leakage of fluid around the piston. A rubber dust boot seals the outer end of the cylinder against dust and dirt. The boot fits around the outer end of either the piston or the brake actuating rod.

When at rest the entire hydraulic system, from the piston(s) in the master cylinder to those in the wheel cylinders or calipers, is full of brake fluid. Upon application of the brake pedal, fluid trapped in front of the master cylinder piston(s) is forced through the lines to the slave cylinders. Here it forces the pistons outward, in the case of drum brakes, and inward toward the disc in the case of disc brakes. The motion of the pistons is opposed by return springs mounted outside the cylinders in drum brakes, and by internal springs or spring seals, in disc brakes.

Upon release of the brake pedal, a spring located inside the master cylinder immediately returns the master cylinder piston(s) to the normal position. The pistons contain check valves and the master cylinder has compensating ports drilled within it. These are uncovered as the pistons reach their normal position. The piston check valves allow fluid to flow toward the wheel cylinders or calipers as the pistons withdraw. Then, as the return springs force the brake pads or shoes into the released position, the excess fluid in the lines is allowed to re-enter the reservoir through the compensating ports.

Dual circuit master cylinders employ two pistons, located one behind the other, in the same cylinder. The primary piston is actuated directly by mechanical linkage from the brake pedal. The secondary piston is actuated by fluid trapped between the two pistons. If a leak de-

Troubleshooting the Brake System

Problem	Cause	Solution
Low brake pedal (excessive pedal travel required for braking action.)	• Excessive clearance between rear linings and drums caused by inoperative automatic adjusters	• Make 10 to 15 alternate forward and reverse brake stops to adjust brakes. If brake pedal does not come up, repair or replace adjuster parts as necessary.
	• Worn rear brakelining	• Inspect and replace lining if worn beyond minimum thickness specification
	• Bent, distorted brakeshoes, front or rear	• Replace brakeshoes in axle sets
	• Air in hydraulic system	• Remove air from system. Refer to Brake Bleeding.
Low brake pedal (pedal may go to floor with steady pressure applied.)	• Fluid leak in hydraulic system	• Fill master cylinder to fill line; have helper apply brakes and check calipers, wheel cylinders, differential valve tubes, hoses and fittings for leaks. Repair or replace as necessary.
	• Air in hydraulic system	• Remove air from system. Refer to Brake Bleeding.
	• Incorrect or non-recommended brake fluid (fluid evaporates at below normal temp).	• Flush hydraulic system with clean brake fluid. Refill with correct-type fluid.
	• Master cylinder piston seals worn, or master cylinder bore is scored, worn or corroded	• Repair or replace master cylinder
Low brake pedal (pedal goes to floor on first application—o.k. on subsequent applications.)	• Disc brake pads sticking on abutment surfaces of anchor plate. Caused by a build-up of dirt, rust, or corrosion on abutment surfaces	• Clean abutment surfaces
Fading brake pedal (pedal height decreases with steady pressure applied.)	• Fluid leak in hydraulic system	• Fill master cylinder reservoirs to fill mark, have helper apply brakes, check calipers, wheel cylinders, differential valve, tubes, hoses, and fittings for fluid leaks. Repair or replace parts as necessary.
	• Master cylinder piston seals worn, or master cylinder bore is scored, worn or corroded	• Repair or replace master cylinder
Decreasing brake pedal travel (pedal travel required for braking action decreases and may be accompanied by a hard pedal.)	• Caliper or wheel cylinder pistons sticking or seized	• Repair or replace the calipers, or wheel cylinders
	• Master cylinder compensator ports blocked (preventing fluid return to reservoirs) or pistons sticking or seized in master cylinder bore	• Repair or replace the master cylinder
	• Power brake unit binding internally	• Test unit according to the following procedure: (a) Shift transmission into neutral and start engine (b) Increase engine speed to 1500 rpm, close throttle and fully depress brake pedal (c) Slow release brake pedal and stop engine (d) Have helper remove vacuum check valve and hose from power unit. Observe for backward movement of brake pedal. (e) If the pedal moves backward, the power unit has an internal bind—replace power unit

Troubleshooting the Brake System (cont.)

Problem	Cause	Solution
Spongy brake pedal (pedal has abnormally soft, springy, spongy feel when depressed.)	• Air in hydraulic system • Brakeshoes bent or distorted • Brakelining not yet seated with drums and rotors • Rear drum brakes not properly adjusted	• Remove air from system. Refer to Brake Bleeding. • Replace brakeshoes • Burnish brakes • Adjust brakes
Hard brake pedal (excessive pedal pressure required to stop vehicle. May be accompanied by brake fade.)	• Loose or leaking power brake unit vacuum hose • Incorrect or poor quality brakelining • Bent, broken, distorted brakeshoes • Calipers binding or dragging on mounting pins. Rear brakeshoes dragging on support plate. • Caliper, wheel cylinder, or master cylinder pistons sticking or seized • Power brake unit vacuum check valve malfunction • Power brake unit has internal bind • Master cylinder compensator ports (at bottom of reservoirs) blocked by dirt, scale, rust, or have small burrs (blocked ports prevent fluid return to reservoirs). • Brake hoses, tubes, fittings clogged or restricted • Brake fluid contaminated with improper fluids (motor oil, transmission fluid, causing rubber components to swell and stick in bores • Low engine vacuum	• Tighten connections or replace leaking hose • Replace with lining in axle sets • Replace brakeshoes • Replace mounting pins and bushings. Clean rust or burrs from rear brake support plate ledges and lubricate ledges with molydisulfide grease. **NOTE:** If ledges are deeply grooved or scored, do not attempt to sand or grind them smooth—replace support plate. • Repair or replace parts as necessary • Test valve according to the following procedure: (a) Start engine, increase engine speed to 1500 rpm, close throttle and immediately stop engine (b) Wait at least 90 seconds then depress brake pedal (c) If brakes are not vacuum assisted for 2 or more applications, check valve is faulty • Test unit according to the following procedure: (a) With engine stopped, apply brakes several times to exhaust all vacuum in system (b) Shift transmission into neutral, depress brake pedal and start engine (c) If pedal height decreases with foot pressure and less pressure is required to hold pedal in applied position, power unit vacuum system is operating normally. Test power unit. If power unit exhibits a bind condition, replace the power unit. • Repair or replace master cylinder **CAUTION:** Do not attempt to clean blocked ports with wire, pencils, or similar implements. Use compressed air only. • Use compressed air to check or unclog parts. Replace any damaged parts. • Replace all rubber components, combination valve and hoses. Flush entire brake system with DOT 3 brake fluid or equivalent. • Adjust or repair engine

Troubleshooting the Brake System (cont.)

Problem	Cause	Solution
Grabbing brakes (severe reaction to brake pedal pressure.)	• Brakelining(s) contaminated by grease or brake fluid	• Determine and correct cause of contamination and replace brakeshoes in axle sets
	• Parking brake cables incorrectly adjusted or seized	• Adjust cables. Replace seized cables.
	• Incorrect brakelining or lining loose on brakeshoes	• Replace brakeshoes in axle sets
	• Caliper anchor plate bolts loose	• Tighten bolts
	• Rear brakeshoes binding on support plate ledges	• Clean and lubricate ledges. Replace support plate(s) if ledges are deeply grooved. Do not attempt to smooth ledges by grinding.
	• Incorrect or missing power brake reaction disc	• Install correct disc
	• Rear brake support plates loose	• Tighten mounting bolts
Dragging brakes (slow or incomplete release of brakes)	• Brake pedal binding at pivot	• Loosen and lubricate
	• Power brake unit has internal bind	• Inspect for internal bind. Replace unit if internal bind exists.
	• Parking brake cables incorrrectly adjusted or seized	• Adjust cables. Replace seized cables.
	• Rear brakeshoe return springs weak or broken	• Replace return springs. Replace brakeshoe if necessary in axle sets.
	• Automatic adjusters malfunctioning	• Repair or replace adjuster parts as required
	• Caliper, wheel cylinder or master cylinder pistons sticking or seized	• Repair or replace parts as necessary
	• Master cylinder compensating ports blocked (fluid does not return to reservoirs).	• Use compressed air to clear ports. Do not use wire, pencils, or similar objects to open blocked ports.
Vehicle moves to one side when brakes are applied	• Incorrect front tire pressure	• Inflate to recommended cold (reduced load) inflation pressure
	• Worn or damaged wheel bearings	• Replace worn or damaged bearings
	• Brakelining on one side contaminated	• Determine and correct cause of contamination and replace brakelining in axle sets
	• Brakeshoes on one side bent, distorted, or lining loose on shoe	• Replace brakeshoes in axle sets
	• Support plate bent or loose on one side	• Tighten or replace support plate
	• Brakelining not yet seated with drums or rotors	• Burnish brakelining
	• Caliper anchor plate loose on one side	• Tighten anchor plate bolts
	• Caliper piston sticking or seized	• Repair or replace caliper
	• Brakelinings water soaked	• Drive vehicle with brakes lightly applied to dry linings
	• Loose suspension component attaching or mounting bolts	• Tighten suspension bolts. Replace worn suspension components.
	• Brake combination valve failure	• Replace combination valve
Chatter or shudder when brakes are applied (pedal pulsation and roughness may also occur.)	• Brakeshoes distorted, bent, contaminated, or worn	• Replace brakeshoes in axle sets
	• Caliper anchor plate or support plate loose	• Tighten mounting bolts
	• Excessive thickness variation of rotor(s)	• Refinish or replace rotors in axle sets
Noisy brakes (squealing, clicking, scraping sound when brakes are applied.)	• Bent, broken, distorted brakeshoes	• Replace brakeshoes in axle sets
	• Excessive rust on outer edge of rotor braking surface	• Remove rust

Troubleshooting the Brake System (cont.)

Problem	Cause	Solution
Noisy brakes (squealing, clicking, scraping sound when brakes are applied.) (cont.)	• Brakelining worn out—shoes contacting drum of rotor	• Replace brakeshoes and lining in axle sets. Refinish or replace drums or rotors.
	• Broken or loose holdown or return springs	• Replace parts as necessary
	• Rough or dry drum brake support plate ledges	• Lubricate support plate ledges
	• Cracked, grooved, or scored rotor(s) or drum(s)	• Replace rotor(s) or drum(s). Replace brakeshoes and lining in axle sets if necessary.
	• Incorrect brakelining and/or shoes (front or rear).	• Install specified shoe and lining assemblies
Pulsating brake pedal	• Out of round drums or excessive lateral runout in disc brake rotor(s)	• Refinish or replace drums, re-index rotors or replace

velops in front of the secondary pistons, it moves forward until it bottoms against the front of the master cylinder, and the fluid trapped between the pistons will operate the rear brakes. If the rear brakes develop a leak, the primary piston will move forward until direct contact with the secondary piston takes place, and it will force the secondary piston to actuate the front brakes. In either case, the brake pedal moves farther when the brakes are applied and less braking power is available.

All dual-circuit systems incorporate switch which senses either line pressure or fluid level. This system will warn the driver when only half of the brake system is operational.

In some disc brake systems, this valve body also contains a metering valve and, in some cases, a proportioning valve. The metering valve keeps pressure from traveling to the disc brakes on the front wheels until the brake shoes on the rear wheels have contacted the drum, insuring that the front brakes will never be used alone. The proportioning valve controls the pressure to the rear brakes avoiding rear wheel lock-up during very hard braking.

DISC BRAKES

CAUTION: *Brake pads contain asbestos, which has been determined to be a cancer causing agent. never clean the brake surfaces with compressed air! Avoid inhaling any dust from any brake surface! When cleaning brake surfaces, use a commercially available brake cleaning fluid.*

Instead of the traditional expanding brakes that press outward against a circular drum, disc brake systems utilize a cast iron disc with brake pads positioned on either side of it. An easily seen analogy is the hand brake arrangement on a bicycle. The pads squeeze onto the rim of the bike wheel, slowing its motion. Automobile disc brakes use the identical principal but apply the braking effort to a separate disc instead of the wheel.

The disc or rotor is a one-piece casting mounted just inside the wheel. Some discs are one solid piece while others have cooling fins between the two braking surfaces. These vented rotors enable air to circulate between the braking surfaces cooling them quicker and making them less sensitive to heat buildup and fade. Disc brakes are only slightly affected by dirt and water since contaminants are thrown off by the centrifugal action of the rotor or scraped off by the pads. Also, the equal clamping action of the two brake pads tend to ensure uniform, straight-line stops, although unequal application of the pads between the left and right wheels can cause a vicious pull under braking. All disc brakes are inherently self-adjusting.

There are three general types of disc brakes:

The fixed caliper design uses two pistons mounted on either side of the rotor (in each side of the caliper). The caliper is mounted rigidly and does not move. This is a very efficient brake system but the size of the caliper and its mounts adds weight and bulk to the car.

The sliding and floating designs are quite similar. In fact, these two types are often lumped together. In both designs, one is moved into contact with the rotor by hydraulic force. The caliper, which is not held in a fixed position, moves slightly, bringing the other pad into contact with the rotor. There are various methods of attaching floating calipers. Some pivot at the bottom or top, and some slide on mounting bolts. Many uneven brake wear problems can be caused by dirty or seized slides or pivots.

DRUM BRAKES

CAUTION: *Brake shoes contain asbestos, which has been determined to be a cancer causing agent. never clean the brake surfaces with Compressed air! Avoid inhaling any dust from any brake surface! When cleaning brake surfaces, use a commercially available brake cleaning fluid.*

Drum brakes employ two brake shoes mounted on a stationary backing plate. These shoes are positioned inside a circular cast iron drum which rotates with the wheel. The shoes are held in place by springs; this allows them to slide toward the drum (when they are applied) while keeping the linings and drums in alignment. The shoes are actuated by a wheel cylinder which is mounted at the top of the backing plate. When the brakes are applied, hydraulic pressure forces the wheel cylinder's two actuating links outward. Since these links bear directly against the top of the brake shoes, the tops of the shoes are then forced outward against the inside of the drum. This action forces the bottoms of the two shoes to contact the brake drum by rotating the entire assembly slightly (known as servo action). When the pressure within the wheel cylinder is relaxed, return springs pull the shoes away from the drum.

Most modern drum brakes are designed to self-adjust during application when the vehicle is moving in reverse. This motion caused both shoes to rotate very slightly with the drum, rocking an adjusting lever, thereby causing rotation of the adjusting screw by means of a star wheel. This on-board adjustment system reduces the need for maintenance adjustments but most drivers don't back up enough to keep the brakes properly set.

POWER BRAKE BOOSTER

Virtually all cars today use a vacuum assisted power brake system to multiply the braking force and reduce pedal effort. Since vacuum is always available when the engine is operating, the system is simple and efficient. A vacuum diaphragm is located on the front of the master cylinder and assists the driver in applying the brakes, reducing both the effort and travel he must put into moving the brake pedal.

The vacuum diaphragm housing is connected to the intake manifold by a vacuum hose. A check valve is placed at the point where the hose enters the diaphragm housing, so that during periods of low manifold vacuum brakes assist will not be lost.

Depressing the brake pedal closes off the vacuum source and allows atmospheric pressure to enter on one side of the diaphragm. This causes the master cylinder pistons to move and apply the brakes. When the brake pedal is released, vacuum is applied to both sides of the diaphragm and springs return the diaphragm and master cylinder pistons to the released position.

If the vacuum supply fails, the brake pedal rod will contact the end of the master cylinder actuator rod and the system will apply the brakes without any power assistance. The driver will notice that much higher pedal effort is needed to stop the car and that the pedal feels "harder" than usual.

Adjustments

DRUM BRAKES

The rear drum brakes are equipped with automatic adjusters actuated by the brake mechanism. No periodic adjustment of the drum brakes is necessary if this mechanism is working properly. If the pedal travel is greater than normal, it may be due to a lack of adjustment at the rear. In a safe location, drive the car backwards at low speed. While backing, pump the brake pedal slowly several times. (Neither the speed of the car or the speed of pumping the pedal has any effect on the adjustment. The idea is to apply the brakes several times while backing.) Drive forward and check the pedal feel by braking from moderate speed. It may take 2 or 3 passes in reverse to bring the pedal to the correct travel; each brake application moves the adjuster very little. It will take several applications to take up excess clearance.

If brake shoe-to-drum clearance is incorrect and applying and releasing the brakes in reverse does not adjust it properly, the parts will have to be disassembled for repair.

An alternate method of adjustment can be used when the brakes have been disassembled or when the reversing method does not work.

1. Elevate and safely support the vehicle. If only the rear wheels are elevated, block the front wheels with chocks. Once the vehicle is firmly on stands, release the parking brake.

2. Remove the rear wheels.

3. Remove the brake drum. It will not come off if the parking brake is applied.

CAUTION: *Brake pads and shoes contain asbestos, which has been determined to be a cancer causing agent. Never clean the brake surfaces with compressed air! Avoid inhaling any dust from brake surfaces! When cleaning brakes, use commercially available brake cleaning fluids.*

4. If the brake drum cannot be removed easily:

   a. Insert a screwdriver through the hole in the backing plate and hold the adjusting lever away from the star wheel.

   b. Using another screw driver or a brake adjusting tool, turn the wheel to reduce the tension (increase the clearance) on the brake shoes.

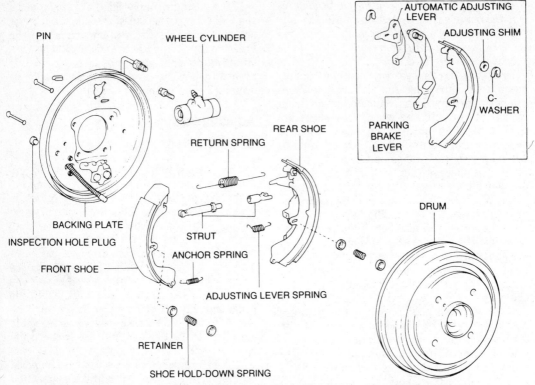

Exploded view of the rear drum brake assembly. The strut is also called the adjustor

5. Use a brake drum measuring tool with both inside diameter and outside diameter capability (GM Tool J–22364–01 or equivalent). Measure the inside diameter of the brake drum and record the reading.

6. Measure the diameter of the brake shoe assemble at the friction surface. Use the adjusting wheel to adjust the brake shoes until the diameter of the shoes is either 0.60mm (Prizm) or 0.33mm (Nova) less than the diameter of the drum. This small clearance is important; over-adjusted brakes cause drag and premature wear on the shoes.

7. Install the brake drum(s) and install the rear wheel(s).

8. Apply the parking brake and lower the car to the ground.

BRAKE PEDAL

The correct adjustment of the brake pedal height, free play and reserve distance is critical to the correct operation of the brake system.

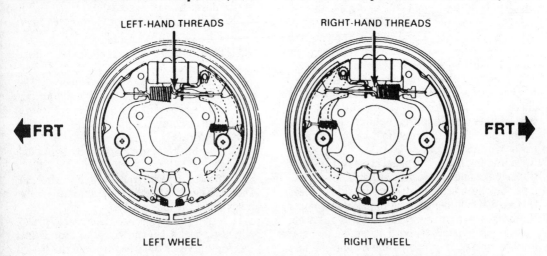

Rear drum brake assemblies. Note that the adjustors are threaded differently on each side

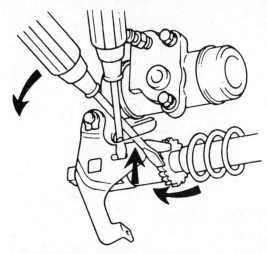

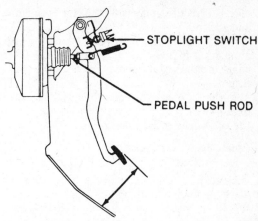

STOPLIGHT SWITCH

PEDAL PUSH ROD

Pedal height

Backing off the adjustor

These three measurements inter-relate and should be performed in sequence.

Pedal Height

1. Measure the pedal height from the top of the pedal pad to the floor. Correct distances are: Nova, 147-157mm and Prizm, 134-149mm.

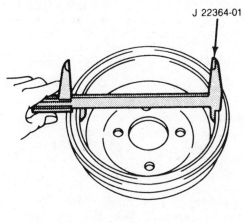

J 22364-01

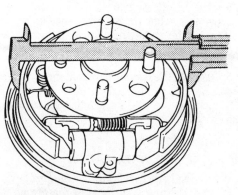

Measuring the diameters of the drum and shoe assemblies. GM tool shown

2. If it is necessary to adjust the pedal height, loosen the brake light switch and back it off so that some clearance exists between it and the pedal arm.

NOTE: *On Novas, it may be necessary to remove the lower dash trim panel and air duct for access.*

3. Adjust the pedal height by loosening the locknut and turning the pedal pushrod.

4. Return the brake light switch to a position in which it lightly contacts the stopper on the pedal arm.

Pedal Freeplay

5. With the engine off, depress the brake pedal several times until there is no vacuum held in the booster.

6. The freeplay distance is between the "at rest" pedal position and the position at which beginning of pedal resistance is felt. This represents the distance the pedal pushrod moves before actuating the booster air valve. If there is no freeplay, the car goes down the road with a slight vacuum leak and the brakes slightly ap-

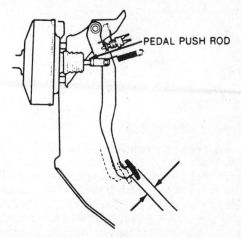

PEDAL PUSH ROD

Pedal free play

plied. Correct freeplay is 3-6mm for both Nova and Prizm.

7. If adjustment is necessary, adjust the pedal pushrod to give the correct clearance. After adjusting the pedal freeplay, recheck the pedal height.

8. Double check the adjustment of the brake light switch; it should trigger the lights just at the end of the pedal freeplay.

Pedal Reserve Distance

9. With the transaxle in **PARK** or **NEUTRAL** and the parking brake fully released, start the engine and apply normal braking effort to the pedal. Depress the pedal fully, but don't try to put it through the floor.

10. While the pedal is depressed, have a helper measure the distance from the top of the pedal pad to the floor. This distance is the extra travel available to the pushrod if it must work without vacuum assist or if the brakes are worn or severely out of adjustment. If the pedal height and pedal freeplay are correctly adjusted, the pedal reserve distance must be at least 65mm for Nova or 55mm for Prizm. The reserve distance can be greater than specified but must not be less. If the reserve distance is less than specification, the brake system must be diagnosed for leaks or component failure.

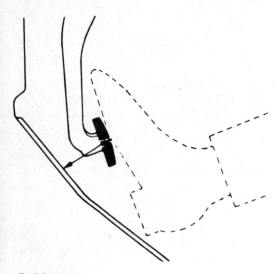

Pedal reserve

Brake Light Switch

The brake light switch is located at the top of the pedal arm. It is the switch which turns the brake lights on when the brakes are applied. The plunger type switch is held in the off position by the normal position of the brake pedal; when the pedal moves during brake application, the switch plunger moves forward and the brake lights are brought on.

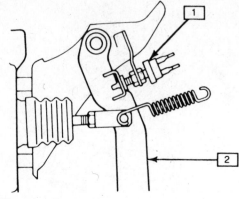

| 1 | STOPLAMP SWITCH |
| 2 | BRAKE PEDAL |

Location of brake lamp switch

The switch is almost always the first place to look for the cause of the brake lights flickering over bumps or staying on without use of the brakes. If the brake lights fail to work with the brakes applied, check the fuse first and then check the switch.

REMOVAL AND INSTALLATION

1. Remove the wiring from the switch terminals. Put a piece of tape over each exposed wiring connector; one wire terminal may be "hot" even though the ignition is off. If it accidentally touches metal, a fuse will blow.

NOTE: *On Novas, it may be necessary to remove the lower dash trim panel and air duct for access.*

2. Loosen the locknut closest to the brake pedal arm. Unscrew the switch from the nut and remove it from the bracket.

3. Install the new switch and tighten the retaining nuts finger tight when the switch plunger is lightly compressed against the stopper on the pedal.

4. Connect an ohmmeter across the terminals of the switch. Move the brake pedal and check the on–off behavior of the switch. Adjust the switch so that the switch comes on at the bottom of the pedal freeplay. This brings the brake lights on just as the brakes apply but no sooner.

5. Tighten the locknuts to hold the switch in position.

6. Remove the tape and connect the wiring to the switch.

Master Cylinder

REMOVAL AND INSTALLATION

WARNING: *Be careful not to spill brake fluid on the painted surfaces of the vehicle; it will damage the paint. If spillage occurs, rinse the area immediately with water.*

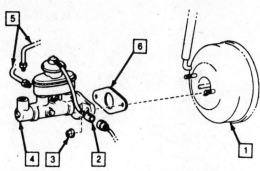

1. BOOSTER
2. CONNECTOR
3. NUT 13 N·m (9 FT.-LB.)
4. MASTER CYLINDER
5. BRAKE TUBES 15 N·m (11 FT.-LB.)
6. GASKET

Removing the brake master cylinder

Handle the steel brake lines very carefully. Once they are bent or kinked, they cannot be straightened.

1. Disconnect the negative battery cable.
2. Clean the area at the reservoir and brake lines to prevent entry of dirt into the system.
3. Disconnect the wiring to the brake fluid level switch. Release the wiring from any clips.
4. On Prizm vehicles, remove the air intake duct.
5. Use a syringe or turkey baster to remove the fluid from the reservoir. Store the fluid in a clean glass jar with a lid.
6. Disconnect the brake lines from the master cylinder. Plug or tape the lines immediately to keep dirt and moisture out of the system.
7. Remove the retaining nuts holding the master cylinder to the brake booster.
8. Remove the three-way union from the booster stud.
9. Remove the master cylinder from the studs.
10. Remove the seal or gasket from the booster.
11. When reinstalling, always use a new gasket or seal and install the master cylinder to the booster. On Nova vehicles, confirm that the "UP" mark on the master cylinder boot is in the correct position.
12. Install the three-way union bracket over the stud and install the retaining nuts finger tight.
13. Connect the brake lines to the master cylinder. Make certain each fitting is correctly threaded and tighten each fitting 1–2 turns. The job is made easier by having a small amount of movement available at the master cylinder mounting studs.
14. Tighten the master cylinder retaining nuts to 9.5 ft. lbs. (115 INCH lbs.)
15. Tighten the brake line fittings to 11 ft. lbs. Do not overtighten these fittings.

16. On Prizm vehicles, install the air intake duct.
17. Connect the wiring to the brake fluid sensing switch and attach any wiring clips.
18. Fill the master cylinder reservoir.
19. Bleed the brakes.
20. Connect the negative battery cable

OVERHAUL

1. Remove master cylinder from the car. Remove the cap and strainer from the reservoir.
2. Remove the set screw and remove the reservoir.
3. Mount the cylinder in a vise.
4. Remove the two grommets from the cylinder.
5. Using a screwdriver or similar tool, push the pistons all the way into the bore and remove the piston stopper bolt with its gasket.
6. Hold the piston into the bore and remove the snapring with snapring pliers.
7. Place a rag on two wooden blocks. Remove the master cylinder from the vise and tap the cylinder flange between the blocks until the piston tip protrudes.
8. Remove the piston by pulling it straight out.

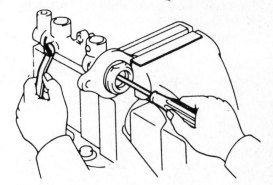

Removing the stopper bolt

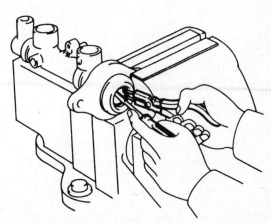

To remove the snapring, the piston must be pushed into the bore

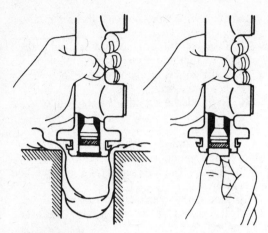

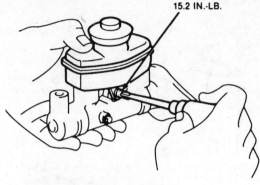

15.2 IN.-LB.

Tightening the reservoir set screw

Lightly tapping the flanges on protected blocks will release the pistons

WARNING: *If the piston is removed at an angle, the cylinder bore may become damaged.*

9. Inspect all parts of the pistons, grommets and bore for any sign of wear, cuts, corrosion or scoring. Check the inlet port and return port for obstructions. Use compressed air to clear any dirt or foreign matter from the area.

10. Apply clean brake fluid to the rubber parts of the pistons.

11. Insert the 2 springs and pistons straight into the bore. Do not angle them during installation.

WARNING: *Be careful not to damage the rubber lips on the pistons.*

12. Install the snapring while pushing in the piston.

13. Push the pistons all the way in and install the piston stopper bolt and gasket. Tighten it to 7 ft. lbs.

14. Install the 2 grommets.

15. Install the cap and strainer onto the reservoir, then press the reservoir into position on the cylinder.

1. Strainer
2. Cap
3. Reservoir
4. Brake fluid switch wiring
5. No. 2 piston and spring
6. No. 1 piston and spring
7. Snapring
8. Seal
9. Cylinder housing
10. Reservoir set screw
11. Gasket
12. Piston stopper bolt
13. Reservoir grommets (seals)

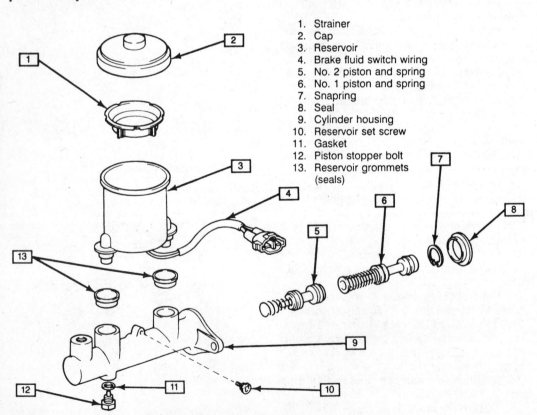

Master cylinder component—Prizm shown, Nova similar

16. Install the set screw while pushing on the reservoir. Tighten the screw to 15 INCH lbs.

NOTE: *There may be a slight bit of play in the reservoir after the set screw is installed. This is normal and no washers or spacers should be installed.*

17. Reinstall the master cylinder.

Power Brake Booster (Vacuum Booster)

REMOVAL AND INSTALLATION

1. Disconnect the negative battery cable.
2. On Prizm vehicles, remove the top of the air cleaner and the intake duct. Remove the charcoal canister mounting nuts.
3. Remove the brake master cylinder from the booster.
4. Remove the vacuum hose from the booster.
5. Inside the car, disconnect the pedal return spring. Disconnect the clip and the clevis pin.
6. Remove the brake booster retaining nuts. It will be helpful to have a helper support the booster while the nuts are loosened.
7. Remove the booster from the engine compartment.
8. When reinstalling, have a helper hold the booster in position while you install the retaining nuts. Tighten the nuts to 9.5 ft. lbs. (115 INCH lbs.)
9. Install the clevis pin and clip, then install the pedal return spring.
10. Connect the vacuum hose to the booster.
11. Install the master cylinder onto the booster and tighten the nuts to 9.5 ft. lbs. (115 INCH lbs.)
12. On Prizm vehicles, install the charcoal canister mounting bolts and install the air cleaner top and intake duct.
13. Connect the negative battery cable.
14. Bleed the brake system.

Brake System Valves
PROPORTIONING VALVE

The proportioning valve is located on the center of the firewall under the hood. Except for leakage or impact damage, it rarely needs replacement. If it must be removed, all 5 brake lines must be labeled and removed and the valve removed from its mount. Clean the fittings before removal to prevent dirt from entering the ports. After the lines are reconnected and carefully tightened to 11 ft. lbs., the entire brake system must be bled.

VACUUM CHECK VALVE

The brake vacuum check valve allows vacuum to flow out of the brake booster but will not allow back-flow. This maintains a supply of vacuum within the booster during periods of low engine vacuum. The valve can be removed from the hose by hand. Once removed, the valve can be tested by gently blowing through it. It should allow airflow in one direction but not the other. When installing a new valve, make sure it is positioned so that the air can flow from the booster to the engine. Most replacement valves have an arrow showing the direction of airflow.

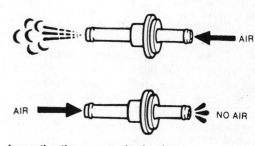

Inspecting the vacuum check valve

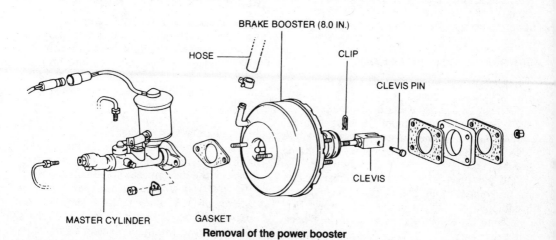

Removal of the power booster

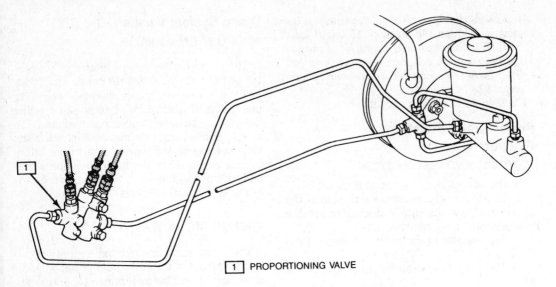

☐1☐ PROPORTIONING VALVE

Brake Hoses

INSPECTION

1. Inspect the lines and hoses in a well lighted area. Use a small mirror to allow you to see concealed parts of the hose or line. Check the entire length and circumference of each line or hose.

2. Look for any sign of wear, deformation, corrosion, cracking, bends, swelling or thread damage.

3. The slightest sign of leakage requires immediate attention.

4. Check all clamps for tightness and check that all lines and hoses have sufficient clearance from moving parts and heat sources.

5. Check that any lines passing through grommets pass through the center of the grommet and are not forced against the side of the hole. Relieve any excess tension.

6. Some metal lines may contain spring-like coils. These coils absorb vibration and prevent the line from cracking under strain. Do not attempt to straighten the coils or change their diameter.

REMOVAL AND INSTALLATION

1. Elevate and safely support the vehicle.
2. Remove the wheel.
3. Clean all dirt from the hose junctions.
4. Place a catch pan under the hose area.
5. Using 2 wrenches, disconnect the flexible hose from the steel brake line at the strut assembly.
6. If equipped with disc brakes, disconnect the brake hose union bolt at the brake caliper. If equipped with drum brakes, disconnect the hose from the steel pipe running to the wheel cylinder.

7. Remove the hose retaining clips and remove the hose from the vehicle.

8. If the system is to remain disconnected for more than the time it takes to swap hoses, tape or plug the line and caliper to prevent dirt and moisture from entering.

9. Install the new brake hose into the retaining clips.

10. Connect the hose to the caliper (disc brakes) and tighten the union bolt to 22 ft. lbs. or connect the hose to the short line running into the wheel cylinder and tighten the fitting to 11 ft. lbs.

11. Connect the steel brake line to the hose at the strut. Start the threads by hand and make sure the joint is properly threaded before tightening. Tighten the fitting to 11 ft. lbs.

12. Install the wheel.
13. Bleed the brake system.
14. Lower the car to the ground.

Bleeding the Brake System

It is necessary to bleed the hydraulic system any time system has been opened or has trapped air within the fluid lines. It may be necessary to bleed the system at all four brakes if air has been introduced through a low fluid level or by disconnecting brake pipes at the master cylinder.

If a line is disconnected at one wheel only, generally only that brake needs bleeding. If lines are disconnected at any fitting between the master cylinder and the brake, the system served by the disconnected pipe must be bled.

WARNING: *Do not allow brake fluid to splash or spill onto painted surfaces; the paint will be damaged. If spillage occurs, flush the area immediately with clean water.*

1. Fill the master cylinder reservoir to the "MAX" line with brake fluid and keep it at least half full throughout the bleeding procedure.

2. If the master cylinder has been removed or disconnected, it must be bled before any brake unit is bled. To bleed the master cylinder:

   a. Disconnect the front brake line from the master cylinder and allow fluid to flow from the front connector port.

   b. Reconnect the line to the master cylinder and tighten it until it is fluid tight.

   c. Have a helper press the brake pedal down one time and hold it down.

   d. Loosen the front brake line connection at the master cylinder. This will allow trapped air to escape, along with some fluid.

   e. Again tighten the line, release the pedal slowly and repeat the sequence (steps c–d–e) until only fluid runs from the port. No air bubbles should be present in the fluid.

   f. Final tighten the line fitting at the master cylinder to 11 ft. lbs.

   g. After all the air has been bled from the front connection, bleed the master cylinder at the rear connection by repeating steps a–e.

3. Place the correct size box-end or line wrench over the bleeder valve and attach a tight-fitting transparent hose over the bleeder. Allow the tube to hang submerged in a transparent container of clean brake fluid. The fluid must remain above the end of the hose at all times, otherwise the system will ingest air instead of fluid.

4. Have an assistant pump the brake pedal several times slowly and hold it down.

5. Slowly unscrew the bleeder valve (¼–½ turn is usually enough). After the initial rush of air and fluid, have the assistant slowly release the brake pedal. When the pedal is released, tighten the bleeder.

6. Repeat Steps 4 and 5 until no air bubbles are seen in the hose or container. If air is constantly appearing after repeated bleedings, the system must be examined for the source of the leak or loose fitting.

7. If the entire system must be bled, begin with the right rear, then the left front, left rear and right front brake in that order. After each brake is bled, check and top off the fluid level in the reservoir.

WARNING: *Do not reuse brake fluid which has been bled from the brake system.*

8. After bleeding, check the pedal for "sponginess" or vague feel. Repeat the bleeding procedure as necessary to correct.

FRONT DISC BRAKES

CAUTION: *Brake pads and shoes contain asbestos, which has been determined to be a cancer causing agent. Never clean the brake surfaces with compressed air! Avoid inhaling any dust from brake surfaces! When cleaning brakes, use commercially available brake cleaning fluids.*

Disc Brake Pads
WEAR INDICATORS

The front disc brake pads are equipped with a metal tab which will come into contact with the disc after the friction surface material has worn near its usable minimum. The wear indicators make a constant, distinct metallic sound that should be easily heard. (The sound has been described as similar to either fingernails on a blackboard or a field full of crickets.) The key to recognizing that it is the wear indicators and not some other brake noise is that the sound is heard when the car is being driven WITHOUT the brakes applied. It may or may not be present under braking is heard during normal driving.

It should also be noted that any disc brake system, by its design, cannot be made to work silently under all conditions. Each system includes various shims, plates, cushions and brackets to supress brake noise but no system can completely silence all noises. Some brake

ROTOR DISC   PAD WEAR INDICATOR

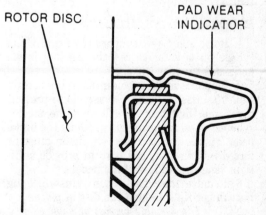

Brake bleeding   **Disc brake pad wear indicator**

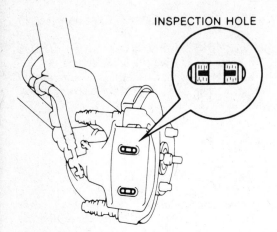

Disc brake pad inspection

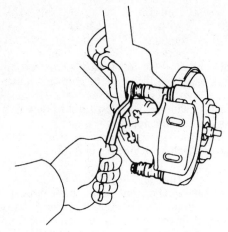

Removing the front caliper mounting bolts

noise–either high or low frequency–can be considered normal under some conditions. Such noises can be controlled and perhaps lessened, but cannot be totally eliminated.

INSPECTION

The front brake pads may be inspected without removal. With the front end elevated and supported, remove the wheel(s). Unlock the steering column lock and turn the wheel so that the brake caliper is out from under the fender.

View the pads—inner and outer—through the cut-out in the center of the caliper. Remember to look at the thickness of the pad friction material (the part that actually presses on the disc) rather than the thickness of the backing plate which does not change with wear.

Remember that you are looking at the profile of the pad, not the whole thing. Brake pads can wear on a taper which may not be visible through the window. It is also not possible to check the contact surface for cracking or scoring from this position. This quick check can be helpful only as a reference; detailed inspection requires pad removal.

REMOVAL AND INSTALLATION

1. Raise and safely support the front of the vehicle on jackstands. Set the parking brake and block the rear wheels.

2. Siphon a sufficient quantity of brake fluid from the master cylinder reservoir to prevent the brake fluid from overflowing the master cylinder when removing or installing the brake pads. This is necessary as the piston must be forced into the cylinder bore to provide sufficient clearance to install the pads.

3. Remove the wheel, then reinstall 2 lug nuts finger tight to hold the disc in place.

NOTE: *Disassemble brakes one wheel at a time. This will prevent parts confusion and*

also prevent the opposite caliper piston from popping out during pad installation.

4. Remove the two caliper mounting bolts and then remove the caliper from the mounting bracket. Position the caliper out of the way and support it with wire so it doesn't hang by the brake line.

NOTE: *It may be necessary to rock the caliper back and forth a bit in order to reposition the piston so it will clear the brake pads.*

5. Remove the 2 brake pads, the 2 wear indicators, the 2 anti-squeal shims, the 4 support plates and the 2 anti squeal springs. Disassemble slowly and take note of how the parts fit together. This will save much time during reassembly.

6. Inspect the brake disc (both sides) for scoring or gouging. Measure the disc for both thickness and run-out. Complete inspection procedures are given later in this section.

7. Inspect the pads for remaining thickness and condition. Any sign of uneven wear, cracking, heat checking or spotting is cause for replacement. Compare the wear of the inner pad to the outer pad. While they will not wear at exactly the same rate, the remaining thickness should be about the same on both pads. If one is heavily worn and the other is not, suspect either a binding caliper piston or dirty slides in the caliper mount.

8. Examine the two caliper retaining bolts and the slide bushings in which they run. Everything should be clean and dry. If cleaning is needed, use spray solvents and a clean cloth. Do not wire brush or sand the bolts–this will cause grooves in the metal which will trap more dirt. Check the condition of the rubber dust boots and replace them if damaged.

9. Install the pad support plates onto the mounting bracket.

10. Install new pad wear indicators onto each

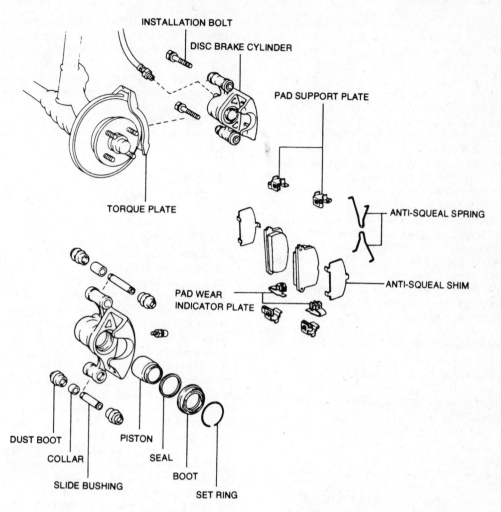

Exploded view of the front disc brake assembly

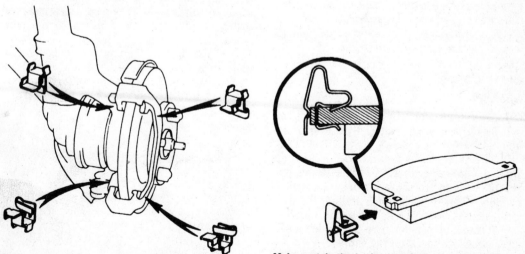

Correct placement of the support plates

Make certain the brake wear indicators are correctly installed

pad, making sure the arrow on the tab points in the direction of disc rotation.

11. Install new anti-squeal pads to the back of the pads.

12. Install the pads into the mounting bracket and install the anti-squeal springs.

13. Use a caliper compressor, a C-clamp or large pair of pliers to slowly press the caliper piston back into the caliper. If the piston is frozen, or if the caliper is leaking hydraulic fluid, the caliper must be overhauled or replaced.

14. Install the caliper assembly to the mounting plate. Before installing the retaining bolts, apply a thin, even coating of anti-seize compound to the threads and slide surfaces. Don't use grease or spray lubricants; they will not hold up under the extreme temperatures generated by the brakes. Tighten the bolts to 18 ft. lbs.

15. Remove the 2 lugs holding the disc in place and install the wheel.

16. Lower the vehicle to the ground. Check the level of the brake fluid in the master cylinder reservoir; it should be at least to the middle of the reservoir.

17. Depress the brake pedal several times and make sure that the movement feels normal. The first brake pedal application may result in a very "long" pedal due to the pistons being retracted. Always make several brake applications before starting the vehicle. Bleeding is not usually necessary after pad replacement.

18. Recheck the fluid level and add to the "MAX" line if necessary.

NOTE: *Braking should be moderate for the first 5 miles or so until the new pads seat correctly. The new pads will bed best if put through several moderate heating and cooling cycles. Avoid hard braking until the brakes have experienced several long, slow stops with time to cool in between. Taking the time to properly bed the brakes will yield quieter operation, more efficient stopping and contribute to extended brake life.*

Brake Caliper

REMOVAL

1. Raise and safely support the front of the vehicle on jackstands. Set the parking brake and block the rear wheels.

2. Siphon a sufficient quantity of brake fluid from the master cylinder reservoir to prevent the brake fluid from overflowing the master cylinder when removing or installing the calipers. This is necessary as the piston must be forced into the cylinder bore to provide sufficient clearance to install the caliper.

3. Remove the wheel, then reinstall 2 lug nuts finger tight to hold the disc in place.

NOTE: *Disassemble brakes one wheel at a time. This will prevent parts confusion and also prevent the opposite caliper piston from popping out during installation.*

4. Disconnect the hose union at the caliper. Use a pan to catch any spilled fluid and immediately plug the disconnected hose.

5. Remove the two caliper mounting bolts and then remove the caliper from the mounting bracket.

OVERHAUL

6. Drain the remaining fluid from the caliper.

7. Carefully remove the dust boot from around the piston.

8. Pad the inside arms of the caliper with rags. Apply compressed air into the brake line port; this will force the piston out.

CAUTION: *Do not place fingers in front of the piston in an attempt to catch it or protect it when applying compressed air. Injury can result. Use just enough air pressure to ease the piston out of the bore.*

9. Remove the seal from the inside of the caliper bore. Check all the parts for wear, scoring, deterioration, cracking or other abnormal conditions. Corrosion — generally caused by water in the system — will appear as white deposits on the metal, similar to what may be found on an old aluminum storm door on your house. Pay close attention to the condition of the inside of the caliper bore and the outside of the piston. Any sign of corrosion or scoring requires new parts; do not attempt to clean or resurface either face.

10. The caliper overhaul kit will, at minimum, contain new seals and dust boots. A good kit will contain a new piston as well, but you may have to buy the piston separately. Any time the caliper is disassembled, a new piston is highly recommended in addition to the new seals.

11. Clean all the components to be reused with an aerosol brake solvent and dry them thoroughly. Take any steps necessary to eliminate moisture or water vapor from the parts.

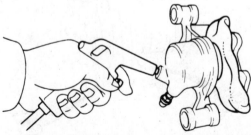

Use just enough air to ease the piston out of the caliper. Keep fingers out of the way of the piston

12. Coat all the caliper components with fresh brake fluid from a new can.

NOTE: *Some repair kits come with special assembly lubricant for the piston and seal. Use this lubricant according to directions with the kit.*

13. Install the piston seal and piston into the caliper bore. This is an exacting job; the clearances are very small. Make sure that the seal is seated in its groove and that the piston is not cocked when inserted into the bore.

14. Install the dust boot and its clip or ring.

15. Install the slide bushings and rubber boots onto the caliper if they were removed during disassembly.

INSTALLATION

16. Use a caliper compressor, a C-clamp or large pair of pliers to slowly press the caliper piston back into the caliper.

17. Install the caliper assembly to the mounting plate. Before installing the retaining bolts, apply a thin, even coating of anti-seize compound to the threads and slide surfaces. Don't use grease or spray lubricants; they will not hold up under the extreme temperatures generated by the brakes. Tighten the bolts to 18 ft. lbs.

18. Install the brake hose to the caliper. Always use a new gasket and tighten the union to 17 ft. lbs.

19. Bleed the brake system.

20. Remove the 2 lugs holding the disc in place and install the wheel.

21. Lower the vehicle to the ground. Check the level of the brake fluid in the master cylinder reservoir; it should be at least to the middle of the reservoir.

Brake Rotor

REMOVAL AND INSTALLATION

1. Elevate and safely support the car. If only the front end is supported, set the parking brake and block the rear wheels.

2. Remove the wheel.

3. Remove the brake caliper from its mount and suspend it out of the way. Don't disconnect the hose and don't let the caliper hang by the hose. Remove the brake pads with all the clips, shims, etc.

4. Install all the lug nuts to hold the rotor in place. If the nuts are open at both ends, it is helpful to install them backwards (tapered end out) to secure the disc. Tighten the nuts a bit tighter than finger tight, but make sure all are at approximately the same tightness.

5. Perform the run-out and thickness measurements explained in "Inspection". Run-out must be measured with the rotor mounted on

the car. Thickness measurements can be made either on or off the car.

6. Remove the two bolts holding the caliper mounting bracket to the steering knuckle. These bolts will be tight. Remove the 4 lug nuts holding the rotor.

7. Remove the bracket from the knuckle. Before removing the rotor, make a mark on the rotor indexing one wheel stud to one hole in the rotor. This assures the rotor will be re-installed in its original position, serving to eliminate minor vibrations in the brake system.

8. When reinstalling, make certain the rotor is clean and free of any particles of rust or metal from resurfacing. Observe the index mark made earlier and fit the rotor over the wheel lugs. Install 2 lug nuts to hold it in place.

9. Install the caliper mounting bracket in position and tighten its bolts to 65 ft. lbs.

10. Install the brake pads and the hardware.

11. Install the caliper. Tighten the mounting bolts to 18 ft. lbs.

12. Install the wheel and lower the car to the ground.

INSPECTION

Run-out

NOTE: *Before measuring the run-out on the front discs, confirm that the front wheel bearing play is within specification.*

1. Elevate and safely support the car. If only the front end is supported, set the parking brake and block the rear wheels.

2. Remove the wheel.

3. Remove the brake caliper from its mount and suspend it out of the way. Don't disconnect the hose and don't let the caliper hang by the hose. Remove the brake pads with all the clips, shims, etc.

4. Install all the lug nuts to hold the rotor in place. If the nuts are open at both ends, it is helpful to install them backwards (tapered end out) to secure the disc. Tighten the nuts a bit tighter than finger tight, but make sure all are at approximately the same tightness.

5. Mount a dial indicator with a magnetic or universal base on the strut so that the tip of the indicator contacts the rotor about ½ in. from the outer edge.

6. Zero the dial indicator. Turn the rotor one complete revolution and observe the total indicated run-out.

7. If the run-out exceeds 0.15mm (Nova) or 0.09mm (Prizm), clean the wheel hub and rotor mating surfaces and remeasure. If the run-out still exceeds maximum, remove the rotor and remount it so that the wheel studs now run through different holes. If this re-indexing does not provide correct run-out measurements, the

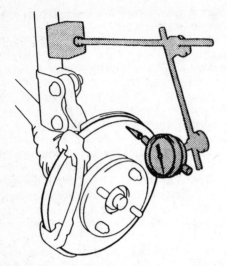

Measuring rotor run-out

rotor should be considered warped beyond use and either resurfaced or replaced.

Thickness

The thickness of the rotor partially determines its ability to withstand heat and provide adequate stopping force. Every rotor has a minimum thickness established by the manufacturer. This minimum measurement must not be exceeded. A rotor which is too thin may crack under braking; if this occurs the wheel can lock instantly, resulting in sudden loss of control.

If any part of the rotor measures below minimum thickness, the disc must be replaced. Additionally, a rotor which needs to be resurfaced may not allow sufficient cutting before reaching minimum. Since the allowable wear from new to minimum is about 1mm, it is wise to replace the rotor rather than resurface it.

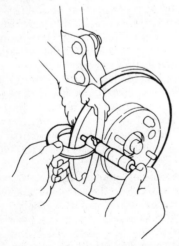

Never reuse a rotor which is below minimum thickness

Thickness and thickness variation can be measured with a micrometer capable of reading to one ten-thousandth inch. All measurements must be made at the same distance in from the edge of the rotor. Measure at four equally spaced points around the disc and record the measurements. Compare each measurement to the minimum thickness specifications in the chart at the end of this chapter.

Compare the four measurements to each other and find the difference between each pair. A rotor varying by more than 0.013mm can cause pedal vibration and/or front end vibration during stops. A rotor which does not meet these specifications should be resurfaced or replaced.

Condition

A new rotor will have a smooth even surface which rapidly changes during use. It is not uncommon for a rotor to develop very fine concentric scoring (like the grooves on a record) due to dust and grit being trapped by the brake pad. This slight irregularity is normal, but as the grooves deepen, wear and noise increase and stopping may be affected. As a general rule, any groove deep enough to snag a fingernail during inspection is cause for action or replacement.

Any sign of blue spots, discoloration, heavy rusting or outright gouges require replacement of the rotor. If you are checking the disc on the car (such as during pad replacement or tire rotation) remember to turn the disc and check both the inner and outer faces completely. If anything looks questionable or requires consideration, choose the safer option and replace the rotor. The front brakes are a critical system and must be maintained at 100% reliability.

Any time a rotor is replaced, the pads should also be replaced so that the surfaces mate properly. Since brake pads should be replaced in axle sets (both front or rear wheels), consider replacing both rotors instead of just one. The restored feel and accurate stopping make the extra investment worthwhile.

REAR DRUM BRAKES

CAUTION: *Brake pads and shoes contain asbestos, which has been determined to be a cancer causing agent. Never clean the brake surfaces with compressed air! Avoid inhaling any dust from brake surfaces! When cleaning brakes, use commercially available brake cleaning fluids.*

Brake Drums
REMOVAL AND INSTALLATION

1. Elevate and safely support the vehicle. If only the rear wheels are elevated, block the

front wheels with chocks. Once the vehicle is firmly on stands, release the parking brake.

2. Remove the rear wheel.

3. Make an index mark showing the relationship between one wheel lug and one hole in the drum. This will allow the drum to be reinstalled in its original position.

4. Tap the drum with a rubber mallet or wooden hammer handle. Remove the brake drum. It will not come off if the parking brake is applied. If the brake drum cannot be removed easily:

    a. Insert a screwdriver through the hole in the backing plate and hold the adjusting lever away from the star wheel.

    b. Using another screw driver or a brake adjusting tool, turn the star wheel to reduce the tension (increase the clearance) on the brake shoes.

WARNING: *Do not apply the brake pedal while the drum is removed.*

5. Before reinstalling the drum, perform the measurements and adjustments explained in the "Adjustments" section earlier in this chapter.

6. Reinstall the drum, observing the matchmarks made earlier. Keep the drum straight while installing it; if it goes on crooked it can damage the brake shoes.

7. Install the wheel.

8. Lower the car to the ground.

9. Test drive the car at safe speeds and in a safe location to check the pedal feel and brake function. Adjust as necessary.

INSPECTION

1. Clean the drum.

2. Inspect the drum for scoring, cracks, grooves and out-of-roundness. Measure it to determine maximum diameter. A cracked drum must be replaced; do not attempt to weld a drum.

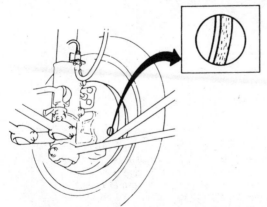

One brake shoe on each rear wheel can be checked through the inspection hole, but a complete inspection requires removing the brake drums

3. Light scoring may be removed by dressing the drum with fine emery cloth. If brake linings are replaced, always resurface a grooved drum.

4. Heavy scoring will require the use of a brake drum lathe to turn the drum.

NOTE: *During manufacture, weights are used to balance brake drums. These weights must not be removed. After a drum is refinished or if there are vibration problems not traceable to wheel balance, the brake drums should be checked for balance. This can be done on most off-vehicle balancers; a bubble balancer is particularly handy for this check. If the drum is out of balance, it must be replaced.*

Brake Shoes
INSPECTION

An inspection hole is provided in the backing plate of each rear wheel which allows the brakes to be checked without removing the drum. Remove the hole plug and check the lining thickness through the hole. If below minimum, the shoes will need replacement. Always replace the plug after checking and make certain it is properly seated and tight.

It should be obvious that this method doesn't provide a lot of information about how the brakes are wearing since it only shows one part of one shoe, but is a quick and easy first check. The only way to see the friction faces of the shoes is to remove the brake drums. No generalities can be drawn between the left and right side shoes, so both drums must be removed to perform a proper inspection.

With the drums removed:

1. Liberally spray the entire brake assembly with aerosol brake cleaner. Do not use other solvents, compressed air or a dry brush.

2. Measure the thickness of the friction surface on each shoe at several different locations. If any measurement is below the minimum thickness, replace all the shoes as a set.

3. Check the contact surfaces closely for any signs of scoring, cracking, uneven or tapered wear, discoloration or separation from the backing plate. Anything that looks unusual requires replacement.

4. If the shoes are in otherwise good condition except for glazing (a shiny, hard surface), the glaze may be removed by light sanding with emery cloth. Also lightly sand the inside of the drum to de-glaze its surface. Do not attempt to rub out grooves or ridges; this is best done with a resurfacing lathe. After sanding the components wash them thoroughly with aerosol brake cleaner to remove any grit.

REMOVAL AND INSTALLATION

NOTE: *The brake shoes can be removed and replaced using everyday hand tools, but the use of brake spring tools and assorted specialty tools makes the job much easier. These common brake tools are available at low cost and can greatly reduce working time.*

1. Elevate and safely support the vehicle. If only the rear wheels are elevated, block the front wheels with chocks. Once the vehicle is firmly on stands, release the parking brake.

2. Remove the rear wheel.

3. Make an index mark showing the relationship between one wheel lug and one hole in the drum. This will allow the drum to be reinstalled in its original position.

4. Tap the drum with a rubber mallet or wooden hammer handle. Remove the brake drum. It will not come off if the parking brake is applied. If the brake drum cannot be removed easily:

    a. Insert a screwdriver through the hole in the backing plate and hold the adjusting lever away from the star wheel.

    b. Using another screw driver or a brake

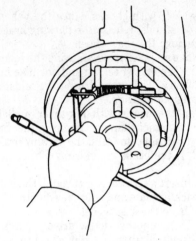

Removing the return spring with a T-shaped brake spring tool

adjusting tool, turn the star wheel to reduce the tension (increase the clearance) on the brake shoes.

WARNING: *Do not apply the brake pedal while the drum is removed.*

5. Remove the return spring.

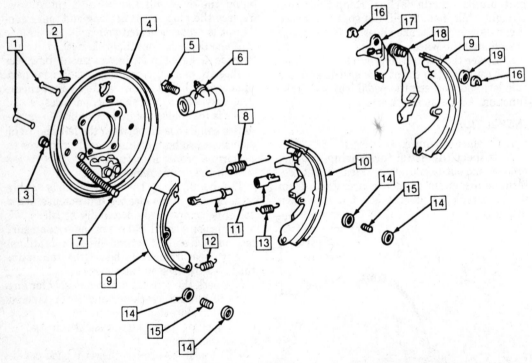

1. Holddown pin	8. Return spring	15. Hold down spring
2. Plug	9. Front (leading) shoe	16. "C" washer
3. Inspection hole plug	10. Rear (trailing) shoe	17. Adjusting lever
4. Backing plate	11. Strut (adjuster)	18. Parking brake lever
5. Bolt	12. Anchor spring	19. Shim
6. Wheel cylinder	13. Adjusting lever spring	
7. Parking brake cable	14. Retainer	

Rear brake components

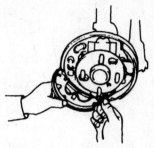

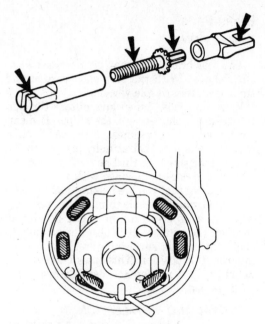

Areas to be lubricated during reassembly

6. Disconnect and remove the retainers, hold down springs and pins.

7. Remove the anchor spring.

8. Use a pair of pliers to disconnect the parking brake cable from the parking brake lever.

9. Remove the adjusting lever spring.

10. Remove the shoes and adjuster as a unit.

11. Disassemble the adjustor, the parking brake lever and the automatic adjuster lever. The "C" washer holding the shoe to the adjuster may need to be spread a little before removal.

12. Clean all the parts with aerosol brake solvent. Do not use other solvents.

13. Closely inspect all the parts. Any part of doubtful strength or quality must be replaced.

14. Before reinstallation, apply high-temperature grease to the points at which the brake shoes contact the backing plate and to both the contact and pivot points on the adjuster strut.

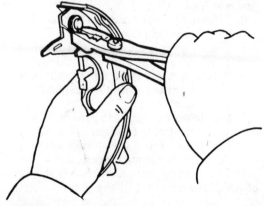

Installing the C-washer

Install the front shoe by engaging the spring, when swinging the shoe into position

15. Install the parking brake lever and automatic adjusting lever to the rear (trailing) shoe.

16. Install a new C-washer and use pliers to close it. Do not bend it more than necessary to hold in place.

17. Install the adjuster (strut) and return spring in place on the rear shoe and install the adjusting lever spring.

WARNING: *Do not allow oil or grease to get on the lining surface.*

18. Using pliers, connect the parking brake cable to the lever.

19. Pass the parking brake cable through the notch in the anchor plate.

20. Set the rear shoe in place with the end of the shoe inserted in the wheel cylinder and the adjuster in place.

21. Install the hold-down spring, retainers and pin.

22. Install the anchor spring between the front (leading) and rear shoe.

23. Position the front shoe with the end of the shoe inserted in the wheel cylinder and the adjuster in place.

24. Install the hold-down spring, retainers and pin.

25. Connect the return spring.

26. Measure both the brake diameter and the drum diameter as explained in "Adjustments" and adjust the brake shoes to the proper clearance.

27. Install the drum. Install the wheel.

28. Lower the car to the ground.

29. While not absolutely required, bleeding the brakes is recommended after replacing shoes.

Wheel Cylinders
REMOVAL AND INSTALLATION

If wheel cylinders are leaking or seized, they should be replaced. The units are inexpensive enough to make replacement a better choice than repair. Even if the pistons and seals can be replaced, the internal bore can rarely be restored to perfect condition. A faulty repair can

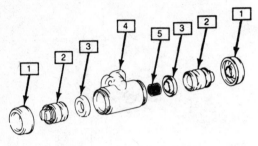

1. Boot   4. Cylinder body
2. Piston   5. Spring
3. Piston cup

Wheel cylinder components

reduce braking effort on the wheel or cause a leak which soaks the brake shoes in fluid.

When inspecting the cylinders on the car, the rubber boots must be lifted carefully and the inner area checked for leaks. A very slight moistness – usually coated with dust – is normal, but any accumulation of fluid is evidence of a leak and must be dealt with immediately.

1. Remove the rear brake shoes and hardware.

2. Using a line wrench if possible, disconnect the brake line from the back of the cylinder. This joint may be dirty or corroded. Clean it off and apply penetrating oil if necessary. Do not allow the threaded fitting to twist the brake line. Plug or tape the brake line to prevent leakage.

3. Remove the two bolts holding the wheel cylinder to the backing plate. Loosen these gently to prevent breaking the bolts.

4. Remove the wheel cylinder from the backing plate. Drain the remaining fluid into a container.

5. Install the new cylinder onto the backing plate and tighten the mounting bolts to 7.5 ft. lbs. (90 INCH lbs.).

6. Carefully reinstall the brake line and tighten it to 11 ft. lbs.

7. Reinstall the shoes and hardware.

8. Install the brake drum and wheel.

9. Bleed the brake system. Repeated bleedings may be needed to eliminate all the air within the line and cylinder.

REAR DISC BRAKES

CAUTION: *Brake pads and shoes contain asbestos, which has been determined to be a cancer causing agent. Never clean the brake surfaces with compressed air! Avoid inhaling any dust from brake surfaces! When cleaning brakes, use commercially available brake cleaning fluids.*

Brake Pads

INSPECTION

The rear brake pads may be inspected without removal. With the rear end elevated and supported, remove the wheel(s).

View the pads – inner and outer – through the cut-out in the center of the caliper. Remember to look at the thickness of the pad friction material (the part that actually presses on the disc) rather than the thickness of the backing plate which does not change with wear.

Remember that you are looking at the profile of the pad, not the whole thing. Brake pads can wear on a taper which may not be visible through the window. It is also not possible to check the contact surface for cracking or scoring from this position. This quick check can be helpful only as a reference; detailed inspection requires pad removal.

REMOVAL AND INSTALLATION

1. Raise and safely support the rear of the vehicle on jackstands. Block the front wheels.

2. Siphon a sufficient quantity of brake fluid from the master cylinder reservoir to prevent the brake fluid from overflowing the master cylinder when removing or installing the brake pads. This is necessary as the piston must be forced into the cylinder bore to provide sufficient clearance to install the pads.

3. Remove the wheel, then reinstall 2 lug nuts finger tight to hold the disc in place.

NOTE: *Disassemble brakes one wheel at a time. This will prevent parts confusion and also prevent the opposite caliper piston from popping out during pad installation.*

4. Remove the mounting (lower) bolt from the mounting bracket. Do not remove the caliper from the main (upper) pin.

5. Lift the caliper from the bottom so that it hinges upward on the upper pin. Use a piece of wire to hold the caliper up. Do not allow the brake hose to become twisted or kinked during this operation.

6. Remove the brake pads with their shims, springs and support plates.

7. Check the rotor thickness and run-out following the procedures explained under Front Disc Brakes in this chapter. Refer to the Specifications Chart at the end of this chapter for the correct measurements.

8. Install new pad support plates to the lower sides of the mounting bracket.

9. Install new anti-rattle springs to the upper side of the mounting bracket.

10. Install a new anti-squeal shim to the back of each pad and install the pads onto the mounting bracket. Install the pads so that the wear indicator is at the top side.

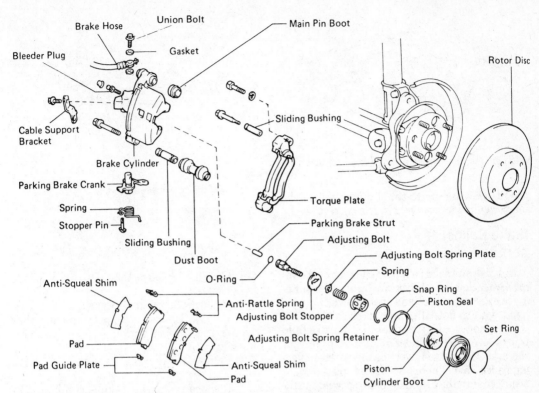

Brake Hose — Union Bolt — Main Pin Boot

Rotor Disc

Bleeder Plug — Gasket

Cable Support Bracket — Sliding Bushing

Brake Cylinder — Torque Plate

Parking Brake Crank — Parking Brake Strut

Spring — Adjusting Bolt

Stopper Pin — Adjusting Bolt Spring Plate

Sliding Bushing — Spring

Dust Boot — Snap Ring

Anti-Squeal Shim — Piston Seal

O-Ring — Anti-Rattle Spring

Adjusting Bolt Stopper — Set Ring

Pad — Adjusting Bolt Spring Retainer

Pad Guide Plate — Anti-Squeal Shim — Piston

Pad — Cylinder Boot

Rear disc brake components

11. Use GM Tool J-37149 or its equivalent to slowly turn the caliper piston clockwise while pressing it into the bore until it locks.

12. Lower the caliper so that the pad protrusion fits into the piston stopper groove.

13. Install the mounting bolt and tighten it to 14 ft. lbs.

14. Install the rear wheel.

15. Depress the brake pedal once or twice to take up the excess piston play.

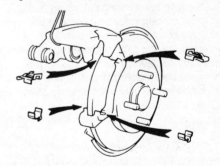

Installing support plates and anti-rattle shims

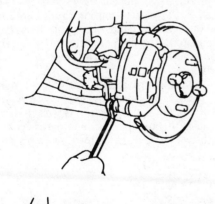

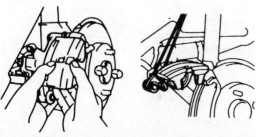

Correct method of raising the rear caliper for access to the pads

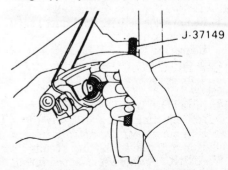

J-37149

Using the GM tool to retract the rear caliper piston

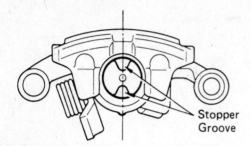

Align the stopper groove with the pad protrusion

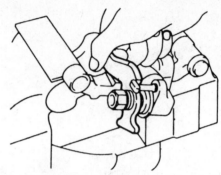

Removing the parking brake crank

16. Lower the car to the ground and fill the master cylinder reservoir to the correct level.

Brake Caliper

REMOVAL

1. Raise and safely support the rear of the vehicle on jackstands. Block the front wheels. Remove the rear wheel and install two lug nuts hand tight to hold the rotor in place.

2. Siphon a sufficient quantity of brake fluid from the master cylinder reservoir to prevent the brake fluid from overflowing when replacing pads. This is necessary as the piston must be forced into the cylinder bore to provide sufficient clearance to install the pads.

3. Place a container under the caliper assembly to catch spillage. Disconnect the union bolt holding the brake hose to the caliper. Plug or tape the hose immediately.

4. Remove the clip from the parking brake cable and remove the cable.

5. Remove the caliper mounting bolt.

6. Lift the caliper up and remove the parking brake pin clip.

7. Push on the parking brake crank (arm) to relieve the tension and remove the pin.

8. Slide the caliper off the upper pin.

9. Remove the brake pads, springs and clips.

OVERHAUL

WARNING: *The use of the correct special tools or their equivalent is REQUIRED for this procedure!*

10. Remove the slide bushings and dust boots.

11. Remove the set ring and dust boot from the caliper piston.

12. Using GM Tool J-37149 or its equivalent, remove the caliper piston from the bore.

13. Remove the seal from the inside of the caliper bore.

14. Install GM Tool J-37150 or its equivalent onto the adjusting bolt and lightly tighten it with a 14mm socket. Do not overtighten the tool; damage to the spring may result.

WARNING: *Always use this tool during disassembly. The spring may fly out, causing*

personal injury and/or damage to the caliper bore!

15. Remove the snapring from the caliper bore.

16. Carefully remove the adjusting bolt and disassemble it.

17. Remove the parking brake strut.

18. Remove the cable support bracket, then remove the torsion spring from the parking brake crank.

19. Remove the parking brake crank from the caliper.

20. Remove the parking brake crank boot by tapping it lightly on the metal portion of the boot. Do not remove the boot unless it is to be replaced.

21. Use a pin punch to tap out the stopper pin.

22. Check all the parts for wear, scoring, deterioration, cracking or other abnormal conditions. Corrosion — generally caused by water in the system — will appear as white deposits on the metal. Pay close attention to the condition of the inside of the caliper bore and the outside of the piston. Any sign of corrosion or scoring requires new parts; do not attempt to clean or resurface either face.

23. The caliper overhaul kit will, at minimum, contain new seals and dust boots. A good kit will contain a new piston as well, but you may have to buy the piston separately. Any time the caliper is disassembled, a new piston is

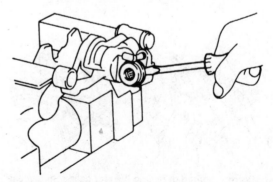

Removing the parking brake crank boot

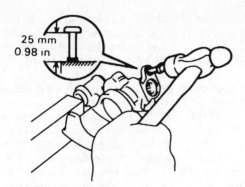

Installing the stopper pin

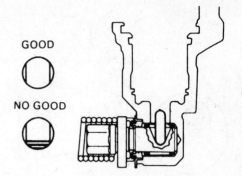

GOOD

NO GOOD

Installation of parking brake strut

highly recommended in addition to the new seals.

24. Clean all the components to be reused with an aerosol brake solvent and dry them thoroughly. Take any steps necessary to eliminate moisture or water vapor from the parts.

25. Coat all the caliper components with fresh brake fluid from a new can.

NOTE: *Some repair kits come with special assembly lubricant for the piston and seal. Use this lubricant according to directions with the kit.*

26. Install the stopper pin into the caliper until the pin extends 25mm.

27. Install the parking brake crank boot. Use a 24mm socket to tap the boot to the caliper.

28. Install the parking brake crank onto the caliper. Make certain the crank boot is securely matched to the groove of the crank seal.

29. Install the cable support bracket. Press the surface of the bracket flush against the wall of the caliper and tighten the bolt to 34 ft. lbs.

30. Check that the clearance between the parking brake crank and the cable support is 6mm.

31. Install the torsion spring.

32. Inspect the crank sub-assembly, making sure it touches the stopper pin.

33. Install the parking brake strut. Before adjusting the strut, adjust the rollers of the needle roller bearing so they do not catch on the caliper bore.

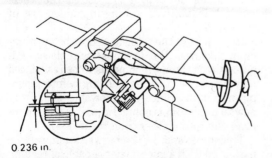

0.236 in.

Installing the cable support bracket

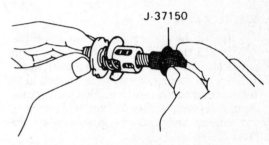

J-37150

Assembly of the adjusting bolt; GM tool shown

34. Install a new O-ring on the adjusting bolt.

35. Install the stopper, plate, spring, and spring retainer onto the adjusting bolt. Use Tool J-37150 and hand tighten the assembly. Make certain the inscribed portion of the stopper faces upward. Align the notches of the spring retainer with the notches of the stopper.

36. Install the adjusting bolt assembly into the cylinder.

37. Install snapring into the bore. Make certain the gap in the ring faces toward the bleeder side.

38. Pull up on the adjusting bolt by hand to make certain it does not move.

39. Move the parking brake crank by hand and make certain adjusting bolt moves smoothly.

40. Install a new piston seal in the caliper bore.

41. Install the piston into the caliper bore. Using Tool J-37149 or its equivalent, slowly screw the piston clockwise until it will not descend any further.

42. Align the center of the piston stopper groove with the positioning marks of the caliper bore.

43. Install the piston dust boot and its set ring.

44. Install a new boot on the main (upper) caliper pin. Use a 21mm socket to press in the new boot.

45. Install the slide bushings and boots onto the caliper.

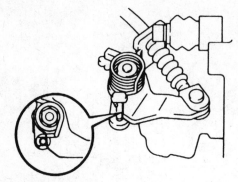

Checking the parking brake crank

INSTALLATION

46. Install the brake pads, springs and clips.
47. Install the caliper assembly to the main pin. Before installing the retaining bolts, apply a thin, even coating of anti-seize compound to the threads and slide surfaces. Don't use grease or spray lubricants; they will not hold up under the extreme temperatures generated by the brakes.
48. Install the caliper mounting bolt and tighten it to 14 ft. lbs.
49. Install the parking brake clip.
50. Install the brake hose to the caliper. Always use new gaskets and tighten the union to 22 ft. lbs.
51. Bleed the brake system.
52. To automatically adjust the parking brake, pull up on the lever several times, then release the lever and step on the brake pedal.
53. Double check that the parking brake crank touches the stopper.
54. Install the rear wheel and lower the car to the ground.

Brake Rotor

REMOVAL

1. Raise and safely support the rear of the vehicle on jackstands. Block the front wheels.
2. Siphon a sufficient quantity of brake fluid from the master cylinder reserve to prevent the brake fluid from overflowing when removing or installing the brake pads. This is necessary as the piston must be forced into the cylinder bore to provide sufficient clearance to install the pads.
3. Remove the wheel.
   NOTE: *Disassemble brakes one wheel at a time. This will prevent parts confusion and also prevent the opposite caliper piston from popping out during pad installation.*
4. Remove the mounting (lower) bolt from the mounting bracket.
5. Lift the caliper from the bottom so that it hinges upward on the upper pin and slide the caliper off the pin. Use a piece of wire to hold the caliper out of the way. Do not disconnect the brake hose and do not allow the brake hose to become twisted or kinked during this operation.
6. Remove the brake pads with their shims, springs and support plates.
7. If the rotor is to be measured, install all the lug nuts to hold the rotor in place. If the nuts are open at both ends, it is helpful to install them backwards (tapered end out) to secure the disc. Tighten the nuts a bit tighter than finger tight, but make sure all are at approximately the same tightness. Follow the measurement and inspection procedures listed under "INSPECTION".
8. Remove the mounting bolts holding the mounting bracket to the rear axle carrier.
9. Remove the lug nuts and remove the rotor.

INSPECTION

Run-out

1. Mount a dial indicator with a magnetic or universal base on the strut so that the tip of the indicator contacts the rotor about ½ in. from the outer edge.
2. Zero the dial indicator. Turn the rotor one complete revolution and observe the total indicated run-out.
3. If the run-out exceeds 0.15mm, clean the wheel hub and rotor mating surfaces and remeasure. If the run-out still exceeds maximum, remove the rotor and remount it so that the wheel studs now run through different holes. If this re-indexing does not provide correct run-out measurements, the rotor should be considered warped beyond use and either resurfaced or replaced.

Thickness

The thickness of the rotor partially determines its ability to withstand heat and provide adequate stopping force. Every rotor has a minimum thickness established by the manufacturer. This minimum measurement must not be exceeded. A rotor which is too thin may crack under braking; if this occurs the wheel can lock instantly, resulting in sudden loss of control.

If any part of the rotor measures below minimum thickness, the disc must be replaced. Additionally, a rotor which needs to be resurfaced may not allow sufficient cutting before reaching minimum. Since the allowable wear from new to minimum is about 1mm, it is wise to replace the rotor rather than resurface it.

Thickness and thickness variation can be measured with a micrometer capable of reading to one ten-thousandth inch. All measurements must be made at the same distance in from the edge of the rotor. Measure at four equally spaced points around the disc and record the measurements. Compare each measurement to the minimum thickness specifications in the chart at the end of this chapter.

Compare the four measurements to each other and find the difference between each pair. A rotor varying by more than 0.013mm can cause pedal vibration and/or front end vibration during stops. A rotor which does not meet these specifications should be resurfaced or replaced.

Condition

A new rotor will have a smooth, even surface which rapidly changes during use. It is not uncommon for a rotor to develop very fine concentric scoring (like the grooves on a record) due to dust and grit being trapped by the brake pad. This slight irregularity is normal, but as the grooves deepen, wear and noise increase and stopping may be affected. As a general rule, any groove deep enough to snag a fingernail during inspection is cause for action or replacement.

Any sign of blue spots, discoloration, heavy rusting or outright gouges require replacement of the rotor. If you are checking the disc on the car (such as during pad replacement or tire rotation) remember to turn the disc and check both the inner and outer faces completely. If anything looks questionable or requires consideration, choose the safer option and replace the rotor. The brakes are a critical system and must be maintained at 100% reliability.

Any time a rotor is replaced, the pads should also be replaced so that the surfaces mate properly. Since brake pads should be replaced in axle sets (both front or rear wheels), consider replacing both rotors instead of just one. The restored feel and accurate stopping make the extra investment worthwhile.

INSTALLATION

1. Place the rotor in position over the studs and install two lug nuts finger tight to hold it in place.
2. Install the mounting plate to the rear axle

carrier and tighten the mounting bolts to 34 ft. lbs.

3. Install the brake pads, springs and clips.
4. Carefully mount the caliper onto the upper slide pin.
5. Use GM Tool J-37149 or its equivalent to slowly turn the caliper piston clockwise while pressing it into the bore until it locks.
6. Lower the caliper so that the pad protrusion fits into the piston stopper groove.
7. Install the mounting bolt and tighten it to 14 ft. lbs.
8. Remove the lug nuts holding the disc, install the rear wheel and install all the lug nuts.
9. Depress the brake pedal once or twice to take up the excess piston play.
10. Lower the car to the ground and fill the master cylinder reservoir to the correct level. Final tighten the lug nuts.

PARKING BRAKE

Cables

REMOVAL AND INSTALLATION

1. Elevate and safely support the car. If only the rear wheels are elevated, block the front wheels. Release the parking brake after the car is supported.
2. Remove the rear wheel(s).
3. If equipped with drum brakes, remove the brake drum and remove the brake shoes.
4. If equipped with disc brakes, remove the clip from the parking brake cable and remove the cable from the caliper assembly.
5. If equipped with drum brakes, remove the parking brake retaining bolts at the backing plate.
6. Remove any exhaust heat shields which interfere with the removal of the cable.
7. Remove the 2 cable clamps.
8. Disconnect the cable retainer.
9. Remove the cable from the equalizer (yoke).
10. When reinstalling, fit the end of the new

Brake Specifications

Years	Models	Brake Disc			Brake Drum		Lining Minimum Thickness	
		Original Thickness	Minimum Thickness	Maximum Run-out	Max. Inside Dia.	Wear Limit	Front	Rear
1985–88	Nova	0.551	0.492	0.0059	7.874	7.913	0.039	0.039
1988	Nova 4A-GE	F 0.354 R 0.354	0.315 0.315	0.0059 0.0059	—	—	0.039	0.039
1989–90	Prizm	0.709	0.669	0.0035	7.874	7.913	0.039	0.039

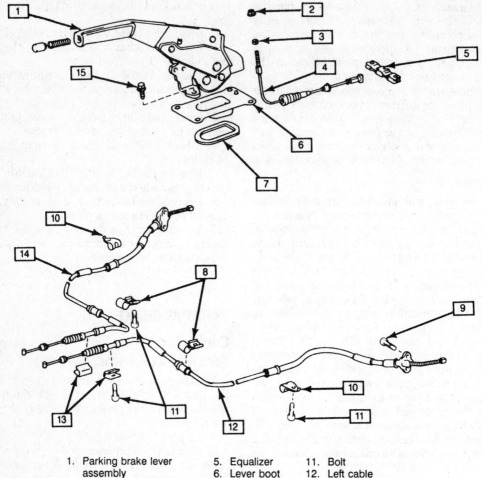

1. Parking brake lever
   assembly
2. Lock nut
3. Parking brake adjuster
   nut
4. Front cable
5. Equalizer
6. Lever boot
7. Shield
8. Clamp
9. Bolt
10. Clamp
11. Bolt
12. Left cable
13. Retainer clamp
14. Right cable
15. Lever retaining bolt

Parking brake cable assembly

cable into the equalizer and make certain it is properly seated.

11. Install the cable retainer, and, working along the length of the cable, install the clamps.
   NOTE: *Make certain the cable is properly routed and does not contain any sharp bends or kinks.*

12. Feed the cable through the backing plate and install the retaining bolts.

13. If equipped with disc brakes, connect the cable to the arm and install the clip.

14. If equipped with drum brakes, re-install the shoes. The cable will be connected to the shoes during the installation process.

15. Reinstall the wheel(s) and lower the car to the ground.

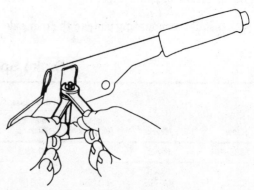

Loosen the locknut on the cable and before adjusting cable tension

ADJUSTMENT

Pull the parking brake lever all the way up and count the number of clicks. The correct range is 4–7 clicks before full application. A system which is too tight or too loose requires adjustment.

NOTE: *Before adjusting the parking brake cable, make certain that the rear brake shoe-to-drum clearance is correct.*

1. Remove the center console box.
2. At the rear of the handbrake lever, loosen the locknut on the brake cable.
3. Turn the adjusting nut until the parking brake travel is correct.
4. Tighten the locknut.
5. Reinstall the console.

Body

10

EXTERIOR

Doors

WARNING: *The doors are heavier than they appear. Support the door from the bottom and use a helper to support the door during removal and installation.*

REMOVAL AND INSTALLATION

Front Doors

NOVA

1. Remove the door check pin.
2. Remove the rear view mirror assembly as follows:
   a. Remove the cover to expose the screw.
   b. Remove the screw and lift off the mirror assembly.
3. If equipped with power door locks, remove the door trim panel and disconnect the lock wiring harness.
4. Check for any other wiring (speakers, courtesy lights, etc.) running between the door and the body.
5. Carefully outline the hinge location on the door.

On Novas, remove the hinge-to-door bolts

6. Support the door and remove the hinge-to-door bolts.
7. Lift the door away from the body. Place the door on cloths or an old blanket to protect the paint from scuffing.
8. Support the door and install the hinge bolts snugly.
9. Once the bolts are snug, move the door on the hinge bolts until the hinge aligns with the marks made during removal.
10. Support the door in its aligned position and tighten the hinge-to-door bolts.
11. Connect any wiring which was disconnected during removal.
12. Install the mirror assembly.
13. Install the door check pin.
14. Align the door.

PRIZM

1. Remove the pin from the door check arm.
2. Disconnect any wiring running between the door and body. The door pad may require removal to gain access to connectors.
3. Inside the front wheel well, remove the screws holding the rear portion of the wheelhousing cover and remove the cover. This gives access to the inside rear of the front fender.
4. With the door supported from the bottom and held by a helper, remove the 12mm hinge-to-body bolts.
   NOTE: *Unless the hinge is to be replaced, do not loosen the hinge-to-door bolts.*
5. Lift the door away from the body. Place the door on cloths or an old blanket to protect the paint from scuffing.
6. To reinstall, support the door in place and install the hinge bolts. Do not final-tighten any bolt until all are in place and snug.
7. Connect any wiring which was disconnected during removal.
8. Install the door check pin.

9. Install the wheelwell liner and install its screws.

Rear Doors

The rear doors on both Nova and Prizm are removed in approximately the same manner as the respective front door. On Novas, the hinge is disconnected from the door; on Prizms, the hinge is disconnected from the body. Don't forget to disconnect any wiring running from the door before removal.

ADJUSTMENT/ALIGNMENT

When checking for door alignment, look carefully at each seam between the door and body. The gap should be constant and even all the way around the door. Pay particular attention to the door seams at the corners farthest from the hinges; this is the area where errors will be most evident. Additionally, the door should pull against the weatherstrip when latched to seal out wind and water. The contact should be even all the way around and the stripping should be about half compressed.

The position of the door can be adjusted in 3 dimensions: fore and aft, up and down, in and out. The primary adjusting points are the door-to-hinge bolts. While the hinge is firmly mounted on the body, the door bolts may be loosened and the door repositioned. Once in the correct alignment, tighten the hinge bolts.

As explained above, the primary door adjustments are carried out at the hinge bolts at the forward end of each door. Further adjustment for closed position and for smoothness of latching may be made at the latch plate or striker. This piece is located at the rear edge of the door and is attached to the bodywork of the car; it is the piece the door engages when closed.

Although the striker or latchplate may differ on various models or from front to rear, the procedure for adjusting is the same:

1. Loosen the large cross-point screw(s) holding the striker. Know in advance that these bolts will be very tight; an impact screwdriver is a very handy tool for this job–make sure you use the correct size bit.

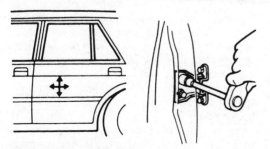

Rear door adjustment

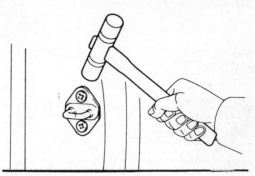

One method of adjusting the striker after the bolts are loosened

2. With the bolts just loose enough to allow the striker to move if necessary, hold the outer door handle in the released position and close the door. The striker will move into the correct location to match the doorlatch. Open the door and tighten the mounting bolts. The striker may be adjusted towards or away from the center of the car, thereby pulling the door tighter to the body if needed.

NOTE: *Do not attempt to correct height variations (sag) by adjusting the striker.*

3. After the striker bolts have been tightened, open and close the door several times. Observe the motion of the door as it engages the striker; it should continue its straight-in motion and not deflect up or down as it hits the striker.

Check the feel of the latch during opening and closing. It must be smooth and linear, without any trace of grinding or binding during engagement and release.

It may be necessary to repeat the striker adjustment procedure several times (and possibly adjust the hinges) before the correct door-to-body match is produced.

Hood

REMOVAL AND INSTALLATION

NOTE: *It is advisable to use two people while removing the hood from the vehicle. The hood is lightweight metal and can be easily damaged by twisting or dropping it.*

1. Open the hood and support with the prop rod.

2. Mark the hinge location on the hood.

3. Disconnect the windshield washer lines running to the hood. Disconnect the underhood light if so equipped.

4. Remove the bolts attaching the hood to the hood hinges.

5. Remove the hood assembly, lifting it off the hood prop.

6. Reinstall the hood by placing it in position and installing the hinge bolts. Tighten the bolts

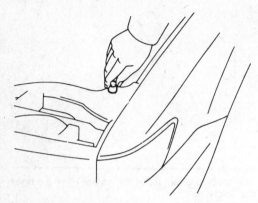

Adjust the hood height by turning the rubber bumper

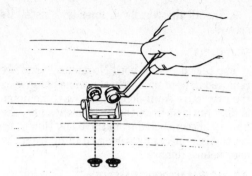

Removing the hatchback lid-to-hinge bolts

snug but not tight. Move the hood until the matchmarks made during removal align with the hinges.

7. Check the hood to fender alignment and adjust the hood position as needed. When the hood is properly positioned, tighten the hinge bolts.

8. Reconnect the washer lines and any wiring which was disconnected.

9. Check the hood latch operation and adjust as necessary. The closed height of the hood is adjusted by turning the rubber stoppers to raise or lower them.

10. When properly aligned, the closed hood has even seams on each side and sits at the same height as the fenders.

Hatch or Trunk Lid
REMOVAL AND INSTALLATION

In all cases the hatch or trunk lid is removed by separating the lid from the hinge. Certain rules must be observed:

1. Two people are absolutely required for safe and efficient removal. Some components are heavy and/or bulky. Damage or injury may result from improper removal.

2. Although the lid may be supported by springs or struts, always install a prop to support the lid.

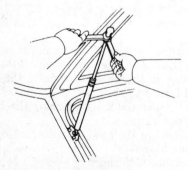

Removing the hatchback support strut

3. On hatchbacks, the support (gas strut) must be disconnected from the lid before removal. The hatch is heavy; make sure an assistant supports it before removing the strut.

4. Trunk lid hinges are supported by 2 torsion rods (spring rods) running between the hinges. These rods SHOULD NOT BE DISCONNECTED during removal of the lid.

5. Outline the position of the hinge with pencil or marker. Pad or cover the surrounding area so that the paint is not damaged during removal.

6. Check carefully for any wiring harnesses or hoses running from the body to the lid and disconnect them before removal.

7. Make sure that both ends of the lid are well supported before removing the final bolt. The lid may slip and cause damage.

8. Place the lid on cloths or a padded surface to prevent scuffing. Do not stand a hatchback lid on edge and do not allow it to rest on the glass.

9. When reinstalling, position the lid to the car and install the bolts snug but not tight. Move the lid until the matchmarks made during removal align.

10. Tighten the mounting bolts.

11. If reinstalling a hatchback lid, connect the strut to the lid.

12. Connect the wiring and hoses as necessary.

13. Align the lid with the body.

ALIGNMENT

With the trunk lid or hatchback down and latched, check the lid-to-body gap all the way around. It should be even in width and the lid should sit flush to the other body panels. Check the corners farthest from the hinges; this is where any errors will be most visible.

If adjustment is necessary, loosen the lid-to-hinge bolts and reposition the lid. Tighten the bolts and recheck alignment. If vertical adjustment is required, shims or washers must be added or removed between the lid and the hinge to raise or lower the lid.

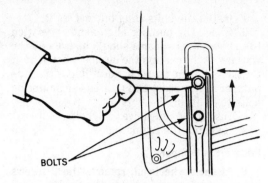

Loosen the hinge bolts to adjust the trunk lid

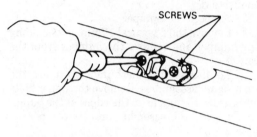

Adjusting the hatchback striker

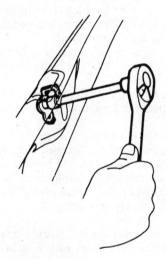

Trunk lid striker adjustment

The lid striker is adjustable. Loosen the nuts or bolts just enough to allow motion in the striker. Close the lid and let the latch move the striker into a matching position. Open the lid and tighten the striker. Double check the striker position by opening and closing the lid a few times. Chances are good that the striker adjustment will not come out right the first time. Continue adjusting it for the best feel when closing (no drag or grinding) and ease of release. The latch should hold to the striker without binding; there should be almost no tension on the key when used to release the lid.

Bumpers
REMOVAL AND INSTALLATION

The bumpers, front or rear, are actually assemblies. The outer surface is the cover or fascia, behind which is found the absorbent material (foam block or honeycomb lattice) and the reinforcing steel bar. The components cannot be removed separately; the entire assembly must be removed from the car and then broken down into individual pieces.

CAUTION: *The bumper assemblies are heavy. Always support the bumper from below in at least two places before removing the last bolts. Never lie under the bumper while removing it.*

Nova Front Bumper

1. Remove the headlamp assemblies.
2. Remove the grille.
3. Remove the upper bumper retaining bolts.
4. Support the bumper.
5. Remove the lower bumper bolts and remove the bumper assembly.
6. The fascia may be removed by removing the nuts, bolts and lower retainer. Pay close attention to the location of any washers or shims during diassembly. They must be reinserted in their original location.
7. Inspect the reinforcing bar closely for any sign of twisting, crushing or deformation. Check the mounting bars for straightness. Do not attempt to straighten any bent metal components; they must be replaced.

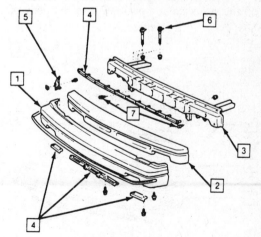

1. Bumper cover (fascia)
2. Absorber
3. Reinforcing bar
4. Retainer
5. Reinforcement
6. Upper mounting bolts
7. Lower mounting bolts

Nova front bumper components

8. Reassemble the fascia and absorber to the bar and tighten the nuts and bolts.

9. With a helper, place the bumper assembly on the supports and position it to the front of the car.

10. Install the lower bolts snug but not tight, then install the upper bolts snugly.

11. Check the bumper alignment in relation to the bodywork. Seams should be even all the way across the car and the bumper should be at the same height on both sides. Reposition the bumper as necessary and tighten the mounting bolts, lower ones first, to 70 ft. lbs.

12. Install the grille.

13. Install the headlight assemblies.

Nova Rear Bumper

1. Open the trunk lid and lift the padding or carpet out of the way.

2. Remove the plugs to gain access to the bumper retaining bolts.

3. Support the bumper.

4. Remove the bumper bolts.

5. The fascia may be removed by removing the nuts, bolts and lower retainer. Pay close attention to the location of any washers or shims during disassembly. They must be reinserted in their original location.

6. Inspect the reinforcing bar closely for any sign of twisting, crushing or deformation. Check the mounting bars for straightness. Do not attempt to straighten any bent metal components; they must be replaced.

7. Reassemble the fascia and absorber to the bar and tighten the nuts and bolts.

8. With a helper, place the bumper assembly on the supports and position it to the body of the car.

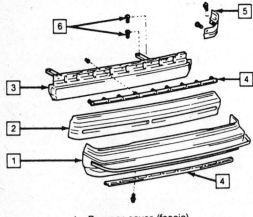

1. Bumper cover (fascia)
2. Absorber
3. Reinforcing bar
4. Retainer
5. Reinforcement
6. Mounting bolts

Nova rear bumper assembly

9. Install the bolts snug but not tight.

10. Check the bumper alignment in relation to the bodywork. Seams should be even all the way across the car and the bumper should be at the same height on both sides. Reposition the bumper as necessary and tighten the mounting bolts to 70 ft. lbs.

11. Install the plugs over the bolts.

12. Reinstall the trunk mat.

Prizm Front Bumper

1. At each wheelwell, remove the 2 screws holding the bumper cover to the fender.

2. Disconnect the turn signal wiring connectors.

3. Support the bumper.

4. Remove the 2 vertical 17mm bolts holding the bumper and remove the bumper from the car.

5. To disassemble the bumper, remove the turn signal assemblies. Remove the upper bolts and the lower nuts from the edges of the bumper. Separate the assembly into its component pieces.

6. Inspect the reinforcing bar closely for any sign of twisting, crushing or deformation. Check the mounting bars for straightness. Do not attempt to straighten any bent metal components; they must be replaced.

7. Reassemble the fascia and absorber to the bar and tighten the nuts and bolts. Install the turn signal lamps.

8. With a helper, place the bumper assembly on the supports and position it to the body of the car.

9. Install the bolts snug but not tight.

10. Check the bumper alignment in relation to the bodywork. Seams should be even all the way across the car and the bumper should be at the same height on both sides. Reposition the bumper as necessary and tighten the mounting bolts to 70 ft. lbs.

11. Connect the turn signal wiring harnesses.

12. Install the 2 screws at each wheelwell.

Prizm Rear Bumper

1. At each wheelwell, remove the 2 screws holding the bumper cover to the fender.

2. Remove the 2 nuts on each side holding the bumper mounting posts to the bodywork.

3. Support the bumper.

4. Remove the 4 nuts (14mm) holding the bumper to the frame of the car and remove the bumper assembly.

5. To remove the bumper cover, remove the 7 nuts from the lower edge and remove the six bolts from inside the upper perimeter of the bumper.

6. Inspect the reinforcing bar closely for any sign of twisting, crushing or deformation.

CHILTON'S
AUTO BODY
REPAIR TIPS

Tools and Materials • Step-by-Step Illustrated Procedures
How To Repair Dents, Scratches and Rust Holes
Spray Painting and Refinishing Tips

the metal a little at a time. Get the panel as straight as possible before applying filler.

1 This dent is typical of one that can be pulled out or hammered out from behind. Remove the headlight cover, headlight assembly and turn signal housing.

2 Drill a series of holes ½ the size of the end of the dent puller along the stress line. Make some trial pulls and assess the results. If necessary, drill more holes and try again. Do not hurry.

3 If possible, use a body hammer and block to shape the metal back to its original contours. Get the metal back as close to its original shape as possible. Don't depend on body filler to fill dents.

4 Using an 80-grit grinding disc on an electric drill, grind the paint from the surrounding area down to bare metal. Use a new grinding pad to prevent heat buildup that will warp metal.

5 The area should look like this when you're finished grinding. Knock the drill holes in and tape over small openings to keep plastic filler out.

6 Mix the body filler (see Body Repair Tips). Spread the body filler evenly over the entire area (see Body Repair Tips). Be sure to cover the area completely.

7 Let the body filler dry until the surface can just be scratched with your fingernail. Knock the high spots from the body filler with a body file ("Cheesegrater"). Check frequently with the palm of your hand for high and low spots.

8 Check to be sure that trim pieces that will be installed later will fit exactly. Sand the area with 40-grit paper.

9 If you wind up with low spots, you may have to apply another layer of filler.

10 Knock the high spots off with 40-grit paper. When you are satisfied with the contours of the repair, apply a thin coat of filler to cover pin holes and scratches.

11 Block sand the area with 40-grit paper to a smooth finish. Pay particular attention to body lines and ridges that must be well-defined.

12 Sand the area with 400 paper and then finish with a scuff pad. The finished repair is ready for priming and painting (see Painting Tips).

Materials and photos courtesy of Ritt Jones Auto Body, Prospect Park, PA.

REPAIRING RUST HOLES

There are many ways to repair rust holes. The fiberglass cloth kit shown here is one of the most cost efficient for the owner because it provides a strong repair that resists cracking and moisture and is relatively easy to use. It can be used on large and small holes (with or without backing) and can be applied over contoured areas. Remember, however, that short of replacing an entire panel, no repair is a guarantee that the rust will not return.

1 Remove any trim that will be in the way. Clean away all loose debris. Cut away all the rusted metal. But be sure to leave enough metal to retain the contour or body shape.

2 Grind away all traces of rust with a 24-grit grinding disc. Be sure to grind back 3-4 inches from the edge of the hole down to bare metal and be sure all traces of paint, primer and rust are removed.

3 Block sand the area with 80 or 100 grit sandpaper to get a clear, shiny surface and feathered paint edge. Tap the edges of the hole inward with a ball peen hammer.

4 If you are going to use release film, cut a piece about 2-3″ larger than the area you have sanded. Place the film over the repair and mark the sanded area on the film. Avoid any unnecessary wrinkling of the film.

5 Cut 2 pieces of fiberglass matte to match the shape of the repair. One piece should be about 1″ smaller than the sanded area and the second piece should be 1″ smaller than the first. Mix enough filler and hardener to saturate the fiberglass material (see Body Repair Tips).

6 Lay the release sheet on a flat surface and spread an even layer of filler, large enough to cover the repair. Lay the smaller piece of fiberglass cloth in the center of the sheet and spread another layer of filler over the fiberglass cloth. Repeat the operation for the larger piece of cloth.

7 Place the repair material over the repair area, with the release film facing outward. Use a spreader and work from the center outward to smooth the material, following the body contours. Be sure to remove all air bubbles.

8 Wait until the repair has dried tack-free and peel off the release sheet. The ideal working temperature is 60°-90° F. Cooler or warmer temperatures or high humidity may require additional curing time. Wait longer, if in doubt.

9 Sand and feather-edge the entire area. The initial sanding can be done with a sanding disc on an electric drill if care is used. Finish the sanding with a block sander. Low spots can be filled with body filler; this may require several applications.

10 When the filler can just be scratched with a fingernail, knock the high spots down with a body file and smooth the entire area with 80-grit. Feather the filled areas into the surrounding areas.

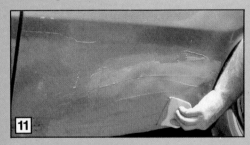

11 When the area is sanded smooth, mix some topcoat and hardener and apply it directly with a spreader. This will give a smooth finish and prevent the glass matte from showing through the paint.

12 Block sand the topcoat smooth with finishing sandpaper (200 grit), and 400 grit. The repair is ready for masking, priming and painting (see Painting Tips).

Materials and photos courtesy Marson Corporation, Chelsea, Massachusetts

PAINTING TIPS

Preparation

1 SANDING — Use a 400 or 600 grit wet or dry sandpaper. Wet-sand the area with a ¼ sheet of sandpaper soaked in clean water. Keep the paper wet while sanding. Sand the area until the repaired area tapers into the original finish.

2 CLEANING — Wash the area to be painted thoroughly with water and a clean rag. Rinse it thoroughly and wipe the surface dry until you're sure it's completely free of dirt, dust, fingerprints, wax, detergent or other foreign matter.

3 MASKING — Protect any areas you don't want to overspray by covering them with masking tape and newspaper. Be careful not get fingerprints on the area to be painted.

4 PRIMING — All exposed metal should be primed before painting. Primer protects the metal and provides an excellent surface for paint adhesion. When the primer is dry, wet-sand the area again with 600 grit wet-sandpaper. Clean the area again after sanding.

Painting Techniques

P aint applied from either a spray gun or a spray can (for small areas) will provide good results. Experiment on an old piece of metal to get the right combination before you begin painting.

SPRAYING VISCOSITY (SPRAY GUN ONLY) — Paint should be thinned to spraying viscosity according to the directions on the can. Use only the recommended thinner or reducer and the same amount of reduction regardless of temperature.

AIR PRESSURE (SPRAY GUN ONLY) — This is extremely important. Be sure you are using the proper recommended pressure.

TEMPERATURE — The surface to be painted should be approximately the same temperature as the surrounding air. Applying warm paint to a cold surface, or vice versa, will completely upset the paint characteristics.

THICKNESS — Spray with smooth strokes. In general, the thicker the coat of paint, the longer the drying time. Apply several thin coats about 30 seconds apart. The paint should remain wet long enough to flow out and no longer; heavier coats will only produce sags or wrinkles. Spray a light (fog) coat, followed by heavier color coats.

DISTANCE — The ideal spraying distance is 8"-12" from the gun or can to the surface. Shorter distances will produce ripples, while greater distances will result in orange peel, dry film and poor color match and loss of material due to overspray.

OVERLAPPING — The gun or can should be kept at right angles to the surface at all times. Work to a wet edge at an even speed, using a 50% overlap and direct the center of the spray at the lower or nearest edge of the previous stroke.

RUBBING OUT (BLENDING) FRESH PAINT — Let the paint dry thoroughly. Runs or imperfections can be sanded out, primed and repainted.

Don't be in too big a hurry to remove the masking. This only produces paint ridges. When the finish has dried for at least a week, apply a small amount of fine grade rubbing compound with a clean, wet cloth. Use lots of water and blend the new paint with the surrounding area.

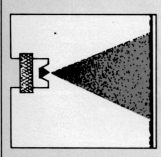

WRONG

Thin coat. Stroke too fast, not enough overlap, gun too far away.

CORRECT

Medium coat. Proper distance, good stroke, proper overlap.

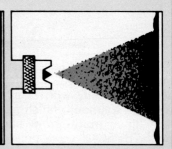

WRONG

Heavy coat. Stroke too slow, too much overlap, gun too close.

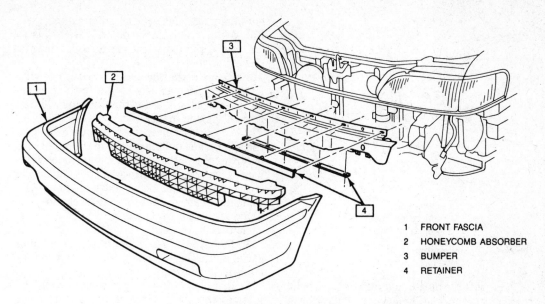

1	FRONT FASCIA
2	HONEYCOMB ABSORBER
3	BUMPER
4	RETAINER

Prizm front bumper assembly

Check the mounting bars for straightness. Do not attempt to straighten any bent metal components; they must be replaced.

7. Reassemble the fascia and absorber to the bar and tighten the nuts and bolts.

8. With a helper, place the bumper assembly on the supports and position it to the body of the car.

9. Install the mounting bolts snug but not tight.

10. Check the bumper alignment in relation to the bodywork. Seams should be even all the way across the car and the bumper should be at the same height on both sides. Reposition the bumper as necessary and tighten the mounting bolts.

11. Install the nuts holding the mounting posts to the bodywork.

12. Install the 2 screws at each wheelwell.

Mirrors

REMOVAL AND INSTALLATION

Outside Mirrors

1. Remove the screw holding the remote control knob to the shaft. The screw may be concealed under a cap which can be popped off with a small tool.

2. Use a flat-bladed tool to carefully pry off the triangular plastic cover. Don't damage the plastic and don't break the plastic clip underneath.

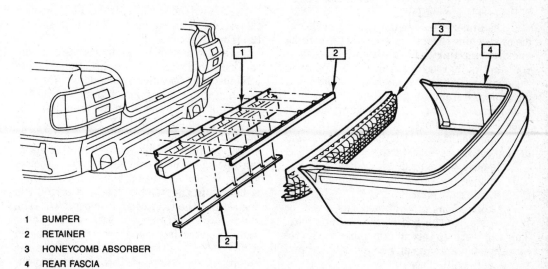

1	BUMPER
2	RETAINER
3	HONEYCOMB ABSORBER
4	REAR FASCIA

Prizm rear bumper components.

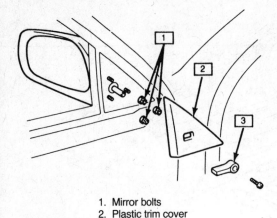

1. Mirror bolts
2. Plastic trim cover
3. Adjustment knob

Door mirror components

3. Support the mirror and remove the 3 bolts holding it to the door. Remove the mirror from the car.

4. When reinstalling, hold the mirror in position and install the 3 bolts. Before tightening the bolts, make certain the mirror is properly seated and mates flush to the door. The slightest gap will cause wind noise when the car is moving.

5. Install the triangular bezel.

6. Install the remote control knob and its retaining screw.

Antenna

NOTE: *The mast and cable are one piece. If the mast is damaged or broken, the entire antenna assembly including the cable must be replaced.*

REMOVAL AND INSTALLATION

1. Remove the console side panel, to the right of the accelerator pedal.

2. Disconnect the antenna cable from the radio by reaching through the back of the console and disconnecting the cable from its socket. If you can't quite reach or release the cable, the radio will have to be loosened in the dash and disconnected from the front.

3. Remove the two screws holding the hood release lever and move the lever out of the way.

4. Remove the lower left dashboard trim and disconnect the speaker wiring.

5. Remove the left side kick panel.

6. Remove the retaining screw and remove the left side cowl trim.

7. Attach a long piece of mechanic's wire or heavy string to the end of the antenna wire. This will track up through the pillar as you remove the old antenna and be available to pull the new line into place.

8. Remove the two attaching screws at the

antenna mast. Remove the antenna and carefully pull the cable up the pillar. Use a helper to insure the end inside the car does not snag or pull other wires.

9. Remove the mechanic's wire or twine from the old cable and attach it to the new cable. Make sure it is tied so that the plug will stay straight during installation

10. With your helper, feed the new cable into the pillar while pulling gently on the guide wire or string. Route the antenna cable properly under the dash, making sure it will not foul on the steering column or pedal linkages. Route the cable high enough that there is no chance of it hanging around the driver's feet. Use tape or cable ties to secure it.

11. Remove the guide line from the antenna cable. Route the antenna into the radio and install the connector.

12. Install the attaching screws holding the mast to the pillar. Make sure the screws are properly threaded and that both the screws and their holes are free of dirt or corrosion. A poor connection at these screws can affect antenna and radio performance.

13. Install the left side cowl trim and the left side kick panel.

14. Connect the speaker wiring and install the lower left dashboard trim.

15. Install the hood release lever.

16. Install the console side panel.

INTERIOR

Door Panels

REMOVAL AND INSTALLATION

1. Remove the small screw holding the plastic trim bezel at the inside door release. Slide the trim off the handle.

2. On Prizm models, disconnect the rod from the door handle and remove the handle. Before attempting to disconnect the rod, note that the retaining clip can be released from the rod and pivoted out of the way. The rod then lifts free.

3. If not equipped with electric windows, remove the window winder handle. This can be tricky, but not difficult. Install a piece of masking tape on the door trim panel to show the position of the handle before removal. The handle is held onto the winder axle by a spring clip shaped like the Greek letter omega: "Ω". The clip is located between the back of the winder handle and the door pad. It is correctly installed with the legs pointing along the length of the winder handle. There are three common methods of removing the clip:

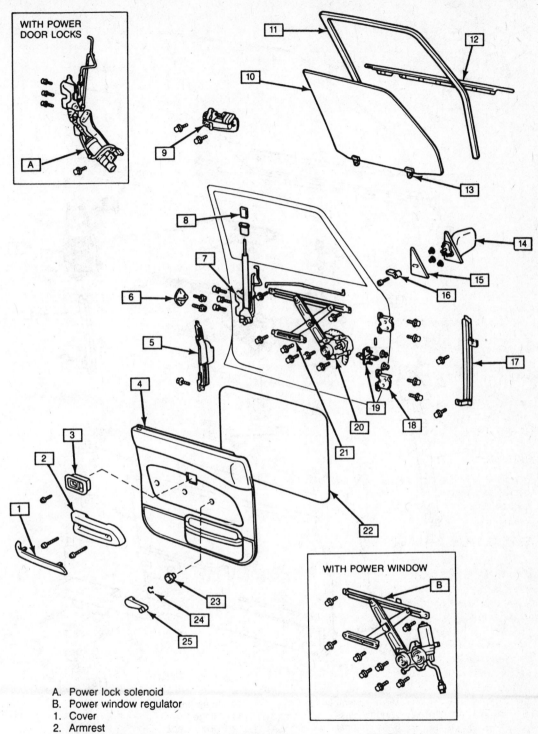

WITH POWER DOOR LOCKS

A

WITH POWER WINDOW

B

A. Power lock solenoid
B. Power window regulator
1. Cover
2. Armrest
3. Inner door handle
4. Door trim panel
5. Rear lower door frame
6. Striker
7. Door latch/lock
8. Lock knob
9. Outer handle and lock cylinder
10. Window glass
11. Glass run
12. Door belt molding
13. Glass channel
14. Side mirror
15. Cover
16. Adjustment knob
17. Front lower door frame
18. Door hinge
19. Door check arm
20. Window regulator
21. Equalizer arm.
22. Water deflector
23. Plate
24. Spring clip
25. Window winder handle

Prizm front door assembly

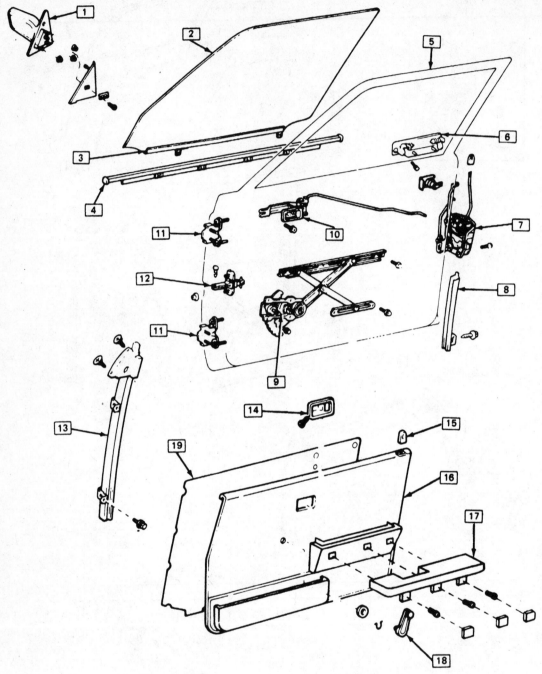

1. Mirror assembly
2. Window glass
3. Sash channel
4. Door belt molding
5. Door assembly
6. Outer handle
7. Door latch/lock assembly
8. Rear run channel guide
9. Window regulator
10. Inner handle
11. Hinge
12. Door check
13. Front run channel guide
14. Inner handle bezel
15. Lock knob
16. Door trim panel
17. Armrest
18. Window winder handle
19. Water deflector shield

Nova front door assembly

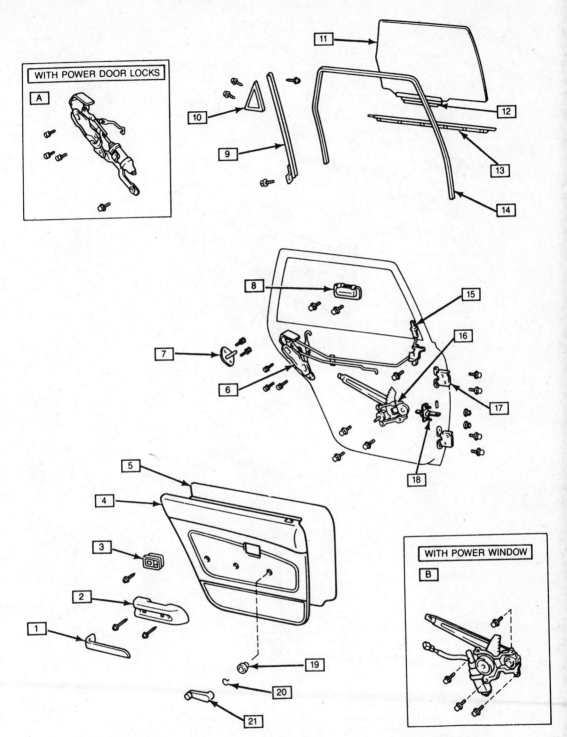

A. Door lock solenoid
B. Power window regulator
1. Cover
2. Armrest
3. Inner handle
4. Trim panel
5. Water deflector
6. Door latch/lock

7. Striker
8. Outer handle
9. Rear lower frame
10. Rear guide seal
11. Window glass
12. Glass channel
13. Belt molding
14. Glass run

15. Lock knob
16. window regulator
17. Hinge
18. Door check arm
19. Plate
20. Spring clip
21. Regulator arms

Prizm rear door components

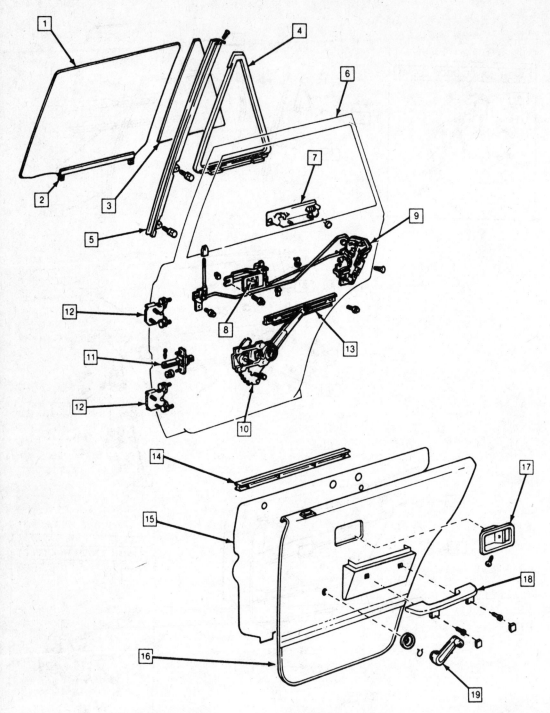

1. Window glass
2. Sash channel
3. Stationary window
4. Weather strip
5. Run channel guide
6. Door assembly
7. Outer handle
8. Inner handle
9. Door latch/lock
   assembly
10. Window regulator
11. Door check
12. Hinge
13. Lift arm bracket
14. Door belt molding
15. Water deflector
16. Trim panel
17. Inner handle bezel
18. Armrest
19. Window winder handle

Nova rear door components

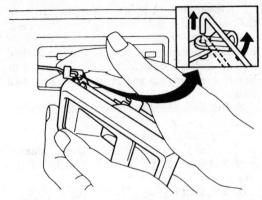

Disconnecting the Prizm door handle

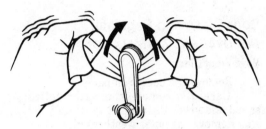

One method of removing the window winder clip

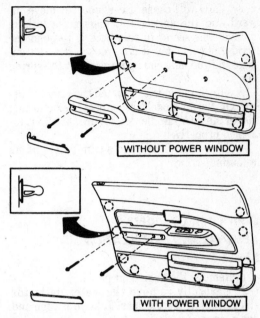

WITHOUT POWER WINDOW

WITH POWER WINDOW

Removing the front door inner panels. Rear panels similar

a. Use a door handle removal tool. This inexpensive slotted and toothed tool can be fitted between the winder and the panel and used to push the spring clip free.

b. Use a rag or piece of cloth and work it back and forth between the winder and door panel. If constant upward tension is kept, the clip will be forced free. Keep watch on the clip as it comes free; it may get lost as it pops out.

c. Straighten a common paper clip and bend a very small J-hook at the end of it. Work the hook down from the top of the winder and engage the loop of the spring clip. As you pull the clip free, keep your other hand over the area. If this is not done, the clip will depart for undisclosed locations, never to be seen again.

4. Remove the armrest retaining bolts and remove the armrest. The bolts may be concealed under various trim pieces. On cars with power windows, the front part of the armrest is bonded to the door panel and cannot be removed.

5. On Novas, the outside remote control mirror must be removed before removing the front door panels.

6. Using a broad, flat-bladed tool—not a screwdriver—begin gently prying the door pad away from the door. You are releasing plastic inserts from plastic seats. There are 8–10 of them around the door.

7. When all the clips are released, lift up on the panel to release the lip at the top of the door. This may require a bit of jiggling to loosen the panel; do so gently and don't damage the panel.

8. Once the panel is free of all its mounts, check behind it before removing it from the door. Disconnect any wiring and then remove the panel.

WARNING: *Behind the trim panel is a plastic sheet taped or glued to the door. This is a water shield and must be intact to prevent water entry into the car. It must be securely attached at its edges and not be ripped or damaged. Small holes or tears can be patched with waterproof tape applied to both sides of the liner.*

9. When reinstalling, connect any disconnected wiring and align the upper edge of the panel along the top of the door first. Make sure its left–right positioning is correct and tap it into place with the heel of your hand.

10. Make sure that the plastic clips align with their holes. Use the heel of your hand to gently pop the clips into position.

11. Reinstall the armrest and tighten the bolts. Install the bolt cover (trim) pieces.

12. Install the window winder handle if not equipped with power windows. Place the spring clip into the slot on the handle. (Remember to position it so the legs point along the length of the winder.) Align the handle with the tape mark made earlier and put the winder over the end of the axle. Use the heel of your hand to give the center of the winder a short, sharp

blow. This will cause the winder to move inward and the spring will engage its locking groove. The secret to this trick is to push the winder straight on; if it's crooked it won't engage and you may end up hunting for the spring clip.

13. On Nova models, reinstall the remote mirror. On Prizm models, reconnect the actuating rod to the door handle. Make sure the clip is installed properly.

14. Install the door handle trim bezel and its retaining screw.

Door Lock Cylinders

REMOVAL AND INSTALLATION

Nova

1. Remove the door trim panel.
2. Carefully remove the water deflector shield from inside the door. Take your time and don't rip it.
3. Disconnect the link rod running between the lock cylinder and the lock/latch mechanism.
4. The lock is held to the door by a horseshoe shaped retaining clip. Slide the clip free of the lock and remove the cylinder from the outside of the door.
5. Install the new cylinder and install the clip. The retaining clip has a slight bend in it and will install under tension. Do not attempt to straighten the clip.
6. Connect the link rod.
7. Install the water deflector shield, making sure that it is intact and firmly attached all the way around.
8. Reinstall the door trim panel.

Prizm

1. Remove the door trim panel.
2. Carefully remove the water deflector shield from inside the door. Take your time and don't rip it.

3. Disconnect the link rods running between the lock cylinder and the lock/latch mechanism.
4. Remove the two bolts holding the door handle to the door and remove the handle and lock from the outside. The cylinder and door handle are one piece and must be replaced as a unit.
5. Install the lock and handle and tighten the bolts.
6. Connect the link rods.
7. Install the water deflector shield, making sure that it is intact and firmly attached all the way around.
8. Reinstall the door trim panel.

Door Glass and Regulator

REMOVAL AND INSTALLATION

Nova Front Glass

1. Remove the door trim panel.
2. Carefully remove the water deflector shield and lower the window glass fully.
3. Remove the outer weatherstrip.
4. Remove the sash channel mounting bolts.
5. Carefully remove the glass through the top of the door.
6. Remove the window regulator mounting bolts and remove the regulator
7. If the window glass is to be replaced:
   a. Remove the sash channel from the glass.
   b. Apply a solution of soapy water to the sash channel.
   c. Install the channel to the new glass using a plastic or leather mallet to tap the sash into place. Note that the sash channel must

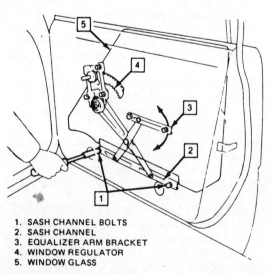

1. SASH CHANNEL BOLTS
2. SASH CHANNEL
3. EQUALIZER ARM BRACKET
4. WINDOW REGULATOR
5. WINDOW GLASS

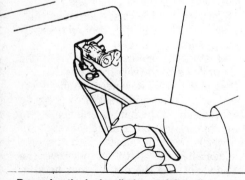

Removing the lock cylinder retaining clip

Removing the sash channel mounting bolts

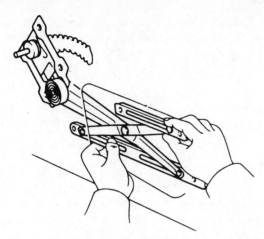

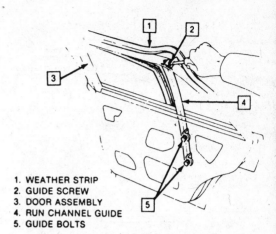

1. WEATHER STRIP
2. GUIDE SCREW
3. DOOR ASSEMBLY
4. RUN CHANNEL GUIDE
5. GUIDE BOLTS

Remove the regulator assembly through the access hole in the door

Removing Nova rear door run channel guide

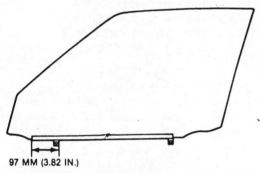

97 MM (3.82 IN.)

Correct placement of the regulator sash channel is critical to proper glass alignment

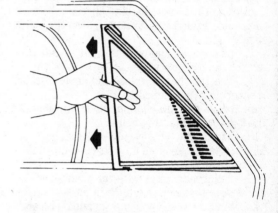

be exactly positioned on the glass or the bolt holes will not align at reinstallation.

8. Install the regulator and tighten the bolts evenly.

9. Install the window glass and install the sash channel mounting bolts.

10. Wind the window slowly up and down and observe its movement and alignment. The position of the glass can be adjusted by moving the equalizing arm bracket up or down. Make small adjustments and work for a perfectly aligned window.

11. Install the outer weatherstrip.

12. Install the water deflector, making sure it is intact and properly sealed.

13. Install the door trim panel.

Nova Rear Glass

NOTE: *The movable window glass cannot be removed without removing the fixed glass.*

1. Remove the door trim panel.

2. Carefully remove the water deflector shield and lower the window glass fully.

3. Remove the outer weatherstrip.

Removing Nova fixed rear glass

4. Partially remove the door weatherstrip to remove the run channel guide upper retaining screw.

5. Remove the rubber or felt run channel.

6. Remove the 2 lower run channel guide bolts and remove the guide.

7. Pull the fixed glass forward and remove it. Place it in a safe and protected location, away from the work area.

8. Remove the sash channel bolts.

9. Carefully remove the glass through the top of the door.

10. Remove the window regulator mounting bolts and remove the regulator.

11. If the window glass is to be replaced:

   a. Remove the sash channel from the glass.

   b. Apply a solution of soapy water to the sash channel.

   c. Install the channel to the new glass using a plastic or leather mallet to tap the sash into place. Note that the sash channel must

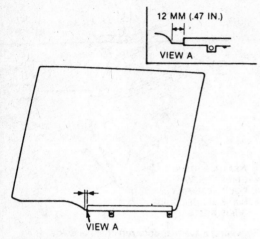

VIEW A

12 MM (.47 IN.)

VIEW A

Correct placement of sash channel on Nova rear glass

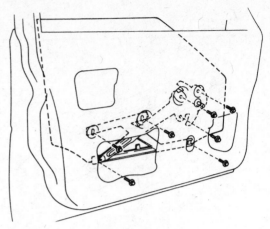

Prizm front door window regulator

be exactly positioned on the glass or the bolt holes will not align at reinstallation.

12. Install the regulator and tighten the bolts evenly.

13. Install the window glass and install the sash channel mounting bolts.

14. Reinstall the fixed glass and make certain it is correctly positioned.

15. Install the run channel guide and install the two lower retaining bolts.

16. Install the felt or rubber run channel. Make certain there are no twists or kinks in the channel.

17. Install the top screw in the channel guide and secure the door weatherstrip.

18. Wind the window slowly up and down and observe its movement and alignment. The position of the glass can be adjusted by moving the equalizing arm bracket up or down. Make small adjustments and work for a perfectly aligned window.

19. Install the outer weatherstrip.

20. Install the water deflector, making sure it is intact and properly sealed.

21. Install the door trim panel.

Prizm Front Glass

1. Remove the door trim panel.

2. Carefully remove the water deflector shield and lower the window glass fully.

3. Remove the glass channel mounting bolts.

4. Remove the window glass by lifting it through the top of the door.

5. Disconnect the window regulator as follows:

   a. For power windows, disconnect the electrical connector and remove the 4 mounting bolts. The regulator will be removed with the motor attached.

   b. For manual windows, remove the 3 mounting bolts.

6. Remove the two mounting bolts holding the equalizer arm bracket.

7. Remove the window regulator.

CAUTION: *If the motor is to be removed from the power window regulator, install a large stopper bolt through the regulator frame before removing the motor. When the motor is removed, the spring loaded gear will be disengaged, causing the gear to rotate until the spring is unwound. Install the stopper bolt to prevent possible injury by the spinning gear.*

8. Before installing the regulator assembly, apply a light coat of lithium grease to the sliding surfaces and pivot points of the regulator. Do not apply grease to the spring.

9. Install the regulator:

   a. With power windows, install the 4 mounting bolts and connect the motor wiring.

   b. With manual windows, install the 3 mounting bolts.

10. Install the bolts holding the equalizer arm bracket.

11. Place the glass into the door and install the glass channel retaining bolts.

12. Adjust the door glass by moving the equalizer arm up or down as necessary to get the window level in the frame.

13. Install the water deflector, making sure it is intact and properly sealed.

14. Install the door trim panel.

Prizm Rear Glass

1. Remove the door trim panel.

2. Carefully remove the water deflector shield and lower the window glass fully.

3. Remove the glass from the regulator arm.

4. Loosen the window weatherstrip at the rear edge of the glass run channel.

5. Remove the screws holding the top and bottom of the rear channel guide.

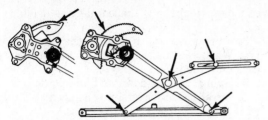

Points to be lubricated before installing Prizm front or rear regulator. Do not lubricate the spiral spring

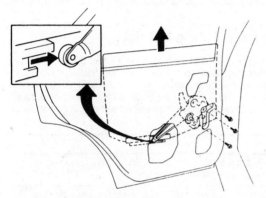

Prizm rear door glass regulator

6. Lift the door weatherstrip and remove the screws holding the (black) window filler panel.

7. Remove the door glass by pulling it upward.

8. If equipped with power windows, disconnect the motor wiring connector.

9. Remove the bolts holding the regulator and remove the regulator.

CAUTION: *If the motor is to be removed from the power window regulator, install a large stopper bolt through the regulator frame before removing the motor. When the motor is removed, the spring loaded gear will be disengaged, causing the gear to rotate until the spring is unwound. Install the stopper bolt to prevent possible injury by the spinning gear.*

10. Before installing the regulator assembly, apply a light coat of lithium grease to the sliding surfaces and pivot points of the regulator. Do not apply grease to the spring.

11. Install the regulator and tighten the mounting bolts evenly.

12. If equipped with power windows, connect the wiring to the motor.

13. Install the glass into the door and connect it to the regulator.

14. Install the black window filler panel and its 2 screws.

15. Install the rear glass guide channel.

16. Install the window weatherstrip.

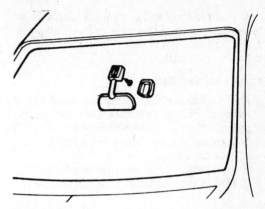

Inside mirror

17. Install the water deflector, making sure it is intact and properly sealed.

18. Install the door trim panel.

Inside Mirror
REMOVAL AND INSTALLATION

The inside mirror is removed by carefully prying off the plastic cover and removing the retaining bolts. The inside mirror is designed to break loose from the roof mount if it receives moderate impact. If the mirror has come off due to impact, it can usually be remounted by installing a new mirror base rather than an entire new mirror. If the glass is cracked, the mirror must be replaced.

Seats
REMOVAL AND INSTALLATION
Front Seats

The front seats of both the Nova and Prizm are removed by disconnecting the 4 mounting bolts holding the seat to the floor rails. The bolts may be under plastic covers which can be popped off with a small tool. The seat assembly will come out of the car complete with the tracks and adjuster. When reinstalling the seat, make certain that the bolts are properly threaded and tightened to 27 ft. lbs. Seat mounting and retention is a critical safety item. Never attempt to alter the mounts or the seat tracks.

Rear Bench Seat Cushion

1. Pull forward on the seat cushion releases. These are small levers on the lower front of the cushion.

2. Pull upward on the front of the seat cushion and rotate it free. It is not retained or bolted under the seat back.

3. To reinstall, fit the rear of the cushion into place under the seat back.

4. Push inward and downward on the front of the cushion until the releases lock into place. Make sure the seat is locked into place and the releases are secure.

Rear Bench Seat Back

NOTE: *The seat bottom cushion need not be removed for this procedure, but access is improved with the cushion removed.*

1. Remove the two lower bolts holding the seat back to the body.

2. Pull outward and push upward on the bottom edge of the seat back. This will release the seat back from the L-shaped hangers holding it.

3. Remove the seat back from the car.

4. When reinstalling, carefully fit the seat back onto the hangers.

5. Swing the back down and into place.

6. Install the lower retaining bolts and tighten them to 3.5 ft. lbs. (42 INCH lbs.)

Split/Folding Rear Seat Cushion

1. At the front lower edge of the seat cushion, remove the 2 bolts holding the seat cushion

How to Remove Stains from Fabric Interior

For rest results, spots and stains should be removed as soon as possible. Never use gasoline, lacquer thinner, acetone, nail polish remover or bleach. Use a 3′ x 3″ piece of cheesecloth. Squeeze most of the liquid from the fabric and wipe the stained fabric from the outside of the stain toward the center with a lifting motion. Turn the cheesecloth as soon as one side becomes soiled. When using water to remove a stain, be sure to wash the entire section after the spot has been removed to avoid water stains. Encrusted spots can be broken up with a dull knife and vacuumed before removing the stain.

Type of Stain	How to Remove It
Surface spots	Brush the spots out with a small hand brush or use a commercial preparation such as K2R to lift the stain.
Mildew	Clean around the mildew with warm suds. Rinse in cold water and soak the mildew area in a solution of 1 part table salt and 2 parts water. Wash with upholstery cleaner.
Water stains	Water stains in fabric materials can be removed with a solution made from 1 cup of table salt dissolved in 1 quart of water. Vigorously scrub the solution into the stain and rinse with clear water. Water stains in nylon or other synthetic fabrics should be removed with a commercial type spot remover.
Chewing gum, tar, crayons, shoe polish (greasy stains)	Do not use a cleaner that will soften gum or tar. Harden the deposit with an ice cube and scrape away as much as possible with a dull knife. Moisten the remainder with cleaning fluid and scrub clean.
Ice cream, candy	Most candy has a sugar base and can be removed with a cloth wrung out in warm water. Oily candy, after cleaning with warm water, should be cleaned with upholstery cleaner. Rinse with warm water and clean the remainder with cleaning fluid.
Wine, alcohol, egg, milk, soft drink (non-greasy stains)	Do not use soap. Scrub the stain with a cloth wrung out in warm water. Remove the remainder with cleaning fluid.
Grease, oil, lipstick, butter and related stains	Use a spot remover to avoid leaving a ring. Work from the outisde of the stain to the center and dry with a clean cloth when the spot is gone.
Headliners (cloth)	Mix a solution of warm water and foam upholstery cleaner to give thick suds. Use only foam—liquid may streak or spot. Clean the entire headliner in one operation using a circular motion with a natural sponge.
Headliner (vinyl)	Use a vinyl cleaner with a sponge and wipe clean with a dry cloth.
Seats and door panels	Mix 1 pint upholstery cleaner in 1 gallon of water. Do not soak the fabric around the buttons.
Leather or vinyl fabric	Use a multi-purpose cleaner full strength and a stiff brush. Let stand 2 minutes and scrub thoroughly. Wipe with a clean, soft rag.
Nylon or synthetic fabrics	For normal stains, use the same procedures you would for washing cloth upholstery. If the fabric is extremely dirty, use a multi-purpose cleaner full strength with a stiff scrub brush. Scrub thoroughly in all directions and wipe with a cotton towel or soft rag.

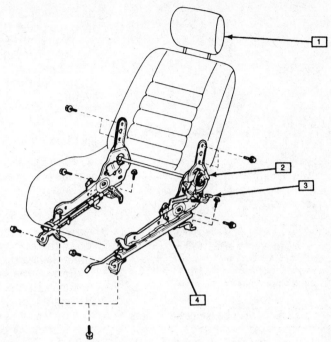

1. Head restraint
2. Recliner mechanism
3. Recliner actuator handle
4. Seat adjuster

Prizm front seat components. Nova similar

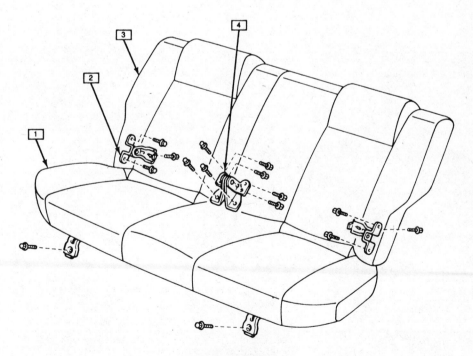

1. Rear seat cushion
2. Side hinge
3. Seat back
4. Center hinge

Split/folding rear seat components

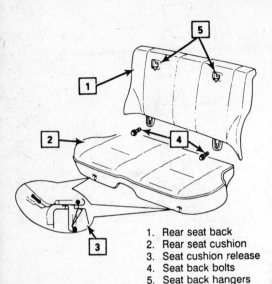

1. Rear seat back
2. Rear seat cushion
3. Seat cushion release
4. Seat back bolts
5. Seat back hangers

Rear bench seat components

to the body. The bolts may be concealed under carpeting or trim pieces.

2. Pull upward on the front of the seat cushion and rotate it free. It is not retained or bolted under the seat back.

3. To reinstall, fit the rear of the cushion into place under the seat back.

4. Push inward and downward on the front of the cushion until it is in place and the bolt holes align.

5. Install the retaining bolts and tighten them.

Split/Folding Rear Seat Back

1. Push the seat back forward into a folded position.

2. Remove the carpeting from the rear of the seat back.

3. At the side hinge, remove the bolt holding the seat back to the hinge.

4. At the center hinge, remove the 2 bolts holding the seat back to the hinge.

5. Remove the seat back from the car.

6. Reinstall the seat back and install the bolts finger tight.

7. Tighten the side hinge bolt to 13 ft. lbs.

8. Tighten the center hinge bolts to 5.4 ft. lbs. (65 INCH lbs.)

9. Install the carpeting and trim on the rear of the seat back.

Mechanic's Data

11

1":254mm
10.16mm
TAX
Liter
Parts
Overhaul

General Conversion Table

Multiply By	To Convert	To	
		LENGTH	
2.54	Inches	Centimeters	.3937
25.4	Inches	Millimeters	.03937
30.48	Feet	Centimeters	.0328
.304	Feet	Meters	3.28
.914	Yards	Meters	1.094
1.609	Miles	Kilometers	.621
		VOLUME	
.473	Pints	Liters	2.11
.946	Quarts	Liters	1.06
3.785	Gallons	Liters	.264
.016	Cubic inches	Liters	61.02
16.39	Cubic inches	Cubic cms.	.061
28.3	Cubic feet	Liters	.0353
		MASS (Weight)	
28.35	Ounces	Grams	.035
.4536	Pounds	Kilograms	2.20
—	To obtain	From	Multiply by

Multiply By	To Convert	To	
		AREA	
.645	Square inches	Square cms.	.155
.836	Square yds.	Square meters	1.196
		FORCE	
4.448	Pounds	Newtons	.225
.138	Ft./lbs.	Kilogram/meters	7.23
1.36	Ft./lbs.	Newton-meters	.737
.112	In./lbs.	Newton-meters	8.844
		PRESSURE	
.068	Psi	Atmospheres	14.7
6.89	Psi	Kilopascals	.145
		OTHER	
1.104	Horsepower (DIN)	Horsepower (SAE)	.9861
.746	Horsepower (SAE)	Kilowatts (KW)	1.34
1.60	Mph	Km/h	.625
.425	Mpg	Km/1	2.35
—	To obtain	From	Multiply by

Tap Drill Sizes

National Coarse or U.S.S.

Screw & Tap Size	Threads Per Inch	Use Drill Number
No. 5	40	39
No. 6	32	36
No. 8	32	29
No. 10	24	25
No. 12	24	17
1/4	20	8
5/16	18	F
3/8	16	5/16
7/16	14	U
1/2	13	27/64
9/16	12	31/64
5/8	11	17/32
3/4	10	21/32
7/8	9	49/64

National Coarse or U.S.S.

Screw & Tap Size	Threads Per Inch	Use Drill Number
1	8	7/8
1 1/8	7	63/64
1 1/4	7	1 7/64
1 1/2	6	1 11/32

National Fine or S.A.E.

Screw & Tap Size	Threads Per Inch	Use Drill Number
No. 5	44	37
No. 6	40	33
No. 8	36	29
No. 10	32	21

National Fine or S.A.E.

Screw & Tap Size	Threads Per Inch	Use Drill Number
No. 12	28	15
1/4	28	3
6/16	24	1
3/8	24	Q
7/16	20	W
1/2	20	29/64
9/16	18	33/64
5/8	18	37/64
3/4	16	11/16
7/8	14	13/16
1 1/8	12	1 3/64
1 1/4	12	1 11/64
1 1/2	12	1 27/64

Drill Sizes In Decimal Equivalents

Inch	Decimal	Wire	mm
1/64	.0156		.39
	.0157		.4
	.0160	78	
	.0165		.42
	.0173		.44
	.0177		.45
	.0180	77	
	.0181		.46
	.0189		.48
	.0197		.5
	.0200	76	
	.0210	75	
	.0217		.55
	.0225	74	
	.0236		.6
	.0240	73	
	.0250	72	
	.0256		.65
	.0260	71	
	.0276		.7
	.0280	70	
	.0292	69	
	.0295		.75
	.0310	68	
1/32	.0312		.79
	.0315		.8
	.0320	67	
	.0330	66	
	.0335		.85
	.0350	65	
	.0354		.9
	.0360	64	
	.0370	63	
	.0374		.95
	.0380	62	
	.0390	61	
	.0394		1.0
	.0400	60	
	.0410	59	
	.0413		1.05
	.0420	58	
	.0430	57	
	.0433		1.1
	.0453		1.15
3/64	.0465	56	
	.0469		1.19
	.0472		1.2
	.0492		1.25
	.0512		1.3
	.0520	55	
	.0531		1.35
	.0550	54	
	.0551		1.4
	.0571		1.45
	.0591		1.5
	.0595	53	
	.0610		1.55
1/16	.0625		1.59
	.0630		1.6
	.0635	52	
	.0650		1.65
	.0669		1.7
	.0670	51	
	.0689		1.75
	.0700	50	
	.0709		1.8
	.0728		1.85

Inch	Decimal	Wire	mm
	.0730	49	
	.0748		1.9
	.0760	48	
	.0768		1.95
5/64	.0781		1.98
	.0785	47	
	.0787		2.0
	.0807		2.05
	.0810	46	
	.0820	45	
	.0827		2.1
	.0846		2.15
	.0860	44	
	.0866		2.2
	.0886		2.25
	.0890	43	
	.0906		2.3
	.0925		2.35
	.0935	42	
3/32	.0938		2.38
	.0945		2.4
	.0960	41	
	.0965		2.45
	.0980	40	
	.0981		2.5
	.0995	39	
	.1015	38	
	.1024		2.6
	.1040	37	
	.1063		2.7
	.1065	36	
	.1083		2.75
7/64	.1094		2.77
	.1100	35	
	.1102		2.8
	.1110	34	
	.1130	33	
	.1142		2.9
	.1160	32	
	.1181		3.0
	.1200	31	
	.1220		3.1
1/8	.1250		3.17
	.1260		3.2
	.1280		3.25
	.1285	30	
	.1299		3.3
	.1339		3.4
	.1360	29	
	.1378		3.5
	.1405	28	
9/64	.1406		3.57
	.1417		3.6
	.1440	27	
	.1457		3.7
	.1470	26	
	.1476		3.75
	.1495	25	
	.1496		3.8
	.1520	24	
	.1535		3.9
	.1540	23	
5/32	.1562		3.96
	.1570	22	
	.1575		4.0
	.1590	21	
	.1610	20	

Inch	Decimal	Wire & Letter	mm
	.1614		4.1
	.1654		4.2
	.1660	19	
	.1673		4.25
	.1693		4.3
	.1695	18	
11/64	.1719		4.36
	.1730	17	
	.1732		4.4
	.1770	16	
	.1772		4.5
	.1800	15	
	.1811		4.6
	.1820	14	
	.1850	13	
	.1850		4.7
	.1870		4.75
3/16	.1875		4.76
	.1890		4.8
	.1890	12	
	.1910	11	
	.1929		4.9
	.1935	10	
	.1960	9	
	.1969		5.0
	.1990	8	
	.2008		5.1
	.2010	7	
13/64	.2031		5.16
	.2040	6	
	.2047		5.2
	.2055	5	
	.2067		5.25
	.2087		5.3
	.2090	4	
	.2126		5.4
	.2130	3	
	.2165		5.5
7/32	.2188		5.55
	.2205		5.6
	.2210	2	
	.2244		5.7
	.2264		5.75
	.2280	1	
	.2283		5.8
	.2323		5.9
	.2340	A	
15/64	.2344		5.95
	.2362		6.0
	.2380	B	
	.2402		6.1
	.2420	C	
	.2441		6.2
	.2460	D	
	.2461		6.25
	.2480		6.3
1/4	.2500	E	6.35
	.2520		6.
	.2559		6.5
	.2570	F	
	.2598		6.6
	.2610	G	
	.2638		6.7
17/64	.2656		6.74
	.2657		6.75
	.2660	H	
	.2677		6.8

Inch	Decimal	Letter	mm
	.2717		6.9
	.2720	I	
	.2756		7.0
	.2770	J	
	.2795		7.1
	.2810	K	
9/32	.2812		7.14
	.2835		7.2
	.2854		7.25
	.2874		7.3
	.2900	L	
	.2913		7.4
	.2950	M	
	.2953		7.5
19/64	.2969		7.54
	.2992		7.6
	.3020	N	
	.3031		7.7
	.3051		7.75
	.3071		7.8
	.3110		7.9
5/16	.3125		7.93
	.3150		8.0
	.3160	O	
	.3189		8.1
	.3228		8.2
	.3230	P	
	.3248		8.25
	.3268		8.3
21/64	.3281		8.33
	.3307		8.4
	.3320	Q	
	.3346		8.5
	.3386		8.6
	.3390	R	
	.3425		8.7
11/32	.3438		8.73
	.3445		8.75
	.3465		8.8
	.3480	S	
	.3504		8.9
	.3543		9.0
	.3580	T	
	.3583		9.1
23/64	.3594		9.12
	.3622		9.2
	.3642		9.25
	.3661		9.3
	.3680	U	
	.3701		9.4
	.3740		9.5
3/8	.3750		9.52
	.3770	V	
	.3780		9.6
	.3819		9.7
	.3839		9.75
	.3858		9.8
	.3860	W	
	.3898		9.9
25/64	.3906		9.92
	.3937		10.0
	.3970	X	
	.4040	Y	
13/32	.4062		10.31
	.4130	Z	
	.4134		10.5
27/64	.4219		10.71

Inch	Decimal	mm
	.4331	11.0
7/16	.4375	11.11
	.4528	11.5
29/64	.4531	11.51
15/32	.4688	11.90
	.4724	12.0
31/64	.4844	12.30
	.4921	12.5
1/2	.5000	12.70
	.5118	13.0
33/64	.5156	13.09
17/32	.5312	13.49
	.5315	13.5
35/64	.5469	13.89
	.5512	14.0
9/16	.5625	14.28
	.5709	14.5
37/64	.5781	14.68
	.5906	15.0
19/32	.5938	15.08
39/64	.6094	15.47
	.6102	15.5
5/8	.6250	15.87
	.6299	16.0
41/64	.6406	16.27
	.6496	16.5
21/32	.6562	16.66
	.6693	17.0
43/64	.6719	17.06
11/16	.6875	17.46
	.6890	17.5
45/64	.7031	17.85
	.7087	18.0
23/32	.7188	18.25
	.7283	18.5
47/64	.7344	18.65
	.7480	19.0
3/4	.7500	19.05
49/64	.7656	19.44
	.7677	19.5
25/32	.7812	19.84
	.7874	20.0
51/64	.7969	20.24
	.8071	20.5
13/16	.8125	20.63
	.8268	21.0
53/64	.8281	21.03
27/32	.8438	21.43
	.8465	21.5
55/64	.8594	21.82
	.8661	22.0
7/8	.8750	22.22
	.8858	22.5
57/64	.8906	22.62
	.9055	23.0
29/32	.9062	23.01
59/64	.9219	23.41
	.9252	23.5
15/16	.9375	23.81
	.9449	24.0
61/64	.9531	24.2
	.9646	24.5
31/32	.9688	24.6
	.9843	25.0
63/64	.9844	25.0
1	1.0000	25.4

GLOSSARY OF TERMS

AIR/FUEL RATIO: The ratio of air to gasoline by weight in the fuel mixture drawn into the engine.

AIR INJECTION: One method of reducing harmful exhaust emissions by injecting air into each of the exhaust ports of an engine. The fresh air entering the hot exhaust manifold causes any remaining fuel to be burned before it can exit the tailpipe.

ALTERNATOR: A device used for converting mechanical energy into electrical energy.

AMMETER: An instrument, calibrated in amperes, used to measure the flow of an electrical current in a circuit. Ammeters are always connected in series with the circuit being tested.

AMPERE: The rate of flow of electrical current present when one volt of electrical pressure is applied against one ohm of electrical resistance.

ANALOG COMPUTER: Any microprocessor that uses similar (analogous) electrical signals to make its calculations.

ARMATURE: A laminated, soft iron core wrapped by a wire that converts electrical energy to mechanical energy as in a motor or relay. When rotated in a magnetic field, it changes mechanical energy into electrical energy as in a generator.

ATMOSPHERIC PRESSURE: The pressure on the Earth's surface caused by the weight of the air in the atmosphere. At sea level, this pressure is 14.7 psi at 32°F (101 kPa at 0°C).

ATOMIZATION: The breaking down of a liquid into a fine mist that can be suspended in air.

AXIAL PLAY: Movement parallel to a shaft or bearing bore.

BACKFIRE: The sudden combustion of gases in the intake or exhaust system that results in a loud explosion.

BACKLASH: The clearance or play between two parts, such as meshed gears.

BACKPRESSURE: Restrictions in the exhaust system that slow the exit of exhaust gases from the combustion chamber.

BAKELITE: A heat resistant, plastic insulator material commonly used in printed circuit boards and transistorized components.

BALL BEARING: A bearing made up of hardened inner and outer races between which hardened steel ball roll.

BALLAST RESISTOR: A resistor in the primary ignition circuit that lowers voltage after the engine is started to reduce wear on ignition components.

BEARING: A friction reducing, supportive device usually located between a stationary part and a moving part.

BIMETAL TEMPERATURE SENSOR: Any sensor or switch made of two dissimilar types of metal that bend when heated or cooled due to the different expansion rates of the alloys. These types of sensors usually function as an on/off switch.

BLOWBY: Combustion gases, composed of water vapor and unburned fuel, that leak past the piston rings into the crankcase during normal engine operation. These gases are removed by the PCV system to prevent the buildup of harmful acids in the crankcase.

BRAKE PAD: A brake shoe and lining assembly used with disc brakes.

BRAKE SHOE: The backing for the brake lining. The term is, however, usually applied to the assembly of the brake backing and lining.

BUSHING: A liner, usually removable, for a bearing; an anti-friction liner used in place of a bearing.

BYPASS: System used to bypass ballast resistor during engine cranking to increase voltage supplied to the coil.

CALIPER: A hydraulically activated device in a disc brake system, which is mounted straddling the brake rotor (disc). The caliper contains at least one piston and two brake pads. Hydraulic pressure on the piston(s) forces the pads against the rotor.

CAMSHAFT: A shaft in the engine on which are the lobes (cams) which operate the valves. The camshaft is driven by the crankshaft, via a belt, chain or gears, at one half the crankshaft speed.

CAPACITOR: A device which stores an electrical charge.

CARBON MONOXIDE (CO): a colorless, odorless gas given off as a normal byproduct of combustion. It is poisonous and extremely dangerous in confined areas, building up slowly to toxic levels without warning if adequate ventilation is not available.

CARBURETOR: A device, usually mounted on the intake manifold of an engine, which mixes the air and fuel in the proper proportion to allow even combustion.

CATALYTIC CONVERTER: A device installed in the exhaust system, like a muffler, that converts harmful byproducts of combustion into carbon dioxide and water vapor by means of a heat-producing chemical reaction.

CENTRIFUGAL ADVANCE: A mechanical method of advancing the spark timing by using flyweights in the distributor that react to centrifugal force generated by the distributor shaft rotation.

CHECK VALVE: Any one-way valve installed to permit the flow of air, fuel or vacuum in one direction only.

CHOKE: A device, usually a moveable valve, placed in the intake path of a carburetor to restrict the flow of air.

CIRCUIT: Any unbroken path through which an electrical current can flow. Also used to describe fuel flow in some instances.

CIRCUIT BREAKER: A switch which protects an electrical circuit from overload by opening the circuit when the current flow exceeds a predetermined level. Some circuit breakers must be reset manually, while other reset automatically

COIL (IGNITION): A transformer in the ignition circuit which steps of the voltage provided to the spark plugs.

COMBINATION MANIFOLD: An assembly which includes both the intake and exhaust manifolds in one casting.

COMBINATION VALVE: A device used in some fuel systems that routes fuel vapors to a charcoal storage canister instead of venting them into the atmosphere. The valve relieves fuel tank pressure and allows fresh air into the tank as fuel level drops to prevent a vapor lock situation.

COMPRESSION RATIO: The comparison of the total volume of the cylinder and combustion chamber with the piston at BDC and the piston at TDC.

CONDENSER: 1. An electrical device which acts to store an electrical charge, preventing voltage surges.
 2. A radiator-like device in the air conditioning system in which refrigerant gas condenses into a liquid, giving off heat.

CONDUCTOR: Any material through which an electrical current can be transmitted easily.

CONTINUITY: Continuous or complete circuit. Can be checked with an ohmmeter.

COUNTERSHAFT: An intermediate shaft which is rotated by a mainshaft and transmits, in turn, that rotation to a working part.

CRANKCASE: The lower part of an engine in which the crankshaft and related parts operate.

CRANKSHAFT: The main driving shaft of an engine which receives reciprocating motion from the pistons and converts it to rotary motion.

CYLINDER: In an engine, the round hole in the engine block in which the piston(s) ride.

CYLINDER BLOCK: The main structural member of an engine in which is found the cylinders, crankshaft and other principal parts.

CYLINDER HEAD: The detachable portion of the engine, fastened, usually, to the top of the cylinder block, containing all or most of the combustion chambers. On overhead valve engines, it contains the valves and their operating parts. On overhead cam engines, it contains the camshaft as well.

DEAD CENTER: The extreme top or bottom of the piston stroke.

DETONATION: An unwanted explosion of the air fuel mixture in the combustion chamber caused by excess heat and compression, advanced timing, or an overly lean mixture. Also referred to as "ping".

DIAPHRAGM: A thin, flexible wall separating two cavities, such as in a vacuum advance unit.

DIESELING: A condition in which hot spots in the combustion chamber cause the engine to run on after the key is turned off.

DIFFERENTIAL: A geared assembly which allows the transmission of motion between drive axles, giving one axle the ability to turn faster than the other.

DIODE: An electrical device that will allow current to flow in one direction only.

DISC BRAKE: A hydraulic braking assembly consisting of a brake disc, or rotor, mounted on an axle, and a caliper assembly containing, usually two brake pads which are activated by hydraulic pressure. The pads are forced against the sides of the disc, creating friction which slows the vehicle.

DISTRIBUTOR: A mechanically driven device on an engine which is responsible for electrically firing the spark plug at a predetermined point of the piston stroke.

DOWEL PIN: A pin, inserted in mating holes in two different parts allowing those parts to maintain a fixed relationship.

DRUM BRAKE: A braking system which consists of two brake shoes and one or two wheel cylinders, mounted on a fixed backing plate, and a brake drum, mounted on an axle, which revolves around the assembly. Hydraulic action applied to the wheel cylinders forces the shoes outward against the drum, creating friction and slowing the vehicle.

DWELL: The rate, measured in degrees of shaft rotation, at which an electrical circuit cycles on and off.

ELECTRONIC CONTROL UNIT (ECU): Ignition module, module, amplifier or igniter. See Module for definition.

ELECTRONIC IGNITION: A system in which the timing and firing of the spark plugs is controlled by an electronic control unit, usually called a module. These systems have not points or condenser.

ENDPLAY: The measured amount of axial movement in a shaft.

ENGINE: A device that converts heat into mechanical energy.

EXHAUST MANIFOLD: A set of cast passages or pipes which conduct exhaust gases from the engine.

FEELER GAUGE: A blade, usually metal, of precisely predetermined thickness, used to measure the clearance between two parts. These blades usually are available in sets of assorted thicknesses.

F-Head: An engine configuration in which the intake valves are in the cylinder head, while the camshaft and exhaust valves are located in the cylinder block. The camshaft operates the intake valves via lifters and pushrods, while it operates the exhaust valves directly.

FIRING ORDER: The order in which combustion occurs in the cylinders of an engine. Also the order in which spark is distributed to the plugs by the distributor.

FLATHEAD: An engine configuration in which the camshaft and all the valves are located in the cylinder block.

FLOODING: The presence of too much fuel in the intake manifold and combustion chamber which prevents the air/fuel mixture from firing, thereby causing a no-start situation.

FLYWHEEL: A disc shaped part bolted to the rear end of the crankshaft. Around the outer perimeter is affixed the ring gear. The starter drive engages the ring gear, turning the flywheel, which rotates the crankshaft, imparting the initial starting motion to the engine.

FOOT POUND (ft.lb. or sometimes, ft. lbs.): The amount of energy or work needed to raise an item weighing one pound, a distance of one foot.

FUSE: A protective device in a circuit which prevents circuit overload by breaking the circuit when a specific amperage is present. The device is constructed around a strip or wire of a lower amperage rating than the circuit it is designed to protect. When an amperage higher than that stamped on the fuse is present in the circuit, the strip or wire melts, opening the circuit.

GEAR RATIO: The ratio between the number of teeth on meshing gears.

GENERATOR: A device which converts mechanical energy into electrical energy.

HEAT RANGE: The measure of a spark plug's ability to dissipate heat from its firing end. The higher the heat range, the hotter the plug fires.

HUB: The center part of a wheel or gear.

HYDROCARBON (HC): Any chemical compound made up of hydrogen and carbon. A major pollutant formed by the engine as a byproduct of combustion.

HYDROMETER: An instrument used to measure the specific gravity of a solution.

INCH POUND (in.lb. or sometimes, in. lbs.): One twelfth of a foot pound.

INDUCTION: A means of transferring electrical energy in the form of a magnetic field. Principle used in the ignition coil to increase voltage.

INJECTION PUMP: A device, usually mechanically operated, which meters and delivers fuel under pressure to the fuel injector.

INJECTOR: A device which receives metered fuel under relatively low pressure and is activated to inject the fuel into the engine under relatively high pressure at a predetermined time.

INPUT SHAFT: The shaft to which torque is applied, usually carrying the driving gear or gears.

INTAKE MANIFOLD: A casting of passages or pipes used to conduct air or a fuel/air mixture to the cylinders.

JOURNAL: The bearing surface within which a shaft operates.

KEY: A small block usually fitted in a notch between a shaft and a hub to prevent slippage of the two parts.

MANIFOLD: A casting of passages or set of pipes which connect the cylinders to an inlet or outlet source.

MANIFOLD VACUUM: Low pressure in an engine intake manifold formed just below the throttle plates. Manifold vacuum is highest at idle and drops under acceleration.

MASTER CYLINDER: The primary fluid pressurizing device in a hydraulic system. In automotive use, it is found in brake and hydraulic clutch systems and is pedal activated, either directly or, in a power brake system, through the power booster.

MODULE: Electronic control unit, amplifier or igniter of solid state or integrated design which controls the current flow in the ignition primary circuit based on input from the pickup coil. When the module opens the primary circuit, the high secondary voltage is induced in the coil.

NEEDLE BEARING: A bearing which consists of a number (usually a large number) of long, thin rollers.

OHM: (Ω) The unit used to measure the resistance of conductor to electrical flow. One ohm is the amount of resistance that limits current flow to one ampere in a circuit with one volt of pressure.

OHMMETER: An instrument used for measuring the resistance, in ohms, in an electrical circuit.

OUTPUT SHAFT: The shaft which transmits torque from a device, such as a transmission.

OVERDRIVE: A gear assembly which produces more shaft revolutions than that transmitted to it.

OVERHEAD CAMSHAFT (OHC): An engine configuration in which the camshaft is mounted on top of the cylinder head and operates the valve either directly or by means of rocker arms.

OVERHEAD VALVE (OHV): An engine configuration in which all of the valves are located in the cylinder head and the camshaft is located in the cylinder block. The camshaft operates the valves via lifters and pushrods.

OXIDES OF NITROGEN (NOx): Chemical compounds of nitrogen produced as a byproduct of combustion. They combine with hydrocarbons to produce smog.

OXYGEN SENSOR: Used with the feedback system to sense the presence of oxygen in the exhaust gas and signal the computer which can reference the voltage signal to an air/fuel ratio.

PINION: The smaller of two meshing gears.

PISTON RING: An open ended ring which fits into a groove on the outer diameter of the piston. Its chief function is to form a seal between the piston and cylinder wall. Most automotive pistons have three rings: two for compression sealing; one for oil sealing.

PRELOAD: A predetermined load placed on a bearing during assembly or by adjustment.

PRIMARY CIRCUIT: Is the low voltage side of the ignition system which consists of the ignition switch, ballast resistor or resistance wire, bypass, coil, electronic control unit and pick-up coil as well as the connecting wires and harnesses.

PRESS FIT: The mating of two parts under pressure, due to the inner diameter of one being smaller than the outer diameter of the other, or vice versa; an interference fit.

RACE: The surface on the inner or outer ring of a bearing on which the balls, needles or rollers move.

REGULATOR: A device which maintains the amperage and/or voltage levels of a circuit at predetermined values.

RELAY: A switch which automatically opens and/or closes a circuit.

RESISTANCE: The opposition to the flow of current through a circuit or electrical device, and is measured in ohms. Resistance is equal to the voltage divided by the amperage.

RESISTOR: A device, usually made of wire, which offers a preset amount of resistance in an electrical circuit.

RING GEAR: The name given to a ring-shaped gear attached to a differential case, or affixed to a flywheel or as part a planetary gear set.

ROLLER BEARING: A bearing made up of hardened inner and outer races between which hardened steel rollers move.

ROTOR: 1. The disc-shaped part of a disc brake assembly, upon which the brake pads bear; also called, brake disc.
2. The device mounted atop the distributor shaft, which passes current to the distributor cap tower contacts.

SECONDARY CIRCUIT: The high voltage side of the ignition system, usually above 20,000 volts. The secondary includes the ignition coil, coil wire, distributor cap and rotor, spark plug wires and spark plugs.

SENDING UNIT: A mechanical, electrical, hydraulic or electromagnetic device which transmits information to a gauge.

SENSOR: Any device designed to measure engine operating conditions or ambient pressures and temperatures. Usually electronic in nature and designed to send a voltage signal to an on-board computer, some sensors may operate as a simple on/off switch or they may provide a variable voltage signal (like a potentiometer) as conditions or measured parameters change.

SHIM: Spacers of precise, predetermined thickness used between parts to establish a proper working relationship.

SLAVE CYLINDER: In automotive use, a device in the hydraulic clutch system which is activated by hydraulic force, disengaging the clutch.

SOLENOID: A coil used to produce a magnetic field, the effect of which is produce work.

SPARK PLUG: A device screwed into the combustion chamber of a spark ignition engine. The basic construction is a conductive core inside of a ceramic insulator, mounted in an outer conductive base. An electrical charge from the spark plug wire travels along the conductive core and jumps a preset air gap to a grounding point or points at the end of the conductive base. The resultant spark ignites the fuel/air mixture in the combustion chamber.

SPLINES: Ridges machined or cast onto the outer diameter of a shaft or inner diameter of a bore to enable parts to mate without rotation.

TACHOMETER: A device used to measure the rotary speed of an engine, shaft, gear, etc., usually in rotations per minute.

THERMOSTAT: A valve, located in the cooling system of an engine, which is closed when cold and opens gradually in response to engine heating, controlling the temperature of the coolant and rate of coolant flow.

TOP DEAD CENTER (TDC): The point at which the piston reaches the top of its travel on the compression stroke.

TORQUE: The twisting force applied to an object.

TORQUE CONVERTER: A turbine used to transmit power from a driving member to a driven member via hydraulic action, providing changes in drive ratio and torque. In automotive use, it links the driveplate at the rear of the engine to the automatic transmission.

TRANSDUCER: A device used to change a force into an electrical signal.

TRANSISTOR: A semi-conductor component which can be actuated by a small voltage to perform an electrical switching function.

TUNE-UP: A regular maintenance function, usually associated with the replacement and adjustment of parts and components in the electrical and fuel systems of a vehicle for the purpose of attaining optimum performance.

TURBOCHARGER: An exhaust driven pump which compresses intake air and forces it into the combustion chambers at higher than atmospheric pressures. The increased air pressure allows more fuel to be burned and results in increased horsepower being produced.

VACUUM ADVANCE: A device which advances the ignition timing in response to increased engine vacuum.

VACUUM GAUGE: An instrument used to measure the presence of vacuum in a chamber.

VALVE: A device which control the pressure, direction of flow or rate of flow of a liquid or gas.

VALVE CLEARANCE: The measured gap between the end of the valve stem and the rocker arm, cam lobe or follower that activates the valve.

VISCOSITY: The rating of a liquid's internal resistance to flow.

VOLTMETER: An instrument used for measuring electrical force in units called volts. Voltmeters are always connected parallel with the circuit being tested.

WHEEL CYLINDER: Found in the automotive drum brake assembly, it is a device, actuated by hydraulic pressure, which, through internal pistons, pushes the brake shoes outward against the drums.

ABBREVIATIONS AND SYMBOLS

A: Ampere

AC: Alternating current

A/C: Air conditioning

A-h: Ampere hour

AT: Automatic transmission

ATDC: After top dead center

μA: Microampere

bbl: Barrel

BDC: Bottom dead center

bhp: Brake horsepower

BTDC: Before top dead center

BTU: British thermal unit

C: Celsius (Centigrade)

CCA: Cold cranking amps

cd: Candela

cm^2: Square centimeter

cm^3, cc: Cubic centimeter

CO: Carbon monoxide

CO_2: Carbon dioxide

cu.in., in^3: Cubic inch

CV: Constant velocity

Cyl.: Cylinder

DC: Direct current

ECM: Electronic control module

EFE: Early fuel evaporation

EFI: Electronic fuel injection

EGR: Exhaust gas recirculation

Exh.: Exhaust

F: Fahrenheit

F: Farad

pF: Picofarad

μF: Microfarad

FI: Fuel injection

ft.lb., ft. lb., ft. lbs.: foot pound(s)

gal: Gallon

g: Gram

HC: Hydrocarbon

HEI: High energy ignition

HO: High output

hp: Horsepower

Hyd.: Hydraulic

Hz: Hertz

ID: Inside diameter

in.lb.; in. lb.; in. lbs: inch pound(s)

Int.: Intake

K: Kelvin

kg: Kilogram

kHz: Kilohertz

km: Kilometer

km/h: Kilometers per hour

$k\Omega$: Kilohm

kPa: Kilopascal

kV: Kilovolt

kW: Kilowatt

l: Liter

l/s: Liters per second

m: Meter

mA: Milliampere

mg: Milligram

mHz: Megahertz

mm: Millimeter

mm^2: Square millimeter

m^3: Cubic meter

MΩ: Megohm

m/s: Meters per second

MT: Manual transmission

mV: Millivolt

μm: Micrometer

N: Newton

N-m: Newton meter

NOx: Nitrous oxide

OD: Outside diameter

OHC: Over head camshaft

OHV: Over head valve

Ω: Ohm

PCV: Positive crankcase ventilation

psi: Pounds per square inch

pts: Pints

qts: Quarts

rpm: Rotations per minute

rps: Rotations per second

R-12: A refrigerant gas (Freon)

SAE: Society of Automotive Engineers

SO$_2$: Sulfur dioxide

T: Ton

t: Megagram

TBI: Throttle Body Injection

TPS: Throttle Position Sensor

V: 1. Volt; 2. Venturi

μV: Microvolt

W: Watt

∞: Infinity

<: Less than

>: Greater than

Index

Chilton's Repair & Tune-Up Guides

The Complete line covers domestic cars, imports, trucks, vans, RV's and 4-wheel drive vehicles.

RTUG Title	Part No.
AMC 1975-82	7199
Covers all U.S. and Canadian models	
Aspen/Volare 1976-80	6637
Covers all U.S. and Canadian models	
Audi 1970-73	5902
Covers all U.S. and Canadian models.	
Audi 4000/5000 1978-81	7028
Covers all U.S. and Canadian models including turbocharged and diesel engines	
Barracuda/Challenger 1965-72	5807
Covers all U.S. and Canadian models	
Blazer/Jimmy 1969-82	6931
Covers all U.S. and Canadian 2- and 4-wheel drive models, including diesel engines	
BMW 1970-82	6844
Covers U.S. and Canadian models	
Buick/Olds/Pontiac 1975-85	7308
Covers all U.S. and Canadian full size rear wheel drive models	
Cadillac 1967-84	7462
Covers all U.S. and Canadian rear wheel drive models	
Camaro 1967-81	6735
Covers all U.S. and Canadian models	
Camaro 1982-85	7317
Covers all U.S. and Canadian models	
Capri 1970-77	6695
Covers all U.S. and Canadian models	
Caravan/Voyager 1984-85	7482
Covers all U.S. and Canadian models	
Century/Regal 1975-85	7307
Covers all U.S. and Canadian rear wheel drive models, including turbocharged engines	
Champ/Arrow/Sapporo 1978-83	7041
Covers all U.S. and Canadian models	
Chevette/1000 1976-86	6836
Covers all U.S. and Canadian models	
Chevrolet 1968-85	7135
Covers all U.S. and Canadian models	
Chevrolet 1968-79 Spanish	7082
Chevrolet/GMC Pick-Ups 1970-82 Spanish	7468
Chevrolet/GMC Pick-Ups and Suburban 1970-86	6936
Covers all U.S. and Canadian 1/2, 3/4 and 1 ton models, including 4-wheel drive and diesel engines	
Chevrolet LUV 1972-81	6815
Covers all U.S. and Canadian models	
Chevrolet Mid-Size 1964-86	6840
Covers all U.S. and Canadian models of 1964-77 Chevelle, Malibu and Malibu SS; 1974-77 Laguna; 1978-85 Malibu; 1970-86 Monte Carlo; 1964-84 El Camino, including diesel engines	
Chevrolet Nova 1986	7658
Covers all U.S. and Canadian models	
Chevy/GMC Vans 1967-84	6930
Covers all U.S. and Canadian models of 1/2, 3/4, and 1 ton vans, cutaways, and motor home chassis, including diesel engines	
Chevy S-10 Blazer/GMC S-15 Jimmy 1982-85	7383
Covers all U.S. and Canadian models	
Chevy S-10/GMC S-15 Pick-Ups 1982-85	7310
Covers all U.S. and Canadian models	
Chevy II/Nova 1962-79	6841
Covers all U.S. and Canadian models	
Chrysler K- and E-Car 1981-85	7163
Covers all U.S. and Canadian front wheel drive models	
Colt/Challenger/Vista/Conquest 1971-85	7037
Covers all U.S. and Canadian models	
Corolla/Carina/Tercel/Starlet 1970-85	7036
Covers all U.S. and Canadian models	
Corona/Cressida/Crown/Mk.II/Camry/Van 1970-84	7044
Covers all U.S. and Canadian models	

RTUG Title	Part No.
Corvair 1960-69	6691
Covers all U.S. and Canadian models	
Corvette 1953-62	6576
Covers all U.S. and Canadian models	
Corvette 1963-84	6843
Covers all U.S. and Canadian models	
Cutlass 1970-85	6933
Covers all U.S. and Canadian models	
Dart/Demon 1968-76	6324
Covers all U.S. and Canadian models	
Datsun 1961-72	5790
Covers all U.S. and Canadian models of Nissan Patrol; 1500, 1600 and 2000 sports cars; Pick-Ups; 410, 411, 510, 1200 and 240Z	
Datsun 1973-80 Spanish	7083
Datsun/Nissan F-10, 310, Stanza, Pulsar 1977-86	7196
Covers all U.S. and Canadian models	
Datsun/Nissan Pick-Ups 1970-84	6816
Covers all U.S. and Canadian models	
Datsun/Nissan Z & ZX 1970-86	6932
Covers all U.S. and Canadian models	
Datsun/Nissan 1200, 210, Sentra 1973-86	7197
Covers all U.S. and Canadian models	
Datsun/Nissan 200SX, 510, 610, 710, 810, Maxima 1973-84	7170
Covers all U.S. and Canadian models	
Dodge 1968-77	6554
Covers all U.S. and Canadian models	
Dodge Charger 1967-70	6486
Covers all U.S. and Canadian models	
Dodge/Plymouth Trucks 1967-84	7459
Covers all 1/2, 3/4, and 1 ton 2- and 4-wheel drive U.S. and Canadian models, including diesel engines	
Dodge/Plymouth Vans 1967-84	6934
Covers all 1/2, 3/4, and 1 ton U.S. and Canadian models of vans, cutaways and motor home chassis	
D-50/Arrow Pick-Up 1979-81	7032
Covers all U.S. and Canadian models	
Fairlane/Torino 1962-75	6320
Covers all U.S. and Canadian models	
Fairmont/Zephyr 1978-83	6965
Covers all U.S. and Canadian models	
Fiat 1969-81	7042
Covers all U.S. and Canadian models	
Fiesta 1978-80	6846
Covers all U.S. and Canadian models	
Firebird 1967-81	5996
Covers all U.S. and Canadian models	
Firebird 1982-85	7345
Covers all U.S. and Canadian models	
Ford 1968-79 Spanish	7084
Ford Bronco 1966-83	7140
Covers all U.S. and Canadian models	
Ford Bronco II 1984	7408
Covers all U.S. and Canadian models	
Ford Courier 1972-82	6983
Covers all U.S. and Canadian models	
Ford/Mercury Front Wheel Drive 1981-85	7055
Covers all U.S. and Canadian models Escort, EXP, Tempo, Lynx, LN-7 and Topaz	
Ford/Mercury/Lincoln 1968-85	6842
Covers all U.S. and Canadian models of FORD Country Sedan, Country Squire, Crown Victoria, Custom, Custom 500, Galaxie 500, LTD through 1982, Ranch Wagon, and XL; MERCURY Colony Park, Commuter, Marquis through 1982, Gran Marquis, Monterey and Park Lane; LINCOLN Continental and Towne Car	
Ford/Mercury/Lincoln Mid-Size 1971-85	6696
Covers all U.S. and Canadian models of FORD Elite, 1983-85 LTD, 1977-79 LTD II, Ranchero, Torino, Gran Torino, 1977-85 Thunderbird; MERCURY 1972-85 Cougar,	

continued on next page

continued on next page

RTUG Title	Part No.	RTUG Title	Part No.
1983-85 Marquis, Montego, 1980-85 XR-7; LINCOLN 1982-85 Continental, 1984-85 Mark VII, 1978-80 Versailles		Mercedes-Benz 1974-84 Covers all U.S. and Canadian models	6809
Ford Pick-Ups 1965-86 Covers all 1/2, 3/4 and 1 ton, 2- and 4-wheel drive U.S. and Canadian pick-up, chassis cab and camper models, including diesel engines	6913	Mitsubishi, Cordia, Tredia, Starion, Galant 1983-85 Covers all U.S. and Canadian models	7583
		MG 1961-81 Covers all U.S. and Canadian models	6780
Ford Pick-Ups 1965-82 Spanish	7469	Mustang/Capri/Merkur 1979-85 Covers all U.S. and Canadian models	6963
Ford Ranger 1983-84 Covers all U.S. and Canadian models	7338	Mustang/Cougar 1965-73 Covers all U.S. and Canadian models	6542
Ford Vans 1961-86 Covers all U.S. and Canadian 1/2, 3/4 and 1 ton van and cutaway chassis models, including diesel engines	6849	Mustang II 1974-78 Covers all U.S. and Canadian models	6812
		Omni/Horizon/Rampage 1978-84 Covers all U.S. and Canadian models of DODGE omni, Miser, 024, Charger 2.2; PLYMOUTH Horizon, Miser, TC3, TC3 Tourismo; Rampage	6845
GM A-Body 1982-85 Covers all front wheel drive U.S. and Canadian models of BUICK Century, CHEVROLET Celebrity, OLDSMOBILE Cutlass Ciera and PONTIAC 6000	7309		
		Opel 1971-75 Covers all U.S. and Canadian models	6575
GM C-Body 1985 Covers all front wheel drive U.S. and Canadian models of BUICK Electra Park Avenue and Electra T-Type, CADILLAC Fleetwood and deVille, OLDSMOBILE 98 Regency and Regency Brougham	7587	Peugeot 1970-74 Covers all U.S. and Canadian models	5982
		Pinto/Bobcat 1971-80 Covers all U.S. and Canadian models	7027
		Plymouth 1968-76 Covers all U.S. and Canadian models	6552
GM J-Car 1982-85 Covers all U.S. and Canadian models of BUICK Skyhawk, CHEVROLET Cavalier, CADILLAC Cimarron, OLDSMOBILE Firenza and PONTIAC 2000 and Sunbird	7059	Pontiac Fiero 1984-85 Covers all U.S. and Canadian models	7571
		Pontiac Mid-Size 1974-83 Covers all U.S. and Canadian models of Ventura, Grand Am, LeMans, Grand LeMans, GTO, Phoenix, and Grand Prix	7346
GM N-Body 1985-86 Covers all U.S. and Canadian models of front wheel drive BUICK Somerset and Skylark, OLDSMOBILE Calais; and PONTIAC Grand Am	7657	Porsche 924/928 1976-81 Covers all U.S. and Canadian models	7048
		Renault 1975-85 Covers all U.S. and Canadian models	7165
GM X-Body 1980-85 Covers all U.S. and Canadian models of BUICK Skylark, CHEVROLET Citation, OLDSMOBILE Omega and PONTIAC Phoenix	7049	Roadrunner/Satellite/Belvedere/GTX 1968-73 Covers all U.S. and Canadian models	5821
		RX-7 1979-81 Covers all U.S. and Canadian models	7031
GM Subcompact 1971-80 Covers all U.S. and Canadian models of BUICK Skyhawk (1975-80), CHEVROLET Vega and Monza, OLDSMOBILE Starfire, and PONTIAC Astre and 1975-80 Sunbird	6935	SAAB 99 1969-75 Covers all U.S. and Canadian models	5988
		SAAB 900 1979-85 Covers all U.S. and Canadian models	7572
		Snowmobiles 1976-80 Covers Arctic Cat, John Deere, Kawasaki, Polaris, Ski-Doo and Yamaha	6978
Granada/Monarch 1975-82 Covers all U.S. and Canadian models	6937	Subaru 1970-84 Covers all U.S. and Canadian models	6982
Honda 1973-84 Covers all U.S. and Canadian models	6980	Tempest/GTO/LeMans 1968-73 Covers all U.S. and Canadian models	5905
International Scout 1967-73 Covers all U.S. and Canadian models	5912	Toyota 1966-70 Covers all U.S. and Canadian models of Corona, MkII, Corolla, Crown, Land Cruiser, Stout and Hi-Lux	5795
Jeep 1945-87 Covers all U.S. and Canadian CJ-2A, CJ-3A, CJ-3B, CJ-5, CJ-6, CJ-7, Scrambler and Wrangler models	6817		
		Toyota 1970-79 Spanish	7467
		Toyota Celica/Supra 1971-85 Covers all U.S. and Canadian models	7043
Jeep Wagoneer, Commando, Cherokee, Truck 1957-86 Covers all U.S. and Canadian models of Wagoneer, Cherokee, Grand Wagoneer, Jeepster, Jeepster Commando, J-100, J-200, J-300, J-10, J20, FC-150 and FC-170	6739	Toyota Trucks 1970-85 Covers all U.S. and Canadian models of pick-ups, Land Cruiser and 4Runner	7035
		Valiant/Duster 1968-76 Covers all U.S. and Canadian models	6326
		Volvo 1956-69 Covers all U.S. and Canadian models	6529
Laser/Daytona 1984-85 Covers all U.S. and Canadian models	7563	Volvo 1970-83 Covers all U.S. and Canadian models	7040
Maverick/Comet 1970-77 Covers all U.S. and Canadian models	6634	VW Front Wheel Drive 1974-85 Covers all U.S. and Canadian models	6962
Mazda 1971-84 Covers all U.S. and Canadian models of RX-2, RX-3, RX-4, 808, 1300, 1600, Cosmo, GLC and 626	6981	VW 1949-71 Covers all U.S. and Canadian models	5796
		VW 1970-79 Spanish	7081
Mazda Pick-Ups 1972-86 Covers all U.S. and Canadian models	7659	VW 1970-81 Covers all U.S. and Canadian Beetles, Karmann Ghia, Fastback, Squareback, Vans, 411 and 412	6837
Mercedes-Benz 1959-70 Covers all U.S. and Canadian models	6065		
Mereceds-Benz 1968-73 Covers all U.S. and Canadian models	5907		

Chilton's Repair & Tune-Up Guides are available at your local retailer or by mailing a check or money order for **$13.95** plus **$3.25** to cover postage and handling to:

Chilton Book Company
Dept. DM
Radnor, PA 19089

NOTE: When ordering be sure to include your name & address, book part No. & title.